GLOBE FEARON

LITERATURE

TEACHER'S EDITION

■ *Purple Level* ■

PROGRAM REVIEWERS

Kathy Babigian, Coordinator, Tioga Literacy Center, Fresno, California
Pat Bartholomew, M.A., Reading Specialist, Milton, Ohio
Jennifer Dilks-Mundt, English Teacher, Brant Rock, Massachusetts
Ann Fitzgerald, M.A., Education Director, Southshire Community School,
    North Bennington, Vermont
Pat Miller, M.A., Reading/English/Language Arts Supervisor, Prince Georges County
    Public Schools, Maryland
Artie P. Norton, English Teacher, Suffern, New York
Timothy Rasinski, Professor of Curriculum and Instruction, Kent State University, Kent, Ohio
Cynthia Saska, M.A., Professor of English, University of Texas, San Antonio, Texas
Margaret-Mary Sulentic, Ph.D., Assistant Professor of Literacy, Department of Curriculum
    and Instruction, University of Southern Mississippi, Hattiesburg, Mississippi
Dr. Helen W. Taylor, Director of Programs K-12 Curriculum and Instruction, Portsmouth City
    Public Schools, Virginia

CONSULTANTS

Dr. Virginia Bryg; Josephine Gemake, Ph.D.; Alfred Schifini, Ph.D.; Deborah Walker; Robert
    Wandberg, Ph.D.

Supervising Editor/Team Leader: Karen McCollum
Editors: Ayanna Taylor, Amy Greenberg, Theresa McCarthy
Editorial Developer: Pearson Education Development Group
Marketing Assistant: Kate Krimsky
Production Editor: Travis Bailey
Associate Production Editors: Amy Benefiel, Alia Lesser
Senior Designer: Angel Weyant
Manufacturing Buyer: Mark Cirillo
Cover and Interior Design/Production: Pearson Education Development Group
Photo Research: Pearson Education Development Group

ABOUT THE COVER

The Workers on the Cart, Alberto Magnelli. Musee National d'Art Moderne, Paris, France/
Bridgeman Art Library. Alberto Magnelli was a pioneer in abstract art, the defining style of the
20th century. Abstractionists have challenged themselves to capture the unseen aspects of nature
and the heroic capacities of individuals and society. What does Magnelli's painting of workers on a
cart say about the human spirit?

ISBN 0-130-23564-4
Printed in the United States of America

3 4 5 6 7   08 07 06 05 04

Globe Fearon
Pearson Learning Group

1-800-321-3106
www.pearsonlearning.com

CONTENTS

UNIT 1 *Looking at Love*

CONTENTS

UNIT 5 *Heroes*

UNIT 6 *Generations*

Making Literature Accessible to All Students

Globe Fearon Literature is a comprehensive high school literature program that meets the needs of all students.

- *Adapted selections provide accessibility.*

- *Model lessons promote independent reading.*

- *Reading skill instruction is included with every selection.*

PURPLE LEVEL
Literature Organized by Theme

GREEN LEVEL
Literature from Around the World

■ STUDENT EDITION

- Skillful adaptations of the more difficult selections offer accessibility.
- Model selections guide students to become independent active readers.
- Reading skill instruction is provided with every selection.

■ TEACHER'S EDITION

- Teaching strategies are provided at point-of-use.
- An easy-to-follow three-step lesson plan for each selection saves time.
- Additional activities for ESL students and cooperative learning groups help teachers meet individual needs.

■ TEACHER'S RESOURCES

- This resource is offered in two formats: print and CD-ROM.
- Over 400 reproducibles help you to reinforce, extend, and assess understanding.
- Scoring rubrics and evaluation guides provide support for alternative assessment.
- Answer keys to all ancillaries save time.
- **CD-ROM** includes correlations to national and many state standards for reading and language arts.

■ ADDITIONAL ANCILLARIES

- Comprehension and Vocabulary Workbook
- Language Enrichment Workbook
- Answer Key

SILVER LEVEL
American Literature

GOLD LEVEL
British Literature

▪ *Purple Level* ▪

LITERATURE ORGANIZED BY THEME
UNITS

Looking at Love
The Unknown
Suspense
Discoveries
Heroes
Generations

Exciting unit openers capture students' interest.

Unit Openers explore ideas related to the unit theme and discuss how the selections relate to one another.

Motivating questions help students activate prior knowledge to promote comprehension.

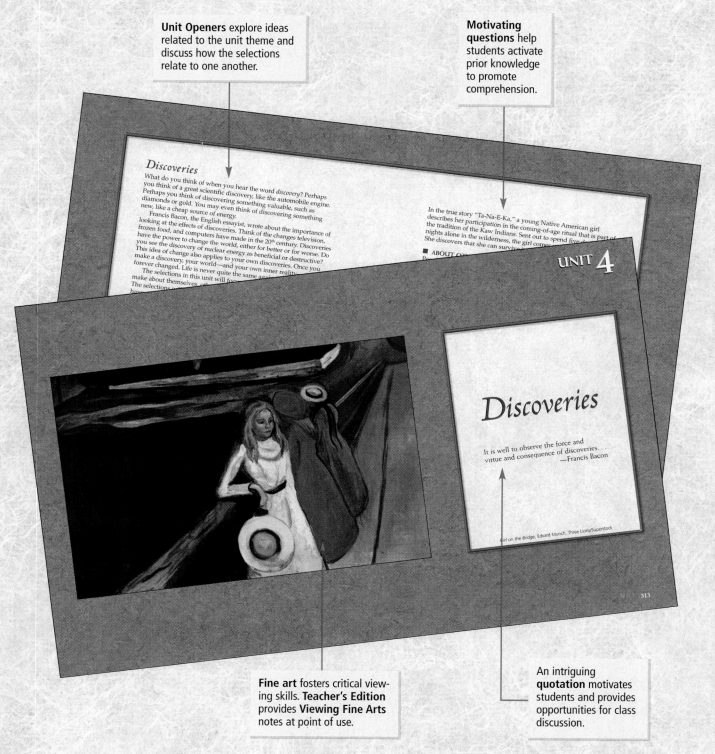

Discoveries

What do you think of when you hear the word *discovery*? Perhaps you think of a great scientific discovery, like the automobile engine. Perhaps you think of discovering something valuable, such as diamonds or gold. You may even think of discovering something new, like a cheap source of energy.

Francis Bacon, the English essayist, wrote about the importance of looking at the effects of discoveries. Think of the changes television, frozen food, and computers have made in the 20th century. Discoveries have the power to change the world, either for better or for worse. Do you see the discovery of nuclear energy as beneficial or destructive? This idea of change also applies to your own discoveries. Once you make a discovery, your world—and your own inner reality— forever changed.

The selections in this unit will focus . . .

The selections in this unit will focus on . . .

make about themselves . . .
hav . . .

In the true story "Ta-Na-E-Ka," a young Native American girl describes her participation in the coming-of-age ritual that is part of the tradition of the Kaw Indians. Sent out to spend five nights alone in the wilderness, the girl comes . . . She discovers that she can surviv . . .

■ ABOUT O . . .
P . . .

UNIT **4**

Discoveries

It is well to observe the force and
virtue and consequence of discoveries. . . .
—Francis Bacon

Girl on the Bridge, Edvard Munch. Three Lions/Superstock

313

Fine art fosters critical viewing skills. **Teacher's Edition** provides **Viewing Fine Arts** notes at point of use.

An intriguing **quotation** motivates students and provides opportunities for class discussion.

Model selections guide students to become independent readers.

Focus on lessons discuss the elements of a particular genre—fiction, nonfiction, poetry, or drama—to promote student understanding.

Model selections provide margin notes to help students become active readers.

Focus ON FICTION

Short stories are a very popular form of fiction. Why? Short stories are so concentrated that they can have a lot of impact in just a few pages. The conciseness of a short story also provides the chance for a clear examination of the four basic elements of fiction. These are plot, characters, setting, and theme.

Plot Plot is usually the most obvious element of a short story. Many people think of it first when they talk about a story: the telling of one event after another to form a series of actions ... through **exposition**, or written ... background

Second, the writer can tell you indirectly about a character by describing what the character says, or how the character acts. This information portrays the character, too, but you must use some imagination to fit the pieces into the overall description.

Usually a writer uses both methods. In "Appointment in Baghdad," you learn that one character is a young man. That is **direct information**. You also learn that he rushes into the Sultan's palace "out of breath and wild with excitement." That is **indirect information**, giving you clues to his general state of mind and how he reacts in certain situations.

Setting A third element of a short story is setting. You can probably guess that setting includes where a story takes place, but it also includes when a story happens. Additionally, it can include ... ral events, such as a blizzard or a hurricane. ... es in this unit have a variety of settings. ... in modern-day New York, ... Middle East

MODEL

Death on a Pale Horse, William Blake. Fitzwilliam Museum, University of Cambridge/Bridgeman Art Library

118 ■ Unit 2

APPOINTMENT AT NOON

by Eric Frank Russell

Henry Curran was big, busy, and successful. He had no patience with people who weren't successful. He had the build of a fighter and the soul of a tiger. His time was worth a thousand bucks an hour. He knew of nobody who was worth more.

And crime did not pay? "Bah!" said Henry Curran. The law of the jungle paid off. Henry Curran had learned that nice people are soft people, and that smiles are made to be slapped.

Entering his large office with the fast, heavy step of a big man in fighting shape, Henry threw his hat onto a hook. He glanced at the wall clock. He noted that it was ten minutes to twelve.

Seating himself in the large chair behind his desk, he kept his eyes on the door. His wait lasted about ten seconds. Frowning at the thought of it, Curran reached over and pushed a red button on his big desk.

"What's wrong with you?" he snapped when Miss Reed came in. "You get worse every day. Old age creeping over you or something?"

She paused. She was tall, neat, and steady. She faced him across the desk, her eyes showing a touch of fear. Curran hired to work for him only people he knew too much about.

FOCUS ON FICTION STUDY HINTS

The main character is introduced right away. His traits are described directly as well as indirectly.

Note the writer's statement of the setting. The office's location and the date do not matter. The description of Henry Curran acts as exposition. Now, with background information and setting provided, the plot begins to unfold.

The second character of the story is introduced. Notice how information about Miss Reed tells us more about Curran.

Appointment at Noon ■ 119

Study Hints guide students as they read by pointing out important elements of the genre.

Each selection includes strategies to help students master essential skills.

*A **clear and predictable** format promotes understanding of concepts.*

The **Learn About** feature explains a key literary element of each selection.

Learn About

THEME

A **theme** is an idea or message in a story, play, or poem. It is possible for a piece of literature to have several themes. Only one of these, however, will be the main theme. For example, in the story "The Gold Medal," the main theme is Amanda's discovery of her true self apart from the roles people tried to impose on her. A less important theme, or **subtheme**, is the dilemma of an African American girl in a society that is made up mostly of white people.

You can often recognize the theme of a story by thinking, "Why did the author write this story, play, or poem?" As you read "Thank You, M'am," ask yourself:

1. What message does Langston Hughes wish to convey?
2. How does the story communicate this message?

WRITING CONNECTION

Imagine that you are a short-story writer. What kind of a theme might you choose? Write a paragraph in which you describe a theme that is meaningful to you. (For example, you might want to write about standing up for someone who is being teased.) Discuss how you would handle the theme and the message you would communicate.

READING FOCUS

Make Predictions When you make predictions, you try to guess what will happen in a story before it actually happens. Confirming your predictions is one way to measure how well you understand the story. Revising predictions helps you summarize what has happened so far and adds to your enjoyment. Your own experience can help you make predictions about a story. Jot down your predictions. Compare them to what happens in the story. Then make new predictions based on what you have read.

THANK YOU, M'AM

by Langston Hughes

She was a large woman with a large purse that had everything in it but hammer and nails. It had a long strap, and she carried it slung across her shoulder. It was about eleven o'clock at night, and she was walking alone, when a boy ran up behind her and tried to snatch her purse. The strap broke with the sudden single tug the boy gave it from behind. But the boy's weight and the weight of the purse combined caused him to lose his balance.

slung (SLUNG) hung; made to swing loosely

The **Reading Focus** provides critical reading support to increase comprehension.

Writing activities help students connect the elements of literature to their lives.

Purpose-setting questions focus students' reading.

Defined words at the bottom of the page help students build vocabulary without losing track of their reading.

Review the Selection ensures mastery of skills.

Understand the Selection contains three-tiered questions that prompt recall and higher-order thinking skills.

Write About the Selection provides process-writing opportunities.

The **Think About** section reviews and reinforces the literary skill taught in the lesson.

Develop Your Vocabulary reinforces students' understanding of key vocabulary.

Review the Selection

UNDERSTAND THE SELECTION

Recall

1. What is the opening incident?

2. Where does Mrs. Jones take the boy?

3. What does Mrs. Jones give the boy at the end of the story?

Infer

4. What can you infer about the boy's parents?

5. What argument does Mrs. Jones use when the boy begs her to turn him loose?

6. In what kind of house does Mrs. Jones live?

7. What hint in the story tells you that Mrs. Jones did not always behave herself when she was young?

Apply

8. Why do you think the boy does not run from Mrs. Jones's house when he has the chance?

9. What will the boy do with the money?

10. Predict whether or not you think the boy will behave himself from now on.

Respond to Literature

What do Mrs. Jones and the boy discover about each other? Do you think discoveries like this can happen in real life?

WRITE ABOUT THE SELECTION

Suppose that many years have passed and that the boy in "Thank You, M'am" is an adult. How do you think he would remember his encounter with Luella Bates Washington Jones? Write a paragraph in which the boy (now grown up) tells about Mrs. Jones.

Prewriting Take a few minutes to brainstorm about the details you want to include in your paragraph. Decide how old you want the boy to be and what the circumstances of his life are (such as rich, poor, successful, in jail).

Writing Use the ideas from your brainstorming session to write a paragraph from the adult boy's point of view. Be sure to make clear the boy's feelings about Mrs. Jones and the incident with the purse. Also, make clear what effect, if any, the incident had on the boy as he grew older. Base your paragraph on Langston Hughes's message to the readers in the story.

Revising You can make your paragraph more effective by adding specific details from the story as seen from the boy's point of view. Rearrange phrases and eliminate boring words to make your story come alive.

Proofreading Check your paragraph for errors in spelling, usage, and mechanics. Add periods or other end marks to correct run on sentences. Make sure that every sentence ends with a period, question mark or exclamation mark.

THINK ABOUT THEME

When thinking about the theme of a story, it is important not to confuse theme with plot. The **plot** of a story is what happens in the story, while the **theme** is the message or main idea of the story. Stories with different plots might have the same theme.

1. What is the theme of "Thank You, M'am"?

2. Do you agree with the message of the story?

3. Why do you think Mrs. Jones treated the boy the way she did?

4. What did Mrs. Jones hope her encounter with the boy would accomplish?

5. In general, do you think that people like Mrs. Jones tend to make other people better, or that others just take advantage of them?

READING FOCUS

Make Predictions As you read "Thank You, M'am," you were able to make, confirm, and revise predictions. How were your predictions about the title and the characters confirmed? Did you have to revise any of your other predictions? If so, how?

DEVELOP YOUR VOCABULARY

A **synonym** is a word that has the same or almost the same meaning as another word. For example, the boy in "Thank You, M'am" tries to *snatch* Mrs. Jones's purse. Two words that are synonyms for *snatch* are the words *take* and *grab*.

Review these words from "Thank You, M'am" and other stories in this unit. Write at least one synonym for each word. Then write an original paragraph that uses the words from the list.

1. slung
2. frail
3. barren
4. gingerly
5. quaver
6. zealously
7. surmised
8. acrid
9. shrewdest
10. horrendous

Respond to Literature helps students relate the selection to their own experiences through discussion or writing.

Reading Focus questions assess students' mastery of the reading skill.

Unit Review includes literature-based activities and test-preparation strategies.

Writing activities allow students to explore key elements of literature through process writing.

Vocabulary and **grammar** reviews reinforce language skills.

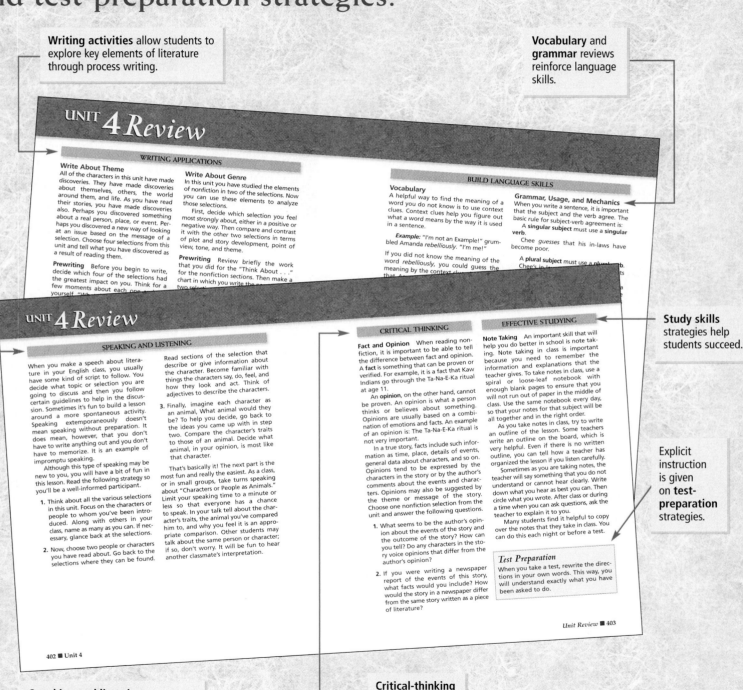

UNIT 4 Review

WRITING APPLICATIONS

Write About Theme
All of the characters in this unit have made discoveries. They have made discoveries about themselves, others, the world around them, and life. As you have read their stories, you have made discoveries also. Perhaps you discovered something about a real person, place, or event. Perhaps you discovered a new way of looking at an issue based on the message of a selection. Choose four selections from this unit and tell what you have discovered as a result of reading them.

Prewriting   Before you begin to write, decide which four of the selections had the greatest impact on you. Think for a few moments about each one. Ask yourself, "Wh...

Write About Genre
In this unit you have studied the elements of nonfiction in two of the selections. Now you can use these elements to analyze those selections.

First, decide which selection you feel most strongly about, either in a positive or negative way. Then compare and contrast it with the other two selections in terms of plot and story development, point of view, tone, and theme.

Prewriting   Review briefly the work that you did for the "Think About . . ." for the nonfiction sections. Then make a chart in which you write the ... two selecti...

BUILD LANGUAGE SKILLS

Vocabulary
A helpful way to find the meaning of a word you do not know is to use context clues. Context clues help you figure out what a word means by the way it is used in a sentence.

Example: "I'm not an Example!" grumbled Amanda *rebelliously.* "I'm me!"

If you did not know the meaning of the word *rebelliously,* you could guess the meaning by the context clu... that A...

Grammar, Usage, and Mechanics
When you write a sentence, it is important that the subject and the verb agree. The basic rule for subject-verb agreement is:
A **singular subject** must use a **singular verb**.

Chee *guesses* that his in-laws have become poor.

A **plural subject** must use a **plural verb**.
Chee's in-la...

UNIT 4 Review

SPEAKING AND LISTENING

When you make a speech about literature in your English class, you usually have some kind of script to follow. You decide what topic or selection you are going to discuss and then you follow certain guidelines to help in the discussion. Sometimes it's fun to build a lesson around a more spontaneous activity. Speaking extemporaneously doesn't mean speaking without preparation. It does mean, however, that you don't have to write anything out and you don't have to memorize. It is an example of impromptu speaking.

Although this type of speaking may be new to you, you will have a bit of fun in this lesson. Read the following strategy so you'll be a well-informed participant.

1. Think about all the various selections in this unit. Focus on the characters or people to whom you've been introduced. Along with others in your class, name as many as you can. If necessary, glance back at the selections.

2. Now, choose two people or characters you have read about. Go back to the selections where they can be found.

Read sections of the selection that describe or give information about the character. Become familiar with things the characters say, do, feel, and how they look and act. Think of adjectives to describe the characters.

3. Finally, imagine each character as an animal, What animal would they be? To help you decide, go back to the ideas you came up with in step two. Compare the character's traits to those of an animal. Decide what animal, in your opinion, is most like that character.

That's basically it! The next part is the most fun and really the easiest. As a class, or in small groups, take turns speaking about "Characters or People as Animals." Limit your speaking time to a minute or less so that everyone has a chance to speak. In your talk tell about the character's traits, the animal you've compared him to, and why you feel it is an appropriate comparison. Other students may talk about the same person or character; if so, don't worry. It will be fun to hear another classmate's interpretation.

CRITICAL THINKING

Fact and Opinion   When reading nonfiction, it is important to be able to tell the difference between fact and opinion. A **fact** is something that can be proven or verified. For example, it is a fact that Kaw Indians go through the Ta-Na-E-Ka ritual at age 11.

An **opinion,** on the other hand, cannot be proven. An opinion is what a person thinks or believes about something. Opinions are usually based on a combination of emotions and facts. An example of an opinion is: The Ta-Na-E-Ka ritual is not very important.

In a true story, facts include such information as time, place, details of events, general data about characters, and so on. Opinions tend to be expressed by the characters in the story or by the author's comments about the events and characters. Opinions may also be suggested by the theme or message of the story. Choose one nonfiction selection from the unit and answer the following questions.

1. What seems to be the author's opinion about the events of the story and the outcome of the story? How can you tell? Do any characters in the story voice opinions that differ from the author's opinion?

2. If you were writing a newspaper report of the events of this story, what facts would you include? How would the story in a newspaper differ from the same story written as a piece of literature?

EFFECTIVE STUDYING

Note Taking   An important skill that will help you do better in school is note taking. Note taking in class is important because you need to remember the information and explanations that the teacher gives. To take notes in class, use a spiral or loose-leaf notebook with enough blank pages to ensure that you will not run out of paper in the middle of class. Use the same notebook every day, so that your notes for that subject will be all together and in the right order.

As you take notes in class, try to write an outline of the lesson. Some teachers write an outline on the board, which is very helpful. Even if there is no written outline, you can tell how a teacher has organized the lesson if you listen carefully.

Sometimes as you are taking notes, the teacher will say something that you do not understand or cannot hear clearly. Write down what you hear as best you can. Then circle what you wrote. After class or during a time when you can ask questions, ask the teacher to explain it to you.

Many students find it helpful to copy over the notes that they take in class. You can do this each night or before a test.

> #### Test Preparation
> When you take a test, rewrite the directions in your own words. This way, you will understand exactly what you have been asked to do.

Unit Review ■ 403

402 ■ Unit 4

Study skills strategies help students succeed.

Explicit instruction is given on **test-preparation** strategies.

Speaking and listening activities help students analyze literature through oral interpretation.

Critical-thinking activities increase understanding of literature.

The Teacher's Edition provides strategies at point of use.

Concise **Selection Objectives** are highlighted for quick reference.

Lesson Resources list additional program components that reinforce skills.

About the Author notes provide background information about the author of each selection.

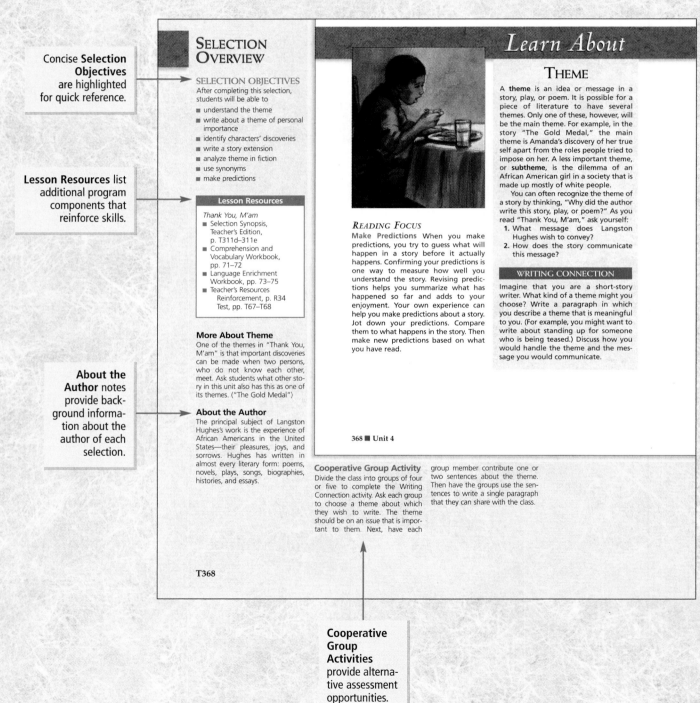

SELECTION OVERVIEW

SELECTION OBJECTIVES
After completing this selection, students will be able to
- understand the theme
- write about a theme of personal importance
- identify characters' discoveries
- write a story extension
- analyze theme in fiction
- use synonyms
- make predictions

Lesson Resources

Thank You, M'am
- Selection Synopsis, Teacher's Edition, p. T311d–311e
- Comprehension and Vocabulary Workbook, pp. 71–72
- Language Enrichment Workbook, pp. 73–75
- Teacher's Resources Reinforcement, p. R34 Test, pp. T67–T68

More About Theme
One of the themes in "Thank You, M'am" is that important discoveries can be made when two persons, who do not know each other, meet. Ask students what other story in this unit also has this as one of its themes. ("The Gold Medal")

About the Author
The principal subject of Langston Hughes's work is the experience of African Americans in the United States—their pleasures, joys, and sorrows. Hughes has written in almost every literary form: poems, novels, plays, songs, biographies, histories, and essays.

READING FOCUS
Make Predictions When you make predictions, you try to guess what will happen in a story before it actually happens. Confirming your predictions is one way to measure how well you understand the story. Revising predictions helps you summarize what has happened so far and adds to your enjoyment. Your own experience can help you make predictions about a story. Jot down your predictions. Compare them to what happens in the story. Then make new predictions based on what you have read.

Learn About

THEME
A **theme** is an idea or message in a story, play, or poem. It is possible for a piece of literature to have several themes. Only one of these, however, will be the main theme. For example, in the story "The Gold Medal," the main theme is Amanda's discovery of her true self apart from the roles people tried to impose on her. A less important theme, or **subtheme**, is the dilemma of an African American girl in a society that is made up mostly of white people.

You can often recognize the theme of a story by thinking, "Why did the author write this story, play, or poem?" As you read "Thank You, M'am," ask yourself:
1. What message does Langston Hughes wish to convey?
2. How does the story communicate this message?

WRITING CONNECTION
Imagine that you are a short-story writer. What kind of a theme might you choose? Write a paragraph in which you describe a theme that is meaningful to you. (For example, you might want to write about standing up for someone who is being teased.) Discuss how you would handle the theme and the message you would communicate.

368 ■ Unit 4

Cooperative Group Activity
Divide the class into groups of four or five to complete the Writing Connection activity. Ask each group to choose a theme about which they wish to write. The theme should be on an issue that is important to them. Next, have each group member contribute one or two sentences about the theme. Then have the groups use the sentences to write a single paragraph that they can share with the class.

T368

Cooperative Group Activities provide alternative assessment opportunities.

Easy-to-follow three-step lesson format accompanies every selection.

THANK YOU, M'AM

by Langston Hughes

She was a large woman with a large purse that had everything in it but hammer and nails. It had a long strap, and she carried it slung across her shoulder. It was about eleven o'clock at night, and she was walking alone, when a boy ran up behind her and tried to snatch her purse. The strap broke with the sudden single tug the boy gave it from behind. But the boy's weight and the weight of the purse combined caused him to lose his balance.

---

slung (SLUNG) hung; made to swing loosely

Thank You, M'am ■ 369

TEACHING PLAN

INTRODUCE

Motivation
Ask students if they have ever had a chance encounter with a stranger that proved to be unusual. Relate their responses to the encounter between the boy and Luella Bates Washington Jones.

Purpose-Setting Question
How would you react if someone younger than you tried to take your purse or wallet?

READ

Literary Focus:
Theme
Encourage students to consider how the characters feel about and act toward each other as the story progresses. Ask: What do the characters discover about and learn from each other? Help students use their responses to identify the theme of the selection.

Reading Focus:
Make Predictions
Tell students that writers give clues that can help them predict. Look at the title. Ask: Is there a clue in the title to what might happen in the story? Think about dialogue or behavior that surprises you. Ask: Does it change any of your previous predictions? Think about surprising plot developments. Ask: Why did this happen? What will happen next?

CLOSE

Have students complete Review the Selection on pages 330–331.

1. **Introduce** provides ideas to motivate students and help them set a purpose for reading.

2. **Read** includes strategies to help students master the literary and reading skills in the selection.

3. **Close** references Review the Selection pages that provide opportunities for practice, application, and assessment.

Develop Vocabulary Skills
Write on the chalkboard sentences that use the vocabulary words footnoted in the story. Ask students to determine from the context what they think each word means. Discuss the meanings of the words in preparation for the students' reading of the selection.

ESL Activity

Invite pairs of students to read the story aloud as a dialogue. You may wish to have them photocopy the story twice and highlight one character's lines on each copy. Remind them that they should read only the words and sentences that appear in quotation marks. Encourage them to read through their own lines once alone. As they do, they should think about what the character is feeling and put appropriate expression into their spoken lines. After the pairs have read together, ask two volunteers to read the dialogue to the entire class.

T369

Activities and strategies for **building vocabulary skills** are included for each selection.

ESL Activities help teachers meet the diverse needs of today's classrooms.

Reading comprehension and vocabulary skills are reinforced for each selection.

The **Comprehension and Vocabulary Workbook** highlights vocabulary in each selection. Reading comprehension activities are provided to strengthen your students' understanding of each selection.

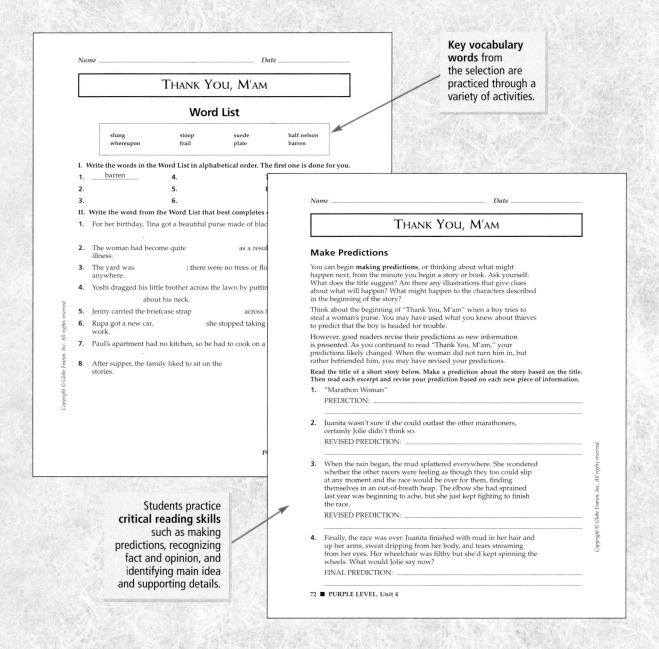

Key vocabulary words from the selection are practiced through a variety of activities.

Name _____ Date _____

THANK YOU, M'AM

Word List

| slung | stoop | suede | half nelson |
| whereupon | frail | plate | barren |

I. Write the words in the Word List in alphabetical order. The first one is done for you.

1. barren   4.   7.
2.   5.   8.
3.   6.

II. Write the word from the Word List that best completes

1. For her birthday, Tina got a beautiful purse made of blac

2. The woman had become quite _____ as a resul illness.

3. The yard was _____; there were no trees or flo anywhere.

4. Yoshi dragged his little brother across the lawn by puttin _____ about his neck.

5. Jenny carried the briefcase strap _____ across h

6. Rupa got a new car, _____ she stopped taking work.

7. Paul's apartment had no kitchen, so he had to cook on a

8. After supper, the family liked to sit on the _____ stories.

Name _____ Date _____

THANK YOU, M'AM

Make Predictions

You can begin **making predictions**, or thinking about what might happen next, from the minute you begin a story or book. Ask yourself: What does the title suggest? Are there any illustrations that give clues about what will happen? What might happen to the characters described in the beginning of the story?

Think about the beginning of "Thank You, M'am" when a boy tries to steal a woman's purse. You may have used what you knew about thieves to predict that the boy is headed for trouble.

However, good readers revise their predictions as new information is presented. As you continued to read "Thank You, M'am," your predictions likely changed. When the woman did not turn him in, but rather befriended him, you may have revised your predictions.

Read the title of a short story below. Make a prediction about the story based on the title. Then read each excerpt and revise your prediction based on each new piece of information.

1. "Marathon Woman"
   PREDICTION: _____

2. Juanita wasn't sure if she could outlast the other marathoners, certainly Jolie didn't think so.
   REVISED PREDICTION: _____

3. When the rain began, the mud splattered everywhere. She wondered whether the other racers were feeling as though they too could slip at any moment and the race would be over for them, finding themselves in an out-of-breath heap. The elbow she had sprained last year was beginning to ache, but she just kept fighting to finish the race.
   REVISED PREDICTION: _____

4. Finally, the race was over. Juanita finished with mud in her hair and up her arms, sweat dripping from her body, and tears streaming from her eyes. Her wheelchair was filthy but she'd kept spinning the wheels. What would Jolie say now?
   FINAL PREDICTION: _____

72 ■ PURPLE LEVEL, Unit 4

Students practice **critical reading skills** such as making predictions, recognizing fact and opinion, and identifying main idea and supporting details.

Comprehensive support helps you manage your diverse classrooms.

*The **Language Enrichment Workbook** meets a wide range of student needs. The activities are ideal for students with limited English proficiency or for those who need extra support with language arts skills.*

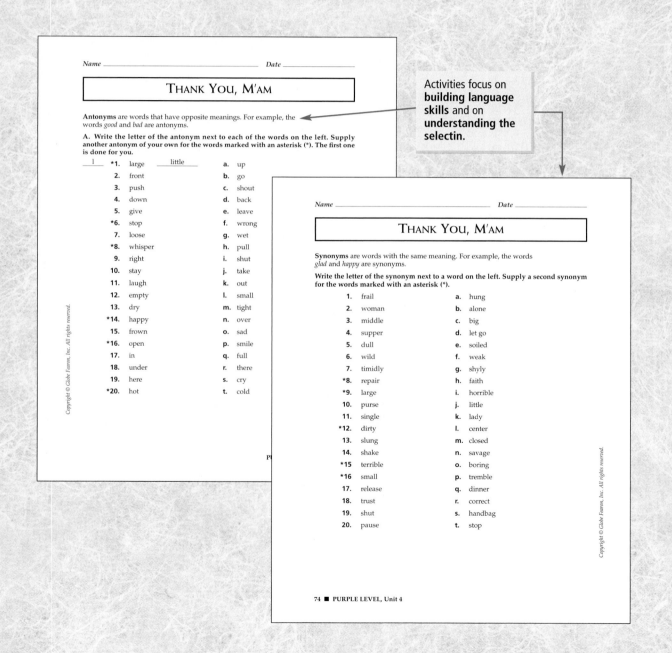

Name _____ Date _____

THANK YOU, M'AM

Antonyms are words that have opposite meanings. For example, the words *good* and *bad* are antonyms.

A. Write the letter of the antonym next to each of the words on the left. Supply another antonym of your own for the words marked with an asterisk (*). The first one is done for you.

l	*1.	large	little		a.	up
	2.	front			b.	go
	3.	push			c.	shout
	4.	down			d.	back
	5.	give			e.	leave
	*6.	stop			f.	wrong
	7.	loose			g.	wet
	*8.	whisper			h.	pull
	9.	right			i.	shut
	10.	stay			j.	take
	11.	laugh			k.	out
	12.	empty			l.	small
	13.	dry			m.	tight
	*14.	happy			n.	over
	15.	frown			o.	sad
	*16.	open			p.	smile
	17.	in			q.	full
	18.	under			r.	there
	19.	here			s.	cry
	*20.	hot			t.	cold

Activities focus on **building language skills** and on **understanding the selectin.**

Name _____ Date _____

THANK YOU, M'AM

Synonyms are words with the same meaning. For example, the words *glad* and *happy* are synonyms.

Write the letter of the synonym next to a word on the left. Supply a second synonym for the words marked with an asterisk (*).

1.	frail		a.	hung
2.	woman		b.	alone
3.	middle		c.	big
4.	supper		d.	let go
5.	dull		e.	soiled
6.	wild		f.	weak
7.	timidly		g.	shyly
*8.	repair		h.	faith
*9.	large		i.	horrible
10.	purse		j.	little
11.	single		k.	lady
*12.	dirty		l.	center
13.	slung		m.	closed
14.	shake		n.	savage
*15	terrible		o.	boring
*16	small		p.	tremble
17.	release		q.	dinner
18.	trust		r.	correct
19.	shut		s.	handbag
20.	pause		t.	stop

TT19

The Teacher's Resources helps tailor instruction to meet individual needs.

The **Teacher's Resources** is offered in print and CD-ROM formats. Resources include:

- Reinforcement worksheets for every selection
- Tests (customizable on CD-ROM)
- Writing Process worksheets
- Grammar, Usage, and Mechanics worksheets
- Literary Analysis worksheets
- Critical Thinking worksheets
- Speaking and Listening worksheets
- Assessment rubrics and answer keys

The **CD-ROM** includes the reproducibles for all four levels of Globe Fearon Literature, complete answer keys, and correlations to national and many state standards.

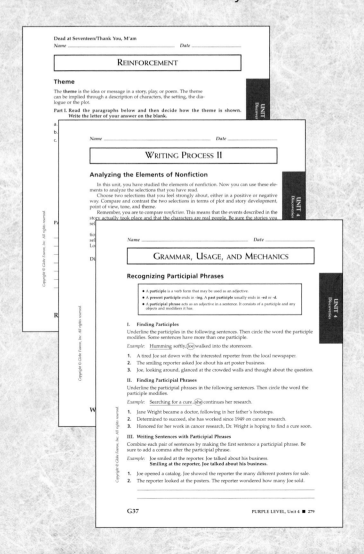

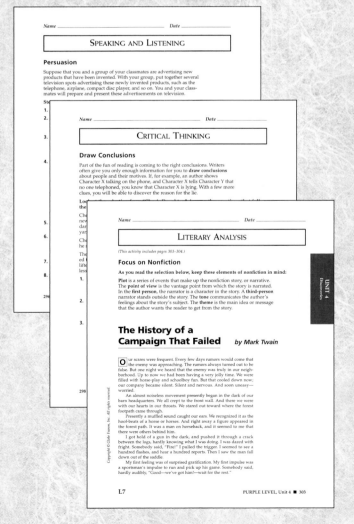

Assessment options and scoring rubrics offer maximum flexibility.

The **Teacher's Resources** provides traditional and alternative assessment options to help teachers assess individual student needs. Included are:

- Selection Tests and Unit Tests in a variety of formats, customizable on CD-ROM

- Writing Rubrics
- Speaking and Listening Rubrics
- Peer and Self-assessment Guides

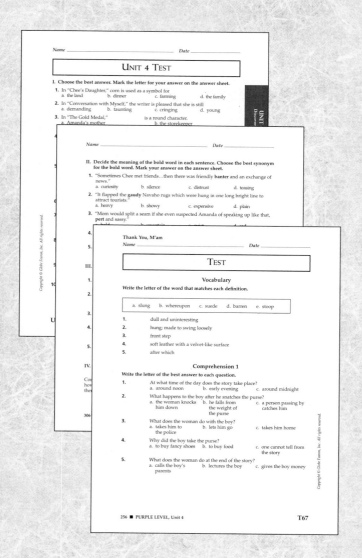

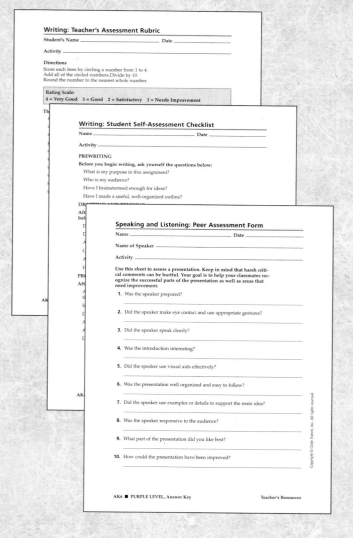

GLOBE FEARON LITERATURE
SCOPE AND SEQUENCE OF SKILLS

- READING COMPREHENSION
- LITERARY SKILLS
- VOCABULARY/WORD ATTACK
- PROCESS WRITING

- GRAMMAR, USAGE, AND MECHANICS
- CRITICAL THINKING
- SPEAKING AND LISTENING

- STUDY SKILLS
- RESEARCH SKILLS
- CRITICAL VIEWING

SCOPE AND SEQUENCE OF SKILLS	PURPLE LEVEL Units	GREEN LEVEL Units	SILVER LEVEL Units	GOLD LEVEL Units
■ READING COMPREHENSION				
Analyze Details	1, 5	4	1, 3, 4	1, 6
Compare and Contrast	1, 6	6	1, 3, 4, 6	2, 5
Distinguish Fact From Opinion	1, 4	4	1, 4, 6	6
Draw Conclusions	1, 2	1	2, 3	3
Evaluate Writer's Purpose	1, 2	4, 6	1, 5	4, 6
Evaluate Writer's Style	3	6	5	4
Identify Cause and Effect	5, 6	1, 2, 3, 6	1, 2, 5	5
Identify Changes in Relationships	5	2, 3		
Identify Main Idea and Supporting Details	4, 5	3, 4	1, 3, 4	6
Identify Mood	2, 6	3	5	4
Identify Persuasive Techniques	1, 5	3	1, 2	
Identify Relationships Between Characters	5, 6	2, 3, 6		
Identify Sequence of Events	5	2	5, 6	5
Identify Tone	1, 3, 6	1, 3	1, 6	3, 4, 5
Interpret Character	2	1, 3, 5	4, 6	2, 3
Make Generalizations		5	1	
Make Inferences	2, 4	1, 3, 5	1, 2, 3, 4, 5, 6	3, 5
Make Judgments	1, 3			1
Paraphrase	1	2, 3	6	5
Predict Outcomes	2, 3, 4	1, 5	4	3
Recognize/Interpret Figurative Language	1, 4, 6	1, 2, 3, 4, 5	2, 3, 4, 5	1, 2, 3, 4, 5, 6
Hyperbole	1	3	1, 2, 3	6
Idioms/Dialect	1		4	3
Imagery	1	3	4, 5	1, 5, 6
Metaphors	1, 6	3, 5	3, 5, 6	2, 3, 4, 6
Personification	1	2, 3, 5	3, 6	2, 3, 6

SCOPE AND SEQUENCE OF SKILLS	PURPLE LEVEL Units	GREEN LEVEL Units	SILVER LEVEL Units	GOLD LEVEL Units
Similes	1, 6	2, 3, 5	3, 5, 6	2, 3, 4, 6
Recognize Symbolism	4	3	4, 5	2, 3, 5
Summarize Text	4	2	6	5
Use Context Clues	1, 3, 5	1, 2, 4, 6	2, 3, 5	4, 5, 6
Use Prior Knowledge	2	2		6
■ LITERARY SKILLS				
Antagonist	3	4	1, 2, 5, 6	4
Author's Purpose	1, 2	3, 4, 6	1, 5, 6	4, 6
Autobiography	4	4	1, 2	6
Biography	1, 2, 3, 4, 5, 6	1, 2, 3, 4, 5, 6	1, 2, 3, 4, 5, 6	1, 2, 3, 4, 5, 6
Characterization	1, 2, 4, 5	1, 2, 3, 4, 5, 6	1, 2, 3, 4, 5, 6	1, 2, 3, 4, 5, 6
Comedy/Humor	1	1, 2, 4, 6	1, 4, 5	3, 5
Conflict	1, 2, 3, 4	1, 2, 3, 4, 6	2, 3, 4, 5	2, 3, 4, 5, 6
Connotation/Denotation	2, 3	5, 6	3, 5	1, 3
Drama	1, 2, 3	1, 3, 6	2, 5	2, 5
Epigram	6	3	1, 2, 3	3, 5
Essay			1, 3, 4	6
Fiction	1, 2, 3, 4, 5, 6	1, 2, 3, 4, 5, 6	1, 2, 3, 4, 5, 6	1, 2, 3, 4, 5, 6
Figures of Speech	1, 2, 3, 4, 5, 6	2, 3, 5	1, 2, 3, 5, 6	1, 2, 3, 4, 5, 6
Alliteration	3, 4	5	3, 5	1, 2
Hyperbole	1	3	1, 2, 3	6
Metaphors	1, 6	3, 5	3, 5, 6	2, 3, 4, 6
Onomatopoeia	3	5	2, 3, 6	5
Personification	1, 2	2, 3, 5	3, 6	3, 4, 6
Similes	1, 6	2, 3, 5	3, 5, 6	2, 3, 4, 6
Flashback	5	1	5	5
Folktales/Fables/Legends		1, 2	1, 2	1, 6
Foreshadowing	1, 2, 5	1, 2	2, 4, 5	5
Imagery	1, 2, 4, 6	2, 3	3, 4, 6	1, 2, 3, 4, 5, 6
Irony	1, 3, 5	2, 3, 6	4, 5	1, 3, 6
Journal/Diary/Letter/Almanac	1	6	1	3
Mood	2, 4	1, 3, 4, 5	1, 4, 5	1, 2, 5
Mystery/Suspense	2, 3, 4	1, 2	2, 5, 6	3, 4, 5
Nonfiction	1, 2, 3, 4, 5	1, 2, 3, 4, 5, 6	1, 2, 3, 4, 6	1, 2, 3, 5, 6
Plot Elements	2, 3, 5	1, 2, 4, 6	2, 3, 4, 5	2, 3, 4, 5, 6
Climax/Turning Point	2, 3, 5	1, 2, 4, 6	2, 3, 4, 5	2, 3, 4
Complication/Conflict	2, 3	1, 2, 4, 6	2, 3, 4, 5	2, 3, 4, 5, 6
Denouement/Conclusion/Resolution	2, 3, 5	1, 2, 4, 6	2, 3, 4	2, 4

SCOPE AND SEQUENCE OF SKILLS	PURPLE LEVEL Units	GREEN LEVEL Units	SILVER LEVEL Units	GOLD LEVEL Units
Exposition	2, 3	2, 4	1, 4	6
Falling Action/Rising Action	2, 3, 5	1, 6	4	4
Poetic Devices/Forms				
Closed Form	5, 6	3, 5	3, 4, 5, 6	2, 3, 4, 5
Open Form	1, 3, 6	3, 5	4, 5, 6	6
Repetition	4	3, 6	3, 5	5
Stanza		3	6	5
Poetry	1, 2, 3, 4, 5, 6	1, 2, 3, 4, 5, 6	1, 2, 5	1, 2, 3, 4, 5, 6
Ballad		3		1
Concrete		5		
Epic/Heroic	5	3		1
Haiku	4	3		
Lyric			2, 5	2
Narrative	2	4		1
Sonnet				2
Point of View	1, 2, 3, 4, 5, 6	1, 2, 3, 4, 5, 6	1, 2, 6	1, 2, 3, 4, 5, 6
Protagonist	3	1, 4		4
Rhyme	1, 2, 4	1, 3, 4, 5	3, 4, 5, 6	1, 2, 3, 4, 5, 6
Rhythm	3, 5, 6	3, 4, 5, 6	1, 2, 3, 5, 6	1, 2, 3, 4, 5
Satire		1		3, 4, 5, 6
Setting	2, 3, 4, 5	1, 2, 3, 4, 6	1, 4, 5, 6	1, 2, 3, 4, 5
Short Story	1, 2, 3	1, 2, 3, 4, 5, 6	2, 4, 5, 6	5, 6
Speaker	4	1, 4	1	
Style/Techniques	1, 2, 3, 4, 5, 6	1, 2, 3, 6	1, 4, 5	2
Surprise Ending	1, 2, 3, 4, 5	1, 2, 6	4, 5	
Symbols/Symbolism	2, 3, 4, 5, 6	1, 3, 4, 5, 6	1, 2, 4, 5, 6	1, 2, 3, 4, 5
Theme	1, 2, 3, 4, 5, 6	1, 2, 3, 4, 5, 6	1, 2, 3, 4, 6	1, 2, 3, 4, 5, 6
Tone/Attitude	1, 3, 4, 5, 6	1, 2, 3, 4, 5, 6	1, 4, 5, 6	1, 2, 3, 4, 5, 6
■ VOCABULARY/WORD ATTACK				
Antonyms	6	1, 2, 5, 6	2, 3, 5, 6	5, 6
Archaic Words	1, 2	1	1	2, 3
Compound Words		3	1	6
Connotation/Denotation	2, 3	5, 6	3, 5	1, 3
Context	1, 3, 4, 5, 6	1, 2, 3, 4, 5, 6	1, 2, 3, 4, 5, 6	1, 2, 4, 5, 6
Contractions	1, 2, 4, 5	3, 4, 5	2, 4	2
Dialect	2		3	3
Dictionary Pronunciation Key	4	2, 3		4
Etymology	2, 5, 6	2, 3	1, 3, 4, 5, 6	1, 2, 3, 5

SCOPE AND SEQUENCE OF SKILLS	PURPLE LEVEL Units	GREEN LEVEL Units	SILVER LEVEL Units	GOLD LEVEL Units
Figurative Language	1, 2, 3, 4, 5, 6	1, 2, 3, 4, 5, 6	2, 3, 4, 5, 6	1, 2, 3, 4, 5, 6
Homographs		3	6	6
Homophones	1, 5, 6	1, 2, 4, 5	2, 3	1, 3, 4
Letter Sounds	1, 2, 4, 6	2, 5	3, 4, 5, 6	1, 2, 4, 5
Meanings of New Words	1, 2, 3, 4, 5, 6	1, 2, 3, 4, 5, 6	1, 2, 3, 4, 5, 6	1, 2, 3, 4, 5, 6
Multiple-Meaning Words	1, 2, 3, 4, 5	1, 2, 3, 5, 6	1, 2, 5, 6	1, 2, 3, 6
Parts of Speech	1, 2, 4, 5, 6	1, 2, 3, 4, 5, 6	1, 2, 3, 4, 5, 6	1, 2, 3, 4, 5, 6
Adjectives	1, 2, 4, 5, 6	4, 5, 6	2, 4, 5, 6	1, 3, 4, 5
Adverbs	4, 5, 6	4, 5, 6	2, 5, 6	1, 3, 4
Conjunctions	2, 6			4
Nouns	1, 2, 3, 4, 5, 6	1, 2, 3	1, 2, 4, 5, 6	1, 2, 3, 4, 5, 6
Prepositions	4			4
Pronouns	1, 3, 4, 6	1, 3, 4, 5	4, 5, 6	2, 4, 5
Verbs	1, 2, 3, 4, 5, 6	1, 2, 3, 4, 5, 6	1, 4, 5, 6	1, 2, 3, 4, 6
Phonetic Respellings	1, 2, 3, 4, 5, 6	1, 2, 3, 4, 5, 6	1, 2, 3, 4, 5, 6	1, 2, 3, 4, 5, 6
Prefixes	2, 6	2, 3, 4, 5, 6	6	4, 5
de-, dis-	2, 6	3		5
fore-		3		
il-	6			5
im-, in-, ir-, non-, un-	2, 6	2, 3, 4, 5, 6	6	4, 5
mis-			6	
pre-		5		
re-		2	6	5
Roots	1, 2, 3, 5	2, 3, 4, 5, 6	1, 2, 6	3, 4, 5
Shades of Meaning	1, 2, 4, 5	1, 2, 4, 5	3, 5, 6	1, 2, 5, 6
Slang	6	3		
Suffixes	1, 2	1, 3, 4, 5, 6	2	1, 2, 4, 5
-able	1		2	
-acy, -cy		3		
-ance, -ence	2	1, 5	2	
-ard	1			
-ation, -tion		4, 5		5
-er, -or		3	2	1
-ery				2
-ful	1		2	4
-hood		6		
-ible		5		
-ic	1			

SCOPE AND SEQUENCE OF SKILLS	PURPLE LEVEL Units	GREEN LEVEL Units	SILVER LEVEL Units	GOLD LEVEL Units
-ion		5	2	
-ish	1			4
-ity	2		2	
-less	1	4, 5, 6	2	
-ly	4	4, 5, 6	2, 5, 6	
-ment		1	2	
-ness	2	4		
-ory			2	
-tude	2			
-ward			2	
Synonyms	1, 2, 3, 4, 5, 6	1, 2, 3, 4, 5, 6	3, 5	1, 2, 5, 6
Technical/Occupational/Jargon		1, 2	5	
Word Parts	1, 2	3	1, 4, 6	6
■ PROCESS WRITING				
Prewriting	1, 2, 3, 4, 5, 6	1, 2, 3, 4, 5, 6	1, 2, 3, 4, 5, 6	1, 2, 3, 4, 5, 6
Brainstorm/Freewrite	1, 2, 3, 4, 5, 6	1, 2, 3, 4, 5, 6	4, 5, 6	1, 2
List:	1, 2, 3, 4, 5, 6	1, 2, 3, 4, 5, 6	1, 2, 3, 4, 5, 6	1, 2, 3, 4, 5, 6
Actions/Events	3	1, 2	2, 3, 6	1, 3, 4, 5
Causes/Conditions/Factors	4	1, 2	4	4
Characters	3, 4, 6	5	1, 5, 6	3, 4
Descriptions	3, 6	2, 3, 5	2, 4, 5, 6	
Emotions/Thoughts	1, 3, 4, 6	1, 2, 3, 5, 6	2, 3, 6	1, 2, 4, 5
Examples/Explanations/Facts	2, 3, 4, 5, 6	2	2	1, 4
Ideas	1, 2, 3, 4, 6	2, 3, 4, 5	1, 2, 4	2, 3, 4, 5
Literary Elements	1, 4, 6	1, 2, 3, 4, 5, 6	2, 3, 5	1, 2, 3, 4, 5
Points/Reactions/Responses	2, 3, 5, 6	2, 3, 6	1, 2	
Questions/Answers/Solutions	2, 3, 5, 6	2, 5, 6	4, 5, 6	1, 2, 4, 5
Reasons	1, 3	1, 2, 3	2, 3, 4, 6	2, 5
Similarities/Differences	1, 3	5		
Words/Phrases	3	3, 5	3, 6	2
Outline	1, 2, 3, 5, 6	1, 2, 3, 4, 5, 6	1, 2, 4, 5, 6	1, 2, 3, 4
Writing	1, 2, 3, 4, 5, 6	1, 2, 3, 4, 5, 6	1, 2, 3, 4, 5, 6	1, 2, 3, 4, 5, 6
Additional Episode	1, 2, 3, 4, 5	1, 2, 3, 4, 5, 6	1, 2, 3, 4, 5	1, 2, 3, 4, 5, 6
Characterization		1, 2	2, 4, 5	
Comparisons	1, 2, 5, 6	1, 3, 4, 5	1, 2, 3, 4, 5, 6	1, 2, 3, 4, 5
Composition	1, 2, 3, 4, 5, 6	1, 2, 3, 4, 5	1, 2, 3, 4, 5, 6	1, 2, 3, 4, 5, 6
Description	1, 2, 3, 4, 5, 6	1, 2, 3, 4, 5, 6	1, 2, 3, 4, 5, 6	1, 2, 3, 4, 5, 6
Dialogue	1, 2, 5, 6	1, 2	1, 2, 3, 5, 6	1, 2, 3, 4, 6

SCOPE AND SEQUENCE OF SKILLS	PURPLE LEVEL Units	GREEN LEVEL Units	SILVER LEVEL Units	GOLD LEVEL Units
Epigram	6	3		3
Essay	3	1, 3, 4, 6	2, 5	1, 2
Explanation	2, 3, 4, 5, 6	1, 2, 3, 4, 5, 6	1, 2, 3, 4, 5, 6	1, 2, 3, 4, 5, 6
Figure of Speech		3		
Firsthand Report	2, 3, 4, 5, 6	1, 2, 3	1, 2, 3, 4, 6	2, 3, 4, 5, 6
Irony/Satire	3	1, 2	4	4
Imagery	1	3	3	4
Journal/Diary Entry	1	1, 3, 6	3	1, 3, 6
Letter	1, 2, 4	2, 3, 4, 5, 6	1, 2, 5	1
Narrative	1	1, 2	1, 2, 3, 4, 6	1, 3, 4, 5, 6
Newspaper Article	2	3, 4, 5	4, 6	1, 6
Notes	1, 2, 3, 4, 5, 6		1, 2, 3, 4	1, 3, 5, 6
Opinion	1, 2, 3, 4, 5, 6	1, 2, 3, 4, 5, 6	1, 2, 3, 4, 5, 6	1, 2, 3, 4, 5
Paragraphs	1, 2, 3, 4, 5, 6	1, 2, 3, 4, 5, 6	1, 2, 3, 4, 5, 6	1, 2, 3, 4, 5, 6
Persuasion	2, 5	1, 2, 3, 4, 5, 6	1, 2, 3, 5, 6	5
Play	3		5	
Poem	1, 2, 4, 5, 6	1, 2, 3, 4, 5, 6	3, 4, 5, 6	1, 2, 4, 5
Review	1, 4, 6	1, 2, 3, 5	1, 3	2, 4, 5, 6
Similes/Metaphors		1, 2	6	2, 3
Speech	3, 5	1, 2	1, 2	4
Story	1, 2, 5, 6	1, 2, 3, 4, 5	1, 2, 3, 4, 6	1, 3, 4, 5, 6
Summary		3	6	5
Television Report	3		1	1
Revising	1, 2, 3, 4, 5, 6	1, 2, 3, 4, 5, 6	1, 2, 3, 4, 5, 6	1, 2, 3, 4, 5, 6
Include:				
Character's Thoughts/Ideas/Feelings	3, 6	1, 2, 4	2, 6	1, 4
Description	1, 2, 5, 6	1, 3, 4	2, 6	3, 5
Details	1, 2, 3, 4, 6	1, 2, 4, 5	1, 2, 4, 5, 6	1, 2, 3, 5, 6
Dialogue	5, 6	3		2, 4
Literary Elements		3	3	
Observations	3	3	3	
Point of View		1		
Quotations	4, 5, 6	1, 5	6	3, 5
Reasons/Examples	3	4, 5	4, 6	2, 4
Topic Sentences	1, 4, 5	2		
Transition Words	4, 5	1, 4, 5		5
Maintain:				
Believability	4	1, 2, 3, 5	5	1, 2

SCOPE AND SEQUENCE OF SKILLS	PURPLE LEVEL Units	GREEN LEVEL Units	SILVER LEVEL Units	GOLD LEVEL Units
Consistency	1, 2, 3, 4, 5, 6	1, 2, 3, 4, 5, 6	1, 2, 3, 5, 6	1, 3
Clarity	1, 2, 3, 4, 6	1, 2, 3, 4, 5, 6	1, 2, 5, 6	1, 2, 3, 4, 5, 6
Order	5	2, 3, 6	5, 6	5
Proofreading	1, 2, 3, 4, 5, 6	1, 2, 3, 4, 5, 6	1, 2, 3, 4, 5, 6	1, 2, 3, 4, 5, 6
Correct:				
Capitalization/Punctuation	1, 2, 3, 4, 5, 6	1, 2, 3, 4, 5, 6	1, 2, 3, 4, 5, 6	1, 2, 3, 4, 5, 6
Grammar	1, 2, 3, 4, 6	1, 2, 3, 4	1, 2, 4, 6	1, 2, 3, 4, 5, 6
Letter/Poetry Form		2, 3		2
Paragraphing	2, 5, 6	1, 3, 4, 5, 6	4	1, 5
Spelling	1, 2, 4, 5, 6	1, 2, 3, 4, 5	1, 2, 3, 5	1, 2, 3, 4, 6
■ GRAMMAR, USAGE, AND MECHANICS				
Adjectives	1, 2, 4, 5, 6	4, 5, 6	2, 4, 5, 6	1
Adverbs	4, 5, 6	4, 5, 6	2, 5, 6	1
Conjunctions	4, 5, 6	4, 5, 6	2, 5, 6	1
Nouns	1	1, 2, 3, 5, 6	5	1, 5, 6
Prepositions	4	5		3
Pronouns	2	3	1	1
Verbs	1, 3, 4	2	2	2
Punctuation	2, 4, 5, 6	1, 3, 6	1, 3, 4, 5, 6	4, 5, 6
Colon/Semicolon	4, 6	6	6	
Commas	6	3, 6	3, 4	4, 5, 6
Quotations	5, 6	1, 6	4, 5	4, 6
Word Series	2, 5, 6	6		5, 6
Sentences	1, 5	2	1, 4, 5	1, 5, 6
Syntax				3
■ CRITICAL THINKING				
Analyze	1, 2, 3, 4, 5, 6	1, 2, 3, 4, 5, 6	1, 2, 3, 4, 5, 6	1, 2, 3, 4, 5, 6
Analyze Analogies		1, 6		
Analyze Details	1	1		
Analyze Syllogisms	3			
Apply	2, 3, 4	1, 2, 4, 5	1, 3, 4, 5	1, 3, 4, 6
Classify/Categorize	2		3, 5	2, 3
Compare and Contrast	1, 4, 5, 6	1, 2, 3, 4, 5, 6	1, 3, 4, 5, 6	2, 3, 5
Distinguish Fact From Opinion	1, 2, 4	4	1, 4, 6	1, 6
Draw Conclusions	1, 2, 3, 4, 5, 6	1, 2, 3, 4, 5, 6	1, 2, 3, 4, 5, 6	1, 2, 3, 4, 5, 6
Evaluate	1, 2, 3, 4	4, 5, 6	1, 2, 3, 4, 5	1, 2, 4, 6
Generalize	1, 6	2, 5	1, 4, 5	4
Infer/Interpret	1, 2, 3, 4, 5, 6	1, 2, 3	2, 3, 4, 5	1, 2, 3, 4

SCOPE AND SEQUENCE OF SKILLS	PURPLE LEVEL Units	GREEN LEVEL Units	SILVER LEVEL Units	GOLD LEVEL Units
Predict	1, 2, 3, 4	1, 2, 3	2, 5	1, 3, 4
Reason Inductively/Deductively	1, 3			
Recognize Cause and Effect	5, 6	1		1, 6
Recognize Character Conflict			2	4
Recognize Order			1, 2, 4	
Summarize	1, 2, 4	1, 2, 4	1, 5	1, 2, 5
Synthesize	4		3, 5	4
■ CRITICAL THINKING AND DRAMA				
Adapt a Play for Movies/Radio/TV	2	1	2, 5	
Compare and Contrast Characters	1, 3	3, 6	2, 5	3, 4, 5
Interpret the Effect of Imagery	1			4
Make Inferences About Characters	1, 2, 3	1, 3, 6	2, 5	2, 3, 4, 5
Predict Outcomes	3	1, 3	2, 5	3, 4
Recognize Cause and Effect	1, 2, 3	1, 3, 6	2, 5	2, 3, 4
Summarize a Play				5
■ CRITICAL THINKING AND FICTION				
Analyze the Effect of Setting	3, 4, 5	1, 2, 3, 4, 6	2, 4, 5, 6	1, 3, 5, 6
Analyze Sequence in a Story	1, 2, 3, 4, 5, 6	1, 2, 3, 4, 5, 6	2, 3, 4, 5, 6	1, 4
Analyze Solutions	2, 3, 5, 6	1, 2, 4	2, 4, 5, 6	6
Compare and Contrast	1, 2, 3, 4, 6	1, 2, 3, 4, 5, 6	1, 2, 3, 4, 5, 6	3, 4, 5, 6
Draw Conclusions	1, 2, 3, 4, 5, 6	1, 2, 3, 4, 5, 6	1, 2, 3, 4, 5, 6	1, 3, 4, 5
Identify Cause and Effect	1, 2, 3, 4, 5, 6		2, 3, 4, 5, 6	1, 3, 4, 5, 6
Identify Exaggeration			1	4, 6
Make Inferences About Characters	1, 2, 3, 4, 5, 6	1, 2, 3, 4, 5, 6	1, 2, 3, 4, 5, 6	1, 3, 4, 5, 6
Paraphrase	2, 3, 5		2, 6	
Recognize Relevant Details	1, 5	4	1, 3	6
Understand Plausibility	1, 2, 3, 4		1, 2, 3	
■ CRITICAL THINKING AND NONFICTION				
Compare and Contrast Words	2, 3, 4	2, 3, 4, 5, 6	1, 2, 4, 6	2, 5
Evaluate Biographical/Autobiographical Subject	4	2, 4	1, 2, 6	6
Evaluate Historical Inferences	4, 5	1	1, 2	1, 3, 5, 6
Find Relevant Evidence	1, 2, 3, 4, 5	1, 2, 3, 4, 5, 6	1, 2, 3, 4, 6	2, 3, 5, 6
Infer Writer's Purpose	2, 3, 4, 5	2, 3, 6	1, 2, 4, 6	2, 5, 6
Recognize Generalizations	3, 4, 5	1, 2, 5, 6	1, 2, 4, 6	5
Recognize Persuasive Techniques	2, 3, 5	3	1, 2, 3	
Separate Details	1, 2, 3, 4, 5	1, 2, 3, 4, 5, 6	1, 2, 3, 4, 6	1, 2, 3, 5, 6
Separate Fact From Opinion	2, 3, 4	1, 2, 3, 4, 5, 6	1, 2, 6	1, 2, 5
Summarize an Essay			1, 4	

SCOPE AND SEQUENCE OF SKILLS	PURPLE LEVEL Units	GREEN LEVEL Units	SILVER LEVEL Units	GOLD LEVEL Units
Understand Sequence of Events	2, 3, 4, 5	2, 3, 4, 5, 6	1, 2, 6	2, 5
■ CRITICAL THINKING AND POETRY				
Interpret Figures of Speech	1, 2 3, 6	2, 3, 5	3, 5, 6	2, 3, 4, 5, 6
Interpret Sensory Words	1		3, 5	5
Interpret Symbols	1, 2, 4, 6	3	3, 4	2, 3, 4
Make Inferences About Speaker	1, 2, 3, 4, 5, 6	1, 2, 3, 4, 5, 6	1, 2, 3, 4, 5, 6	1, 2, 3, 4, 5, 6
Make Inferences About Theme	1, 2, 3, 6	1, 2, 3, 4	1, 2, 5, 6	1, 2, 3, 4, 5, 6
Paraphrase Poetry	1, 2, 3, 4, 6	1, 3, 5, 6	2, 3, 4, 5, 6	1, 2, 3, 4, 5, 6
Recognize Assertions	1, 2, 3, 5	1, 2, 3, 4, 5, 6	1, 2, 3, 5, 6	1, 2, 3, 4, 5, 6
Understand Cause and Effect	1, 2, 3, 4, 5, 6	1, 2, 3, 4, 5, 6	1, 2, 3, 4, 5, 6	1, 2, 3, 4, 5, 6
■ SPEAKING AND LISTENING				
Character Analysis and Interpretation	1, 2, 3, 5, 6	3, 4, 6	4, 5	2, 5
Create Dialogue	1, 2	1, 3	2, 3, 4, 5	3
Create Monologue	3, 5			2, 6
Debate/Panel Discussion	2, 4, 6	1, 2, 3, 4, 5, 6	3, 4, 6	1, 2, 3, 6
Dramatic Reading	6	6	3, 4	1, 2, 4, 5, 6
Fiction Analysis	2		2, 3, 5	2, 3, 4
Folktale		2		
Group Presentation		1, 2, 3, 4, 6	1	5
Interview	1, 2, 3, 4, 5, 6	2, 3, 4, 5		4
Oral Directions			1	3
Oral Interpretation	1, 2, 4, 5	1, 6	1, 2, 3	1, 4
Pantomime		5		1
Persuasive Presentation	2, 3, 4, 5	2	1, 2, 4	1, 3, 5, 6
Poetry/Song	1	2, 3, 6	2, 3, 4, 5, 6	1, 4, 5
Plot/Theme Discussion	3	4	2, 5	
Radio or Television Show	1, 4, 6	2, 3, 4, 5, 6	2, 4, 5	1, 3, 4, 5, 6
Role Play	1, 3, 4, 5, 6	6		4
Speech	4	4	1	3
■ STUDY SKILLS				
Note-Taking	4	4	1	1, 4
Outline	1	4	6	6
Reading Techniques	3, 6	1, 2, 3, 6	1, 2, 4, 6	1, 2, 4, 5, 6
Preview	6	1, 6		1, 5
Identify Main Idea	3	1, 2, 3	1, 4, 6	1, 2, 4, 6
Paraphrase		3	2, 6	
Read Table of Contents	3	3		
Recognize Persuasion/Propaganda	1	3	2	

SCOPE AND SEQUENCE OF SKILLS	PURPLE LEVEL Units	GREEN LEVEL Units	SILVER LEVEL Units	GOLD LEVEL Units
Reference Books	3	6		
Study Habits	1, 2, 3, 4, 5, 6	1, 2, 3, 4, 5, 6	1, 2, 3, 4, 5, 6	1, 2, 3, 4, 5, 6
Summarize	4	3	4, 6	2, 5
Test-Taking Strategies	1, 2, 3, 4, 5, 6	1, 2, 3, 4, 5, 6	1, 2, 3, 4, 5, 6	1, 2, 3, 4, 5, 6
Essay Tests		2		
Objective Tests	5, 6	1		
■ RESEARCH SKILLS				
Almanac/Atlas				6
Dictionary	3	1, 2, 3, 4, 5, 6	1, 2, 3, 4, 5, 6	1, 2, 3, 4, 5, 6
Encyclopedia			1, 5	6
Follow Directions	1, 2, 3, 4, 5, 6	1, 2, 3, 4, 5, 6	1, 2, 3, 4, 5, 6	1, 2, 3, 4, 5, 6
Glossary		2, 5	1	
Note-Taking	4	4, 6	1	
Recognize Persuasion/Propaganda		3	1	
Reference Sources	3		1	1, 6
Thesaurus				2, 5
■ CRITICAL VIEWING				
Analyze and Interpret Art From Other Cultures	4, 6	1, 2, 3, 4, 5	2	6
Interpret Genre Painting		1, 3, 5	2	2, 3, 4
Interpret Impressionist Painting	1	3	4, 6	3, 4, 5, 6
Examine Landscape/Seascape	2, 4, 5	1, 2	2, 3, 4, 5, 6	2, 3, 4, 6
Examine Lithographs			1, 3, 4	
Examine Older Art Forms	6	1		1, 3
Examine Photographic, Photorealistic Art		3	3	5
Examine Portraits	5		1, 2, 5	2, 3, 4
Examine Sketches		5	4	4
Interpret Expressionistic Painting	1	2	2, 4, 6	
Interpret Modern Art	1, 2, 4, 5, 6	1, 4, 5, 6	4	5
Interpret Primitive Art			2, 3	
Interpret Realistic Art	1, 2, 3, 4, 5	5	1, 6	2
Interpret Romantic Art	2, 3		3	2, 4
Interpret Surrealistic and Mystic Art	1, 2	2, 5, 6		6

GLOBE FEARON LITERATURE PROFESSIONAL DEVELOPMENT ARTICLES

Globe Fearon understands the importance of providing quality literature instruction to students. Today's educators must do so while facing the daily challenges of meeting the diverse needs of their students. The following pages contain additional teaching suggestions to help you to tailor instruction to your students' needs. We welcome your comments and suggestions for further staff development ideas. Visit our Web site, *www.globefearon.com*, to share ideas with Globe Fearon and other educators.

CREATING A POSITIVE ENVIRONMENT FOR DIVERSE LEARNERS
(TT33–TT34)

PROMOTING COMPREHENSION THROUGH GUIDED READING LESSONS
(TT35–TT36)

SUCCESSFUL EXPERIENCES IN LITERATURE FOR STUDENTS WITH LIMITED ENGLISH PROFICIENCY (LEP)
(TT37–TT39)

BLOCK SCHEDULING
(TT40–TT43)

CREATING A POSITIVE ENVIRONMENT FOR DIVERSE LEARNERS

By Deborah Walker

The typical classroom includes students who have different ways of learning, understanding what they have just learned, and applying that understanding to other materials and situations.

ADDRESSING THE MIXED-ABILITY CLASSROOM

Teachers today, more than ever before, must accommodate a broad range of student abilities, interests, learning styles, and other special needs. The typical classroom includes students who have different ways of learning, understanding what they have just learned, and applying that understanding to other materials and situations. Students may be highly visual learners, auditory learners, tactile learners, or kinesthetic learners. To add to this complexity, a typical classroom may be comprised of students who have attained different levels of English proficiency. More special-needs students are being mainstreamed into general education classes. All of these factors combine to offer an extraordinary challenge to the educator teaching in an average classroom.

As mandated by the National Education Standards, "All students, regardless of their ability level, learning style, interests, ethnic background, or physical limitations shall have the opportunity to attain high levels of literacy." The message to educators is clear: A variety of learning approaches and activities must be employed to motivate and engage all students in the learning process. This means that teachers must recognize and respond to student diversity and then encourage all students to participate fully in the learning process.

GLOBE FEARON LITERATURE AND THE DIVERSE CLASSROOM

Globe Fearon Literature encourages and provides opportunities for students to be actively involved in the learning process. A flexible textbook, such as *Globe Fearon Literature*, combines teacher-centered instruction, oral reading, discussion opportunities, cooperative group activities, and media and technology. Following the activities in the textbook creates an ideal environment to meet the needs of diverse learners.

Additionally, to address the needs of diverse learners, a mixture of learning tasks or activities should be employed on a regular basis. With *Globe Fearon Literature*, teachers can accommodate and enable students with diverse backgrounds to be successful in a variety of learning situations, such as active inquiry, collaboration, and class interaction. Opportunities for activity-based learning should be provided as often as possible to allow all students an equal chance to succeed. Suggestions for these activities are provided in *Globe Fearon Literature*.

You can achieve a maximum degree of flexibility in the classroom by making a few adjustments to your teaching style, learning environment, and assessments. The lessons in *Globe Fearon Literature* are structured so that every student is given the opportunity to learn. By creating a student-centered environment in your classroom, your lesson plan will focus on a variety of learners—tactile, visual, kinesthetic, and auditory, as well as special-needs and English-as-a-second-language (ESL) students. Your role as teacher becomes that of facilitator, coach, and mentor to your students. You can use *Globe Fearon Literature* to enhance the knowledge of students of all abilities and help all of your students reach their individual potential.

This literature program gives you the opportunity to present a number of assignment options to your students. While all students will read the literature selection, you may assign a variety of additional in-class and homework activities to allow students to demonstrate understanding of the material. You can give students the assignments that best meets their learning styles, ability levels, or interests. For example, one student may describe in detail how a quotation from a poem relates to a piece of fine art in the Student Edition. The student may present his or her proof of understanding orally, in writing, or by using a media presentation. Another student may role-play a character in a literature selection. Class discussion will reveal whether the character is flat or round and help to determine if the assignment was completed successfully. A group of students may work cooperatively to write a screenplay of a story.

One challenge you might have in implementing new strategies for reaching diverse learners is how to assess the outcomes in a meaningful way. Assessments are not based on the traditional percentage of correct information remembered, but on the depth of understanding of the selection that the students demonstrate. Rubrics that include the criteria that you might look for in assessing each student's performance on speaking and listening and writing activities are provided in the Answer Key section of the *Teacher's Resources*. It is useful to give students the criteria ahead of time so that they all know exactly what is expected of them and how the assignment will be assessed. This straightforward method helps students reflect on their preferences, explore their alternatives, organize their learning experiences, and take responsibility for their learning. It also broadens and energizes your teaching style. Reproducible rubrics and forms for student self-assessment and peer assessment are also provided in the Answer Key section of the *Teacher's Resources*.

PROMOTING COMPREHENSION THROUGH GUIDED READING LESSONS

By Josephine Gemake, Ph.D.

There are many ways that students can be guided in their reading of stories, plays, essays, poems, and informational texts. Teachers' choices of methods and activities should factor in students' interests and abilities and the difficulty levels of the texts that they will read and interpret.

The scene is common in today's schools—teachers wondering how to make literature meaningful for students. Of course, there are no absolute answers. The Globe Fearon Literature program, however, offers flexible lesson formats that have been developed with today's students and teachers in mind.

The selections in the program have been carefully chosen to expose students to exemplary pieces of classic and contemporary literature. Each selection is preceded by a concise explanation of a literary element such as tone, theme, character, setting, plot, and so on.

Reading comprehension is a key element of the Globe Fearon Literature program. A Reading Focus feature in every selection helps students become more skillful and strategic readers. Some of the comprehension techniques include making predictions, summarizing and paraphrasing texts, drawing conclusions, and identifying author's purpose.

Information about unfamiliar and difficult words is provided throughout the program. In this way, students can learn the meanings and pronunciations of words at the most relevant time—while they read.

Follow-up questions and writing activities have been designed to deepen students' understanding of the literary work they have read. Students are encouraged to discuss universal themes and how they relate to their own lives.

The Teaching Plan and point-of-use annotations in the Teacher's Edition provide activities and discussion opportunities before, during, and after reading. A description of each section of the Teaching Plan follows.

INTRODUCE

The Motivation activity and the Purpose-Setting Question help teachers guide students to activate prior knowledge and to make connections to real life. These brief activities prompt students to compare and contrast, predict, evaluate, and discuss concepts relevant to the selection they are about to read.

Teachers may also facilitate the development of new ideas by incorporating the following techniques into this section of the lesson:

- **Graphic Organizers** The use of graphic organizers—diagrams that illustrate connections among ideas—helps students to organize their thinking and to relate ideas. These organizers may be webs, maps, timelines, outlines, or idea clusters. Graphic organizers visually display associations and properties of topics. They are also used in vocabulary development to display word relationships.

- **Anticipation or Prediction Guides** To create these guides, a teacher writes statements about selections to be read on a chalkboard or reproducible. Students respond to these statements with predictions about what they think will happen. Statements are written so that thinking is stimulated at the literal, interpretive, and applied levels.

- During prereading time, strategies necessary for reading and interpreting selections are taught. Teacher modeling through "think alouds" is an important part of the procedure in skill development lessons. Think alouds enable students to watch how a teacher uses the selection objectives being taught to gain meaning from the text.

READ

In this section of the Teaching Plan, teachers are given ideas to support two key elements in the Student Edition: the Learn About feature and the Reading Focus feature. Literary skills include analysis of traditional elements of literature such as plot, theme, character, and setting; and of literary techniques such as figurative language, foreshadowing, and flashback. Reading Focus features highlight key comprehension strategies such as recognizing an author's purpose, identifying main idea and supporting details, summarizing and paraphrasing, and drawing conclusions.

Sidenote annotations throughout each selection provide further support for these lesson elements, as well as for critical thinking and discussion.

Teachers can also guide silent-reading comprehension using the following techniques:

- Have students read silently to find answers to questions posed by the teacher.

- Ask students to pose their own questions about events and ideas in the text and to read to find the answers.

- Have students predict, or form hypotheses, about ideas and events that will occur, and have them read to confirm or modify their predictions.

CLOSE

After reading, students complete activities in the Review the Selection section. These activities reinforce and extend ideas developed during lessons. Skills necessary for literary interpretation and appreciation are practiced, and mastery of these skills is evaluated. Vocabulary is recalled and reviewed. Reading skills and literary skills that were introduced at the beginning of a selection are reviewed and reinforced through writing. Students are also encouraged to write personal responses to each selection and to use process writing to complete an assignment.

There are many ways that students can be guided in their reading of stories, plays, essays, poems and informational texts. Teachers' choices of methods and activities should factor in students' interests and abilities and the difficulty level of the texts that they will read and interpret. The techniques described in this article will help students to develop comprehension skills and have the added advantage of being easily adapted in existing curriculum structures.

Successful Experiences in Literature for Students with Limited English Proficiency (LEP)

By Alfed Schifini, Ph.D.
Revised by Dr. Virginia Bryg

All students, including those whose primary language is one other than English, should have access to challenging material and literature. Yet not all students bring the same world knowledge and language skills to school.

Rapid demographic changes in the United States have had a direct impact on public schools. Every year an increased number of students come to school with a primary language other than English. Students with limited English proficiency (LEP) often lack the language skills needed to benefit from instruction geared for English proficient speakers.

All students, including those whose primary language is one other than English, should have access to challenging material and literature. Yet not all students bring the same level of literacy to school. Some LEP students may never have been formally educated in their homelands. Others may have had a rich educational experience and have achieved a high level of literacy in their native language. Finally, teachers may also encounter native speakers of English who demonstrate deficiencies in literacy.

EDUCATIONAL APPROACHES

ENGLISH AS A SECOND LANGUAGE

In recent years, students in U.S. schools who are totally non-English proficient have been able to gain immediate access to literature and basic subject matter through instruction in their native languages while they learn the English language. All LEP students should be provided with a rigorous program of English as a Second Language (ESL). As students' proficiency in English increases, the dependency on primary language instruction decreases. A strong ESL program provides students with the necessary foundation in English and ensures a smooth transition to instruction taught in a mainstream context.

ESL AND CONTENT AREA INSTRUCTION

In addition to beginning-level ESL courses geared toward functional fluency, other ESL classes that incorporate content material, such as math, science, and social studies, have been designed for intermediate ESL speakers. These content-area ESL courses teach the terminology and key requisite concepts needed to provide a broader linguistic and experiential base for second-language learners.

Recent advances in language acquisition theory have made it clear that language is acquired by receiving meaningful input in a low-anxiety environment.

Language is more effectively learned when conscious language learning is not the focus of the lessons. It follows, therefore, that if subject matter can be made comprehensible through a variety of means, such as by demonstrations, visual aids, hands-on material and manipulation of the content, students' language development will be expanded, and requisite subject matter concepts will be acquired.

GLOBE FEARON LITERATURE PROGRAM

The Globe Fearon Literature program provides a sound approach to integrating language development and literature study. It enables students to successfully engage in experiences with literature that are appropriate to their evolving language and literacy levels. The subject matter presented in this language-sensitive fashion not only provides increased familiarity with masterworks of literature, but helps to develop the language skills necessary for academic achievement.

Globe Fearon Literature integrates language and content instruction using a variety of literary selections. Instructional strategies are designed to build on students' prior knowledge of literature. Brainstorming activities enable students to capture the broad meaning of selections before studying details. Vocabulary is acquired through interactive activities that are contextual in nature. Learning strategies such as organizing and summarizing, and a wide range of questioning techniques are included to help prepare students to meet the challenge of cognitively demanding subject matter.

SUGGESTED STRATEGIES

Teachers may consider the following strategies when working with LEP students:

- Simplify the language by using a slow but natural rate of speech, by enunciating clearly, by defining idiomatic expressions and multiple meanings before reading, and by limiting the teaching of vocabulary to those words that are key to the comprehension of the passage to be read.

- Use context clues as often as possible. Context clues give meaning to oral language as well as to written language. Common context clues include paralinguistic clues such as gestures, facial expressions, and acting out meanings; props such as graphs, charts, real objects, bulletin board displays, maps, and timelines; and visual and word associations. Prereading discussions of visuals and other features in the text also aid in student comprehension.

- Check understanding frequently by asking for clarification and expansion of student statements. Use a variety of oral questions that are commensurate with the evolving language proficiency of the students. Provide opportunities for one-on-one interaction between students and between the teacher and students.

- Tap and focus students' prior background knowledge of the theme to be presented in the text by asking open-ended questions, such as: "Have you ever had this experience or been in this situation?" or "How would you feel if _____ happened to you?" Use real objects or visuals to stimulate prereading discussion and provide an opportunity for students to share what they already know about the topic to be read. Allow students to respond in their primary languages, if necessary, while sharing their experiences.

- Create student-centered activities by using different grouping strategies that allow students to try out their newly acquired English skills in a safe environment. By interacting with their peers, students must rephrase their thoughts and correct their own errors so that others can understand them. Pairing LEP students with English proficient students is especially effective.

- Keep in mind that language development is accelerated when students are engaged in activities that enable them to experience success. Direct error correction, especially in the initial stages of acquiring a new language, should be held to a minimum. In cognitively demanding situations, emphasis should be on what is said, rather than on form.

BLOCK SCHEDULING

By Robert Wandberg, Ph.D.

Under the block scheduling format, many teachers report increased student success by using assignments and tasks that take the students deeper into the content.

DEFINING BLOCK SCHEDULING

Many literature and language arts classrooms are moving toward block scheduling as a means of delivering instruction to students. Block scheduling is frequently referred to as a 4-period schedule, a 4 X 4 schedule, or an extended-period schedule. The common threads of block scheduling are single classes that run 70 to 100 minutes rather than the more traditional classes of 45 to 55 minutes.

Block schedules offer several possible varieties. The basic format is four classes per day per term. A student in this schedule typically takes 16 classes (4 classes X 4 terms) in one school year. However, some of these classes may run for two or more terms while others may run only one term. Therefore, in reality, a student may only have 8 to 10 different classes per school year.

Some school schedules combine block and traditional schedules, where some classes, such as chemistry for example, may run for 40 minutes and other classes, such as art, for 80 minutes. Another format of the block schedule is that in which the extended length classes meet every other day. This is often called an A/B schedule. A student in the A/B schedule typically takes six, seven, or eight classes per term.

About one-third of secondary schools in United States are currently operating under some form of a block schedule.

POTENTIAL BENEFITS OF BLOCK SCHEDULING

Why do schools choose a block schedule? There are several reasons:

- to reduce the number of classes a student has during one term
- to decrease the number of classes and students a teacher has during one term
- to increase the opportunities for students to be involved in enrichment or remedial classes
- to increase the opportunities for varied instructional strategies
- to decrease student absenteeism and failure rate
- to increase interdisciplinary, cooperative teaching, and team teaching opportunities
- to increase staff development and curriculum development opportunities

Research continues to assess and evaluate teaching and learning in block schedules. Students in many block schedule schools report more positive attitudes toward school than corresponding students in traditional 7-period schedules. Indicators for this judgment include the following perceptions among students:

- higher degree of student respect and spirit within their school

- better behavior and more positive relationships among students in school

- greater respect for teachers and more positive student-teacher relationships

- a greater feeling of personal safety in school

- an increased interest and engagement in classes

- an increased level of student involvement in classroom activities

- decreased student frustrations related to homework

Teachers in block schedule schools also report more favorable attitudes about their schedule than do teachers in traditional 7-period schools. Indicators for this judgment include a belief that the block schedule

- allows teachers to do their job more effectively

- allows teachers to know their students better

- allows teachers to work equally as hard but experience less stress

- facilitates student achievement

- improves student behavior

- provides a quality educational experience for students

- provides the opportunity for more teacher collaboration

- provides feelings of respect and support from colleagues and administrators

- provides teachers the opportunity to use varied, instructionally effective strategies

Under the block scheduling format, many teachers report increased student success by using assignments and tasks that take the students deeper into the content. These assignments and tasks, developed by the teachers, are typically more student-centered and more "robust" than the assignments and tasks that they had previously used. One of the more common reasons teachers report more student success under the block system is the fact that the block schedule gives them more time for monitoring, guiding, and providing feedback to the student.

DESIGNING LESSONS FOR A BLOCK SCHEDULE

Consider the successful model of an effective block schedule lesson design as shown on page TT42. Although there are justifiable reasons to deviate from the model from time to time, such as to invite special speakers to the class or to perform student assessments, the model is recommended as a foundation for block schedule lesson structure. Listed with each step in the lesson design is the percent of total class time devoted to those activities based on an 80-minute class period.

USING GLOBE FEARON LITERATURE IN A BLOCK SCHEDULE

Here are some types of activities from *Globe Fearon Literature* that can be integrated into the extended class period. Activities such as these can be found in the Teacher's Edition and the Teacher's Resources.

1. Poetry Reading Students take part in a mystery poetry reading. Each student writes a four-line poem about him or herself. Another student reads each one aloud to the class, and the class guesses who wrote it.

2. Literary Seminar Students take part in a literary seminar. The class discusses the selections in the unit. Then students determine why the selections were placed in this unit, and compare and contrast them.

3. Writing Screenplays Students work in cooperative groups. Students play the role of screenwriters. Each group develops one of the unit selections into an exciting screenplay for a movie. The group then pitches its idea to the executive producers (a selected group of students or the entire class). The producers then vote on one or more screenplays to create and perform.

BLOCK SCHEDULE LESSON DESIGN
Percentage of total class time is based on an 80-minute block.

Focus and warm-up
Total time: 4–12 minutes   Teacher role: Leader

5–15%

Focus students' attention on the lesson outcomes and learning expectations; review previous lesson(s); announcements and class management tasks.

Direct teaching
Total time: 2–20 minutes   Teacher role: Leader

5–25%

Provide students with information, insights, and guidance necessary for successful achievement of the lesson outcomes. Methods include multi-media demonstrations, lectures, and guest speakers.

Student performance
Total time: 28–36 minutes   Teacher role: Coach/facilitator

35–45%

Students are actively involved in learning, decision making, and creating personal meaning to the lesson outcome. Activities include student presentations, research, creations, advocacy, inventions, inquiry, analysis, assessment, evaluation, and skill development.

Closure
Total time: 4–12 minutes   Teacher role: Coach/facilitator

15–25%

Students gather/return materials, hand in classwork and previous homework assignments, receive homework assignments, ask clarifying questions, and publish/present their work.

Review
Total time: 12–20 minutes   Teacher role: Coach/facilitator

5–15%

Students summarize class activity and generate plans for subsequent classes, considering timelines, due dates, and future process steps. Activities include journaling, group writing, active questioning, pairing / sharing, summarizing, and planning.

ROBUST LEARNING TASK

Block schedules lend themselves to robust learning tasks. A robust learning task is a student project (assignment) that requires several classes to complete and often requires multiple integrated skills such as decision-making, problem solving, inquiry, self-direction, and communication.

As teachers, we typically have and use established criteria for student performance. Similarly, we should have and use established criteria for the development and creation of robust learning tasks. Nine criteria are suggested. Tasks should be:

Authentic   The task simulates a way information is handled in the world outside of school.

Teachers should ask: What do people outside of school do with this information?

Unbiased   All students, regardless of culture, gender, or learning style, have an opportunity to achieve; the task does not rely on specialized knowledge or narrow interests.

Teachers should ask: Does every student have an opportunity to be successful doing this task?

Constructivist   Students are actively involved in creating meaning for their learning by making decisions about the work.

Teachers should ask: Are my students doing the work and making decisions that determine the meaning for their learning?

Developmental   The task is appropriate to the intellectual, physical, and psychological maturity of the students.

Teachers should ask: Is this work at the appropriate level for my students?

Embedded   The task is an integral part of regular classroom work, not an add-on.

Teachers should ask: Does this task blend into my normal classroom activities?

Focused   The task stays on target to assess the process/concept and topic.

Teachers should ask: Are my students demonstrating the learning called for in the standards and expectations of the course?

Generalizable   The specific skills and knowledge required for the task represent the larger learning required for the content standard.

Teachers should ask: If my students do this robust task, will I be reasonably sure they have the knowledge and skills called for in the standards and expectations of the course?

High in Rigor   The task represents a high learning expectation.

Teachers should ask: Does the robust task represent high expectations for student learning?

Interesting   The task is engaging work for students.

Teachers should ask: Will my students be interested in doing this robust task?

How do your student assignments measure up? Consider adopting some of the strategies and criteria described here to add rigor and robustness to future assignments, especially in a block-scheduling setting. Supply students with the criteria ahead of time to ensure their awareness of the tasks on which they will be assessed.

CRITERIA FOR EVALUATING LITERATURE TEXTBOOKS

Choosing the appropriate literature textbook is a vital part of building a strong language arts program. The textbook must meet the needs of both students and teachers in addition to fulfilling the requirements of local and state curriculum guidelines. The purpose of the following survey is to assist teachers in systematically evaluating the literature materials under consideration. Study each point carefully, and then rank the various textbooks using a rating scale of 0 to 5. You may reproduce this form as needed.

RATING SCALE		TEXTBOOK PUBLISHER
5 = EXCELLENT	2 = POOR	A _____
4 = GOOD	1 = UNSATISFACTORY	B _____
3 = FAIR	0 = NOT APPLICABLE	C _____

STUDENT TEXT	A	B	C
1. Quality of selections			
2. Special study tips for students at the beginning of the book			
3. Balance of traditional and contemporary selections			
4. Appropriate cultural diversity and male/female representation			
5. Variety and balance of genre (fiction, poetry, nonfiction, and drama)			
6. Representation of major types of poetry			
7. Representation of major types of nonfiction			
8. Model lessons that demonstrate reading strategies			
BEFORE EVERY SELECTION			
1. Motivation for reading and purpose-setting questions			
2. Writing activity			
3. Literary skill instruction			
4. Reading skill instruction			
5. Motivating visuals			
DURING EVERY SELECTION			
1. Open layout with easy-to-read text			
2. Visuals that relate to the selection and increase comprehension			
3. Vocabulary definition			
AFTER EVERY SELECTION			
1. Open-ended questions that allow students to respond to literature			
2. Recall, inference, and application questions about the selection			
3. Writing about the selection			
4. Literary skill reinforcement			
5. Reading skill reinforcement			
6. Vocabulary reinforcement			

CONTINUED

STUDENT TEXT (CONTINUED)	A	B	C
UNIT DEVELOPMENT (INTRODUCTION AND CLOSURE ACTIVITIES)			
1. Fine Art that reflects the unit theme or literary period			
2. Opening quote or motivating introduction			
3. Appropriate historical introductions and timelines for chronologically-organized units			
4. Introduction to the unit theme for thematically-organized units			
5. Explicit instruction on effective studying and test preparation			
6. Writing process lesson			
7. Speaking and listening activities			
8. Critical-thinking activities			
9. Support for grammar, usage, and mechanics			
10. Support for test taking			

TEACHER'S EDITION	A	B	C
1. Teaching suggestions at point of use			
2. Flexible teaching opportunities			
3. Professional development articles about key trends and issues in education			
4. Suggestions for activities at various reading levels			
5. Suggestions for cooperative learning activities			
6. Selection synopses and activities			
7. Student motivation activities			
8. Block scheduling strategies			
9. Critical thinking activities			
10. Critical viewing questions and background notes about Fine Art			
11. Background information about authors			
12. ESL-appropriate activities			
13. Enrichment opportunities			
14. Comprehension checks within the selection			
15. Quizzes for each selection			
16. Answers to all review questions in Student Edition			
17. Suggestions for using technology			
18. Related materials listings			

PROGRAM COMPONENTS	A	B	C
1. Vocabulary skills reinforcement worksheets			
2. Literary skills reinforcement worksheets			
3. Reading comprehension skills reinforcement worksheets			
4. Grammar, usage, and mechanics reinforcement worksheets			
5. Critical thinking activities			
6. Writing process activities			
7. Speaking and listening activities			
8. Evaluation rubrics for alternative assessments			
9. Reading in the content areas activities			
10. Selection tests			
11. Unit tests			
12. Answer keys for all worksheets and activities Technology Components			
TECHNOLOGY COMPONENTS			
1. Answer keys to all print components			
2. Tests in a modifiable format			
3. Reinforcement and extension activities			
4. Reinforcement, writing, speaking and listening, and critical thinking worksheets			

OTHER CRITERIA	A	B	C
1. Ease of use			
2. Literature is accessible to all students			
3. Moves students from literal reading to higher level reading in a step-by-step fashion			

ADDITIONAL COMMENTS

_____

_____

_____

_____

_____

THESE OTHER FINE GLOBE FEARON PROGRAMS HELP TEACHERS MEET THE NEEDS OF ALL STUDENTS

Globe Fearon has a strong commitment to providing high-quality reading and literature materials that motivate students. The materials on the following pages may be used as additional resources in your classroom. Visit our website, www.globefearon.com, for more information about these and other Globe Fearon products.

An array of additional Globe Fearon materials may help you to:

- Motivate students and challenge them to accelerate their learning

- Extend independent reading opportunities by providing high-interest literature at accessible reading levels

- Reinforce reading and writing skills

Enrich Your Students' Reading Experiences with High-interest Paperback Anthologies

No two students are alike in their interests or ability levels. Finding high-interest, high-quality reading materials at the appropriate reading level for each student can be a challenge.

The *Globe Reader's Collection* is a set of six anthologies of high-interest fiction, nonfiction, and drama at controlled reading levels. Providing a wide variety of themes, genres, and topics—from mythology to science fiction—this collection can extend your classroom library and enrich your students' reading experiences.

Inspire Your Students' Creativity and Critical Reading Skills

The *Stories and Plays Without Endings* series offers students the opportunity to construct appropriate endings to compelling works of fiction and drama. These books help reinforce critical reading, creative writing, and literary skills, as well as providing ideas for a variety of classroom activities, including independent writing, cooperative learning, Reader's Theater, and group discussion.

Globe Fearon Makes Classic Literature Accessible to Every Student

Literary masterpieces have influenced and inspired generations for decades. By offering three levels of many popular classics, Globe Fearon supports your efforts to make the classics available to all of your students.

■ PACEMAKER CLASSICS

For your students that are reading significantly below grade level, the *Pacemaker Classics* offer classics that have been skillfully adapted to a reading level of 3-4. These adaptations maintain the integrity and intent of the original works. *Pacemaker Classics* also contain an audio component that allows students to listen and read confidently. Comprehension is enhanced through the use of the Study Guide, which provides background information about the time periods, authors, plots, and characters, as well as teaching ideas.

■ GLOBE ADAPTED CLASSICS

Many of your students may be reading slightly below grade level. For these students Globe Fearon offers *Globe Adapted Classics*. These titles have been only slightly abridged to help students comprehend and enjoy classic pieces of literature. Reading reviews and footnotes aid in comprehension. The reading level of *Adapted Classics* varies from 5–8.

■ MASTERWORKS COLLECTION

To extend your literature instruction for students who read on level, Globe Fearon offers the *Masterworks Collection*. These softcover texts allow you to provide your students with original works for independent reading. A *Teacher's Resource Manual* offers additional teaching strategies and discussion questions to enhance comprehension.

Teach Classic Literature to Every Student in Your Class

The Pacemaker Classics and Adapted Classics series feature titles that appeal to the different interests and abilities of your students.

There are a number of ways to motivate your students to read independently and participate in cooperative group activities using these books. Here are a few suggestions.

■ SHAKESPEAREAN PLAYS

Give students the opportunity to explore the timeless themes of Shakespeare's most widely read plays.

PACEMAKER CLASSICS: Hamlet, Julius Caesar, Macbeth, A Midsummer Night's Dream, and Romeo and Juliet

ADAPTED CLASSICS: Hamlet, Julius Caesar, Macbeth, Othello, and Romeo and Juliet

■ CLASSIC PLAYS

Engage students in a drama genre study, have them conduct Reader's Theater, or challenge them to write a movie screenplay based on these classic plays.

PACEMAKER CLASSICS: Antigone, Cyrano de Bergerac, A Doll's House

ADAPTED CLASSICS: A Raisin in the Sun, A Doll's House, The Importance of Being Earnest (new)

■ A WORLD OF ADVENTURE

Invite students to work in small groups or pairs to create chain of events charts, to rewrite the endings, or to dramatize important scenes from these classic adventure tales.

PACEMAKER CLASSICS: The Adventures of Huckleberry Finn, The Adventures of Tom Sawyer, The Call of the Wild, The Deerslayer, Gulliver's Travels, The Last of the Mohicans, Moby Dick, Robinson Crusoe, The Sea-Wolf, 20,000 Leagues Under the Sea, The Three Musketeers, Treasure Island, Two Years Before the Mast

ADAPTED CLASSICS: The Adventures of Huckleberry Finn, The Adventures of Tom Sawyer, The Call of the Wild, Gulliver's Travels, Moby Dick, 20,000 Leagues Under the Sea, Treasure Island

■ MYSTERIOUS TALES

Mysteries provide opportunities to sharpen reasoning skills, to make and revise predictions, to rewrite story endings, and to write character sketches.

PACEMAKER CLASSICS: The Adventures of Sherlock Holmes, Dracula, Dr. Jekyll and Mr. Hyde, Tales of Edgar Allan Poe, Frankenstein, The Hound of the Baskervilles, The House of the Seven Gables, O. Henry, The Phantom of the Opera, The Turn of the Screw

ADAPTED CLASSICS: The Adventures of Sherlock Holmes, Tales of Edgar Allan Poe, Frankenstein, O. Henry, The Phantom of the Opera

GLOBE FEARON CLASSICS: Accessible Literature for All Students

THE ADVENTURES OF HUCKLEBERRY FINN
- Pacemaker Classic Reading Level 3-4
  Book, Audiocassette, Study Guide
- Adapted Classic Reading Level 5-6
  Book, TRM*
- Masterworks (Unabridged)
  Book, TRM*

THE ADVENTURES OF SHERLOCK HOLMES
- Pacemaker Classic Reading Level 3-4
  Book, Study Guide
- Adapted Classic Reading Level 6-7
  Book, TRM*

THE ADVENTURES OF TOM SAWYER
- Pacemaker Classic Reading Level 3-4
  Book, Audiocassette, Study Guide
- Adapted Classic Reading Level 6-7
  Book, TRM*

ALL QUIET ON THE WESTERN FRONT
- Pacemaker Classic Reading Level 3-4
  Book, Audiocassette, Study Guide
- Adapted Classic Reading Level 5-6
  Book, TRM*

ANNE FRANK: THE DIARY OF A YOUNG GIRL
- Pacemaker Classic Reading Level 3-4
  Book, Audiocassette, Study Guide
- Adapted Classic Reading Level 6
  Book, TRM*

ANTIGONE
- Pacemaker Classic Reading Level 3-4
  Book, Audiocassette, Study Guide

AROUND THE WORLD IN 80 DAYS
- Pacemaker Classic Reading Level 3-4
  Book, CD-ROM, Study Guide
- Adapted Classic Reading Level 5-6
  Book, TRM*

BEOWULF
- Adapted Classic Reading Level 7-8
  Book, TRM*

THE CALL OF THE WILD
- Pacemaker Classic Reading Level 3-4
  Book, Audiocassette, Study Guide
- Adapted Classic Reading Level 6-7
  Book, TRM*

THE CANTERBURY TALES
- Pacemaker Classic Reading Level 3-4
  Book, Study Guide
- Adapted Classic Reading Level 4-5
  Book, TRM*

A CHRISTMAS CAROL
- Pacemaker Classic Reading Level 3-4
  Book, Audiocassette, Study Guide
- Adapted Classic Reading Level 7-8
  Book, TRM*

CRIME AND PUNISHMENT
- Pacemaker Classic Reading Level 3-4
  Book, Audiocassette, Study Guide

CYRANO DE BERGERAC
- Pacemaker Classic Reading Level 3-4
  Book, Audiocassette, Study Guide

DAVID COPPERFIELD
- Pacemaker Classic Reading Level 3-4
  Book, Audiocassette, Study Guide

THE DEERSLAYER
- Pacemaker Classic Reading Level 3-4
  Book, Audiocassette, Study Guide

A DOLL'S HOUSE
- Pacemaker Classic Reading Level 3-4
  Book, Audiocassette, Study Guide
- Adapted Classic Reading Level 5-6
  Book, TRM*

DR. JEKYLL AND MR. HYDE
- Pacemaker Classic Reading Level 3-4
  Book, Audiocassette, Study Guide

DRACULA
- Pacemaker Classic Reading Level 3-4
  Book, Audiocassette, Study Guide

ETHAN FROME
- Pacemaker Classic Reading Level 3-4
  Book, Audiocassette, Study Guide
- Adapted Classic Reading Level 4-5
  Book, TRM*

FRANKENSTEIN
- Pacemaker Classic Reading Level 3-4
  Book, Audiocassette, Study Guide
- Adapted Classic Reading Level 4-5
  Book, TRM*

THE GOOD EARTH
- Pacemaker Classic Reading Level 3-4
  Book, Audiocassette, Study Guide

THE GRAPES OF WRATH
- Pacemaker Classic Reading Level 3-4
  Book, Audiocassette, Study Guide
- Adapted Classic Reading Level 5-6
  Book, TRM*

GREAT EXPECTATIONS
- Pacemaker Classic Reading Level 3-4
  Book, Audiocassette, Study Guide
- Adapted Classic Reading Level 6-7
  Book, TRM*

GULLIVER'S TRAVELS
- Pacemaker Classic Reading Level 3-4
  Book, Audiocassette, Study Guide
- Adapted Classic Reading Level 5-6
  Book, TRM*

HAMLET
- Pacemaker Classic Reading Level 3-4
  Book, Audiocassette, Study Guide
- Adapted Classic Reading Level 5-6
  Book, TRM*
- Masterworks (Unabridged)
  Book, TRM*

HEART OF DARKNESS
- Pacemaker Classic Reading Level 3-4
  Book, Audiocassette, Study Guide
- Adapted Classic Reading Level 5-6
  Book, TRM*

THE HOUND OF THE BASKERVILLES
- Pacemaker Classic Reading Level 3-4
  Book, Audiocassette, Study Guide

THE HOUSE OF THE SEVEN GABLES
- Pacemaker Classic Reading Level 3-4
  Book, Audiocassette, Study Guide

THE HUNCHBACK OF NOTRE DAME
- Pacemaker Classic Reading Level 3-4
  Book, Audiocassette, Study Guide

THE IMPORTANCE OF BEING EARNEST
- Pacemaker Classic Reading Level 3-4
  Book, CD-ROM, Study Guide
- Adapted Classic Reading Level 4-5
  Book, TRM*

JANE EYRE
- Pacemaker Classic Reading Level 3-4
  Book, Audiocassette, Study Guide
- Adapted Classic Reading Level 4-5
  Book, TRM*

JULIUS CAESAR
- Pacemaker Classic Reading Level 3-4
  Book, Audiocassette, Study Guide
- Adapted Classic Reading Level 5-6
  Book, TRM*
- Masterworks (Unabridged)
  Book, TRM*

THE JUNGLE (SINCLAIR)
- Pacemaker Classic Reading Level 3-4
  Book, Audiocassette, Study Guide
- Adapted Classic Reading Level 7-8
  Book, TRM*

THE JUNGLE BOOK (KIPLING)
- Pacemaker Classic Reading Level 3-4
  Book, Audiocassette, Study Guide

LAST OF THE MOHICANS
- Pacemaker Classic Reading Level 3-4
  Book, Audiocassette, Study Guide

*Teacher's Resource Manual

LES MISÉRABLES
- Adapted Classic Reading Level 7-8
  Book, TRM*

LITTLE WOMEN
- Pacemaker Classic Reading Level 3-4
  Book, Study Guide
- Adapted Classic Reading Level 5-6
  Book, TRM*

LORD JIM
- Pacemaker Classic Reading Level 3-4
  Book, CD–ROM, Study Guide
- Adapted Classic Reading Level 5-6
  Book, TRM*

MACBETH
- Pacemaker Classic Reading Level 3-4
  Book, Audiocassette, Study Guide
- Adapted Classic Reading Level 5-6
  Book, TRM*
- Masterworks (Unabridged)
  Book, TRM*

THE MAYOR OF CASTERBRIDGE
- Pacemaker Classic Reading Level 3-4
  Book, Audiocassette, Study Guide

A MIDSUMMER NIGHT'S DREAM
- Pacemaker Classic Reading Level 3-4
  Book, Audiocassette, Study Guide

MOBY DICK
- Pacemaker Classic Reading Level 3-4
  Book, Audiocassette, Study Guide
- Adapted Classic Reading Level 5-6
  Book, TRM*

THE MOONSTONE
- Pacemaker Classic Reading Level 3-4
  Book, Audiocassette, Study Guide

MY ANTONIA
- Adapted Classic Reading Level 7-8
  Book, TRM*

NARRATIVE OF THE LIFE OF FREDERICK DOUGLASS
- Pacemaker Classic Reading Level 3-4
  Book, Audiocassette, Study Guide
- Adapted Classic Reading Level 5-6
  Book, TRM*

O. HENRY
- Pacemaker Classic for Reading Level 3-4
  Book, Study Guide
- Adapted Classic for Reading Level 7-8
  Book, TRM*

O PIONEERS!
- Pacemaker Classic Reading Level 3-4
  Book, Audiocassette, Study Guide

THE ODYSSEY
- Pacemaker Classic Reading Level 3-4
  Book, Study Guide
- Adapted Classic Reading Level 5-6
  Book, TRM*

OLIVER TWIST
- Pacemaker Classic Reading Level 3-4
  Book, Audiocassette, Study Guide
- Adapted Classic Reading Level 5-6
  Book, TRM*

OTHELLO
- Adapted Classic Reading Level 5-6
  Book, TRM*

THE PHANTOM OF THE OPERA
- Pacemaker Classic Reading Level 3-4
  Book, Audiocassette, Study Guide
- Adapted Classic Reading Level 7-8
  Book, TRM*

PRIDE AND PREJUDICE
- Pacemaker Classic Reading Level 3-4
  Book
- Adapted Classic Reading Level 7-8
  Book, TRM*

THE PRINCE AND THE PAUPER
- Pacemaker Classic Reading Level 3-4
  Book, Audiocassette, Study Guide

A RAISIN IN THE SUN
- Adapted Classic Reading Level 7-8
  Book, TRM*

THE RED BADGE OF COURAGE
- Pacemaker Classic Reading Level 3-4
  Book, Audiocassette, Study Guide
- Adapted Classic Reading Level 7-8
  Book, TRM*
- Masterworks (Unabridged)
  Book, TRM*

ROBINSON CRUSOE
- Pacemaker Classic Reading Level 3-4
  Book, Audiocassette, Study Guide

ROMEO AND JULIET
- Pacemaker Classic Reading Level 3-4
  Book, Audiocassette, Study Guide
- Adapted Classic Reading Level 5-6
  Book, TRM*
- Masterworks (Unabridged)
  Book, TRM*

THE SCARLETT LETTER
- Pacemaker Classic Reading Level 3-4
  Book, Audiocassette, Study Guide
- Adapted Classic Reading Level 7-8
  Book, TRM*

THE SEA-WOLF
- Pacemaker Classic Reading Level 3-4
  Book, Audiocassette, Study Guide

SILAS MARNER
- Pacemaker Classic Reading Level 3-4
  Book, Study Guide
- Adapted Classic Reading Level 5-6
  Book, TRM*

THE STORY OF MY LIFE: HELEN KELLER
- Pacemaker Classic Reading Level 3-4
  Book, CD-ROM, Study Guide
- Adapted Classic Reading Level 4-5
  Book, TRM*

TALES OF EDGAR ALLAN POE
- Pacemaker Classic Reading Level 3-4
  Book, Audiocassette, Study Guide
- Adapted Classic Reading Level 4-5
  Book, TRM*

A TALE OF TWO CITIES
- Pacemaker Classic Reading Level 3-4
  Book, Audiocassette, Study Guide
- Adapted Classic Reading Level 5-6
  Book, TRM*
- Masterworks (Unabridged)
  Book, TRM*

THINGS FALL APART
- Adapted Classic Reading Level 7-8
  Book, TRM*

THE THREE MUSKETEERS
- Pacemaker Classic Reading Level 3-4
  Book, Audiocassette, Study Guide

THE TIME MACHINE
- Pacemaker Classic Reading Level 3-4
  Book, Audiocassette, Study Guide

TREASURE ISLAND
- Pacemaker Classic Reading Level 3-4
  Book, Audiocassette, Study Guide
- Adapted Classic Reading Level 5-6
  Book, TRM*

THE TURN OF THE SCREW
- Pacemaker Classic Reading Level 3-4
  Book, Audiocassette, Study Guide

20,000 LEAGUES UNDER THE SEA
- Pacemaker Classic Reading Level 3-4
  Book, Audiocassette, Study Guide
- Adapted Classic Reading Level 4-5
  Book, TRM*

TWO YEARS BEFORE THE MAST
- Pacemaker Classic Reading Level 3-4
  Book, Audiocassette, Study Guide

UP FROM SLAVERY
- Pacemaker Classic Reading Level 3-4
  Book, CD-ROM, Study Guide
- Adapted Classic Reading Level 4-5
  Book, TRM*

THE WAR OF THE WORLDS
- Pacemaker Classic for Reading Level 3-4
  Book, Audiocassette, Study Guide

WUTHERING HEIGHTS
- Pacemaker Classic Reading Level 3-4
  Book, Audiocassette, Study Guide
- Masterworks (Unabridged)
  Book, TRM*

Other Outstanding Globe Fearon Products Provide Additional Reading Skill Support

Developing strategies for reading and comprehending literature means helping students grow as readers.

To assist those students who need additional support in developing skills and strategies for comprehension, critical thinking, and test taking, Globe Fearon can offer a range of in-depth supplemental reading materials.

- **Reading in the Content Areas:** Strategies for Reading Informational Text in Science, Math and Social Studies

- **Reading for Proficiency:** Preparation for State and Standardized Reading Tests

- **Be a Better Reader:** Comprehension, Decoding, and Study Skills

For Students Who Need Additional Instruction, Globe Fearon Offers Writing Skill Support

Extending literature means encouraging students to respond to literature or to use literature as a model for their own writing.

For students who need additional support in developing skills for persuasive or expository writing, practicing process writing, and test taking, Globe Fearon can provide a range of additional materials.

- **Writer's Toolkit:** Interactive Software to Build Writing Skills
- **Writing Across the Curriculum:** Writing in Response to Literature

- **Success in Writing:** Applications of Process Writing
- **Writing for Proficiency:** Preparation for State and Standardized Writing Tests

GLOBE FEARON

LITERATURE

▪ *Purple Level* ▪

PROGRAM REVIEWERS

Kathy Babigian, Coordinator, Tioga Literacy Center, Fresno, California
Pat Bartholomew, M.A., Reading Specialist, Milton, Ohio
Jennifer Dilks-Mundt, English Teacher, Brant Rock, Massachusetts
Ann Fitzgerald, M.A., Education Director, Southshire Community School,
    North Bennington, Vermont
Pat Miller, M.A., Reading/English/Language Arts Supervisor, Prince Georges County
    Public Schools, Maryland
Artie P. Norton, English Teacher, Suffern, New York
Timothy Rasinski, Professor of Curriculum and Instruction, Kent State University, Kent, Ohio
Cynthia Saska, M.A., Professor of English, University of Texas, San Antonio, Texas
Margaret-Mary Sulentic, Ph.D., Assistant Professor of Literacy, Department of Curriculum
    and Instruction, University of Southern Mississippi, Hattiesburg, Mississippi
Dr. Helen W. Taylor, Director of Programs K-12 Curriculum and Instruction, Portsmouth City
    Public Schools, Virginia

CONSULTANTS

Dr. Virginia Bryg; Josephine Gemake, Ph.D.; Alfred Schifini, Ph.D.; Deborah Walker; Robert
    Wandberg, Ph.D.

Supervising Editor/Team Leader: Karen McCollum
Editors: Ayanna Taylor, Amy Greenberg, Theresa McCarthy
Editorial Developer: Pearson Education Development Group
Marketing Assistant: Kate Krimsky
Production Editor: Travis Bailey
Associate Production Editors: Amy Benefiel, Alia Lesser
Senior Designer: Angel Weyant
Manufacturing Buyer: Mark Cirillo
Cover and Interior Design/Production: Pearson Education Development Group
Photo Research: Pearson Education Development Group

ABOUT THE COVER

The Workers on the Cart, Alberto Magnelli. Musee National d'Art Moderne, Paris, France/
Bridgeman Art Library. Alberto Magnelli was a pioneer in abstract art, the defining style of the
20th century. Abstractionists have challenged themselves to capture the unseen aspects of nature
and the heroic capacities of individuals and society. What does Magnelli's painting of workers on a
cart say about the human spirit?

ISBN 0-130-23562-8
Printed in the United States of America

3 4 5 6 7   08 07 06 05 04

Globe
Fearon
Pearson Learning Group

1-800-321-3106
www.pearsonlearning.com

Preview

UNIT 1 *Looking at Love*

iv ■ Contents

Writing • Vocabulary • Grammar, Usage, and Mechanics
Speaking and Listening • Critical Thinking • Effective Studying
• Test Preparation

UNIT 2 *The Unknown*

Writing • Vocabulary • Grammar, Usage, and Mechanics
Speaking and Listening • Critical Thinking • Effective Studying
• Test Preparation

UNIT 3 *Suspense*

Writing • Vocabulary • Grammar, Usage, and Mechanics
Speaking and Listening • Critical Thinking • Effective Studying
• Test Preparation

UNIT 4 *Discoveries*

UNIT 5 *Heroes*

Writing • Vocabulary • Grammar, Usage, and Mechanics
Speaking and Listening • Critical Thinking • Effective Studying
• Test Preparation

UNIT 6 Generations

References

How to Use This Book

Welcome to *Globe Fearon Literature*. As you read this textbook, you will learn about many new worlds. By reading literature you can experience the past and the future, and you can learn about people—how they feel and how they think.

To get the most out of this book, you will need to become an active reader. Active readers think about reading materials before they begin, during, and after they read.

TIPS FOR IMPROVING YOUR READING

Before You Read
- Think about the title of the selection. What does it tell you about the topic? What do you already know about the topic?
- Determine the genre of the selection. For example—if the selection is a poem, ask yourself, "How will this be different from reading an essay or short story?"
- Set a purpose for reading. What do you think you will learn by reading this selection?

As You Read
- Predict what you think will happen next. Then pause occasionally and ask yourself if your predictions were correct.
- Form questions about what you are reading. For example, ask yourself, "What idea is the author trying to convey?"
- When you encounter a word you are unfamiliar with, use the help that Globe Fearon Literature gives you. Difficult words are defined at the bottom of the page they appear on.

After You Read
Consider the following questions:
- Did the selection end the way you anticipated?
- What did you learn from reading this selection?
- How does this selection relate to others you have read?

THE BOOK IS ORGANIZED TO HELP YOU

Your literature book has been organized into units. Each unit is introduced with a piece of fine art and a quote. Look at these pages. What do you think this unit will be about?

The next two pages of the unit give you a preview of what to expect. These two pages will help you set the stage for reading and understanding the selections. You may want to refer back to these pages as you read through the unit.

The "Focus On" feature gives you some tips to help you understand specific genres of literature, such as fiction or poetry You will notice that each Model selection has blue notes in the margin. These are study hints to help you read actively. The notes relate back to the "Focus On" feature. The notes will help you identify key elements of the genre. Later, you can look for similar elements in other selections as you read independently.

Before each selection, you will be introduced to a reading skill, a literary skill, and a writing activity. The reading skill will help you understand what you are reading. The literary skill will call your attention to elements of literature. The writing activity will help you relate the literature to your own life.

There are review questions at the end of each selection. These questions help you think about what you have just read. They will also help you relate this selection to others that you may have read.

Globe Fearon Literature was created for you. Reading literature can be one of the most rewarding experiences you can ever have. There are new worlds to explore and exciting people to meet. It's all here. So, let's begin. . .

UNIT ACTIVITY

A Continuing Unit Project: Creating Journals

Explain to students that a journal is like a diary. It is a way of recording the events of their lives, as well as the feelings and thoughts that they experience. Point out that writing in a journal is similar to writing to a friend. Very often, problems and feelings become much clearer once they have been examined. Writing in a journal can also help a person decide what is or is not really important.

Have students keep a personal journal as they read this unit. Encourage students to relate each selection that they read to events and feelings in their own lives. You may wish to have students write in their journals every day, or you may ask them to write only after reading each selection. The important thing is that the response to each selection should be integrated with the student's life and experience. Ask students to be especially aware of selections that seem to relate to their personal experiences. For example, a student who has just broken up with a boyfriend or girlfriend may find special meaning in one of the poems about ending a romance.

You may wish to allow some class time for journal writing, or you may wish to have students do their writing as a homework assignment. Some general questions that will help students in writing their entries include:

What is the most important thing that happened to you today?

Did you do anything today that was unusual or outside of your normal routine?

What kind of mood are you in? Did anything happen today that caused you to have strong feelings?

Given the kind of day that you had, how did the selection affect you? How does the selection relate to events happening in your life right now?

Does the selection bring up memories of past experiences? What are those memories?

Did you have any other thoughts and feelings about the selection?

If your class requires more structure, you may wish to pose a question for each selection. Some possible questions include:

■ **"The Locket"/"The Kiss"**
How do you feel when you find something you thought you had lost for good? Do you agree with the saying that "love is blind"?

■ **"Love" An African American Folk Poem**
What do you think love is like?

■ **"First Person Demonstrative"**
Do you sometimes have trouble expressing your feelings?
What do you do instead?

■ **"What Is Once Loved"**

■ **"Spring"**
What have you learned from a past relationship that you try not to repeat again?

■ **"Luckiest Time of All"** from *The Lucky Stone*
Do you believe in love at first sight? Explain.

■ **"Stepping Out with My Baby"**
How is the relationship between a parent or guardian and a child different from other relationships?

■ from *The Tragedy of Romeo and Juliet*
Have you ever loved or wanted to be friends with someone who was not acceptable to your family or peer group? What did you do?

■ **"Greyday"**

■ **"Here—Hold My Hand"**

■ **"Finis"**
How do you feel when you are separated from the people you love?

How do you feel when a relationship changes or comes to an end?

Have you ever lied about something and later regretted it ?

What problems in the world, your school, or your community make you unhappy?

Give each student a choice as to whether or not you will read the journal. Yet another option is to have students exchange journals with classmates of their choice.

After the unit has been completed, have students discuss their journal writing assignment. Did they find it difficult or pleasurable? What did they learn about themselves and the selections? Ask for volunteers to share one or two of their journal entries with the class.

SELECTION SYNOPSIS

In "The Locket," on the eve of a battle, a young Confederate soldier talks to his messmates about his lucky charm, a locket given to him by the girl he loves. Following the battle, a priest who has come to pray for the dead finds the locket on a dead soldier and returns it to the girl along with a letter describing the scene. In Louisiana some time later, the girl, who is in deep mourning, goes for a carriage ride with her neighbor, who is the soldier's father. She is affected by the beauty of the spring day and contrasts it sharply with her own sense of loss. Her neighbor, a judge, urges her to remove her black veil and asks her if she believes in miracles. When they reach the neighbor's house, the miracle happens—she is reunited with the soldier! He tells her that the locket had been stolen from him the night before the battle.

In the second story, "The Kiss," a wealthy young man and a young woman are casually conversing. He obviously loves her, but she loves only his wealth. Another young man suddenly enters the room and, not seeing the wealthy young man in the shadows, kisses the girl impulsively and familiarly. The wealthy man leaves abruptly, and the woman scolds the intruder. Later at a party, she takes the wealthy young man aside and concocts a story about the intruder's being an old family friend, which he believes. Her story is so convincing that he proposes. At their wedding, the intruder approaches the woman saying that her husband told him to kiss her, as an old family friend. As she eagerly awaits his kiss, he tells her that he no longer kisses women. She realizes that she cannot have everything.

SELECTION ACTIVITY

"The Locket" is fiction, but the Civil War setting of the story is real. In this activity, students will conduct research to gain information about what life was like during the Civil War and how the war affected personal relationships. In preparation for this activity, gather encyclopedias and reference books containing information about the Civil War and make them available during class time.

To begin the activity, ask students to view the Civil War from an ordinary person's perspective. They want to learn as much as possible about what everyday life was like during the 1860s. Have students suggest some things they would like to know about how the relationships between ordinary people were affected by the war. How might a young soldier away from home for the first time feel? How might a child react to his or her father going off to war? What did soldiers do when they were not fighting? How did people at home cope with daily living?

Next, have the students review the story, "The Locket." Read the first paragraph aloud to the class. Ask the students what the descriptions tell them about life as a soldier. What would it be like to sleep on the ground for months or years or to cook their meals over a camp fire every night? What can they learn from the story about fighting in a Civil War battle? about family and loved ones at home?

At this point, divide the class into small groups. Each group should decide how to proceed with its project and what they want the final format to be. For example, one group may title their project, "Letters to a Husband Fighting in the War." This group may include a series of letters written by a woman over a period of several years. Other groups may wish to create diary entries. Another group may wish to give an oral presentation in which each group member talks about how the war affected a different person in the same family.

Emphasize to the students as they work that they should be creative and show insight into the effect of war on personal relationships. However, it is important that they use information and facts found during their research.

■ "Love"
An African American folk poem (page 21)

SELECTION SYNOPSIS

The subject matter of this poem is love. The message of the poem is that a lot of significant things can happen in life, but nothing is more important than falling in love.

SELECTION ACTIVITY

Have students work in pairs or groups to create songs and lyrics that reflect the message of this poem. Students can use the actual lines of the poem, or they can create their own lyrics. Tape recorders may be helpful to students as they complete their song. You may also wish to enlist the assistance of a music teacher in your school.

■ "First Person Demonstrative"
by Phyllis Gotlieb (page 26)

SELECTION SYNOPSIS

The subject matter of this poem is the unwillingness of the speaker to express feelings of love. An underlying message of the poem is that the speaker really *wants* to express her feelings.

SELECTION ACTIVITY

Divide the class into small groups. Challenge each group to create a dramatization of this poem. Students may find it helpful to realize that a lot of action is suggested in the figures of speech used by the poet.

■ "What Is Once Loved"
by Elizabeth Coatsworth (page 31)

■ "Spring"
by Carole Gregory Clemmons (page 31)

SELECTION SYNOPSES

The theme of the first poem is that it is possible to hold onto what is loved in one's own thoughts and feelings. The theme of "Spring" is that when a person loves the second time around, certain things may be done differently—but that will cause the lovers to succeed.

SELECTION ACTIVITY

Both of these poems give advice about love. The first poem points out that the love a person has for another can never be taken away. The second poem talks about how one might approach a love relationship the second time around—especially with regard to struggles against domination and the desire to dominate.

Point out to students that the kind of advice given in these poems might appear in a newspaper column such as "Ann Landers" or "Dear Abby." Challenge students to create a "love advice" newspaper column, using one or both of these poems as the "answer" to several letters.

Have the class assist you in deciding how the columns will be written. One way would be for each student or small group to write the letters and answers for a typical column. Another way would be for several students to write letters for another student "advice-giver" to answer. A third way would be for each student in the class to write a letter; then have students randomly pick the letters they will answer in their newspaper columns.

When students have completed their columns, display them on a bulletin board. Allow time for discussion about the similarities and differences in the "love problems" that were written about. Also discuss the various interpretations that may have been given to the two poems.

■ "Luckiest Time of All" from *The Lucky Stone*
by Lucille Clifton (page 35)

SELECTION SYNOPSIS

Mrs. Elzie F. Pickens' great-granddaughter Tee brings her dogwood blooms, which reminds Mrs. Pickens of the Spring day she met her husband. Speaking in realistic dialect, Mrs. Pickens tells Tee about the day she and her friend Ovella went to join a traveling show. Young Elzie accidentally hit a dancing dog on the nose with her lucky stone, was chased by the dog, and caused an uproar. She was rescued by a "fast-runnin hero" who demonstrated his kindness and gentleness and helped her find her lucky stone. When Tee remarks that the stone was not lucky on that day, Mrs. Pickens says it was the luckiest day of all because it was the day she met Mr. Amos Pickens.

SELECTION ACTIVITY

"The Luckiest Time of All" is written in a realistic Southern dialect. The story of dialects in the United States and how they came to be is an interesting one. Many books on this subject are readily available in libraries in the 427.973 area. (Several good examples are listed below.) You might divide the class into groups and give each group a particular dialect to research such as those of the Ozark or Appalachian Mountains, Virginia Tidewater, Pennsylvania, Southern lowlands, or Louisiana.

Have each group prepare a presentation of its results, including samples of the dialect, a map showing where it is (or was) spoken, and information about the origins of the dialect.

Resources:

The American Language by H.L. Mencken
The Miracle of Language by Richard Lederer
American Dialects by Lewis Herman
American Talk by Robert Hendrickson
I hear America Talking by Stuart Flexner
Listening to America by Stuart Flexner
How to Talk American by Jim Cretty
Down in the Holler by Vance Randolph

■ "Stepping Out With My Baby"
by Paul Reiser (page 43)

SELECTION SYNOPSIS

Paul Reiser describes taking his baby son for a first-time walk to the mailbox. As they arrive at the mailbox, Reiser is an unsure, anxious father, determined to do the best for his son. He relies on the "voice" of his wife in his head, which tells him to talk to the baby. Through a humorous series of trials and errors, he finally decides to demonstrate how to mail a letter as he talks to the baby. The baby seems to enjoy the squeaky mailbox noise, which makes Reiser happy and inspires him to tell the baby more and more. The baby gives him a big smile, and Reiser realizes that the baby has no idea what he has been talking about but likes him anyway.

SELECTION ACTIVITY

Paul Reiser gave his infant some information about the history and operation of the postal service and also shared some opinions about operating a mailbox and mailbox schedules. Although the postal service is part of our everyday lives, few people really know how it oper-

ates or what changes in its technology have taken place in recent years. Invite a postal-service worker to the class as a guest speaker. Before the event, discuss with students what they would like to know about the postal service and help students prepare questions. Share these with your speaker ahead of time. When planning the event, allow time for a question-and-answer period after the speaker's presentation. As an alternate activity, have small groups of students research the history and operations of the U.S. Postal Services through personal interviews, encyclopedias, and the internet.

■ from *The Tragedy of Romeo and Juliet*
by William Shakespeare (page 49)

SELECTION SYNOPSIS

The story of Romeo and Juliet takes place in Verona, Italy. Two prominent families, the Capulets and the Montagues, have had a long-standing feud. Lately, new violence has erupted. When the first act of the play opens, Romeo Montague is unhappy because he is in love with a woman named Rosaline, who does not love him. Romeo's friend Benvolio tells him not to worry—he can meet some pretty girls at a party being given by Capulet. Because of the feud between the families, Romeo must go to the party in disguise. It is at this party that he meets Capulet's daughter, Juliet. Juliet is supposed to marry a young man named Paris, but she is drawn to Romeo. Romeo and Juliet fall in love almost at once. They know, in a certain sense, that their love is doomed because of the family feud, but their passion is so great that they vow to go on loving. In the second act of the play, Romeo goes to Friar Lawrence, a Catholic priest. The friar agrees to marry the pair, hoping that the marriage will end the fighting between the families.

The marriage takes place secretly in Friar Lawrence's private room. In Act III, there is a terrible fight between the Capulets and the Montagues. Romeo's friend Mercutio is killed, and Romeo, in his distress, kills the Capulet who killed his friend. Romeo is banished from the city for murder and is thus separated from Juliet. Meanwhile, Juliet's parents tell her that she must marry Paris in three days. Juliet feels she must kill herself. Friar Lawrence, however, comes up with a plan. He tells Juliet that she will take a potion that will make her appear dead. Her body will be taken to the Capulet family tomb, and there Romeo will meet her. When the potion wears off, the two lovers will flee to another city. The plan goes awry when a letter from Friar Lawrence informing Romeo of the plan does not reach him in time. Romeo hears only of Juliet's supposed death and vows that if she is dead, he, too, must die. Romeo goes to the tomb, and, seeing that Juliet appears to be dead, takes a bottle of poison and dies. When Juliet awakens and realizes what has happened, she stabs herself and also dies. When the parents of both lovers arrive at the tomb, they find that their grief is greater than the hatred that exists between their families. The feud is ended as Capulet extends his hand to Montague, and Montague vows to build a statue in honor of Romeo's beloved Juliet.

SELECTION ACTIVITY

In this activity, students will become familiar with the story and music of *West Side Story*, a musical that became popular in the 1960s. Many of the songs from *West Side Story* are still popular today.

If possible, obtain a video or rental film of the movie version of *West Side Story*. Show the film to your class. (You may need to do this over several class periods since the film is about two hours long.) You may also wish to borrow from the library the book of the musical, as well as a copy of the musical score and a record or tape cassette of the songs. Your school music teacher may be able to help you obtain some of these items.

Explain to students that the plot of *West Side Story* is similar to that of *Romeo and Juliet*—only the setting is different. In *West Side Story*, Tony, of Italian descent, and Maria, of Puerto Rican descent, fall in love. They quickly discover that their love is doomed because their friends and siblings are members of rival gangs in New York City's Upper West Side.

Once students have viewed the film and have had a chance to look at the other materials you have obtained, divide the class into small groups. Ask each group to choose some aspect of *West Side Story* to use as a basis for a group project. Some possible group projects include:

1. A paper and/or oral presentation comparing and contrasting the setting, theme, plot, and characters of *West Side Story* and *Romeo and Juliet*.
2. A presentation of several of the songs from the musical, using instruments such as guitar or piano, as well as singing. This project could include teaching one of the songs to the class.

3. A dramatization of one or more of the scenes from *West Side Story*, with or without the music.

After each group has had a chance to present its project to the class, close the activity with a discussion about the timelessness of Shakespeare's plot and how human nature seems to have changed very little in the last 400 years. Encourage students to share experiences they may have had in which they were caught between two families or groups who were in conflict with each other.

■ **"Greyday"**
by Maya Angelou (page 81)

■ **"Here—Hold My Hand"**
by Mari Evans (page 81)

■ **"Finis"**
by Waring Cuney (page 82)

SELECTION SYNOPSES

These three poems deal with some of the sad and frustrating aspects of romantic love. In "Greyday," the speaker is sad because her lover is away. The speaker in "Here—Hold My Hand" is frustrated because verbal communication does not seem to work with the person she loves. The poem "Finis" speaks rather wistfully about a relationship in which two people have drifted apart—one of them vowing never again to love "overmuch."

SELECTION ACTIVITY

Have students read the short biography of Maya Angelou on page 83. Then have students read at least a portion of Angelou's well-known autobiography, *I Know Why the Caged Bird Sings*. Have students write a short summary of what they have read. Since this book was made into a screenplay, it may be possible to obtain a film or video version that can be shown to the class. If this is the case, show the screenplay and then have students discuss the various events that were important in the life of this writer.

■ **"Housecleaning"**
by Nikki Giovanni (page 87)

■ **"Where Have You Gone"**
by Mari Evans (page 87)

SELECTION SYNOPSES

Both of these poems deal with the end of a relationship. The viewpoint of the speakers, however, is quite different in each poem. The speaker in "Housecleaning" is the one who has decided to end the relationship. It is clear from the tone of the poem that the speaker has no regrets and has not had to struggle very much to come to this decision. In "Where Have You Gone," the speaker is the one who has been left by another. The speaker is suffering a great deal and feels very much the victim. One can infer from the poem that the person who left did so very abruptly and perhaps without warning.

SELECTION ACTIVITY

Most students have probably listened at least once to a radio talk show. A popular format for these shows is to have a well-known psychologist or other expert in human behavior on the air live for a certain period of time. During this time, listeners call in and talk to the expert. Usually the purpose of these calls is to obtain advice about a personal problem. Most of the problems center around human relationships. Very often, the expert uses a person's call to give the audience general advice about a particular type of situation.

Divide the class into small groups. Tell each group that their assignment is to present a ten- to fifteen-minute segment from a radio talk show. Encourage them to let their imaginations run freely. The only restriction is that at least one of the speakers in the poems in this selection must be used as a telephone caller.

Discuss with students how the two speakers represent two different personality types. For example, the speaker in "Housecleaning" seems to have no trouble ending a relationship, finding it as simple as cleaning out the refrigerator or sweeping the house. One gets the feeling that this speaker's life will go on as usual without the relationship. The speaker in the second poem, on the other hand, is a typical victim. She has been abandoned by her lover (whom she still loves) and has lost out on at least part of her financial support. She faces problems that are both emotional and practical. It is likely that she will suffer for awhile before pulling her life back together—unless her lover returns.

Ask students to think about what each speaker might say when calling a radio talk show for advice. For example, perhaps the speaker in "Housecleaning" is being criticized by friends for being cold-hearted or irresponsible and calls to justify her behavior. Perhaps the speaker in the second poem feels overwhelmed by her problems, or she may want advice on how to get her lover back. An interesting variation on the theme is the possibility that the speaker in "Where Have You Gone" has been abandoned by the speaker in "Housecleaning." If this is the case, she might complain that her lover acted as if getting rid of her were no different than vacuuming the rug.

Have each group present their finished talk show segments to the class. An interesting extension or variation of this activity would be to have one student act as an expert who is on the air and have other students spontaneously "call in." In this version of the activity, both the calls and the expert's responses would be unrehearsed.

■ **"Where Are You Now, William Shakespeare?"**
by M. E. Kerr (page 91)

SELECTION SYNOPSIS

The Shakespeare in the title of this autobiographical sketch is a ten-year-old playmate of Marijane, the narrator. A bit of a tomboy, Marijane likes to climb trees and ride bicycles with Billy. But she also likes to play house with a neighborhood girl named Dorothy. The game is always essentially the same: The girls are preparing dinner for their movie-star husbands. Dorothy always prepares a dinner of meat loaf and mashed potatoes for Spencer Tracy. Marijane varies her menu and changes the movie star from time to time. All of this is before the girls go to see *Brother Rat* starring Ronald Reagan. Both girls fall in love with Reagan, and the dinner preparations in the playhouse become tense. Both girls decide to write to Reagan. In hopes of getting a better letter than her friend, Marijane tells Reagan that she is crippled and has to go to his movies in a wheelchair. When Reagan's reply comes, Marijane's father learns of her trick. He forces her to confess her lie to her idol in another letter.

SELECTION ACTIVITY

In this activity, students will write their own versions of the letter that Marijane's father made her write to Ronald Reagan. Students can work in pairs to create their letters, or they can work individually.

Discuss briefly with students some of the things that the letter might contain. Also remind them that it is being written by a ten-year-old child, not a teenager or an adult. The style of the letter should reflect the way a ten-year-old would speak.

After students have completed their letters, have them "send" them to a classmate to read. Ask each student to imagine being Ronald Reagan reading the letter. It time permits, you may wish to have students respond to the letters as they think Ronald Reagan might have responded to Marijane.

■ **"I Dream a World"**
by Langston Hughes (page 101)

■ **"Reflections"**
by Vanessa Howard (page 101)

SELECTION SYNOPSES

The subject matter of both poems is the many social problems that cloud our world. The tone of each poem, however, is quite different. The speaker in "I Dream a World" hopes for a day when things will be better—when all people will be free and when love will be in evidence everywhere. Although he sees the problems at hand, he also sees them as solvable. The speaker in "Reflections" is much less optimistic. If she hopes for a better world, she does not say so. She speaks only of the negative things that she sees: hate, sorrow, and war. She feels that the world is in such bad shape that it should run away and hide.

SELECTION ACTIVITY

Many social and economic problems affect the world in which we live. In this activity, students will choose a current social problem and determine some ways in which the problem might be solved or changed.

Begin by having the class suggest some important social concerns. These concerns may be local or national. For example, perhaps there is a crisis in your town because there is not enough housing senior citizens can afford. Perhaps your city is concerned about drug traffic or large numbers of homeless people. People all over the country may be concerned about terrorist activity and its impact on airline flights, or about crime, or about the lack of equality between people that still exists in many places. List on the chalkboard all of the students' ideas.

Ask each student or group of students to choose one social problem that interests them. Then have them complete these four steps.

1. Define the problem and its scope. This means reading newspaper and magazine articles or using current reference sources.
2. Find out what is already being done to eliminate the problem. This would include any laws that have been passed or that are pending, and any volunteer or professional organizations that have been set up to work on the problem.
3. Express your own ideas about what more could or should be done about this problem. How do you feel about what is being done so far?
4. Offer several suggestions of contributions the average person can make right now to eliminate this problem. This might include volunteering time, donating money, writing a letter to a Congressperson, voting for certain laws, or encouraging adults to vote for them.

Have each student or group present their information to the class in the form of an oral report. Encourage the class to respond to each presentation. Emphasize the significance of this activity by saying it is important to identify problems and to be optimistic about their solutions. It is also important, however, to take practical and informed action against a problem.

STUDENT READING LIST

Mazer, A. N. *Working Days: Short Stories About Teenagers at Work.* Persea Bks., 1997.

Nardo, Don. *Readings on Romeo and Juliet.* Greenhaven, 1997.

Pilling, Ann (comp.) *Love Stories.* CIP, 1997.

Breslin, Rosemary. *Not Exactly What I Had in Mind: An Incurable Love Story.* Villard, 1997.

Hill, Christine. *Langston Hughes: Poet of the Harlem Renaissance.* Enslow, 1997.

Allenbaugh, Kay. *Chocolate for a Woman's Heart: 77 Stories of Love, Kindness and Compassion to Nourish Your Soul and Sweeten Your Dreams.* Simon & Schuster, 1997.

From Globe Fearon Educational Publisher

African American Poetry
Pacemaker Classics and Adapted Classics
Romeo and Juliet William Shakespeare

UNIT 1
Overview

UNIT OBJECTIVES

After completing this unit, students will be able to

- understand the elements of poetry
- understand tone and theme
- use context clues in defining new words
- further develop the plot or characters of a story
- describe abstract feelings in writing
- identify and use images
- recognize slang and archaic usage
- find homophones and synonyms

UNIT SELECTIONS

The theme of this unit is love. The selections are organized into several categories.

- **"The Locket,"** (p. 5) and **"The Kiss,"** (p. 13) are two stories about two very different kinds of love

  LITERARY SKILL: point of view

  READING SKILL: draw conclusions

  VOCABULARY: use synonyms effectively

  WRITING: compare and contrast

- **"Love,"** (p. 21) is an African American folk poem that warns of the pitfalls of falling in love.

  LITERARY SKILL: rhyme

  READING SKILL: understand idioms

  VOCABULARY: words as nouns or verbs

  WRITING: a description of love

- **"First Person Demonstrative,"** (p. 26) This model selection is a modern-day look at what's expected when you fall in love.

  LITERARY SKILL: elements of poetry

  READING SKILL: understand figurative language

  VOCABULARY: figurative expressions

  WRITING: humor

- **"What is Once Loved"** and **"Spring,"** (p. 31) deal with the lasting influence of love.

  LITERARY SKILL: figures of speech

  READING SKILL: compare and contrast

  VOCABULARY: contractions

  WRITING: abstract thoughts or feelings

- **"Luckiest Time of All,"** (p. 35) is a story of a lucky mistake.

  LITERARY SKILL: dialect

  READING SKILL: identify the author's purpose

  VOCABULARY: antonyms

  WRITING: magazine article

- **"Stepping Out With My Baby,"** (p. 43) is a humorous account of a father and son on an outing.

  LITERARY SKILL: point of view

  READING SKILL: distinguish fact from opinion

  VOCABULARY: root words

  WRITING: instructions

- **from *The Tragedy of Romeo and Juliet,*** (p. 49) No unit on love would be complete without *Romeo and Juliet.* An adapted version with the play's important scenes is offered here.

  LITERARY SKILL: figures of speech

  READING SKILL: recognize imagery

  VOCABULARY: archaic words

  WRITING: a letter of advice

Looking at Love

How do I love thee? Let me count the ways.
—Elizabeth Barrett Browning

Birthday, Marc Chagall, 1915. Oil on cardboard, 31¾ × 39¼".
Collection, The Museum of Modern Art, New York
Acquired through the Lillie P. Bliss Bequest.

1

Introducing the Unit Theme

Elizabeth Barrett is addressing her husband-to-be, Robert Browning, in the quotation opening this unit. What might the answer to her question be? How many ways are there to love people? Explore with the class various kinds of love: love for a parent, love for a boyfriend or girlfriend, love for a movie star, love for a pet, love for people suffering misfortune. Does the word "love" mean the same thing to all people?

Viewing Fine Art

Marc Chagall (1889–1985) was born in Belarus and lived most of his life in France and the United States. He lived nearly a century, and in that century profound changes happened in all aspects of life, including art. Chagall's style is linked with the modern art movements of Cubism and Surrealism; some of his works are considered the earliest examples of the latter movement. *Birthday* is an example. Surrealism gives free expression to the unconscious, and the viewer is asked to interpret the message behind the artist's use of unconventional forms. Ask: Is the man in *Birthday* swept off his feet in an expression of love for a woman on her birthday? How are we affected by his snake-like twisting? What does their kiss signify?

■ **"Greyday," "Here—Hold My Hand," and "Finis,"** (p. 81)
Love lost through separation is described in three poems.

LITERARY SKILL: imagery

READING SKILL: paraphrase poetry

VOCABULARY: use context clues

WRITING: images that express feelings

■ **"Housecleaning" and "Where Have You Gone,"** (p. 87)
show two approaches on what to do when a relationship ends.

LITERARY SKILL: tone in poetry

READING SKILL: compare and contrast

VOCABULARY: slang

WRITING: reply to a poem in first person

■ **"Where Are You Now, William Shakespeare?"**
(p. 91) A look at young love is presented.

LITERARY SKILL: tone in nonfiction

READING SKILL: analyze details

VOCABULARY: homophones

WRITING: a reply of friendship

■ **"I Dream a World" and "Reflections,"** (p. 101)
Two poems describe love in the real world.

LITERARY SKILL: theme

READING SKILL: recognize simile and personification

VOCABULARY: synonyms

WRITING: a poem in first person

RELATED MATERIALS

1. *Maya Angelou: Creativity with Bill Moyers.* [Video, Public Affairs TV, Zenger.] An interview with the famous poet.

2. *I Know Why the Caged Bird Sings.* [Audiotape, Random House.] Maya Angelou reads from her book of the same title.

3. *Romeo and Juliet.* [CD-ROM, Stratford Studios, Zenger.] The timeless play on CD.

4. *Romeo and Juliet.* [Paramount: Paramount Home Video, 1968; directed by Franco Zeffirelli.] A video based on the Shakespearean love story.

5. *Meet the Newbery Author: Betsy Byars.* [Video, SRA School Group, Follett, 1991.] A visit with the popular young adult author.

6. *If I Love You, Am I Trapped Forever?* [Audiotape, Random House] by M. E. Kerr.

7. *Poetry and Reflections.* [Audiotape, New York, Caedmon] performed by Langston Hughes. A Collection of poetry spoken by the famous American poet.

8. *Chagall.* [Video, Media Basic Video.] A video showing the artist's work.

9. *Master Poets Collection.* Video Library Collection. Works by popular poets.

10. The following Web sites may also be helpful. Please note that some Internet addresses change frequently. These are the latest versions:

On Beauty and Love. . . , Gary N. Boone's homepage, Prose and Poetry at *http://www.cc.gatech.edu/ grads/b/Gary.N.Boone/ beauty_and_love.html*

Passions in Poetry, Poems for the People, Poems by the people at *http://www.netpoets.com/*

Looking at Love

Why do writers always write about love? Why do singers always sing about love?

It must be because love is a theme always on people's minds.

Do we know, however, what love is? The poet Elizabeth Barrett Browning was able to count the ways she loved someone.

Are we all so lucky? Does everyone find love? What happens when we lose love? Is love for friends, family, and the world a totally different kind of love from what is felt between a boy and a girl?

The selections in this unit are about love and its power over people.

■ LOVE FOUND

What do we mean by "true love"? Are there different kinds of love? "The Locket" and "The Kiss" explore these questions.

"Love," an African American folk poem, describes love as "a lizard" and calls it "the great fall." The poem is simple and direct, yet powerful.

Poet Phyllis Gotlieb knows she loves someone in "First Person Demonstrative," but she is unable to do all the little things people expect from someone in love. Elizabeth Coatsworth reintroduces romance in "What Is Once Loved," while Carole Gregory Clemmons in "Spring" thinks she will be more realistic about "second" love.

"Luckiest Time of All" was the time Mrs. Pickens met Mr. Pickens. "Stepping Out with My Baby" tells about some of the foolish things we do for love.

A classic love story in the English language is William Shakespeare's *The Tragedy of Romeo and Juliet*. An adaptation appears here. Romeo

Inspiration Point, Classic Romance Poetry at *http://www.inspirationpoint. com/ippoetry.htm* and Juliet are bound by love. Their families are divided by hate. Love is found, but lost in death.

■ LOVE LOST

You can become depressed when you are apart from someone you love or love begins to unravel, as Maya Angelou shows in the poem "Greyday." Mari Evans tries to cope with not being able to communicate with someone you love in "Here—Hold My Hand."

Waring Cuney in "Finis" sees love ending and warns that the next time he will not love "overmuch." In "Housecleaning," Nikki Giovanni would end a relationship in the same way she cleans house. Mari Evans in "Where Have You Gone" feels lonely and hurt.

■ LOVE FOR FRIENDS AND FAMILY

Shakespeare reappears in M.E. Kerr's "Where Are You Now, William Shakespeare?" However, this is not the Shakespeare of *Romeo and Juliet*. The characters are even younger than Romeo and Juliet were. As you read it, ask who the characters really love.

■ LOVE FOR THE WORLD

The last two poems in the unit, "I Dream A World" by Langston Hughes and "Reflections" by Vanessa Howard, talk about love (and hate) between different kinds of people rather than just love between individuals. How do you translate your feelings of love for individuals into love for people of different races and countries?

What is love? Come, discover!

Discussing the Unit Theme

Write on the chalkboard or overhead projector the word "LOVE." Ask students for words often paired with love. You could start by listing "love lost" or "puppy love." See how many expressions the class can brainstorm. After you have a list, look at the phrases and discuss how love is thought of in many different ways.

Cooperative Group Activity

In the Introducing the Unit Theme section, students were asked to discuss the meaning of love in the context of the Elizabeth Barrett Browning poem and to discuss different kinds of love. Divide the class into small groups and ask them to list what kinds of love they think are most important. For example, is love for one's country more important than love for one's family? Is love of peace more important than love for an important public figure? Is love for a pet more important than love for a friend?

SELECTION OVERVIEW

SELECTION OBJECTIVES

After completing this selection, students will be able to

- understand point of view
- relate an incident from the third-person point of view
- discuss whether love can have different meanings for different people
- compare and contrast characters' motivations and actions
- understand the advantages and disadvantages of third-person point of view
- revise sentences with unfamiliar words
- draw conclusions

Lesson Resources

The Locket/The Kiss
- Selection Synopsis, Teacher's Edition, p. TT58
- Comprehension and Vocabulary Workbook, pp. 1–2
- Language Enrichment Workbook, p. 1
- Teacher's Resources Reinforcement, p. R1 Test, pp. T1–T2

More About the Unit Theme

Love means different things to different people. When an author is an observer, he or she is able to show what is in the minds of different characters. Alert students to different meanings of love as shown by the thoughts of different characters.

About the Author

Kate Chopin (1851–1904) grew up in St. Louis, Missouri, and suffered personal losses during the Civil War. "The Locket" reflects her first-hand knowledge of this conflict. Most of her writing, however, focuses on women's concerns and approaches to life. One such approach is explored in "The Kiss."

Learn About

The Letter, Mary Cassatt. Courtesy of the Library of Congress

READING FOCUS

Draw Conclusions An author often uses a character's words or thoughts to reveal something about that character's emotions. You can use what the author tells you, and what you know from your own experience, to draw conclusions about a character's emotions. Drawing conclusions helps you better understand characters and what motivates them.

POINT OF VIEW

Have you ever read a story and wished you knew what the characters were thinking?

If the author tells the story as an outside observer, he or she can reveal different characters' actions and thoughts. If the author assumes a role in the story, he or she can tell the story only from the perspective of that role.

The position from which a story is told is called **point of view**. Telling the story as an outside observer is called **third-person** point of view. If a story is written in third-person point of view, the author uses the pronouns *he*, *she*, and *they* rather than *I*. The storyteller in third-person point of view is an observer of the action but not a participant in it.

Third-person writing can be very informative. The author can choose to tell you about different characters' thoughts and help you to understand their motives.

As you read both "The Locket" and "The Kiss," ask yourself:

1. How do you know the story's point of view?
2. How does the story's point of view contribute to your understanding of the characters?

WRITING CONNECTION

Think of something interesting or amusing that recently happened to you or someone you know. Write three sentences about it using the third-person point of view. Remember to use the pronouns *he*, *she*, and *they*.

Viewing Fine Art

Mary Cassatt (1844–1926) was an American expatriate who lived in Paris. She was strongly influenced by Degas and by Japanese design. Her delicate studies of women and children were carefully constructed with the asymmetrical balance Western artists had admired in Japanese prints.

Above, for example, the interesting patterns of wallpaper and dress are set off by the strong geometric design of the brown wall, desk edge, and chair. Ask: Does this painting seem to capture the mood of a specific time period? Why?

Cooperative Group Activity

Have students work in pairs throughout this oral exercise. Begin by having one partner tell a story in first-person point of view, using the pronoun *I*. The other partner retells the same story in the third-person point of view, using the pronouns *he*, *she*, and *they*. Then have the partners switch roles.

The Locket

ADAPTED

by Kate Chopin

PART 1

One night in autumn a few men were gathered about a fire on the slope of a hill. They belonged to a small group of Confederate forces and were waiting for orders to march. Their gray uniforms were old and worn out. One of the men was heating something in a tin cup over the fire. Two were lying down a little distance away, and a fourth was trying to read a letter and had come close to the light. He had unbuttoned a good bit of his flannel shirt.

"What's that you have around your neck, Ned?" asked one of the other men.

Ned—or Edmond—did not reply. He went on reading his letter.

"Is it your sweetheart's picture?"

"It's no girl's picture," said the man at the fire. He had removed his tin cup and was stirring its contents with a small stick. "It's a charm—some kind of lucky piece that's supposed to keep him out of trouble. That's how come Frenchy got promoted and never got a scratch since he's been here. Hey, French! Am I right?" Edmond looked up from his letter.

"What is it?" he asked.

"Isn't that a lucky charm you got around your neck?"

"It must be, Nick," returned Edmond with a smile. "I don't know how I could have gone through this year and a half without it."

The letter he was reading had made Edmond heartsick and homesick. He stretched out on his back and looked straight up at

---

Confederate (kun FED uh raht) during the Civil War, a supporter of the South

The Locket ■ 5

Develop Vocabulary Skills
Divide the class into six groups. Assign five new words to each. The groups look the words up in the dictionary, and use each new word in a sentence.

ESL Activity
Have students consider the following questions: Have you ever thought you would like to live in a different time? What period of time would you choose and why? If you fell in love, what would you want the other person to be like?

TEACHING PLAN

INTRODUCE

Motivation
("The Locket") Ask students if they have a small possession to which they are very attached. Does the possession have a special meaning or sentiment? Ask: How would you feel if you lost it?

("The Kiss") Ask students what the saying "You can't have your cake and eat it, too" means to them. Ask: Have you ever had to choose one thing over an equally important thing? What helped you make your decision? How did you feel?

Purpose-Setting Question
What kind of love is expressed in these stories?

READ

Literary Focus:
Point of View
The author establishes point of view right away to give the reader information about the setting and characters. Discuss with students how the third-person point of view can present a wide variety of details about the different characters.

Reading Focus:
Draw Conclusions
Tell students that an author often reveals important information about a character through descriptions of their thoughts and actions. ("The Locket") Ask: What details does the author give about Edmond (Ned)? What is he doing? What is he thinking? What conclusions can you draw about him? Discuss the importance he attaches to the locket.

("The Kiss") Ask: What do the girl's thoughts in the fourth paragraph tell about her feelings towards Brantain? Do you think her reason for deciding to accept his proposal predicts a happy marriage?

CLOSE

Have students complete Review the Selection on pages 18–19.

T5

the blinking stars. But he was not thinking of them nor of anything but a certain spring day when a girl was saying good-bye to him. He could see her as she took from her neck the locket that she put around his own. It was an old-fashioned locket bearing pictures of her father and mother with their names and the date of their marriage. It was her most precious earthly possession. Edmond could feel again the folds of the girl's soft white gown. He could picture her as she circled her fair arms about his neck. Her sweet face, pained by the thought of parting, appeared before him as vividly as life. He turned over, burying his face in his arm. There he lay, still and motionless.

The darkness of night with its semblance of peace settled upon the camp. He dreamed that the fair Octavie brought him a letter. He had no chair to offer her and was pained and embarrassed at the condition of his clothing. He was ashamed of the poor food he had to offer her.

He dreamed of a serpent coiling around his throat. When he tried to grasp it, it glided away from his clutch. Then he was awakened by a great deal of noise.

"Get up! You! Frenchy!" Nick was shouting in his face. There was what appeared to be a scramble and a rush rather than any smooth movement. The hillside was alive with clatter and motion. Lights suddenly appeared among the pines. In the east the dawn was unfolding out of the darkness. Its glimmer was still dim in the plain below.

"What's it all about?" wondered a big black bird perched in the top of the tallest tree. He was an old and wise bird, yet he was not wise enough to guess what it was all about. So all day long he kept blinking and wondering.

The noise reached far out over the plain and across the hills. It awoke the little babes that were sleeping in their cradles. The smoke curled up toward the sun and shadowed the plain. The stupid birds thought it was going to rain, but the wise one knew better.

"They are children playing a game," thought he. "I shall know more about it if I watch long enough."

Literary Focus:
Point of View
How does the author use the third-person point of view to present a clear picture of the scene? How does this influence your understanding of Edmond's feelings?

Critical Thinking:
Analyze
What do you think the big black bird is seeing? Why do you think the author chose to present this scene through the bird's thoughts?

---

semblance (SEHM bluns) outward appearance or show

The Locket ■ 7

By night they had all vanished away with their noise and smoke. Then the old bird fluffed his feathers. At last he had understood! With a flap of his great, black wings he shot downward, circling toward the plain.

A man was picking his way across the plain. He was dressed as a priest. His mission was to bring the consolations of religion to any of the men who might still be alive. A young man accompanied him, carrying a bucket of water.

There were no wounded here. They had all been taken away. But the retreat had been hurried, and the vultures and the priest would have to look to the dead.

---

consolations (KAHN suh LAY shunz) the acts of comforting in time of sorrow

There was a soldier—a mere boy—lying with his face to the sky. His hands were clutching the grass on either side. His fingernails were stuffed with earth and bits of grass that he had gathered in his despairing grasp upon life. His musket was gone. He was hatless and his face and clothing were dirty. Around his neck hung a gold chain and locket. The priest, bending over him, removed it from the dead soldier's neck. He had grown used to the terrors of war and could face them without flinching, but its sorrows, somehow, always brought the tears to his old, dim eyes.

The church bells were ringing half a mile away. The priest and the young man knelt and murmured together the evening prayers and a prayer for the dead.

PART 2

Back in Louisiana, where Octavie lived, the peace and beauty of a spring day had fallen upon the earth like a blessing. Along the leafy road, which skirted the narrow stream near her house, rumbled an old-fashioned carriage, much the worse for hard and rough usage over country roads and lanes. The fat, black horses went in a slow, measured trot in spite of the constant urging on the part of the fat coachman. Within the vehicle were seated the fair Octavie and her old friend and neighbor, Judge Pillier. He had come to take her for a morning drive.

Octavie wore a plain black dress. A narrow belt held it at the waist. Its sleeves were gathered into close-fitting wristbands. She had discarded her hoop skirt and appeared not unlike a nun. Beneath the folds of her clothing was the old locket. She never displayed it now. It had returned to her sanctified in her eyes. It seemed to have been made precious as material things sometimes are by being forever identified with a significant moment in one's life.

A hundred times she had read over the letter with which the locket had come back to her. No later than that morning she had again pored over it. As she sat beside the window, smoothing the letter out upon her knee, heavy and spiced odors stole in to her with the songs of birds and the humming of insects in the air.

---

musket (MUHS kut) an old type of firearm, now replaced by the rifle
sanctified (SANK tuh fyd) set apart as holy

The Locket ■ 9

Reading Focus:
Draw Conclusions
What do you think happened to Edmond? Why do you think so?

Critical Thinking:
Analyze
The priest weeps over the "sorrows" of war. Ask: Whose sorrows might the priest be thinking about?

Literary Focus:
Plot
The author shifts the scene of the story to a description of Octavie in Louisiana. She seems to be dressed in mourning clothes. Ask: How do you know who Octavie is? Why is she now wearing the locket?

Enrichment
Explain to students that during the time period of this story, people who had suffered the loss of one close to them were expected to dress very conservatively for at least a year. They were also expected to avoid recreation and most social gatherings.

She was so young and the world was so beautiful that there came over her a sense of unreality as she read again and again the priest's letter. He told of that autumn day drawing to its close, with the gold and the red fading out of the west, and the night gathering its shadows to cover the faces of the dead. Oh! She could not believe that one of those dead was her own! A spasm of resistance and rebellion seized and swept over her. Why was the spring here with its flowers and its warm breath if he was dead! Why was she here! What further had she to do with life and the living!

Octavie had experienced many such moments of despair, but a blessed resignation had never failed to follow. This feeling of acceptance then fell upon her like a mantle and enveloped her.

"I shall grow old and quiet and sad like poor Aunt Tavie," she murmured to herself as she folded the letter and put it back in the desk. Already she gave herself a modest little air like her Aunt Tavie. She walked with a slow glide, unconsciously imitating Mademoiselle Tavie, whom some youthful sorrow had robbed of earthly joys while leaving her with the illusions of youth.

As she sat in the old carriage beside the father of her dead beloved, Octavie again felt the terrible sense of loss. The soul of her youth clamored for its rights, for its share in the world's glory and joy. She leaned back and drew her veil a little closer about her face. It was an old black veil of her Aunt Tavie's. A whiff of dust from the road had blown in. She wiped her cheeks and her eyes with her soft, white handkerchief, a homemade handkerchief, made from one of her old fine petticoats.

"Will you do me the favor, Octavie," requested the judge in his usual courteous tone, "to remove that veil. It seems out of harmony, somehow, with the beauty and promise of the day."

The young girl obediently yielded to her old companion's wish. She unpinned the black veil from her bonnet, folded it neatly, and laid it upon the seat in front of her.

"Ah! That is better, far better!" he said in a tone expressing great relief. "Never put it on again, dear." Octavie felt a little hurt, as if he wished to keep her from sharing the sorrow that had been

---

resignation (reh zig NAY shun) patient acceptance

Literary Focus:
Point of View

Ask: How does the third-person point of view allow the reader to understand Octavie's view of her future?

Critical Thinking:
Infer

Octavie thinks about and even imitates "poor Aunt Tavie." Ask: What do you think might have caused Aunt Tavie to dress and act the way she did?

Reading Focus:
Draw Conclusions

Edmond's father, the judge, reacts with relief when Octavie obediently removes her veil. Ask: What does the judge's reaction say about his hopes for Octavie's future?

placed upon all of them. Again she drew forth the old homemade handkerchief.

They had left the big road and turned into a level plain which used to be an old meadow. There were clumps of thorn trees here and there, gorgeous in their spring beauty. Some cattle were grazing off in the distance in spots where the grass was tall and thick. At the far end of the meadow was the towering lilac hedge that lined the lane leading to Judge Pillier's house. The scent of its heavy blossoms met them like a soft and tender embrace of welcome.

As they neared the house the old gentleman placed an arm around the girl's shoulders. Turning her face up to him he said, "Do you not think that on a day like this, miracles might happen? When the whole earth is full of life, does it not seem to you, Octavie, that heaven might for once relent and give us back our dead?" He spoke very low, softly, and impressively. In his voice was an unusual trembling, and there was excitement in every line of his face. She gazed at him with eyes that were full of pleading and a certain terror of joy.

They had been driving through the lane with the towering hedge on one side and the open meadow on the other. The horses had somewhat quickened their lazy pace. As they turned into the avenue leading to the house, a whole choir of birds suddenly sang a melodious greeting from their leafy hiding places.

There was the old gray house with its sloping roof. Amid the blur of green, and dimly, she saw familiar faces and heard voices as if they came from far across the fields. Suddenly Edmond was holding her. She felt the beating of his heart against her and the agonizing joy of his kisses. The spirit of life and the awakening spring had given back the soul to her youth and told her to rejoice.

It was many hours later that Octavie pulled out the locket and looked at Edmond with a questioning appeal in her glance.

"It was the night before a battle," he said. "In the hurry of the fight, and the falling back the next day, I never missed it till the battle was over. I thought of course I had lost it in the heat of the struggle, but it was stolen."

relent (ruh LEHNT) to become gentler or more compassionate

Critical Thinking:
Compare and Contrast
Compare and contrast Judge Pillier's mood with Octavie's mood as they approach the house. Ask: How might this foreshadow future events?

Literary Focus:
Description
The author describes the end of the ride and approach to the house. Ask: How does this description alter the mood of the story?

"Stolen," she shuddered. She thought of the dead soldier with his face uplifted to the sky in an agony of prayer.

Edmond said nothing, but he thought of his messmate—the one who had lain far back in the shadow, the one who had said nothing.

The Kiss

ADAPTED

by Kate Chopin

It was still quite light out of doors, but inside, with the curtains drawn and the low fire sending out a dim, uncertain glow, the room was full of deep shadows.

Brantain sat in one of these shadows. It had overtaken him and he did not mind. The darkness gave him the courage to keep his eyes fastened as ardently as he liked upon the girl who sat in the firelight.

She was very good-looking, with the fine, rich coloring that true brunettes often have. She was quite calm, as she gently stroked the satiny coat of the cat that lay curled in her lap. She occasionally sent a slow glance into the shadow where her companion sat. They were talking low, of ordinary things that plainly were not the things that occupied their thoughts.

She knew that he loved her. He was an honest fellow who didn't have enough guile to conceal his feelings, and he had no desire to do so. For the past two weeks he had sought her company eagerly and persistently. She was confidently waiting for him to declare himself and she meant to accept him. The rather unattractive Brantain was enormously rich. Even though she didn't especially like him, she liked and required all the things that his wealth could give her.

During one of the pauses between their talk of the last tea and the next party, the door opened. A young man whom Brantain knew quite well entered. The girl turned her face toward him. A stride or two brought him to her side, and he bent over her chair. Before she could suspect what he would do, for she did not realize that he had not seen her visitor, he pressed a warm kiss upon her lips.

---

ardently (AR dent lee) with great enthusiasm and eagerness
guile (GYL) the use of cunning; slyness

The Kiss ■ 13

Literary Focus:
Point of View
The third-person point of view reveals the thoughts and actions of the two characters in the opening scene. Ask: What do the two characters think of each other?

Reading Focus:
Draw Conclusions
Ask: What will Brantain probably think about the action of the young man who enters suddenly?

Brantain slowly arose. The girl arose, too, but quickly. The newcomer stood between them, a little amusement and some challenge struggling with the confusion in his face.

"I believe," stammered Brantain, "I see that I have stayed too long. I—I had no idea—that is, I must wish you good-bye." He was holding his hat with both hands, and probably did not see that she was extending her hand to him. Her presence of mind had not completely deserted her, but she could not have trusted herself to speak.

After Brantain had gone, the other man spoke. "Hang me if I saw him sitting there, Nattie! I know it must have been awkward for you. But I hope you'll forgive me this once—this very first break. Why, what's the matter?"

"Don't touch me! Don't come near me," she returned angrily. "What do you mean by entering the house without ringing?"

"I came in with your brother, as I often do," he answered coldly, explaining himself. "We came in the side way. He went upstairs and I came in here hoping to find you. The explanation is simple enough and ought to prove to you that I didn't mean any harm. But do say that you forgive me, Nathalie," he pleaded, softening.

"Forgive you! You don't know what you are talking about. Let me pass. It depends on—a good deal whether I ever forgive you."

At that next party which she and Brantain had been talking about, she approached the wealthy young man with a delicious frankness of manner when she saw him there.

"Will you let me speak to you a moment or two, Mr. Brantain?" she asked with a sweet but perturbed smile. He seemed extremely unhappy. But when she took his arm and walked away with him, seeking a quiet corner, the expression on his face changed. A ray of hope seemed to mingle with his look of almost comical misery. She was apparently very outspoken.

"Perhaps I should not have approached you, Mr. Brantain. But—but, oh, I have been very uncomfortable, almost miserable, since what happened the other afternoon. When I thought how you might have misinterpreted it, and believed things . . ." As she spoke, hope was clearly overcoming the misery in Brantain's round, guileless face. Nathalie continued, "Of course, I know it is

---

stammered (STAM urd) in speaking, repeated the same sound without meaning to
perturbed (pur TURBD) greatly disturbed or alarmed

The Kiss ■ 15

Critical Thinking:
Infer
Ask: What can you infer about the relationship between Nathalie and the young man who kissed her?

Discussion
Ask: Why do you think Nathalie is so angry with the young man?

Literary Focus:
Point of View
Ask: How does the third-person point of view help the reader understand Brantain's feelings?

Reading Focus:
Draw Conclusions

On page 15, the author describes Brantain's face as "guileless." What does this quality indicate about the possible success of Nathalie's persuasive speech?

Discussion

Ask: What do you think of Nathalie's story and her acting ability? Do you think Brantain will believe and forgive her?

Critical Thinking:
Interpret

Ask: Do you think Nathalie was surprised by Harvy's response to her at the end? Were you?

nothing to you, but for my own sake I do want you to understand that Mr. Harvy is an intimate friend of long standing. Why, we have always been like cousins——like brother and sister, I may say. He is my brother's most intimate associate and often thinks that he is entitled to the same privileges as the family. Oh, I know it is ridiculous, uncalled for, to tell you this—it is undignified, even." She was almost weeping as she spoke. "But it makes so much difference to me what you think of—of me." Her voice had grown very low and agitated. The misery had all but disappeared from Brantain's face.

"Then you do really care what I think, Miss Nathalie? May I call you Miss Nathalie?" They turned into a long, dim corridor that was lined on either side with tall, graceful plants. They walked slowly to the very end of it. When they turned to walk back, Brantain's face was radiant and hers was triumphant.

◆ ◆ ◆ ◆ ◆ ◆ ◆ ◆

Harvy was among the guests at the wedding. He sought Nathalie out in a rare moment when she stood alone.

"Your husband," he said, smiling, "has sent me over to kiss you."

A quick blush suffused her face and round polished throat. "I suppose it's natural for a man to feel and act generously on an occasion of this kind. He tells me he doesn't want his marriage to interrupt that pleasant closeness that has existed between you and me. I don't know what you've been telling him," said Harvy with an insolent smile, "but he has sent me here to kiss you."

She felt like a chess player who, by the clever handling of his pieces, sees the game going his way. Her eyes were bright and tender with a smile as they glanced up into his. Her lips looked hungry for the kiss which they invited.

"But, you know," he went on quietly, "I didn't tell him so—it would have seemed ungrateful—but I can tell you. I've stopped kissing women. It's dangerous."

Well, she had Brantain and his million left. A person can't have everything in this world. It was a little unreasonable of her to expect it.

---

suffused (suh FYOOSD) spread through or over, as with a color, liquid, or light
insolent (IN suh lunt) deliberately rude or insulting

16 ■ Unit 1

The Kiss ■ 17

Mini Quiz

Write the following questions on the chalkboard or overhead projector and call on students to fill in the blanks. Discuss the answers with the class.

1. "The Locket" takes place during the _____.

2. A _____ returned the locket to Octavie.

3. Edmund tells Octavie that the locket was _____ before the battle.

4. When Harvy kisses her, Nathalie is afraid _____.

5. Nathalie marries Brantain for his _____.

Answers
1. Civil War
2. priest
3. stolen
4. Brantain will not marry her
5. wealth (money)

UNDERSTAND THE SELECTION

Answers

1. A priest visiting the battlefield takes the locket from a body and returns it.
2. Edmond is the judge's son.
3. Nathalie wants to marry Brantain for his wealth.
4. The thief thought it was a lucky charm that would protect him in the battle.
5. Judge Pillier knows that Edmond is alive. He seems happy and tells Octavie to remove her mourning veil.
6. Nathalie is choosing marriage for wealth rather than for love.
7. Brantain gladly believes Nathalie is telling him the truth and loves only him.
8. Sample answer: I would be angry that his action caused grief for others but sad because he thought the locket would protect him.
9. Sample answer: No, I would not have believed her because I saw the way Harvy kissed her earlier.
10. Sample answer: Octavie will be happier because she truly loved Edmond.

Respond to Literature

Students' answers will vary. Explore their answers by asking them to define and perhaps categorize different kinds of love.

WRITE ABOUT THE SELECTION

Prewriting

Ask students to consider relationships they have had with good friends. What made them successful? List students' answers on the chalkboard. Then, draw a Venn diagram on the chalkboard. Label one circle "Octavie/Edmond" and label the other circle "Nathalie/Brantain." Suggest to students that they copy the diagram in their notebooks. They should list the qualities of each relationship that are different in the circles. The qualities that are the same for both couples can be listed in the area where the two circles intersect.

UNDERSTAND THE SELECTION

Recall

1. Who finds the locket and returns it to Octavie?
2. What is the relationship between Edmond and Judge Pillier?
3. Why does Nathalie want to marry Brantain?

Infer

4. What must the thief of the locket have believed about it?
5. What must the judge know that Octavie does not? How do you know?
6. What choice is Nathalie making when she scolds Harvy?
7. Describe Brantain's feelings when Nathalie tells him about her relationship with Harvy.

Apply

8. How do you feel about the soldier who stole the locket?
9. If you were Brantain, would you have believed Nathalie's explanation of her relationship to Harvy? Why?
10. Who do you think will have a happier marriage, Octavie or Nathalie? Why?

> ### Respond to Literature
> These stories suggest that "love" can mean different things to different people. Do you agree with this idea? Explain.

WRITE ABOUT THE SELECTION

Use what you have read to compare and contrast these relationships: Octavie/Edmond and Nathalie/Brantain. How would each character define "love"? Which couple will probably be happier in the future? Come up with your own definition for a successful relationship between two people.

Prewriting List the qualities you feel are necessary for a good relationship, such as a marriage. Then brainstorm for descriptions of Octavie and Edmond as shown through their thoughts and actions. Write down any details that reveal their emotions, motivations, and hopes. Do the same for Nathalie and Brantain.

Writing Use your prewriting notes to define a successful relationship. Then write a paragraph about each couple, comparing and contrasting their personal qualities and attitudes toward love and relationships. End with a paragraph which answers the question: which couple will be happier in the future?

Revising Did you state your own definition of a successful relationship, such as a marriage? Did you make use of your prewriting notes to compare and contrast Octavie's and Nathalie's relationships? Whose relationship, if any, is a success according to your definition? Is this the couple you picked to have a happy future?

Proofreading Reread what you have written and check for errors. Have you capitalized the first word of every sentence and all proper nouns?

Writing

Circulate as students work individually. Explain that the author's use of the third-person point of view should help them to understand the thoughts of the characters.

Revising

Point out passages in the stories that illustrate how the characters feel about each other. Discuss why people might have different ideas about what is important in a relationship.

Proofreading

Have students work in pairs and exchange papers for proofreading.

THINK ABOUT POINT OF VIEW

The third-person point of view allows the author to observe all aspects of the story. The author can then choose to tell the reader not only what the characters are doing and saying but also what they are thinking. This helps the reader to understand their motivations.

1. Look at the paragraphs in "The Locket" in which the author tells the thoughts of the bird viewing the battle scene. What does the bird's confusion reveal to you about the scene?

2. The author describes the beauty of spring while also telling of Octavie's sorrowful thoughts. What effect does this contrast have on Octavie?

3. How would this story be different if told from Edmond's point of view?

4. Early in "The Kiss" the author reveals Nathalie's thoughts about Brantain. How does this make you feel about what she later tells him about Harvy?

5. If Nathalie had told this entire story, what might be her final line?

READING FOCUS

Draw Conclusions Do you think Brantain may ever regret marrying Nathalie? Do you think he may discover her reason for marrying him? How might he feel? Use details from the story to explain your conclusion.

DEVELOP YOUR VOCABULARY

Both of these stories use some unfamiliar vocabulary for which we have more common words. Different words that have the same meaning are called **synonyms**.

The definitions of unfamiliar words were given in the stories, but do you understand how these words are used?

Below are several sentences from the stories. Each has at least one unfamiliar word. Rewrite the sentences substituting a more common synonym or phrase for the unfamiliar word. You may have to rearrange the parts of the sentences.

1. The darkness of night with its *semblance* of peace settled upon the camp.

2. When the whole earth is full of life, does it not seem . . . that heaven might for once *relent* and give us back our dead?

3. He was an honest fellow who didn't have enough *guile* to conceal his feelings.

4. A quick blush *suffused* her face and round polished throat.

5. "I don't know what you've been telling him," said Harvy with an *insolent* smile, "but he has sent me here to kiss you."

Review the Selection ■ 19

READING FOCUS

Sample Answer
Brantain may regret marrying Nathalie if she begins spending a lot of money. He might realize that she is more fond of his money than of him. He has already seen her kissing someone else, and this may also make him suspicious.

SELECTION OVERVIEW

SELECTION OBJECTIVES

After completing this selection, students will be able to

- understand rhyme
- see how rhymes are used in everyday life
- talk about feelings associated with love
- write a description of love
- analyze different kinds of rhymes
- recognize words used as both nouns and verbs
- understand idioms

Lesson Resources

Love, An African American Folk Poem

- Selection Synopsis, Teacher's Edition, p. TT59
- Comprehension and Vocabulary Workbook, pp. 3–4
- Language Enrichment Workbook, pp. 2–3
- Teacher's Resources Reinforcement, p. R2 Test, pp. T3–T4

More About Rhymes

"End rhyme" occurs when similar-sounding words are at the end of lines. "Internal rhyme" occurs when these words are within lines. There are many different rhyming patterns in poetry. The pattern in this folk poem, for example, is broken only once. Also, certain rhyming patterns within a set number of lines make up a specific form of poem. A limerick, for example, contains five lines; the end-of-line rhyming pattern is first-second-fifth lines, and third-fourth lines.

Background Notes

Folk poems might be new to students, but folk songs are probably not. Real folk songs, like folk poems, have obscure origins; little is known about who wrote the lyrics. Today, the definition of a folk song is often stretched to include a new, contemporary style of music, but authentic folk music still endures and continues to come from "the folk."

READING FOCUS

Understand Idioms An idiom is an expression that has a different meaning from the dictionary definition of its words. For example, if you fall for a trick, you know you don't literally fall. You can look at the context to determine another meaning.

Idioms are often used in poetry to express a particularly strong feeling, and they can enhance the overall tone of the poem. Look for idioms as you read the poem. If you are not sure whether or not an expression is an idiom, think of the dictionary definitions of the words in the phrase.

Learn About

RHYME

Many, but not all, poems are written in rhyme. Why is rhyme a popular technique?

Our brains seem to remember things that are repeated. Rhyme is the repeating of the same sound, so this repetition says to us "Hey, take notice of this and remember!"

The next selection is a **folk poem**, a term that refers to poetry that has unknown origins and an unknown author. It was told among African Americans, and no doubt rhyme helped people remember its message.

The pairing of words by rhyme can help to communicate the feeling and meaning of a poem. An imaginative rhyme can make you smile or nod with immediate understanding.

As you read the folk poem, ask:

1. What are the rhymes, and where do they occur in the poem?
2. Do the rhymes occur regularly?

WRITING CONNECTION

Rhymes are all around us, not just in poetry. Suppose that you work for an advertising company. You have just been told to write a rhyme that advertises a product. Choose a product, and write a rhyming advertisement for it.

Develop Vocabulary Skills

Write the new vocabulary word, *gizzard*, on the chalkboard or overhead projector. Ask students to guess why the poet may have used it in a poem about love. (You may want to hint at an end-rhyme association with *lizard*.)

ESL Activity

Have students work in pairs or groups to choose a product. Then brainstorm a list of rhyming adjectives that describe that product. You may want to have them begin by finding rhyming words that describe a familiar object, such as a desk or a book.

Cooperative Group Activity

Have groups of four or five students share their lines from the Writing Connection. Ask each group to pick what it considers the best rhyme. Write these rhymes on the board. As a class analyze which lines would most effectively sell a product. Have students save their rhymes for the next Cooperative Group Activity.

Love

an African American folk poem

Love is a funny thing
Shaped like a lizard,
Run down your heartstrings
And tickle your gizzard.

You can fall from a mountain,
You can fall from above,
But the great fall is
When you fall in love.

Folk Singer, Charles White. Courtesy Heritage Gallery, Los Angeles.
Harry Belafonte Collection

gizzard (GIZ-urd) [Colloq.] the stomach; usually a humorous usage

Love ■ 21

Mini Quiz

Write the following questions on the chalkboard or overhead projector and call on students to fill in the blanks. Discuss the answers with the class.

1. This selection is a _____ poem.

2. Love, shaped like a lizard, _____ _____ a person's heartstrings.

3. Love can tickle your _____.

4. Two places you can fall from are _____ and _____.

5. The great fall is _____ _____ _____ _____.

Answers

1. folk
2. runs down
3. gizzard
4. a mountain, above
5. when you fall in love

TEACHING PLAN

INTRODUCE

Motivation

Ask students what animal they would choose to help describe the way love affects people? For example, can you compare love with a dog, a cat, or even—as in the next selection—with a lizard?

Purpose-Setting Question

How does love make you feel?

READ

Literary Focus:
Rhyme

Have students say the rhyming words. Invite them to supply other end-rhymed lines that could be used instead.

Reading Focus:
Understand Idioms

Have students read the poem through without stopping, just for the sheer fun of its language. Then go through the poem line by line and point out the use of idioms. What is the literal meaning of lines like, "Run down your heartstrings," and "When you fall in love"? What meaning does the author wish to convey by using these expressions?

CLOSE

Have students complete Review the Selection on pages 22–23.

Viewing Fine Art

Charles White (1918–1979) was an African American artist who made many illustrations, prints, and paintings on subjects relating to African American history. Among his illustrations are the "I Have a Dream" series. White was widely honored during his lifetime. Ask: What would you say the mood of the picture is? Do you think the mood of the picture fits the mood of the poem? Explain.

UNDERSTAND THE SELECTION

Answers

1. A lizard is compared to love.
2. The heart and the gizzard are mentioned.
3. Falling in love is the greatest fall.
4. The theme of this poem is love, and what it's like.
5. By comparing love to a lizard, the author makes love seem slippery, fast, and ticklish.
6. No, they don't exist; they are an image for emotions.
7. The author uses the word "funny" to mean "strange" or "unpredictable."
8. Sample answer: I'd compare it to a bear—hungry, very cute, and warm.
9. The word "fall" is used to create a feeling of downward motion.
10. When you fall you may feel out of control, as you do when you're in love.

Respond to Literature

Ask students whether they like the feeling of being swept off their feet by emotion, or whether love is like a painful accident. Have they ever been swept away by another emotion—such as pride, or anger? What do the feelings caused by these emotions have in common?

WRITE ABOUT THE SELECTION

Prewriting

Encourage students to consider all kinds of images for a comparison to love. Suggest some ideas such as a snowstorm, a high-tension wire, falling leaves.

Writing

Circulate as students work individually. For those who need assistance, guide them into focusing on the relationship between love and the thing they've chosen to compare it to.

Revising

Discuss as a class when rhyme is effective. Point out to students that rhymes created simply for the sake of rhyming rather than for connecting ideas are usually distracting to the reader.

Proofreading

Once students have proofread their own papers, have them write a list of 10 words they used in their poems. Before exchanging the list with a partner, they can purposely misspell a word. Their partner then looks for every misspelled word and tries to spell it correctly. The writer gets a point for every misspelled word that isn't caught.

UNDERSTAND THE SELECTION

Recall

1. Love is compared to an animal in the poem. What animal is it?
2. Two parts of the body are mentioned in the poem. What are they?
3. According to the poem, what is the greatest fall of all?

Infer

4. What is the theme of the poem?
5. Why do you think love is compared to an animal?
6. What is meant by "heartstrings"? Do they really exist?
7. The poem calls love "a funny thing." What is meant by "funny"?

Apply

8. If you had to describe how love felt, what description might you use?
9. How is falling from a mountain or from "above" like falling in love?
10. Why do you think the word "fall" is used to describe what happens when you first love someone?

Respond to Literature

Do you believe people "fall" in love or is it an old-fashioned idea? Have you ever fallen in love? What did it feel like to you?

WRITE ABOUT THE SELECTION

What is love like for you? What can you compare it to?

Maybe it is like a broken-down car that will not start, a stereo set at maximum volume, or an alarm clock that always seems to go off too early. Perhaps you think love is like the flowering plant on your window sill.

What does love look like? How does it affect your attitude toward life? How does it make you feel?

Write your own description of love by comparing it with something real.

Prewriting In the middle of a piece of paper, write down the object that you want to compare love to. Around it, cluster ideas about its connection to love.

Writing Use the cluster to write a paragraph comparing love to this object. Make sure you make clear the connection between the object and love.

Revising Turn your paragraph into poetry. Consider using rhyme to add emphasis or to make imaginative connections between ideas. You may prefer using free verse so that you can form lines and verses in any form. You may want to try writing a concrete poem where the lines form a recognizable shape.

Proofreading Reread what you have written and check for spelling errors. If you are using rhyming words, a mistake in spelling could confuse the reader.

ESL Activity

In the poem the author compares love to a lizard. Have students make a list of emotions that they equate with love. Then make another list of animals that they equate with those emotions. Talk about why they chose certain animals to symbolize certain emotions.

THINK ABOUT RHYME

What counts as a rhyme? Do you consider *thing* and *strings* a rhyme? Most poets would, although strictly speaking the words do not rhyme. The final *s* on *strings* makes the sounds slightly different.

1. **Poetic license** usually allows rhymes between words that "almost" rhyme. Think of an example.

2. Rhymes often occur at the end of lines, but they also can occur within the same line. Find an example of **internal** rhyme.

3. The best rhymes are those that link interesting words or ideas. What is your favorite rhyme in the poem, and why?

4. Eliminate one of the rhymes in the poem by substituting another word. Reread the poem. How does it sound now?

5. Without looking back, try to recite the poem. Which lines, if any, are easiest to remember?

READING FOCUS

Understand Idioms As you read the poem, you were able to recognize the author's use of idioms. Choose one idiom from the poem. How did the use of that idiom enhance the poem?

DEVELOP YOUR VOCABULARY

A **noun** is a word that names a person, place, idea, or object. A **verb** is a word that expresses an action or state of being. Poets often use both forms of a word in a poem to make a connection between two ideas or feelings.

In the poem you have just read, *fall* is used as both a noun and a verb. Which *fall* is a noun and which is a verb?

In the sentences below, decide whether the italicized word in the sentence pairs is a noun or verb. Find the dictionary definition that fits the meaning of the word in the sentence. Then, use both words in original sentences.

1. **a.** You can *fall* from a mountain.
   b. The great *fall* is love.

2. **a.** She took a *turn* down the street.
   b. I *turn* cartwheels when I see her.

3. **a.** *Love* is a book with blank pages.
   b. We *love* creating new things.

4. **a.** The *shape* of my feelings is square.
   b. I *shape* my life around you.

Review the Selection ■ 23

THINK ABOUT RHYME

Sample Answers

1. "There was an old woman tossed up in a basket,
   Seventeen times as high as the *moon*;
   Where she was going I couldn't but ask it,
   For in her hand she carried a *broom*."

2. A lean, clean machine.

3. *Lizard* and *gizzard* because it links two different things.

4. You can fall from a *tree*,
   But the great fall is
   When you fall in *love*.

   Substituting "tree" for "above" eliminates the rhyme with the last word in the poem, "love." Emphasis on "love" is lost.

5. It could be:
   You can fall from a mountain
   You can fall from above,
   But the great fall is,
   When you fall in love.

   Devices other than rhyme make these lines easy to remember. Repetition of "fall" and repetition of sentence structure (except the third line) help these lines to stay in your mind.

DEVELOP YOUR VOCABULARY

Answers

1. (a) verb—to plunge downward by accident
   (b) noun—the result of falling

2. (a) noun—movement in a different direction
   (b) verb—to move in a different direction

3. (a) noun—strong attraction between people
   (b) verb—to like very much to do something

4. (a) noun—the form of something
   (b) verb—to make something into a particular form

READING FOCUS

Sample Answer

I think the idiom "tickle your gizzard" enhances the poem because it catches your attention and is funny. The poem seems to be saying not to take yourself too seriously when you fall in love.

Focus ON POETRY

Discuss with students the ideas contained in the first three paragraphs of the "Elements" section. Then, point out the importance of understanding poetry as a "concentrated" genre: The poet attempts to get more out of less. Language is used creatively and energetically, with the poet sometimes speaking in what might seem like code. A poem must be read several times, the meanings of words and phrases explored, and the connections between ideas made clear.

ELEMENTS OF POETRY

Use the untitled African American folk poem on page 21 to explore the elements of a poem.

Who is the main character in the poem? There is no "I" speaker perhaps because the poem has no one known author. The "you" of the poem refers to the reader.

Where is imagery used? Think of how a lizard running down your heartstrings might feel, and how this enhances the poem.

What is the theme? If students thought of a title for the poem, remind them of it and discuss how it might relate to the theme.

What is the tone? The image of love "shaped like a lizard" helps make it less serious—even though the theme is a serious one.

Can the rhyming structure be improved? Try making the one line that does not rhyme (the one ending in "mountain") rhyme with another line. Does this improve the poem?

What figure of speech is used in the poem? Discuss the comparison of love and a lizard. Do students agree that love can have a shape?

*M*any people do not like poetry. Others think poetry is still the world's most powerful form of communication—whether it be a sixteenth-century Shakespearean sonnet or a modern age lyric by Stevie Wonder.

The poet uses language in a very different way from prose writers. To understand a poet's message, you need to learn the elements of poetry.

Character   Character in poetry refers to the speaker. If the poet uses *I*, you usually learn about the poet him- or herself. The poem can be very personal, as in "Finis." However, sometimes the *I* is a speaker very different from the poet.

Often the poet addresses an unidentified "you," as in "Where Have You Gone." This person is an absent character whom we know only through the speaker.

Imagery   Poets often use language to appeal to any or all of your five senses. They use images to help you see, hear, smell, feel, or taste what they are writing about.

The author of "Greyday" uses images from the Christian religion of "a crown of thorns" and "a shirt of hair" to help you feel the heaviness she is describing.

Theme   The idea or meaning of a poem is its theme. The poems "Reflections" and "I Dream A World" both have themes about the world. In the first, the poet expresses the idea that there is only hate, not love, in the world. The author of the second poem might agree with that idea, but he also expresses hope that "love will bless the earth."

Tone   The poet conveys to you an attitude when writing. That attitude is called tone. Tone is a clue to meaning.

Maybe the tone is earnest yet light-hearted, as in "First Person Demonstrative." The tone also can be sad, as in "Finis."

You can determine a poem's tone by simply asking yourself, "How does this poem make me feel?" Do not be afraid to give more than one answer, for often tone creates many feelings.

Rhyme   Rhyme is repetition of the same sound. If it comes at the end of a line, it is called **end rhyme**. If it comes within a single line, it is called **internal rhyme**.

End rhyme is the more common type. "Love," an African American folk poem uses it. Notice the rhyming of *lizard* and *gizzard*, and *above* and *love*.

Figures of Speech   When you use an expression that says one thing to mean something else, you are using a figure of speech. Common figures of speech are metaphor, simile, personification, and hyperbole.

The author of "Spring" talks about a "wishbone," yet she does not mean that she and her "second man" actually will find a wishbone and make wishes. "Wishbone" is a **metaphor** for the hopes that she and her partner will have.

The comparison of one thing to another through the use of *like* or *as* is a **simile**. In "I Dream a World," for example, *joy* is described as being *like a pearl*.

Another line in "I Dream a World" is an example of **personification**, or the giving of human qualities to nonhuman subjects. In this line the poet talks of a world "where wretchedness will hang its head." The poet has given a human quality to an abstract idea in order to express his idea more forcefully.

Another way to express ideas forcefully is to exaggerate by using **hyperbole**. In "First Person Demonstrative," the poet says she would rather "wrench off an arm than hug you." She uses hyperbole to exaggerate her feelings.

As you read the next selections in this unit, look for the elements of the poems. Ask yourself these questions:

1. How do the elements of poetry such as imagery and figures of speech strengthen a poem?
2. Is the theme of a poem always easy to determine? What can I do if a poem confuses me?

SELECTION OVERVIEW

SELECTION OBJECTIVES

After completing this selection, students will be able to

- understand tone
- describe how they express feelings
- use humor in writing a poem
- understand figurative language

Lesson Resources

First Person Demonstrative
- Selection Synopsis, Teacher's Edition, p. TT59
- Comprehension and Vocabulary Workbook, pp. 5–6
- Language Enrichment Workbook, pp. 4–6
- Teacher's Resources
  Reinforcement, p. R3
  Test, pp. T5–T6
  Literary Analysis, pp. L1–L2

More About the Unit Theme

When love is found, do people begin to take it for granted? Or does love move to a level where two people don't have to demonstrate in outward ways their feelings toward each other?

About the Author

Phyllis Gotlieb is a Canadian writer who writes both poetry and prose. She once said that the most help she ever got in developing her writing was from her husband, a computer scientist.

First Person Demonstrative

by Phyllis Gotlieb

FOCUS ON POETRY STUDY HINTS

Can you imagine anyone heaving a brick rather than saying, "I love you?" The speaker is exaggerating her feelings, using hyperbole.

Notice the speaker's appeal to your sense of touch. She uses imagery to describe how she feels.

The speaker fears showing her emotions. She speaks in first person. Her character is frank and open.

The poet is being sarcastic, making fun of usual expressions about feelings. The tone is serious yet mocking.

The "message" is the theme of the poem. The speaker wants to make sure that the reader "gets" her main idea. If you do not, read it again, she says, in a lighthearted yet earnest tone.

> I'd rather
> heave half a brick than say
> I love you, though I do
> I'd rather
> 5 crawl in a hole than call you
> darling, though you are
> I'd rather
> wrench off an arm than hug you though
> it's what I long to do
> 10 I'd rather
> gather a posy of poison ivy than
> ask if you love me
>
> so if my
> hair doesn't stand on end it's because
> 15 I never tease it
> and if my heart isn't in my mouth it's because
> it knows its place
> and if I
> don't take a bite of your ear it's because
> 20 gristle gripes my guts
> and if you
> miss the message better get new
> glasses and read it twice

posy (POH zee) a flower or bouquet
gristle (GRIS ul) tough, elastic white animal tissue
gripe (GRYP) to cause sharp pain in the bowels

ESL Activity

Have students work with partners to discuss the many ways that feelings can be expressed. Some people share their feelings openly, while others keep them inside. Have the students choose one emotion, such as happiness, to focus on.

Viewing Fine Art

Sometimes called a primitive surrealist, Philip Evergood (1901–1973) is an American artist with a style that combines a kind of social realism with odd and unexpected images. In *Her World* (p. 27) and several other paintings, Evergood depicts the world of certain African Americans. Made in 1948, the painting may symbolize, with its fence and the child behind it, the barriers facing African Americans at that time. Ask: What does the title of this painting suggest to you? How does the painting relate to the poem depicted?

Cooperative Group Activity

Ask students to divide into small groups. Have them read to one another the advertising rhymes they wrote for the previous Writing Connection. Ask the groups, How important is tone in advertising? Then have them choose their best rhyme, present it to the class, and explain how its tone could influence advertising sales.

Her World, Philip Evergood. The Metropolitan Museum of Art, Arthur Hoppock Hearn Fund

First Person Demonstrative ■ 27

Develop Vocabulary Skills

Write the three new vocabulary words—*posy*, *gristle*, and *gripe*—on the chalkboard or overhead projector. Pronounce and define the words, then ask students how these words help establish the tone of the poem.

Mini Quiz

1. The speaker would rather throw a _____ than say "I love you."

2. The word that might make the speaker crawl in a hole is _____.

3. The speaker's _____ doesn't stand on end.

4. Her _____ isn't in her mouth.

5. The speaker suggests anyone not understanding her message should read the poem _____.

Answers

1. brick
2. darling
3. hair
4. heart
5. twice

TEACHING PLAN

INTRODUCE

Motivation

Is it easy to express deep feelings? Discuss with students whether they find it easy or hard to show emotion. Guide the discussion in the direction of love. Ask students whether love is an easy emotion to share, or do they tend, like our next poet, to say "I'd rather heave half a brick than say I love you"?

Purpose-Setting Question

Why is love between a man and woman sometimes very difficult to express?

READ

Literary Focus:
Elements of Poetry

The blue side notes in this selection provide a model for students to understand the literary elements introduced in Focus on Poetry, pages 24–25. Suggest that students notice the nearly identical structures of the lines in the first verse: "I'd rather" followed by a "than" comparison and then a qualifying "though." Only once is the structure broken slightly—in the last three lines the "though" qualifier is gone.

Reading Focus:
Understand Figurative Language

Explain how figures of speech, such as hyperbole, often enhance the message of a poem. In this case, it is clear from the author's exaggerated declarations, such as, "I'd rather wrench off an arm than hug you," that she feels strongly about the subject of her poem.

CLOSE

Have students complete Review the Selection on pages 28–29.

T27

UNDERSTAND THE SELECTION

Answers

1. She would rather crawl in a hole.
2. poison ivy
3. If you don't understand what I mean, get new glasses and read the poem again.
4. Yes—she answers each of her strongly-felt emotions with "though" [I do love you]
5. It's something you want to stay away from at nearly any cost—which is what the speaker says she wants to do when it comes to expressing feelings.
6. They all include parts of the body; they all make fun of common expressions.
7. The speaker is afraid to show her feelings of love.
8. Answers will vary; the speaker gives seven examples to explain that she is afraid to show feelings of love.
9. Sample answer: I'd rather crawl in a hole than call you darling." Darling is something my mother called me when I was 3 years old.
10. Students should be able to identify this as a modern poem because of the contemporary language that is used.

Respond to Literature

Ask students whether reading Gotlieb's poem has changed their minds about expressing their feelings. Do they feel more, or less, secure about voicing their feelings?

WRITE ABOUT THE SELECTION

Prewriting

With the class, draw up a cluster of reactions to a certain feeling, such as pride or joy. Use the chalkboard or overhead projector to write down their responses for use in the next step.

UNDERSTAND THE SELECTION

Recall

1. What would the speaker rather do than call someone "darling"?
2. What plant is mentioned in the poem?
3. What instructions does the speaker give at the end of the poem?

Infer

4. Does the speaker love the person to whom she is talking? Explain.
5. Why do you think poison ivy is mentioned in the poem?
6. What connects all the "if" expressions in the second half of the poem?
7. What is the "message" of the poem?

Apply

8. The theme of the poem is repeated a number of times. Point to at least three examples, and explain them.
9. Which of the statements of the theme seems clearest to you?
10. Do you think this poem was written recently, or a long time ago? Why?

Respond to Literature

Do you show your feelings? Maybe you are like the speaker in "First Person Demonstrative." Perhaps you are somewhere in between. Describe your personal style of expressing feelings.

WRITE ABOUT THE SELECTION

Phyllis Gotlieb uses humor in "First Person Demonstrative," even if the theme of the poem is serious. She exaggerates, using hyperbole to make her point. She mocks, poking fun at figurative expressions that are used to describe strong emotions.

Can you use humor to make some point about your feelings? Write a poem to express your feelings in a humorous way. You may choose a feeling other than love.

Prewriting Pick a feeling, or several feelings, you would like to write about. Write the feelings in the middle of the page. How do having these feelings make you feel? In other words, do you become strong when you are angry or afraid, or shy when you care about someone? Cluster ideas around the feeling or feelings. Think humor!

Writing Use the form of "First Person Demonstrative" to write several lines of poetry about your subject. Substitute your ideas for the poet's, if you like. Study how she uses hyperbole, and see if you can do the same.

Revising Have you used imagery? Add an image appealing to one sense, or try to strengthen any images you have.

Proofreading Writing a poem in the first person means you will be using a lot of pronouns. Reread what you have written and make sure you are using all pronouns correctly, and your verb forms agree. Also, be very careful to check the punctuation in your poem.

Writing

Circulate among the students as they work individually. Repeat to students having trouble that using Gotlieb's structure might make writing easier.

Revising

As a class, think of an image to illustrate one feeling from the class cluster.

Proofreading

Have students circle all pronouns, identify their antecedents, and make sure the verb forms are correct.

ESL Activity

Have students write a single paragraph describing themselves as a more emotional or more controlled person in displaying their feelings. Review the requirements of a paragraph.

THINK ABOUT POETRY

Poetry shares some elements with other types of literature. However, because a poet wants to create a strong feeling with only a few words, he or she also uses special language techniques. The main characters in a poem are usually the speaker and the listener. Poets use images to appeal to their readers' senses. Poems, like stories and plays, have themes—ideas—to communicate. Poets convey their attitudes toward their subjects through tone. Rhyme is the repetition of the same sounds at the ends of words. Poets use rhyme at the end or inside lines of their poems. Figures of speech are expressions that compare two or more unlike things.

1. Who is the speaker in "First Person Demonstrative"? Who is the listener?

2. What is your favorite image in this poem? Explain.

3. What is the poem's theme?

4. What is the tone of the poem? How do you know?

5. Give an example of a figure of speech.

DEVELOP YOUR VOCABULARY

Figurative expressions are groups of words that have a special meaning. The meaning is usually different from the meanings of the individual words.

Phyllis Gotlieb uses several figurative expressions in "First Person Demonstrative."

Below is a list of the figurative expressions that Gotlieb uses in her poem, and some others. What does each mean?

1. hair standing on end

2. heart in your mouth

3. keep an ear to the ground

4. look down your nose at someone

5. put your foot in your mouth

6. cross your fingers

7. to jawbone someone

8. a lump in your throat

9. catch your eye

10. bite your lip

Now write five sentences that use figurative expressions to make a point.

Review the Selection ■ 29

THINK ABOUT POETRY

Answers

1. The speaker is the writer; the listener is the person to whom she is writing.

2. Sample answer: My favorite image is of a posy of poison ivy.

3. Love is the theme.

4. Humorous; she is making fun of herself and the situation with the language and images she uses in the poem.

5. Sample answer: "My heart isn't in my mouth."

DEVELOP YOUR VOCABULARY

Answers

1. fear
2. apprehension
3. pay close attention
4. feel superior to someone
5. say the wrong thing
6. hope for something
7. attempt to persuade by using one's position
8. sentimentality
9. to attract your attention
10. hold back your feelings

Sample sentences:

1. I got a lump in my throat when I saw you the first time.

2. Bob gets embarrassed because he always puts his foot in his mouth.

3. Cross your fingers that the last bus hasn't left.

4. Only tall people should look down their noses at others.

5. Keep your ear to the ground for the next big opportunity.

SELECTION OVERVIEW

SELECTION OBJECTIVES

After completing these selections, students will be able to

- identify and understand figures of speech
- use metaphor in description
- discuss the power of memory to retain emotions
- write a description of a feeling
- give the root words of contractions
- compare and contrast

Lesson Resources

What Is Once Loved/Spring
- Selection Synopses, Teacher's Edition, pp. TT59
- Comprehension and Vocabulary Workbook, pp. 7–8
- Language Enrichment Workbook, pp. 7–8
- Teacher's Resources Reinforcement, p. R4 Test, pp. T7–T8

More About Figures of Speech

Figurative expressions are closely related to figures of speech. Both can be grouped under what is called figurative language, or language that describes things indirectly. The opposite of figurative language is literal language, or language that means exactly what it says. Ask students to identify these examples.

I'm *keeping my fingers crossed* that I win the race.

I *hope* to win the race.

About the Authors

Elizabeth Coatsworth, born 1893 in Buffalo, N.Y., began writing poetry but later turned to children's books and novels. Carole Gregory Clemmons, born in 1945 in Youngstown, Ohio, has worked for *Look* magazine and in educational television. Her poems have been published in such collections as *A Galaxy of Black Writing* (1970).

T30

The Equatorial Jungle, Henri Rousseau. National Gallery of Art, Washington, D.C.

READING FOCUS

Compare and Contrast When you compare and contrast two different pieces of writing, you may find similarities and differences that you did not notice at first. Comparing allows you to see broader themes or similarities in tone, while contrasting may help you to notice differences in smaller details. As you read, try to find as many similarities and differences in the following two poems.

30 ■ Unit 1

Learn About

FIGURES OF SPEECH

Poetry allows you to use language in a free and creative way. Figures of speech give you a special kind of freedom. They allow you, the poet, to make connections between things that normally you might not connect.

The connections allow the reader to transfer knowledge of one thing to another. It is as though you, the writer, are carrying a torch lighting new paths for the reader.

Metaphor is one of the most common figures of speech. A **metaphor** shows the connection between two ideas without using the words "as" or "like." An example is "The sun was a golden shield hung in the sky." Other figures of speech are simile, which compares using the words *like* or *as*; personification, which gives human qualities to nonhuman things; and hyperbole, which exaggerates a quality or element.

As you read "What Is Once Loved" and "Spring," ask yourself:
1. What metaphors are used?
2. What is the purpose of the metaphors?

WRITING CONNECTION

People use figures of speech all the time, both in writing and speaking. Create your own metaphor.

Develop Vocabulary Skills

Since there are no new vocabulary words in these selections you may want to use this opportunity to review new words from previous selections.

Viewing Fine Art

Henri Rousseau (1844–1910) worked as a customs collector to support himself. He was a self-taught artist who created imaginative worlds of giant tropical leaves and mysterious lurking animals. Ask: How does the detail make this scene strikingly real and powerful?

Cooperative Group Activity

After students have worked individually on the Writing Connection, ask them to share their metaphors with a partner. Challenge the partners to think of related metaphors and then present their work to the class. As they work, check that students are using metaphors, not similes.

What Is Once Loved

by Elizabeth Coatsworth

What is once loved
You will find
Is always yours
From that day.
Take it home
In your mind
And nothing ever
Can take it away.

Spring

by Carole Gregory Clemmons

the second man I love,
we'll find the wishbone
and make our wishes,
I won't even try for the strongest end,
because this time when the bone breaks
either way I'll be in.

TEACHING PLAN

INTRODUCE

Motivation
Draw a wishbone on the chalkboard and ask what a wishbone brings to mind. Discuss the symbolism of the wishbone—both as a hope for something and as a contest between two people. Suggest that while only one of the poets likens love to a wishbone, each yearns for love.

Purpose-Setting Question
Does love for somebody stay with you, even after a relationship ends?

READ

Literary Focus:
Figures of Speech
Encourage students to think about common figures of speech. Do figures of speech help them to better express their ideas or feelings? How? Discuss how the author of "Spring" uses the image of a wishbone to express her feelings about love.

Reading Focus:
Compare and Contrast
Both "What Is Once Loved" and "Spring" explore themes of love. However, the point of view of these two poems is different. Ask: How does that affect the tone of each? Does "Spring" seem less formal and more intimate? Why or why not?

CLOSE

Have students complete Review the Selection on pages 32–33.

Comparing Selections
These poems are related because both speakers have already found love. In "What Is Once Loved," the poet couldn't have written the poem without having felt love herself. In "Spring," the poet had found a first love, but that relationship has ended and she is reflecting on what a second love might be like.

Mini Quiz

Write the following questions on the chalkboard or overhead projector and call on students to fill in the blanks. Discuss the answers with the class.

1. When you love something, according to Elizabeth Coatsworth, it is _____ yours.

2. She also advises to take _____ what you once loved.

3. Carole Gregory Clemmons opens her poem by describing the kind of relationship she'll have with the _____ _____ she loves.

4. She and her new man will find a _____.

5. She's sure that eventually the bone they hold will _____.

Answers
1. always
2. home
3. second man
4. wishbone
5. break

UNDERSTAND THE SELECTION

Answers

1. Love, or "what is once loved"
2. "in your mind"
3. "the second man I love"
4. It could be either or both. The past tense is not used for any of the verbs, just the indefinite time adverb "once."
5. The poet uses "home" as a metaphor for the human mind because home is the most personal place we have.
6. It is a metaphor for love and its joys and problems.
7. She won't try to dominate the relationship.
8. It could refer to anything because it's not defined in the poem.
9. Spring represents a new beginning; it is a metaphor for a new love.
10. Sample answer: One break won't necessarily end the relationship. People in love learn they must give and take.

Respond to Literature

Do students agree with what the speaker says in "What Is Once Loved"—that once you love something it is always yours? Discuss memory and other ways in which you "keep" something even when it is gone.

WRITE ABOUT THE SELECTION

Prewriting

Brainstorm as a class. Write on the chalkboard or overhead projector as many feelings as students can think of.

Writing

Circulate as students work individually. For students having difficulty, review their notes with them and discuss ideas they could develop.

UNDERSTAND THE SELECTION

Recall

1. What "is always yours" in "What Is Once Loved"?

2. Where should you keep what "is always yours"?

3. Who will be at the other end of Carole Gregory Clemmons's "wishbone"?

Infer

4. Do you think Elizabeth Coatsworth is talking about lost love or an existing love in "What Is Once Loved"?

5. Explain the phrase "home in your mind" in "What Is Once Loved."

6. What does a wishbone have to do with love in the poem "Spring"?

7. Explain why the speaker says she will not "try for the strongest end" in "Spring".

Apply

8. Does *what* in "What Is Once Loved" refer to people, things, or both?

9. Why do you think Carole Gregory Clemmons chose the title "Spring"?

10. Explain the last line "either way I'll be in" in the poem "Spring."

Respond to Literature

Can you *always* carry in your mind "what is once loved," or is that an exaggeration of the power of memory?

WRITE ABOUT THE SELECTION

What is it like to carry something "in your mind"? It is an odd expression. You can never carry a "thing" in your mind, just abstract thoughts.

Poets try to make abstract thoughts, particularly feelings, become real. You will do the same. How can you turn a feeling into something real? Try using a metaphor; it might help.

Prewriting Brainstorm to find a feeling to describe. Choose one of your ideas, and jot down a few notes about it. Think about what you associate it with: perhaps a specific color, a special place, a wonderful song, or a valued possession. Write about experiences with the feeling, give examples, and compare it to other things.

Writing Use your notes to describe the feeling. Try to write in poetry form, but use prose if you can not.

Revising Have you used a metaphor to describe the feeling? Try to add one if you have not. Make your ideas clear by using specific words and vivid phrases. Eliminate any dull, boring, or overused phrasing.

Proofreading Reread what you have written and check for mistakes in verb-subject agreement. Singular nouns take singular verbs, and plural nouns take plural verbs. Be careful with punctuation at the end of lines if you wrote a poem. You can use punctuation more creatively in poetry, but do not confuse your readers.

Revising

Return to the list of feelings the class brainstormed. Take one of the feelings and ask the class to think of metaphors describing it.

Proofreading

Review verb-subject agreement rules. Point out how punctuation is used in the two poems. Clemmons does not follow strict punctuation and capitalization rules, yet what punctuation she does use is used clearly and effectively.

ESL Activity

Have students use their list of descriptive words and phrases to write a short paragraph about their lost love. Discuss the requirements of a well-written paragraph.

THINK ABOUT FIGURES OF SPEECH

Carole Gregory Clemmons used a metaphor to relate love to a wishbone in "Spring." She also could have used a **simile**, which is distinguished from a metaphor by the use of the words *like* or *as*: "Love is *like* a wishbone."

Phyllis Gotlieb used hyperbole, a figure of speech, again and again in her poem "First Person Demonstrative."

A fourth common figure of speech is **personification**. Human qualities are given to a nonhuman subject in the following example: *The broom stared at my empty hands.*

1. What human qualities are given to the broom in the example above?

2. How can personification be used to describe a car or something a car does?

3. Use a simile to express the kind of love Phyllis Gotlieb describes in "First Person Demonstrative. "

4. Do you think hyperbole is used in "What Is Once Loved"? Think back to your answer to the discussion question in "Review the Selection."

5. Use a metaphor to describe weather.

READING FOCUS

Compare and Contrast As you read "What Is Once Loved" and "Spring," you were able to look for similarities and differences between the two poems. In what ways are the poems similar? In what ways are they different?

DEVELOP YOUR VOCABULARY

A **contraction** is a shortened form of two words. One or more letters have been omitted, and these are replaced by an apostrophe (').

> **Examples: he** + **is** = **he's**
> **they** + **will** = **they'll**

Only one contraction requires a spelling change:

> **will** + **not** = **won't**

Write the two words that have been joined, or contracted, to form the italicized contractions.

1. *We'll* find the wishbone.

2. I *won't* even try for the strongest end.

3. Either way *I'll* be in.

4. *I'd* rather heave a brick than say I love you.

5. If my hair *doesn't* stand on end *it's* because I never tease it.

6. If I *don't* take a bite of your ear *it's* because gristle gripes my guts.

Write an original paragraph or poem that uses five contractions.

Review the Selection ■ 33

Answers
1. the ability to see
2. Sample answer: The car sighed and stalled.
3. Sample answer: Love is like a roller coaster.
4. Sample answer: No. The poet herself isn't exaggerating, although other people might think so.
5. Sample answer: The pea soup fog makes driving hazardous.

DEVELOP YOUR VOCABULARY

Answers
1. We will
2. will not
3. I will
4. I would
5. does not; it is
6. do not; it is

Sample paragraph:
    I won't go to the movie because it doesn't sound very good, and it's late anyhow. I'd rather that we all stay here at the campsite, and go to bed early so we're ready for tomorrow's hike.

READING FOCUS

Sample Answer

The poems are alike in that they both express ideas or themes of love. The poem "Spring" seems more real and personal because it is told in the first person, while "What Is Once Loved" seems more formal or less intimate because it is told in the third person.

SELECTION OVERVIEW

SELECTION OBJECTIVES

After completing this selection, students will be able to

- understand the use of dialect
- write a paragraph using dialect
- analyze and discuss story content
- write a magazine article about an alternate viewpoint
- recognize antonyms and use them in sentences
- identify the author's purpose

Lesson Resources

Luckiest Time of All
- Selection Synopsis, Teacher's Edition, p. TT59
- Comprehension and Vocabulary Workbook, pp. 9–10
- Language Enrichment Workbook, pp. 9–10
- Teacher's Resources Reinforcement, p. R5 Test, pp. T9–T10

More About Dialect

Ask students to discuss dialects in their region of the country. Are they aware of any vocabulary, grammar, or pronunciation differences between their speech and that of a typical TV newscaster? Ask students if they think that the standard English used by the media has had any effect on regional dialects. Ask students how they think regional dialects came about in the first place.

More About the Unit Theme

In this selection, an elderly woman tells about the surprising way she met her first love. Ask students for titles or descriptions of other stories or films that are about people finding love unexpectedly.

READING FOCUS

Identify the Author's Purpose Writers have many reasons for putting words on paper, including a need to express themselves. Most text, though, is written either to describe, entertain, inform, or persuade, or for a combination of these. You can understand the author's purpose by looking at the word choice, tone, and—of course—subject matter. As you read, think about what the author's purpose may be. Jot down details in the selection that reveal the author's purpose.

Learn About

DIALECT

Dialect is a way of speaking that is different from standard English, or the language spoken in the United States. Dialect is the form of the language that is used among a certain group or only in a certain place. Dialects may vary from region to region of a country. For example, people from Maine may use words or pronunciations not used by natives of Texas. Some fiction writers use dialect to create colorful speech. This technique helps give life and personality to the characters in a story. As you read "Luckiest Time of All," notice the southern dialect spoken by Mrs. Elzie F. Pickens. Try to "hear" her talking as you read.

Ask yourself:

1. How does Mrs. Pickens' dialect make her a more realistic and interesting character?
2. What does the use of dialect tell you about the setting?
3. How would the story be different if Mrs. Pickens spoke standard English?

WRITING CONNECTION

Think of someone you know who speaks in a dialect or in some other unique way. Write a paragraph in the "voice" of that person. Then write how the dialect adds a dimension or uniqueness.

Cooperative Group Activity

After students have chosen a "voice" to write from, have them work in pairs to practice speaking in their dialects before they begin writing. After they have written their paragraphs, have students read them to one another and give constructive comments and suggestions.

Luckiest Time of All
from The Lucky Stone

by Lucille Clifton

Mrs. Elzie F. Pickens was rocking slowly on the porch one afternoon when her Great-granddaughter, Tee, brought her a big bunch of dogwood blooms, and that was the beginning of the story.

"Ahhh, now that dogwood reminds me of the day I met your Great-granddaddy, Mr. Pickens, Sweet Tee.

"It was just this time, spring of the year, and me and my best friend Ovella Wilson, who is now gone, was goin to join the Silas Greene. Usta be a kinda show went all through the South, called it the Silas Greene show. Somethin like the circus. Me and Ovella wanted to join that thing and see the world. Nothin wrong at home or nothin, we just wanted to travel and see new things and have high times. Didn't say nothin to nobody but one another. Just up and decided to do it.

TEACHING PLAN

INTRODUCE

Motivation
Ask students what they know about how their parents or grandparents met one another. Did any meetings happen in unusual ways? Discuss whether finding a special person to love is any different today than it was in the past.

Purpose-Setting Question
Do you believe in love at first sight?

READ

Literary Focus:
Dialect
Some students may have difficulties understanding the dialect. Read the story aloud to students, reading expressively and having them read along silently. Direct students to look and listen for dialect in the story. When you finish, encourage students to point out and paraphrase dialogue that is written in dialect. Model paraphrasing for them as needed.

Reading Focus:
Identify the Author's Purpose
As students read, have them ask themselves questions to determine the author's purpose for writing. Suggest they answer these questions: What is the tone? What is the theme? What is the setting? What is the plot? How do these elements reveal the author's purpose?

CLOSE

Have students complete Review the Selection on pages 40–41.

Develop Vocabulary Skills
Write on the board or a transparency the footnoted vocabulary words and their definitions. Point out the words that would be familiar only in certain regions of the country. Discuss other regional terms that students may be unfamiliar with.

ESL Activity
Have groups discuss dialects and styles of language in their countries of origin. As you read the story aloud, pause after each paragraph to see if listeners need clarification.

Background Notes
Historically, some of the best-known dialects in this country have been those of Pennsylvania, the South, the Appalachian and Ozark Mountains, and the Louisiana bayou country. Since even before 1889, when the American Dialect Society was organized, scholars have been fascinated by the origins and word patterns of dialects.

T35

"Well, this day we plaited our hair and put a dress and some things in a croksack and started out to the show. Spring day like this.

"We got there after a good little walk and it was the world, Baby, such music and wonders as we had never had seen! They had everything there, or seemed like.

"Me and Ovella thought we'd walk around for a while and see the show before goin to the office to sign up and join.

"While we was viewin it all we come up on this dancin dog. Cutest one thing in the world next to you, Sweet Tee, dippin and movin and head bowin to that music. Had a little ruffly skirt on itself and up on two back legs twistin and movin to the music. Dancin dancin dancin till people started throwin pennies out of they pockets.

"Me and Ovella was caught up too and laughin so. She took a penny out of her pocket and threw it to the ground where that dog was dancin, and I took two pennies and threw-em both.

"The music was faster and faster and that dog was turnin and turnin. Ovella reached in her sack and threw out a little pin she had won from never being late at Sunday school. And me, laughin and all excited, reached in my bag and threw out my lucky stone!

---

plaited (PLAT ihd) braided
croksack, variation of *croker sack* (KRO kur sak) a bag of rough cloth
    or burlap

36 ■ Unit 1

Critical Thinking:
Predict
Ask: Is the story going to have a happy or sad ending? Why do you think so?

"Well, I knew right off what I had done. Soon as it left my hand it seemed like I reached back out for it to take it back. But the stone was gone from my hand and Lord, it hit that dancin dog right on his nose!

"Well, he lit out after me, poor thing. He lit out after me and I flew! Round and round the Silas Greene we run, through every place me and Ovella had walked before, but now that dancin dog was a runnin dog and all the people was laughin at the new show, which was us!

"I felt myself slowin down after a while and I thought I would turn around a little bit to see how much gain that cute little dog was makin on me. When I did I got such a surprise! Right behind me was the dancin dog and right behind him was the finest fast runnin hero in the bottoms of Virginia.

"And that was Mr. Pickens when he was still a boy! He had a length of twine in his hand and he was twirlin it around in the air just like the cowboy at the Silas Greene and grinnin fit to bust.

"While I was watchin how the sun shined on him and made him look like an angel come to help a poor sinner girl, why, he twirled that twine one extra fancy twirl and looped it right around one hind leg of that dancin dog and brought him low.

"I stopped then and walked slow and shy to where he had

---

bottoms (BAH tumz) low-lying land along a river
twine (TWYN) a thin rope with several strands

Luckiest Time of All ■ 37

picked up that poor dog to see if he was hurt, cradlin him and talkin to him soft and sweet. That showed me how kind and gentle he was, and when we walked back to the dancin dog's place in the show he let the dog loose and helped me to find my stone. I told him how shiny black it was and how it had the letter *A* scratched on one side. We searched and searched and at last he spied it!

"Ovella and me lost heart for shows then and we walked home. And a good little way, the one who was gonna be your Great-granddaddy was walkin on behind. Seein us safe. Us walkin kind of slow. Him seein us safe. Yes." Mrs. Pickens' voice trailed off softly and Tee noticed she had a little smile on her face.

"Grandmama, that stone almost got you bit by a dog that time. It wasn't so lucky that time, was it?"

Tee's Great-grandmother shook her head and laughed out loud.

"That was the luckiest time of all, Tee Baby. It got me acquainted with Mr. Amos Pickens, and if that ain't luck, what could it be! Yes, it was luckier for me than for anybody, I think. Least mostly, I think it."

Tee laughed with her Great-grandmother though she didn't exactly know why.

"I hope I have that kind of good stone luck one day," she said.

"Maybe you will someday," her Great-grandmother said.
And they rocked a little longer and smiled together.

---

acquainted (uh KWAYN tid) known to one another

38 ■ Unit 1

Lucille Clifton (1936–   )

MORE ABOUT
THE AUTHOR

Lucille Clifton is a prolific author. She has received numerous literary awards, including a nomination for the Pulitzer Prize and has also been named Poet Laureate of Maryland.

Many of Clifton's poems condemn racist attitudes and foster African American identity and pride. She is particularly known for the African American experiences that she writes about from the perspective of strong, heroic female characters. Her writing style is purposely simple, and she has received much praise for the genuineness of the dialect in her prose and poetry.

Additional Works

BY LUCILLE CLIFTON

You may wish to suggest these works by Lucille Clifton for additional reading:

Generations: A Memoir, Random House, 1976. This is Clifton's prose autobiography, which was praised for its celebration of an African American family's survival.

Good Times: Poems, Random House, 1969.

The Lucky Stone, (juvenile) illustrations by Dale Payson, Delacorte, 1979.

My Friend Jacob, (juvenile) illustrations by DiGrazia, Dutton, 1980. A young African American boy befriends a mentally challenged teenager.

When (Thelma) Lucille Clifton was a little girl growing up in Depew, New York, she already understood the importance of literature. That was because of her parents, neither of whom had finished elementary school. However, her father often told his four children stories, especially about his ancestors. Her mother wrote poetry filled with feeling, which she read to her children. Lucille Clifton has said, "From Mama I knew one could write as a way to express oneself."

Clifton is best known for her poetry and her children's books. She says her writing is often inspired by her own six children: Sidney, Fredrica, Channing, Gillian, Graham, and Alexia.

Clifton's work is centered on the African American family. She is concerned about the destruction of its youth. She believes that husbands and fathers are necessary family members. Her characters often portray strong and loving women. She says, "I am not interested if anyone knows whether or not I am familiar with big words. I am interested in trying to render big ideas in a simple way."

UNDERSTAND THE SELECTION

Answers

1. her Great-granddaughter, Tee
2. They want to travel and see new things.
3. an angel that has come to help a poor sinner girl
4. Sample answer: She had no more money.
5. He catches up with the running dog and comes to save the girls.
6. Sample answer: Her last name started with an *A*.
7. Sample answer: People had laughed at them and they were tired.
8. Sample answer: a rabbit because she was chased by a dog; sunshine because she was happy
9. Sample answer: a rabbit's foot, a coin, a four-leafed clover
10. They had a happy marriage. Sample answer: I think they had an ideal marriage, one with love and respect.

Respond to Literature

Discuss with students what Elzie's first impressions were of Amos. What did she find out by observing him? What story clues imply that Amos was indeed an especially good man? Ask students how they would decide if someone is kind, gentle, or trustworthy.

WRITE ABOUT THE SELECTION

Prewriting

Review orally with the group how Mrs. Pickens met her future husband. Have students think about what it might be like to be Amos, and then use student suggestions to list a few of Amos's possible observations of Elzie. Have students continue on their own. Write the following headings on the board: *Actions*, *Appearance*, *Personality*. Encourage students to place their responses in the appropriate columns.

UNDERSTAND THE SELECTION

Recall

1. Who does Elzie tell her story to?
2. Why do Elzie and Ovella want to join the Silas Greene show?
3. What does Amos look like in the sunshine?

Infer

4. Why might Ovella have thrown her Sunday-school pin to the dog rather than money?
5. Why does Elzie call Amos a "fast runnin hero"?
6. Why might Elzie's lucky stone have the letter *A* scratched on it?
7. Why do Ovella and Elzie "lose heart" for the show and go home?

Apply

8. What words might Amos use to describe Elzie? Why?
9. Name some objects that you or other people think are lucky.
10. What type of marriage do you think the Pickenses have? How does it compare to your ideas about what marriage should be?

Respond to Literature

Does Elzie's first impression of Amos Pickens last through the years? Do you think love like this can happen in real life?

WRITE ABOUT THE SELECTION

How do you think Amos Pickens would tell the story of meeting his future wife at the Silas Greene show? Would he be as impressed with her as she was with him? Pretend to be a writer assigned to interview Amos Pickens about love at first sight. Write a brief magazine article about the interview with Amos.

Prewriting Re-read the part of the story that tells what happens when Elzie first sees Amos. Think about how the same incident might seem to Amos. Brainstorm to make a quick list of questions to ask Amos, including what he observed about her actions and her personal qualities.

Writing Use the questions from your brainstorming list to write answers from Amos's point of view. Try using some dialect in your writing, since Amos might speak the same way Elzie does. Then write several paragraphs about the Pickens's relationship. Use quotes from Amos in the article.

Revising Look again at the original story to re-check your facts. Can you use more descriptive words or details to make your paragraphs more interesting? Did you use the pronouns *I* and *me* to speak as Amos? If you have used dialect, try reading aloud or to a partner to make sure it sounds realistic.

Proofreading Read through your paragraphs and check for errors. If you have misspelled words on purpose for the dialect, make sure you have spelled them as you want them to sound.

Writing

You might have students who are writing dialect work with partners to practice saying the words aloud before they write them and also to confer with one another on spelling dialectic pronunciations. Remind students to try to think and speak as Amos might.

Revising

Have students check each other's work for interesting descriptive words and make constructive suggestions.

Proofreading

Have students check for errors in punctuation and capitalization. Point out that when dialect is written, these rules still apply.

ESL Activity

It may be better for students to concentrate on writing from Amos's viewpoint rather than on writing dialect. Make sure that students understand that writing dialect is optional. Have students record their ideas in a chain-of-events organizer before they write the article.

THINK ABOUT DIALECT

Dialect is a regional way of speaking that is different from standard English in vocabulary, grammar, and pronunciation. In "Luckiest Time of All" Elzie F. Pickens, who is an elderly woman of rural Virginia, speaks in dialect.

1. Find several words used by Mrs. Pickens that might be unfamiliar to someone from a different region of the country.

2. Words may also be pronounced differently in dialect. Point out several examples in this story.

3. Mrs. Pickens's great-granddaughter doesn't speak the same dialect. Why might this be so?

4. How does the use of dialect bring the events of the story and the character of Mrs. Pickens to life?

READING FOCUS

Identify the Author's Purpose As you read "Luckiest Time of All," you thought about the author's purpose in writing the story. What did you conclude is the author's purpose? List three details from the story that support your conclusion.

DEVELOP YOUR VOCABULARY

Antonyms are words with the opposite or nearly opposite meaning. *Rich* and *poor*, are antonyms. So are *before* and *after*. In the first sentence of "Luckiest Time of All," Mrs. Pickens was rocking slowly. An antonym for *slowly* is *quickly*. Replacing *slowly* with *quickly* would give the phrase an opposite meaning.

Think of a word that is the antonym of the bold word in each sentence below. Then choose one sentence with the antonym as a story starter. Write a short story, keeping in mind that the events and outcome should be different from the selection.

1. Usta be a kinda show went all through the **South**, called it the Silas Greene show.

2. The music was **faster** and **faster** and that dog was turnin and turnin.

3. And a good little way, the one who was gonna be your Great-granddaddy was walkin on **behind**.

THINK ABOUT DIALECT

Answers

1. Words may include: *dogwood, plaited, croksack, lit out, bottoms, twine, spied.*
2. Sample answers: *usta, goin, somethin, dancin*
3. Answers will vary, but should suggest that Tee was exposed to other ways of speaking by TV, radio, films, school, and/or friends, while Mrs. Pickens probably spent her childhood in a small, isolated community.
4. The dialect makes the readers feel that they are really there with the characters. The characters are true to life and their dialect makes the reading more interesting.

DEVELOP YOUR VOCABULARY

Sample Answers

1. North
2. slower
3. ahead

The events in students' short stories should have different outcomes from the selection.

READING FOCUS

Sample Answer

The purpose was to entertain, but the author also described the characters and the Silas Greene show, and even gave a little lesson about love.

SELECTION OVERVIEW

SELECTION OBJECTIVES

After completing this selection, students will be able to

- identify point of view
- write from first-person and third-person viewpoints
- evaluate and discuss story content
- write a step-by-step list of instructions
- recognize root words and use them to define new words
- distinguish fact from opinion

Lesson Resources

Stepping Out With My Baby
- Selection Synopsis, Teacher's Edition, p. TT60
- Comprehension and Vocabulary Workbook, pp. 11–12
- Language Enrichment Workbook, p. 11
- Teacher's Resources Reinforcement, p. R6 Test, pp. T11–T12

More About Point of View

Tell students that "Stepping Out With My Baby" is autobiographical, meaning that it is about the author's personal experience. What do students predict will be the point of view? Why?

About the Author

Paul Reiser (1957–present) was born and raised in New York City. While he was still in high school, he became interested in comedy, and during college he worked in comedy clubs in the summers while completing a degree in music. He graduated from college in 1977 and began working in films in 1980. Since then, he has also starred in two TV sitcoms, including his own creation, "Mad About You." He has also written two books, *Couplehood* and *Babyhood*. His son, Ezra, was born in September, 1994.

READING FOCUS

Distinguish Fact From Opinion A **fact** is a statement that can be proven to be true. An **opinion** is a judgment that cannot be proven true or false. For example, in "Luckiest Time of All," it was a fact that the dancing animal was a dog, but it was an opinion that the dog was cute. Cuteness cannot be proven because it depends on each person's idea of what is cute and what isn't. Before you read this selection, make two columns on a sheet of paper, one for facts and one for opinions. As you read, jot down the facts and opinions you notice.

Learn About

POINT OF VIEW

Point of View is the position from which a story is told. If a story is being told by a character in the story, this is called *first-person point of view*. The character refers to himself or herself as *I* or *me*, and can only tell what he or she experiences, thinks, or knows.

In *third-person point of view*, the narrator is someone outside the story who observes and tells what happens. Sometimes the third-person storyteller is *omniscient*, or all-knowing. The narrator knows everything about the characters—even what they think and feel. In a *limited* third-person point of view, the storyteller knows only the thoughts and feelings of one character.

As you read the next selection, ask yourself these questions:

1. What is the narrator's point of view?
2. How would the story be different if told from a different viewpoint?

WRITING CONNECTION

Write two paragraphs that describe your experiences at school so far today. Write one paragraph using first-person point of view and the other using third-person omniscient point-of-view.

Cooperative Group Activity

As a pre-writing exercise for the Writing Connection, organize students into small groups. Have a student in each group briefly describe his or her day thus far. Then have another group member stand and repeat the story, using *he/she*, *him/her* instead of *I* and *me*. Point out that these are examples of the first-person and third-person viewpoints. Repeat with remaining group members.

Stepping Out with My Baby

by Paul Reiser

Finally we arrive at the mailbox—an exhausting block and a half from home. Dizzy with the victory of arriving at our destination in more or less one piece, I reach into my pocket, retrieve the now sweaty envelopes, and am about to toss them into the mailbox when I hear a voice. It's my wife's voice, echoing in my head.

"Talk to him."

"Hmm?" I say automatically, totally accepting that my wife might in fact be physically standing next to me, just for a follow-up evaluation on my performance.

"Talk to him. Explain to him what you're doing." The voice in my head suggests.

Sometimes I forget that part- talking to my child. Actually *being* with him. When I'm in charge of the kid, I tend to either stare at him like he's a television or drift totally into a world of my own, running through my list of things-I-have-to-do-later-when-I'm-not-taking-care-of-the-kid. Or take the job so seriously I become blinded by the severity of the responsibility, and panic. What I

---

exhausting (eg ZAW sting) very tiring
destination (des tuh NAY shun) a place to which one is going
automatically (aw tuh MAT ihk lee) happening in a regular way
   without planning
severity (suh VAIR uh tee) great strictness or harshness

Stepping Out with My Baby ■ 43

seem to miss is the middle ground- the part where you share, teach, learn, play-the part you can actually enjoy.

"Right. Talk to him. I'll do that. Thanks." I say to myself, and the voice of the Nice Lady in My Head leaves me alone again.

"So." I say to my buckled-up Beautiful Boy. "This is a mailbox."

And in response, he takes a hearty bite out of his little red corduroy clown's terry-cloth head.

"See? Daddy's going to put these letters into the mailbox. See? . . . What else can I tell you . . . The mailbox is blue."

When in doubt, mention the color. They can't get enough of colors, these kids.

"It's a blue mailbox."

Another ferocious bite-and-tug almost removes the corduroy clown's left ear. Clearly the boy is not that interested- I'll just mail the letters.

"Explain to him how it works."

"I tried."

"Try again."

"All right, all right. Quit yelling."

Fortunately, no one sees or hears this violent exchange in my head. (See what I mean? They think I am the guy-with-this-kid, and in fact I'm not only hearing voices but barking back at them.)

"We put the letters in the mailbox, and then the mailman comes and gets them."

Talking to your baby is a lot like being on a first date; you feel like you're either saying too little or too much.

"The postal system was invented by Benjamin Franklin. In Philadelphia. He also invented bifocals."

Probably too much.

"The mailman takes the letters and puts them in a big bag and then he takes them to where they're going. See, this one goes to Aunt Ellen, who sent you that itchy sweater you hate, and this one goes to the Electric Company so they don't shut off our electricity and force us out of our home."

A little too heavy.

"Forget that. That will never happen."

Then, remembering that Demonstrating is always better than

---

ferocious (fuh ROH shus) very fierce or savage
bifocals (BY foh kulz) eyeglasses with parts to correct both near vision and far vision

Explaining. I unbuckle him, scoop him up, and illustrate my letter-mailing technique.

"What you want to do is: Pull down the handle, open the mailbox's mouth, and then you *flick* the letters in. You want to get that nice flicking motion in your wrist . . . And then you pull the mouth open-and-closed a few times, to make sure the letters went down. A lot of people will tell you that doesn't do anything. They're wrong. You *must* check. Otherwise the mailbox will chew up your letter and stick it in a corner where no one can find it for years and years and years."

My son smiles. I pull the handles up and down again. He seems to enjoy the squeaky noise. Who said mailboxes aren't a dynamite activity for youngsters? As we prepare for our return voyage, I wonder if I left anything out.

"Now, you may notice, it says here they pick up at eleven A.M., but between you and me it says the same thing on every mailbox in town at the same time, so I say just throw it in whenever you feel like it-it makes no difference. But you know what? You probably won't be mailing things by yourself for a while, so forget that. The main thing for you to remember, I would say, is: The box is blue. It's a big shiny blue box with a squeaky blue mouth."

As I buckle him back in, my son gives me one of those magnificent, otherworldly smiles, and looks at me as if to say, "Dad, I don't know what you're talking about, but you seem like a very nice man."

---

illustrate (IL uh strayt) to make clear by giving an example
technique (tek NEEK) a way of doing something

Stepping Out with My Baby ■ 45

Mini Quiz

Write the following sentences on the board or overhead projector, and call on students to fill in the blanks. Discuss the answers with the class.

1. The father is going to the _____.

2. His wife wants him to _____ things to the baby.

3. He picks the baby up to _____ his technique.

4. The father tells his son that the mailbox could _____ up your letters.

5. The baby seems to like the _____ noise of the mailbox.

Answers

1. mailbox
2. explain
3. demonstrate
4. chew
5. squeaky

UNDERSTAND THE SELECTION

Answers

1. a block and a half
2. He becomes blinded by the responsibility and panics.
3. He pulls the handle up and down and makes a squeaky noise.
4. Paul Reiser's wife
5. Sample answer: He is so nervous that his hands are sweaty.
6. Sample answer: No. He wouldn't be so worried if he had experience with babies.
7. He is so anxious about taking the baby out.
8. Sample answer: Demonstrating is the better way to teach because the person can connect the words with the actions.
9. Sample answers: operating a concession stand; teaching younger siblings; babysitting
10. Sample answer: I taught my younger brother how to ride a bicycle. First, I told him what to do; then I demonstrated how to ride it.

Respond to Literature

With student suggestions, make a list on the board or overhead projector showing all the things Paul Reiser feared or worried about when he took his baby out. Then, have students discuss which of these would be less scary the next time Reiser and the baby go for a walk. Ask students for examples of things from their own lives they accomplished that at first seemed too hard or things they tried even though they were frightened.

Review the Selection

UNDERSTAND THE SELECTION

Recall

1. How far from home is the mailbox?
2. What happens to the father when he takes the parenting job too seriously?
3. What does the father do with the mailbox that the baby seems to like?

Infer

4. Who is "the Nice Lady" in the father's head?
5. Why are the envelopes sweaty when the father takes them from his pocket?
6. Do you think the father has other children? Explain your answer.
7. Why does the father think of the block-and-a-half walk as a "voyage"?

Apply

8. Do you think explaining or demonstrating is a better way to teach? Explain.
9. What responsibility have you been given that made you nervous at first?
10. What have you taught a baby or younger child to do? How did you do it?

> ### Respond to Literature
> What do you think will happen the next time Paul Reiser takes his son for a walk? Will he still be as anxious? Will he still talk the same way to the baby?

46 ■ Unit 1

WRITE ABOUT THE SELECTION

Paul Reiser tried to show and tell his son in a clear and simple way how to operate a mailbox. Write a numbered list, in order, of the steps needed to operate another simple machine or appliance, such as a toaster, a blender, a washing machine, or a TV set. Keep your directions as brief and clear as possible.

Prewriting   First, decide what object you are going to write about. Choose something with only a few necessary steps for operation. Then, visualize step-by-step what you do to make it work. Think through it again and jot down the steps.

Writing   Give your instruction list a title, such as How to Operate a Toaster. Write down your steps in the order you would do them. Make sure each step describes only one action. Make sure you describe the entire process from beginning to end.

Revising   Carefully read through your instructions, picturing yourself doing each step. Are your instructions clear? Have you left out any steps in the process? Could any of the steps be explained more briefly?

Proofreading   Make sure that every step of your instructions is written in a complete sentence, which begins with a capital letter and ends with a period.

WRITE ABOUT THE SELECTION

Prewriting

With the class, prepare a sample list of steps for covering a textbook. Have student volunteers demonstrate the process and suggest steps. On the board or overhead, write the agreed-upon list. Then have students work individually with their own topics.

Writing

Monitor lists for clarity and brevity. Suggest that students begin each instruction sentence with a verb. Encourage them to think of the reader (or listener) as they write.

Revising

To decide if instructions are clear, have students work in pairs, with each reading his or her instructions aloud to a partner, who pantomimes them.

Proofreading

Have students proofread their own papers and then trade with a partner for a double-check.

T46

THINK ABOUT POINT OF VIEW

You can determine the point of view in a story by looking at the pronouns the narrator uses. *I* and *me* are always used by a first-person narrator, who is a character in the story. The third-person narrator is not a character in the story and therefore uses *he, she, they, it, them, him, her*.

1. Describe the point of view of "Stepping Out With My Baby."

2. If Paul Reiser's baby son could tell the story of the trip to the mailbox, what point of view would the story have?

3. What do you call nonfiction writing by a person telling about his or her real life? Which point of view is most likely to be used in this type of writing?

4. If a bystander observed and described what happened at the mailbox, what would be the point of view?

5. Rewrite a paragraph of the story so that it is told from the third-person omniscient viewpoint.

READING FOCUS

Distinguish Fact from Opinion As you read "Stepping Out With My Baby," you listed some of the facts and opinions you found. On a separate paper, write two paragraphs. Provide the facts in the first paragraph and the opinions in the second.

DEVELOP YOUR VOCABULARY

A **root word** is a word, or a part of a word, that is used to form other words. Often finding the root word can help you figure out the meaning of the entire word.

An example is *physically*. You might not know what it means, but you might know what the root word, *physical*, means. *Physical* means "of or about the body"; *physically* is an adverb that tells that someone reacts with his or her body.

Write the root of each of the following words. Check definitions in a dictionary if you are not sure. Then figure out the meaning of the entire word, and use each word in a sentence.

1. destination
2. automatically
3. evaluation
4. responsibility
5. fortunately
6. exchange
7. bifocals
8. activity
9. beautiful
10. unbuckle

THINK ABOUT POINT OF VIEW

Answers

1. first-person point of view
2. first-person point of view
3. autobiography; first- person point of view
4. It would be first-person viewpoint if the bystander was a character in the story and used *I* and *me*. It would be a third person viewpoint if the bystander was not part of the story.
5. Sample answer: He reached into his pocket, retrieved the sweaty envelopes, and was about to toss them into the mailbox when he heard a voice. It was his wife's voice, echoing in his head.

DEVELOP YOUR VOCABULARY

Sample Answers

1. destine; Our vacation *destination* is Florida.
2. automatic; The clerk *automatically* listed my name on the register.
3. evaluate; After a detailed *evaluation*, the judge dismissed the case.
4. responsible; It is my *responsibility* to water the plants in the yard.
5. fortune; *Fortunately*, I corrected my mistake in time to avoid an accident.
6. change; My friend and I like to *exchange* gifts at the end of the school year.
7. focal; My *bifocals* allow me to see both close up and far away.
8. active; Soccer is an *activity* that requires a good bit of coordination.
9. beauty; The young girl has a *beautiful* smile.
10. buckle; Before you leave the cart, you must *unbuckle* your seat harness.

READING FOCUS

Sample Answer

There are many facts in "Stepping Out With My Baby." For example, the mailbox is a block and a half from home. The father talks to his baby on the way to the mailbox. He is about to toss envelopes into the mailbox when he decides to explain the process to the baby.

Some opinions in the selection are that the walk to the mailbox is exhausting and that talking to a baby is like being on a first date. It is the father's opinion that kids can't get enough of colors and that the baby's sweater is itchy. It is also the father's opinion that demonstrating is always better than explaining.

SELECTION OVERVIEW

SELECTION OBJECTIVES

After completing this selection, students will be able to

- identify similes in literary works
- express a feeling through simile
- discuss the ageless appeal of *Romeo and Juliet*
- write a letter of advice on a serious subject
- analyze the effectiveness of a specific simile
- find definitions for archaic words
- recognize imagery

Lesson Resources

from The Tragedy of Romeo and Juliet
- Selection Synopsis, Teacher's Edition, pp. TT60–TT61
- Comprehension and Vocabulary Workbook, pp. 13–14
- Language Enrichment Workbook, p. 12
- Teacher's Resources Reinforcement, p. R7 Test, pp. T13–T14

More About Figures of Speech

Remind students that figures of speech are words or phrases that are not meant to be interpreted literally. What is meant is *not* exactly what is said. One common figure of speech is a simile. A simile compares two things of different classes by using the words "like" or "as." For example, "I wandered lonely *as* a cloud." Another common figure of speech which compares different things but does *not* use "like" or "as" is a metaphor. An example of a metaphor is "I'm a lonely cloud in the sky." Other figures of speech include personification and hyperbole. Shakespeare's writing is full of figurative language, so encourage students to concentrate on just similes and metaphors. Others will be pointed out, however, and students should be encouraged to understand those as well.

T48

READING FOCUS

Recognize Imagery An author uses imagery to create a vivid picture in the reader's mind. Imagery uses words that will appeal to the reader's sense of sight, smell, taste, hearing, or touch. By appealing to your senses, the author brings details in a story to life and allows you to experience them the way the characters in the story do. Look for imagery as you read this play, and try to recognize which of your senses it appeals to.

48 ■ Unit 1

Learn About

FIGURES OF SPEECH

Figures of speech are expressions that follow a particular form. Two important figures of speech are similes and metaphors. Similes and metaphors are comparisons. They point out similarities between things that ordinarily do not seem similar. **Similes** use *like* or *as* to point out a comparison—*eyes like stars*—while **metaphors** compare without special words—*her eyes are stars*.

Figures of speech add punch to a poem or literary passage; they make literature more powerful and effective.

William Shakespeare is considered by many the greatest English-language writer who ever lived. What makes him stand out among writers is his creative use of language. Among other things, Shakespeare includes many figures of speech in his plays and poems.

As you read the adaptation of *Romeo and Juliet*, ask yourself:

1. How are similes and metaphors used?
2. How do figures of speech enrich the play?

WRITING CONNECTION

Use a simile or metaphor to describe your feelings about reading Shakespeare. Try writing several different ones, and then choose your favorite.

Background Notes

Shakespeare did not create the characters and story of *Romeo and Juliet*. He "borrowed" them from a long narrative poem written by another Englishman, Arthur Broke, who himself had borrowed them from an Italian writer, Bandello. Such borrowing is common throughout history. Shakespeare's version of the "Tragicall Historye" of Romeo and Juliet (as Broke's work was called) differs from previous versions in several respects: It shortens the action from nine months to less than a week; it portrays Juliet as a 14 year old rather than an 18 year old (as in Bandello) or a 16 year old (as in Broke); and it expands Mercutio's role and more fully develops the character of the Nurse.

Cooperative Group Activity

For the Writing Connection activity, have students work in groups to brainstorm ideas about similes and metaphors. To begin, they might want to peruse this book for specific examples by more contemporary writers, such as Langston Hughes and Maya Angelou. Have each group present their work to the class.

from

The Tragedy of
ROMEO and JULIET

ADAPTED
by William Shakespeare

*T*he Tragedy of Romeo and Juliet opens with a chorus providing background that serves as an introduction to the play.

The story takes place in Verona, Italy in the 1500s. Two socially prominent families, the Capulets and the Montagues, have had a long-running feud, and lately new violence has broken out.

The chorus provides some foreshadowing. "A pair of star-crossed lovers," from the opposing families, will lose their lives because of the feud. The only hopeful note is that through their deaths, the families' conflict will end.

The lovers are, of course, Romeo and Juliet. Romeo is the son of Montague; Juliet, the daughter of Capulet. We meet Romeo first—not during the fight that opens the play, but afterwards. He has been off by himself, and he is depressed. He loves a woman, Rosaline, who, unfortunately, does not seem to love him.

A friend, Benvolio, tells him that Rosaline is not so pretty. He promises to show him some much prettier women if he will go to a banquet that evening. He must go in disguise, though, for the banquet is hosted by Capulet.

We meet Juliet as she is preparing for the banquet. Her father is hosting it partly as a way to introduce his daughter to Verona society. She is 14, and her parents think that it is time for her to marry. They hope to match her with Paris, a handsome young

Develop Vocabulary Skills

Nearly 200 new words are introduced in this adapted version of *Romeo and Juliet*. It is unrealistic to expect students to master them all, and many are archaic words that won't benefit a student's active vocabulary. Ask students, as they read the play individually, to study the meaning of new words for better understanding of the passages in which they appear. For an even greater appreciation of the language, a class reading of the play is suggested.

ESL Activity

Have students work in pairs and discuss with their partners some of the movies they may have seen about young love. Have students list three movies that deal with young love. Note whether they ended happily or unhappily. Can they offer explanations why? Discuss and write.

TEACHING PLAN

INTRODUCE

Motivation
One literary critic has noted that the most popular Shakespearean passages among Oxford University students in centuries past have come from *Romeo and Juliet*. Ask students if they recognize any lines from this play. Use Bartlett's *Familiar Quotations*, or another reference book, to point out some famous lines from *Romeo and Juliet*. You may also emphasize that, at fourteen, Juliet was about the same age as the students themselves.

Purpose-Setting Question:
Does love conquer all?

READ

Literary Focus:
Figures of Speech
Encourage students to pay attention to Shakespeare's vivid use of language. The literal meaning of his characters' words is not always the intended meaning. Help students understand the figures of speech that he uses.

Reading Focus:
Recognize Imagery
Explain to students that Shakespeare uses vivid descriptions in his characters' dialogue, which is intended to appeal to the reader's senses. Point out that this play was written hundreds of years ago, yet it is possible to experience the world of Shakespeare's characters. Ask students how imagery helps them to do this.

CLOSE

Have students complete Review the Selection on pages 78–79.

T

Critical Thinking:
Draw Conclusions

Students learned from the introduction that Verona, the city, suffers from the feud of two leading families—the Capulets and Montagues. Ask: What trouble do you think might lie ahead for these two families?

count. Paris has already declared his love for her. Juliet promises to consider him.

We join the action at the banquet, Act I, Scene 5. Use this list of characters to help you identify the players.

CHARACTERS

THREE SERVING MEN	FRIAR LAWRENCE
CAPULET	PARIS
SECOND CAPULET	PARIS' PAGE
ROMEO	BALTHASAR, *Romeo's man*
TYBALT	THREE WATCHMEN
JULIET	A PRINCE, *with* ATTENDANTS
NURSE	LADY CAPULET
BENVOLIO	MONTAGUE
MERCUTIO	

ACT I, SCENE 5

A hall in CAPULET'S *house.*

[*Enter* CAPULET, *his* WIFE, JULIET, TYBALT, NURSE, *and all the* GUESTS *and* GENTLEWOMEN *to the* MASKERS.]

CAPULET: Welcome, gentlemen! Ladies that have their toes
    Unplagued with corns will walk a bout[1] with you.
    Ah, my mistresses, which of you all
    Will now deny to dance? She that makes dainty.[2]
    She I'll swear hath[3] corns. Am I come near ye[4] now?
    Welcome, gentlemen! I have seen the day
    That I have worn a visor and could tell
    A whispering tale in a fair lady's ear.
    Such as would please. 'Tis gone, 'tis gone, 'tis gone.
    You are welcome, gentlemen! Come, musicians, play.

[*Music plays, and they dance.*]

    A hall,[5] a hall! Give room! And foot it, girls.
    More light, you knaves,[6] and turn the tables up,
    And quench the fire; the room is grown too hot.
    Ah, sirrah, this unlooked-for sport comes well.
    Nay,[7] sit; nay, sit, good cousin Capulet;
    For you and I are past our dancing days.
    How long is't now since last yourself and I
    Were in a mask?
SECOND CAPULET: By'r[8] Lady, thirty years.
CAPULET: What, man? 'Tis not so much, 'tis not so much:
    'Tis since the nuptial of Lucentio.
    Come Pentecost[9] as quickly as it will,
    Some five-and-twenty years, and then we masked.
SECOND CAPULET: 'Tis more, 'tis more. His son is elder, sir;
    His son is thirty.

---

nuptial (NUP shul) wedding
[1]**walk a bout:** dance a turn
[2]**makes dainty:** hesitates
[3]**hath:** (*archaic*) has
[4]**ye:** (*archaic*) you
[5]**a hall:** clear the hall for dancing
[6]**knave:** (*archaic*) serving boy or male servant; also sometimes a dishonest,
   deceitful person; a rogue
[7]**nay:** (*archaic*) no
[8]**by'r:** contraction of "by your"
[9]**Pentecost:** Christian holiday fifty days after Easter, marking the descent
   of the Holy Spirit upon Christ's apostles

from The Tragedy of Romeo and Juliet ■ 51

Background Notes
On the entrance of Capulet, a scene notation mentions "to the maskers." Masked balls were a common form of entertainment of the time.

Reading Focus:
Recognize Imagery
When the first act opens, the reader is at once pulled into the world of the characters. Ask: What language does the author use to set this scene and bring it to life?

Literary Focus:
Characterization
How does the author describe the character of Capulet in this dialogue?

Literary Focus:
Figures of Speech

Point out the first simile encountered in this adaptation. It occurs when Romeo, in his opening speech, describes Juliet "as a rich jewel in an Ethiop's ear." It is a classic example of "love at first sight."

Critical Thinking:
Infer

When Capulet says ". . . gentle coz, let him alone," he is putting Tybalt in his place. What can you infer about Capulet's character from this statement?

Literary Focus:
Foreshadowing

Ask: How is Tybalt's bitterness at Romeo's presence a foreshadowing of the trouble that lies ahead?

CAPULET: Will you tell me that?
    His son was but a ward two years ago.
ROMEO [*to a* SERVINGMAN]**:** What lady's that which doth
       enrich the hand
    Of yonder knight?
SERVINGMAN: I know not, sir.
ROMEO: O, she doth teach the torches to burn bright!
    It seems she hangs upon the cheek of night
    As a rich jewel in an Ethiop's[10] ear—
    Beauty too rich for use, for earth too dear!
    So shows a snowy dove trooping with crows
    As yonder lady o'er[11] her fellows shows.
    The measure done, I'll watch her place of stand
    And, touching hers, make blessed my rude hand.
    Did my heart love till now? Forswear[12] it, sight!
    For I ne'er[13] saw true beauty till this night.
TYBALT: This, by his voice, should be a Montague.
    Fetch me my rapier, boy. What! Dares the slave
    Come hither, covered with an antic face,[14]
    To fleer[15] and scorn at our solemnity?
    Now, by the stock and honor of my kin,
    To strike him dead I hold it not a sin.
CAPULET: Why, how now, kinsman? Wherefore[16] storm you so?
TYBALT: Uncle, this is a Montague, our foe,
    A villain, that is hither come in spite
    To scorn at our solemnity this night.
CAPULET: Young Romeo is it?
TYBALT: 'Tis he, that villain Romeo.
CAPULET: Content thee, gentle coz,[17] let him alone.

---

ward (WAWRD) a minor, or someone under the age of 18 or 21
rude (ROOD) crude or rough; also, impolite
rapier (RAY pee ur) sword
hither (HI*TH* ur) to, toward, or here
[10]**Ethiop:** old term for a Black person; short for Ethiopian
[11]**o'er:** shortened form of "over"
[12]**forswear:** (*archaic*) deny
[13]**ne'er:** shortened form of "never"
[14]**antic face:** (*archaic*) strange or funny; an "antic face" is a mask
[15]**fleer:** (*archaic*) sneer or mock
[16]**wherefore:** (*archaic*) why
[17]**coz:** usually "cousin" but used here as a term of address for any relative. Capulet is Tybalt's uncle.

A bears him like a portly gentleman,[18]
And, to say truth, Verona brags of him
To be a virtuous and well-governed youth.
I would not for the wealth of all this town
Here in my house do him disparagement.
Therefore be patient; take no note of him.
It is my will, the which if thou respect,
Show a fair presence and put off these frowns,
An ill-beseeming[19] semblance for a feast.

[Meanwhile, Romeo and Juliet meet.]

ROMEO: If I profane with my unworthiest hand
This holy shrine, the gentle sin is this:
My lips, two blushing pilgrims, ready stand
To smooth that rough touch with a tender kiss.
JULIET: Good pilgrim, you do wrong your hand too much,
Which mannerly devotion shows in this;
For saints have hands that pilgrims' hands do touch,
And palm to palm is holy palmers' kiss.
ROMEO: Have not saints lips, and holy palmers too?
JULIET: Ay, pilgrim, lips that they must use in prayer.
ROMEO: O, then, dear saint, let lips do what hands do!
They pray; grant thou, lest faith turn to despair.
JULIET: Saints do not move,[20] though grant for prayers' sake.
ROMEO: Then move not while my prayer's effect I take.
Thus from my lips, by thine my sin is purged.   *[Kisses her.]*
JULIET: Then have my lips the sin that they have took.
ROMEO: Sin from my lips? O trespass sweetly urged![21]
Give me my sin again.   *[Kisses her.]*

---

portly (PAWRT lee) heavy, but dignified
virtuous (VUR choo us) honorable
disparagement (dih SPAR ij munt) discredit, insult
semblance (SEM bluns) appearance
profane (proh FAYN) show disrespect for holy things
shrine (SHRYN) place of worship or devotion
palmers (PAHM urz) pilgrims
lest (LEST) for fear that
purge (PURJ) get rid of
[18]**A . . . gentleman:** He behaves like a dignified gentleman.
[19]**ill-beseeming:** (*archaic*) inappropriate
[20]**move:** initiate involvement in earthly affairs
[21]**O . . . urged!:** Romeo is saying, in substance, that he is happy. Juliet calls
   his kiss a sin, for now he can take it back—by another kiss.

from The Tragedy of Romeo and Juliet ■ 53

Enrichment
Juliet's mention on first meeting Romeo, of "palm to palm" refers to the pilgrims who carried palms from the Holy Land as proof of their journey.

Literary Focus:
Rhyme
When she tells Romeo that pilgrims must use lips "in prayer," Juliet is clarifying her "Good Pilgrim" address for Romeo. In using end rhyme twice in this address, Juliet is following Romeo's lead. You might want to review the scene for other examples of rhyme. When is rhyme used, and what is its effect?

Reading Focus:
Recognize Imagery
Although an audience watching this play would be able to see much of what the author describes, the language of the play itself still brings the action to life. Ask students what senses the author uses to describe Romeo and Juliet's meeting? Make sure that students recognize the many references to "touch" in their dialogue.

Literary Focus:
Characterization
Ask: What clues to the nurse's character does her speech provide?

JULIET: You kiss by th' book.

NURSE: Madam, your mother craves a word with you.

ROMEO: What is her mother?

NURSE: Marry, bachelor,
    Her mother is the lady of the house,
    And a good lady, and a wise and virtuous.
    I nursed her daughter that you talked withal[22]
    I tell you, he that can lay hold of her
    Shall have the chinks.[23]

ROMEO: Is she a Capulet?
    O dear account! My life is my foe's debt.[24]

BENVOLIO: Away, be gone; the sport is at the best.

ROMEO: Ay,[25] so I fear; the more is my unrest.

CAPULET: Nay, gentlemen, prepare not to be gone;
    We have a trifling foolish banquet towards.[26]
    Is it e'en[27] so?[28] Why then, I thank you all.

---

[22]**withal:** (*archaic*) with

[23]**chinks:** (*archaic*) money

[24]**My life . . . debt:** Since Juliet is a Capulet, Romeo's life is at the mercy of the enemies of his family

[25]**ay:** (*archaic*) yes

[26]**towards:** being prepared

[27]**e'en:** even

[28]**Is . . . so?:** Is it the case that you really must leave?

I thank you, honest gentlemen. Good night.
More torches here! Come on then; let's to bed.
Ah, sirrah,[29] by my fay,[30] it waxes late:
I'll to my rest.   [*Exit all but* JULIET *and* NURSE.]
JULIET: Come hither, nurse. What is yond[31] gentleman?
NURSE: The son and heir of old Tiberio.
JULIET: What's he that now is going out of door?
NURSE: Marry, that, I think, be young Petruchio.
JULIET: What's he that follows here, that would not dance?
NURSE: I know not.
JULIET: Go ask his name—if he is married,
My grave is like to be my wedding bed.
NURSE: His name is Romeo, and a Montague,
The only son of your great enemy.
JULIET: My only love, sprung from my only hate!
Too early seen unknown, and known too late!
Prodigious birth of love it is to me
That I must love a loathèd enemy.
NURSE: What's this? What's this?
JULIET: A rhyme I learnt even now.
Of one I danced withal.   [*One calls within, "Juliet."*]
NURSE: Anon,[32] anon!
Come, let's away; the strangers all are gone.   [*Exit.*]

ACT II

The second act begins again with the chorus. It tells us that Romeo has replaced his love for Rosaline with love for Juliet, and that Juliet is "alike bewitched." It reminds us of the conflict between the families, but notes that "passion lends them [Romeo and Juliet] power."

Benvolio and another of Romeo's friends, Mercutio, discuss Romeo's new state of mind. They, and Romeo, have snuck into Capulet's orchard. Then comes one of the most famous love scenes in literature, the "balcony meeting" between Romeo and Juliet.

---

prodigious (pruh DIJ us) monstrous
loathe (LOH*TH*) detest, hate
[29]**sirrah:** old form of address, usually said to show anger
[30]**fay:** faith
[31]**yond:** yonder; at a distance
[32]**anon:** (*archaic*) immediately, at once; also, very soon

from The Tragedy of Romeo and Juliet ■ 55

Reading Focus:
Recognize Imagery
The dialogue between Juliet and her nurse, and Romeo and his friends is not as rich in imagery as that between Romeo and Juliet. It is in their dialogue that the author paints the most vivid images. Ask: How does this help to bring their feelings for each other to life for the reader?

Critical Thinking:
Infer
Ask: What inferences can you make about the future of Romeo's relationship with Juliet? What led you to make these inferences?

Literary Focus:
Figures of Speech

Have students identify the metaphor Romeo uses to describe Juliet. Have them explain why they think their choice is correct.

Background Notes

Romeo is hiding; Juliet, at the window, is unaware that Romeo is there. The window opens onto a balcony; it is one of Shakespeare's most famous settings.

Reading Focus:
Recognize Imagery

Romeo's speech describing Juliet and her beauty is poetic. Ask: How would this speech be different if the author did not describe Juliet with such vivid imagery? Imagine the speech written in more simple language that does not appeal to your senses. What is lost?

CAPULET'S *orchard.*

ROMEO [*coming forward*]: He jests at scars that never felt a wound.
[*Enter* JULIET *at a window.*]

But soft! What light through yonder window breaks?
It is the East, and Juliet is the sun!
Arise, fair sun, and kill the envious moon.
Who is already sick and pale with grief
That thou her maid art[33] far more fair than she.
Be not her maid, since she is envious.
Her vestal livery is but sick and green,
And none but fools do wear it. Cast it off.
It is my lady! O, it is my love!
O, that she knew she were!
She speaks, yet she says nothing. What of that?
Her eye discourses; I will answer it.
I am too bold; 'tis not to me she speaks:
Two of the fairest stars in all the heaven,
Having some business, do entreat her eyes
To twinkle in their spheres[34] till they return.
What if her eyes were there, they in her head?
The brightness of her cheek would shame those stars
As daylight doth a lamp; her eyes in heaven
Would through the airy region stream so bright
That birds would sing and think it were not night.
See how she leans her cheek upon that hand,
O, that I were a glove upon that hand,
That I might touch that cheek!

JULIET: Ay me!

ROMEO: She speaks.
O, speak again, bright angel, for thou art
As glorious to this night, being o'er my head,
As is a wingèd messenger of heaven

---

vestal (VES tul) virtuous, pure
livery (LIV uh ree) clothing worn by servants
discourses (dis KAWRS iz) utters, talks, communicates
entreat (en TREET) beg, ask earnestly
[33]**art:** (*archaic*) is
[34]**spheres:** orbits

from The Tragedy of Romeo and Juliet ■ 57

Discussion
The illustration at the left suggests that Romeo used an indirect entry into the Capulets' orchard. Why does he do this? What does this risk-taking tell you about Romeo's feelings for Juliet?

Unto the white-upturnèd wond'ring eyes
Of mortals that fall back to gaze on him
When he bestrides the lazy puffing clouds
And sails upon the bosom of the air.

JULIET: O Romeo, Romeo! Wherefore art thou Romeo?[35]
Deny thy father and refuse thy name:
Or, if thou wilt[36] not, be but sworn my love,
And I'll no longer be a Capulet.

ROMEO: [*Aside*] Shall I hear more, or shall I speak at this?

JULIET: 'Tis but thy name that is my enemy.
Thou art thyself, though not[37] a Montague.
What's Montague? It is nor hand, nor foot,
Nor arm, nor face. O, be some other name
Belonging to a man.
What's in a name? That which we call a rose
By any other word would smell as sweet.
So Romeo would, were he not Romeo called.
Retain that dear perfection which he owes[38]
Without that title. Romeo, doff thy name:
And for thy name, which is no part of thee,
Take all myself.

ROMEO: I take thee at thy word.
Call me but love, and I'll be new baptized:
Henceforth I never will be Romeo.

JULIET: What man art thou, thus bescreened in night,
So stumblest on my counsel?[39]

ROMEO: By a name
I know not how to tell thee who I am.
My name, dear saint, is hateful to myself
Because it is an enemy to thee.
Had I it written, I would tear the word.

JULIET: My ears have yet not drunk a hundred words

---

bestride (bih STRYD) sit or mount
bosom (BUUZ um) breast
retain (rih TAYN) hold or keep
doff (DOF) take off or discard
bescreened (bih SKREEND) hidden
[35]**Wherefore . . . Romeo?:** Why are you Romeo, a Montague?
[36]**wilt:** (*archaic*) will
[37]**though not:** even if you were not
[38]**owes:** owns, possesses
[39]**counsel:** here, secret thoughts or plans

Of thy tongue's uttering, yet I know the sound.
Art thou not Romeo, and a Montague?

ROMEO: Neither, fair maid, if either thee dislike.

JULIET: How camest thou hither, tell me, and wherefore?
The orchard walls are high and hard to climb,
And the place death, considering who thou art,
If any of my kinsmen find thee here.

ROMEO: With love's light wings did I o'erperch[40] these walls;
For stony limits cannot hold love out,
And what love can do, that dares love attempt.
Therefore thy kinsmen are no stop to me.

JULIET: If they do see thee, they will murder thee.

ROMEO: Alack[41] there lies more peril in thine eye
Than twenty of their swords! Look thou but sweet,
And I am proof[42] against their enmity.

JULIET: I would not for the world they saw thee here.

ROMEO: I have night's cloak to hide me from their eyes;
And but[43] thou love me, let them find me here.
My life were better ended by their hate
Than death proroguèd, wanting of thy love.

JULIET: By whose direction found'st thou out this place?

ROMEO: By love, that first did prompt me to inquire.
He lent me counsel, and I lent him eyes.
I am no pilot; yet, wert thou as far
As that vast shore washed with the farthest sea,
I should adventure[44] for such merchandise.

JULIET: Thou knowest the mask of night is on my face;
Else would a maiden blush bepaint my cheek
For that which thou hast heard me speak tonight.
Fain[45] would I dwell on form—fain, fain deny
What I have spoke; but farewell compliment![46]
Dost thou love me? I know thou wilt say "Ay";

---

enmity (EN muh tee) hate
prorogued (proh ROHGD) postponed
[40]**o'erperch:** shortened form of "overperch," meaning "fly over"
[41]**alack:** exclamation of surprise or disappointment
[42]**proof:** here, protected with armor
[43]**and but:** unless
[44]**adventure:** here, risk as a voyage
[45]**fain:** (*archaic*) with eagerness, gladly
[46]**compliment:** here, etiquette

from The Tragedy of Romeo and Juliet ■ 59

Literary Focus:
Figures of Speech
When Juliet tells Romeo that "my ears have yet not drunk . . .", it is a good example of the many rhetorical techniques Shakespeare constantly uses: in this instance, it is a *synecdoche*, or using a part to stand for the whole. Ask: What does "ears" represent?

Enrichment
When Romeo says, "With love's light wings . . .", he is saying, in short, "love conquers all."

And I will take thy word. Yet, if thou swear'st,
Thou mayst prove false. At lovers' perjuries,
They say Jove[47] laughs. O gentle Romeo,
If thou dost love, pronounce it faithfully.
Or if thou thinkest I am too quickly won,
I'll frown and be perverse and say thee nay,
So thou wilt woo; but else, not for the world.
In truth, fair Montague, I am too fond,
And therefore thou mayst think my havior[48] light:
But trust me, gentleman, I'll prove more true
Than those that have more cunning to be strange.[49]
I should have been more strange, I must confess,
But that thou overheard'st, ere[50] I was ware,
My truelove passion. Therefore pardon me,
And not impute this yielding to light love,
Which the dark night hath so discovered.

ROMEO: Lady, by yonder blessed moon I vow,
That tips with silver all these fruit-tree tops—

JULIET: O, swear not by the moon, th' inconstant moon,
That monthly changes in her circle orb,
Lest that thy love prove likewise variable.

ROMEO: What shall I swear by?

JULIET: Do not swear at all;
Or if thou wilt, swear by thy gracious self,
Which is the god of my idolatry,
And I'll believe thee.

ROMEO: If my heart's dear love—

JULIET: Well, do not swear. Although I joy in thee,
I have no joy of this contract[51] tonight.
It is too rash, too unadvised, too sudden;
Too like the lightning, which doth cease to be
Ere one can say it lightens. Sweet, good night!
This bud of love, by summer's ripening breath,

---

perverse (pur VURS) here, stubbornly difficult or contrary
impute (im PYOOT) charge to or blame
[47]**Jove:** supreme god in Roman mythology: also called "Jupiter"
[48]**havior:** behavior
[49]**strange:** distant and cold
[50]**ere:** before
[51]**contract:** betrothal

Literary Focus:
Foreshadowing

In Juliet's speech about her love for Romeo she says, "But trust me gentleman, I'll prove more true than those that have more cunning to be strange." Ask: What does this line suggest about events to come?

Reading Focus:
Recognize Imagery

Have students find images of the night in the characters' lines on this page. Ask: How do these images strengthen the romantic atmosphere?

Critical Thinking:
Evaluate
Ask: Does Juliet's declaration of love seem genuine? Why or why not?

May prove a beauteous flow'r when next we meet.
Good night, good night! As sweet repose and rest
Come to thy heart as that within my breast!
ROMEO: O, wilt thou leave me so unsatisfied?
JULIET: What satisfaction canst thou have tonight?
ROMEO: Th' exchange of thy love's faithful vow for mine.
JULIET: I gave thee mine before thou didst request it;
    And yet I would it were to give again.
ROMEO: Wouldst thou withdraw it? For what purpose, love?
JULIET: But to be frank[52] and give it thee again.
    And yet I wish but for the thing I have.
    My bounty[53] is as boundless as the sea,
    My love as deep; the more I give to thee,
    The more I have, for both are infinite,
    I hear some noise within. Dear love, adieu!

                    [NURSE *calls within.*]

---

repose (rih POHZ) rest, or peace of mind
adieu (uh DYOO) French for "goodbye"
[52]**frank:** here, generous
[53]**bounty:** what I have to give

Enrichment
As Juliet hears a noise, she says "Adieu" to Romeo. Thus begin their efforts to leave one another. Parting is never easy when love is found, so Shakespeare draws the scene out.

from The Tragedy of Romeo and Juliet ■ 61

Anon, good nurse! Sweet Montague, be true.
Stay but a little, I will come again.   [*Exit.*]
ROMEO: O blessed, blessed night! I am afeard,
Being in night, all this is but a dream
Too flattering-sweet to be substantial.

[*Enter* JULIET *again.*]

JULIET: Three words, dear Romeo, and good night indeed.
If that thy bent of love be honorable,
Thy purpose marriage, send me word tomorrow
By one that I'll procure to come to thee,
Where and what time thou wilt perform the rite;
And all my fortunes at thy foot I'll lay
And follow thee my lord throughout the world.
NURSE [*within*]: Madam!
JULIET: I come anon.—But if thou meanest not well,
I do beseech thee—
NURSE [*within*]: Madam!
JULIET: By and by[54] I come.—
To cease thy strife[55] and leave me to my grief.
Tomorrow will I send.
ROMEO: So thrive my soul—
JULIET: A thousand times good night!   [*Exit.*]
ROMEO: A thousand times the worse, to want thy light!
Love goes toward love as schoolboys from their books;
But love from love, toward school with heavy looks.
[*Enter* JULIET *again.*]
JULIET: Hist![56] Romeo, hist! O for a falc'ner's[57] voice
To lure this tassel[58] gentle back again!
Bondage[59] is hoarse and may not speak aloud,

---

substantial (sub STAN chul) real
bent (BENT) purpose or inclination
procure (proh KYUUR) obtain, arrange
beseech (bih SEECH) ask earnestly
[54]**By and by:** at once
[55]**strife:** (*archaic*) strong efforts
[56]**hist:** exclamation said to draw attention, like "listen" or "quiet"
[57]**falc'ner:** falconer, or someone who keeps and trains the hawklike
birds known as falcons
[58]**tassel:** a male falcon, properly called a "tiercel"
[59]**bondage:** slavery, or being subjected to someone else. Juliet means
the nearness of her family makes it hard to talk.

Literary Focus:
Figures of Speech
Have students identify the figure of speech in Romeo's last lines on this page. Lead a discussion about the simile's meaning.

Else would I tear the cave where Echo[60] lies
And make her airy tongue more hoarse than mine
With repetition of "My Romeo!"

ROMEO: It is my soul that calls upon my name.
How silver-sweet sound lovers' tongues by night,
Like softest music to attending ears!

JULIET: Romeo!

ROMEO: My sweet?

JULIET: What o'clock tomorrow
Shall I send to thee?

ROMEO: By the hour of nine.

JULIET: I will not fail. 'Tis twenty year till then.
I have forgot why I did call thee back.

ROMEO: Let me stand here till thou remember it.

JULIET: I shall forget, to have thee still stand there,
Rememb'ring how I love thy company.

ROMEO: And I'll stay, to have thee still forget,
Forgetting any other home but this.

JULIET: 'Tis almost morning. I would have thee gone—
And yet no farther than a wanton's bird,
That lets it hop a little from his hand,
Like a poor prisoner in his twisted gyves,[61]
And with a silken thread plucks it back again,
So loving-jealous of his liberty.

ROMEO: I would I were thy bird.

JULIET: Sweet, so would I.
Yet I should kill thee with much cherishing.
Good night, good night! Parting is such sweet sorrow
That I shall say good night till it be morrow.   [*Exit.*]

ROMEO: Sleep dwell upon thine eyes, peace in thy breast!
Would I were sleep and peace, so sweet to rest!
Hence will I to my ghostly friar's[62] close cell,
His help to crave and my dear hap[63] to tell.   [*Exit.*]

---

wanton (WAHN tun) spoiled child
cell (SEL) small room
[60]Echo: in Greek mythology, a nymph whose love for Narcissus made her
    waste away until nothing was left of her but her voice
[61]gyves: chains or fetters
[62]ghostly friar's: spiritual father's
[63]dear hap: good luck or fortune

from The Tragedy of Romeo and Juliet ■ 63

Reading Focus:
Recognize Imagery
Although the reader is not able to actually hear Romeo and Juliet speaking to each other, the author describes the sound of their voices vividly. Have students identify the lines on this page that help them "hear" the young lovers. Ask: Which descriptive words or phrases are most vivid? Explain your answer.

Critical Thinking:
Analyze
Juliet states that "Yet I should kill thee with much cherishing." Can a person be killed by too much love? Discuss.

Literary Focus:
Plot
Up until this point in the play, Romeo and Juliet have known that their families are enemies. But now the conflict between the two families heightens. How does this conflict help the plot's development?

Critical Thinking:
Evaluate
Ask: What was Friar Lawrence's motivation for helping Romeo and Juliet? Do you think he was right to do so? Explain.

Romeo goes to see Friar Lawrence, a Catholic priest. The friar, who knows Romeo well, consents to marry Juliet and him. Friar Lawrence hopes the marriage will end the feud between the Capulets and Montagues.

The marriage takes place, secretly, in Friar Lawrence's cell, or room.

ACT III

Act III brings another confrontation between the Capulets and Montagues. Tybalt and Mercutio fight. Romeo tries to stop them, but only hinders Mercutio, his friend. Tybalt stabs Mercutio. He dies. Romeo, distraught that he had not defended his friend, kills Tybalt.

Romeo is banished from the city for the murder. Juliet hears of the fight, and is overcome with grief: Tybalt, a cousin, has been killed by Romeo, her husband. And now Romeo is exiled.

Both Romeo and Juliet feel banishment from each other is the worst of the tragedies, however. With the help of Friar Lawrence, they spend their wedding night together, and plan for Romeo to leave for the city of Mantua. There, he will wait until tempers cool, Friar Lawrence can arrange a pardon, and the wedding is made public.

The situation, however, is complicated by Juliet's father. He announces that she is to marry Paris in three days. Juliet begs her parents to delay the wedding, but they will not. They order her to obey their wishes.

ACT IV

In Act IV Juliet flees to Friar Lawrence for guidance. She sees no way out of the situation.

Friar Lawrence, though, comes up with a plan. Juliet will take a potion that will make her appear dead. Her body will be taken to the Capulet family tomb. Romeo will be summoned from Mantua and will wait at the tomb while the potion wears off. Reunited, the two lovers can then flee together to Mantua.

ACT V

The plan goes awry, however. In Act V, the letter that Friar Lawrence sends to Romeo informing him of the plan does not reach Romeo in Mantua. Instead, Balthasar, Romeo's old servant, arrives hurriedly in Mantua and tells him he has seen Juliet's body being taken to the Capulet vault for burial. Romeo, thinking her dead, leaves immediately for Verona. He takes with him a bottle of poison. If Juliet is dead, he, too, does not wish to live. The stage is set for the dramatic climax.

SCENE 3

A churchyard: in it a monument belonging to the CAPULETS.

[*Enter* PARIS *and his* PAGE *with flowers and sweet water.*]

PARIS: Give me thy torch, boy. Hence, and stand aloof.
　　Yet put it out, for I would not be seen.

---

aloof (uh LOOF) at a distance, apart

from The Tragedy of Romeo and Juliet ■ 65

Reading Focus:
Recognize Imagery
Point out to students the striking difference between the actual passages from the play, and the summaries. Ask: In what ways does the author's vivid language and imagery contribute color and life to the action?

Discussion
Point out that Romeo and Juliet placed much trust in Friar Lawrence. Ask: Do you think this trust was misplaced? Why or why not?

Under yond yew trees lay thee all along,[64]
Holding thy ear close to the hollow ground.
So shall no foot upon the churchyard tread
(Being loose, unfirm, with digging up of graves)
But thou shalt hear it. Whistle then to me,
As signal that thou hearest something approach.
Give me those flowers. Do as I bid thee, go.

PAGE [*aside*]: I am almost afraid to stand alone
Here in the churchyard; yet I will adventure.[65]   [*Retires.*]
PARIS: Sweet flower, with flowers thy bridal bed I strew
(O woe! thy canopy is dust and stones)
Which with sweet[66] water nightly I will dew;
Or, wanting that, with tears distilled by moans.
The obsequies that I for thee will keep
Nightly shall be to strew thy grave and weep.

[BOY *whistles.*]

The boy gives warning something doth approach.
What cursèd foot wanders this way tonight
To cross[67] my obsequies and true love's rite?
What, with a torch? Muffle me, night, awhile.   [*Retires.*]

[*Enter* ROMEO, *and* BALTHASAR *with a torch, a mattock, and a crow*[68] *of iron.*]

ROMEO: Give me that mattock and the wrenching iron.
Hold, take this letter. Early in the morning
See thou deliver it to my lord and father.
Give me the light. Upon thy life I charge thee,
Whate'er thou hearest or seest, stand all aloof
And do not interrupt me in my course.
Why I descend into this bed of death
Is partly to behold my lady's face.
But chiefly to take thence[69] from her dead finger

---

yew (YOO) a kind of evergreen shrub or small tree
obsequies (OB sih kweez) funeral rites or ceremonies
mattock (MAT uk) a tool like a pickax for loosening soil
[64]**lay . . . along:** lie down flat
[65]**adventure:** chance it
[66]**sweet:** perfumed
[67]**cross:** interrupt
[68]**crow:** here, crowbar
[69]**thence:** (*archaic*) from that place

Literary Focus:
Figures of Speech
Paris refers to Juliet as "Sweet flower." Ask: How is this a metaphor of both figurative and literal meaning?

Reading Focus:
Recognize Imagery
The scene at the graveyard takes place during the night, just as Romeo's secret meetings with Juliet did. Ask: How are the descriptions of the two night settings different? How has the mood changed?

A precious ring—a ring that I must use
In dear employment.[70] Therefore hence, be gone.
But if thou, jealous,[71] dost return to pry
In what I farther shall intend to do,
By heaven, I will tear thee joint by joint
And strew this hungry churchyard with thy limbs.
The time and my intents are savage-wild,
More fierce and more inexorable far
Than empty[72] tigers or the roaring sea.

BALTHASAR: I will be gone, sir, and not trouble ye.

ROMEO: So shalt thou show me friendship. Take thou that.
Live, and be prosperous; and farewell, good fellow.

BALTHASAR [*aside*]: For all this same, I'll hide me hereabout.
His looks I fear, and his intents I doubt.   [*Retires.*]

ROMEO: Thou detestable maw, thou womb of death,
Gorged with the dearest morsel of the earth,
Thus I enforce thy rotten jaws to open.
And in despite[73] I'll cram thee with more food.

[ROMEO *opens the tomb.*]

PARIS: This is that banished haughty Montague
That murd'red my love's cousin—with which grief
It is supposed the fair creature died
And here is come to do some villainous shame
To the dead bodies. I will apprehend him.
Stop thy unhallowèd toil, vile Montague!
Can vengeance be pursued further than death?
Condemnèd villain, I do apprehend thee.
Obey, and go with me; for thou must die.

---

inexorable (in EKS uh ruh bul) unable to change or control
detestable (dih TES tuh bul) hateful
maw (MAW) stomach
womb (WOOM) stomach or uterus; any place that holds or generates
   something else
morsel (MAWR sul) a small piece or bit
haughty (HAWT ee) proud, showing disdain for others
apprehend (ap rih HEND) catch, seize, or arrest
unhallowed (un HAL ohd) unholy
vengeance (VEN juns) revenge
[70]**dear employment:** important business
[71]**jealous:** here, curious; that is, jealous of one's privacy
[72]**empty:** hungry
[73]**in despite:** to spite

from The Tragedy of Romeo and Juliet ■ 67

Literary Focus:
Figures of Speech
Personification is a figure of speech that gives human characteristics to nonhuman objects. Romeo compares the opening of the tomb to a hungry moth with "rotten jaws." Ask: How does this comparison fit the definition of personification?

Critical Thinking:
Compare and Contrast
Ask: How do Romeo and Paris react to the news of Juliet's supposed death?

ROMEO: I must indeed: and therefore came I hither.
    Good gentle youth, tempt not a desp'rate man.
    Fly hence and leave me. Think upon these gone;
    Let them affright thee. I beseech thee, youth,
    Put not another sin upon my head
    By urging me to fury. O, be gone!
    By heaven, I love thee better than myself,
    For I come hither armed against myself.
    Stay not, be gone. Live, and hereafter say
    A madman's mercy bid thee run away.
PARIS: I do defy thy conjurations.
    And apprehend thee for a felon here.
ROMEO: Wilt thou provoke me? Then have at thee, boy!

[*They fight.*]

PAGE: O Lord, they fight! I will go call the watch.

[*Exit.* PARIS *falls.*]

PARIS: O, I am slain! If thou be merciful,
    Open the tomb, lay me with Juliet.   [*Dies.*]
ROMEO: In faith, I will. Let me peruse this face.
    Mercutio's kinsman, noble Count Paris!
    What said my man when my betossèd[74] soul
    Did not attend[75] him as we rode? I think
    He told me Paris should have married Juliet.
    Said he not so, or did I dream it so?
    Or am I mad, hearing him talk of Juliet.
    To think it was so? O, give me thy hand,
    One writ[76] with me in sour misfortune's book!
    I'll bury thee in a triumphant grave.
    A grave? O, no, a lanthorn,[77] slaught'red youth,
    For here lies Juliet, and her beauty makes

---

conjuration (kon juh RAY shun) threatening appeal
felon (FEL un) criminal
provoke (pruh VOHK) excite, irritate, or anger to action
slain (SLAYN) from "slay," to kill
peruse (puh ROOZ) look at or read
[74]**betossed:** upset
[75]**attend:** give attention to
[76]**writ:** (*archaic*) wrote or written
[77]**lanthorn:** structure with windows at the top of a room to admit light; sometimes also used instead of "lantern"

This vault a feasting presence[78] full of light.
Death, lie thou there, by a dead man interred.

[*Lays him in the tomb.*]

How oft when men are at the point of death
Have they been merry! Which their keepers call
A lightning before death. O, how may I
Call this a lightning? O my love, my wife!
Death, that hath sucked the honey of thy breath,
Hath had no power yet upon thy beauty.
Thou art not conquered. Beauty's ensign yet
Is crimson in thy lips and in thy cheeks,
And death's pale flag is not advanced there.
Tybalt, liest thou there in thy bloody sheet?
O, what more favor can I do to thee
Than with that hand that cut thy youth in twain[79]
To sunder his that was thine enemy?

---

interred (in TURD) buried
keepers (KEEP urz) jailers
ensign (EN sun) flag or banner
sunder (SUN dur) break apart or split
[78]**feasting presence:** chamber fit for celebration
[79]**twain:** (*archaic*) two

from The Tragedy of Romeo and Juliet ■ 69

Critical Thinking:
Predict
In Romeo's long soliloquy after the death of Paris, he unknowingly speaks an important truth: Juliet isn't dead. Ask: Had he known, what might have been their fate?

Reading Focus:
Recognize Imagery
Romeo's description of Juliet as she lies in the tomb is similar to his description of her during the balcony scene. She appears to Romeo to be as beautiful in death as she was in life (because in fact, she is still living). Ask: How does the author make Romeo's description more vivid?

Draw students' attention to the author's powerful description of death. Ask: What words or phrases does he use to convey the darkness and dampness of the tomb? Ask students for their reactions to this image.

Enrichment

When Friar Lawrence enters, he calls upon St. Francis, the founder of the order to which he belongs. He is appealing to St. Francis for help.

Forgive me, cousin! Ah, dear Juliet.
Why art thou yet so fair? Shall I believe
That unsubstantial Death is amorous,
And that the lean abhorrèd monster keeps
Thee here in dark to be his paramour?
For fear of that I still will stay with thee
And never from this pallet of dim night
Depart again. Here, here will I remain
With worms that are thy chambermaids. O, here
Will I set up my everlasting rest
And shake the yoke of inauspicious stars
From this world-wearied flesh. Eyes, look your last!
Arms, take your last embrace! And, lips, O you
The doors of breath, seal with a righteous kiss
A dateless[80] bargain to engrossing death!
Come, bitter conduct;[81] come, unsavory guide!
Thou desperate pilot,[82] now at once run on
The dashing rocks thy seasick weary bark!
Here's to my love! [*Drinks*] O true apothecary!
Thy drugs are quick. Thus with a kiss I die.   [*Falls.*]

[*Enter* FRIAR LAWRENCE, *with lanthorn, crow, and spade.*]

FRIAR: Saint Francis be my speed![83] How oft tonight
    Have my old feet stumbled[84] at graves! Who's there?
BALTHASAR: Here's one, a friend, and one that knows you well.
FRIAR: Bliss be upon you! Tell me, good my friend,
    What torch is yond that vainly lends his light

---

amorous (AM uh rus) full of love
abhorred (ab HAWRD) hated, dreaded
paramour (PAR uh muur) lover
pallet (PAL it) bed
inauspicious (in aw SPISH us) unlucky, forecasting misfortune
righteous (RY chus) morally right, virtuous
engrossing (en GROHS ing) taking all one's attention
unsavory (un SAY vuh ree) unpleasant
bark (BAHRK) a small sailing boat
apothecary (uh POTH uh ker ee) someone who prepares and
    dispenses drugs
[80]**dateless:** eternal
[81]**conduct:** here, guide (referring to the poison)
[82]**pilot:** captain (Romeo himself)
[83]**speed:** help
[84]**stumbled:** stumbling was thought to be a bad omen

To grubs and eyeless skulls? As I discern,
It burneth in the Capels' monument.
BALTHASAR: It doth so, holy sir; and there's my master,
One that you love.
FRIAR: Who is it?
BALTHASAR: Romeo.
FRIAR: How long hath he been there?
BALTHASAR: Full half an hour.
FRIAR: Go with me to the vault.
BALTHASAR: I dare not, sir.
My master knows not but I am gone hence,
And fearfully did menace me with death
If I did stay to look on his intents.
FRIAR: Stay then; I'll go alone. Fear comes upon me.
O, much I fear some ill unthrifty[85] thing.
BALTHASAR: As I did sleep under this yew tree here.
I dreamt my master and another fought,
And that my master slew him.
FRIAR: Romeo!
Alack, alack, what blood is this which stains
The stony entrance of this sepulcher?
What mean these masterless[86] and gory swords
To lie discolored by this place of peace?   [*Enters the tomb.*]

Romeo! O, pale! Who else? What, Paris too?
And steeped in blood? Ah, what an unkind[87] hour
Is guilty of this lamentable chance!
The lady stirs.   [JULIET *rises.*]

JULIET: O comfortable[88] friar! Where is my lord?
I do remember well where I should be,
And there I am. Where is my Romeo?

---

grubs (GRUBZ) young wormlike stage of some insects
discern (dih SURN) make out or recognize
sepulcher (SEP ul kur) small chamber used as a tomb
gory (GAWR ee) bloody
lamentable (LAM un tuh bul) distressing, sorrowful
[85]**unthrifty:** (*archaic*) unfortunate
[86]**masterless:** discarded
[87]**unkind:** unnatural
[88]**comfortable:** (*archaic*) comfort-giving

from The Tragedy of Romeo and Juliet ■ 71

Critical Thinking:
Summarize
Ask students to write a summary of the play up to this point. Have a volunteer read his or her summary. Ask the students if they agree with this summary. Discuss why or why not.

Literary Focus:
Foreshadowing
When the friar says that "fear comes upon me," he foreshadows the tragic discovery of the dead lovers. Have students review and discuss other instances of foreshadowing in the play.

Reading Focus:
Recognize Imagery

Romeo's appearance in death is described through Juliet's eyes. She kisses him and notices that his lips are still warm. Ask: In what way is this like Romeo's discovery of her (seemingly) dead body?

Literary Focus:
Figures of Speech

Juliet finds Romeo's dagger and exclaims, "O happy dagger!" Ask: Can a dagger be happy? Why does she describe it this way?

FRIAR: I hear some noise. Lady, come from that nest
    Of death, contagion, and unnatural sleep.
    A greater power than we can contradict
    Hath thwarted our intents. Come, come away.
    Thy husband in thy bosom there lies dead;
    And Paris too. Come, I'll dispose of thee
    Among a sisterhood of holy nuns.
    Stay not to question, for the watch is coming.
    Come, go, good Juliet. I dare no longer stay.
JULIET: Go, get thee hence,[89] for I will not away.   [*Exit* FRIAR.]
    What's here? A cup, closed in my truelove's hand?
    Poison, I see, hath been his timeless[90] end.
    O churl! Drunk all, and left no friendly drop
    To help me after? I will kiss thy lips.
    Haply[91] some poison yet doth hang on them
    To make me die with a restorative.   [*Kisses him.*]
    Thy lips are warm!
CHIEF WATCHMAN [*within*]: Lead, boy. Which way?
JULIET: Yea, noise? Then I'll be brief. O happy[92] dagger!

    [*Snatches* ROMEO'S *dagger.*]

    This is thy sheath: there rust, and let me die.

    [*She stabs herself and falls.*]

    [*Enter* PARIS' BOY *and* WATCH.]

BOY: This is the place. There, where the torch doth burn.
CHIEF WATCHMAN: The ground is bloody. Search about the
    churchyard.
    Go, some of you: whoe'er you find attach.[93]

    [*Exit some of the* WATCH.]

---

contagion (kun TAY jun) spreading disease
thwarted (THWAWRT id) blocked or stopped
churl (CHURL) selfish, mean, rude person
restorative (rih STAWR uh tiv) something that brings back consciousness
    or health generally; a medicine
[89]**hence:** (*archaic*) away from this place
[90]**timeless:** here, too soon
[91]**haply:** perhaps
[92]**happy:** (*archaic*) convenient
[93]**attach:** here, arrest

Pitiful sight! Here lies the County slain:
And Juliet bleeding, warm, and newly dead,
Who here hath lain this two days burièd.
Go, tell the Prince; run to the Capulets;
Raise up the Montagues: some others search.

[*Exit others of the* WATCH.]

We see the ground whereon these woes do lie,
But the true ground[94] of all these piteous woes
We cannot without circumstance[95] descry.

[*Enter some of the* WATCH, *with* ROMEO'S MAN, BALTHASAR.]

SECOND WATCHMAN: Here's Romeo's man. We found him in the
    churchyard.
CHIEF WATCHMAN: Hold him in safety till the Prince come hither.

[*Enter* FRIAR LAWRENCE *and another* WATCHMAN.]

THIRD WATCHMAN: Here is a friar that trembles, sighs, and weeps.
    We took this mattock and this spade from him
    As he was coming from this churchyard's side.
CHIEF WATCHMAN: A great suspicion! Stay[96] the friar too.

[*Enter the* PRINCE *and* ATTENDANTS.]

PRINCE: What misadventure is so early up,
    That calls our person from our morning rest?

[*Enter* CAPULET *and his* WIFE *with others.*]

CAPULET: What should it be, that is so shrieked abroad?
LADY CAPULET: O, the people in the street cry "Romeo,"
    Some "Juliet," and some "Paris": and all run
    With open outcry toward our monument.
PRINCE: What fear is this which startles in your ears?

---

woes (WOHZ) misery, sorrows
descry (dih SKRY) discover, see clearly
[94]ground: cause
[95]circumstance: here, details
[96]stay: here, keep or hold

from The Tragedy of Romeo and Juliet ■ 73

Enrichment

Juliet, now conscious, tells the friar she will "not away." She hopes that Romeo has left at least a drop of poison for her—but he has drunk it all. She kisses him, hoping some poison is left on his lips. Then, when she realizes the nightwatch is coming, she takes Romeo's dagger and kills herself—proving her resolve to join her lover in death.

Critical Thinking:
Compare and Contrast
Both Capulet and Montague lost a child. Have students compare the fathers' reaction to their child's death. Ask: Are there similarities, differences? Discuss.

Reading Focus:
Recognize Imagery
When Capulet arrives at the death scene, he sees that the dagger isn't in the sheath carried by Romeo, but is plunged into his daughter's breast. This is a powerful image. Ask: How might Capulet and his wife have felt upon seeing this?

CHIEF WATCHMAN: Sovereign, here lies the County Paris lain;
  And Romeo dead; and Juliet, dead before,
  Warm and new killed.
PRINCE: Search, seek, and know how this foul murder comes.
CHIEF WATCHMAN: Here is a friar, and slaughtered Romeo's man.
  With instruments upon them fit to open
  These dead men's tombs.
CAPULET: O heavens! O wife, look how our daughter bleeds!
  This dagger hath mista'en, for, lo, his house[97]
  Is empty on the back of Montague.
  And it missheathèd in my daughter's bosom!
LADY CAPULET: O me, this sight of death is as a bell
  That warns my old age to a sepulcher.

[*Enter* MONTAGUE *and others.*]

PRINCE: Come, Montague; for thou art early up
  To see thy son and heir more early down.
MONTAGUE: Alas, my liege, my wife is dead tonight!
  Grief of my son's exile hath stopped her breath.
  What further woe conspires against mine age?
PRINCE: Look, and thou shalt see.
MONTAGUE: O thou untaught! What manners is in this,
  To press before thy father to a grave?
PRINCE: Seal up the mouth of outrage[98] for a while,
  Till we can clear these ambiguities
  And know their spring, their head, their true descent;
  And then will I be general of your woes[99]
  And lead you even to death. Meantime forbear,
  And let mischance be slave to patience.[100]
  Bring forth the parties of suspicion.

---

liege (LEEJ) lord
conspire (kun SPYR) plan and act together secretly
ambiguities (am buh GYOO uh teez) things that are not clear
forbear (fawr BAIR) keep under control, endure
mischance (mis CHANS) misfortune
[97]**house:** sheath
[98]**mouth of outrage:** violent cries
[99]**general . . . woes:** leader in your sorrowing
[100]**let . . . patience:** be patient in the face of misfortune

FRIAR: I am the greatest, able to do least,
  Yet most suspected, as the time and place
  Doth make against me, of this direful murder;
  And here I stand, both to impeach and purge
  Myself condemnèd and myself excused.
PRINCE: Then say at once what thou dost know in this.
FRIAR: I will be brief, for my short date of breath[101]
  Is not so long as is a tedious tale.
  Romeo, there dead, was husband to that Juliet;
  And she, there dead, that's Romeo's faithful wife.
  I married them; and their stol'n marriage day
  Was Tybalt's doomsday, whose untimely death
  Banished the new-made bridegroom from this city;
  For whom, and not for Tybalt, Juliet pined.
  You, to remove that siege of grief from her,
  Betrothed and would have married her perforce
  To County Paris. Then comes she to me
  And with wild looks bid me devise some mean
  To rid her from this second marriage,
  Or in my cell there would she kill herself.
  Then gave I her (so tutored by my art)
  A sleeping potion: which so took effect
  As I intended, for it wrought on her
  The form of death. Meantime I writ to Romeo
  That he should hither come as[102] this dire night
  To help to take her from her borrowed grave,
  Being the time the potion's force should cease,
  But he which bore my letter, Friar John,
  Was stayed by accident, and yesternight
  Returned my letter back. Then all alone
  At the prefixèd hour of her waking
  Came I to take her from her kindred's vault:

Literary Focus:
Plot
With the climax past, the Prince demands an explanation. How does Friar Lawrence's explanation provide plot resolution?

---

direful (DYR ful) terrible, dreadful
impeach (im PEECH) accuse
bridegroom (BRYD groom) groom
potion (POH shun) a drink with special powers, such as medicine or poison
wrought (RAWT) formed or brought about
[101]**date of breath:** term of life
[102]**as:** here, on

from The Tragedy of Romeo and Juliet ■ 75

Reading Focus:
Recognize Imagery
Ask students why the Prince speaks of a glooming peace.

Literary Focus:
Figures of Speech
At the end of the play, the Prince says that even the sun itself will not rise as it hides its head in sadness. Have students identify the figure of speech. Ask: How does this figure of speech convey the families' sorrows?

Critical Thinking:
Analyze
Earlier in the play, the Friar said that he hoped the marriage of Romeo and Juliet would end the feuding between the families. What actually ended the feud between the families? Did love really conquer all in this story? Discuss.

Meaning to keep her closely[103] at my cell
Till I conveniently could send to Romeo.
But when I came, some minute ere the time
Of her awakening, here untimely lay
The noble Paris and true Romeo dead.
She wakes; and I entreated her come forth
And bear this work of heaven with patience;
But then a noise did scare me from the tomb,
And she, too desperate, would not go with me,
But, as it seems, did violence on herself.
All this I know, and to the marriage
Her nurse is privy; and if aught[104] in this
Miscarried by my fault, let my old life
Be sacrificed some hour before his time
Unto the rigor of severest law.
CAPULET: O brother Montague, give me thy hand.
This is my daughter's jointure,[105] for no more
Can I demand.
MONTAGUE: But I can give thee more;
For I will raise her statue in pure gold,
That whiles Verona by that name is known,
There shall no figure at such rate[106] be set
As that of true and faithful Juliet.
CAPULET: As rich shall Romeo's by his lady's lie—
Poor sacrifices of our enmity!
PRINCE: A glooming[107] peace this morning with it brings.
The sun for sorrow will not show his head.
Go hence, to have more talk of these sad things;
Some shall be pardoned, and some punishèd;
For never was a story of more woe
Than this of Juliet and her Romeo.

[*Exit all.*]

---

untimely (un TYM lee) coming before the expected time
privy (PRIV ee) secretly informed
miscarried (mis KAR eed) went wrong
rigor (RIG ur) strictness
[103]**closely:** here, hidden
[104]**aught:** (*archaic*) anything whatever
[105]**jointure:** marriage gift
[106]**rate:** value
[107]**glooming:** cloudy, gloomy

Mini Quiz

Write the following questions on the chalkboard or overhead projector and call on students to fill in the blanks. Discuss the answers with the class.

1. The banquet at which Romeo and Juliet meet is hosted by _____.

2. Juliet's balcony overlooks an _____.

3. In the balcony scene, Romeo and Juliet are interrupted by the _____.

4. Romeo meets _____ at the Capulet grave and kills him.

5. Juliet uses a _____ to kill herself.

Answers
1. Juliet's father, Capulet
2. orchard
3. nurse
4. Paris
5. dagger

William Shakespeare (1564–1616)

William Shakespeare is considered by many to be the greatest playwright, and perhaps the greatest author, of all time. His works show a talent for characterization and poetic expression that have never been equaled.

Shakespeare was born in Stratford-upon-Avon in 1564. Little is known about his early life, except that he was the son of a businessman and probably attended the local grammar school. In 1582 he married Anne Hathaway, and they had three children.

Shakespeare was an actor as well as a playwright, and was a member of a group of actors called Lord Chamberlain's Men. Shakespeare was part owner of the company's theater, the Globe, and he wrote his plays exclusively for this company at the rate of about two a year.

The characters in Shakespeare's plays are the first "modern" dramatic characters—with both strengths and weaknesses. Shakespeare skillfully conveys a sense of his characters' psychological identities, and this is part of the reason why these characters have endured so vividly for so many years.

In the course of his life, Shakespeare wrote over 30 plays and hundreds of sonnets and other poems. Because Shakespeare wrote his plays for performance, he was indifferent about their publication. Many of the plays that were published shortly after his death were reconstructed from memory by actors.

MORE ABOUT THE AUTHOR

Interestingly, Shakespeare's works are so outstanding that some people have refused to believe that an actor with a country background could have written them. While most scholars feel strongly that Shakespeare indeed wrote the plays and poems, at least six other possible authors have been named, including Sir Francis Bacon and Christopher Marlowe.

Additional Works

BY WILLIAM SHAKESPEARE

You may wish to suggest these works by William Shakespeare for additional reading:

Hamlet, The play that has perhaps enjoyed the greatest popularity of all of Shakespeare's works, *Hamlet* is a classic melodrama in the genre of romantic tragedy.

A Midsummer Night's Dream, A fantasy of folklore and fairies, this is one of Shakespeare's most popular comedies. The play's title alludes to the excess, romance, and youthful spirit of midsummer's madness.

Macbeth, Shakespeare's reputation as a brilliant writer of tragedy was established by the time he wrote *Macbeth*. This famous play about ambition and fear is a study of character and character motivations.

King Lear, Shakespeare used ancient British history as a source for characters and events in this tragic play about an aging king and his daughters.

UNDERSTAND THE SELECTION

Answers

1. Tybalt
2. in Friar Lawrence's cell
3. Where is Romeo?
4. He is young, impetuous, and in awe of Juliet's beauty.
5. Romeo is still Juliet's handsome lover, regardless of the fact he is a Montague.
6. She has discovered Romeo is dead. Friar Lawrence wants to hide her, and cover up the failed plan.
7. Sample answer: Friar Lawrence's letters don't get through to Romeo.
8. Sample answer: Many street gangs and political opponents fight for no real reason.
9. Sample answer: The prince should punish no one, for the people who kept the feud alive must now suffer the loss of their beloved children.
10. The drama tells a classic story: two lovers kept apart because of hatred between their families.

Respond to Literature

The theme of *Romeo and Juliet* is timeless. Anyone who has experienced love can appreciate the tragedy in which the two lovers are caught. A modern film version of the story was *West Side Story*. The story has also been turned into a ballet score.

WRITE ABOUT THE SELECTION

Prewriting

Review as a class the roles the various characters play in the story. Ask whether students have any special thoughts or ideas they would like to share about any of the characters.

Writing

Circulate as students work individually. A general theme should be identified in the cluster, and students should organize their letter around it. Discuss this with any students having difficulty.

UNDERSTAND THE SELECTION

Recall

1. Who threatens Romeo at the banquet?
2. Where are Romeo and Juliet married?
3. What is the first question Juliet asks when she awakes in the tomb?

Infer

4. How could Romeo change his love so quickly from Rosaline to Juliet?
5. Explain "That which we call a rose by any other word would smell as sweet."
6. Why does Friar Lawrence suggest Juliet go to a convent of nuns?
7. Chance plays an important part in this story. Give one example.

Apply

8. The Capulets and Montagues fight not for a good reason, but because they are enemies. Give a modern-day example of such conflict.
9. Whom should the prince pardon, and whom should he punish? Why?
10. Why is *Romeo and Juliet* one of the most famous love stories in literature?

Respond to Literature

The story of Romeo and Juliet has been retold many times and sometimes adapted and modernized. Why?

WRITE ABOUT THE SELECTION

During Shakespeare's time, educated people wrote many letters. If you could write a letter of advice to any of the characters in *Romeo and Juliet*, to whom would you write—Romeo, Mercutio, or Juliet? How about giving advice to Tybalt, the friar, or Juliet's nurse? Choose one character with which to correspond and compose a letter.

Prewriting As you choose the character, you will be thinking of things you would like to say to him or her. Write them down in clusters around the character's name. If at first you cannot decide on one character, choose several, make clusters, and then pick the one you think will give you the chance to write the most interesting letter.

Writing Use the cluster to write your letter. Make sure the comments and help you offer are clear. Since you are writing a letter, you need to use the second-person pronouns—*you, yourself*.

Revising You may write in poetry or prose. Whichever form you use, have you thought of trying to make the letter sound "old"? That is, can you make it sound as though it were written by a contemporary of the person to whom you are writing?

Proofreading Reread what you have written and check for mistakes. Pay particular attention to **homophones**, or words that sound alike but are spelled differently. The person reading your letter might think that you are trying to make a joke instead of simply having misspelled something!

Revising

Students might like writing a "parallel" letter that translates their original letter into a letter written with an older style. Explore with students what makes Shakespeare's writing different from modern writing. Much of it comes from the use of archaic words, different verb endings, and a more complicated style. Analyze one or two brief passages to pinpoint these qualities.

Proofreading

Write on the chalkboard or overhead projector some examples of homophones. Then suggest that a few homophones can be found among the new vocabulary words. Show how slight spelling changes can create large differences in meaning.

ESL Activity

Have students review their list of movies from the ESL Activity on page T49 and choose one. Have students write a few sentences discussing whether the movie was realistic or unrealistic, and why they think so.

THINK ABOUT FIGURES OF SPEECH

Let us examine one specific case of Shakespeare's imaginative use of language—**simile**, which uses the words *like* or *as* to compare two different things. Figures of speech like similes add richness to literature. Romeo speaks these lines when he must leave Juliet at the end of the balcony scene:

"Love goes toward love as schoolboys
    from their books;
But love from love, toward school with
    heavy looks."

1. What figure of speech is used?

2. What is being compared?

3. Explain the meaning of the first part of the comparison.

4. Explain the meaning of the second part of the comparison.

5. What adds to the effectiveness of the comparison?

READING FOCUS

Recognize Imagery As you read *Romeo and Juliet* you were able to see how the author used imagery to make the characters, setting, and action of the play come alive. Shakespeare was skilled at creating vivid images by appealing to your senses. What senses in particular did this play appeal to? Provide examples from the play to support your answer.

DEVELOP YOUR VOCABULARY

Shakespeare uses many words that are uncommon today. Sometimes the meaning he intended has dropped out of use, or sometimes the word itself is no longer used.

The words *thou* and *thee* are good examples. They are pronouns, and in Shakespeare's time were used instead of the word *you* to address friends and other close acquaintances. *Thou* is the nominative case, *thee* the objective case, and *thy* or *thine* the possessive case.

The dictionary can help you learn about old word usages. Sometimes it will note that a word, or a particular definition of a word, is **archaic** (abbreviated *arch.*). This means the word, or definition, is rarely used today.

Look up the following words in a dictionary. Write down the definition that fits with Shakespeare's time, and then use the word in a sentence.

1. knave
2. sirrah (or "sirah")
3. doth
4. hither
5. perforce
6. choler

THINK ABOUT FIGURES OF SPEECH

Answers
1. simile
2. love and schoolboys
3. Meeting up with the person you love is like quitting studying.
4. Leaving someone you love is like having to go to school.
5. The use of rhyme—"books" and "looks."

DEVELOP YOUR VOCABULARY

Answers
1. knave; a serving boy or male servant, also a rascal
2. sirrah; old form of address, often used to show contempt; fellow
3. doth; do
4. hither; to, toward, or here
5. perforce; by force, enforced
6. choler; anger

Sample sentences:
1. Remove that knave from this hall!
2. Sirrah, I wish never to see you in my house again!
3. He doth move like a deer chased by dogs.
4. Come hither, boy, and take your punishment.
5. Ambition and greed perforce create trouble.
6. His choler flashed like sparks from a welder's torch.

READING FOCUS

Sample Answer
The author was especially skilled at appealing to the senses of sight and touch. He vividly described how Juliet appeared to Romeo, the quality of her eyes and skin. He also described the softness and color of her skin and lips.

SELECTION OVERVIEW

SELECTION OBJECTIVES

After completing the next three selections, students will be able to

- identify imagery in poetry
- understand how character is revealed through imagery
- use an image to describe something
- express feelings through images
- evaluate images by their appeal to the senses
- paraphrase poetry

Lesson Resources

Greyday/Here–Hold My Hand/ Finis
- Selection Synopses, Teacher's Edition, p. TT61
- Comprehension and Vocabulary Workbook, pp. 15–16
- Language Enrichment Workbook, pp. 13–15
- Teacher's Resources Reinforcement, p. R8 Test, pp. T15–T16

More About Imagery

In the last poetry selection, students studied figurative language. Often, figurative language uses imagery. "Today is as cold as a deep freeze" is an example in which the sense of touch is aroused. Imagery is often used in describing characters. Romeo describes Juliet as "fair sun." In this description, the sense of sight is addressed.

Background Notes

The images in "Greyday" are Christian in origin and symbolize suffering. The first, a crown of thorns, is an allusion to the mock crown pressed on Jesus's head as he was being led to his crucifixion. The second, a hair shirt, alludes to the medieval practice of wearing a rough and irritating shirt (usually made of horsehair or camel's hair) as penance.

Summer Millinery, Charles W. Hawthorne, 1866. (American, 1872–1930) Oil on board, 58½ × 46¾ in. Chrysler Museum of Art, Norfolk, VA Gift of Walter P. Chrysler, Jr. 71.659

READING FOCUS

Paraphrase Poetry When you paraphrase you restate the speaker's experiences and feelings in your own words. Restating the lines or stanzas of a poem will help you to clarify their meaning. As you read the next three poems, practice paraphrasing the lines of each one.

Learn About

IMAGERY

An image is a mental "sensation." You are provided with information that creates a picture that you can see, hear, smell, feel, or taste in your mind. You form this picture with your imagination. The use of language that stimulates these mental pictures is called **imagery**.

Imagery appeals to the senses and helps you experience what a writer is describing. For example, a visual image allows you to "see"; an aural image allows you to "hear." When you read, you are not really seeing or hearing these things, but you can imagine that you are. You experience, in your imagination, what the writer creates.

Poets use all kinds of objects and activities to create images in their poems. In fact, if an image is unexpected or unique, it is usually very effective.

Look for answers to the following questions as you read the poems:

1. Why is imagery a powerful tool?
2. How is imagery used effectively?

WRITING CONNECTION

Using imagery, describe something in your classroom. Try to think of an image that gives a vivid sense of what you are describing.

Viewing Fine Art

Call attention to the details in the painting. Ask: What impression does the posture of the milliner (the person making the hat) give about how she feels? How do the colors add to the imagery?

Cooperative Group Activity

After the Writing Connection, divide students into small groups. Begin by pointing to an object and asking students to think of an image to describe it, if possible. Specify the sense to which the image should appeal. On completion, ask the groups to choose their best image for presentation to the class.

Greyday

by Maya Angelou

The day hangs heavy
loose and grey
when you're away.

A crown of thorns
a shirt of hair
is what I wear.

No one knows
my lonely heart
when we're apart.

Here—Hold My Hand

by Mari Evans

Here
hold my hand
let me touch you
there is
5   nothing
we can
say . . . your
soul
eludes me
10   when I reach
out
your eyes
resent
my need to know
15   you
here
hold my hand
since
there is nothing
20   we can
say

eludes (ih LOODS) avoids or escapes
resent (rih ZENT) to feel or show anger

INTRODUCE

Motivation
Popular songs and folk music often focus on love—especially love lost. Ask students to bring in records or tapes of songs describing the break-up of a relationship. What are the various tones of the lyrics?

Purpose-Setting Question
How can writing poetry ease the pain of love lost?

READ

Literary Focus:
Imagery
Imagery is used to describe "the day" in "Greyday." The day "hangs heavy loose and grey." The author wants the reader to feel the weight of her sorrow due to her partner's absence. Ask students to look for sensory images in all three poems.

Reading Focus:
Paraphrase Poetry
Work with the class to paraphrase each stanza of "Greyday." Allow students to work in pairs or small groups to paraphrase the other two poems in this selection.

CLOSE

Have students complete Review the Selection on pages 84–85.

Develop Vocabulary Skills
Write the new vocabulary words on the chalkboard or overhead projector. Ask for volunteers to use each in a sentence that also contains imagery.

ESL Activity

Have students work in groups to list as many words as possible that describe how a person might feel when love is lost. Have students share their lists with the group. Have them decide if the lists are similar, then compile one large list, embellishing words into phrases as they write.

Literary Focus:
Imagery

Point out to students the image of the moving clouds and the sky that the author uses to open "Finis." Ask: What emotion does this image evoke?

Critical Thinking:
Evaluate

"Magic touch" is a common phrase; it means a special, rare skill. What does it mean in this poem?

Comparing Selections

Have students compare the theme, mood, and imagery in the three poems. Ask: Do all three poems have the same theme? Why do you think as you do? Do all three poems evoke the same mood? Why or why not? Do the three authors use the same type of imagery? Discuss similarities and differences.

Reading Focus:
Paraphrase Poetry

Have students paraphrase the last four lines of "Finis." Ask volunteers to read aloud their paraphrased statements.

FINIS

by Waring Cuney

Now that our love has drifted
To a quiet close,
Leaving the empty ache
That always follows when beauty goes;
5   Now that you and I,
Who stood tiptoe on earth
To touch our fingers to the sky,
Have turned away
To allow our little love to die—
10   Go, dear, seek again the magic touch.
But if you are wise,
As I shall be wise,
You will not again
Love overmuch.

82 ■ Unit 1

Mini Quiz

Write the following questions on the chalkboard or overhead projector and call on students to fill in the blanks. Discuss the answers with the class.

1. The crown mentioned in "Grey-day" is made of _____.

2. In Mari Evans's poem, the sense of _____ is the only way the speaker thinks she can communicate with her partner.

3. Eluding her when she reaches out is her partner's _____.

4. In "Finis," when beauty departs, an _____ remains.

5. The speaker in "Finis" has learned to be _____.

Answers
1. thorns
2. touch
3. soul
4. ache
5. wise

AUTHOR BIOGRAPHY
Maya Angelou (1928–)

When the American choreographer Alvin Ailey was a college student at San Francisco State, he took time away from the books to form a nightclub dance act with a young woman named Marguerite Johnson. Little did the two dancers know that in a few decades, both would be famous—Ailey as the founder of the Alvin Ailey Dance Company and Marguerite Johnson as the celebrated author Maya Angelou.

Twelve years after her partnership with Ailey, Angelou was in Cairo, Egypt as associate editor of the *Arab Observer*. A year later she went to Ghana, where she became a writer for the *Ghanaian Times*

and an assistant administrator at the University of Ghana. In 1966 she returned to the states as a lecturer at the University of California.

Maya Angelou is best known for her autobiography, *I Know Why the Caged Bird Sings*, which was written in 1970. The book tells the moving and often humorous story of her childhood in segregated Arkansas. The book was made into a play for television in 1977.

In addition to her careers as a dancer and a writer, Angelou has worked as a movie and stage actress. She has written plays, books of poetry, and screenplays, and has also composed music.

Author Biography ■ 83

MORE ABOUT THE AUTHOR

What makes a poet? Increased sensitivity to everything in the immediate environment is one ingredient. Where does that sensitivity come from? In the case of Maya Angelou, it could be attributed to the broad range of her experiences, some of which were quite oppressive. Angelou, whose real name is Marguerite Johnson, grew up in Arkansas when segregation between black and white was prevalent. Her account of those years in her autobiography, *I Know Why the Caged Bird Sings,* makes it clear she learned at an early age what pain and survival really mean. Later she lived abroad, in Egypt and Ghana. Adapting to new experiences probably helped her develop a special sensitivity to the world around her.

Additional Works
BY MAYA ANGELOU

You may wish to suggest these works by Maya Angelou for additional reading:

Magic, New York, Clarkson Potter, 1996. An African boy tells about village life in West Africa. Photos by Margaret Courtney-Clarke. (fiction)

On the Pulse of Morning, New York, Random House, 1993. (poetry)

Phenomenal Women: Four Poems Celebrating Women, New York, Random House, 1993. (poetry)

Even the Stars Look Lonesome, New York, Random House, 1993. Angelou talks about her life and views. (autobiography)

UNDERSTAND THE SELECTION

Answers

1. "when you're away"
2. To touch the person she has loved
3. It "has drifted to a quiet close."
4. She describes the day as hanging "grey."
5. They are images, religious in nature, suggesting great pain.
6. No; "your eyes resent my need to know you," suggests the speaker's partner has difficulty communicating.
7. Because the "empty ache" is too hard to bear.
8. The love they once shared reached great heights.
9. She feels hurt, alone, and rejected.
10. No. The first-person character of "Finis" is sensitive, realistic, and more mature.

Respond to Literature

It was Tennyson who asserted that "Tis better to have loved and lost, Than never to have loved at all." Ask students if they agree. Should one experience both the pain and the beauty of love?

WRITE ABOUT THE SELECTION

Prewriting

In this assignment students may use any image they want, including metaphor, to describe the feeling they choose. As a warmup, have the class pick a feeling, and do the "Z" mapping suggested in the Student's Book.

Writing

Circulate as students work individually. Encourage students to try writing poetry; it might be an easier way for them to express feelings.

Revising

On the chalkboard or overhead projector, write the lines from "Finis" that express the desire to reach upward—"Who stood tip-toe on earth To touch our fingers to the sky." Rewrite the phrase using less

---

UNDERSTAND THE SELECTION

Recall

1. When does the day seem grey to the speaker in "Greyday"?
2. Why does the speaker of "Here—Hold My Hand" want to hold hands?
3. How has love ended in "Finis?"

Infer

4. Why did Maya Angelou choose the title "Greyday" for her poem?
5. Explain the images of a "crown of thorns" and "a shirt of hair".
6. Do you think that the two people in "Here—Hold My Hand" can look at each other honestly? Why or why not?
7. Why does the speaker of "Finis" tell his partner not to "love overmuch" again?

Apply

8. What is suggested to you by the lines "Who stood tiptoe on earth to touch our fingers to the sky" in "Finis"?
9. What is the character in "Here—Hold My Hand" feeling?
10. Is the character in "Finis" the same as in "Here—Hold My Hand"? Explain.

Respond to Literature

Is it better to love and then lose that love, rather than never to love at all? Why?

WRITE ABOUT THE SELECTION

Maya Angelou loses love only temporarily in "Greyday," while Mari Evans and Waring Cuney lose their loved ones completely in their poems.

All three poets are trying to capture the feeling of losing love, however. Each does it in his or her unique way, based on feelings.

How do you best express your feelings when writing about something? Do you use the first person? Do you think of images that describe your feelings? Express an important feeling with images.

Prewriting Concentrate on one feeling. Write the feeling at the top left corner of a piece of paper. Now, make a Z from there. Along the line, fill in words or draw pictures that describe your feeling.

Writing Combine your thoughts into a single paragraph or a few lines of poetry. "Translate" any pictures into words, using imagery if you can. Appeal to several different senses, not just sight. Can you make your readers hear, taste, smell, or feel?

Revising Are your words communicating your feeling? Think of changing or adding words that "sharpen" your description. Make every word count!

Proofreading Reread your description and check for unnecessary repetition. Also, check that your punctuation is consistent throughout; for example, Maya Angelou uses only a final period at the end of each verse.

---

expressive words—"Who tried reaching as high as we could toward the sky." Discuss with the class how just a few carefully-chosen words can sharpen an image.

Proofreading

Repetition is not necessarily bad: In "Here—Hold My Hand," several lines are repeated. Unnecessary repetition, however, can be boring. If you chose to write a paragraph, don't say, for example, "several lines are repeated again"; "again" is redundant. As you read for punctuation and spelling, also concentrate on deleting such unnecessary words.

THINK ABOUT IMAGERY

Imagery is one device an author uses to appeal to the senses. Images can be strengthened by appealing to the same sense in different ways or by appealing to a different sense at the same time. Maya Angelou describes the day as hanging "heavy loose and grey." "Heavy" and "loose" appeal to your sense of touch. "Grey" appeals to your sense of sight.

1. Think of an image that describes the hand in "Here—Hold My Hand." To which sense will you appeal?

2. Try to add an image to the description you have just thought of. Appeal to the same or a different sense.

3. None of the three poems has imagery appealing to the senses of hearing, smell, or taste. Why is this so?

4. Is any one sense best for imagery?

5. Think of an image appealing to the sense of hearing, smell, or taste that describes something mentioned in one of the poems.

READING FOCUS

Paraphrase Poetry Paraphrase one of the poems you just read. Then tell how restating the poem in your own words helped to make the meaning clearer.

DEVELOP YOUR VOCABULARY

Context, or the words or phrases surrounding a word, can be an important help in understanding words you do not know. Even when you do know a word, context can help to understand added meaning behind a word.

Look at the word *elude* in "Here—Hold My Hand": "your soul *eludes* me when I reach out." The theme of the poem is falling out of love. The two people cannot communicate anymore. You might guess that *elude* relates to not being able or not wanting to reach something. It does. *Elude* means "to avoid or escape."

Use context to help you write the meaning of the italicized words in the following lines. When you have finished, use a dictionary to check your meanings.

1. "Your eyes *resent* my need to know you. "

2. "The sweetest joy, the wildest *woe* is love. "

3. "Many waters cannot *quench* love, neither can the floods drown it."

THINK ABOUT IMAGERY

Sample Answers
1. tired hand, which appeals to the sense of touch
2. cold, tired hand
3. The lack of communication is an important aspect in the poems, so it's logical that hearing is absent. As to smelling and tasting, it's more likely that these senses would be used to portray love more positively—for example, smelling the flower of love, or tasting the sweet cup of love.
4. No. The best sense is the one that best communicates the writer's thoughts.
5. An image of love in "Finis" might be "a glass with only a scent of the sweet wine that once filled it."

DEVELOP YOUR VOCABULARY

Answers
1. to feel angry or bitter at
2. sorrow
3. to put an end to

READING FOCUS

Sample Answer

I paraphrased "Finis" this way: Now that our love has ended, leaving an empty feeling inside us, now that we, who had once felt on top of the world, have turned our backs on love—Go and find love like ours once was. But if you've learned from our failed love, as I have, you will not try to fall so deeply in love again.

Paraphrasing this poem helped me to understand the lines "who stood tiptoe on earth to touch our fingers to the sky" and to appreciate the overall theme of the pain of lost love.

SELECTION OVERVIEW

SELECTION OBJECTIVES

After completing these selections students will be able to

- see differences of tone in poetry
- analyze how tone affects meaning in everyday speech
- evaluate the tone of a character
- write a reply to the speaker of a poem
- analyze a poet's tone
- compare and contrast

Lesson Resources

Housecleaning/Where Have You Gone
- Selection Synopses, Teacher's Edition, p. TT62
- Comprehension and Vocabulary Workbook, pp. 17–18
- Language Enrichment Workbook, p. 16
- Teacher's Resources Reinforcement, p. R9 Test, pp. T15–T16

More About Tone

Tone was discussed previously in the "First Person Demonstrative" selection. Ask students to recall the tone of that selection. Suggest that the tone of "Housecleaning," one of the following selections, may be similar but the overall message is more harsh. The tone of "Where Have You Gone," is very different. Ask students to determine that difference as they read the next two selections.

ESL Activity

Have students list and define some slang words or expressions from their culture. Use the assignment for a whole-class discussion.

T86

Portrait of Langston Hughes, Winold Reiss. National Portrait Gallery, Gift of W. Tjark Reiss

READING FOCUS

Compare and Contrast Comparing and contrasting two different poems helps you to focus on both the smaller details and the larger themes or messages of the poems. Poems can be very different in tone or theme and still have many characteristics in common. Compare and contrast these two poems to help you to see what makes the poems similar and different.

Learn About

TONE IN POETRY

Writers often have strong opinions about what they are writing. These opinions usually show in the attitude a writer expresses towards his or her subject. This attitude is usually expressed in the **tone** of a selection.

The tone can be lighthearted and mocking. It can be serious and depressing. It can be several things at once.

Poems that have strong tones tell you something about the poet's attitude. The speaker in the poem can say things in a certain way that reveals the poet's opinions about the theme.

Look for answers to the following questions as you read the poems:

1. What is the tone of each of the poems?
2. What creates the tone?

WRITING CONNECTION

Think of a recent conversation you have had with somebody. How did you reveal your opinions, other than by direct comments? Did you use certain words that sounded angry, disappointed, proud, or expressed some other feeling? Did you talk about something else in order to describe your thoughts? Write a few lines of what you said. What kind of tone do the lines have? Why?

Viewing Fine Art

This portrait was painted in the 1920s by Winold Reiss (1886–1953). The subject, Langston Hughes (1902–1967), is a well-known African American poet who wrote several books and poems which brought him considerable attention. Today, Hughes is known as one of the foremost interpreters of the African American experience. Although this portrait is considered a painting, the background gives it a drawing-like quality. Note how Hughes's jacket is different from the background. Ask: Which do you prefer, a drawing or a painting? Why?

Cooperative Group Activity

Use the Writing Connection as background for this activity. Start with a dialogue. Use a definite tone when talking with one student; then vary the tone, but not the dialogue, as you begin talking with another student. Repeat the procedure until students grasp what you're doing. Discuss how different tones affect the message; ask for specific examples of tone as a communicator.

Housecleaning

by Nikki Giovanni

i always liked housecleaning
even as a child
i dug straightening
the cabinets
5   putting new paper on
the shelves
washing the refrigerator
inside out
and unfortunately this habit has
10   carried over and i find
i must remove you
from my life

Anna Washington Derry, Laura Wheeler Waring.
National Museum of American Art, Smithsonian
Institution, Gift of the Harmon Foundation

Where Have You Gone

by Mari Evans

Where have you gone

with your confident
walk with
your crooked smile

5   why did you leave
me
when you took your
laughter
and departed

10   are you aware that
with you
went the sun

all light
and what few stars
15   there were?

where have you gone
with your confident
walk your
crooked smile the
20   rent money
in one pocket and
my heart
in another . . .

Housecleaning/Where Have You Gone ■ 87

UNDERSTAND THE SELECTION

Answers

1. when she was a child
2. a habit
3. "Rent money" and "my heart"
4. It means removing the food before cleaning inside and out.
5. The only way she can end a relationship is to stop it and remove the person from her life; that is the only way she knows, "unfortunately."
6. She distrusts him.
7. Her life is generally depressing; her lover brought some of the few rays of happiness she has known.
8. Sample answer: I thought the poem was going to be sappily romantic; instead it is both sensitive and realistic.
9. She feels robbed or cheated—as if the friend has left with both her heart and her money.
10. She must forget about the person entirely.

ESL Activity

Divide students into pairs. Have each partner write sentences using the words in the Infer questions above. The ask them to check each other's work. Provide help as needed.

Respond to Literature

Two very different responses to the break-up of a relationship are suggested by the poems. One response is a practical "let's get on with life," the other is a realistic reflection tinged with depression. Have students "vote" for the poet they'd like to meet. If you can't discern a pattern in their responses, poll the students for their reasons.

WRITE ABOUT THE SELECTION

Prewriting

As a class discuss possibilities of why the relationship ended. Try to elicit a broad range of responses.

UNDERSTAND THE SELECTION

Recall

1. When did the housecleaner begin to love cleaning?

2. What does she call housecleaning?

3. What "things" were in the friend's pocket when he left?

Infer

4. What does washing the refrigerator "inside out" mean?

5. What does "unfortunately" mean in the next line of "Housecleaning"?

6. What does "crooked smile" tell about the person who walked out?

7. Why does the speaker of "Where Have You Gone" say "what few stars there were" when she describes life?

Apply

8. What did you think the tone of "Where Have You Gone" would be? Did your idea change?

9. How does the speaker in "Where Have You Gone" feel after the friend left?

10. Why must the housecleaner remove someone from her life?

Respond to Literature

If you could meet either speaker from these two poems, which one would you choose to meet? Explain your answer.

WRITE ABOUT THE SELECTION

Why do you think the "you" in the poem "Where Have You Gone" left the speaker? Do you think the person is a good-for-nothing who cheated the speaker? Do you think the speaker did not mention something about how the relationship ended, and that the speaker is as much to blame as the partner for their falling out of love?

Write a "reply" to the speaker of the poem. Present your ideas about why the relationship broke up.

Prewriting   What happened to end the relationship? Answer that question and write it in the middle of a piece of paper. Cluster reasons for the ending and the partner's feelings around it in boxes.

Writing   Read over your cluster and add any new ideas. Decide what reasons you will use in your response. Assemble your information into a few lines of poetry. See if you can keep the same style as Mari Evans. Write in the first person.

Revising   Pay attention to tone. Is your attitude toward the ending of the relationship clear? Are you happy, sad, relieved, or happy-go-lucky? Does your poem reflect this?

Proofreading   If you have kept the same style as Mari Evans, you will have no punctuation or capital letters. However, what words would be capitalized and what punctuation would there be in "normal" writing? Make notes in the margin to indicate the correct style.

Writing

Circulate as students work individually. Check to see that students are writing poetry and from a first-person point of view.

Revising

Using some of the responses from the "Prewriting" exercise, discuss how tone can be used to convey the partner's feelings. What specific words or figures of speech could be used?

Proofreading

Have students write a "correct" version of their poem, with proper punctuation and capitalization. For students who didn't use Evan's style, encourage them to produce another version that doesn't use punctuation or capitalization.

THINK ABOUT TONE

Tone is the overall attitude a writer brings to his or her work. Tone gives you a clue about what a writer feels about the subject and theme.

1. Read the opening of "Where Have You Gone" without "crooked" before "smile." Does the tone seem different?

2. How do the lines "the rent money in one pocket and my heart in another" make you feel? Do they tell anything about the speaker?

3. "Where Have You Gone" ends with an **ellipsis**, three periods in a row. Does this add to the tone of the poem? How?

4. Tone is often best created when you do not say directly how you feel. Does the speaker in "Housecleaning" say directly how she feels? How do you think she feels?

5. What do you think people mean by the expression "the tone of your voice"?

READING FOCUS

Compare and Contrast Tell how the tone and themes of the two poems are alike or different. How did comparing and contrasting the two poems help you to better understand each one?

DEVELOP YOUR VOCABULARY

Words used informally to mean something other than their usual, accepted definitions are called **slang**.

An example is *dug* in "Housecleaning": "I dug straightening the cabinets."

The usual definition of *dug* is "made a hole." This definition does not fit in the context of the poem, however. The poet means the slang definition of *dug*, which is "liked."

Dictionaries usually give definitions for slang. When you look up the word, the slang definition is usually given following the notation "slang." Make sure that you look under root words (under *dig* for *dug*, for example).

What are the slang definitions of the italicized words in these sentences? Check them in a dictionary.

1. The lead drummer plays *cool*.

2. She *aced* the test with ease.

3. His one-man show *bombed*.

4. Jimmy *beat* the robbery charge.

5. Hey, let's *rap* about this first.

6. "*Split!* Cat's here!" said the mice.

THINK ABOUT TONE

Answers

1. Yes; cynical distrust is gone.
2. Combining money and love makes the speaker seem poorer but wiser, or doubly cheated.
3. The ellipsis makes the poem's speaker seem unsure, still searching for an answer, maybe ready to ask more questions.
4. No, her feelings are hidden in her description of efficiency and cleanliness. She wants simply to get on with life, no questions asked.
5. Your true feelings. Tone expresses your attitude.

DEVELOP YOUR VOCABULARY

Answers

1. very well
2. did well, or got an "A" grade
3. failed
4. avoided the penalties associated with something
5. have a serious, sometimes long talk
6. leave

READING FOCUS

Sample Answer

Both poems had a somewhat sarcastic tone. But when I contrasted the two poems, I found that "Housecleaning," had a brisker, more practical feel to it, while "Where Have You Gone" seemed more melancholy and bitter. Comparing the poems made me see how they both dealt with themes of lost love.

SELECTION OVERVIEW

SELECTION OBJECTIVES

After completing this selection, students will be able to

- understand tone in a nonfiction work
- evaluate the tone of a written opinion
- record a personal feeling for critical examination of tone
- write a letter as a character in a story
- give examples of homophones
- analyze details

Lesson Resources

Where Are You Now, William Shakespeare?
- Selection Synopsis, Teacher's Edition, p. TT62
- Comprehension and Vocabulary Workbook, pp. 19–20
- Language Enrichment Workbook, p. 17
- Teacher's Resources Reinforcement, p. R10 Test, pp. T17–T18

More About Tone

So far, tone has been discussed only in connection with poetry. Now students will have a chance to examine tone in a short story. The first thing to know is that whether in poetry or prose, tone is the same: It is the writer's *attitude* toward the subject he or she has chosen.

The Breakfast Room, Pierre Bonnard Collection, The Museum of Modern Art, New York. Given anonymously.

READING FOCUS

Analyze Details Authors supply details to provide information about the characters, setting, tone or plot of a piece of writing. Analyzing the details in a story will help you to understand the author's attitude toward the subject matter. Look carefully at how the author describes characters and events. Does the author seem to be having fun? Does the author express sorrow or anger?

TONE IN NONFICTION

Like a poet writing a poem, when a writer tells a story what he or she thinks about the subject is very important. If a writer thinks the subject is funny, his or her attitude will probably be humorous. If a writer thinks the subject is serious, the attitude will be earnest.

A writer often sends "messages" to you, the reader, hinting how he or she feels about the subject. How those messages are expressed is also very important, for it reveals the writer's attitude toward you.

These attitudes—toward the subject and toward you—make up **tone**. Tone is all the unstated understandings between the writer and you about what the writer is trying to do.

As you read "Where Are You Now, William Shakespeare?", ask yourself:

1. What is the author's attitude toward the subject?
2. What is the author's attitude toward the reader?

WRITING CONNECTION

Write a short paragraph on something you feel strongly about. Exchange papers with a partner. Read your partner's paragraph, and determine its tone. Discuss with your partner your evaluation.

90 ■ Unit 1

Viewing Fine Art

Pierre Bonnard (1867–1947) began his career as an impressionist, favoring heavy paint and short brushstrokes. In the 20th century he developed a new style showing intimate and subtle interior scenes. Ask: What gives the feeling of intimacy in this scene?

Cooperative Group Activity

Before starting, have five or six different newspaper editorials available for distribution. Divide the class into five groups, and give one editorial to each group. Save one for demonstration purposes. Point out that editorials are different from news stories: Editorials express opinions. While news stories strive to be objective, editorials are subjective. (You may want to read an example from your editorial.) Emphasize that the tone of an editorial often tells as much about the writer's opinion as the words themselves. Examine your editorial with the class to determine its tone. Then ask the groups to examine the tone of their editorials and report to the class. Ask each group: How does the tone affect content? Follow up this activity by assigning the Writing Connection.

Where Are You Now, William Shakespeare?

by M. E. Kerr

My very first boyfriend was named William Shakespeare. This was his real name, and he lived over on Highland Hill, about a block from my house.

I often went to his house to get him, or I met him down in the empty lot on Alden Avenue, or over at Hoopes Park, where we caught sunfish and brought them from the pond in bottles of murky water with polliwogs.

Marijane is ten [my father wrote in his journal]. *She plays with boys and looks like one.*

This was true.

My arms and knees were full of scabs from falls out of trees and off my bicycle. I was happiest wearing the pants my brother'd grown out of, the vest to one of my father's business suits over one of my brother's old shirts, Indian moccasins, and a cap. Everything I said came out of the side of my mouth, and I strolled around with my fists inside my trouser pockets.

---

murky (MUR kee) clouded; unclear
journal (JUR nul) daily record; diary
stroll (STROHL) walk in a leisurely way

Develop Vocabulary Skills
Have students work in pairs. Tell them that all the new vocabulary words are nouns or verbs—except "murky." Ask one partner to learn all the new nouns, the other partner all the verbs. They then "quiz" each other to see if they've mastered pronunciations and definitions.

ESL Activity
Pair students according to English proficiency. Have the partners write original sentences using the words from the Develop Vocabulary Skills exercise. Have the partners share their sentences with the class.

TEACHING PLAN

INTRODUCE

Motivation
Ask students to remember their first "crush." What was it like? Have them share as much as they are willing, especially the humorous side. Then introduce the character Marijane. She's only ten, has a boyfriend with an awesome name, and loves to climb trees.

Purpose-Setting Question
Does love look the same to you now as it did five years ago?

READ

Literary Focus:
Tone in Nonfiction
The author's description of Marijane's neighborhood, appearance, and clothing makes her a believable character. Have students tell how vivid description helps to set the humorous tone of the story.

Reading Focus:
Analyze Details
The last paragraph on this page is very specific and humorous. The author seems to view herself and her actions as a young girl with a sense of humor. Ask students to find details that support this inference as they read the rest of the story.

CLOSE

Have students complete Review the Selection on pages 98–99.

Reading Focus:
Analyze Details
Ask: What does it reveal about the writer's and Billy's character to name their future child—when they're only 10 years old.

Enrichment
Parents are usually heroes to ten-year-olds, aren't they? Pay attention to the mention of heroes and presidents. The theme will emerge again.

This did not faze Billy Shakespeare, whose eyes lit up when he saw me coming, and who readily agreed that when we married we'd name our first son Ellis, after my father, and not William after him.

"Because William Shakespeare is a funny name," I'd say.

"It isn't funny. It's just that there's a famous writer with the same name," he'd say.

"Do you agree to Ellis Shakespeare then?"

"Sure, if it's all right with your father."

"He'll be pleased," I'd tell Billy.

Around this time, I was always trying to think of ways to please my father. (The simplest way would have been to wear a dress and a big hair ribbon, stay out of trees, stop talking out of the side of my mouth, and act like a girl . . . but I couldn't have endured such misery even for him.)

Billy Shakespeare accepted the fact early in our relationship, that my father was my hero. He protested only slightly when I insisted that the reason my father wasn't President of the United States was that my father didn't want to be.

That was what my father told me, when I'd ask him why he wasn't President. I'd look at him across the table at dinner, and think, he knows more than anybody knows, he's handsome, and he gets things done—so he ought to be President. If he was, I'd think, there'd be no problems in the world.

Sometimes I'd ask him: "Daddy, why aren't you President of the United States?"

His answer was always the same.

"I wouldn't want that job for anything. We couldn't take a walk without Secret Service men following us. Do you think we could go up to the lake for a swim by ourselves? No. There'd be Secret Service men tagging along. It'd ruin our lives. It'd end our privacy. Would you want that?"

Billy Shakespeare would say, "He's not President because nobody elected him President."

"He won't let anyone elect him," I'd answer. "He doesn't want Secret Service men around all the time."

"I'm not sure he could *get* elected," Billy would venture.

"He could get elected," I'd tell Billy. "He doesn't want to! We like our privacy."

"Okay." Billy'd give in a little. "But he never tried getting elected, so he really doesn't know if he could."

I'd wave that idea away with my dirty hands. "Don't worry. He'd be elected in a minute if he wanted to be. You don't know *him*."

Billy Shakespeare's other rivals for my attention were movie stars. I'd write Clark Gable and Henry Fonda and Errol Flynn, and they'd send back glossy photos of themselves and sometimes letters, too.

---

faze (FAYZ) confuse; weaken
endure (en DUUR) put up with
venture (VEN chur) proceed onward; risk
rival (RY vul) one who wants the same thing as another person

These photographs and letters were thumbtacked to the fiberboard walls of a playhouse my father had built for me in our backyard.

When I did play with a girl, the game was always the same: getting dinner ready for our husbands. I had an old set of dishes back in the playhouse, and my girl friend and I played setting the table for dinner. During this game, Billy Shakespeare was forgotten. When my husband came through the playhouse door, he would be one of the movie stars pinned to the wall.

I played this game with Dorothy Spencer, who lived behind our house.

She was a tall redhead who looked like a girl, and who always had it in her head to fix meat loaf with mashed potatoes for a movie star named Spencer Tracy.

I changed around a lot—the menu as well as the movie star—but Dorothy stuck to meat loaf with mashed for Spencer.

I'd be saying, "Well, Clark is a little late tonight and the turkey is going to be overdone," or "Gee, Henry isn't here yet and the ham is going to be dried up." But Dorothy would persist with "Spencer's going to love this meat loaf when he gets here. I'll wait until I hear his footsteps to mash the potatoes."

Billy Shakespeare was jealous of this game and tried his best to ruin it

The Letter, Pierre Bonnard. National Gallery of Art, Washington, D.C., Chester Dale Collection

with reality.

He'd say, "What are two famous movie stars doing living in the same house?"

He'd say, "How come famous movie stars only have a one-room house with no kitchen?"

But Dorothy Spencer and I went on happily playing house, until the movie *Brother Rat* came to town.

That was when we both fell in love with the movie star Ronald Reagan.

Suddenly we were both setting the table for the same movie star—different menus, but the same husband.

---

fiberboard (FY bur bawrd) building material made from compressed wood chips
persist (pur SIST) say over and over; keep on going
reality (ree AL uh tee) actual fact

Where Are You Now, William Shakespeare? ■ 93

"You've always stuck to meat loaf and mashed for Spencer!" I said angrily. "Now you want my Ronald!"

"He's not *your* Ronald," she said.

"It's my playhouse, though," I reminded her.

"But I won't play if I can't have Ronald," she said.

"We both can't have Ronald!" I insisted.

We took the argument to her mother, who told us to pretend Ronald Reagan was twins. Then we could both have him.

"He isn't twins, though," Dorothy said.

"And if he is," I put in, "I want the real Ronald, and not his twin."

Our game came to a halt, but our rivalry did not. Both of us had written to Ronald Reagan and were waiting for his reply.

"No matter what he writes her," I told Billy Shakespeare, "my letter from him will be better."

"You might not even get a letter," Billy said. "She might not get one either. "

"She might not get one," I said, "but I will."

"You don't know that," Billy said.

"Do you want to know why I know I'll get one?" I asked him.

I made him cross his heart and hope to die if he told anyone what I'd done.

Billy was a skinny little kid with big eyes that always got bigger when I was about to confess to him something I'd done.

"Crossmyheartandhopetodie," he said very fast. "What'd you do?"

"You know that Ronald Reagan isn't like any of the others," I said.

"Because Dorothy Spencer likes him, too."

"That's got nothing to do with it!" I said. "He's just different. I never felt this way about another movie star."

"Why?"

"*Why?* I don't know why! That's the way love is."

"Love?" Billy said.

"Yes. What did you think made me write him that I was a crippled child, and had to go to see him in a wheelchair?"

"Oh migosh!" Billy exclaimed. "Oh migosh!"

"I had to get his attention somehow."

"Oh migosh!"

"Just shut up about it!" I warned him. "If word gets out I'll know it's you."

Dorothy Spencer was the first to hear from Ronald Reagan. She didn't get a letter, but she got a signed photograph.

"Since I heard from him first," she said, "he's my husband."

"Not in my playhouse!" I said.

"He wrote me back first," she said.

"Just wait," I said.

"I don't have to wait," she said. "I'm setting the table for him in my own house."

"It's not even your house, it's your father's," I said. "At least when he's married to me, we'll have our own house."

---

rivalry (RY vul ree) competition; trying to get the same thing as another

"He's married to me now," she said.

"We'll see about that," I said.

I was beginning to get a panicky feeling as time passed and no mail came from Ronald Reagan. You'd think he'd write back to a crippled child first . . . . Meanwhile Dorothy was fixing him meat loaf and mashed at her place.

I had pictures of him cut out of movie magazines scotch-taped to my bedroom walls. I went to sleep thinking about him, wondering why he didn't care enough to answer me.

The letter and photograph from Ronald Reagan arrived on a Saturday.

I saw the Hollywood postmark and let out a whoop, thereby attracting my father's attention.

"What's all the excitement?"

I was getting the photograph out of the envelope. "I got a picture from Ronald Reagan!"

"Who's he?"

"Some movie star," my mother said.

By that time I had the photograph out. My heart began to beat nervously as I read the inscription at the bottom. "To a brave little girl, in admiration, Ronald Reagan."

"What does it say?" my father said.

"Nothing, it's just signed," I said, but he already saw what it said as he stood behind me looking down at it.

"Why are you a brave little girl?" he asked.

"How do I know?" I said.

"There's a letter on the floor," said my mother.

"That's my letter," I said, grabbing it. "Why are you considered a brave little girl?" my father said again. "Why does *he* admire *you*?"

I held the letter to my chest. "Those are just things they say," I said.

"They say you're *brave*?" my father said.

"Brave or honest or any dumb thing," I said weakly.

"Read the letter, Marijane," said my father.

I read the letter to myself,

Dear Marijane,
Thank you for your letter.
Remember that a handicap can be a challenge.
Always stay as cheerful as you are now.
Yours truly,
Ronald Reagan

"What does it say?" my mother asked. "Just the usual," I said. "They never say much."

"Let me see it, brave little girl," my father said.

"It's to me."

"Marijane . . ." and he had his hand out.

After my father read the letter, and got the truth out of me concerning my correspondence with Ronald Reagan, he told me what I was to do.

What I was to do was to sit down immediately and write Ronald Reagan, telling him I had lied. I was to add that I thanked God for my good health. I was to return both the letter and the photograph.

---

correspondence (kawr uh SPON duns) exchange of letters

Where Are You Now, William Shakespeare? ■ 95

Background Notes

Ronald Reagan, 40th President of the United States, was asked when he left office in 1988 how he would most like to be remembered. He replied, "As a movie actor." Reagan was a radio sports announcer before going to Hollywood, where he starred in "B" grade movies that were popular. Many think his best performance was in *Kings Row*.

No Saturday in my entire life had ever been so dark.

My father stood over me while I wrote the letter in tears, convinced that Ronald Reagan would hate me all his life for my deception. I watched through blurred eyes while my father took my letter, Ronald Reagan's letter, and the signed photograph, put them into a manila envelope, addressed it, sealed it, and put it in his briefcase to take to the post office.

For weeks and weeks after that, I dreaded the arrival of our postman. I was convinced a letter'd come beginning,

Dear Marijane,
    How very disappointed I am in you. . . .

"I don't think he'll write back," Billy Shakespeare told me. "I don't think he'll want anything more to do with you."

That ended getting dinner for movie stars in my playhouse.

I told Dorothy Spencer that I'd outgrown all that.

Three years after I wrote Ronald Reagan that letter, I slumped way down in my seat in humiliation as I watched him lose a leg in the movie *King's Row*. . . . I was sure he thought of the little liar from upstate New York who'd pretended she was crippled.

Many, many years later, the man I always thought should be President of the United States was dead, and Ronald Reagan was President of the United States.

I didn't vote for him.

I heard Dorothy Spencer got married, and I envision her making meat loaf and mashed for her husband.

The only remaining question is,
Where are you now,
               William Shakespeare?

Discussion
Was Marijane's father right in making her apologize and send back the letter and photograph?

Literary Focus:
Plot
The resolution to the conflict in the story is Marijane's decision to put her "getting dinner for movie stars" game behind her. The author shares what has happened to her friend Dorothy and to Ronald Reagan. Ask: What question does she leave unresolved? Does this make the story less enjoyable? Why?

Reading Focus:
Analyze Details
Marijane still remembers her letter to Ronald Reagan, and the lie she told, three years later. Ask: What clue to understanding the kind of person that she is does this give you?

---

deception (dih SEP shun) trick; act of deceiving

Where Are You Now, William Shakespeare? ■ 97

Mini Quiz

Write the following questions on the chalkboard or overhead projector and call on students to fill in the blanks. Discuss the answers with the class.

1. Marijane thought her father could easily become _____.

2. Marijane and the other girls always played _____.

3. Dorothy Spencer's first movie-star love was _____.

4. Marijane wrote Ronald Reagan and told him she was _____.

5. Marijane told Dorothy Spencer she stopped hosting dinners for movie stars because she has _____ all that.

Answers
1. President of the United States
2. getting dinner ready for their husbands
3. Spencer Tracy
4. crippled
5. outgrown

UNDERSTAND THE SELECTION

Answers

1. Marijane's father, Ellis
2. meat loaf with mashed (potatoes)
3. Ronald Reagan lost a leg, and she was sure he'd thought of "the little liar from upstate New York who'd pretended she was crippled."
4. She is ten years old, looks and plays like a boy, wants to marry William Shakespeare or any of a number of movie actors.
5. She thought he would reply faster and that he would express greater love than in his answer to Dorothy.
6. It is what they imagined a wife's main job to be, and the way that women were supposed to show love for their husbands.
7. He was jealous of it; why should he give up his "wife" to some movie actor?
8. Answers will vary. Many students will recognize Marijane's dishonesty and her father's attempt to make her face up to it.
9. Answers will vary. Students should recognize that more than hero-worship of a child for her father is necessary to qualify for the office.
10. Answers will vary. Marijane does not give us the answer to this question. We can only conjecture.

Respond to Literature

What do students think of a 10-year-old falling for Ronald Reagan? Ask why we often worship from afar, getting crushes on people we don't really know, such as movie stars.

WRITE ABOUT THE SELECTION

Prewriting

As a class, brainstorm ideas about the life William Shakespeare might now be leading. Ask students to imagine where they will be, what they will be doing, and with whom they'll be in twenty years.

UNDERSTAND THE SELECTION

Recall

1. Who did Marijane and Billy plan to name their first child after?
2. What meal did Dorothy Spencer always like to serve Spencer Tracy?
3. Why did Marijane slump in her seat when she saw the film *King's Row*?

Infer

4. Describe Marijane.
5. Why did Marijane write Ronald Reagan that she was crippled?
6. Why do you think Marijane and Dorothy always played the same "game" with their actor husbands?
7. What was Billy Shakespeare's reaction to the dinner game Marijane and Dorothy played?

Apply

8. Would you have reacted in the same way to Marijane's letter to Ronald Reagan as her father did? Explain.
9. Do you think Marijane's father would have made a good president?
10. Why do you think Marijane did not vote for Ronald Reagan as president?

Respond to Literature

Were you in love with anyone when you were ten years old? Who and why?

98 ■ Unit 1

WRITE ABOUT THE SELECTION

Where do you think Marijane's friend, William Shakespeare, is now? Marijane decides to find out. She asks old high school friends what has become of him, she writes some letters to addresses she has been given, and one day a letter with the return address marked "William Shakespeare" arrives. What do you think the letter says?

Assume that you are William Shakespeare. What would you say to an old friend who wonders what you are doing?

Prewriting What are you, William Shakespeare, doing now? Are you married? Do you have a family? What is your job? How do you now feel about the relationship you and Marijane had many years before? Make some notes, and organize your ideas into paragraphs using an informal outline.

Writing Write your letter to Marijane, using the informal outline. Write as much as you want. Remember, you have not seen or talked to Marijane in years.

Revising What is the tone of your letter? Is it consistent with how you imagine William Shakespeare to be now? Make any changes to make clear your attitude toward him and the reader. Remember letters include inside addresses, dates, salutations, and closings. Add them if you do not have them.

Proofreading Reread your letter and check for errors. Make sure transitions from one paragraph to the next are clear. A good letter is well-organized.

Writing

Circulate as students work individually. Remind them that this is a letter, and must be written in first-person. Stress that although a letter can be "chatty," it must still be well-organized.

Revising

There are actually three levels of tone at play in the letter. First, the student's attitude toward William. Second, the student's attitude toward the actual reader. Third, William's attitude toward Marijane. Discuss with students how these tones are expressed in their letters.

Proofreading

Have students exchange letters and check for correct punctuation, paragraphing, and spelling.

ESL Activity

Have students of like cultures meet in groups. Ask them to make a list of celebrities they admire. Then ask the whole class to discuss the lists. Point out similarities.

THINK ABOUT TONE

A writer sets the tone of a story in many ways. The **tone** can be set through the choice of individual words, the use of certain phrases, detailed descriptions, or by including or omitting specific things.

1. The title of this selection sounds like a trick. Yet M.E. Kerr says in the first paragraph no trick is involved. How does she do this? What does this say about her attitude toward the reader?

2. M.E. Kerr offers a detailed description in the fifth paragraph of herself at age ten. What is the tone?

3. M.E. Kerr gives her father's reason why he did not want to be president. What is the effect of this information?

4. The first time Marijane tells about Dorothy's meal she calls it "meat loaf with mashed potatoes." After that she calls it "meat loaf with mashed." How does that change make you feel?

5. How does the use of the phrase "Crossmyheartandhopetodie" affect tone?

READING FOCUS

Analyze Details While reading this story you were able to analyze details about the characters, tone, or plot. Based on those details, what do you think the overall tone of the story is? What is the author's attitude toward the subject matter of the story?

DEVELOP YOUR VOCABULARY

Homophones are words that sound alike but have different spellings and different meanings.

Examples: son-sun days-daze flour-flower

In each sentence below is at least one word that has a homophone. Find the word, and give its homophone.

1. We would name our first son Ellis.

2. This did not faze Billy Shakespeare.

3. This was his real name.

4. Is it all right with your father?

5. She wanted to please my father.

6. I wanted a Ronald Reagan photograph.

7. We had been playing house.

8. Dorothy served Spencer meat loaf.

9. She also gave him mashed potatoes.

10. They were in love.

11. We loved these little games.

12. My hair never had a ribbon.

THINK ABOUT TONE

Answers

1. She says bluntly William Shakespeare was her first boyfriend's "real name." The straightforward remark makes readers feel they'll be treated honestly by the writer.
2. Again, honesty—and also the ability to stand back from the subject, which is herself, and laugh.
3. The writer shows she is being honest, and can re-create the mind of a child. It's realistic. It's also funny, as are many things a 10-year-old thinks.
4. Sample answer: The writer uses the informal description to let you know she doesn't take all this too seriously.
5. Sample answer: It helps create a sense of realism, because this is how people really talk; but it's also funny, because we don't often think about how we talk.

DEVELOP YOUR VOCABULARY

Answers

1. son—sun
2. faze—phase
3. real—reel
4. right—write
5. to—too—two
6. I—eye
7. been—bin
8. meat—meet
9. him—hymn
10. in—inn
11. we—wee
12. hair—hare

READING FOCUS

Sample Answer

The tone of the story was humorous. The author described herself in a funny way and included details about the silly things she said and did, such as the clothes she wore. She seemed to think that the reader also would find these details funny so it was like she was sharing a joke with the reader.

SELECTION OVERVIEW

SELECTION OBJECTIVES

After completing these selections, students will be able to

- understand theme
- determine the theme of a poem
- discuss an abstract ideal
- write a reply to the theme a poet expresses
- find clues to help determine theme
- use synonyms
- recognize simile and personification

Lesson Resources

I Dream a World/Reflections
- Selection Synopses, Teacher's Edition, p. TT63
- Comprehension and Vocabulary Workbook, pp. 21–22
- Language Enrichment Workbook, p. 19
- Teacher's Resources Reinforcement, p. R11 Test, p. T19–T20

More About Theme

Remind students that theme is an element of poetry, as well as short stories and drama. (Its role in these other genres will be discussed in Units 2 and 3.) Theme is important in poetry because it can help the reader understand specific images and the choice of certain words or phrases. It it the thread that binds all the elements in a poem together.

About the Author

Langston Hughes is one of the most famous poets of the Harlem Renaissance of the 1920s. Many African Americans moved north in the early years of the 20th century, searching for good-paying jobs. Harlem, named for a Dutch city and once just a little village in northern Manhattan, was where many African Americans settled. The concentration of African Americans in a place

that allowed relatively free expression of ideas led to a stream of creative art—in music, dance, and literature. Hughes, like African American writers of the Harlem Renaissance, tried to look objectively at life and make sense of the African American experience.

Learn About

READING FOCUS

Recognize Simile and Personification
A simile makes a comparison between two different things, using the words *like* or *as*. Personification gives human characteristics to non-human objects or ideas. For example, in "I Dream a World," the author describes a world where "wretchedness will hang its head." As you read, look at the way similes and personification strengthen the poems and the authors' messages.

THEME

Did you ever get to the end of a poem and ask, "What does it mean?" You reread the poem, maybe two or three times. You look up definitions for all the unfamiliar words. You examine each line to understand its meaning, but still you are in doubt.

Now you sit back and try to get the "bigger" picture. You are searching for the "theme" of the poem. The **theme** of a poem is its main idea or meaning.

Perhaps the theme is about the difficulty in expressing love, as in "First Person Demonstrative," or it may be about the ending of a relationship, as in "Finis." Theme can be anything the poet chooses.

The poems you have read so far in this unit have been about love between individual people. The last two poems are a bit different.

As you read them, look for answers to the following questions:

1. How are they different from the other poems in this unit?
2. What is the theme of each of the two poems?

WRITING CONNECTION

Songs are often lyric poetry. Write the lyrics of a song you like; then, in a sentence or two, explain the theme.

Develop Vocabulary Skills

Have students make flashcards of the new words and their pronunciation. Ask students to use the words in the writing assignment for this selection or writing assignments in the next unit.

Cooperative Group Activity

Have students work in pairs to discuss the theme of their Writing Connection activity. They should explain to their partner, in precise terms, how they determined theme.

I Dream a World

by Langston Hughes

I dream a world where man
No other man will scorn,
Where love will bless the earth
And peace its paths adorn.
5 I dream a world where all
Will know sweet freedom's way,
Where greed no longer saps the soul
Nor avarice blights our day.
A world I dream where black or white,
10 Whatever race you be,
Will *share* the bounties of the earth
And every man is free,
Where wretchedness will hang its head,
And joy, like a pearl,
15 Attend the needs of all mankind.
Of such I dream—
Our world!

Reflections

by Vanessa Howard

If the world looked in a looking glass,
It'd see back hate, it'd see back war and it'd see
    back sorrow,
It'd see back fear.
If the world looked in a looking glass, it'd run
    away with shame, and hide.

---

adorn (uh DAWRN) to beautify or embellish
greed (GREED) a great desire for wealth or material things
avarice (AV uh ris) greed
blights (BLYTS) destroys, disappoints, frustrates

I Dream a World/Reflections ■ 101

Mini Quiz

Write the following questions on the chalkboard or overhead projector and call on students to fill in the blanks. Discuss the answers with the class.

1. "I Dream A World" is written in _____-person point of view.

2. Hughes dreams _____ will adorn earth's paths.

3. Hughes hopes all races will one day _____ the bounties of the earth.

4. "Reflections" is written in _____-person point of view.

5. Howard writes about the world looking into a _____ _____.

Answers
1. first
2. peace
3. share
4. third
5. looking glass

INTRODUCE

Motivation
Point out to students that there is a U.S. postage stamp with the word "LOVE" printed on it . Ask students, Does "LOVE" seem like a funny thing to put on a stamp? Isn't love supposed to be something personal? Or can love between people exist anywhere in the world? Does love conquer all, or, as our next poets suggest, must human beings first rid themselves of hate?

Purpose-Setting Question
Is love or hate the dominant force in the world?

READ

Literary Focus:
Theme
Although these two poems have very different tones, they share a similar theme. Both explore the theme of the condition of the world that we live in. Ask what is missing from the theme of "Reflections" that is present in "I Dream a World."

Reading Focus:
Recognize Simile and Personification
Discuss the fact that simile involves a direct comparison with the use of *like* or *as*, and have students look for an example in the first poem. Explain that personification gives human characteristics to non-human objects or ideas, and have students look for examples. Ask students to look for a line that tells about an idea that shows a feeling of shame.

CLOSE

Have students complete Review the Selection on pages 102–103.

Comparing Selections
Have students compare the selections as to theme, mood, and use of figures of speech. Ask them to tell which comparison helps them to better understand the poems and why.

UNDERSTAND THE SELECTION

Answers

1. people of all races
2. a pearl
3. hate, war, sorrow, or fear
4. The other poems were about love between individuals; "you" indicated the two-person relationship. These last two poems are about love—or the lack of love—between groups of people, such as the black and white races.
5. There are problems with the world the way it is, but we can dream of a better world.
6. She wants the world to look in a looking glass to see the reality in its own reflection.
7. The world is a place not of love, but of hate.
8. They both have as part of their theme the lack of love in the world.
9. "I Dream A World" expresses hope for a better world, "Reflections" expresses no hope.
10. Sample answers: Both might have had sad lives, but Hughes must have had some experiences that made him feel people have some good in them. Howard seems to be filled only with bitterness.

Respond to Literature

Hughes expresses hope, Howard only anger. Even though someone feels there is little love in the world, can hope create love? Encourage students to share their feelings on this topic.

 ## WRITE ABOUT THE SELECTION

Prewriting

Use students' answers to *Respond to Literature* as a class brainstorming session.

Writing

Circulate as students work individually. Using Howard's style will make writing easier, but some students may wish to experiment with other styles.

Revising

As a class, discuss the strong words that Howard uses—"hate," "war," "fear," etc. Point out that these words create sharp pictures in the reader's mind and help to communicate the poem's theme.

Proofreading

Point out that both Hughes and Howard follow capitalization and punctuation rules in their poems. Compare them with previous selections, such as "Housecleaning" and "Where Have You Gone." Do capitalization and punctuation help or hinder in communicating a poem's theme?

Review the Selection

UNDERSTAND THE SELECTION

Recall

1. Who does the speaker of "I Dream A World" hope will one day share the earth's bounties?

2. The speaker of "I Dream A World" compares the "joy" he is dreaming about to something. What is it?

3. Name at least two things the speaker in "Reflections" feels the world would see in a looking glass.

Infer

4. Speakers in other poems in this unit have addressed a "you." These two poems do not. Why?

5. What is the theme of "I Dream A World"?

6. Why is the title of Vanessa Howard's poem "Reflections"?

7. What is the theme of "Reflections"?

Apply

8. How are the themes similar?

9. How are these themes different?

10. What do you think the poets are like? What kind of lives do they have?

Respond to Literature

Explain which of these poems more accurately presents your view of the world and the love in it.

WRITE ABOUT THE SELECTION

Vanessa Howard uses personification when she describes the world looking in a mirror. The world cannot "look" into a mirror. It also cannot "run" or "hide." Only people can do that.

The mirror is a way for the poet to talk about what she feels exists in the world. Since a mirror reflects only what is there, the technique adds a touch of reality to her opinions.

What do you think the world would see if it looked in a mirror? Vanessa Howard thinks it would see hate, war, sorrow, and fear. Do you agree?

Write what you think would be in the mirror if the world looked at itself.

Prewriting Draw a frame around a blank sheet of paper. Suppose that it is a mirror. Write some words or phrases in the mirror describing what the world would see.

Writing Turn your words and phrases into a poem. You can use the same style Vanessa Howard did, or you can try something different.

Revising What is the theme of your poem? Is it clear? Add any words or phrases that will help to make the meaning clear. Eliminate any words or phrases that are confusing.

Proofreading Have you used any contractions in your poem? Check to make sure that you have spelled them correctly. Be sure to be consistent with your capitalization and punctuation.

THINK ABOUT THEME

There are many clues you can look for when you are searching for theme.

1. Does the poet use negative or positive words? **Negative words** make you feel hopeless and sad. **Positive words** make you feel hopeful and happy. Look at "I Dream A World" and "Reflections." Make a list of key words, and mark them with a + or −.

2. What is the tone of each poem? What is each poet's attitude toward his and her respective subject?

3. Is there any form of humor (such as hyperbole or irony) in either of the poems? Are the poets speaking "straight," or are they hiding meaning?

4. Look at the titles of the poems. Explain how "I Dream A World" and "Reflections" relate to the themes.

5. Use your feelings as a guide to finding the theme. How do you feel when you read these two poems?

READING FOCUS

Recognize Simile and Personification
Provide an example of simile and personification in the two poems. Tell how these figures of speech enhance the poems.

DEVELOP YOUR VOCABULARY

Synonyms are words having the same or nearly the same meaning. Langston Hughes uses *greed* in one line of his poem, and *avarice* in the next. Both mean "a great desire for wealth or material things." They are synonyms.

Synonyms are very useful if you are trying to rhyme. You can choose a synonym that rhymes with another word, rather than one that does not.

Use a dictionary to find synonyms for the following words as they are used in "I Dream A World." Then use each in a sentence.

1. scorn
2. bless
3. adorn
4. sap
5. blight
6. bounties
7. wretchedness
8. attend

Review the Selection ■ 103

Answers

1. "I Dream A World": dream (+), scorn (−), love (+), bless (+), peace (+), adorn (+), sweet (+), freedom (+), greed (−), sap (−), avarice (−), blights (−), share (+), wretchedness (−), joy (+), pearl (+).
"Reflections": hate (−), war (−), sorrow (−), fear (−), run away (−), shame (−), hide (−).

2. "I Dream A World": the tone is realistic but hopeful. "Reflections": the tone is pessimistic.

3. There is no humor in either poem. The poets speak candidly. The lightheartedness is in some of the figurative language in Hughes's poem.

4. "I Dream A World": the title expresses hope. "Reflections": the poet is reflecting on the world's condition and reporting back, like a mirror, what she feels it is.

5. "I Dream A World": hopeful "Reflections": hopeless

 DEVELOP YOUR VOCABULARY

Answers

1. spurn
2. smile on
3. beautify
4. weaken
5. poison
6. riches
7. suffering
8. serve

Sample sentences:

1. He spurned his opponent's handshake.
2. Good will smiles on the earth at Christmas.
3. Generosity beautifies understanding.
4. Jealousy weakens love.
5. Her criticisms poison our atmosphere of cooperation.
6. Nature, he thought, surrounds us with riches.
7. No child should have to endure the suffering caused by famine and disease.
8. "The butler will serve your every need," the hostess said to her guest.

READING FOCUS

Sample Answer

An example of a simile: "And joy, like a pearl," (from "I Dream a World"). Personification from "Reflections": ". . . the world looked in a looking glass . . ." Both figures of speech make the poems more interesting and help to get the authors' messages across.

Unit Review Resources

TEACHER'S RESOURCES

- Writing Process, pp. W1–W12
- Grammar, Usage, and Mechanics, pp. G1–G12
- Speaking and Listening, pp. S1–S6
- Critical Thinking, pp. C1–C6
- Choose from Reading in the Content Areas, pp. RCA1–RCA72
- **Standardized Test Preparation**
  Unit 1 Test, pp. UT1–UT2

WRITING APPLICATIONS

Write About Theme

Prewriting: On the chalkboard or overhead projector, write the titles of the selections. Ask students for short descriptions of the theme of each. Reviewing the themes will help students choose one selection and focus their thoughts on it.

 Writer's Toolkit CD-ROM
Encourage students to use the Story Wheels (Writing Tools, Choosing a Topic) to complete the Prewriting activity.

Writing: Circulate among students as they work individually. You could point out that many songs use an A-A-B-A format: the melody is stated and repeated, then a variation is introduced, and finally the melody is restated. Thinking of the musical organization of a song might help students in writing the lyrics.

Revising: Ask students to write titles for their songs. They should reflect the theme.

Proofreading: Have a partner read the song lyrics and tell what he or she thinks the message of the song is. If it isn't clear, have the writer check punctuation.

WRITING APPLICATIONS

Write About Theme

You have just been hired by a record company to write songs. Your first assignment is to write a love song.

You panic. What can you write about? Then you remember that you once read a series of stories and poems on love in English class. Themes come back to you: love lost; love found; love for friends, family, the world.

You have not been told whether the music has already been written for the song. You could write the words for a tune you already know or for a tune not yet composed.

Prewriting   Think back on the stories and poems. Which "message" did you like the best? Choose one poem or story, and think about the feelings presented in it. Write them down, quickly, with some ideas on how to describe the feelings. Decide on point of view for the song.

Writing   Assemble your material as a song. Think about other love songs you know. What makes their lyrics effective? Think of each verse as a paragraph.

Revising   Make sure that your song has stuck to the feeling that you want to describe. The theme should be clear.

Proofreading   Check that you have used commas and semicolons to make your ideas easy to understand.

Write About Genre

This unit has helped you see the elements of poetry, or how a poem is put together. You now should be better able to analyze poetry, to state what you like and do not like, and give reasons for your opinion.

Choose two poems in the unit, one that you did like and one that you did not. You will figure out why you formed these opinions by looking at the elements involved in each poem.

Prewriting   Review the work you did for the "Think About . . . " sections in this unit. Then make a chart with the name of the selections you have chosen at the top and the elements of poetry down the side: character, imagery, theme, tone, rhyme, and figures of speech. Reread each poem. Write down character, theme, and tone. Look for other elements in each poem: imagery, rhyme, and figures of speech. Note if they are present.

Writing   Look at your chart and determine how one element or the other makes you like or dislike a poem. Were you disappointed by the theme? Was there a lot of good imagery? Was the tone appealing? Write why that was important to you.

Revising   Make sure each paragraph has a topic sentence that expresses the paragraph's main idea.

Proofreading   Reread your writing for errors in spelling, punctuation, and mechanics. Neatly insert any changes.

Write About Genre

Prewriting: Use the information from the Prewriting portion of the previous writing assignment to review the various poems. Discuss as a class what students liked and what they didn't like.

Writing: Circulate as students work individually. Picking the most important factor that influenced their opinion of the poem will give students focus for their critiques. They should include information about other factors, as well.

Revising: Have students write the central idea of each paragraph. Is there a topic sentence in the paragraph that reflects this idea?

 Writer's Toolkit CD-ROM
Encourage students to use the Unity and Coherence Checker (Writing Tools, Revising/Editing) to complete the Revising activity.

Proofreading: After students have proofread their own papers, have them exchange papers with a partner for a second review. A new draft should be written if the partner finds a number of errors.

Vocabulary

Suffixes are often used to turn nouns into adjectives. Notice in this sentence how the suffix *-ful* is added to the noun *success* to form the adjective *successful*: Henry Curran was big, busy, and successful.

If you know how a particular suffix is used, you can often figure out the meaning of the new word.

-ful = having the quality of
-ic = characteristic of
-less = without
-able = able to or having
-ard = possessing something to excess
-ish = characteristic of or tending toward something

Try to define each italicized adjective by examining the root noun and suffix. Remember that spellings sometimes change slightly when a suffix is added. Check your definition in a dictionary. Then write your own sentence using each word.

1. She spoke in an *apologetic* voice.
2. "I do not care if he is *armless*," he said.
3. She had a *sorrowful* look.
4. My time is *valuable*.
5. A *haggard* look was on her face.
6. "He is sixteen, but he is *smallish*," she said.
7. My dog looks *pathetic* after her bath.

Grammar, Usage, and Mechanics

Verbs must always agree with their subjects. Singular subjects take singular verbs, and plural subjects take plural verbs.

You must be careful to match a verb with its subject and not other words in the sentence.

You must remember that "there" is never the subject of a sentence. The verb of a sentence beginning with "there" matches the subject, which comes after the verb.

Here are some examples of correct verb-subject agreement:

Examples: All snowflakes are six-sided. The question on verbs is a good one. There are the buses.

Correct the verb-subject agreement errors in these sentences.

1. It are always one or the other with you innocent victims.
2. Why, I never were in Springfield in my life!
3. Her father own the bank.
4. There is lots of nickel-plated shoehorns in there.
5. Underneath the pigeonholes were a row of three brass-knobbed, little drawers.
6. My hand and shirt cuff was streaked with old dust.

Unit Review ■ 105

Grammar, Usage, and Mechanics

Answers

1. It *is* always one or the other with you innocent victims.
2. Why, I *was* never in Springfield in my life!
3. Her father *owns* the bank.
4. There *are* lots of nickel-plated shoehorns in there.
5. Underneath the pigeonholes *was* a row of three brass-knobbed, little drawers.
6. My hand and shirt cuff *were* streaked with old dust.

Here are examples of some difficult verb-subject questions. Write these sentences on the chalkboard and point out why the subject/verb agreement may not be what is expected.

1. The car, as well as the truck and the bus, has influenced our lifestyles. (The "as well" phrase doesn't make the subject plural. It remains "car.")
2. My friend and teacher is Miss Durmacher. ("friend" and "teacher" refer to the same person.)
3. Either Bill or I has to go. ("either-or" doesn't make the subject plural.)
4. Either Bill or the boys have to go. (The verb should agree with the nearest subject, in this case "boys.")
5. The number of apples on a single tree is never the same. ("number" is singular here; one definite number is meant.)
6. A number of the apples have to be thrown out because they're spoiled. (Changing from a definite to indefinite article before "number" changes the sense of "number"—it's now plural.)

Cooperative Group Activity

Have students ever encountered verb-subject problems which they couldn't figure out? Have the class make a list. If you're comfortable with verb-subject agreement rules, ask students to try to "stump" you with their questions.

BUILD LANGUAGE SKILLS

Vocabulary

Answers

1. sounding like an apology
2. without arms
3. full of sorrow
4. having value
5. gaunt, pale
6. tending toward being small for his age
7. pitiful

Sentences will vary.

More About Word Attack: Here are some general spelling rules students might find helpful.

1. If a suffix begins with a vowel, drop the final "e" of the root word. Example: usable

2. If the suffix begins with a consonant, retain the final "e." Example: useful

Cooperative Group Activity

Have students work in pairs to look back at the selections and find other adjectives using the suffixes defined in this exercise. Give them 10 minutes and see how many examples each pair can find.

SPEAKING AND LISTENING

Motivation

Prepare a poem that you can recite to the class. It needn't be from this unit, and it needn't be long. Reciting it from memory should allow you to concentrate on dramatic emphasis and eye contact.

Teaching Strategy

With the students, go through the steps of preparing for reading a poem. You could outline the steps on the chalkboard or overhead projector, noting the goal of each practice "read."

Evaluation Criteria

Evaluate the students' readings of the poems they've chosen by marking pluses, minuses, or checks on these points:

1. correct pronunciation of words
2. expressive pronunciation of words or phrases used in alliteration, onomatopoeia, or similar devices
3. attention to punctuation
4. projection, including eye contact with audience
5. proper pacing; speed is appropriate to the poem's theme

You could give this checklist to students and have them evaluate a recording of their reading before they make their class presentation.

SPEAKING AND LISTENING

When you select a poem to read aloud, it should be one that you especially like. If you like it, you will be able to read it in such a way that your audience will like it, too.

Reading poems aloud is much different than reading other types of literature aloud. Most poems have so much emotion that they require certain procedures so the reader and the audience enjoy the poem.

Practice the following steps before you read the poem of your choice.

1. Read the poem to yourself.

2. Read the poem again. Determine the subjects of the verbs and the antecedents of the pronouns. This will help you understand what the poem is about.

3. Pay attention to words that you may not be familiar with. Check their definitions and pronunciations to ensure understanding of the poem.

4. Read the poem aloud softly and slowly so you hear the sounds of the words. This will help the meaning of the poem to set in.

5. Now read the poem once again. This time pay particular attention to the punctuation. Remember, most poetry is written in sentences just as prose is. The way a poem is punctuated tells you how it should be read. Pause when necessary!

6. Practice reading the poem in front of a mirror. Decide when to look at your audience. You want to maintain some eye contact not just out of courtesy, but also because looking forward will help project your voice.

7. Ask a friend or a family member to listen to you read the poem. If someone is not available, use a tape recorder so you can listen to your delivery. Concentrate on reading the poem just loud enough and just slow enough for your audience to enjoy. Think about improvements as you listen to yourself. Then read the poem again if you decide on any changes.

Once you have prepared yourself for this assignment, choose a poem or part of a poem from this unit. Follow the procedures above so you can successfully read your poem to a group or your entire class. Limit your reading to approximately two minutes. There is no need to be nervous if you are prepared adequately. Enjoy yourself!

Career Connection

Shakespearean plays are drama at its best. A student who enjoyed *from The Tragedy of Romeo and Juliet* might want to investigate a career in the theater—not just as an actor or actress, but as one of the numerous technical people who work behind the scenes to put on the play. An example would be someone involved in lighting. This person should have an artistic sense of emphasizing people's actions through the use of light. He or she must also have technical training in how lights are set up and operated. Direct experience is often just as useful as specialized, advanced education. On-the-job training can easily be gained by volunteering to help with local stage productions. A high school education and a general interest in the theater are necessary.

CRITICAL THINKING

Reasoning Inductive and deductive reasoning are used to make conclusions based on evidence.

In **inductive reasoning**, you begin with evidence and arrive at a conclusion. Here is an example of inductive reasoning: The desk lamp in your room goes out. You replace the bulb with a new one. The lamp still does not work. You try another new bulb. Still no luck. Something is wrong with the lamp, you conclude.

In **deductive reasoning**, you reason the other way: You begin with a conclusion that is generally accepted as true. You consider the evidence of a situation, and make a conclusion based on whether the evidence fits the conclusion with which you started. Here is an example: Animals with six legs are insects. You see an animal with six legs. You conclude, therefore, that the animal is an insect.

You must be careful to reason correctly. Incorrect inductive reasoning leads to hasty generalization, and incorrect deductive reasoning leads to unsound conclusions. A hasty generalization is a statement made about a whole group on the basis of a few examples. For example: *teenagers are poor drivers and cause most accidents.* Unsound conclusions result when facts and evidence are not true. For example: *John is qualified to be class president because he has run for other offices.*

Look back at the selections in this unit, and find one example each of inductive and deductive reasoning. Explain the reasoning process.

EFFECTIVE STUDYING

Studying Poetry It is sometimes helpful to step back from what you are reading to get the bigger picture.

When you study a poem, read it straight through once without stopping. This first quick read will give you an idea about character, tone, and theme. It will also put things in context, which could give you clues to parts of the poem you do not understand.

Then go back and read the poem again. Stop whenever you do not understand a word or phrase, and find its meaning. Look for imagery, figures of speech, and rhyme. Take the poem apart, but think how all the elements fit together.

Then step back and get the bigger picture. Read the poem again, straight through. The poet's message now should be loud and clear.

Choose one poem from this book. Use these techniques and write a paragraph analyzing it.

Test Preparation

When answering test questions about a poem, be sure to read the poem several times before answering the questions. Use the strategies listed above.

Unit Review ■ 107

Teaching Strategy

The technique of stepping back to get the big picture is applicable not only to reading poetry but to all types of literature. Review the following steps with the class.

1. Read the poem straight through once without stopping.

2. Read the poem slowly, stopping to define and check the pronunciation of unfamiliar words, looking for imagery, figures of speech, and rhyme.

3. Read the poem again, straight through, to fit all the pieces back together.

Have students discuss how to apply these steps to another selection in the unit that is not poetry. Ask students to discuss how this strategy helped them understand the selection.

CRITICAL THINKING

Sample Answer

"When you're twenty-four and a bachelor, you usually figure you'll be married before much longer." The speaker starts with a general principle—that people who are twenty-four and single usually get married—and reasons that he'll be married before too long.

UNIT ACTIVITY

A Continuing Unit Project:
Travel Poster

The theme of this unit is the unknown. Many of the stories and poems describe places, either real or imaginary. All of the selections describe a state of mind or an unreal place. The unit offers an excellent opportunity for students to create travel posters that express the setting, mood, or inner reality of the poems and stories that they read.

Explain to students that they are to be literary travel agents. It is their job to plan and advertise a tour of the Unknown. In order to do this, they must create travel posters that will make people want to "visit" each selection in the unit. The poster can focus on an actual place, such as Baghdad in the first selection. The poster can advertise a mysterious-looking house for rent, as in "The Judge's House." The poster can advertise the opportunity to see an unusual character in action, such as the ghosts described in "The Great Amherst Mystery." Or the poster can entice the traveler to visit the scene of a story or poem while it is taking place (for example, the police station while Mrs. Stevenson is talking to Sergeant Duffy in *Sorry, Wrong Number*).

Discuss with students some characteristics of a good travel poster. Obtain from a local travel agent some posters and travel brochures to display on the wall. Point out that the most important aspect of a travel poster is an eye-catching picture or photograph. Students who are less artistically inclined can cut pictures from magazines or photocopy pictures from books. Also point out that a travel poster should communicate some information in words. The poster should name the place that is pictured and have a phrase or sentence that will make a person want to go there. (For example, "Listen in on a murder being planned!")

Have students create a travel poster after reading each selection. Some general questions to help them get started include:

What is the setting of this selection? What would it be like to go there?

What parts of the story might be especially exciting for a visitor to experience firsthand?

What places or people exist in the characters' imaginations?

What is the mood of the selection? Can you recreate this mood as if it were an actual place?

What character or characters might a visitor enjoy seeing in action?

If students need more specific guidance, ask questions such as the following for each selection.

■ **"Appointment in Baghdad"**
Would you like to be in Baghdad when Death meets the young man?

■ **"Appointment at Noon"**
Where do you think Henry Curran's visitor came from?

■ **"Incident in a Rose Garden"**
Would you like to visit a rose garden where Death meets the Master?

■ **"Boy in the Shadows"**
What story could you unravel if you visited Jayse's grave?

■ ***Sorry, Wrong Number***
How would you like to be on Second Avenue in New York City when Mrs. Stevenson is murdered?

■ **"Thus I Refute Beelzy"**
Can you create the place in Small Simon's mind where Mr. Beelzy exists?

■ **"hist, whist"/"Overheard on a Saltmarsh"**
Would you enjoy seeing a variety of ghost things?

■ **"The Judge's House"**
What would it be like to tour a haunted house?

- **"The Listeners"/"Eldorado"**
  What would it be like to visit Eldorado?

- **"The Loch Ness Monster"**
  How would you like to spend a few days at Expedition Headquarters?

- **"The Great Amherst Mystery"**
  What would it be like to go to Esther Cox's house and watch "Maggie" and "Bob" in action?

After the travel posters have been completed, display them around the classroom. Discuss with students how various interpretations may have been given to each selection. Also discuss with students how they found this assignment. Were certain selections easier to make posters for than others? For which selection did they most enjoy making a poster? Why?

- **"Appointment in Baghdad"**
  Traditional version retold by Edith Wharton (page 113)

SELECTION SYNOPSIS

This very short story takes place in and around the palace of the Sultan in Damascus. One morning, the Sultan's most valued assistant comes in and asks for the Sultan's fastest horse. He says that he must escape to Baghdad. When the Sultan asks the young man why he is in such a rush, he replies that he has just seen Death in the palace garden, and he must escape at once. The Sultan gives the young man the horse, then goes into the garden to ask Death why he frightened his assistant. In a twist of irony, Death informs the Sultan that he was surprised to see the young man in the garden because he has an appointment to meet him tonight in Baghdad.

SELECTION ACTIVITY

In this activity, students will research the setting of the story, which is Damascus. They will also research the city where Death would meet the young man, which is Baghdad. The purpose of the research will be to locate the cities geographically, to learn something about the history of these cities, and to get a feel for the old Middle East. Students should also be able to give an approximate time period for the story based on the following factors (students should discover these connections for

themselves; the information is given here only as a teacher's guide).

1. A main character in the story is the Sultan. A sultan is a ruler of a Muslim state. Rulers in the Ottoman Empire (Turks) were sultans.
2. The city of Damascus, which was a center of early Christianity, was captured by the Arabs in A.D. 635 and became Islamic. After 750 B.C., it was held by many conquerors; then was seized by the Turks (Ottoman Empire) in 1516. It remained under Turkish rule until 1918, when it came under British control.
3. The city of Baghdad was founded in A.D. 762. It became an Islamic city and was ruled by a monarch, called a caliph. It became part of the Ottoman Empire in 1638 and remained so until the British took control in 1917.

It seems reasonable to assume that this story could have taken place in the Ottoman Empire between the mid-1600s and the end of the nineteenth century. Once students have found this information, have them learn as much as they can about life in the Middle East during this period. (You may find it helpful to agree on a certain period of time to research, perhaps the nineteenth century.) Have students work in groups or pairs to learn about such aspects of life as trade, dress, life in the city, art, social structures in the family, marriage, or political structures. Students should also prepare a map showing the relative location of the two cities. The map should show the geography of the Middle East as it was then rather than as it is today.

After students have completed their research, have each group or pair display its information in the form of a chart or poster. Display the charts and posters, along with the maps, around the classroom.

- **"Appointment at Noon"**
  by Eric Frank Russell (page 119)

SELECTION SYNOPSIS

Henry Curran is a ruthless but very successful businessman, who has nothing but contempt for the law and accepted standards of behavior. The story begins when he enters his office at 11:50 A.M. After barking a few commands to his secretary, he learns from her that a visitor is waiting to see him. The visitor claims to have an appointment with Curran at two minutes to twelve. Curran snorts that he has made no appointment, but his curiosity is aroused when he learns that the visitor accurately predicted the time at which he would return to the office. He agrees to see the stranger, who is ushered in at three minutes to twelve. The stranger is Death personified, and a minute later Henry Curran keeps his appointment.

SELECTION ACTIVITY

In this activity, students will write an obituary of Henry Curran as it might appear in a newspaper. Begin the activity by collecting and displaying some well-written obituaries from local and national newspapers. Aim to present obituaries that are full-length articles rather than just listings or short entries.

Discuss with students the things that are included in an obituary. The most essential and obvious are name, date of death, age at time of death, occupation, cause of death (if known), where the person lived, and the names of surviving family members. A more lengthy obituary may include the person's early life, major events in the person's career, what has been said or written about the person, the person's major contribution to society, some quotations by the person, a discussion of the person's character and personality, or a discussion of any controversy surrounding the person.

Explain to students that usually the better known a person is, the more complete the obituary will be. Also point out that an obituary writer may give a feel for the person being written about, making that person very vivid and real to the reader. An obituary writer should not express an opinion about the person, but the writer can use facts skillfully to convey a certain impression.

Since Henry Curran is described as "big" and "successful," it is likely that his obituary would be quite substantial. Although certain things about Henry Curran are made clear in the story, much of the information needed for an obituary will have to be composed by the students. Students must also deal with the fact that, according to the story, Curran's death took place in a rather unusual way. Some questions that students might ask themselves as they write their obituaries include:

How would a newspaper describe Henry Curran's "cause of death"?

Would anyone interview his secretary to find out exactly how Curran died?

Who are Curran's survivors? Do you think he had a family? Sisters or brothers? Parents? Do you think he had any friends?

Where do you think Curran lived? In a small town? In the city?

How was Curran known in the area where he lived?

Do you think there would be any controversy surrounding Curran's death? Might some people think that he was done in by underworld figures?

When students have completed the assignment, ask for volunteers to read their obituaries aloud. Discuss the similarities and differences in the ways in which students view Henry Curran.

■ "Incident in a Rose Garden"
by Donald Justice (page 123)

SELECTION SYNOPSIS

Like the two selections that precede it, the theme of this poem is death. In this case, a gardener is frightened when he meets Death in the rose garden. The gardener tells his master, who confronts Death for scaring the gardener only to learn that the person Death wants is not the gardener but the master himself.

SELECTION ACTIVITY

Have students work in groups of three to dramatize the text of this selection. Assign one student the role of the gardener, another the role of the master, and another the role of Death. Death should be costumed as described in the poem; each group can decide how to costume the other characters. Have each group perform its dramatization for the class.

■ "Boy in the Shadows"
by Margaret Ronan (page 127)

SELECTION SYNOPSIS

Irene and Ernest Platt retire to a small house in the foothills of the Ozarks. Irene plants a garden, and as she works in it, she notices a thin, hollow-eyed boy watching her. He disappears, only to return a day or so later with his mother, a haggard-looking woman of about forty. She offers Irene the boy's services as a gardener and a handyman for $2 a day to be paid to her. The boy, Jayse, is to live in a small shed near the garden, and his mother is to bring him his meals. Irene is warned not to feed Jayse, who has a "finicky stomach." Jayse is an excellent worker, but he never speaks to the Platts. Time passes, and

Jayse begins to look even more emaciated than before. Irene, determined to feed Jayse a decent meal, cooks ham and eggs. When she sets it before the silent boy, he eats a few bites and then strides out of the house and into the woods. The next day, Jayse's mother demands to know what Irene fed Jayse. Irene demands to be taken to Jayse. His mother leads Irene to a half-opened grave near her cabin. There Irene sees Jayse's body. His mother explains that Jayse and his father died of pneumonia two years before. She "wished them back" because she needed their help, but only Jayse returned. She tells Irene that one cannot feed the dead salt because it makes them forget everything except the last place they rested. The salt in the food Irene gave Jayse has caused him to return to his grave, which he will never leave again.

SELECTION ACTIVITY

Jayse's mother takes Irene Platt to see Jayse's body in a half-opened grave. Ask students to assume that the grave is eventually closed and that tombstone is placed over it. What might be written on that tombstone? Might there be a picture or symbol of some kind carved on the stone?

Have each student create a tombstone for Jayse. Students should draw their tombstones on pieces of posterboard. Display the finished tombstones on a bulletin board.

■ *Sorry, Wrong Number*
by Lucille Fletcher (page 137)

SELECTION SYNOPSIS

Mrs. Stevenson is a neurotic, bedridden, physically handicapped woman. One day, when she attempts to call her husband's office, she overhears two men on another line plotting a murder. Alarmed and excited, she asks the telephone operator to try to trace the overheard call. When these efforts fail, she calls the police and demands a citywide search for the killers. As she reports the call to the desk sergeant, Mrs. Stevenson begins to realize that many of the details fit her own situation. A telephone call from Western Union tells her that her husband, whom she has been expecting home, has gone to Boston on business. His telegram says that he was unable to reach her by telephone because her line was busy. Now quite upset, Mrs. Stevenson calls a nearby hospital in hopes of hiring a practical nurse for the night. During this call, she realizes that it is almost the moment at which the murder is to be committed. She also hears the downstairs phone being lifted. She hangs up and dials the operator again, asking for the police. When the call is put through and the desk sergeant answers again, George, the hired killer, says, "Sorry, wrong number" and hangs up.

SELECTION ACTIVITY

In this activity, students will write a news story about the murder of Mrs. Stevenson as it might appear in a New York City newspaper. An important question for students to consider is, How much information about the murder will be known to the media by the time the story is written?

Point out that, as readers of the play, students have "inside information" about the murder. The writer has allowed them to know exactly what is happening and why. Once the murder is committed, however, the facts may become difficult for the authorities to discover.

Encourage students to recall what they know about the crime from the play

Then ask these questions: Do you think that the police and news media will realize what happened? Do you think that it will be apparent that Mr. Stevenson played an important part in the crime? Do you think that George will get caught, or do you think that the identity of the murderer will remain a mystery? What about Sergeant Duffy? Will he be criticized for not taking Mrs. Stevenson's telephone calls seriously? Will he have learned enough from her calls to help catch the murderer? In the beginning of the story, the men on the telephone say that they want the murder to look like a robbery. Do you think that the police and news media will be deceived?

Students' news stories should include a headline, for example, "Eastside Woman Murdered—Police Suspect Husband Involved in Crime." Give students the option of writing one news story or a series of stories. The series might be very effective if the clues about the murder become evident over a period of time. Students who wish to write a series might enjoy working in pairs or small groups in which members take turns writing articles.

When students have completed their stories, make a bulletin board display in the form of newspaper pages. Title the display "The Murder of Mrs. Stevenson."

■ "Thus I Refute Beelzy"
by John Collier (page 155)

SELECTION SYNOPSIS

Small Simon is a young boy who spends all of this time playing in a small garden house. Small Simon's mother complains that he always comes inside tired and nervous. Small Simon's father, who calls himself Big Simon, believes that children should choose for themselves what they want to do. Big Simon becomes upset, however, when Small Simon claims to have a playmate that is made up; Small Simon insists that he is real. The conflict escalates, and Small Simon is sent upstairs. Big Simon soon follows with the intention of punishing Small Simon. Small Simon insists that Mr. Beelzy will protect him from harm. Shortly after Big Simon goes upstairs, Small Simon's mother and her guest hear a terrible sound. They rush upstairs, only to find on the stairs a man's shoe with the foot still in it.

SELECTION ACTIVITY

A minor character in this story is Betty, who appears to be a guest of Mrs. Carter. Betty seems quite familiar with the Carter family, yet she does not play a central role in the action.

Ask students to be Betty and to be in the Carter home when this story takes place. Then ask them to write a letter to a friend, describing what happened on this particular afternoon. Tell students that, while their descriptions must not contradict anything that is stated in the story, they are free to add to and elaborate on the story in any way they wish. They should also develop as much as possible the character of Betty, making it clear how she feels about what she is witnessing.

When students have completed the assignment, have them exchange letters with a classmate to read. Then ask for several volunteers to share their letters with the class.

■ "hist, whist"
by E. E. Cummings (page 163)

■ "Overheard on a Saltmarsh"
by Harold Monro (page 164)

SELECTION SYNOPSES

The subject matter of both poems is the world of supernatural beings. The poem, "hist, whist" describes a variety of "ghostthings." "Overheard on a Saltmarsh" describes a squabble between a nymph and a goblin over a set of green glass beads.

SELECTION ACTIVITY

In this activity, students will work in teams to create a play for children based on one or both of the poems in this selection.

Begin by discussing with students how the subject matter and language of these poems might appeal to children. Point out that the poems would be especially appealing around Halloween, when children naturally begin thinking about ghosts and other supernatural creatures.

Give students time to suggest some of the ways these poems might be used to create a play. For example, the encounter between the nymph and the goblin in "Saltmarsh" could be very effectively acted out. The special words and sounds in "hist, whist" could be made into a song, or spoken aloud in choral reading. "hist, whist" would also lend itself well to dance, perhaps with some of the words and sounds being spoken or sung as accompaniment. Students might also create dialogue to be spoken by the various creatures in this poem.

Encourage each team to create scenery and costumes for their performance as time permits. Have each team perform their children's theater for other members of the class. Then try to arrange for all or some of the teams to perform for children. You might try calling nearby preschools and elementary schools, as well as day care centers and children's hospitals.

■ "The Judge's House"
by Bram Stoker (page 169)

SELECTION SYNOPSIS

Sometime in the 1890's, British university student Malcolm Malcolmson rents an old, vacant house in the village of Benchurch. His goal is to have a quiet place to study for his exams. One hundred years earlier, the house had been owned by a much-feared judge known for his harsh rulings and cruel treatment of prisoners. Some townspeople help Malcolmson move in while hinting about the house's sinister reputation.

Late one night Malcolm hears rats scratching behind the walls, and an enormous rat with an evil glare sits on a large chair near the fireplace. He chases the rat, which escapes up a rope to the house's alarm bell. Malcolmson notices that the rope is unusually flexible for its age and could be used to hang someone. A local doctor tells Malcolmson that the rope to the alarm bell was the hangman's rope used for the judge's victims.

The next night the experience with the rat is repeated, although Malcolmson doesn't seem frightened. Malcolmson becomes curious about the very grimy paintings on the wall and asks his housekeeper to clean them. The paintings depict the judge in that very room. Malcolmson's studying is again interrupted when the huge rat reappears and gnaws the hanging rope in two. The severed rope falls to the floor, and the rat vanishes. The judge's likeness disappears from a portrait and reappears before Malcolmson, knotting the rope into a noose. The judge pursues Malcolmson with the noose in his hands, cutting off any avenue of escape. Malcolmson freezes in fear. The judge throws the noose over the petrified Malcolmson's head and stands him on a chair. He then ties the ends of the rope back together and pulls away the chair. The resultant ringing of the alarm bell summons the townspeople, who arrive too late to save Malcolmson. The judge's portrait now wears an evil smile.

SELECTION ACTIVITY

Discuss with students how the news of Malcolmson's death might affect the townspeople of Benchurch. Students will work in small groups to create newspaper articles to report this event. Divide the class into small groups. Each group is to write an article about Malcolmson's death for the Benchurch local newspaper. The articles should include the *who, what, when, where,* and *why* typical of all effective newspaper reports. Challenge students to come up with interesting and relevant headlines for their articles.

Remind students that they must limit their reportings to what outside observers can deduce from the situation. However, encourage students to create quotes from some of the townspeople in their articles to lend authenticity. Enough information about Mrs. Witham (the inn's landlady), Mrs. Dempster (Malcolmson's housekeeper), and Dr. Thornhill is provided in the story to enable students to infer what they might say about the situation.

When students have completed the assignment, have a representative from each group read their article to the class. Discuss the effectiveness of each article.

If you wish, you might have students use the computer lab to design a final layout of the newspaper and display it on the classroom bulletin board.

■ "The Listeners"
by Walter de la Mare (page 181)

■ "Eldorado"
by Edgar Allan Poe (page 183)

SELECTION SYNOPSES

"The Listeners" tells of a traveler on horseback, who comes to a house in the forest at night and knocks on the door. It appears that he has come to keep a promise made long before. No one answers his call, and the house appears to be empty. The poem suggests that it is filled with phantom listeners, who are probably spirits of the people who once lived in the house. After staying a short time, the traveler rides away. The poem "Eldorado" describes an aging knight who has spent his life searching for "Eldorado," a kind of Camelot. For advice, the knight consults a pilgrim shadow, who tells him to continue to ride on in his search for Eldorado.

SELECTION ACTIVITY

The poem "Eldorado" is similar to the novel *Don Quixote* by Cervantes, for both works describe a person's quest for the ideal. Have students read excerpts from this novel and report on what they have read.

Students may also enjoy learning about the popular musical based on *Don Quixote*, called *The Man of La Mancha*. You may wish to obtain a CD or a cassette tape of the songs from this show to play for the class. You may also be able to obtain a video of the movie version of this musical.

■ "The Loch Ness Monster"
by John McPhee (page 187)

SELECTION SYNOPSIS

In this real-life story, the narrator has joined an expedition formed to sight and positively identify the Loch Ness Monster. This story is primarily expository, with the senior crew member, Skelton, relating many details about the Monster to the reader. Through the conversations with the narrator, Skelton tells about his experiences at Expedition Headquarters. He relates information about past sightings of the Loch Ness Monster, its physical appearance, and many of its behavioral patterns. The reader is able to get a sense of Skelton's burning desire to one day know exactly what the creature is. The reader can sense, however, based on the Monster's long history of elusiveness, that Skelton might never really know.

SELECTION ACTIVITY

Reading "The Loch Ness Monster" will probably heighten the students' interest in what the Loch Ness Monster really is. On the chalkboard, develop a list of questions pertaining to the Monster. Allow the students to offer any valid questions they might have. Then, if necessary, suggest a few questions of your own. Some possible questions might be:

Does the Loch Ness Monster really exist?
What does the Monster look like?
Where does the Monster live?
What kind of food does it eat?
Why is it so hard to actually spot the Monster?

After you and the class have developed a list of 8–10 questions, break the class into groups of 5 or 6. Have each group research the questions in the school library. After the research is completed, have a spokesperson from each group lead a discussion about the answers they found.

■ **"The Great Amherst Mystery"**
by Walter Hubbell (page 201)

SELECTION SYNOPSIS

This nonfiction selection describes the strange story of Esther Cox, a young woman who becomes the target of the activities of ghosts, or poltergeists. The reporter who goes to verify the story (he is the author of the selection) claims not to believe in ghosts, but says afterward that this experience made him a believer.

SELECTION ACTIVITY

In this activity, students will work in groups to present a television round-table discussion. The topic of the discussion will be "Poltergeists—Are They For Real?"

Have students use the selection by Walter Hubbell as the basis for their discussion. Students may do additional research on the topic, but this need not be mandatory. Encourage each group to use characters from the selection as members of the round-table. These could include the reporter Walter Hubbell, Dr. Carritte, Esther's sister Jennie, the Teeds, and Esther Cox herself. The round-table should also include one or two other characters that the students create—perhaps a noted psychologist who does not believe in ghosts, or an expert on ESP who definitely does. An interesting twist to the round-table would be to have the ghosts "Maggie" and "Bob" appear.

Set a time limit for each group's round-table discussion; about twenty minutes. After each presentation, have the class discuss the effectiveness of the dialogue and any general conclusions reached in the discussion. Also have students evaluate how well their classmates have used the facts and opinions presented in the selection.

STUDENT READING LIST

Brooke, William. *Teller of Tales.* 1994, Harper Collins.

Ellis, Sarah. *Back of Beyond: Stories of the Supernatural*, 1997, S&S.

Poe, Edgar Allan. *The Fall of the House of Usher and Other Tales*, New York: New American Library. 1960.

Shusterman, Neal. *Mindtwisters: Stories to Shred Your Head.* 1997, Tor.

San Souci, Robert D. *Even More Short & Shivery: Thirty Spine-Tingling Stories.* 1997, Delacorte.

From Globe Fearon Educational Publisher

Pacemaker Classics
    Dracula by Bram Stoker
    The Moonstone by Wilkie Collins
    The Time Machine by H. G. Wells
Globe Reader's Collection
    Eight Science Fiction Stories

UNIT 2
Overview

UNIT OBJECTIVES

After completing this unit, students will be able to

- understand the four basic elements of a short story: plot, character, setting, and theme
- recognize elements in a poem that are similar to elements in a short story
- use a dictionary to understand words based on a foreign language and words that are archaic
- understand the meaning of words having suffixes or prefixes by finding the root word
- write accurate, detailed descriptions
- recognize how good exposition is crafted
- edit their own writing more effectively
- use facts to support opinions

UNIT SELECTIONS

The theme of this unit is the unknown: unexplained and mysterious creatures and events.

- **"Appointment in Baghdad"** (p. 113) presents death as a real person.
  LITERARY SKILL: foreshadowing
  READING SKILL: draw conclusions
  VOCABULARY: comparison of adjectives
  WRITING: thoughts and actions of main characters

- **"Appointment at Noon"** (p. 119) and **"Incident in a Rose Garden"** (p.123) are other works that personify death. These are the model selections.
  LITERARY SKILL: elements of poetry
  READING SKILL: make inferences
  VOCABULARY: using suffixes
  WRITING: descriptions

- **"Boy in the Shadows"** (p. 127) is set in the Ozark Mountains. This story tells an eerie tale about superstitions.
  LITERARY SKILL: character
  READING SKILL: make predictions
  VOCABULARY: use flashcards to build vocabulary

WRITING: epitaphs
- **"Sorry, Wrong Number"** (p. 137) is a drama about a telephone conversation and a mysterious murder.
  LITERARY SKILL: conflict
  READING SKILL: make inferences from conversation

VOCABULARY: negative words
WRITING: news stories
- **"Thus I Refute Beelzy"** (p. 155) is a story in which a boy's fantasies are pitted against a father's reason.
  LITERARY SKILL: plot
  READING SKILL: analyze characters' responses
  VOCABULARY: draw inferences
  WRITING: create a postscript

- **"hist, whist,"** by E. E. Cummings (p. 163) and **"Overheard on a Salt Marsh"** (p. 164) by Harold Monro, depict imaginary creatures.
  LITERARY SKILL: sound segments
  READING SKILL: identify mood
  VOCABULARY: synonyms
  WRITING: descriptions of settings

Have students discuss whether the opening quotation—"We are such stuff as dreams are made on"—can be applied to the unknown. Then, point out examples of the unknown that students will read about in this unit: death, unexplainable sightings of a prehistoric animal, and documented evidence of spirits. Next, stress the problem of proving, scientifically, the actual existence of the unknown.

Viewing Fine Art

Henri Rousseau (1844–1910) was a French customs officer who began painting as an adult with no training. He is known as a "primitive" painter because his work is simple, uncluttered by formal artistic conventions. Mystery pervades "The Sleeping Gypsy," as it does in many of his paintings. Ask: Is the lion real, or is it what the gypsy is dreaming? Where does the scene take place?

The Unknown

We are such stuff
As dreams are made on.
—William Shakespeare

The Sleeping Gypsy, 1897, Henri Rousseau. Oil on canvas, 51" X 6'7". Collection, The Museum of Modern Art, New York. Gift of Mrs. Simon Guggenheim

- **"The Judge's House"** (p. 169) In this story, a student seeks a quiet place to study, but finds himself in a haunted house.
  LITERARY SKILL: theme
  READING SKILL: use prior knowledge
  VOCABULARY: revise archaic words and phrases
  WRITING: write a story in the first person

- **"The Listeners"** (p. 181) and **"Eldorado"** (p. 183) are poems that touch on the supernatural as travelers search for the unobtainable.
  LITERARY SKILL: narrative poetry
  READING SKILL: draw conclusions
  VOCABULARY: archaic verb forms
  WRITING: poetry to prose

- **"The Loch Ness Monster"** (p. 187) is a true story of people whose lives are spent studying and searching for the Loch Ness monster.
  LITERARY SKILL: exposition
  READING SKILL: evaluate the writer's purpose
  VOCABULARY: American/British English differences
  WRITING: focused description

- **"The Great Amherst Mystery"** (p. 201) is the story of one man's search for the "truth" about poltergeists.
  LITERARY SKILL: persuasion
  READING SKILL: make inferences about setting
  VOCABULARY: borrowed words
  WRITING: develop a convincing argument

UNIT 2 Overview

RELATED MATERIALS

1. ***Edgar Allan Poe: A Light and Enlightening Look.*** [Video, Media Consultants, 1996.] This is a different look at Poe.

2. ***Classic Chilling Tales,*** v. 1 and v. 2. [Audiotape, Naxos International, 1995.] Here is another source of tales involving the unknown.

3. ***Creatures of the Night.*** [Video, DK Vision, 1998.] More looks at the unknown are available through this video.

4. ***Loch Ness Discovered.*** [Video, Discovery Channel, Special Interest Video Collection.] This video examines the history behind the possibility of a Loch Ness creature and also looks at the fascinating ecology of the lake itself.

5. ***"Appointment at Noon"*** and ***"Incident in a Rose Garden" Poetry of Death; Part II*** [Spectrum Educational Media, Inc.] These can reinforce the text presentation.

6. The following Web sites may also be helpful. Please note that some Internet addresses change frequently. These are the latest versions:

   Mysteries and the Unknown at *http://www.serve.com/shadows/mystery.htm*

   The Linkoping Science Fiction and Fantasy Archive; Ray Bradbury at *http://sf.www.lysator.liu.se/sf_archives/sf-texts/authors/B/Bradbury%2CRay.mbox*

   e. e. cummings biography, poems, other links at *http://www.imsa.edu/~junkee/cummmings.html*

The Unknown

Have you ever had the feeling there are "things" out there that you know nothing about?

The conflict between what is known and what is unknown is a common theme in literature. William Shakespeare suggests that you yourself might be nothing more than dreams. Are you then part of the unknown?

Throughout time, writers have created stories and poems about the unknown. As you read a few of them in this unit, try to keep an open mind about the existence of mysterious, unexplainable things.

■ MATTERS OF LIFE AND DEATH

One part of the unknown that may always remain a mystery is death. Yet writers have tried for centuries to understand death and make it "come alive."

In the first two selections, "Appointment in Baghdad," a folktale that originated long ago in the Middle East, and "Appointment at Noon," Death is an actual person who comes to claim victims whose time on earth has run out. The same theme appears in the poem "Incident in a Rose Garden."

Can people come back from the dead? In the story "Boy in the Shadows," Irene and Ernest Platt wonder about their hired hand; how can his thinness, his listlessness, and his odd manner be explained?

Modern city life abounds with all sorts of fears. What if you were to overhear a phone conversation concerning a murder? In "Sorry, Wrong Number," a woman is faced with just that situation and she tries to do something to prevent the crime. What steps would you take if you were aware of a similar situation?

■ MYSTERIES WITHIN

When you were young, did you have imaginary playmates that you thought were real?

Small Simon is sure that an imaginary companion he calls "Mr. Beelzy" really exists in "Thus I Refute Beelzy." His father, Big Simon, tries to convince him otherwise. Big Simon's logic has no effect on the boy, and the story has a mysterious conclusion.

E. E. Cummings shows his remarkable skill in using language creatively as he conjures images of ghosts, witches, goblins, and toads in the poem "hist, whist." "Overheard on a Saltmarsh" describes a tussle between mysterious night creatures over green glass beads stolen from the moon.

In "The Judge's House," a student finds himself in a frightening situation. Looking for a quiet place to study, he rents an old house that used to belong to a judge. He ignores warnings that the house is haunted and is later threatened by the ghost of the judge. Why do you think some people choose to ignore warnings about potential dangers?

"The Listeners" and "Eldorado" tell of travelers who are searching. They seem to be chasing dreams.

■ COULD IT BE REAL?

In a world of technology you might feel that unknown or unexplainable things are not worth thinking about.

But what do you do when sincere, trustworthy observers provide evidence that suggests you are wrong?

"The Loch Ness Monster" and "The Great Amherst Mystery" take a reasonable, logical approach toward explaining the unexplainable and solving certain mysteries. Both stories suggest that while it's good to be skeptical, you should keep an open mind.

Discussing the Unit Theme

After they read the full commentary on the unknown, present a topic to students that falls in the realm of the "unknown," such as UFOs. Ask students to name any facts about UFOs. For example, it is a fact that many people the world over have reported UFO sightings. Then, encourage discussion of why, in the course of evaluating evidence, it is often difficult—as with UFOs—to separate fact from hearsay.

Cooperative Group Activity

Have students name other "unknown" topics. Write them on the board. Divide the class into small groups. Assign one of the topics to each group. Ask the groups if they can reach a consensus on whether they believe in their assigned topic. Have group members give reasons for their agreement or dissent. As the groups make their class presentations, have a student record both facts and opinions; save them for the end of the unit.

SELECTION OBJECTIVES

After completing this selection, students will be able to

- recognize foreshadowing
- utilize foreshadowing in humorous dialogue
- discuss the idea of fate
- develop a fuller description of a character's thoughts and actions
- understand the use of foreshadowing
- make comparisons of adjectives
- make inferences
- draw conclusions

Lesson Resources

Appointment in Baghdad
- Selection Synopsis, Teacher's Edition, p. T107c
- Comprehension and Vocabulary Workbook, pp. 23–24
- Language Enrichment Workbook, pp. 20–21
- Teacher's Resources Reinforcement, p. R12 Test, pp. T21–T22

More About Foreshadowing

Help students see that foreshadowing is similar to a weather prediction or an introduction to a book; we are told indirectly about what is to come. Ask students for examples of foreshadowing in other narrative art forms, such as films.

Viewing Fine Art

Mystical artists of the United States, like their romantic counterparts in Europe, depicted exotic, emotional, and literary events. Albert Pinkham Ryder (1847–1917) was an imaginative artist of dramatic and mystical scenes, like the one shown on page 113. Ask: What do you think this painting says about death?

T112

Learn About

FORESHADOWING

Hints or clues about what will happen in a story are called **foreshadowing**. You can take these hints or clues and make a prediction about how the story will develop. Through this technique, the author prepares you for the action ahead.

Good foreshadowing provides just enough information to give you a general idea of what will happen, but not enough to give away the ending.

As you read "Appointment in Baghdad," ask yourself these questions:

1. Does the author use foreshadowing?
2. How can foreshadowing be used to predict what will happen at the end of the story?

WRITING CONNECTION

Foreshadowing is often used in jokes. Through foreshadowing, the joke teller gives you clues as to what the "punch line" will be. You make a prediction, but usually it is wrong. When the punch line is finally told, surprise turns to humor. Think of a joke that uses foreshadowing and write it down as a dialogue.

READING FOCUS

Draw Conclusions An author does not always state directly why certain events in a story take place, or why characters do certain things.

Often readers must draw their own conclusions. To do this, use clues that the author gives about events and characters and what you already know. Try to draw conclusions as you read by asking questions about why certain events take place and why characters behave as they do.

112 ■ Unit 2

Develop Vocabulary Skills

Write the words *Baghdad* and *Damascus* on the board. Point out that names of cities and other places often evoke feelings or attitudes. Ask students to name some places and the feelings they associate with those places. Ask why an author would choose place names carefully, and why Baghdad and Damascus might be chosen for a story such as this one.

ESL Activity

Have students work in small groups or pairs to identify foreshadowing in "Appointment in Baghdad," predict the ending, and compare the ending with their prediction.

Cooperative Group Activity

For the Writing Connection activity, divide students into groups. Have each student tell a joke that uses foreshadowing. Have the group choose the joke that shows the best use of foreshadowing and discuss their reasoning. Have them write the joke as dialogue, assign parts, and present it to the class.

Appointment in Baghdad

traditional version
retold by Edith Wharton

The Race Track (Death on a Pale Horse), Albert Pinkham Ryder.
c. 1886–1908. (American, 1847–1917) Oil on canvas,
70.5 × 90 cm. ©The Cleveland Museum of Art, 2000.
Purchase from the J. H. Wade Fund, 1928.8

One morning the Sultan was resting in his palace in Damascus.[1] Suddenly the door flew open, and in rushed a young man, out of breath and wild with excitement. The Sultan sat up alarmed, for the young man was his most skillful assistant.

"I must have your best horse!" the youth cried out. "There is little time! I must fly at once to Baghdad!"[2]

The Sultan asked why the young man was in such a rush.

"Because," came the hurried reply, "just now, as I was walking in the palace garden, I saw Death standing there. And when Death saw me, he raised his arms in a frightening motion. Oh, it was horrible! I must escape at once!"

The Sultan quickly arranged for the youth to have his fastest horse. And no sooner had the young man thundered out through the palace gate, than the Sultan himself went into the garden. Death was still there.

The Sultan was angry. "What do you mean?" he demanded. "What do you mean by raising your arms and frightening my young friend?"

"Your Majesty," Death said calmly, "I did not mean to frighten him. You see, I raised my arms only in surprise. I was astonished to see him here in your garden, for I have an appointment with him tonight in Baghdad."

---

[1]**Damascus:** an important Middle Eastern city, now capital of Syria
[2]**Baghdad:** an important city in the old Middle East, now capital of Iraq

Appointment in Baghdad ■ 113

UNDERSTAND THE SELECTION

Answers

1. at the Sultan's place in Damascus
2. the Sultan's "most skillful assistant"
3. He raised them in surprise because he was astonished to see the young man in Damascus instead of Baghdad, where he had an appointment with him that night.
4. The young man interpreted Death raising his arms as a sign that Death had come to claim him.
5. to get to Baghdad, where he felt he would be safe from Death
6. He is angry, he confronts Death, Death explains that he had expected to see the young man in Baghdad, not Damascus.
7. It is a reference to an inevitable meeting between Death and the young man.
8. Answers will vary. Sample: I would be scared, too, and try to get away.
9. Answers will vary. Sample: He is a much older man than the young assistant, and he might think that he and Death are bound to meet soon anyhow.
10. to illustrate that we cannot escape death

Respond to Literature

The quotation from Shakespeare that opens this unit ("We are such stuff as dreams are made on") is from Act IV, scene 1 of the *The Tempest*. Shakespeare is suggesting that in life, we all might be nothing more than actors on a stage. The script describes our fate, and we can do nothing to change it. Ask students why the notion of fate has persisted in literature for hundreds, even thousands of years.

WRITE ABOUT THE SELECTION

Prewriting

Use students' suggestions to create a drawing on the chalkboard or overhead transparency.

UNDERSTAND THE SELECTION

Recall

1. Where does the story take place?
2. Who is the young man who rushes in asking to borrow a horse?
3. Why did Death raise his arms when he encountered the young man?

Infer

4. Why did Death's actions frighten the young man?
5. Why did the young man want a horse?
6. Describe what happens when the Sultan goes out to the palace garden.
7. What is the significance of the word "Appointment" in the title?

Apply

8. Suppose that you are the young man and you have seen Death in the palace garden. How would you react?
9. The Sultan seems to be a brave man to go out to the palace garden and confront Death. Is this part of the story hard for you to believe?
10. What is the point of this story?

Respond to Literature

Is there such a thing as fate? Are all of our actions predetermined, and we are like players on a stage acting out parts? Explain your answers.

WRITE ABOUT THE SELECTION

What do you think the young man thought when he saw Death in the palace garden? Many thoughts must have raced through his mind when he encountered the figure.

Suppose that you are the young man. Write what happened and what you thought when you were walking in the garden and first saw Death.

Prewriting Draw a quick sketch of the garden to help you visualize the scene before describing it in words. Place the young man in the scene, and mark where he sees Death. Then write a few words next to the man to describe his thoughts just before he met Death, at the moment he met Death, and immediately after their encounter. Finally, try to draw a picture of Death.

Writing Use your picture and notes to write one or several paragraphs to describe what happened in the garden. Remember to use first-person point of view so that your description fits into the rest of the story.

Revising Try to write in the same style as Edith Wharton, using short sentences and simple, direct language. Consider adding specific details and vivid words to make your paragraph really come alive.

Proofreading As you reread what you have written, check carefully that references to the character Death begin with a capital letter. If you have included direct conversation, make sure you have followed the rules of punctuation.

Writing

Allow students to work on their descriptions individually. Circulate, asking about the sketches they have made in order to prompt ideas on details to include.

Revising

Have students revise working in small groups. Each student reads his or her description aloud to the group, and group members offer feedback. Remind students that the description should be written in first person.

Proofreading

Have students continue working in small groups. Ask them to exchange papers for proofreading. Students should ask for explanations from their partner, another student, or the teacher if they do not understand a suggested change.

THINK ABOUT FORESHADOWING

What makes "Appointment in Baghdad" such a good short story? It is short—even for a short story—but that is not all. Let us look again at expectations of what will happen, what really happens, and foreshadowing. The writer's skillful use of foreshadowing—hints or clues that suggest what might happen—lead you to expect a certain outcome.

1. After the young man rides off on the horse, what do you expect will happen?

2. How was that expectation formed?

3. How does the story end?

4. Look back at the story again. Are there hints about what will happen?

5. Do you feel the writer has played a trick on you with the ending to the story? Explain your answer.

READING FOCUS

Draw Conclusions As you read the story, you were able to draw conclusions about certain events and why they occurred. Name one such event and the conclusion you drew from it.

DEVELOP YOUR VOCABULARY

The comparative and superlative forms of almost all one-syllable adjectives are formed by adding *er* and *est*.

Some two-syllable adjectives are formed in the same way, but others are formed, (like all adjectives of more than two syllables) by adding *more* and *most*.

fast	faster	fastest
skillful	more skillful	most skillful

Some adjective forms are irregular:

good	better	best

If you are in doubt about adjective forms, check the dictionary.

Give the forms for these adjectives:

1. fresh
2. many
3. plain
4. beautiful
5. dear

6. pretty
7. friendly
8. thin
9. humble
10. contented

Review the Selection ■ 115

ESL Activity

Discuss the prefixes *super* and *un*. Examples are *superman*, *supermarket*, *unwanted*, and *unhappy*. Have students find three examples of other words using the prefixes *super* and *un*. Make up sentences using the words, then ask what the prefixes *super* and *un* mean.

Guide students through the discussion of a short story's elements by writing the four elements on the chalkboard or an overhead transparency and listing key words associated with each element. (For example, list "when" and "where" under "Setting.") You might want to show that these elements are found in any story, not just a short story, by referring to other texts students have read. Stress that sometimes one particular element is much more important than another.

ELEMENTS OF FICTION

Revisit "Appointment in Baghdad" on page 113 to explore the elements of fiction. Create a four-column chart on the chalkboard with the following headings: **characters**, **setting**, **plot**, **theme**. Ask students for specific examples of each. Start with **characters**. Elicit from students the names of the three characters. Write them in the appropriate column. Add short descriptions of each if you wish. Then ask students to identify the **setting** of the story. Have students guess what time the story takes place and add that to the chart.

Draw a simple flow-chart under the heading **plot**. Have students tell what happened in the story. Enter the information in proper order on the flow chart. Identify actions with labels such as "complication," "rising action," and "climax."

End with theme. Help students formulate a one-sentence statement of theme. Write this statement under **theme**.

Focus ON FICTION

Short stories are a very popular form of fiction. Why?

Short stories are so concentrated that they can have a lot of impact in just a few pages. The conciseness of a short story also provides the chance for a clear examination of the four basic elements of fiction. These are plot, characters, setting, and theme.

Plot   Plot is usually the most obvious element of a short story. Many people think of it first when they talk about a story: the telling of one event after another to form a series of actions leading to a conclusion.

The plot is usually introduced through **exposition**, or written interpretation, by the author. Exposition provides background information for the actions that will take place in the story.

As the action unfolds, a complication arises. The **complication** is like a question demanding an answer. It keeps the story moving, as you wonder what will happen next. Sometimes the answer ends the story, or it can lead to another question.

As the plot develops, the action rises. **Rising action** leads to a crisis with a climax at the end, or near the end, of the story. **Climax** is the peak of the action.

If the story continues beyond the climax, the action falls. The plot develops further, but only to resolve a final question. The **falling action** ends in **resolution**.

When you read a story quickly, you are probably unaware of all those plot developments. Try to keep them in mind as you read the next selections, especially "Thus I Refute Beelzy," when you'll be studying plot developments in detail.

Characters   The characters are the people in a short story. They act, or are acted upon, as the plot develops.

You learn about characters in two ways. First, the writer might tell you directly whether a certain character is clever, mean, bold or shy. The writer is creating **traits** that describe the character.

Second, the writer can tell you indirectly about a character by describing what the character says or how the character acts. This information portrays the character, too, but you must use some imagination to fit the pieces into the overall description.

Usually a writer uses both methods. In "Appointment in Baghdad," you learn that one character is a young man. That is **direct information**. You also learn that he rushes into the Sultan's palace "out of breath and wild with excitement." That is **indirect information**, giving you clues to his general state of mind and how he reacts in certain situations.

Setting A third element of a short story is setting. You can probably guess that setting includes where a story takes place, but it also includes when a story happens. Additionally, it can include natural events, such as a blizzard or a hurricane.

The short stories in this unit have a variety of settings. "Of Missing Persons" takes place in modern-day New York, while "Appointment in Baghdad" takes place in the Middle East long ago.

Theme Theme is the fourth element of a short story.

A writer usually has a reason for telling us a story. He or she chooses a subject, and then develops plot, setting, and characters. What the writer wants you to learn from the story is the theme. It is the story's idea or message.

"Appointment in Baghdad" has a single, clear theme: Death cannot be avoided.

Sometimes a short story has more than one theme. Sometimes there is no theme of real importance, or the theme is not clear.

As you read the selections in this unit, look for the elements of the short stories. Ask yourself these questions:
1. Which elements are the easiest to identify and understand? Which are the hardest?
2. Are elements more important in some stories than in others?

Focus on Fiction ■ 117

Real-Life Application

Ask students to think of a "story" from a song, the movies, a TV show, or perhaps even an advertisement. Then have them identify the elements of the story. If they think an element is missing, such as the setting, help them understand that sometimes the element may be inferred from context clues, that is, from language that merely suggests the setting.

SELECTION OVERVIEW

SELECTION OBJECTIVES

After completing the next two selections, students will be able to

- understand the elements of a short story
- relate the theme to their own lives
- use personification in describing death
- see similarities between elements in short stories and poems
- recognize how certain suffixes change adjectives into nouns
- make inferences

Lesson Resources

Appointment at Noon
Incident in a Rose Garden
- Selection Synopses, Teacher's Edition, pp. T107c–107d
- Comprehension and Vocabulary Workbook, pp. 25–26
- Language Enrichment Workbook, pp. 22–23
- Teacher's Resources Reinforcement, p. R13 Test, pp. T23–T24 Literary Analysis, pp. L3–L4

More About the Unit Theme

In the previous story, Death was personified as a gracious but sure figure. How might Death be portrayed in a more modern story?

Background Notes

Henry Curran is a caricature of the prototypical American business-man: big, busy, successful, impatient, and ruthless. Romanticism has no place in his life. Traditionally, businessmen have been viewed negatively in American literature. Sinclair Lewis vilified the small-town businessman in the novel *Babbitt*, and Arthur Miller showed the emptiness of a salesman's life in *Death of a Salesman*.

Death on a Pale Horse, William Blake. Fitzwilliam Museum, University of Cambridge/Bridgeman Art Library

118 ■ Unit 2

Viewing Fine Art

William Blake (1757–1827) was a poet, painter, and engraver. His works frequently express dramatic subjects and feelings. (His major sources were the Bible, Milton, and Dante.) Ask students to speculate on who the three figures are and what they are doing.

Cooperative Group Activity

Divide students into groups. Have each student tell a different story from his or her choice in the Real-Life Application section. Ask each student to make a chart listing all the elements of his or her chosen story. Then, as they tell their story to the group, have them point out at least one element that can be deduced from context clues only.

APPOINTMENT AT NOON

by Eric Frank Russell

Henry Curran was big, busy, and successful. He had no patience with people who weren't successful. He had the build of a fighter and the soul of a tiger. His time was worth a thousand bucks an hour. He knew of nobody who was worth more.

And crime did not pay? "Bah!" said Henry Curran.

The law of the jungle paid off. Henry Curran had learned that nice people are soft people, and that smiles are made to be slapped.

Entering his large office with the fast, heavy step of a big man in fighting shape, Henry threw his hat onto a hook. He glanced at the wall clock. He noted that it was ten minutes to twelve.

Seating himself in the large chair behind his desk, he kept his eyes on the door. His wait lasted about ten seconds. Frowning at the thought of it, Curran reached over and pushed a red button on his big desk.

"What's wrong with you?" he snapped when Miss Reed came in. "You get worse every day. Old age creeping over you or something?"

She paused. She was tall, neat, and steady. She faced him across the desk, her eyes showing a touch of fear. Curran hired to work for him only people he knew too much about.

FOCUS ON FICTION
STUDY HINTS

The main character is introduced right away. His traits are described directly as well as indirectly.

Note the writer's statement of the setting. The office's location and the date do not matter. The description of Henry Curran acts as exposition. Now, with background information and setting provided, the plot begins to unfold.

The second character of the story is introduced. Notice how information about Miss Reed tells us more about Curran.

Appointment at Noon ■ 119

TEACHING PLAN

INTRODUCE

Motivation
Ask students what connection there might be, if any, between this story and the previous one. The titles are nearly identical, substituting a time for a place. (Both time and place are part of a setting.) Whet their appetites further by noting that both stories have three characters.

Purpose-Setting Question
How can the passage of time (in "Appointment at Noon," just 8 minutes) be used to help tell a story?

READ

Literary Focus:
Elements of Fiction
The blue side notes in this annotated lesson provide a model for students to understand the literary elements introduced in Focus on Fiction, pages 116–117. A number of interesting expressions are used such as "His time was worth a thousand bucks an hour," "the law of the jungle paid off," "smiles are made to be slapped." Discuss with students how these expressions reveal character.

Reading Focus:
Make Inferences
Explain that asking questions is a helpful strategy to use when making inferences. Suggest that students use the elements of fiction as a general guide to asking questions about characters. As they read, they might ask themselves: What is happening? Why? Why would this character say or do this?

CLOSE

Have students complete Review the Selection on pages 124–125.

Develop Vocabulary Skills
Write on the chalkboard or a transparency the definitions for the footnoted vocabulary in the story. Then read each new vocabulary word and ask students to match the word with the correct definition. This exercise can be done as an entire class or with students working individually.

ESL Activity

Death is viewed differently in many cultures. Have small groups discuss how the death of someone is viewed in their culture. Suggest that they discuss these questions: "Is death viewed as a positive or negative thing in your culture?" "What kinds of ceremonies do you have when people die?" "Are there any stories that people tell to try to teach about death?" Tell students to look for similarities between views of death expressed in this story and their own cultural traditions.

This is the plot complication.

The third character, the uninvited guest, is described indirectly. Despite this description, he is pretty mysterious. This mystery creates tension. Further hints about him heighten the mystery.

"I'm sorry, Mr. Curran, I was—"

"Never mind the excuse. Be faster—or else! Speed's what I like. SPEED—SEE?"

"Yes, Mr. Curran."

"Has Lolordo phoned in yet?"

"No, Mr. Curran."

"He should be through by now if everything went all right." He looked at the clock again, tapping angrily on his desk. "If he's made a mess of it and the mouthpiece comes on, tell him to forget about Lolordo. He's in no position to talk, anyway. A little time in jail will teach him not to be stupid."

"Yes, Mr. Curran. There's an old—"

"Shut up till I've finished. If Michaelson calls up and says the *Firefly* got through, phone Voss and tell him without delay! And I mean without delay! That's important!" He thought for a moment. Then he finished, "There's that meeting downtown at twelve-twenty. God knows how long it will go on. If they want trouble, they can have it! If anyone asks, you don't know where I am. You don't expect me back before four."

"But, Mr. Curran—"

"You heard what I said. Nobody sees me before four."

"There's a man already here," she got out in an apologetic voice. "He said you have an appointment with him at two minutes to twelve."

"And you fell for a joke like that?" He studied her with a cutting smile.

"I can only repeat what he said. He seemed quite sincere."

"That's a change," snapped Curran. "Sincerity in *my* office? He's got the wrong address. Go tell him to spread himself across the tracks. "

"I said you were out and didn't know when you would return. He took a seat and said he'd wait because you would be back at ten to twelve."

Without knowing it, both suddenly stared at the clock. Curran lifted an arm and looked at his wristwatch to check the instrument on the wall.

---

mouthpiece (MOUTH pees) slang for criminal lawyer
apologetic (uh POL uh JET ik) filled with apology; suggesting that one is sorry
sincerity (sin SER uh tee) honesty; quality of being sincere

120 ■ Unit 2

"That's what the scientific bigbrains would call precognition. I call it a lucky guess. One minute either way would have made him wrong. That guy ought to bet money on the horses." He made a gesture of dismissal. "Push him out—or do I have to get the boys to do it for you?"

"That wouldn't be necessary. He is old and blind."

"I don't care if he's armless and legless—that's *his* tough luck. Give him the rush."

Obediently she left. A few moments later she was back. She had the sorrowful look of a person whose job forced her to face Curran's anger.

"I'm terribly sorry, Mr. Curran. He insists that he has a date with you for two minutes to twelve. He is to see you about a personal matter of great importance."

Curran scowled at the wall. The clock said four minutes to twelve. He spoke with purpose.

"I know no blind man and I don't forget appointments. Throw him down the stairs."

She hesitated, standing there wide-eyed. "I'm wondering whether—"

"Out with it!"

"Whether he's been sent to you by someone else, someone who'd rather he couldn't tell who you were by sight."

He thought it over and said, "Could be. You use your brains once in a while. What's his name?"

"He won't say."

"Nor state his business?"

"No."

"H'm! I'll give him two minutes. If he's trying to get money for some church or something he'll go out through the window. Tell him my time is valuable and show him in."

She went away and brought back the visitor. She gave him a chair. The door closed quietly behind her. The clock said three minutes before the hour.

Curran sat back and looked at his guest, finding him tall, thin, and white-haired. The old man's clothes were black, a deep,

The action continues to rise. Note how time has become very important to the story.

The visitor now confronts Henry Curran. What can you infer about the old man from the description?

Critical Thinking:
Interpret
Discuss Death's blindness. Ask: Why is death blind? Is it a hindrance or a help?

Reading Focus:
Make Inferences
Ask: What can you infer about the visitor? Why do you think his eyes are sorry for what they see?

---

precognition (pree kog NISH un) knowledge of future events
scowled (SKOULD) frowned and looked angry

Appointment at Noon ■ 121

somber black. They set off the bright, blue, unseeing eyes staring from his colorless face.

Those strange eyes were the old man's most noticeable feature. They were odd, as if somehow they could look *into* the things they could not look at. And they were sorry—sorry for what they saw.

For the first time in his life, Henry Curran felt a little alarmed. He said, "What can I do for you?"

"Nothing," replied the other. "Nothing at all."

His voice was like an organ. It was low, no more than a whisper, and with its sounding a queer coldness came over the room. He sat there unmoving and staring at whatever a blind man can see. The coldness increased, became bitter. Curran shivered despite himself. He frowned and got a hold on himself.

"Don't take up my time," advised Curran. "State your business or get out."

"People don't take up time. Time takes up people."

"Just what do you mean? Who are you?"

"You know who I am. Every man is a shining sun to himself, until he is dimmed by his dark companion."

"You're not funny," said Curran, freezing.

"I am never funny."

The tiger light blazed in Curran's eyes as he stood up. He placed a thick, firm finger near his desk button.

"Enough of this nonsense! What d'you want?"

Suddenly holding out a lengthless, dimensionless arm, the man whispered sadly, "You!"

And Death took him.

At exactly two minutes to twelve.

---

somber (SOM bur) gloomy and dark; very sad
dimensionless (duh MEN shun les) without dimensions, or size that can be measured in length, height, or width

Incident in a Rose Garden

by Donald Justice

GARDENER: Sir, I encountered Death
Just now among our roses.
Thin as a scythe he stood there.

Notice how this poem shares elements with the short story. The title and the first two lines establish the setting.

5   I knew him by his pictures.
He had his black coat on,
Black gloves, a broad black hat.

The poem has characters, like a short story.

I think he would have spoken,
Seeing his mouth stood open.
Big it was, with white teeth.

10   As soon as he beckoned, I ran.
I ran until I found you.
Sir, I am quitting my job.

The plot has developed from the very first line of the poem. Now the plot complication appears.

15   I want to see my sons
Once more before I die.
I want to see California.

MASTER: Sir, you must be that stranger
Who threatened my gardener.
This is my property, sir.
I welcome only friends here.

20 DEATH: Sir, I knew your father.
And we were friends at the end.

As for your gardener,
I did not threaten him.
Old men mistake my gestures.

25   I only meant to ask him
To show me to his master.
I take it you are he?

The theme emerges in the climax. What is the theme?

scythe (SYTH) a long, curved blade fixed at an angle to a long, bent handle and used to cut down grass or grain

Incident in a Rose Garden ■ 123

UNDERSTAND THE SELECTION

Answers

1. at ten minutes to twelve
2. He thinks that he wants a contribution to "some church or something."
3. black
4. He was a businessman of some sort because he is so preoccupied with money and time. We do not know exactly what kind of business, though.
5. "Tall, neat, and steady." A bit fearful of Curran, but persistent because she insists on making Curran see the visitor in the waiting room. Clever, because she thinks that maybe a blind man had been sent to Curran by somebody who did not want the man to recognize Curran.
6. "Old" represents the passing of time, "blind" represents a lack of prejudice as to who dies when—everybody's time comes at some point. The old, blind man is a perfect personification of Death.
7. It is the gardener's master that Death is after, not the gardener. There is no real need for Death to speak to the gardener.
8. One talks about an appointment at a place, the other an appointment at a time. Both involve setting, but in different ways. Time and place do not matter when it comes to Death's arrival.
9. Sample answer: There is some foreshadowing: the title itself, for instance, but also the continual emphasis on time, and Curran's nervousness about time. When Death walks into Curran's office, even Henry Curran felt a little alarmed.
10. Gardens are symbols of life and cultivated security. That Death encounters his victims in gardens underlines the theme that Death takes us all, no matter who or where we are.

UNDERSTAND THE SELECTION

Recall

1. When did Henry Curran enter his office?

2. Before the visitor enters Curran's office, what does Curran think about him?

3. What color were Death's clothes?

Infer

4. What was Curran's profession?

5. Describe Miss Reed.

6. Why is the visitor in "Appointment at Noon" old and blind?

7. Why did Death not speak to the gardener in "Incident in a Rose Garden"?

Apply

8. Discuss the difference in titles between "Appointment in Baghdad" and "Appointment at Noon."

9. Did "Appointment at Noon" turn out the way you expected? Was there any foreshadowing to help you?

10. Why do you think both "Appointment in Baghdad" and "Incident in a Rose Garden" include gardens for settings?

Respond to Literature

"Appointment in Baghdad," "Appointment at Noon," and "Incident in a Rose Garden" show Death as being uninterested in the ages of his "victims." Why?

WRITE ABOUT THE SELECTION

If you had to describe Death as a person, what would you say? Is Death a man or a woman? Does it look like a person? Do only certain parts look like a person? Can Death talk? Can it hear, feel, smell, and touch? What does it wear? Does it carry anything?

Assume that you are writing a story and Death is a character. Write a description of Death.

Prewriting Using clusters, answer the questions above. Add any other information that helps to provide an accurate description of what you think Death looks like. Make a sketch or illustration of the character Death if that will stimulate your imagination.

Writing Use the information in the clusters and your drawing to write your description. You may introduce another character if you want to use conversation to build the description, but Death must remain the central figure.

Revising You want your readers to have as clear a picture as possible of how you imagine Death to be. Can you add any similes to make the description more vivid? Think about using sensory details: description that appeals to the senses of sight, sound, smell, feeling, or taste.

Proofreading Reread what you have written and check that all sentences end with a punctuation mark. Check also that Death as a character always begins with a capital *D*.

Respond to Literature

You will want to treat this question with sensitivity. Young people who have experienced the death of a close friend or relative—or heard on TV the mounting number of casualties among young people—may not want to share their feelings. Small groups could be used to prompt discussion before opening the topic for general class consideration.

WRITE ABOUT THE SELECTION

Prewriting

Make a cluster on the chalkboard or overhead transparency of the characteristics of Death in any of the last three selections. Where given, include all their physical traits to show exactly how death is personified.

Writing

Circulate among the students as they work individually on their descriptions. Check to see that they are using their cluster ideas as prompts in describing the personification of death.

THINK ABOUT FICTION

Were you surprised that the poem "Incident in a Rose Garden" was similar to "Appointment at Baghdad"? Were you surprised that a poem could seem like a short story because it shares the same elements?

1. List all of the similar elements of fiction in "Incident in a Rose Garden" and "Appointment at Baghdad."

2. List the differences between the two.

3. Point to things that are missing in the poem as compared to the story.

4. Why do you think some elements are missing in the poem as compared to the story?

5. Which of these three selections is your favorite? Why?

DEVELOP YOUR VOCABULARY

Many times suffixes are added to adjectives to make them nouns:

patient + -ence = patience

If you know the suffix and the root word you can figure out the meaning.

-ence = act, quality, or result of
-ity = state, character, condition of
-ness = state or quality of being
-tude = state or quality of being

Define each italicized noun by determining the root adjective and suffix. Check your definition in a dictionary. Then write your own sentence using each word.

1. "*Sincerity* in my office?" he snapped.

2. Did he state his *business*?

3. A queer *coldness* came over the room.

4. Her *certitude* was a real advantage.

5. "*Capability* is the thing!" he said.

Review the Selection ■ 125

THINK ABOUT FICTION

Answers

1. similarities: characters, setting, plot (until the end), theme
2. The plot ends differently; the setting in the poem is not as specific as in the story. (We can surmise that it is somewhere in America because the gardener wants to go to California to see his sons.)
3. Full descriptions of characters, tension caused by drawing out the plot complication, greater expansion on the theme are all lacking in the poem.
4. The poem is shorter than the story.
5. Answers will vary. Sample: "Appointment in Baghdad" because I was completely fooled by the ending. It really made me stop and think.

DEVELOP YOUR VOCABULARY

Answers

1. sincere + ity = quality of being sincere
   Tom always found Bill's sincerity convincing.
2. busy + ness = state of being busy
   His business kept him on the go all the time.
3. cold + ness = state of being cold
   Coldness accompanied the accused man into the courtroom.
4. certain + tude = quality of being certain
   His certitude borders on stubbornness.
5. capable + ity = character of being capable
   We all admired his capability in computer programming.

Revising

You may want to have students work cooperatively in small groups to think of similes that describe death. They can share the similes they have used in their descriptions, or together, they can think of new ones. Leave time for students to work individually on revising.

Proofreading

Emphasize that common nouns, such as "death," are capitalized whenever they are clearly personified, as in "I encountered Death just now."

ESL Activity

Have students work in small groups. Have them write several adjectives that describe each group member. Then have them use the suffixes *ence*, *ity*, *ness*, and *tude* to change as many of the adjectives to nouns as possible.

SELECTION OVERVIEW

SELECTION OBJECTIVES

After completing this selection, students will be able to

- evaluate character traits when describing an event
- analyze character developed through description of traits and actions
- write an epitaph of someone
- use flashcards to build vocabulary skills
- make predictions

Lesson Resources

Boy in the Shadows
- Selection Synopsis, Teacher's Edition, pp. T107d–107e
- Comprehension and Vocabulary Workbook, pp. 27–28
- Language Enrichment Workbook, pp. 25–27
- Teacher's Resources Reinforcement, p. R14 Test, pp. T25–T26

More About Character

Write on the chalkboard or overhead transparency, "Vote For Your Favorite Character!" Ask students for a list of nominees who might fit the description; limit their choices to well-known, public figures. Then ask students: Do they really know what the character is like? What are his/her special traits? Urge students to be very specific in their comments, and remind them that good writers build character not through generalities but by focusing on small details.

Background Notes

The Ozarks, also called the Ozark Mountains or the Ozark Plateau, cover an area of 50,000 square miles in Missouri, Arkansas, Illinois and Kansas. The mountains are low—1,500 to 2,500 feet—but the area remained isolated and remote for many years. Even today it is considered very rural. In his book, *Blue Highways*, William Least Heat Moon writes about an interesting experience he had in the Ozarks.

READING FOCUS

Make Predictions You can often predict the outcome of a story by paying attention to the clues that the author provides. Clues can also help you determine character's motives, the story's theme, and how conflicts might be resolved. As you read, watch for clues about characters and events that will help you to predict the story's outcome.

CHARACTER

Stories are about characters who may not be real but are probably drawn from real life. A character is often modeled after a real human being with all the good and bad traits that people can have. A story usually revolves around the problems the main character or characters have.

Writers can develop characters directly by telling you what they look like or what they are thinking. Characters also can be developed indirectly through their actions or their speech. Good characters make you care about their problems.

As you read "Boy in the Shadows," ask yourself these questions:

1. How might dialogue between characters reveal their traits?
2. Where do actions reveal character?

WRITING CONNECTION

Suppose you are on vacation. You meet someone who is interesting, and you want to write about him or her in a letter to a friend. Describe the person through an event in which the character traits of that person are revealed.

126 ■ Unit 2

Cooperative Group Activity

Pair off students to help them complete the Writing Connection activity. Then have them pretend that they are returning home from vacation on a bus. Soon, they begin talking to the person sitting next to them; each tells the other about "a character" they have met. Encourage students to use direct description—of actions, dialogue, setting—in telling about their character. As you take note of students' dialogues during the activity, you might want to choose several of the more effective conversations for class presentation.

Boy in the Shadows

by Margaret Ronan

Is it true that love is stronger than death? That the human spirit can survive the grave? Perhaps the answer can be found in the strange experience of Irene and Ernest Platt.

The Platts had always lived in cities, but when Ernest retired, they decided they wanted to spend the rest of their lives in the country. They bought a small house tucked away on the lower slopes of the Ozarks.[1] Irene at once planted a vegetable garden. With what she could grow, and a trip once a week to the supermarket in the nearest town, they should have all the food they needed.

Food was the first thing she thought of when she saw the boy. She had been working in the garden when she became aware that someone was watching her. She raised her eyes, and there, standing at the edge of the field, was the boy—a thin, hollow-eyed boy wearing faded jeans and no shoes.

Irene raised her hand and waved, but the boy did not wave back. Perhaps he doesn't have the strength to wave, she thought to herself. He was very thin, and his ribs showed plainly.

The boy stood there a few more minutes. Then, as if he had seen all he wanted to, he turned and slipped away—vanishing among the thicket of trees at the edge of the field.

Two days later he was back. With him was a haggard-looking woman of about 40. When she saw Irene, she came straight up to the fence. The boy lagged slightly behind, head hanging listlessly.

"Are you the lady who bought this place?" the woman asked.

"I'm Mrs. Platt," replied Irene. "What can I do for you?"

"I've come about what we can do for you, Ma'am," replied the woman firmly. "This here's my son, Jayse. He's a good worker and a lot stronger than he looks. He'll work for you, do your garden and your chores, for two dollars a day."

---

thicket (THIK it) bushes or small trees growing close together
haggard (HAG urd) thin and worn from too much worry or pain
listlessly (LIST lis lee) in a tired, inactive way
[1]**Ozarks:** mountains that run through Arkansas and Missouri, Oklahoma, and Illinois

Boy in the Shadows ■ 127

TEACHING PLAN

INTRODUCE

Motivation
On a relief map of the United States, point out to students where the Ozarks are. Discuss what it would be like to move to a rural, mountainous area, such as the Ozarks, after spending one's life in cities (as the Platt couple have in this selection). Elicit ideas on what the people might be like, and how they might differ from "city folks."

Purpose Setting Questions
If someone related a strange incident by referring to the unknown or to supernatural events, what would be your reaction?

READ

Literary Focus: *Characters*
Point out that in the introductory physical description of Jayse, he is a mysterious figure. Contrast the way the Platts were introduced.

Reading Focus: *Make Predictions*
Tell students that as they read they should ask themselves why Jayse behaves as he does, and how his behavior affects the Platts. Have students make predictions about what is wrong with Jayse after reading the first few pages of the story. Have them revise their predictions as the story progresses and as they gather more information.

CLOSE

Have students complete Review the Selection on pages 134–135.

Develop Vocabulary Skills
Many of the footnoted vocabulary words in this selection can be used to describe people. Go over each footnote with students, illustrating the words in sentences; then call the volunteers to give other examples.

ESL Activity
Have students work in pairs. Students should describe a person to their partners (someone both students know, such as a teacher or fellow student), listing their character traits. The partner must try to guess who the person is based upon the description.

Literary Focus:
Character

Why does Jayse not talk? Why does his mother insist on setting the conditions by which he will work and live at the Platts? How are the characters of both Jayse and his mother being developed?

Reading Focus:
Make Predictions

Remind students that every time Mrs. Platt decides to help Jayse, Jayse's mother comes up with a logical excuse for her not to. Ask: Why do you think Jayse's mother does this? Is she forcing Mrs. Platt to confront her about Jayse? The reader can see that Mrs. Platt is growing more and more curious about Jayse. Ask: How will this affect the outcome of the story?

Irene was about to say that she didn't need any help, that she enjoyed doing her own chores. But the sight of Jayse's thin, dangling arms and hollow-cheeked face stopped her.

"He's very young—and he doesn't look strong," she began, but the woman held up a work-scarred hand to stop her.

"He's 16," she said, "but he's small-ish and looks younger. And he's a lot stronger than he looks, like I said. You won't have no cause for complaint. Jayse's a good worker."

"All right," said Irene. Two dollars a day wasn't much, and having Jayse on her own ground would give her a chance to feed him properly. "All right. That will be fine. Jayse can come at ten every morning and go home at five. I'll give him his dinner at noon." She turned to the boy. "Will that be all right with you, Jayse?"

Jayse didn't answer. Irene wondered if he had even heard her, for he kept his head down, never raising his eyes. His mother beckoned Irene to one side and spoke in a low voice. "No, Ma'am. I don't want Jayse traveling back and forth. We live a fair distance from here. He can sleep in that little shed there. And don't you be worrying about feeding him. I'll come every day and bring his food. He's got a finicky stomach. I know just what he can eat and I'll fix it for him. When I come, you can give me his two dollars."

"But what about Jayse?" Irene asked. "If he's working for the money, shouldn't I pay it to him?"

The woman shook her head. "You don't understand. I need that money to feed my other children. Jayse's pa is dead, and now the boy is the only one who can go out to work. He wants to do it to help us out. You won't be sorry you took him on. He's a good worker, is Jayse. He never gets tired, never complains. You'll see."

"Well, all right, but I don't think he should sleep in the shed. I could fix up a room in the house."

"No, Ma'am. Jayse wouldn't care for that. He's a poor sleeper and he wouldn't want to think he might disturb you. The shed will be fine."

So Jayse came to work for the Platts. Irene soon found that the claims his mother had made were true. Jayse never complained and never seemed to get tired. No matter how early Irene and Ernest got up in the morning, the boy was already at work, feeding the chickens, tending the garden. Gradually, Irene let him take over some of the cleaning chores in the house, and once she showed him what she wanted done, she never had to remind him to do it.

"He's a wonder," she told Ernest, "but he's not like a boy at all. He's like . . . like a machine. Do you know he's never said a word to me. He never even looks at me, only at the ground."

Ernest grunted. "All I know is that the kid gives me the creeps. Maybe he can't talk. And if you ask me, he's not all there mentally."

Irene shook her head. "No, he isn't

---

finicky (FIN ik ee) fussy; very hard to please
creeps (KREEPS) feeling of fear or horror

stupid. It's more as though he's walking around in his sleep."

"Well, the price is right," said Ernest. "In fact, it's wrong—two dollars a day is ridiculous for the work he's doing. Let's raise it to four. I'm not crazy about having Jayse around, but let's see if a raise gets some reaction from him."

Why should it? Irene wondered. Jayse never touched the money he earned. Every day, shortly before noon, he would stop what he was doing. Then he would stand, eyes lowered, head turned slightly to one side as though listening. A few minutes later his mother would appear from the wooded thicket, carrying his dinner in a covered tin plate. She would wait until Irene handed her Jayse's daily wages, then lead him to the shed and sit with him while he ate.

"Why won't she let me feed him?" Irene asked furiously. "I've seen the stuff she brings him—it's some kind of mush. That's not decent food for a boy who works as hard as he does. I think he's even thinner than he was when he first came here."

Ernest had to agree. The bones of Jayse's face were more prominent. When the boy bent over the hoe in the garden, his knobby spine was plainly outlined under his thin T-shirt.

Irene decided to try again. "I want to give Jayse a hot meal every day," she told his mother. "Otherwise I can't let him go on working here the way he does. He's getting thinner all the time. I'm afraid he'll get sick."

There was a frightened glitter in the woman's eyes. "You don't understand, Mrs. Platt. Jayse's like his father. He can't eat the food you and I can eat. He can't take salt—his system can't handle it. Please, Ma'am, let things be. Don't say you won't let him stay. He's the only one the kids and I can depend on. Without what he earns here, his brothers and sisters will starve."

Irene gave in. "All right, he can stay. I must admit he's a wonderful worker—but he doesn't seem happy about being with us. He never smiles or laughs. And he's never said a word to either my husband or myself."

The woman shrugged. "It don't mean anything, Ma'am. Jayse's different. He don't feel things the way most kids do. All he cares about is helping me and the other kids. Don't worry about him. He's doing what he wants to do."

But *is* it what he wants? Irene wondered. She stood at her bedroom window later. She could see the shed where Jayse slept—but he wasn't asleep. He was sitting in the doorway, arms resting slackly on his knees, staring unmovingly into the moonlit night.

"Something's wrong," she said aloud.

"What are you talking about?" her husband asked sleepily.

"Jayse. I've been watching him for half an hour. He's never moved so much as a muscle. With the day he's put in, you'd think he'd have gone to sleep

---

prominent (PROM uh nunt) easy to see; standing out
knobby (NOB ee) lumpy
slackly (SLAK lee) loosely

hours ago. But no—he's just sitting there."

Ernest got up and came to stand at her side. "I could have told you that. He always sits there at night. As far as I know, he never sleeps. I'll admit he's one spooky kid—but he's not really bothering anyone, is he?"

No one but me, Irene thought. As the days wore on, the sight of the boy wrung her heart. His skin, which had been pale, was now yellow and shiny. There were discolored patches on his forehead, cheekbones, and along the ridge of his nose. Even more disquieting, his movements seemed to be slower and more labored.

"Aren't you feeling well, Jayse?" she asked. But the boy only ducked his head and brushed past her. Uneasily, she went to her husband. "Look at Jayse. I think he's sick. He's moving around like an old man."

Ernest peered at Jayse, who was slowly cutting grass. "You're right. What are those dark patches on his skin?"

"I don't know, but I'm sure of one thing. He's going under from malnutrition. I don't care what his mother says—I'm going to get some decent food into him. And tomorrow you can drive him into town to see the doctor."

Protein! Irene thought. Jayse needed some high grade protein, and fast. She went into the kitchen and began to prepare a hearty meal of ham and eggs. That, plus plenty of milk and apple pie, should help.

When it was ready she called Jayse and brought him into the kitchen. "Sit down at the table," she told him. "I've made you a special dinner because you've been here three months today. That's cause for celebration."

Jayse took one bite of the food, then another. He chewed the ham slowly, and swallowed. Then he put down his fork and rose from the table.

"What's the matter?" Irene asked anxiously. "Where are you going?"

But he had already gone. The kitchen door closed behind him. Irene ran to the door and flung it open. The boy had already reached the line of trees that bordered the property. He was moving with long, steady strides. She called his name, but he never looked back.

"Leave him alone," said Ernest, who had just come into the kitchen. "He's going home. His mother was probably right. You shouldn't have given him that food."

Irene slept badly that night. She was up before dawn, walking about the garden. As she feared, Jayse had not come back. But shortly before noon, his mother appeared.

She walked straight up to Irene, her mouth fixed in a hard line. "You did it,

---

disquieting (dis KWY ut ing) disturbing; worrisome
labored (LAY burd) not easy; done with effort
malnutrition (mal noo TRISH un) poor health condition caused by not having enough of the right kinds of food
strides (STRYDZ) long steps

Albert's Son, Andrew Wyeth. Nasjonalgalleriet, Oslo

Journey, Morris Graves. Collection of The Whitney Museum of American Art

Literary Focus:
Plot
The plot reaches a climax when Jayse's mother discovers that Mrs. Platt has fed Jayse. Ask: Has Mrs. Platt realized what is happening, or does she still seem ignorant of Jayse's mysterious condition?

Reading Focus:
Make Predictions
Jayse's mother's reaction to finding out that he has eaten ham and eggs seems extreme. Ask: What can you infer from her reaction? What do you think has happened to Jayse?

didn't you? You fed my boy after I told you not to. What did you give him to eat?"

"Ham and eggs," replied Irene. "Good food, the kind he needed."

"Ham. . ." the woman whispered, "so salty. . . ." Then her voice rose to a shriek. "You're a fool, a meddling fool! Why couldn't you leave well enough alone?"

"I'm sorry if my cooking made Jayse sick," Irene retorted angrily, "but he was starving to death in front of me. I couldn't let it go on. My husband and I will pay any medical bills and see that a doctor takes care of him. Now I want you to take me to him or we will have to notify the authorities."

For a moment the woman was silent, then she began to laugh mirthlessly. "Yes, Ma'am. I'll take you to him. You come with me and see what you've done."

She turned and Irene followed her

---

authorities (uh THAWR uh teez) people with official power
mirthlessly (MURTH lis lee) without humor

through the stretch of woods. For half an hour they climbed through the scraggy foothills. Finally they came to a shabby house where three young children sat listlessly on the stoop. But when Irene stopped, the woman took her arm and pulled her on.

"Isn't that your home?" asked Irene. "Isn't Jayse there?"

The woman shook her head and went on. Presently they came to another stand of trees. Beyond lay an open space with grass-covered mounds. Some of the mounds had wooden markers; others had none.

"What is this place?" Irene cried frantically.

"Old graveyard," replied the woman. "Nobody—hardly nobody uses it anymore. Over here, Ma'am." She pointed to one mound. Irene saw with horror that great tufts of grass had been torn from it, and that someone had tried to scoop a hollow in the dry dirt underneath.

Nothing could have made her go close to the mound. But from where she stood she could see what lay in it—a shriveled, withered something dressed in worn jeans and a stained T-shirt.

"There's Jayse," said the woman. "There's where you sent him. He and his pa died two years ago, that bad winter, of pneumonia. I wished them back, but only Jayse came. He knew I needed him, you see. He wanted to take care of me. He was a good boy, always."

"I don't understand," Irene whispered.

But the woman wasn't listening. She talked on, as if to herself. "I had to take special care of him. You can't feed the dead salt, you know. It makes them forget everything but the last place they rested. That's why Jayse had to come here. Now he won't leave it again, ever."

scraggy (SKRAG ee) rough and uneven
tufts (TUFTS) bunches of grass or hair
shriveled (SHRIV uld) dried up
pneumonia (noo MOHN yuh) disease of the lungs

Boy in the Shadows ■ 133

Critical Thinking:
Generalize
Ask students to discuss how the story might apply to broader areas of potential conflict such as well-to-do versus poor, urban versus rural, or rationalism versus belief in the supernatural.

Mini Quiz

Write on the chalkboard or overhead projector the following questions and call on students to fill in the blanks. Discuss the answers with the class.

1. One of the first things Irene Platt did when they moved to the Ozarks was to plant a _____.

2. Jayse was _____ years old.

3. Mrs. Platt paid Jayse _____ a day.

4. Jayse had worked at the Platts for _____ before Mrs. Platt gave him a meal.

5. Some graves in the cemetery by Jayse's family's house were identified with _____.

Answers
1. vegetable garden
2. 16
3. two dollars
4. three months
5. wooden markers

UNDERSTAND THE SELECTION

Answers

1. to the Ozarks
2. "food without salt"
3. ham and eggs, milk and apple pie
4. The Ozarks still contain remote areas, providing a good setting for strange happenings.
5. the Platts' questions about who Jayse is and why he acts so strangely
6. She laughed "mirthlessly," meaning without humor; she was laughing with grief and anger.
7. Jayse, his mother claims, had come back from the dead. The dead can't eat salt, she says, because they forget everything except the last place they rested—which for Jayse was the grave he had been buried in when he died.
8. Sample answer: Yes, he needed to work to help his family.
9. Sample answer: I would like to have Jayse as a friend because it would be an opportunity to learn about the supernatural world.
10. Sample answer: The story of a return from the dead is so hard to believe that it borders on being a folk tale. On the symbolic level, however, belief is not important. On this level the story could be interpreted as symbolizing the family.

Respond to Literature

Students might think that Jayse's mother was evil, but she was also concerned about feeding her other children. Irene Platt appears to be good, but, inadvertently, she caused Jayse's death.

WRITE ABOUT THE SELECTION

Prewriting

Here is an opportunity for a cooperative learning activity that begins outside the class. Have students work in pairs or groups to brainstorm things that are included in epitaphs on tombstones. At this point, have them list only the main points of the epitaph for background for their own writing. Suggest that they avoid, "Here lies . . . " Perhaps a comment about Jayse's youth would make a good opening.

Writing

You could allow students to work in the same pairs or groups to examine how their brainstorming list compares to the epitaph they have written. Did they include all the necessary items? Then students can work individually on their descriptions.

Revising

Remind students that epitaphs should be short and to the point. Suggest that they reread the epitaphs and delete all unnecessary words.

Proofreading

Ask students to proofread each other's work.

UNDERSTAND THE SELECTION

Recall

1. Where did the Platts retire?
2. What kind of food did Jayse's mother insist that Jayse eat?
3. What food did Irene Platt prepare for Jayse?

Infer

4. How does the setting contribute to the story?
5. What is the "complication" to the plot that keeps the story going?
6. Why do you think Jayse's mother began to laugh when Irene Platt asked to be taken to see the sick Jayse?
7. Explain the significance of Jayse eating the salty food.

Apply

8. Would you have hired Jayse if you had been Irene Platt? Explain your answer.
9. Would you have liked to have had Jayse for a friend?
10. What is your opinion of the story? Is it believable literally? Symbolically?

Respond to Literature

Does this story have any evil characters or does each character show both good and evil traits? Explain your answer.

WRITE ABOUT THE SELECTION

Years ago, interesting information about a person and his or her life might be inscribed on a headstone marking his or her grave. This was called an epitaph. It could be written in poetry or prose. Suppose Jayse's mother and the Platts have decided to mark Jayse's grave with a headstone and to inscribe something on it. What should they write?

Prewriting Draw a headstone. Next to the headstone, write a list of what you would like to mention about Jayse. Decide if you will write in poetry or prose. Remember that tombstones are not very big, so you cannot write much.

Writing Use your list to write the inscription. Try several versions of your message and decide which you like the best. Write it on the headstone you have drawn. You must keep your epitaph short and to the point.

Revising If you wrote in verse, would rhyming help improve the inscription? Synonyms can be used to make rhymes. If you wrote in prose, would a simile or metaphor help? They were commonly used in inscriptions on old headstones.

Proofreading Reread what you have written and check to make sure all words are spelled correctly. Your inscription will be chiseled into stone, and there must be no mistakes. Use a dictionary to check any words you are not sure of. Because of limited space, delete all unnecessary words.

THINK ABOUT CHARACTER

Margaret Ronan tells us about Jayse directly by describing traits and indirectly by telling how he acted in situations. Each description adds to the mystery surrounding him.

1. In the third paragraph, how is Jayse described? What is your impression of him?

2. In the fourth and fifth paragraphs, what do we learn about Jayse?

3. What do we learn about Jayse from his mother's introduction?

4. When Jayse arrives for work at the Platts, more description is given. Which impression of Jayse seems correct, Mrs. Platt's initial impression or the one given by Jayse's mother?

5. Action tells us more about Jayse after he eats Mrs. Platt's dinner. Explain.

READING FOCUS

Make Predictions As you read, you were able to use clues to make predictions about what would happen next in the story and what the final outcome would be. What prediction did you make about the outcome of the story? What clues helped you make this prediction?

DEVELOP YOUR VOCABULARY

A good way to learn and to remember vocabulary words is to use flashcards. Write the words below on a card. On the back of the card, write the definition and an original sentence.

Use the cards to exercise your vocabulary skills. If you are working alone, shuffle the cards, choose one, and give the definition. Go through all the cards, putting aside those for which you need more practice.

You can also practice your vocabulary skills by first looking at the definitions and then giving the correct words. If working with a partner, you can use the same methods.

1. listless
2. work-scarred
3. hollow-eyed
4. hollow-cheeked
5. haggard-looking
6. disquieting
7. finicky
8. creepy
9. knobby
10. spooky

DEVELOP YOUR VOCABULARY

Answers

1. listless—tired, inactive; Jayse seemed listless as his mother introduced him.
2. work-scarred—affected by the difficulties of work; Work-scarred hands held high, the women in the textile mill yelled for a pay increase.
3. hollow-eyed—having deep-set eyes or dark areas under the eyes; He got out of bed, hollow-eyed from lack of sleep.
4. hollow-cheeked—having sunken cheeks; The workers were hollow-cheeked after being trapped for seventy-two hours in the tunnel.
5. haggard-looking—looking thin and worn from too much work, worry, or pain; The haggard-looking doctor left the operating room.
6. disquieting—disturbing, worrisome; The most disquieting thing about this case is the lack of witnesses.
7. finicky—fussy, very hard to please; Are you a finicky eater who is hard to please?
8. creepy—creating a feeling of fear or horror; A creepy feeling swept over me when I entered the old house.
9. knobby—lumpy; "Knobby Knees," the townspeople called Smith; but after he won the marathon, he became "Nimble Ned."
10. spooky—frightening; The costume Gertie wore last Halloween wasn't very spooky.

READING FOCUS

Sample Answer

I predicted that Jayse would disappear. The clues were that he never spoke, that he never seemed to sleep, and that he kept looking worse and worse.

THINK ABOUT CHARACTER

Answers

1. He is described directly—thin, hollow-eyed, wearing faded jeans, barefoot. One impression is that he comes from a poor family and is not well fed.

2. He does not seem very friendly. He might be weak from hunger.

3. She says he is hardworking and is stronger than he looks and never complains.

4. The one given by Jayse's mother. He works hard and never complains.

5. He simply gets up and leaves the house. He becomes an even more mysterious character.

ESL Activity

On page 128, paragraph 10, which begins "So Jayse . . . ," is written in the past tense. Have students work in pairs to change the verbs from past tense to present tense.

SELECTION OBJECTIVES

After completing this selection, students will be able to

- understand conflict
- describe a conflict in a story they have already read
- conduct an interview
- understand minor conflicts in stories
- form negative words
- make inferences from conversation

Lesson Resources

Sorry, Wrong Number
- Selection Synopsis, Teacher's Edition, p. T107e
- Comprehension and Vocabulary Workbook, pp. 29–30
- Language Enrichment Workbook, pp. 29–30
- Teacher's Resources Reinforcement, p. R15 Test, pp. T27–T28

More About Conflict

Literature reflects real conflicts in everyday life. They may be the grand conflicts of nations and political leaders, or the personal conflicts of a parent and child. Ask students for real-life examples of different kinds of conflict: between people, within a single person, between people and things, and between people and nature. Write them on the chalkboard or an overhead transparency.

Background Notes

Sorry, Wrong Number was written for radio. Today, radio dramas are a seldom-used genre, but at one time they were a staple of family entertainment. People would gather around a big "wireless" to hear renditions of well-known plays, new plays, and serials. Perhaps the most famous radio adaptation was Orson Welles's production of *War of the Worlds*—the story of a Martian

Learn About

READING FOCUS

Make Inferences From Conversation
Readers can sometimes learn about the characters, plot, and setting of a story through characters' conversations. In a play, almost all of the plot's developments may be revealed through conversation. The play does not give the reader details about the characters or the plot. The reader must make inferences about these elements from the conversation, or dialogue. As you read, pay close attention to the dialogue so that you can see what it reveals about the characters and the plot.

CONFLICT

The plot in literature often focuses on **conflict**, or the meeting of opposing forces. The conflict can be between people, within a single person, between people and things, or between people and nature. A work of literature may contain more than one kind of conflict, but usually only one is the main conflict.

In drama, the conflict can be physical, psychological, or, most often, a combination of the two. Usually, conflict in a play is easier to identify than in fiction because you can see the clash of personalities on stage or infer it from dialogue on the page.

As you read "Sorry, Wrong Number," ask yourself these questions:

1. What conflicts are in the play?
2. What is the main conflict?

WRITING CONNECTION

Think back on the selections you have read in this unit or the previous unit. Describe the main conflict in one of the selections and tell how it is resolved. If there were other lesser conflicts in the same selection, write them down in a sentence or two.

invasion of Earth. So realistic was the broadcast, it drew national headlines the next day. Some of the better known serials were *The Shadow* and *I Love a Mystery*. Television put an end to radio drama. Some shows, such as *The Lone Ranger*, were turned into TV programs.

Cooperative Group Activity

Have students work in groups of three. First, ask them to do the Writing Connection activity by themselves, and then report to their group. Group members should be asked for feedback on each conflict description, as well as its resolution. Encourage students to consult the text, especially if disagreement arises.

Sorry, Wrong Number

ADAPTED

by Lucille Fletcher

CHARACTERS

MRS. STEVENSON	SERGEANT DUFFY
OPERATOR	THIRD OPERATOR
FIRST MAN	WESTERN UNION
SECOND MAN (GEORGE)	INFORMATION
CHIEF OPERATOR	WOMAN
SECOND OPERATOR	

ACT I

(SOUND: *Number being dialed on phone; busy signal.*)

MRS. STEVENSON (*a complaining, self-centered person*): Oh—dear! (*Slams down receiver. Dials* OPERATOR.)

OPERATOR: Your call, please?

MRS. STEVENSON: Operator? I've been dialing Murray Hill 4-0098 now for the last three quarters of an hour, and the line is always busy. But I don't see how it *could* be busy that long. Will you try it for me, please?

OPERATOR: Murray Hill 4-0098? One moment, please.

MRS. STEVENSON: I don't see how it could be busy all this time. It's my husband's office. He's working late tonight, and I'm all alone here in the house. My health is very poor—and I've been feeling so nervous all day—

OPERATOR: Ringing Murray Hill 4-0098.

---

self-centered (SELF SENT urd) selfish; concerned with oneself

Sorry, Wrong Number ■ 137

Reading Focus:
Make Inferences from Conversation

From the stage directions and her telephone dialogues, the reader can make inferences about the kind of person Mrs. Stevenson is. Ask students if her plight is believable; that is, can they think that a person—at home in bed alone and ill—would speak as she does?

Critical Thinking:
Analyze

Have students analyze the conversation between the two men. Who could they be? What could they be planning? What clues lead students to think this?

Enrichment

You could suggest that a student research how crossed telephone connections occur. Why, for example, is a background conversation sometimes heard when you are making a call.

(SOUND: *Phone buzz. It rings three times. Receiver is picked up at other end*)

MAN: Hello.

MRS. STEVENSON: Hello? (*A little puzzled.*) Hello. Is Mr. Stevenson there?

MAN (*into phone, as though he had not heard*): Hello. (*Louder.*) Hello.

SECOND MAN (*slow, heavy voice, faintly foreign accent*): Hello.

FIRST MAN: Hello, George?

GEORGE: Yes, sir.

MRS. STEVENSON (*louder and more commanding, to phone*): Hello. Who's this? What number am I calling, please?

FIRST MAN: We have heard from our client. He says the coast is clear for tonight.

GEORGE: Yes, sir.

FIRST MAN: Where are you now?

GEORGE: In a phone booth.

FIRST MAN: Okay. You know the address. At eleven o'clock the private patrolman goes around to a place on Second Avenue for a break. Be sure that all the lights downstairs are out. There should be only one light visible from the street. At eleven fifteen a subway train crosses the bridge. It makes a noise in case her window is open and she should scream.

MRS. STEVENSON (*shocked*): Oh—*hello!* What number is this, please?

GEORGE: Okay. I understand.

FIRST MAN: Make it quick. As little blood as possible. Our client does not wish to make her suffer long.

GEORGE: A knife okay, sir?

FIRST MAN: Yes. A knife will be okay. And remember—remove the rings and bracelets, and the jewelry in the bureau drawer. Our client wishes it to look like simple robbery.

GEORGE: Okay. I get—
(SOUND: *A soft buzzing signal.*)

MRS. STEVENSON (*clicking phone*): Oh! (*Soft buzzing signal continues. She hangs up.*) How awful! How unspeakably—

(SOUND: *Dialing. Phone buzz.*)

---

client (KLY unt) person who pays for a duty performed
unspeakably (un SPEEK uh blee) horribly; not to be spoken of

OPERATOR: Your call, please?

MRS. STEVENSON (*uptight and breathless, into phone*): Operator, I—I've just been cut off.

OPERATOR: I'm sorry, madam. What number were you calling?

MRS. STEVENSON: Why—it was supposed to be Murray Hill 4-0098, but it wasn't. Some wires must have crossed—I was cut into a wrong number—and—I've just heard the most dreadful thing—a—a murder—and—(*As an order*) Operator, you'll simply have to retrace that call at once.

OPERATOR: I beg your pardon, madam—I don't quite—

MRS. STEVENSON: Oh—I know it was a wrong number, and I had no business listening—but these two men—they were cold-blooded fiends—and they were going to murder somebody—some poor innocent woman—who was all alone—in a house near a bridge. We've got to stop them—we've got to—

OPERATOR (*patiently*): What number were you calling, madam?

MRS. STEVENSON: That doesn't matter. This was a *wrong* number. And *you* dialed it. And we've got to find out what it was—immediately!

OPERATOR: But—madam—

MRS. STEVENSON: Oh, why are you so stupid? Look, it was obviously a case of some little slip of the finger. I told you to try Murray Hill 4-0098 for me—you dialed it—but your finger must have slipped—and I was connected with some other number—and I could hear them, but they couldn't hear me. Now, I simply fail to see why you couldn't make that same mistake again—on purpose—why you couldn't *try* to dial Murray Hill 4-0098 in the same careless sort of way—

OPERATOR (*quickly*): Murray Hill 4-0098? I will try to get it for you, madam.

MRS. STEVENSON: *Thank* you.

(*Sound of ringing; busy signal.*)

OPERATOR: I am sorry. Murray Hill 4-0098 is busy.

MRS. STEVENSON (*madly clicking receiver*): Operator. Operator.

OPERATOR: Yes, madam.

---

cold-blooded fiends (KOHLD blud id FEENDZ) very wicked people without mercy

Literary Focus:
Foreshadowing
Mrs. Stevenson tells the operator that she overheard two men plan a murder. Point out to students the stress revealed in her broken sentences to the operator. Suggest, without revealing the plot, that this conversation she has overheard could be important. Ask if this could be foreshadowing.

MRS. STEVENSON (*angrily*): You *didn't* try to get that wrong number at all. I asked explicitly. And all you did was dial correctly.

OPERATOR: I am sorry. What number were you calling?

MRS. STEVENSON: Can't you, for once, forget what number I was calling, and do something specific? Now I want to trace that call. It's my civic duty—it's *your* civic duty—to trace that call—and to apprehend those dangerous killers—and if *you* won't—

OPERATOR: I will connect you with the Chief Operator.

MRS. STEVENSON: *Please!*

(*Sound of ringing.*)

CHIEF OPERATOR (*a cool pro*): This is the Chief Operator.

MRS. STEVENSON: Chief Operator? I want you to trace a call. A telephone call. Immediately. I don't know where it came from, or who was making it, but it's absolutely necessary that it be tracked down. Because it was about a murder. Yes, a terrible, cold-blooded murder of a poor innocent woman—tonight—at eleven fifteen.

CHIEF OPERATOR: I see.

MRS. STEVENSON (*high-strung, demanding*): Can you trace it for me? Can you track down those men?

CHIEF OPERATOR: It depends, madam.

MRS. STEVENSON: Depends on what?

CHIEF OPERATOR: It depends on whether the call is still going on. If it's a live call, we can trace it on the equipment. If it's been disconnected, we can't.

MRS. STEVENSON: Disconnected?

CHIEF OPERATOR: If the parties have stopped talking to each other.

MRS. STEVENSON: Oh—but—but of course they must have stopped talking to each other by *now*. That was at least five minutes ago—and they didn't sound like the type who would make a long call.

CHIEF OPERATOR: Well, I can try tracing it. Now—what is your name, madam?

---

explicitly (ik SPLIS it lee) very clearly
specific (spuh SIF ik) definite; exact
civic (SIV ik) having to do with good citizenship
apprehend (ap rih HEND) seize; arrest

140 ■ Unit 2

T140

MRS. STEVENSON: Mrs. Stevenson. Mrs. Elbert Stevenson. But—
listen—

CHIEF OPERATOR (*writing it down*): And your telephone number?

MRS. STEVENSON (*more bothered*): Plaza 4-2295. But if you go on
wasting all this time—

CHIEF OPERATOR: And what is your reason for wanting this call
traced?

MRS. STEVENSON: My reason? Well—for heaven's sake—isn't it
obvious? I overheard two men—they're killers—they're planning to murder this woman—it's a matter for the police.

CHIEF OPERATOR: Have you told the police?

MRS. STEVENSON: No. How could I?

CHIEF OPERATOR: You're making this check into a private call purely as a private individual?

MRS. STEVENSON: Yes. But meanwhile—

CHIEF OPERATOR: Well, Mrs. Stevenson—I seriously doubt whether
we could make this check for you at this time just on your
say-so as a private individual. We'd have to have something
more official.

Sorry, Wrong Number ■ 141

Literary Focus:
Conflict

Mrs. Stevenson appears to be getting nowhere with the Chief Operator. Ask: Is this due to a problem
between the two women, or is it
due more to a struggle that Mrs.
Stevenson is having with her own
fear and frustration?

Critical Thinking:
Evaluate

Have students evaluate the Chief
Operator's approach to the problem
as opposed to Mrs. Stevenson's. Is
the operator's behavior a reflection
of her personal character or the
duties of her job?

MRS. STEVENSON: Oh, for heaven's sake! You mean to tell me I can't report a murder without getting tied up in all this red tape? Why, it's perfectly idiotic. All right, then. I *will* call the police. (*She slams down receiver.*) Ridiculous!
(*Sound of dialing.*)

CHIEF OPERATOR: Your call, please?

MRS. STEVENSON (*very annoyed*): The Police Department—*please.*

SECOND OPERATOR: Ringing the police department.
(*Rings twice. Phone is picked up.*)

SERGEANT DUFFY: Police department. Precinct 43. Duffy speaking.

MRS. STEVENSON: Police department? Oh. This is Mrs. Stevenson— Mrs. Elbert Smythe Stevenson of 53 North Sutton Place. I'm calling to report a murder.

DUFFY: Eh?

MRS. STEVENSON: I mean—the murder hasn't been committed yet. I just overheard plans for it over the telephone . . . over a wrong number that the operator gave me. I've been trying to trace down the call myself, but everybody is so stupid— and I guess in the end you're the only people who could *do* anything.

DUFFY (*not too impressed*): Yes, ma'am.

MRS. STEVENSON (*trying to impress him*): It was a perfectly *definite* murder. I heard their plans distinctly. Two men were talking, and they were going to murder some woman at eleven fifteen tonight—she lived in a house near a bridge.

DUFFY: Yes, ma'am.

MRS. STEVENSON: And there was a private patrolman on the street. He was going to go around for a break on Second Avenue. And there was some third man—a client—who was paying to have this poor woman murdered—They were going to take her rings and bracelets—and use a knife—Well, it's unnerved me dreadfully—and I'm not well—

DUFFY: I see. When was all this, ma'am?

Reading Focus:
Make Inferences from Conversation
As Mrs. Stevenson relates the details of the conversation she overheard to the Sergeant, what does she realize about the description of the neighborhood? What can you infer from this?

---

red tape (RED TAYP) needless complications of official rules
precinct (PREE singkt) division of a city for police control
unnerved (un NURVD) took away courage; terrified

MRS. STEVENSON: About eight minutes ago. Oh . . . (relieved) then you *can* do something? You do understand—

DUFFY: And what is your name, ma'am?

MRS. STEVENSON (*losing patience*): Mrs. Stevenson. Mrs. Elbert Stevenson.

DUFFY: And your address?

MRS. STEVENSON: 53 North Sutton Place. *That's* near a bridge, the Queensborough Bridge, you know—and *we* have a private patrolman on our street—and Second Avenue—

DUFFY: And what was that number you were calling?

MRS. STEVENSON: Murray Hill 4-0098. But—that wasn't the number I overheard. I mean Murray Hill 4-0098 is my husband's office. He's working late tonight, and I was trying to reach him to ask him to come home. I'm an invalid, you know—and it's the maid's night off—and I *hate* to be alone—even though he says I'm perfectly safe as long as I have the telephone beside my bed.

DUFFY (*trying to end it*): Well, we'll look into it, Mrs. Stevenson, and see if we can check it with the telephone company.

MRS. STEVENSON (*using more patience*): But the telephone company said they couldn't check the call if the parties had stopped talking. I've already taken care of *that*.

DUFFY: Oh, yes?

MRS. STEVENSON (*getting bossy*): Personally I feel you ought to do something far more immediate and drastic than just check the call. What good does checking the call do, if they've stopped talking? By the time you track it down, they'll already have committed the murder.

DUFFY: Well, we'll take care of it, lady. Don't worry.

MRS. STEVENSON: The whole thing calls for a search—a complete and thorough search of the whole city. I'm very near a bridge, and I'm not far from Second Avenue. And I know *I'd* feel a whole lot better if you sent around a radio car to *this* neighborhood at once.

DUFFY: And what makes you think the murder's going to be committed in your neighborhood, ma'am?

---

invalid (IN vuh lid) sick person
drastic (DRAS tik) forceful; severe

Sorry, Wrong Number ■ 143

Critical Thinking:
Apply
When forced to summarize for Sgt. Duffy what she has overheard, Mrs. Stevenson begins to apply the information to her own situation. Ask: What words show her thought process? How could you use this strategy to try to guess what will happen in a story?

Literary Focus:
Conflict
The overbearing nature of Mrs. Stevenson's character comes across in many ways as the story unfolds. As an example, she asks for a search of "the whole city" which seems unreasonable. Ask: Could her request be a clue to a possible conflict between her husband and herself?

MRS. STEVENSON: Oh, I don't know. The coincidence is so horrible. Second Avenue—the patrolman—the bridge—

DUFFY: Second Avenue is a very long street, ma'am. And do you happen to know how many bridges there are in the city of New York alone? Not to mention Brooklyn, Staten Island, Queens, and the Bronx? And how do you know there isn't some little house out on Staten Island—on some little Second Avenue you've never heard about? How do you know they were even talking about New York at all?

MRS. STEVENSON: But I heard the call on the New York dialing system.

DUFFY: How do you know it wasn't a long-distance call you overheard? Telephones are funny things. Look, lady, why don't you look at it this way? Supposing you hadn't broken in on that telephone call? Supposing you'd got your husband the way you always do? Would this murder have made any difference to you then?

MRS. STEVENSON: I suppose not. But it's so inhuman—so cold-blooded—

DUFFY: A lot of murders are committed in this city every day, ma'am. If we could do something to stop 'em, we would. But a clue of this kind that's so vague isn't much more use to us than no clue at all.

MRS. STEVENSON: But surely—

DUFFY: Unless, of course, you have some reason for thinking this call is phony—and that someone may be planning to murder *you?*

MRS. STEVENSON: *Me?* Oh, no, I hardly think so. I—I mean—why should anybody? I'm alone all day and night—I see nobody except my maid Eloise—she's a big two-hundred-pounder—she's too lazy to bring up my breakfast tray—and the only other person is my husband Elbert—he's crazy about me—adores me—waits on me hand and foot—he's scarcely left my side since I took sick twelve years ago—

DUFFY: Well, then, there's nothing for you to worry about, is there? And now, if you'll just leave the rest of this to us—

---

coincidence (koh IN suh duns) two or more related events accidentally happening at the same time
vague (VAYG) unclear

Reading Focus:
Make Inferences from Conversation

Ask: What clues does the author give about the nature of Mrs. Stevenson's relationship with her husband? Is the realization that she could be the victim of the crime beginning to dawn on her?

MRS. STEVENSON: But what will you *do?* It's so late—it's nearly eleven o'clock.

DUFFY (*firmly*): We'll take care of it, lady.

MRS. STEVENSON: Will you broadcast it all over the city? And send out squads? And warn your radio cars to watch out—especially in suspicious neighborhoods like mine?

DUFFY (*more firmly*): Lady, I *said* we'd take care of it. Just now I've got a couple of other matters here on my desk that require my immediate—

MRS. STEVENSON: Oh! (*She slams down receiver hard.*) Idiot. (*Looking at phone nervously.*) Now, why did I do that? Now he'll think I am a fool. Oh, why doesn't Elbert come home? *Why* doesn't he?

(*Sound of dialing operator.*)

Sorry, Wrong Number ■ 145

Discussion
Is Sgt. Duffy doing his job properly? His comments may be reassuring, but is his callous manner appropriate?

Literary Focus:
Conflict
It seems that Mrs. Stevenson has come into conflict with everyone she has spoken to on the phone. Ask: How might she avoid these conflicts?

OPERATOR: Your call, please?

MRS. STEVENSON: Operator, for heaven's sake, will you ring that Murray Hill 4-0098 number again? I can't think what's keeping him so long.

OPERATOR: Ringing Murray Hill 4-0098. (*Rings. Busy signal.*) The line is busy. Shall I—

MRS. STEVENSON (*nastily*): I can hear it. You don't have to tell me. I know it's busy. (*Slams down receiver.*) If I could only get out of this bed for a little while. If I could get a breath of fresh air—or just lean out the window—and see the street—(*The phone rings. She answers it instantly.*) Hello. Elbert? Hello. Hello. Hello. Oh, what's the *matter* with this phone? *Hello? Hello?* (*Slams down receiver. The phone rings again, once. She picks it up.*) Hello? Hello— Oh, for heaven's sake, who is this? Hello, Hello, *Hello.* (*Slams down receiver. Dials operator.*)

THIRD OPERATOR: Your call, please?

MRS. STEVENSON (*very annoyed and commanding*): Hello, operator. I don't know what's the matter with this telephone tonight, but it's positively driving me crazy. I've never seen such inefficient, miserable service. Now, look. I'm an invalid, and I'm very nervous, and I'm *not* supposed to be annoyed. But if this keeps on much longer—

THIRD OPERATOR (*a young, sweet type*): What seems to be the trouble, madam?

MRS. STEVENSON: Well, everything's wrong. The whole world could be murdered, for all you people care. And now, my phone keeps ringing—

OPERATOR: Yes, madam?

MRS. STEVENSON: Ringing and ringing and ringing every five seconds or so, and when I pick it up, there's no one there.

OPERATOR: I am sorry, madam. If you will hang up, I will test it for you.

MRS. STEVENSON: I don't want you to test it for me. I want you to put through that call—whatever it is—at once.

OPERATOR (*gently*): I am afraid that is not possible, madam.

---

inefficient (in ih FISH unt) wasteful of time or energy; poorly run

MRS. STEVENSON (*storming*): Not possible? And why may I ask?

OPERATOR: The system is automatic, madam. If someone is trying to dial your number, there is no way to check whether the call is coming through the system or not—unless the person who is trying to reach you complains to the particular operator—

MRS. STEVENSON: Well, of all the stupid, complicated—! And meanwhile *I've* got to sit here in my bed, *suffering* every time that phone rings, imagining everything—

OPERATOR: I will try to check it for you, madam.

MRS. STEVENSON: Check it! Check it! That's all anybody can do. Of all the stupid, idiotic . . . ! (*She hangs up.*) Oh—what's the use . . . (*Instantly* MRS. STEVENSON's *phone rings again. She picks up the receiver. Wildly.*) Hello. HELLO. Stop ringing, do you hear me? Answer me? What do you want? Do you realize you're driving me crazy? Stark, staring—

MAN (*dull, flat voice*): Hello. Is this Plaza 4-2295?

MRS. STEVENSON (*catching her breath*): Yes. Yes. This is Plaza 4-2295.

MAN: This is Western Union. I have a telegram here for Mrs. Elbert Stevenson. Is there anyone there to receive the message?

MRS. STEVENSON (*trying to calm herself*): I am Mrs. Stevenson.

WESTERN UNION (*reading flatly*): The telegram is as follows: "Mrs. Elbert Stevenson. 53 North Sutton Place, New York, New York. Darling. Terribly sorry. Tried to get you for last hour, but line busy. Leaving for Boston 11 P.M. tonight on urgent business. Back tomorrow afternoon. Keep happy. Love. Signed. Elbert."

MRS. STEVENSON (*shocked, to herself*): Oh—no—

WESTERN UNION: That is all, madam. Do you wish us to deliver a copy of the message?

MRS. STEVENSON: No—no, thank you.

WESTERN UNION: Thank you, madam. Good night. (*He hangs up phone.*)

MRS. STEVENSON (*Softly, to phone*): Good night. (*She hangs up slowly, suddenly bursting into tears.*) No—no—it isn't true! He couldn't do it. Not when he knows I'll be all alone. It's some trick—some fiendish—(*She dials operator.*)

---

stark (STAHRK) absolutely; totally
fiendish (FEEN dish) savagely cruel

Sorry, Wrong Number ■ 147

Literary Focus:
Plot
The story continues to build toward a climax. Ask students if the realization that Mr. Stevenson himself will not be coming home is further indication that Mrs. Stevenson is in danger.

OPERATOR (*coolly*): Your call, please?

MRS. STEVENSON: Operator—try that Murray Hill 4-0098 number for me just once more, please.

OPERATOR: Ringing Murray Hill 4-0098. (*Call goes through. We hear ringing at other end. Ring after ring.*)

MRS. STEVENSON: He's gone. Oh, Elbert, how could you? How could you—? (*She hangs up phone, sobbing with pity to herself, turning nervously.*) But I can't be alone tonight. I can't. If I'm alone one more second—I don't care what he says—or what the expense is—I'm a sick woman—I'm entitled—(*She dials Information.*)

INFORMATION: This is Information.

MRS. STEVENSON: I want the telephone number of Henchley Hospital.

INFORMATION: Henchley Hospital? Do you have the address, madam?

MRS. STEVENSON: No. It's somewhere in the seventies, though. It's a very small, private, and exclusive hospital where I had my appendix out two years ago. Henchley. H-E-N-C—

INFORMATION: One moment, please.

MRS. STEVENSON: Please—hurry. And please—what *is* the time?

INFORMATION: I do not know, madam. You may find out the time by dialing Meridian 7-1212.

MRS. STEVENSON (*angered*): Oh, for heaven's sake! Couldn't you—?

INFORMATION: The number of Henchley Hospital is Butterfield 7-0105, madam.

MRS. STEVENSON: Butterfield 7-0105. (*She hangs up before she finishes speaking, and immediately dials number.*)
(*Phone rings.*)

WOMAN (*middle-aged, solid, firm, practical*): Henchley Hospital, good evening.

MRS. STEVENSON: Nurses' Registry.

WOMAN: Who was it you wished to speak to, please?

MRS. STEVENSON (*bossy*): I want the Nurses' Registry at once. I want a trained nurse. I want to hire her immediately. For the night.

---

entitled (en TYT uld) have as a claim or right; empowered
exclusive (ik SKLOO siv) private and expensive
registry (REJ is tree) department where registers, or lists, are kept

148 ■ Unit 2

WOMAN: I see. And what is the nature of the case, madam?

MRS. STEVENSON: Nerves. I'm very nervous. I need soothing—and companionship. My husband is away—and I'm—

WOMAN: Have you been recommended to us by any doctor in particular, madam?

MRS. STEVENSON: No. But I really don't see why all this catechizing is necessary. I want a trained nurse. I was a patient in your hospital two years ago. And after all, I *do* expect to *pay* this person—

WOMAN: We quite understand that, madam. But registered nurses are very scarce just now—and our superintendent has asked us to send people out only on cases where the physician in charge feels it is absolutely necessary.

MRS. STEVENSON (*growing very upset*): Well, it *is* absolutely necessary. I'm a sick woman. I—I'm very upset. Very. I'm alone in this house—and I'm an invalid—and tonight I overheard a telephone conversation that upset me dreadfully. About a murder—a poor woman who was going to be murdered at eleven fifteen tonight—in fact, if someone doesn't come at once—I'm afraid I'll go out of my mind—(*Almost off handle by now.*)

WOMAN (*calmly*): I see. Well, I'll speak to Miss Phillips as soon as she comes in. And what is your name, madam?

MRS. STEVENSON: Miss Phillips. And when do you expect her in?

WOMAN: I really don't know, madam. She went out to supper at eleven o'clock.

MRS. STEVENSON: Eleven o'clock. But it's not eleven yet. (*She cries out.*) Oh, my clock has stopped. I thought it was running down. What time is it?

WOMAN: Just fourteen minutes past eleven.
(*Sound of phone receiver being lifted on same line as* MRS. STEVENSON'S. *A click.*)

MRS. STEVENSON (*crying out*): What's *that*?

WOMAN: What was what, madam?

MRS. STEVENSON: That—that click just now—in my own telephone? As though someone had lifted the receiver off the hook of the extension phone downstairs—

---

catechizing (KAT uh kyz ing) asking many questions

Sorry, Wrong Number ■ 149

Critical Thinking:
Apply
Is hiring a private nurse a reasonable solution to Mrs. Stevenson's problem? Ask students what they would do in her situation.

Literary Focus:
Plot
The action rises quickly at the climactic moment—Mrs. Stevenson calls the hospital. Ask: What will happen now? Will all the previous clues be realized?

Literary Focus:
Plot

What a cool criminal George is! He even has the presence of mind to make up an excuse to the police department about the telephone call. Ask: What do you think the police will do next? Are you left believing that Mr. Stevenson was responsible for the crime?

WOMAN: I didn't hear it, madam. Now—about this—

MRS. STEVENSON (*scared*): But *I* did. There's someone in this house. Someone downstairs in the kitchen. And they're listening to me now. They're—(*Hangs up phone. In a hushed voice.*) I won't pick it up. I won't let them hear me. I'll be quiet—and they'll think—(*with growing terror*) But if I don't call someone now—while they're still down there—there'll be no time. (*She picks up receiver. Soft buzzing signal. She dials operator. Ring twice*)

OPERATOR (*a slow, lazy voice*): Your call, please?

MRS. STEVENSON (*a desperate whisper*): Operator, I—I'm in desperate trouble—I—

OPERATOR: I cannot hear you, madam. Please speak louder.

MRS. STEVENSON (*Still whispering*): I don't dare. I—there's someone listening. Can you hear me now?

OPERATOR: Your call, please? What number are you calling, madam?

MRS. STEVENSON (*desperately*): You've got to hear me. Oh, please. You've got to help me. There's someone in this house. Someone who's going to murder me. And you've got to get in touch with the—(*Click of receiver being put down in* MRS. STEVENSON'S *home. Bursting out wildly.*) Oh, there it is—he's put it down—he's put down the extension—he's coming—(*She screams.*) He's coming up the stairs—(*Wildly.*) Give me the police department—(*Screaming.*) The police!

OPERATOR: Ringing the police department.

(*Phone is rung. We hear sound of a subway train coming nearer. On second ring,* MRS. STEVENSON *screams again, but roaring of train drowns out her voice. For a few seconds we hear nothing but roaring of train, then dying away, phone at police headquarters ringing.*)

DUFFY: Police department. Precinct 43. Duffy speaking. (*Pause.*) Police department. Duffy speaking.

GEORGE: Sorry. Wrong number. (*Hangs up.*)

Mini Quiz

Write on the chalkboard or overhead projector the following questions and call on students to fill in the blanks. Discuss the answers with the class.

1. George is to make things look like a _____ took place.

2. Mrs. Stevenson thought she overheard the men's call because the operator _____.

3. When she insists on tracing the calls, the operator connects Mrs. Stevenson with _____.

4. The man who answers at the police department is _____.

5. The one call Mrs. Stevenson does receive when she is alone is from _____.

Answers
1. robbery
2. misdialed the number
3. the chief operator
4. Sgt. Duffy
5. a Western Union operator

AUTHOR BIOGRAPHY
Lucille Fletcher (1912–   )

If you look in the mystery section of your local library, you are bound to find at least one book by Lucille Fletcher. Noted as a writer of plays, screenplays, and novels, Fletcher is most famous for her suspense classic, "Sorry, Wrong Number." This work was originally written as a radio play, then later adapted as a novel, TV play, and motion picture.

Born in Brooklyn, New York, Lucille Fletcher attended the public schools there, then later received her bachelor of arts degree from Vassar College in Poughkeepsie. She is married to the novelist Douglass Wallop, who is best known for his book, *The Year the Yankees Lost the Pennant*. Speaking of her life at the time her two daughters were growing up, Ms. Fletcher referred to her writing as a "hobby"—then admitted that "the major part of my life is spent in housekeeping and cooking meals."

MORE ABOUT THE AUTHOR

Lucille Fletcher is a mystery writer, but solving the mystery is not the main emphasis of her works. She is more concerned with the mystery and fear that the main character experiences. She is also a master at giving the story an unexpected twist.

Additional Works
BY LUCILLE FLETCHER

You may wish to suggest these works by Lucille Fletcher for additional reading:

Eighty Dollars to Stamford. Novel

Night Watch, 1972. Drama

The Hitch-Hiker, 1952. Drama

UNDERSTAND THE SELECTION

Answers

1. Her husband is working late at his office.

2. The operator's finger "slipped" when she dialed her husband's office number, and she was connected with another number.

3. The operator says she can not do a trace at the request of a private individual—"we'd have to have something more official."

4. The operator has a social responsibility to try to prevent someone from being harmed.

5. because she overheard the two men saying that the murder would take place at 11:15 P.M.

6. He reminds her that the location the men described could have been any one of a number of places in and even beyond New York. He points out that if her phone call had gone through, she would not have overheard anything, and what difference would the murder have made to her then?

7. First, Mr. Stevenson's message that he will not be home is a signal to us of her increasing vulnerability. Second, once we realize who is to be murdered, we begin to think that Mr. Stevenson is the "client" who has ordered the murder.

8. Answers will vary. Sample: Precinct stations in New York receive many frantic calls every night, and not all can be taken seriously. On the other hand, his rationale for Mrs. Stevenson's not worrying about the murder because it apparently does not involve her is a good example of look-the-other-way cynicism.

9. Answers will vary. Sample: One advantage is that noise, such as dial tones, ringings, and subway train rumbles, heighten the tension of the story. A disadvantage could be that we can not see Mrs. Stevenson's reactions.

10. Answers will vary. Sample: It's uncomfortable to overhear a private conversation because you may hear things, especially about yourself, that you don't want to hear.

UNDERSTAND THE SELECTION

Recall

1. Why is Mrs. Stevenson home alone?

2. How did she get the wrong number?

3. Why is the chief operator unwilling to trace the call?

Infer

4. Why is it the operator's "civic duty" to trace the wrong-number call?

5. Why is Mrs. Stevenson so concerned about the time?

6. How does the policeman try to reassure Mrs. Stevenson?

7. What complications are added to the plot by the telegram?

Apply

8. Do you think Sgt. Duffy handled Mrs. Stevenson's call responsibly?

9. What are the advantages and disadvantages to hearing this on the radio rather than seeing it on stage?

10. Have you ever overheard a private conversation? What was it like to be an eavesdropper?

Respond to Literature

How would you feel if your only way of communicating with the outside world was by telephone?

WRITE ABOUT THE SELECTION

Newspapers almost always report murders. Sometimes the report is long, sometimes short. However, a good reporter will try to learn from everyone who might know something about what happened.

Think of yourself as a reporter. Mrs. Stevenson is murdered, and you must write a story about the murder. You learn that a Sgt. Duffy took a call from Mrs. Stevenson shortly before the killing. You talk with him, and his information forms the basis of your story.

Prewriting Look at a newspaper story reporting a crime. Notice how it is constructed with the important facts first. Make an informal outline of your story about Mrs. Stevenson's murder.

Writing Use your informal outline to write the news story. Make sure you include comments from Sgt. Duffy.

Revising Is your story written in the third person? Is it objective? Make sure that your own opinion is not in the story. Rely instead on the people you interviewed to develop the theme of your story.

Proofreading Reread what you have written and check for errors. If you have quoted Sgt. Duffy, make sure punctuation and capitalization for the quotations are correct. Also be sure that all your sentences end with periods, quotation marks or exclamation marks. Check interior punctuation as well.

Respond to Literature

Students may cite examples of adults who are home-bound because of illness or disability. Ask them to put themselves in the place of these people and describe how they think they would feel.

WRITE ABOUT THE SELECTION

Prewriting

Obtain a newspaper story about a murder. Make an overhead transparency of it, or make photocopies for students. Have students work cooperatively in groups outlining it; then ask one group to present to the class its outline.

Writing

Circulate as students work individually. Suggest that direct quotations from officials or witnesses add credibility to a story.

THINK ABOUT CONFLICT

Conflict results from opposing forces—interpersonal, environmental, social, or internal—that drive the plot in many kinds of literature. *Sorry, Wrong Number* contains a number of examples of conflict.

1. What is the main conflict of the story? Who is the conflict between?

2. Conflicts can also be implied, rather than directly stated or described. Do you think there is an implied conflict between Mr. and Mrs. Stevenson?

3. What are some examples of conflict between people in this drama?

4. Is there an example of conflict between people and nature?

5. The final conflict in this story acts as the resolution of the plot. It is the main force behind the story. What is this conflict?

READING FOCUS

Make Inferences From Conversation As you read, you learned a great deal about Mrs. Stevenson from her conversations on the phone. What inference did you make about her relationship with her husband? What things about her conversations led you to make this inference?

DEVELOP YOUR VOCABULARY

Some words are formed by adding prefixes that reverse the meaning. Some common negative prefixes are: *un-, in-, im-, dis-, non-*.

Find one word in the sentence that you can make into a negative word. Then use the new negative word in a sentence.

1. Thank you for your efficient service.

2. I appreciate your courteous behavior.

3. "It's possible," she said, "that I made a mistake."

4. The plane became visible as it emerged from the clouds.

5. He was wise to bring an umbrella on such a cloudy day.

6. I'm glad I can count on you to be reliable.

7. I need someone to give me attention.

Review the Selection ■ 153

SELECTION OBJECTIVES

After completing this selection, students will be able to

- understand plot
- outline the plot of a personal story
- discuss imaginary characters
- create a postscript to the story
- understand the role of rising action in a plot
- infer meaning from a verb that describes a direct response
- analyze characters' responses

Lesson Resources

Thus I Refute Beelzy
- Selection Synopsis, Teacher's Edition, p. T107f
- Comprehension and Vocabulary Workbook, pp. 31–32
- Language Enrichment Workbook, pp. 31–32
- Teacher's Resources Reinforcement, p. R16 Test, pp. T29–T30

More About Plot

Write on the chalkboard or overhead projector the words: *exposition*, *complication*, *crisis*, *climax*, and *resolution*. Using a story the class has read recently, outline the plot according to these five major developments

More About the Unit Theme

In this selection a child comes in touch with the unknown and accepts it. His father, on the other hand, refutes it.

Background Notes

"Thus I Refute Beelzy" was written by a British author. There are British word usages, such as "chap" for "friend," and the names "Big Simon" and "Small Simon." The similar names are supposed to show a bond between father and son, yet they seem to live in different worlds.

The Sphinx and the Milky Way, Charles Burchfield. Munson-Williams-Proctor Institute Museum of Art

READING FOCUS

Analyze Characters' Responses In order to understand the characters in a story, use the information the author gives you plus your own experience. Avoid making guesses about characters that are not supported by details.

Learn About

PLOT

The events in a short story are called the plot. A story's **plot** is its skeleton—the framework that holds it together. It consists of exposition, complication, rising action, climax, and usually resolution. Try to think of a plot as a series of problems that the main character has to overcome. For instance, at the beginning of "The Love Letter" (Unit 1), Jake Belknap has a big decision to make: Should he or should he not try to contact Helen Elizabeth Worley?

Here are two other plot questions Jake confronts in "The Love Letter."
1. How can Jake contact her and how can Helen reply?
2. What are the implications of these letters in the lives of Helen and Jake?

As you read "Thus I Refute Beelzy," think about these questions:
1. What are the plot questions?
2. How do they correspond to the stages of the plot?

WRITING CONNECTION

Review a favorite story you have read in this book. List the plot questions. Which question leads to the climax?

154 ■ Unit 2

Viewing Fine Art

Charles Burchfield (1893–1967) was an American painter who was part mystic and part realist. Though his pictures often depict particularly American places, he made them into visions that were mysterious and moody and filled with symbols and portents. In this painting, he presents an image of a summer night, in which the stars, moths, small insects, and giant flowers seem to revel in the moonlight. Ask students to give their quick overall impression of the picture, then to search for and describe details that support their impressions.

Cooperative Group Activity

Have students work in pairs to complete the Writing Connection activity. Some students may find it helpful to draw a "road map" of their story first and then identify the plot questions. Have one student read the questions and the other student read the corresponding answers.

THUS I REFUTE BEELZY

ADAPTED

by John Collier

"There goes the tea bell," said Mrs. Carter. "I hope Simon hears it."

They looked out from the window of the drawing room. The long yard, agreeably neglected, ended in a waste plot. Here a little summer house was passing close by beauty on its way to complete decay. This was Simon's retreat: it was almost completely screened by the tangled branches of the apple tree and the pear tree, planted too close together, as they always are in suburban yards. They caught a glimpse of him now and then, as he strutted up and down, mouthing and gesticulating, performing all the solemn mumbo jumbo of small boys who spend long afternoons at the forgotten ends of long gardens.

"There he is, bless him," said Betty.

"Playing his game," said Mrs. Carter. "He won't play with the other children any more. And if I go down there—the temper! He comes in tired out."

"He doesn't have his sleep in the afternoons?" asked Betty.

"You know what Big Simon's ideas are," said Mrs. Carter. "'Let him choose for himself,' he says. That's what he chooses, and he comes in as white as a sheet."

"Look. He's heard the bell," said Betty. The expression was justified, though the bell had ceased ringing a full minute ago. Small Simon stopped in his parade exactly as if its tinny ring had at that moment reached his ear. They watched him perform certain ritual sweeps and scratchings with his little stick, and come lagging over the hot and flaggy grass toward the house.

Mrs. Carter led the way down to the playroom or garden room, which was

---

gesticulating (jes TIK yoo layt ing) making motions, as in attracting attention or speaking
ritual (RICH oo ul) a set pattern

Thus I Refute Beelzy ■ 155

Literary Focus:
Setting

Ask students to try to form a mental picture of the playroom, complete with the Van Gogh reproduction over the mantel.

Critical Thinking:
Analyze

What are students' initial impressions of Mr. Carter? Does he seem cold, aloof, silly, condescending? Ask them to point to specific details to explain their impressions.

also the tearoom for hot days. It had been the huge scullery of this tall Georgian house. Now the walls were cream-washed, there was coarse blue net in the windows, canvas-covered armchairs on the stone floor, and a reproduction of Van Gogh's "Sunflowers" over the mantelpiece.

Small Simon came drifting in, and gave Betty a routine greeting. His face was an almost perfect triangle, pointed at the chin, and he was paler than he should have been. "The little elf child!" cried Betty.

Simon looked at her. "No," said he.

At that moment the door opened, and Mr. Carter came in, rubbing his hands. He was a dentist, and washed them before and after everything he did. "You!" said his wife. "Home already!"

"Not unwelcome, I hope," said Mr. Carter, nodding to Betty. "Two people cancelled their appointments: I decided to come home. I said, I hope I am not unwelcome."

"Silly!" said his wife. "Of course not."

"Small Simon seems doubtful," continued Mr. Carter. "Small Simon, are you sorry to see me at tea with you?"

"No, Daddy."

"No what?"

"No, Big Simon."

"That's right. Big Simon and Small Simon. That sounds more like friends, doesn't it? At one time little boys had to call their father 'sir.' If they forgot—a good spanking. On the bottom, Small Simon! On the bottom!" said Mr. Carter,

washing his hands once more with his invisible soap and water.

The little boy turned crimson with shame or rage.

"But now, you see," said Betty, to help, "you can call your father whatever you like."

"And what," asked Mr. Carter, "has Small Simon been doing this afternoon, while Big Simon has been at work?"

"Nothing," muttered his son.

"Then you have been bored," said Mr. Carter. "Learn from experience, Small Simon. Tomorrow, do something amusing, and you will not be bored. I want him to learn from experience, Betty. That is my way, the new way."

"I have learned," said the boy, speaking like an old tired man, as little boys so often do.

"It would hardly seem so," said Mr. Carter. "If you sit on your behind all the afternoon, doing nothing. Had *my* father caught me doing nothing, I would not have sat very comfortably."

"He played," said Mrs. Carter.

"A bit," said the boy, shifting on his chair.

"Too much," said Mrs. Carter. "He comes in all nervy and dazed. He ought to have his rest."

"He is six," said her husband. "He is a reasonable being. He must choose for himself. But what game is this, Small Simon, that is worth getting nervy and dazed over? There are very few games as good as all that."

"It's nothing," said the boy.

---

scullery (SKUL er ee) a room for cleaning and storing dishes and pots

156 ■ Unit 2

Allegory, Ben Shahn. Collection of the Modern Art Museum of Fort Worth. Estate of Ben Shahn/Licensed by VAGA, New York, NY

"Oh, come," said his father. "We are friends, are we not? You can tell me. I was a Small Simon once, just like you, and played the same games you play. Of course there were no airplanes in those days. With whom do you play this fine game? Come on, we must all answer civil questions, or the world would never go round. With whom do you play?"

"Mr. Beelzy," said the boy, unable to resist.

"Mr. Beelzy?" said his father, raising his eyebrows inquiringly at his wife.

"It's a game he makes up," said she.

"Not makes up," cried the boy. "Fool!"

"That is telling stories," said his mother. "And rude as well. We had better talk of something different."

"No wonder he is rude," said Mr. Carter. "If you say he tells lies, and then insist on changing the subject. He tells you his fantasy: you create a guilt feeling. What can you expect? A defense mechanism. Then you get a real lie."

---

civil (SIV ul) here, polite
fantasy (FAN tuh see) something imagined
mechanism (MEK uh niz um) a system whose parts work together like a machine.
   Here, a psychological system of defense

Thus I Refute Beelzy ■ 157

Reading Focus:
*Analyze Characters'
Responses*

Ask: Does Small Simon really believe that Mr. Beelzy exists, or is he just rebelling against his father? What details support your response?

Discussion

"He loves me," says Small Simon of Mr. Beelzy. Is Small Simon perhaps suggesting that his family does not love him?

Critical Thinking:
Evaluate

When Mr. Carter tries to explain Mr. Beelzy as a childish fantasy, his reasoning seems to be impeccable. Yet he seems so distant from his son, so cold and condescending. Ask: Is this an appropriate way for a father to talk to a 6-year-old son?

"Like in *These Three*," said Betty. "Only different, of course. *She* was an unblushing little liar."

"I would have made her blush," said Mr. Carter, "in the proper part of her anatomy. But Small Simon is in the fantasy stage. Are you not, Small Simon? You must make things up."

"No I don't," said the boy.

"You do," said his father. "And because you do, it is not too late to reason with you. There is no harm in a fantasy, old chap. There is no harm in a bit of make-believe. Only you have to know the difference between daydreams and real things, or your brain will never grow. It will never be the brain of a Big Simon. So come on. Let us hear about this Mr. Beelzy of yours. Come on. What is he like?"

"He isn't like any thing," said the boy.

"Like nothing on earth," said his father. "That's a terrible fellow."

"I'm not frightened of him," said the child, smiling. "Not a bit."

"I should hope not," said his father. "If you were, you would be frightening yourself. I am always telling people, older people than you are, that they are just frightening themselves. Is he a funny man? Is he a giant?"

"Sometimes he is," said the little boy.

"Sometimes one thing, sometimes another," said his father. "Sounds pretty vague. Why can't you tell us just what he's like?"

"I love him," said the small boy. "He loves me."

"That's a big word," said Mr. Carter. "That might be better kept for real things, like Big Simon and Small Simon."

"He is real," said the boy, passionately. "He's not a fool. He's real."

"Listen," said his father. "When you go down to the yard there's nobody there. Is there?"

"No," said the boy.

"Then you think of him inside your head, and he comes."

"No," said Small Simon. "I have to do something with my stick."

"That doesn't matter."

"Yes, it does."

"Small Simon, you are being obstinate," said Mr. Carter. "I am trying to explain something to you. I have been longer in the world than you have, so naturally I am older and wiser. I am explaining that Mr. Beelzy is a fantasy of yours. Do you hear? Do you understand?"

"Yes, Daddy."

"He is a game. He is a 'let's-pretend.'"

The little boy looked down at his plate, smiling resignedly.

"I hope you are listening to me," said his father. "All you have to do is say, 'I have been playing a game of let's-pretend. With someone I make up, called Mr. Beelzy.' Then no one will say you tell lies, and you will know the difference between dreams and reality. Mr. Beelzy is a daydream."

The little boy still stared at his plate.

"He is sometimes there and sometimes not there," pursued Mr. Carter.

anatomy (uh NAT uh mee) here, body

"Sometimes he's like one thing, sometimes another. You can't really see him. Not as you see me. I am real. You can't touch him. You can touch me. I can touch you." Mr. Carter stretched out his big, white, dentist's hand, and took his little son by the shoulder. He stopped speaking for a moment and tightened his hand. The little boy sank his head still lower.

"Now you know the difference," said Mr. Carter, "between a pretend and a real thing. You and I are one thing; he is another. Which is the pretend? Come on. Answer me. Which is the pretend?"

"Big Simon and Small Simon," said the little boy.

"Don't!" cried Betty, and at once put her hand over her mouth, for why should a visitor cry "don't" when a father is explaining things in a scientific and modern way?

"Well, my boy," said Mr. Carter, "I have said you must be allowed to learn from experience. Go upstairs. Right up to your room. You shall learn whether it is better to reason, or to be perverse and obstinate. Go up. I shall follow you."

"You are not going to beat the child?" cried Mrs. Carter.

"No," said the little boy. "Mr. Beelzy won't let him."

"Go on up with you," shouted his father.

Small Simon stopped at the door. "He said he wouldn't let anyone hurt me," he whimpered. "He said he'd come like a lion, with wings on, and eat them up."

"You'll learn how real he is," shouted his father at him. "If you can't learn it at one end, you shall learn it at the other. I'll have your breeches down. I shall finish my cup of tea first, however," said he to the two women.

Neither of them spoke. Mr. Carter finished his tea, and unhurriedly left the room, washing his hands with his invisible soap and water.

Mrs. Carter said nothing. Betty could think of nothing to say. She wanted to be talking: she was afraid of what they might hear.

Suddenly it came. It seemed to tear the air apart. "Good God!" she cried. "What was that? He's hurt him." She sprang out of her chair, her silly eyes flashing behind her glasses. "I'm going up there," she cried, trembling.

"Yes, let us go up," said Mrs. Carter. "Let us go up. That was not Small Simon."

It was on the second-floor landing that they found the shoe, with the man's foot still in it, like that morsel of a mouse which sometimes falls unnoticed from the side of the jaws of the cat.

---

perverse (pur VURS) wrong, improper
obstinate (OB stuh nut) stubborn
morsel (MAWR sul) small piece

Thus I Refute Beelzy ■ 159

Mini Quiz

Write on the chalkboard or overhead projector the following questions and call on students to fill in the blanks. Discuss the answers with the class.

1. Small Simon's retreat was hidden by the tangled branches of a _____ tree and an _____ tree.

2. The playroom or garden room doubled as a _____ in hot weather.

3. Mr. Carter works as a _____.

4. At first, Mr. Carter thinks Small Simon has been _____ all day.

5. Small Simon calls Mr. Beelzy with a _____.

Answers
1. pear, apple
2. tearoom
3. dentist
4. bored
5. stick

UNDERSTAND THE SELECTION

Answers

1. in a little summer house at the end of the Carters' long yard
2. He is a dentist and must have clean hands.
3. He wants him to learn by experience that it is better to reason then to be stubborn and to insist on something that can not be true.
4. It gives background and sets the stage for the story.
5. No; in the beginning of the story Mrs. Carter expresses worry that Simon chooses to play alone, and that he seems scared and tired—"white as a sheet"—after he has been playing at his retreat.
6. His father wants to know more about what he is doing at the retreat.
7. His father thinks Simon is making things up and is in a fantasy stage, while Simon insists his game is real.
8. Sample answer: No; families should talk about rules together so that everyone understands what the rules are.
9. Sample answer: The crisis must come to a climax, but physical violence is not the only resolution possible.
10. Answers will very. Sample: I wish the story continued in order to provide a clearer resolution.

Respond to Literature

Students should see the roles that imagination and belief play in our lives. Many young children have imaginary friends, but Small Simon seemed to take his belief in Mr. Beelzy to the extreme.

WRITE ABOUT THE SELECTION

Prewriting

Draw on the chalkboard or overhead projector a plot development map with the points "exposition," "complication," "crisis," "climax," and "final resolution." Connect each point with a line to indicate flow.

UNDERSTAND THE SELECTION

Recall

1. Where did Simon play?

2. Why is Mr. Carter always washing his hands?

3. What does Mr. Carter hope to accomplish by punishing Simon?

Infer

4. What do you think is the purpose of all the description in the beginning?

5. Do you think Mrs. Carter agrees with her husband's idea of letting Simon "choose for himself"? Explain.

6. What complicates the plot question: What is Simon doing at his retreat?

7. What is the main conflict?

Apply

8. Mrs. Carter seems to allow her husband to determine what Simon can and cannot do. Do you think that is good?

9. Assume that you are Mr. Carter. Would you treat Simon the way he does?

10. Do you like the way the story ends? Would you have ended it differently?

> ### Respond to Literature
> Explain why Simon's invention of Mr. Beelzy is unusual.

WRITE ABOUT THE SELECTION

What do you think happened on the second floor when Mr. Carter went to punish Simon? Do you think Mr. Beelzy actually existed and devoured Mr. Carter, or do you think there is a more rational explanation?

Write a postscript to the story, describing what happened. Think of the postscript as continuing the resolution of the story and as being like a short story itself.

Then consider the plot question: What has happened to Mr. Carter? You might want to start with some exposition, perhaps just a sentence or two describing the second floor of the house. Next, begin your answer to the plot question. Present a brief complication that is followed quickly by crisis, climax, and a final resolution.

Prewriting Map your short, short story. Show all the plot development points, and make notes on how you will reach each one.

Writing Use the map to write your postscript. Make sure the plot question is answered.

Revising The author uses vivid language. Can you add a simile or metaphor to add color to your postscript? Check also for redundancy. Your postscript should be tightly written.

Proofreading If you used dialogue in the resolution, be sure each speaker's lines are a separate paragraph. Also check for errors in spelling, usage, and mechanics.

Writing

Circulate as students work individually. Check plot maps and determine if students are using them as rough outlines.

Revising

Divide students into groups and have them look for similes and metaphors in the story.

Proofreading

Have students work in pairs. The writer starts reading his or her postscript aloud, noting a new paragraph to the partner. The partner then checks for a paragraph mark and returns the paper for final copying.

ESL Activity

Have students discuss what may have happened to Big Simon at the end of the story. Then have them work in pairs to write a paragraph or two resolving the story. What has happened to Big Simon? Small Simon? Will Small Simon continue playing with Mr. Beelzy?

THINK ABOUT PLOT

Rising action builds excitement in a story. The events of a story are called the plot. Plot begins with exposition, then moves to complications where rising action builds excitement. The action reaches a crisis, and then something gives in the climax.

1. What is the first sign of resistance from Simon to his father's questions about the game he plays?

2. Simon gives in by answering his father's question about whom he plays with. What is Simon's answer, and why is it important?

3. How does the crisis build?

4. How do you learn that the climax has been reached?

5. In one short paragraph after the climax, there is the falling action of the resolution. What happens in the resolution?

READING FOCUS

Analyze Characters' Responses As you read, you used the characters' responses to analyze their thoughts and feelings. What responses gave you insight into Small Simon's character?

DEVELOP YOUR VOCABULARY

John Collier sometimes uses different verbs when he tells who says something. Instead of simply saying, "he said," for example, he sometimes says, "he cried." These different verbs give us clues about the state of mind of the person talking. For example:

"I'm going up there," she said.
"I'm going up there," she cried.

The first sentence is neutral. The second sentence tells us the speaker is upset.

Look at the following sentences. Make sure you understand what the italicized verb means, and explain, in a sentence, how it tells us something about the speaker.

1. "Nothing," *muttered* his son.

2. "He is sometimes there and sometimes not there," *pursued* Mr. Carter.

3. "He said he wouldn't let anyone hurt me," he *whimpered*.

4. "Go on up with you," *shouted* his father.

Answers

1. When his father asks, "But what game is this, Small Simon, that is worth getting nervy and dazed over?" Simon replies simply, "It's nothing."

2. Answer: "Mr. Beelzy." It introduces the character that increasingly becomes the focus of conflict between Mr. Carter and Simon.

3. Mr. Carter wants Simon to admit that Mr. Beelzy is just a fantasy, and Simon refuses. The stage for the final confrontation is set when little Simon says "Big Simon and Small Simon" are "the pretend," implying Mr. Beelzy is real.

4. We are told about a horrible scream from the second floor, where Mr. Carter had gone to punish Simon.

5. We are told—somewhat mysteriously—that a shoe with a man's foot in it was found on the second floor.

DEVELOP YOUR VOCABULARY

Sample Answers

1. muttered—spoke indistinctly, often with the intent of complaining. It reveals that Small Simon is not really interested in telling his father what he has been doing.

2. pursued—continued with a specific purpose in mind. It indicates that Mr. Carter wants to continue his line of questioning until he achieves the result he wants.

3. whimpered—made low, broken sounds, as in crying or in fear. Small Simon is frightened.

4. shouted—spoke in a loud voice. Here, shouting indicates impatience and anger.

READING FOCUS

Sample Answer

Small Simon does not seem to get along well with his father. He turns crimson with shame or rage in response to one of his father's speeches. He says that Big Simon and Small Simon are pretend. He is so passionate about Mr. Beelzy that he calls his mother a fool when she suggests Mr. Beelzy is not real. His father does not understand him or listen to him. Small Simon may have invented Mr. Beelzy in order to have someone to talk to and to accept him in a way that his father does not seem to. He can also act out his anger with Mr. Beelzy. Maybe with his father gone he'll be less angry. Then he would no longer need Mr. Beelzy.

SELECTION OVERVIEW

SELECTION OBJECTIVES
After completing the next two selections, students will be able to

- understand the use of sound segments
- identify alliteration and onomatopoeia
- see how poetry allows free use of the imagination
- describe the setting of the story in a poem
- recognize rhyme as a sound segment
- differentiate among synonyms often used for supernatural beings
- identify mood

Lesson Resources

hist, whist
Overheard on a Saltmarsh
- Selection Synopses, Teacher's Edition, p. T107f
- Comprehension and Vocabulary Workbook, pp. 33–34
- Language Enrichment Workbook, pp. 33–34
- Teacher's Resources Reinforcement, p. R17 Test, pp. T31–T32

More About Sound Segments
The Shakespeare quotation that opens this unit uses alliteration: "We are such stuff as dreams are made on." The alliteration may consist of only one repetition (the "s" in "such stuff"), yet it is effective in providing extra stress. Sound segments are not confined only to literature. One example of onomatopoeia is the word "ping-pong." It is exactly how the game sounds when it is being played.

More About the Authors
See more about E. E. Cummings on page T165.

Harold Monro was one of the English Georgian poets, taking their name from George V, and writing poetry inspired by nature and the English countryside. One of Monro's goals was to make poetry more accessible to the general public. Therefore, he published anthologies of Georgian poetry and founded the Poetry Bookshop in London in 1912.

The Three Witches, Henri Fuseli. The Granger Collection

READING FOCUS
Identify Mood Poems often have a certain mood. They may be humorous, scary, or sad, for example. Details in the poem such as sounds, time of day, or weather help create the mood. The poet rarely states directly what the mood of the poem is. It is up to the reader to identify the mood from the details in the poem. As you read, pay attention to details in order to identify the mood.

Learn About

SOUND SEGMENTS

Poets use segments—vowel sounds and consonant sounds—in patterns to link sounds with meanings or ideas. In descriptive poetry, segments may even combine with rhythm to imitate something being described. The most common ways poets use sound segments are alliteration, onomatopoeia, and assonance.

The repetition of the initial sound of words, for example, *great grow the grizzlies*, is called **alliteration**. A word prounounced out loud that sounds the same as the sound it is describing is called **onomatopoeia**. An example is the *roar* of a lion. When a poet repeats a vowel sound in a line of poetry, he or she is using **assonance**. "Tis hard to say if greater want of skill."

As you read the two poems, ask yourself these questions:

1. Where are alliteration and assonance used?
2. Where is onomatopoeia used?

WRITING CONNECTION

Use alliteration or assonance in a sentence describing something you have done recently. Write a follow-up sentence using onomatopoeia.

Viewing Fine Art
Henry Fuseli (1741–1825) was a Swiss artist of the romantic style. Here, the three witches from Shakespeare's *Macbeth* are pictured in Fuseli's dramatic style of highlighted faces against the black background of an eerie night. Ask: What do you think the witches are doing?

Cooperative Group Activity
To extend the Writing Connection activity, ask students to work in pairs and research some famous quotations that use either alliteration or onomatopoeia. Direct them to a book such as *Bartlett's Familiar Quotations*.

Mist Fantasy, J. E. H. MacDonald. Art Gallery of Ontario

hist, whist

by E. E. Cummings

hist whist	whisk look out for the old woman
little ghostthings	with the wart on her nose
tip-toe	what she'll do to yer
twinkle-toe 20	nobody knows
5 little twitchy	for she knows the devil ooch
witches and tingling	the devil ouch
goblins	the devil
hob-a-nob hob-a-nob	ach the great
little hoppy happy 25	green
10 toad in tweeds	dancing
tweeds	devil
little itchy mousies	devil
with scuttling	devil
eyes rustle and run and 30	devil
15 hidehidehide	wheeEEE
whisk	

---

scuttling (SKUT ling) moving quickly

hist, whist ■ 163

Develop Vocabulary Skills

Write on the chalkboard or overhead projector the three new vocabulary words and ask for a single sentence that uses all three.

Viewing Fine Art

A Canadian artist, J.E.H. MacDonald (1873–1932) was a leader of a group of painters in Toronto who felt that their painting should reflect their Canadian nationality. They turned away from the subjects and styles of the past to depict landscapes of their country. MacDonald's poetic and moody paintings of Canadian scenery brought him both criticism for his "nationalism" and praise for his expression of the "moods, character, and spirit of the country." Ask: Does the scene depict a place you would like to visit? Explain.

Comparing Selections
Have students compare the characters in "hist, whist" and in "Overheard on a Saltmarsh." Who are the characters? How are they revealed to the reader?

Literary Focus:
Sound Segments
Ask students to find examples of alliteration in this poem.

Reading Focus:
Identify Mood
Ask students what is the mood of "Overheard on a Saltmarsh." Ask for details that support their response.

OVERHEARD ON A SALTMARSH

by Harold Monro

Nymph, nymph, what are your beads?
Green glass, goblin. Why do you stare at them?
Give them me.

No.

5   Give them me. Give them me.

No.

Then I will howl all night in the reeds,
Lie in the mud and howl for them.

Goblin, why do you love them so?

10 They are better than stars or water,
Better than voices of winds that sing,
Better than any man's fair daughter,
Your green glass beads on a silver ring.

Hush, I stole them out of the moon.

15 Give me your beads, I desire them.

No.

I will howl in a deep lagoon
For your green glass beads, I love them so.
Give them me. Give them.

20   No.

---

nymph (NIMF) a minor nature goddess in Greek and Roman myths
lagoon (luh GOON) a shallow body of water, usually connected to a larger one

164 ■ Unit 2

AUTHOR BIOGRAPHY
E. E. Cummings (1894–1962)

Edward Estlin Cummings was born in Cambridge, Massachusetts, on October 14, 1894. He graduated from Harvard University with a major in English and classics, and spent a part of his life as a volunteer in the army. Cummings' name often appears with lower case spelling—the result of a mistaken belief that the author legally changed his name to lower case letters only.

The unusual punctuation of his name is appropriate, for Cummings is noted for his unique use of punctuation, word forms, and topography.

Words such as "puddle-wonderful" and "mud-luscious" roll from his pen like little jewels. Phrases such as "nonsufficiently inunderstood" seem to sum up feelings more accurately than ordinary language ever could. And his unusual arrangement of words on a page gives Cummings' poetry a visual, as well as a verbal, meaning.

In addition to being a poet, Cummings was a painter, novelist, and playwright. In all of his works, Cummings reveals his disillusionment with most people and celebrates the value of the individual.

Author Biography ■ 165

MORE ABOUT THE AUTHOR

During the First World War, Cummings worked as an ambulance driver in France, but was sent to a prison camp by the French authorities, an experience that he described in his novel, *The Enormous Room*. Cummings was sent to the prison camp for his outspoken anti-war sentiments.

Additional Works
BY E. E. CUMMINGS

You may wish to suggest these works by E. E. Cummings for additional reading:

E. E. Cummings Complete Poems 1904–1962, New York, Liveright Publishing Corp., 1991. A comprehensive collection of Cummings' poetry.

E. E. Cummings Selected Poems, New York, Liveright Publishing Corp., 1994. In addition to poetry and biographical information about Cummings, the book also contains black and white plates of his art and photographs.

The Little Tree, New York, Crown Publishers, 1987. A child's Christmas poem written by Cummings and illustrated by Deborah Kogan Ray.

Mini Quiz

Write on the chalkboard or overhead projector the following questions and call on students to fill in the blanks. Discuss the answers with the class.

1. The creatures that "tip-toe" in E. E. Cummings's poem are _____.

2. The creatures that are twitchy are _____.

3. The creatures that are itchy are _____.

4. The goblin in Harold Monro's poem promises to howl all night in _____.

5. The beads are on a _____.

Answers
1. ghostthings
2. witches
3. mousies
4. the reeds
5. silver ring

UNDERSTAND THE SELECTION

Answers

1. toads
2. a wart on her nose
3. from "out of the moon"
4. He wants to include all sorts of mysterious, supernatural things in his poem, not just ghosts.
5. We should avoid her because, as is the case with witches, she "knows the devil" and might even do devilish things herself.
6. A lagoon is a body of water. Mud contains water and reeds grow in water.
7. Simple greed: They both want the same thing.
8. Answers will vary. Sample: the old woman with the wart on her nose; she sounds ugly, unpredictable and evil.
9. Answers will vary. Sample: Throughout history many women have been branded unfairly as witches.
10. The moon represents mystery, and so do the beads.

Respond to Literature

Witches, goblins, and nymphs are mysterious and formless. Writing about them allows free use of the imagination. Ask students if they can think of other examples of supernatural beings from poems.

 ## WRITE ABOUT THE SELECTION

Prewriting

Explore with the class what a saltmarsh is. Find its dictionary definition, and contrast it with the definition for a marsh. Look for a picture of a saltmarsh in an encyclopedia or science book.

Writing

As you circulate among the students working individually, reinforce the idea of appealing to one of the senses for description. Help them think of how it would be to smell salt air or touch a reed.

Revising

Caution students that alliteration must not be taken too far (for example, too many repetitions of the same sound), and onomatopoeia must be accurate.

Proofreading

Have students make flashcards of any words they misspell so they can review them.

Review the Selection

UNDERSTAND THE SELECTION

Recall

1. What wears tweeds in "hist, whist"?

2. What distinctive feature does the old woman have in the same poem?

3. Where did the nymph's green glass beads come from in Monro's poem?

Infer

4. Why does Cummings use the word "ghostthings" rather than just "ghosts"?

5. Why does Cummings tell the reader to "look out for the old woman with the wart on her nose"?

6. What do the places where the goblin will howl have in common in Monro's poem?

7. What causes the conflict between the nymph and the goblin?

Apply

8. Explain which character in "hist, whist" is least appealing to you.

9. Do you think the stereotype of the old woman with the wart is fair?

10. What is significant about the fact that the nymph's green glass beads came from the moon?

Respond to Literature

Why do you think poets like to write about mysterious things?

WRITE ABOUT THE SELECTION

You have been asked by poet Harold Monro to provide an introduction to his poem "Overheard on a Saltmarsh." The introduction does not have to be long. You just need to describe the setting of the poem.

Prewriting   You first need to make sure you understand what a saltmarsh is. Consult a dictionary if you are not sure. Then visualize standing in a saltmarsh. What would it feel like, smell like, and look like? What sounds would you hear? Write on your paper the five senses "touch," "smell," "sight," "hearing," and "taste." Under each, list several sensations.

Writing   Choose from your list of sensations the best ones that provide a vivid description of a saltmarsh. Keep in mind the content and theme of the poem. You may write in poetry or prose. Make sure your thoughts are well-organized.

Revising   Can you use alliteration or onomatopoeia anywhere in your description? Remember that these techniques are not limited to poetry. Add more sensory details and vivid words to make your introduction come alive. And eliminate any dead words or phrases that could make your description seem boring.

Proofreading   Reread your description to check for errors. Make sure there are no misspellings. Alliteration, onomatopoeia, and other techniques require that you spell correctly. Otherwise the reader is confused and the effect you want to create is lost.

ESL Activity

Have students work in pairs to compile lists of sensations that fall under the categories of the five senses. Have them organize their lists into two categories: favorite sensations, and least favorite sensations.

THINK ABOUT SOUND SEGMENTS

Poets use sound segments to link vowel and consonant sounds with ideas. Alliteration repeats consonant sounds while assonance is repetition of vowel sounds. Onomatopoetic words imitate real sounds.

1. Look at the description in "hist, whist" of how "little ghostthings" walk. What technique is this?

2. Identify the onomatopoeia in "Overheard on a Saltmarsh."

3. Cummings likes to play with words. The very first line of the poem is a good example. What is going on here?

4. Find a good example of assonance.

5. How do sound segments help make these poems more interesting?

READING FOCUS

Identify Mood As you read these two poems you were able to identify the different moods in each poem based on details provided. Briefly describe the mood of each poem. Support your response with details from each poem.

DEVELOP YOUR VOCABULARY

Words that mean the same thing are called synonyms. Below are some words from the poems. Consult your dictionary for their precise definitions. Then write a synonym for each. If you can't find a good synonym, make up one, then give a definition for your new word.

1. toad
2. ghostthing
3. wart
4. howl
5. lagoon
6. reeds
7. desire
8. deep

THINK ABOUT SOUND SEGMENTS

Answers

1. "tip-toe twinkle-toe" is alliteration.
2. the verb "howl"
3. Words are used nonsensically and when pronounced they are mysterious-sounding. They also rhyme, which creates a sort of cadence to the opening.
4. ooch, ouch, and ach
5. In "hist, whist," sound segments help to create a playful, light mood—one that is reminiscent of childhood ghost stories and creepy creatures. In "Overheard on a Saltmarsh," sound segments emphasize the mystery of the night through sounds, colors, and images.

DEVELOP YOUR VOCABULARY

Sample Answers

1. frog
2. goblin
3. bump
4. cry
5. pond
6. grasses
7. crave
8. low

READING FOCUS

Sample Answer

The mood of "hist, whist" is playful. It makes you think of little kids trying to work themselves into being scared. Words and phrases such as "little ghostthings," "little twitchy witches," "little hoppy happy toad," "little itchy mousies" keep the mood light. The mood in "Overheard on a Saltmarsh" is mysterious and a little scary, with one creature waiting to take something from another creature. The goblin repeatedly asks for the nymph's beads and threatens to howl all night. The nymph has stolen the beads from the moon.

SELECTION OVERVIEW

SELECTION OBJECTIVES

After completing this selection, students will be able to

- identify theme
- relate a writer's purpose to a story's theme
- discuss people's beliefs in the supernatural
- write a story in the first person
- recognize different methods for developing theme
- replace archaic words and phrases
- use prior knowledge to understand a story

Lesson Resources

The Judge's House
- Selection Synopsis, Teacher's Edition, pp. T107f–107g
- Comprehension and Vocabulary Workbook, pp. 35–36
- Language Enrichment Workbook, pp. 35–36
- Teacher's Resources Reinforcement, p. R18 Test, pp. T33–T34

More About Theme

The theme of a story is sometimes stated explicitly, but often readers must infer it by examining other elements of the story. Students might benefit from thinking of theme as the final piece in a jigsaw puzzle; its shape and message are determined largely by the other pieces.

About the Author

Bram Stoker (1846–1912) is best known for his masterwork *Dracula*, which has been dramatized and reproduced in countless forms since its publication in 1897. Born and raised in Ireland, Stoker followed his father's advice and trained to be a civil servant, but he loved writing and drama and began to write both horror stories and dramatic criticism while working in Dublin Castle. When offered a managerial position

in a theater in London, Stoker resigned from civil service, moved to London, and continued to write while working in the theater. *Dracula* was completed during this time. After the theater closed, Stoker supported himself solely by his writing, although none of his later works ever achieved the success of *Dracula*. Stoker's biographer called him "one of the least known authors of one of the best known books ever written."

READING FOCUS

Use Prior Knowledge When you use prior knowledge to help you understand a story, you use what you know from your own experience and what you know based on what the author has already told you. As you read, use what you already know to help you understand the new events that are occurring and to understand the characters' behaviors.

THEME

Why do we tell stories? Usually it is because we have an important message to relate to our listeners or readers. The central message of a story is called the **theme**.

Sometimes the theme of a story is stated directly. More often, however, the theme is implied, or suggested. The reader must look for clues in the story to discover the theme. Writers often reveal the theme through the words and actions of the characters and through the events in the story. For example, in the selection you are about to read, the main character decides to ignore the warnings of others about the dangers of the judge's house. What theme or message is the writer trying to convey through this character's actions?

As you read "The Judge's House," ask yourself the following questions:

1. What is the theme of this story?
2. What details in the story reveal the theme?

WRITING CONNECTION

At some point in your life, you have probably been asked to tell a story. Think about one such story. What was your purpose in telling it? What was the theme of the story?

ESL Activity

Discuss with students some popular television shows or movies, or widely known stories, such as fairy tales. Have students try to guess what the themes or messages of these stories are.

Cooperative Group Activity

To extend the Writing Connection activity, students could meet in the same pairs as those for the "road map" exercise accompanying the "Thus I Refute Beelzy" selection. Have the listener state the theme of the story that the narrator has related. If the narrator disagrees, the students should discuss their different interpretations and reach a consensus.

T168

The Judge's House

by Bram Stoker

When it was almost time for his examinations, Malcolm Malcolmson went away to study. He wanted to find a quiet little town where there would be nothing to distract him. He bought a ticket for the first town that he did not know on the local time table.

At the end of a three-hour trip he was in Benchurch. He went straight to the one inn that the sleepy town contained and got a room for the night. He looked around the next day to find a place even quieter and more isolated than "The Good Traveler." There was only one place that he liked, and it was certainly quiet. It was an old rambling house with heavy gables. Its windows were unusually small and set higher than was usual in such houses. It was surrounded with a high brick wall. It looked more like a fortress than an ordinary house.

From the post office he got the name of the agent. He was a friendly old gentleman, delighted that anyone would be willing to live in the house.

"To tell the truth," said he, "I would be happy to let anyone have the house rent free for a term of years. This would get the people around here used to the idea of seeing it inhabited. It has been empty for so long that some kind of absurd prejudice has grown up around it. This can best be changed if it is occupied, if only by a scholar like yourself, who wants its quiet for a time."

Malcolmson did not ask the agent about the "absurd prejudice." He knew he would get more information on that subject later. He paid his rent, got the name of an old woman who would probably keep house for him, and came away with the keys in his pocket. He then went to the landlady of the inn, Mrs. Witham, and asked her advice about what he might need at the house. She threw up her hands in amazement when he told her where he was going.

"Not the Judge's House!" she said. She then told him that the house had belonged to a judge more than a hundred

---

gables (GAY bulz) the triangular top part of an outer wall between the sides of a sloped roof
absurd (ab SURD) unreasonable; ridiculous

The Judge's House ■ 169

Develop Vocabulary Skills
Group the new vocabulary words by part of speech: nouns, verbs, adjectives, and adverbs. Divide the class into four groups and assign a list to each group to report on the words and use the words in sentences.

TEACHING PLAN

INTRODUCE

Motivation
Discuss this well-known quote from Shakespeare's *Julius Caesar*: "The evil that men do lives after them; / The good is oft interred with their bones." Have students paraphrase this quote in their own words and provide examples of historical figures or people in the news today to whom it applies.

Purpose-Setting Question
How would you feel about living in a house that some people think is haunted?

READ

Literary Focus:
Theme
Have students create a four-column chart with the following headings: plot (events), characters, setting, and theme. As students read, have them note how the first three elements in the story help reveal the theme.

Reading Focus:
Use Prior Knowledge
To help students tap their prior knowledge, have them create a KWL chart. In the K (know) column, ask them to list what they already know about or associate with the following: old abandoned houses, rats, students or young people, and judges. In the W (what I want to learn) column, students should list several questions they hope will be answered. As they read, they will fill in the last column of the chart and compare their assumptions in the K column with the events in the story.

CLOSE

Have students complete Review the Selection on pages 178–179.

Critical Thinking:
Analyze

Ask: What do Malcolmson's actions and responses to Mrs. Witham reveal about his personality?

years ago. This judge was held in great terror because of his harsh sentences and his hostility to the prisoners. As to what there was against the house itself she could not tell. She had often asked, but no one seemed to know. There was a general feeling that there was something, though. "If you were my boy, you wouldn't sleep there a night!" The good woman was so kind in her intentions that Malcolmson was touched. He told her how much he appreciated her interest.

Then he said, "But, my dear Mrs. Witham, you need not worry about me! A man who is studying for an important test has too much to think of to be disturbed by rumors." Mrs. Witham then kindly offered to see after what he would need, and he went himself to look for the old woman who had been recommended to him as a daytime housekeeper.

He got to the Judge's House with her a few hours later. There, he found Mrs. Witham with several men and boys carrying packages. There was also a man with a bed, for she said, though tables and chairs might be all very well, a bed that hadn't been aired for perhaps fifty years was not proper for young bones to lie on.

After looking through the whole house, Malcolmson decided to settle in the large dining room, which was big enough to serve all his needs. Mrs. Witham, with the aid of the housekeeper, Mrs. Dempster, unpacked. Malcolmson saw that Mrs. Witham had kindly sent from her own kitchen enough food to last for a few days. Before going, she turned at the door and said, "Perhaps, sir, because it is so drafty, you should put one of those big screens around your bed at night. Although I must say I would die myself if

I were to be shut in with all kinds of-of 'things' that put their heads around the sides or over the top to look at me!" The very idea was too much for her nerves, and she fled immediately.

Mrs. Dempster sniffed in a superior manner as the landlady disappeared. She said that for her own part, she wasn't afraid of all the bogies in the kingdom. "There are no 'things' to fear. Rats is bogies, I tell you, and bogies is rats. An old house like this has plenty of them. Don't you get to think anything else!"

"Mrs. Dempster," said Malcolmson, "I'm sure you are right!"

"I know I am, sir. Don't fear anything, and you'll get all the solitude you want here." She got to work with her cleaning. By nightfall, when Malcolmson returned from his walk, he found the room swept and tidied, a fire burning in the old hearth, the lamp lit, and the table spread for supper. "This is comfort, indeed," he said, as he rubbed his hands.

After supper, he got out his books, put fresh wood on the fire, and began studying. He went on without pause until eleven o'clock, when he stopped for a while to fix the fire and to make himself a cup of tea. As he sipped his hot tea, he enjoyed his sense of isolation. It was then that he began to notice for the first time what noise the rats were making.

"Surely," he thought, "they cannot have been at it all the time I was reading. Otherwise, I would have noticed it!" When the noise increased, he was sure that it was really new. It was clear that at first the rats had been frightened at the presence of a stranger and the light of fire and lamp. As the time went on, they had grown bolder and were now acting as they usually did.

How busy they were! Up and down behind the old wainscot, over the ceiling and under the floor they raced and gnawed and scratched! Malcolmson smiled to himself as he remembered Mrs. Dempster's words, "Rats is bogies, and bogies is rats!"

He looked forward to another long spell of work to be done before the night was past. He allowed himself the luxury of a good look around the room. He took his lamp in one hand, and went all around. There were some old pictures on the walls, but they were coated so thick with dust and dirt that he could not see any detail. Here and there he saw some crack or hole blocked for a moment by the face of a rat with its bright eyes glittering in the light. In an instant it was gone, and a squeak and a scamper followed.

The thing that struck him most, however, was the rope of the great alarm bell on the roof. It hung down in a corner of the room to the right of the fireplace. He pulled a carved oak chair up close to the hearth and sat down to his last cup of tea. When this was done he sat back at the table and got to work. He soon got as used to the noise made by the rats as one does to the ticking of a clock. He became so involved with his work that everything else passed away from him.

---

bogies (BOH geez) real or imaginary things that startle or frighten
wainscot (WAYNS koht) a facing for the walls in a room, usually made of wood paneling

The Judge's House ■ 171

Reading Focus:
Use Prior Knowledge
During a break in his studying, Malcolm notices the activity of the rats and smiles as he remembers Mrs. Dempster's words. Ask: Did Malcolmson's reaction to the rats surprise you? Explain. How would you behave in this situation?

T171

Just before dawn, he suddenly looked up. The noise of the rats had stopped. Indeed it seemed to him that the very quiet was what had disturbed him. As he looked around, he was suddenly startled. There on the carved oak chair at the right of the fireplace sat an enormous rat, glaring at him. Malcolmson made a motion to it, but it did not move. He pretended to throw something, and it still did not move. Instead, it showed its great white teeth angrily. Its cruel eyes shone in the lamplight.

Malcolmson felt amazed. He seized the poker from the hearth and ran at it to kill it. Before he could strike it, the rat jumped to the floor and ran up the rope of the alarm bell. It disappeared in the darkness beyond the range of the lamp. Instantly, strange to say, the noisy scampering of the rats in the wainscot began again.

By this time, Malcolmson's mind was quite off the problem. A rooster outside told him of the approach of morning, and he went to bed and to sleep.

By the time he woke up, Mrs. Dempster had already tidied up the room, got his breakfast ready, and tapped on the screen around his bed. He went out for a morning walk, stopping by to see Mrs. Witham and to thank her for her kindness. As they talked, he told her about the rats and about the one who had sat in the oak chair.

"Mercy on us," said Mrs. Witham. "Sitting on a chair by the fireside! Take care, sir! He could be dangerous!" Malcolmson broke into a hearty laugh.

"You needn't laugh, sir. You young folks thinks it easy to laugh at things that makes older ones shudder. Never mind, sir! I hope you'll laugh all the time. It's what I wish you myself!"

172 ■ Unit 2

"Oh, forgive me!" said Malcolmson. "Don't think me rude, but the idea was too much for me—that a big rat could be dangerous!" At the thought he laughed again.

That evening, the scampering of the rats began earlier. How they squeaked and scratched and gnawed! In spite of the noise, Malcolmson got more and more involved in his work.

All at once everything became silent. The silence was as of the grave. He remembered what happened the night before, and he looked at the chair by the fireside. Then a very odd sensation thrilled through him.

There, on the great old carved oak chair beside the fireplace sat the same enormous rat, steadily glaring at him.

He took a book and flung it at the rat. The book was badly aimed, and the rat did not stir. Again the poker performance of the previous night was repeated. Again, the rat fled up the rope of the alarm bell. Strangely too, this was instantly followed by the renewal of the noise made by the general rat community. As on the previous night, Malcolmson could not see at what part of the room the big rat disappeared, for his lamp left the upper part of the room in darkness.

Looking at his watch he found it was close to midnight. He made up the fire and made himself a pot of tea. He worked for a few hours and then took a break. He sat on the great carved oak chair before the fire. He began to think that he would like to know where the rat had disappeared to, for he thought he might set a rat trap in the morning. He lit another lamp and placed it so that it would shine into the right corner of the wall by the fireplace. He lifted up the rope of the alarm bell and placed the end of it on the table. As he handled it he could not help but notice how flexible it was, especially for such a strong rope, and one not in use. "You could hang a man with it," he thought to himself. When he was ready, he looked around, and thought, "Now, my friend, I think we shall learn something about you next time you come."

He went back to his studies and was soon deep in thought. Again he was distracted suddenly. There was that sudden silence, followed by a slight movement of the rope. As he looked he saw the great rat drop from the rope onto the oak chair and sit there glaring at him. Malcolmson flung a book at it. The rat dodged the book, as he dodged the next three. At last, as Malcolmson stood with another book ready to throw, the rat squeaked and seemed afraid. Malcolmson threw it and struck the rat. It gave a terrified squeak, ran up the back of the chair, and ran up the rope of the alarm bell. Malcolmson kept his eyes on the rat and saw it disappear through a hole in one of the pictures that hung on the wall.

As Malcolmson picked up his books, he noticed that the one that had hit the rat was the Bible his mother had given him. "What an odd coincidence," he murmured to himself. He tried to work some more but was not able to concentrate. At the first streak of dawn, he went to bed.

Literary Focus:
Theme and Character
Ask: What emotion does Malcolmson begin to feel in the third paragraph? How might this emotion relate to the theme of the story?

Critical Thinking:
Infer
Lead students in a discussion about the forces of good and evil. Ask: Why is it a coincidence that Malcolmson hits the rat with the Bible?

---

coincidence (koh IN suh duns) two or more related events accidentally happening at the same time

The Judge's House ■ 173

Literary Focus:
Theme and Setting
Explain to students the significance of the setting to the story. The impending storm is part of the setting. Ask: What does the storm symbolize or represent in the story? How does the storm help the writer present the theme?

Mrs. Dempster woke him late in the morning. His first request surprised her. "Mrs. Dempster, when I am out today, I'd like you to get the steps and dust or wash those pictures, especially the third one from the fireplace. I want to see what they are."

On his way back from his morning walk, he stopped in to see Mrs. Witham. She introduced him to her visitor, a Dr. Thornhill. They talked about the Judge's House and about what had happened the previous two nights. After listening to Malcolmson's story, Dr. Thornhill asked, "The rat always went up the rope of the alarm bell?"

"Always."

"I suppose you know," said the doctor after a pause, "what the rope is?"

"No!"

"It is the very rope which the hangman used for all the victims of the Judge's anger!"

At this, Mrs. Witham fainted. As the doctor took care of her, Malcolmson looked at his watch and realized that it was close to his dinner hour. He left before she completely recovered.

When Mrs. Witham was herself again, she asked the doctor why he had said that to Malcolmson. "I wanted to draw his attention to the bell rope. He may get in the night some strange fright. If he does, I want him to pull that rope. All alone as he is, it will give us warning. We may reach him in time to help. I shall be sitting up late tonight and shall keep my ears open. Do not be alarmed if Benchurch gets a surprise before morning."

"Oh, Doctor, what do you mean?"

"I mean this: possibly—even probably—we shall hear the great alarm bell from the Judge's House tonight."

When Malcolmson got home, he found that Mrs. Dempster had already left. He was glad to see that the place was tidy. For a few minutes after his entrance, the noise of the rats ceased. But soon they began again. He was glad to hear them, for he thought of the strange fact that they were quiet only when that big rat came on the scene.

After dinner, Malcolmson sat down to work, determined to make the best use of his time. For an hour or so he worked. Then his thoughts began to wander. The wind outside had turned into a storm. The house, solid though it was, seemed to shake, and the storm roared and raged through its many chimneys and gables, producing strange, unearthly sounds.

As Malcolmson listened to it, he remembered the doctor's words about the rope. He went over to the corner of the fireplace and took it in his hand to look at it. As he stood there, he lost himself in thinking about the victims and about the grim wish of the Judge to have such a ghastly relic in his house. Soon he felt a sort of tremor in the rope, as if something were moving along it.

Looking up, Malcolmson saw the great rat coming slowly down towards him, glaring at him steadily. He dropped the rope, and the rat turned and ran up the rope again and disappeared. It

---

relic (REH lik) something that remains from what has disappeared or been destroyed
tremor (TREH mur) a quick, constant shaking or trembling

occurred to Malcolmson that he had not looked at the pictures, as he had meant to. He held up a lamp and stood opposite the third picture from the fireplace on the right side, where he had seen the rat disappear on the previous night.

The picture had been dusted and washed and now stood out clearly. It was of a Judge dressed in his robes. His face was strong and without mercy. He looked evil, crafty, and cruel. The eyes were quite bright and had an evil expression. They looked exactly like the eyes of the great rat. As he looked at them, Malcolmson realized that the rat was peering out through a hole in the corner of the picture. He also realized that the other rats had stopped making any noise.

In the picture, the Judge was seated in a big carved oak chair on the right side of a great stone fireplace. In the corner a rope hung down from the ceiling, its end lying coiled on the floor. With a feeling of horror, Malcolmson recognized the scene of the very room he was in. Then he looked over to the corner of the fireplace. With a loud cry, he dropped the lamp.

There, in the Judge's chair, with the rope hanging behind, sat the rat with the Judge's eyes. Except for the howling of the storm outside, there was silence.

The fallen lamp brought Malcolmson back to reality. Luckily the lamp was of metal, so the oil was not spilled. He picked it up and got it started again. Then he thought for a moment. "This will not do," he said to himself. "I'm becoming a crazy fool. This must stop! My nerves have been getting into a strange state. I'll be all right now. I shall not be such a fool again."

The Judge's House ■ 175

Reading Focus:
Use Prior Knowledge
This is a critical section of the story. Discuss the significance of the similarities between the rat and the Judge. Have students note what they would like to learn as a result of the comparison between the rat and the Judge.

Critical Thinking:
Evaluate

Ask: What do you know about Malcolmson that makes his ability to return to work under these circumstances seem logical?

Critical Thinking:
Analyze

Ask: What aspects of Malcolmson's character make him an ideal victim for the Judge?

Literary Focus:
Setting

Ask: What elements of the setting contribute to the increasing horror of this scene?

He sat down to his work. An hour later, he noticed the sudden stillness. The wind was still howling outside, but inside there was no sound. Soon Malcolmson heard a thin, squeaking noise, very faint. It came from the corner of the room where the rope hung down. In the dim light, he saw the great rat clinging to the rope and gnawing it. The rope was nearly gnawed through. He could see the lighter color where the strands were laid bare. As he looked, the job was completed. The cut end of the rope fell clattering to the floor. For an instant the great rat remained like a tassel at the end of the rope, which now began to sway to and fro. Malcolmson felt for a moment a pang of terror as he thought that now the possibility of calling anyone from the town to his assistance was cut off. He threw a book at the rat. Before the book could hit it, the rat dropped off and struck the floor with a soft thud. It darted away and disappeared in the darkness of the shadows of the room.

Malcolmson decided then and there to hunt for the rat. He took off the green shade of the lamp to insure a wider spreading light. As he did so, the gloom of the upper part of the room was lit. In the light, the pictures on the wall stood out boldly. From where he stood, Malcolmson saw right opposite to him the third picture on the wall from the right of the fireplace. He rubbed his eyes in surprise, and then a great fear began to come upon him.

The background was as before, with chair and fireplace and rope. But the figure of the Judge had disappeared.

Malcolmson, almost in a chill of horror, turned slowly around. He began to shake and tremble. His strength seemed to have left him, and he couldn't move. He could only see and hear.

There, on the carved oak chair in the room sat the Judge in his robes, with his eyes glaring, and a smile of triumph on the cruel mouth. He lifted with his hands a black cap. Malcolmson felt as if the blood was running from his heart, as one does in moments of prolonged suspense. There was a singing in his ears. Outside, he could hear the roar and howl of the storm. Then came the striking of midnight by the great chimes in the center of town. As the clock struck, so the look of triumph on the Judge's face intensified. At the last stroke of midnight he placed the black cap on his head.

Slowly and deliberately the Judge rose from his chair and picked up the piece of the rope of the alarm bell that lay on the floor. He drew it through his hands as if he enjoyed its touch. Then deliberately he began to knot one end of it, fashioning it into a noose. Then he began to move along the table on the opposite side to Malcolmson, keeping his eyes on him until he had passed him.

When the Judge stood in front of the door, Malcolmson began to feel that he was trapped and tried to think of what he should do. He saw the Judge approach, still keeping between him and the door. Then the Judge raised the noose and threw it toward him. Malcolmson moved to one side, saw the rope fall beside him, and heard it hit the floor. Again the Judge

---

deliberately (dah LIH bur ayt lee) in an unhurried, slow, and steady manner

raised the noose and threw it toward him. This went on many times. Each time the student managed to evade the noose.

The Judge never seemed discouraged, but seemed to be playing as a cat does with a mouse.

At last in despair, Malcolmson looked around him. The lamp seemed to have blazed up. At the many rat-holes and chinks and crannies of the wainscot he saw the rats' eyes. He saw that the rope of the great alarm bell was laden with rats. Every inch of it was covered with them.

More and more were pouring through the small hole in the ceiling, so that with their weight the bell was beginning to sway.

It swayed until the clapper touched the bell. The sound was but a tiny one, but the bell was only beginning to sway, and it would increase.

At the sound the Judge looked up, and a scowl of anger crossed his face. His eyes fairly glowed like hot coals, and he stamped his foot with a sound that seemed to make the house shake. A dreadful peal of thunder broke overhead as he raised the rope again. The rats kept running up and down the rope as though working against time. This time, instead of throwing it, the judge drew close to Mal-

colmson. He held open the noose. As he came closer, there seemed something paralyzing in his very presence. Malcolmson stood rigid as a corpse. He felt the Judge's icy fingers touch his throat as he adjusted the rope. The noose tightened—tightened. Then the Judge, taking the rigid form of the student in his arms, carried him over and placed him standing in the oak chair. Stepping up beside him, he put his hand up and caught the end of the swaying rope of the alarm bell. As he raised his hands, the rats fled squeaking. They disappeared through a hole in the ceiling. Taking the end of the noose which was around Malcolmson's neck, he tied it to the hanging bell rope. Then, descending, he pulled away the chair.

◆◆◆◆◆◆◆

When the alarm bell of the Judge's House began to sound, a crowd soon gathered and hurried to the spot. They knocked loudly at the door, but there was no reply. Then they burst in the door and poured into the great dining room, the doctor at the head.

There at the end of the rope of the great alarm bell hung the body of the student. On the face of the Judge in the picture was a malignant smile.

Reading Focus:
Use Prior Knowledge
Have students review their KWL charts. Ask: Were you able to predict the ending to this story? What hints about Malcolmson's fate did you notice earlier in the story?

---

evade (ee VAHD) to keep away from; avoid
rigid (RIH jihd) stiff
malignant (muh LIHG nunt) evil

The Judge's House ■ 177

Mini Quiz

Write on the chalkboard or overhead projector the following questions and call on students to fill in the blanks. Discuss the answers with the class.

1. Malcolmson goes to Benchurch in order to _____.

2. Malcolmson hires _____ to be his housekeeper

3. Malcolmson's work is interrupted by the noise of _____.

4. Mrs. Witham _____ when she hears about the Judge's hanging rope.

5. _____ disappeared from the portrait.

Answers
1. study
2. Mrs. Dempster
3. rats
4. faints
5. The Judge

UNDERSTAND THE SELECTION

Answers

1. He wanted a quiet place to study for his exams.
2. He was known to give harsh and cruel punishments.
3. He wanted to warn Malcolmson about possible danger.
4. He is practical, realistic, and calm.
5. The storm suggests something horrible will happen. Dr. Thornhill predicted that they would hear the alarm bell.
6. She does not believe in "bogies" or the dangers in the Judge's house.
7. The theme is that the evil works of a person can live on even after the person has died.
8. Answers will vary. Sample answer: Yes, I was told not to go hiking in the woods alone. I did it anyway and got lost for several hours. It was dark before I found my way back home.
9. Answers will vary. Sample answer: I probably would have left as soon as the rats appeared. At least I would have tried to trap the big rat.
10. Answers will vary. Sample answer: Young people tend not to be afraid of dangerous situations. Older people are more cautious and protective of others.

Respond to Literature

Sample Answer

Old houses can be dark and gloomy and often make strange creaking sounds. I can understand why some people might think these houses are haunted by ghosts. I, however, don't believe in haunted houses because I live in an old house, and it is not scary at all.

WRITE ABOUT THE SELECTION

Prewriting

Have the class work together to locate and discuss the places in "The Judge's House" where Mrs. Dempster is mentioned. Make a list of these events on the chalkboard. Discuss how to begin the story.

UNDERSTAND THE SELECTION

Recall

1. Why did Malcolmson go to Benchurch?
2. Why did the people of Benchurch fear the Judge?
3. Why does Dr. Thornhill tell Malcolmson about the bell rope?

Infer

4. How would you describe Malcolmson's personality?
5. What events did the author use to help the reader predict the ending?
6. In what way is Mrs. Dempster like Malcolmson?
7. What is the theme of this story?

Apply

8. Have you ever, like Malcolmson, ignored the advice of others? What happened as a result?
9. Would you have stayed in the house if you were Malcolmson? What would you have done differently if you had been in Malcolmson's position?
10. Based on this story, how do young people react differently to danger than older people?

Respond to Literature

Why do some people believe in haunted houses? Do you believe in them? Why or why not?

WRITE ABOUT THE SELECTION

Telling a story from a different point of view can drastically change it. Mrs. Dempster, Malcolmson's housekeeper, does not seem to be superstitious or fearful. You are Mrs. Dempster. Explain the events of the story from her point of view.

Prewriting Reread the parts of the story where Mrs. Dempster appears. Make a list of what she does and says. Then think about the end of the story. Assume that she is part of the crowd that finds Malcolmson's body. What do you think she would say and do now?

Writing Begin your story when Mrs. Dempster first meets Malcolmson. Include her observations of Malcolmson and of Mrs. Witham. Use your prewriting list to guide you through the rest of the story, especially the end. Think of how Mrs. Dempster might interpret what the crowd sees when they enter the house. Remember to write in the first person point of view. Use the pronoun *I*.

Revising Reread your story. Keep in mind that Mrs. Dempster is not at all superstitious. Think about how such a person would view the events of the story and describe them. Include some dialogue between Mrs. Dempster and some of the more superstitious characters, like Mrs. Witham and Dr. Thornhill to make your story livelier.

Proofreading Make sure you have used the first person and have spelled the characters' names correctly. Check for correct use of quotation marks in the dialogue.

Writing

As students work individually, circulate among them, checking to see that they are writing in the first person. Suggest places in which dialogue could be used.

Revising

Have students work in pairs to revise their stories. Remind students to check their partner's work for the following: vivid word choice, correct use of quotation marks, and the use of first-person narration.

Proofreading

After students have proofread their own texts, have them exchange texts. If any mistakes are found, they should be corrected. The corrected text is then passed on to another reader. If more mistakes are found, the procedure is repeated. A text cannot be considered completed until a reader approves it.

THINK ABOUT THEME

Theme is the main idea or message in a story or play. One theme of "The Judge's House" is that the evil workings of a person continue long after the person dies. This theme is developed in a number of ways.

1. One way the theme of "The Judge's House" is developed is through the setting. How is the house described when Malcolmson first arrives?

2. Mrs. Witham tells Malcolmson that the Judge, who was greatly feared by the townspeople, lived in the house more than a hundred years ago. How does this fact contribute to the theme?

3. Dialogue is also used to develop theme. Find an example.

4. Plot is also used to develop theme. Explain how.

5. The story ends with this sentence: "On the face of the Judge in the picture was a malignant smile." How does this sentence reinforce the theme?

READING FOCUS

Use Prior Knowledge As you read this story, you were able to draw from your own experiences and from early events in the story to make predictions. How did your prior knowledge help you to anticipate the outcome of the story?

DEVELOP YOUR VOCABULARY

Language changes over time. Many words that we use in everyday speech were unknown a hundred years ago. Likewise, many common words used at the time this story was written are no longer used today.

Below are some sentences from the story. Each contains a word or phrase that is not in common use today. These words are italicized in the sentences. Rewrite the sentences by replacing the italicized words with words we would use today. Use a dictionary as needed.

1. ". . . a bed that hadn't been aired for perhaps fifty years was not proper for *young bones to lie on*."

2. "She said that for her own part, she wasn't afraid of *all the bogies in the kingdom*."

3. "Up and down behind the old *wainscot*, over the ceiling and under the floor they raced and gnawed and scratched!"

4. "Mrs. Dempster, . . . I'd like you to get *the steps* and dust or wash those pictures."

5. "Then deliberately he began to knot one end of it [the rope], *fashioning it* into a noose."

Review the Selection ■ 179

SELECTION OVERVIEW

SELECTION OBJECTIVES

After completing these two selections, students will be able to

- understand the elements of narrative poetry
- recognize many nursery rhymes as narrative poems
- examine the quests of other literary figures
- rewrite a narrative poem as a short story
- see the advantages of using poetry in narratives
- recognize and define archaic verb forms
- draw conclusions

Lesson Resources

The Listeners
Eldorado
- Selection Synopses, Teacher's Edition, p. T107g
- Comprehension and Vocabulary Workbook, pp. 37–38
- Language Enrichment Workbook, pp. 37–38
- Teacher's Resources Reinforcement, p. R19 Test, pp. T35–T36

More About Narrative Poetry

Narrative poems are often much longer than these two selections. Longfellow's "The Midnight Ride of Paul Revere," for example, describes many aspects of the Boston patriot's famous trip to warn colonists of British soldiers on the march.

More About the Unit Theme

De la Mare's poem has remained a mystery to readers over the years. That is part of its appeal. The Traveller's question, "Is there anybody there?", is an effort to discover who the listeners are. Poe's poem is more straightforward. It is reminiscent of medieval tales of the search for the Holy Grail.

READING FOCUS

Draw Conclusions When you draw conclusions, you have to decide why certain events take place or why characters do certain things. You can use details in stories and poems and your own experience to draw conclusions about unstated events or actions. Drawing conclusions helps you to understand characters' motivations and why certain events occur. As you read, use what you know and what the author tells you to draw conclusions.

NARRATIVE POETRY

Many poems are written simply to give you an impression or feeling about the subject. They have no real story to tell. Other poems, however, do tell a story. They are like short, short stories written in verse.

Poems that tell a story are called **narrative poems**. They have the elements of a short story—setting, characters, plot, and theme. These elements may not be as well developed as in a short story, however, since a poem is usually shorter.

Why do authors tell stories in poetry rather than prose? That is a question to keep in mind as you read the next two selections. Remember that techniques such as imagery, rhyme, personification, and metaphor can often be used to best advantage in poetry.

As you read "The Listeners" and "Eldorado," ask yourself:
1. What are the poems' elements?
2. What would the story be like if it were in prose rather than poetry?

WRITING CONNECTION

Nursery rhymes, which are poems, are usually a form of narrative poetry. Think of a nursery rhyme. Tell its plot in a paragraph or two.

About the Authors

Walter de la Mare was a British poet and novelist. Born in 1873, he received a royal grant in 1908 which made it possible for him to devote himself completely to his writing. De la Mare is known as a poet for both adults and children. Inclusion of the fantasy world gives a charm to his poems.

Poe is now considered one of the most important figures in American literature, but during his life his work did not receive critical acclaim. Much of his work was viewed as very strange. He led a sad life; his father deserted the family when Edgar was 18 months old, his mother died when he was 2, and he himself died at the age of 40.

Cooperative Group Activity

Have students work in small groups to complete the Writing Connection activity. Distribute copies of the same nursery rhymes to each group. Have each group read its plot summaries to the class. Compare and contrast the summaries.

The Listeners

by Walter de la Mare

"Is there anybody there?" said the Traveller,
    Knocking on the moonlit door;
And his horse in the silence champed the grasses
    Of the forest's ferny floor:
5   And a bird flew up out of the turret,
    Above the Traveller's head:
And he smote upon the door again a second time;
    "Is there anybody there?" he said.
But no one descended to the Traveller;
10   No head from the leaf-fringed sill
Leaned over and looked into his grey eyes,
    Where he stood perplexed and still.
But only a host of phantom listeners
    That dwelt in the lone house then
15 Stood listening in the quiet of the moonlight
    To that voice from the world of men:
Stood thronging the faint moonbeams on the dark stair,
    That goes down to the empty hall,
Hearkening in an air stirred and shaken
20   By the lonely Traveller's call.
And he felt in his heart their strangeness,
    Their stillness answering his cry,
While his horse moved, cropping the dark turf,
    'Neath the starred and leafy sky;
25 For he suddenly smote on the door, even
    Louder, and lifted his head:—
"Tell them I came, and no one answered,
    That I kept my word," he said.
Never the least stir made the listeners,

---

champed (CHAMPT) bit or chewed, usually impatiently
turret (TUR it) small tower on top of a building
smote (SMOHT) pounded; struck
perplexed (pur PLEKST) confused; puzzled
host (HOHST) large group
thronging (THRAWNG ing) crowding; jostling
cropping (KROP ing) biting off the tops
turf (TURF) short grass

The Listeners ■ 181

TEACHING PLAN

INTRODUCE

Motivation
Read aloud to the class another de la Mare or Poe poem. A good choice would be Poe's "Annabel Lee." It is straightforward and talks of young love. Point out that Poe's wife, Virginia, was 14 when they married.

Purpose-Setting Question
Have you ever been sure that something was there, searched and searched for it, but never found it.

READ

Literary Focus:
Narrative Poetry
Although "The Listeners" and "Eldorado" are quite short, the authors manage to include a great amount of detail into a small amount of space. Have students create a four-column chart for each poem with the following headings: *setting, characters, plot, theme.* As students read the poems, have them complete the charts.

Reading Focus:
Draw Conclusions
Have students draw upon their own experiences and on clues in the poems to draw conclusions about why the Traveller has come to the house and receives no response to his knocking and why the knight consults a pilgrim shadow and how he responds.

CLOSE

Have students complete Review the Selection on pages 184–185.

Develop Vocabulary Skills
Ask students to make flashcards of the new vocabulary words and to use each word in a sentence.

ESL Activity

Select a few common examples of narrative poetry. Have students work in groups. Assign one poem to each group. Have students identify the elements of fiction in their poem, and discuss these as a class.

Gustave Klimt (1863–1918) was an Austrian painter who had begun his career as a decorator. His interest in patterns and decorative design appears in much of his painting. His use of metallic paints and mosaic-like patterns gave his famous portraits of Viennese women a Byzantine quality. Later he used these same techniques to express humanity's inner most feelings of violence and huddled bodies and symbolic figures of anguish. In some paintings, like the scene here, he turned to mythical symbolism. The knight riding into the flower-filled field can be seen as a tin figure marching blindly off to war and destruction through a maze of decorative flowers. Ask: What does the title of this painting indicate about the knight? Does the knight represent all people? Could the knight represent both the Traveller and the knight in Eldorado?

Literary Focus:
Narrative Poetry
Have students discuss "The Listeners" as if it were a painting. Ask: What images are created by the details in the poem?

The Battle of Life (*Golden Knight*), Gustave Klimt, Galerie St. Etienne, New York

30   Though every word he spake
        Fell echoing through the shadowiness of the still house
            From the one man left awake:
        Ay, they heard his foot upon the stirrup,
            And the sound of iron on stone,
35   And how the silence surged softly backward,
        When the plunging hoofs were gone.

---

surged (SURJD) rolled; swelled up

ELDORADO

by Edgar Allan Poe

Gaily bedight,
A gallant knight,
In sunshine and in shadow,
Had journeyed long,
5   Singing a song,
In search of Eldorado.

But he grew old—
This knight so bold—
And o'er his heart a shadow
10 Fell, as he found
No spot of ground
That looked like Eldorado.

And, as his strength
Failed him at length
15 He met a pilgrim shadow—
"Shadow," said he,
"Where can it be—
This land of Eldorado?"

"Over the Mountains
20 Of the Moon,
Down the Valley of the Shadow,
Ride, boldly ride,"
The shade replied,
"If you seek for Eldorado!"

---

bedight (bih DYT) adorne
Eldorado (el duh RAH doh) a fabled place full of money-making opportunities

Eldorado ■ 183

Mini Quiz

Write on the chalkboard or overhead projector the following questions and call on students to fill in the blanks. Discuss the answers with the class.

1. "The Listeners" takes place _____.

2. A _____ flew from the turret of the house when the Traveller knocked.

3. The Traveller knocked on the door of the house _____ times.

4. A shadow fell over the knight's heart in "Eldorado" when he _____.

5. The pilgrim shadow told the knight to _____.

Answers
1. at night
2. bird
3. three
4. grew old and failed to find Eldorado
5. continue riding to find Eldorado

UNDERSTAND THE SELECTION

Answers

1. It is somewhere in the forest (because his horse eats grass from the "forest's ferny floor").
2. He rides away.
3. from "a pilgrim shadow"
4. spirits, because the traveler is described as having a voice "from the world of men," which implies that the Listeners are not of this world. Also, they are described as "phantom" listeners.
5. Because he felt "their stillness answering his cry"; somebody or something was inside the house.
6. His search began when he was young because he had "journeyed long."
7. He became discouraged and depressed.
8. Answers will vary. Sample: It was frightening. I felt like somebody was watching me, but I could not see them.
9. Knights are symbols of idealistic searches for things that may not exist.
10. Answers will vary. Sample: Yes, because he has searched his whole life for it and won't give up until he finds it.

Respond to Literature

Discuss with students how often in literature a character searches for a place or a thing that they think will make their life better. Many times it is what they learn about themselves or about life while on this journey that truly matters.

WRITE ABOUT THE SELECTION

Prewriting

Divide the class into four groups. Assign a verse to each. Ask them to translate troublesome words or phrases: for example, "gaily bedight" in verse 1, or "as his strength failed him at length" in verse 3. Then have the group turn its verse into prose.

Writing

Students should work individually. They already have one verse converted to prose. Circulate among students as they work, offering additional help.

Revising

It might help students if they think each verse converts to one paragraph. The transitions then should be smooth, as Poe's verses link together nicely.

Proofreading

Discuss as a class the use of punctuation in poems as compared to prose. Remind students of the extreme liberties taken by E. E. Cummings. Point out that poetry usually allows freer expression, and that it allows for less stringent punctuation rules.

Cooperative Group Activity

After they complete the Write About the Selection activity, have students gather in small groups and read their prose to group members. Have groups discuss how the prose differs from the poem. Ask: Which differences do you consider positive? Which do you consider negative?

Review the Selection

UNDERSTAND THE SELECTION

Recall

1. Where is the house the traveler stopped at in "The Listeners"?
2. What does the traveler do at the end of the poem?
3. From whom did the knight in "Eldorado" ask directions?

Infer

4. Who do you think the listeners are?
5. Why did the traveler knock on the door a third time?
6. When do you think the knight in "Eldorado" began his search?
7. What does Poe mean by the lines "And o'er his heart a shadow fell"?

Apply

8. Have you ever been in an empty building but felt as if someone else were there? Explain.
9. Why do you think a knight is used as the character in "Eldorado"?
10. Will the knight ever find Eldorado?

Respond to Literature

Can you think of other characters in books you have read who are like the knight in "Eldorado"? What are they looking for?

WRITE ABOUT THE SELECTION

Let us go back to a question asked in the opening discussions of these selections. Why do authors sometimes tell stories in poetry when they could write in prose? Maybe you can find an answer by experimenting with the Edgar Allan Poe poem. Like every narrative poem, it has all the elements of a short story. Rewrite Poe's poem as a short story.

Prewriting Make sure you understand all the words and phrases in the poem. Use a dictionary if you are not sure of any meanings. Then freewrite about the events in the poem to flesh out the narrative with details.

Writing The poem is a natural outline for your story. Use it and your freewriting to write your version, changing the poetry to prose. Do a stanza at a time. Each stanza could be one paragraph. You will probably need to add details and even events to make your tale logical and enjoyable.

Revising Read your story through without stopping to make any changes or corrections. Does it read smoothly? Is the theme as clear as in the original poem? Check the transitions between paragraphs. Then go back and make any changes you think are needed.

Proofreading Reread your story and check for errors. Make sure you use correct punctuation, particularly at the ends of sentences. The poem uses many dashes, which you should not use for end punctuation in your prose story.

THINK ABOUT NARRATIVE POETRY

A narrative poem tells a story. The poem will have elements similar to a short story —plot, setting, characters, and theme. In addition, narrative poems can have other poetic elements. The structures of "Eldorado" and "The Listeners" show one of the strengths of using poetry to tell a story.

1. What is the plot of the two poems?

2. Describe the main characters in "The Listeners" and "Eldorado." How are they similar?

3. What is the setting of "The Listeners"? Of "El Dorado"? What do the settings have in common?

4. Explain the themes of both poems in your own words.

5. Rhythm and rhyme together can give a poem a distinctive feeling. What feeling do they create in these poems?

READING FOCUS

Draw Conclusions For each poem that you read, describe one conclusion that you drew about a character or an event. What clues in the poem helped you come to this conclusion?

DEVELOP YOUR VOCABULARY

You often find odd verbs and verb forms in poems. This might be because the poet is trying to find one word to rhyme with another. Perhaps, as in the case of "The Listeners," it might be because the poem was written about a long time ago when different verbs and verb forms were used commonly.

An example of an old verb is the word *smote,* which appears twice in the poem. A dictionary can help you understand both its meaning and whether it still is used.

Here is the entry:
smote (smōt) v., past tense of *smite.*

If you look up *smite,* you will find all the forms of the verb. You will find also that *smite* as a verb meaning "to hit or strike hard" is "Now Rare."

Choose five old verbs from the poems. Then use them in original sentences. Use a dictionary to find the present/past tenses and definitions of these "old" verbs.

THINK ABOUT NARRATIVE POETRY

Answers

1. They tell about a traveler and a knight who encounter spirits on their journeys through life.

2. The Traveller is a lonely man of unspecified age who remains faithful to a promise he made. The knight is a gaily dressed old man who remained true to his quest for Eldorado. Both are travelers who remain faithful to their quest; both come across spirits.

3. The setting of "The Listener" is outside a lone house in a forest. "Eldorado" takes place on an unspecified road. Both are mysterious, unknown settings.

4. Answers will vary. Students may identify loneliness, search for fulfillment or faith.

5. A feeling of endless searching because of the regular repetition of stress and sound.

DEVELOP YOUR VOCABULARY

Sample Answers

1. dwelt—The birds dwelt in the forest where the tallest trees were.

2. hearkening—Hearkening to the sound of the bells, we all ran toward the church.

3. spake—Every word he spake meant nothing to us.

4. gaily—We rode to the party on horseback, with the bells jingling gaily.

5. gallant—The gallant young man helped the woman across the puddle.

READING FOCUS

Sample Answer

In "The Listeners," the listeners are ghosts. They are called "phantom listeners." They are not from the world of men; they have a strangeness. In "Eldorado," the pilgrim shadow tells the knight he will find Eldorado when he dies—when he goes to the great beyond over the mountains of the moon and through the valley of the shadow (of death).

ESL Activity

Have students work to complete the writing assignment. Native speakers should help ESL students with difficult vocabulary in the poems. Encourage students to add unfamiliar words.

SELECTION OBJECTIVES

After completing this selection, students will be able to

- understand exposition
- write a description in the style of a reporter
- focus their descriptive writing
- recognize other types of composition in combination with exposition
- see differences between American and British English
- evaluate the writer's purpose

Lesson Resources

The Loch Ness Monster
- Selection Synopsis, Teacher's Edition, pp. T107g–T107h
- Comprehension and Vocabulary Workbook, pp. 39–40
- Language Enrichment Workbook, pp. 39–40
- Teacher's Resources
  Reinforcement, p. R20
  Test, pp. T37–T38

More About Exposition

Students might understand better the meaning of exposition if you point out its root word, "expose." News reporters like to "expose" corruption, you could note, as an illustration of the principle of exposition. An "exposé" (the noun form, pronounced ex-poh-ZAY) is nothing more than giving background information that describes or explains facts and ideas.

About the Author

John McPhee has a special connection with Great Britain: His ancestors were from the Hebrides, the islands north of Scotland, and he studied for a year at Cambridge University. He calls himself "fundamentally . . . a working journalist," a profession in which he received rigorous training while working for *Time* magazine.

READING FOCUS

Evaluate the Writer's Purpose Every author has a purpose for writing. The purpose may be to inform, to entertain, or to persuade the reader. The way they present information is the way you can determine their purpose. As you read, look for factual, humorous, or persuasive details. This will help you decide the author's purpose. It is up to the reader to decide the writer's purpose.

Learn About

EXPOSITION

Exposition is one of the four types of nonfiction composition. Often when you are asked to write an essay in science or history about types of animals or the causes of World War I, you are writing exposition. The purpose of **exposition** is to explain something to your readers.

While exposition can exist in a form of its own, it is often combined with other types of writing. Exposition can be used to support arguments in persuasive writing, and descriptive writing can blend with exposition to offer examples that explain an important point.

As you read the next selection, ask yourself these questions:

1. What is John McPhee explaining to his readers?
2. What other types of writing does the author use in this essay?

WRITING CONNECTION

Think about something you really enjoy or something that you are good at doing. Use exposition to explain about your "something" to a reader who knows very little about your subject. What do your readers really need to understand?

Background Notes

Major highways in Britain use the prefixes "M" or "A." "M" stands for motorway, a four-lane road (called a dual carriageway in Britain). "A" roads are other major roads (usually two lanes), and "B" roads are minor roads (two lanes).

Cooperative Group Activity

Have students discuss in groups what their talents are. As a prewriting exercise for the Writing Connection, encourage students to write down some things they would like their readers to know about their talents.

THE LOCH NESS MONSTER

ADAPTED

by John McPhee

The road—the A-82—stayed close to the lake, often on ledges that had been blasted into the mountainsides. The steep forests continued, broken now and again, on one shore or the other, by fields of fern, clumps of bright-yellow shrubs and isolated stands of cedar. Along the far shore were widely separated houses and farms, which to the eyes of a traveller appeared almost unbelievably green and fertile after the spare desolation of some of the higher glens. We came to the top of the rise and suddenly saw, on the right-hand side of the road, on the edge of a

---

glens (GLENZ) narrow, secluded valleys

The Loch Ness Monster ■ 187

Develop Vocabulary Skills

McPhee does not write simply, and even though this story has been adapted students should expect challenging vocabulary. Introduce the new words in a "vocabulary bee." Divide the class into two teams, and as in a spelling bee, ask students in turn for the correct definition of the word.

Background Note

"Loch" is a Scottish word for "lake." Loch Ness, about 25 miles long but very narrow, is in the northern third of Scotland, about 100 miles due north of Glasgow.

ESL Activity

Find the location of Loch Ness on a map and show it to the students. See if they can find other lochs in the area and discuss why they are a likely place for this mysterious creature to live.

TEACHING PLAN

INTRODUCE

Motivation
Find a copy of a purported photograph of the Loch Ness Monster. Discuss with students the problems of verifying the existence of something many people doubt.

Purpose-Setting Question
Can this unbiased reporting prove that a phenomenon such as the Loch Ness Monster really exists?

READ

Literary Focus:
Exposition
The author of "The Loch Ness Monster" is clearly explaining something to his readers, but he draws no conclusions of his own along the way. Instead, he presents facts and observations as he gathers them and allows the reader to make up his or her own mind. Ask: What is the author trying to explain to the reader? Is he direct in his explanations?

Reading Focus:
Evaluate the Writer's Purpose
Discuss with students possible reasons someone would write about the Loch Ness Monster. An author might present facts to inform readers or provide his own opinions to persuade them. As students read, have them watch for evidence of McPhee's purpose. To help, have them divide a sheet of paper into two columns headed *Existence of Monster* and *Nonexistence of Monster*. As students read, have them record details that reveal his purpose.

CLOSE

Have students complete Review the Selection on pages 198–199.

Literary Focus:
Exposition

Ask students to note the sensory detail about the landscape and people that McPhee mixes in with his explanation of the work being done. Ask: How does this make the story more real and engaging?

high meadow that sloped sharply a considerable distance to the lake, a cluster of caravans and other vehicles, arranged in the shape of a C, with an opening toward the road—much like a circle of covered wagons formed for protection against savage attack. All but one or two of the vehicles were painted bright lily-pad green. The compound, in its compact half acre, was surrounded by a fence, to keep out, among other things, sheep, which were grazing all over the slope in deep-green turf among buttercups, daisies, and thistles. Gulls above beat hard into the wind, then turned and planed toward the south. Gulls are inland birds in Scotland, there being so little distance from anywhere to the sea. A big fireplace had been made from rocks of the sort that were scattered all over the meadow. And on the lakeward side a platform had been built, its level high position emphasizing the slope of the hill, which dropped away below it. Mounted on the platform was a thirty-five-millimeter motion-picture camera with an enormous telephoto lens. From its point of view, sticking out at two hundred feet above the lake, the camera could take in a dazzling scene that covered thousands of acres of water.

This was Expedition Headquarters, the principal field station of the Loch Ness Phenomena Investigation Bureau—dues five pounds per annum,[1] life membership one hundred pounds, tax on donations recoverable under covenant.[2] Those who join the bureau receive newsletters and annual reports, and are allowed to participate in the fieldwork if they so desire. I turned into the compound and parked between two bright-green reconditioned old London taxis. The central area had long since been worn grassless and was covered at this moment with fine-grain dust. People were coming and going. The place seemed rather public, as if it were a depot. No one even halfway interested in the natural history of the Great Glen would think of driving up the A-82 without stopping in there. Since the A-82 is the principal route between Glasgow and Inverness,[3] it is not surprising that the apparently amphibious creature as yet unnamed, the so-called Loch Ness Monster, has been seen not only from the highway but on it.

The atmosphere around the headquarters suggested a scientific frontier and also a boom town, much as Cape Canaveral and Cocoa Beach do. There were, as well, hints of show business and fine arts. Probably the one word that might have been applied to everyone present was adventurer. There was, at any

---

caravans (KAR uh vanz) in Great Britain, camping trailers
telephoto (TEL uh foht oh) a camera lens that is able to make faraway things appear large
amphibious (am FIB ee us) able to live on land and in water
[1]**dues five pounds per annum:** amount of British money per year that it costs to belong
[2]**tax on donations recoverable by covenant:** Taxes paid on donations will be refunded
[3]**Glasgow and Inverness:** cities in southern and northern Scotland

rate, nothing really laboratorial about the place, although the prevailing mood seemed to be one not of holiday but of matter-of-fact application and patient dedication. A telephone call came in that day, to the caravan that served as an office, from a woman who owned an inn south of Inverarigaig, on the other side of the lake. She said that she had seen the creature that morning just forty yards offshore—three humps, nothing else to report, and being very busy just now, thank you very much, good day. This was recorded, with no particular display of excitement, by an extremely attractive young woman who appeared to be in her late twenties, an artist from London who had missed but one summer at Loch Ness in seven years. She wore sandals, dungarees, a black pullover, and gold earrings. Her name was Mary Piercy, and her toes were painted pink. The bulletin board where she recorded the sighting resembled the kind used in railway stations for the listing of incoming trains.

The office walls were decorated with photographs of the monster in various postures basking, cruising, diving, splashing, looking up questioningly. A counter was covered with some of the essential publications: the bureau's annual report (twenty-nine sightings the previous year), J. A. Carruth's *Loch Ness and Its Monster* (The Abbey Press, Fort Augustus), Tim Dinsdale's *Loch Ness Monster* (Routledge and Kegan Paul, London), and a report by the joint Air Reconnaissance Center of the Royal Air Force on a motion picture of the monster swimming about half a mile on the lake's surface. These books and documents could, in turn, lead the interested reader to less available but nonetheless highly important works such as R. T. Gould's *The Loch Ness Monster and Others* and Constance Whyte's *More Than a Legend*.

My children looked over the photographs with absorption but not a great deal of awe, and they bought about a dozen postcards with glossy prints of a picture of the monster—three humps showing, much the same sight that the innkeeper had described—that had been taken by a man named Stuart, directly across the lake from Urquhart Castle. The three younger girls then ran out into the meadow and began to pick daisies and buttercups. Their mother and sister sat down in the sun to read about the creature in the lake, and to write postcards. We were on our way to Inverness, but with no need to hurry. "Dear Grammy, we came to see the monster today."

From the office to the camera-observation platform to the caravan that served as a pocket cafeteria, I wandered around among the crew, was offered and accepted tea, and squinted with imaginary experience up and down the lake, where the water had grown even rougher. Among the crew at the time were two

---

basking (BASK ing) warming oneself pleasantly, as in sunlight
reconnaissance (rih KON uh sens) quick survey of information

The Loch Ness Monster ■ 189

Critical Thinking:
Analyze
Point out the use of specific example to illustrate a point McPhee wants to make, that the prevailing mood was not one of holiday but of application and patient dedication. For example, he mentions a counter covered with essential bibliography. Ask: Why does he make this distinction? What is he trying to make clear to the reader about the work being done?

Reading Focus:
Evaluate the Writer's Purpose
McPhee writes down practically everything he sees, down to the titles, authors, and publishers of books on display. The books are references which he can consult later if he wants more information on the monster. Ask: Why does he present these details to the reader? What does this reveal about his purpose?

Canadians, a Swede, an Australian, three Americans, two Englishmen, a Welshman, and one Scot. Two were women. When I asked one of the crew members if he knew what jobs some of the others had when they were not at Loch Ness, he said, "I'm not sure what they are. We don't go into that." This was obviously a place where now was all that mattered, and in such surroundings it is distinctly pleasant to accept that approach to things. Nonetheless, I found that I couldn't stick completely to this principle, and I did find out that one man was a medical doctor, another a farmer, another a retired naval officer, and that several were students, as might be expected. The daily watch begins at four in the morning and goes on, as one fellow put it, "as long as we can stand up." It has been the pattern among the hundreds of sightings reported that the early-morning hours are the most promising ones. Camera stations are manned until ten at night, dawn and sunset being so close to midnight at that latitude in summer, but the sentries tend to thin out with the lengthening of the day. During the autumn, the size of the crew reduces almost to one.

One man lives at the headquarters all year long. His name is Clem Lister Skelton. "I've been staring at that piece of water since five o'clock," he said, while he drank tea in the mess caravan.

"Is there a technique?" I asked him.

"Just look," he said. "Look. Run your eye over the water in one quick skim. What we're looking for is not hard to see. You just sit and sort of gaze at the loch, that's all. Mutter a few incantations. That's all there is to do. In wintertime, very often, it's just myself. And of course one keeps a very much more perfunctory watch in the winter. I saw it once in a snowstorm, though, and that was the only time I've had a clear view of the head and neck. The neck is obviously very mobile. The creature was quite big, but it wasn't as big as a seventy-foot MFV. Motor fishing vessel. I'd been closer to it, but I hadn't seen as much of it before. I've seen it eight times. The last time was in September. Only the back. Just the sort of upturned boat, which is the classic view of it."

Skelton drank some more tea, and refilled a cup he had given me. "I must know what it is," he went on. "I shall never rest peacefully until I know what it is. Some of the largest creatures in the world are out there, and we can't name them. It may take ten years, but we're going to identify the genus. Most people are not as fanatical as I, but I would like to see this through to the end, if I don't get too broke first."

Skelton is a tall, informed man, English, with reddish hair that is uncombed in long strings from the thinning crown of his head. In outline, Skelton's life

---

technique (tek NEEK) method of doing something
incantations (in kan TAY shunz) magical words used in enchantment
perfunctory (pur FUNK tuh ree) routine; superficial
genus (JEE nus) main subdivision of a family of closely related species
fanatical (fuh NAT ih kul) incredibly devoted, to the point of being unreasonable

190 ■ Unit 2

Literary Focus:
Character
The long passage about Skelton provides an insight into what motivates the people who run the Loch Ness Phenomena Investigation Bureau. Ask: What do you learn about the Bureau members' motivation?

there in the caravan on the edge of the high meadow over the lake, in a place that must be uncorrectably gloomy during the wet rains of winter, seemed cagelike and hopeless to me—unacceptably lonely. The impression he gave was of a man who had drawn a circle around himself many hundreds of miles from the rest of his life. But how could I know? He was saying that he had flown Supermarine Spitfires[4] for the R.A.F. during the Second World War. His father had been a soldier, and when Skelton was a boy, he lived, as he put it, "all over the place." As an adult, he became first an actor, later a writer and director of films. He acted in London in plays like *March Hare* and *Saraband for Dead Lovers*. One film he directed was, in his words, "a dreadful thing called *Saul and David*." These appearances on the surface apparently did not occur so frequently that he needed to do nothing else for a livelihood. He also directed, in the course of many years, several hundred educational films. The publisher who distributed some of these films was David James, a friend of Skelton's, and at that time a Member of Parliament.[5] James happened to be, as well, the founder of the Loch Ness Phenomena Investigation Bureau—phenomena, because, for breeding purposes, there would have to be at least two monsters living in the lake at any one time, probably more, and in fact two had on occasion been sighted at the same time. James asked Skelton if he would go up to the lake and give the bureau the benefit of his technical knowledge of movie cameras. "Anything for a laugh," Skelton had said to James. This was in the early nineteen-sixties. "I came for a fortnight," Skelton said now, in the caravan. "And I saw it. I wanted to know what it was, and I've wanted to know what it was ever since. I thought I'd have time to write up here, but I haven't. I don't do anything now except hunt this beast."

Skelton talked on about what the monster might be—a magnified newt, a long-necked variety of giant seal, still existing *Elasmosaurus*. Visitors wandered by in groups outside the caravan, and unexplained strangers kept coming in for tea. In the air was a feeling, utterly hidden by the relative permanence of the place, of a country carnival on a two-night stand. The caravans themselves, in their placement, suggested a section of a carnival. I remembered a woman shouting to attract people to a big caravan on a carnival midway one night in May in New Jersey. That was some time ago. I must have been nineteen. The woman, who was standing on a small platform, was fifty or sixty, and she was trying to get people to go into the caravan to see big jungle cats, I suppose, and brown bears—"Ferocious Beasts," at any rate, according to block lettering on the side of the caravan. A steel cage containing a

---

fortnight (FAWRT nyt) two weeks
newt (NOOT) small salamander found in damp places
[4]**Supermarine Spitfires** for the **R.A.F.:** Fighter planes for the British Royal Air Force
[5]**Parliament:** The national legislative body of Great Britain

small black bear had been set up on two sawhorses outside the caravan—a fragment to suggest what might be found on a large scale inside.

So young that it was no more than two feet from nose to tail, the bear was engaged in desperate motion, racing along one side of the cage from corner to corner, striking the steel bars bluntly with its nose. Whirling then tossing its head over its shoulder like a racing swimmer, it turned and bolted crazily for the opposite end. Its eyes were deep red and shining in a kind of full-sighted blindness. It had gone mad there in the cage and its motion, rhythmic and tortured, never stopped, back and forth, back and forth, the head tossing with each jarring turn. The animal skinned its sides on the steel bars as it ran. Hair and skin had scraped from its sides so that pink flesh showed in the downpour of the carnival arc lights. Blood drained freely through the thinned hair of its belly and dropped onto the floor of the cage. What had a paralyzing effect on me was the animal's almost perfect and now involuntary rhythm—the wild toss of the head after the crash into the corner, the turn, the scraping run, the crash again at the other end, never stopping, regular—the exposed interior of some brutal and living time piece.

Beside the cage, the plump, critical woman, red-faced, red-nosed, kept shouting to the crowds, but she said to me, leaning down with her eyes bloodshot,

"Why don't you move on, sonny, if you ain't going to buy a ticket? Beat it. Come on, now. Move on."

"I argue about what it is," Skelton said. "I'm inclined to think it's a giant slug, but there is an amazingly impressive theory for its being a worm. You can't rule out that it's one of the big dinosaurs, but I think this is more wishful thinking than anything else." In the late nineteen-thirties, a large and strange-looking footprint was found along the shore of Loch Ness. It was carefully studied by various people and was assumed, for a time, to be an impression from a foot or flipper of the monster. Eventually, the print was identified. Someone who owned the preserved foot of a hippopotamus had successfully brought off a trick that put layers of mockery and incredibility over the creature in the lake for many years. The Second World War further turned aside any serious interest that amateurs or naturalists might have taken. Sightings continued, however, in a regular pattern, and finally, in the early nineteen-sixties, the Loch Ness Phenomena Investigation Bureau was established. "I have no plans whatever for leaving," Skelton said. "I am prepared to stay here ad infinitum. All my worldly goods are here."

A dark-haired young woman had stepped into the caravan and poured herself a cup of tea. Skelton, introducing her to me, said, "If the beast has done nothing else, it has brought me a wife.

---

slug (SLUG) a small animal like a snail, but without such a hard, outer shell
ad infinitum (ad in fuh NYT um) Latin phrase meaning forever

The Loch Ness Monster ■ 193

Reading Focus:
Evaluate the Writer's Purpose
McPhee uses the placement of the caravans as the link to a description of a New Jersey carnival midway. Ask students to look for a broader meaning. What is his purpose in linking the two scenes?

Critical Thinking:
Classify
Skelton names three kinds of animals that the monster might be. Ask: Are there other animals that the creature could logically be? Discuss reasons for including some possibilities and eliminating others.

She was studying Gaelic and Scottish history at Edinburgh University, and she walked into the glen one day, and I said, 'That is the girl I am going to marry.'" He gestured toward a window of the caravan, which framed a view of the hills and the lake. "The Great Glen is one of the most beautiful places in the world," he continued. "It is peaceful here. I'd be happy here all my life, even if there were nothing in the loch. I've even committed the unforgivable sin of going to sleep in the sun during a flat calm. With enough time, we could shoot the beast with a crossbow, and a line, and get a bit of skin. We could also shoot a small transmitter into its hide and learn more than we know now about its habits and characteristics. "

The creature swims with remarkable speed, as much as 12 to 18 mph when it is really moving. It makes no noise other than sudden splashes, but it is apparently responsive in a highly sensitive way to sound. A shout, an approaching engine, any loud report, will send it into an immediate dive, and this shyness is in large part the cause of why it can't be found, and therefore of its mystery. Curiously, though, the echoing sound was what apparently brought the creature wide attention, for the first series of frequent sightings occurred in 1933, when A-82 was blasted into the cliffsides of the western shore of the lake. Immense boulders kept falling into the depths, and shock waves from dynamite repeatedly ran through the water, causing the creature to lose confidence in its environment and to alter, at least temporarily, its shy and preferred nightlife. In that year it was first observed on land, perhaps attempting to seek a way out forever from the blasts that had alarmed it. A couple named Spicer saw it, near Inverarigiag, and later described its long, serpent-like neck, followed by an awkward hulk of a body, lurching toward the lake and disappearing into high undergrowth as they approached.

With the exception of one report recorded in the sixth century, which said that a monster (fitting the description of the current creatures in the lake) had killed a man with a single bite, there have been no other examples of savagery on its part. To the contrary, its sensitivity to people seems to be sharp, and it keeps a wide margin between itself and mankind. In all likelihood, it feeds on fish and particularly on eels, of which there are millions in the lake. Loch Ness is unparalleled in eel-fishing circles, and has drawn commercial eel fishermen from all over the United Kingdom. The monster has been observed with its neck bent down in the water, like a swan feeding. When the creatures die, they apparently settle into the seven-hundred-foot floor of the lake, where the temperature is always forty-two degrees Fahrenheit—so cold that the lake is known for never

---

Gaelic (GAYL ik) A Celtic language spoken in Scotland and Ireland
crossbow (KRAWS boh) a kind of bow that is set flat for firing
transmitter (trans MIT ur) radio device that sends out signals

Discussion
Ask students if they think this is a photo of the Loch Ness Monster. Have them support their opinions with passages from the selection.

Critical Thinking:
Infer
Point out the clause "there was something inconvenient about the monster's actual appearance." Ask: What is McPhee actually saying? Why wouldn't McPhee simply say, "Unfortunately, it looked like a monster"?

Literary Focus:
Exposition
The writer does an excellent job of explaining what the creature looks like and how it moves. Ask: How might the descriptions have changed had this been a fictional account?

giving up its dead. Loch Ness never freezes, despite its high latitude, so if the creature breathes air, as has seemed apparent from the reports of observers who have watched its mouth rhythmically opening and closing, it does not lose access to the surface in winter. It clearly prefers the smooth, sunbaked waters of summer, however, as it seems to love to bask in the sun, like an upturned boat, slowly rolling, plunging, squirming around with what can only be taken as pleasure. By observers' reports, the creature has two pairs of side flippers, and when it swims off, tail thrashing, it leaves behind it a trail of water as impressive as the track of a small warship. When it dives from a still position, it unexplainably goes down without leaving a bubble. When it dives as it swims, it leaves on the surface a churning signature of foam.

Skelton leaned back against the wall of the caravan in a lazy and calm posture. He was wearing a dark blue tie that was monogrammed in small block letters sewn with white thread—L.N.I. (Loch Ness Investigation). Above the monogram and embroidered also in white thread was a small picture of the monster—humps rising regularly, head high, tail extending in back. Skelton gave the tie a tap with one hand. "You get this with a five-pound membership," he said.

The sea-serpent effect given by the white thread on the tie was less a cartoon-like drawing than an attempt toward a naturalistic sketch. As I studied it there, framed on Skelton's chest, the thought occurred to me that there was something inconvenient about the monster's actual appearance. In every sense except possibly the sense that involves cruelty, the creature in Loch Ness is indeed a monster. An average taken from many films and sightings gives its mature length at about forty feet. Its general appearance is very unattractive, in the sense in which reptiles are repulsive to many human beings, and any number of people might find difficulty in accepting a creature that looks like the one that was slain by St. George.[6] Its neck, about six feet long, column-like, powerfully muscled, is the neck of a serpent. Its head, scarcely broader than the neck, is a serpent's head, with uncompromising, lens-shaped eyes. Sometimes as it swims it holds its head and neck erect. The creature's mouth is at least a foot wide. Its body rises and falls with the waves. Its skin glistens when wet and appears coarse, spotted, gray, and elephant-like when exposed to the air long enough to become dry. The tail, long and column-like, stretches back to something of a point. It seemed to me, sitting there at Headquarters, that the classical, mythical, dragon likeness of this living thing—the modified dinosaur, the fantastically exaggerated newt—was an obstacle to the work of the investigation bureau. The bureau has no real interest in what the monster resembles or calls to mind but a great deal in what it actually is. Their goal is a final and positive identification of the genus.

---

[6]**St. George:** Christian saint who supposedly killed a large dragon.

"What we need is a good, lengthy, basking sighting," Skelton said. "We've had one long surfacing—twenty-five minutes. I saw it. Opposite Urquhart Castle. We only had a twelve-inch lens then, at four and a half miles. We have thirty-six-inch lenses now. We need a long, clear, close-up—in color."

My children had watched, some months earlier, the killing of a small snake on a lawn in Maryland. About eighteen inches long, it came out from a basement-window well, through a covering screen of redwood, and was noticed with shouts and shrieks by the children and a young retriever that barked at the snake and leaped about it in a circle. We were the weekend guests of another family, and eight children in all crowded around the snake, which had been gliding slowly across the lawn during the moments after it had been seen, but had now stopped and was turning its head from side to side in apparent indecision. Our host hurried into his garage and came running back to the lawn with a long shovel. Before he killed the snake, his wife urged him not to. She said the snake could not possibly be poisonous. He said, "How do you know?" The children, mine and theirs, looked back and forth from him to her. The dog began to bark more rapidly and at a higher pitch.

"It has none of the markings. There is nothing triangular about its head," she told him.

"That may very well be," he said. "But you can't be sure."

"It is *not* poisonous. Leave it alone. Look at all these children."

"I can't help that."

"It is *not* poisonous."

"How do you know?"

"I know."

He hit the snake with the flat of the shovel, and it twisted. He hit it again. It kept moving. He hit it a third time, and it stopped. Its underside, whitish green, turned up. The children moved in for a closer look.

The Loch Ness Monster ■ 197

Reading Focus: Evaluate the Writer's Purpose

The ending is not about the Loch Ness Monster but about the killing of a snake in Maryland. Ask: What is the purpose of the anecdote?

Mini Quiz

Write on the chalkboard or overhead projector the following questions and call on students to fill in the blanks. Discuss the answers with the class.

1. The A-82 highway runs between _____ and _____.

2. The one sighting of the monster that occurred the day McPhee visited came from a woman who owned an _____.

3. The crew of observers starts looking for the monster at _____.

4. The only clear view Clem Lister Skelton had of the monster's head and neck was during a _____.

5. The footprint found in the 1930s was not of the monster but of a _____.

Answers

1. Glasgow, Inverness
2. inn
3. 4 A.M.
4. snowstorm
5. hippopotamus

UNDERSTAND THE SELECTION

Answers

1. They were like covered wagons circled to guard against attack.
2. Cape Canaveral and Cocoa Beach
3. a sixth-century report, when the monster supposedly "killed a man with a single bite"
4. He wants to convey the impression of this being an actual observer with a camera recording everything he sees.
5. to make the essay more interesting, and believable, and give the work of the Loch Ness Expedition more validity
6. The children's lackadaisical attitude is not unlike the mood of methodical curiosity of the members of the Loch Ness Phenomena Investigation Bureau.
7. The Expedition Headquarters area reminds McPhee of a "country carnival on a two-night stand." The bear show is described because of the manner in which the barker tried to get people interested in seeing the show. Pay up (meaning get interested) or get out is the message at both Loch Ness and New Jersey.
8. Answers will vary. Sample: Send in teams of divers to look for the monster.
9. He writes in a neutral tone that makes it difficult to tell if he believes or not.
10. Answers will vary. Sample: There have been many sightings, and McPhee shows that the people hunting the monster are not crazy but sincere and dedicated.

Respond to Literature

Lake monster sightings have also been reported in North America: in Lake Champlain between Vermont and New York, and in Lake Memphremagog between Vermont and Quebec, Canada. This could corroborate the existence of lake monsters, or simply be the result of the power of suggestion. People are often quick to label creatures that are unfamiliar as being "monsters". Fear can make people exaggerate what they have seen, rather than taking the time to understand it.

UNDERSTAND THE SELECTION

Recall

1. Describe the cluster of trailers.

2. What two places does Expedition Headquarters remind McPhee of?

3. What is the only report of the monster's hurting people?

Infer

4. Why do you think McPhee writes in first-person point of view?

5. Why does McPhee include so many details in his story?

6. Why do you think McPhee describes what his children did when they looked at the Expedition exhibits?

7. Explain the significance of the story about the New Jersey carnival show.

Apply

8. Standing all day next to a camera seems an inefficient way to track the monster. Do you have any better ideas?

9. Do you think John McPhee believes the Loch Ness Monster exists? Explain.

10. Do you believe the Loch Ness Monster exists? Give some reasons.

Respond to Literature

Why do some people believe creatures like Nessie and Bigfoot exist?

WRITE ABOUT THE SELECTION

John McPhee is an expert nonfiction writer. You can learn from the way he writes, particularly his use of exposition.

In the selection opening, you were asked to explain about something you enjoyed or are good at. Look again at what you wrote. Do you have any ideas for improving it?

Prewriting   Think of a reason or purpose for telling about your hobby or talent. McPhee always has a purpose for his writing. What is the purpose of yours? Will you entertain, inform, persuade? Write that purpose at the top of your paper. Then freewrite for five minutes on your topic.

Writing   Keeping the purpose in mind, use any parts of what you have written already to write a new explanation. Add new details, or focus in on one or two important features.

Revising   Look at a single descriptive paragraph in McPhee's story. Then read your paragraph. Can you borrow any of McPhee's techniques to improve your writing? Make sure you vary sentence structures. Too many sentences constructed in the same way can bore readers.

Proofreading   Reread your description and check that you have used initial capital letters for all proper nouns: the name of your school, football team, school newspaper, and so forth. Check the spelling of each proper noun you include.

WRITE ABOUT THE SELECTION

Prewriting

Encourage students to think of a specific feeling they have when they see the school building. How can their descriptions relay this feeling?

Writing

As students work individually, circulate and ask to see their first draft (from the selection opening). Ask how they are improving on it.

Revising

Work cooperatively as a class to review a paragraph in McPhee's story. The annotations point out two particularly well-done descriptive paragraphs.

Proofreading

Review basic capitalization rules with the class. Ask for examples from students' descriptions to illustrate the rules.

THINK ABOUT EXPOSITION

This selection uses more description and exposition than any other selection you've read so far. The purpose of exposition is to explain something. While it can be used by itself, it is often combined with other types of composition. McPhee combines exposition and description but other writers blend persuasion or narration with exposition.

1. How does the story begin? What feeling do you have after reading the first paragraph?

2. Look at the third paragraph which talks about the atmosphere of the headquarters. How does McPhee describe it? What does he explain with his description?

3. Why do you think McPhee provides names of books about the monster in the next paragraph?

4. Why is it important for McPhee to try to report about the "adventurers'" jobs?

5. What is John McPhee explaining to his readers?

READING FOCUS

Evaluate the Writer's Purpose As you read, you were able to ask questions about why the author presented certain information and why he used a certain style of writing. What do you think the author's purpose in writing this story was? Did he achieve the results he wanted?

DEVELOP YOUR VOCABULARY

People in Britain sometimes use different words for things than do people in the United States. For example, the *hood* of a car is called a *bonnet* in Britain and what Americans call the *trunk* is the *boot* to the British. Some words commonly used in Britain are not used in the United States. *Fortnight*, for example, means two weeks. People in the United States do not usually use this word.

You can check for alternative or new meanings of words in the dictionary. If a word is used mainly in Britain rather than the U.S., the note [Chiefly Brit.] will come before the definition. Knowing about the background of a new word can help you understand a selection.

Use a dictionary to help you find definitions people in Britain might have for these words. Then use the words in sentences.

1. caravan	6. hoover
2. chips	7. goods
3. crisp	8. lorry
4. boot	9. petrol
5. nappy	10. holiday

Review the Selection ■ 199

DEVELOP YOUR VOCABULARY

Answers

1. camping trailer—We are taking our caravan to the lake.
2. french fries—I love chips and hamburgers.
3. potato chip—Do not give me a single crisp! I am on a diet!
4. trunk of a car—Put the suitcase in the boot, will you?
5. diaper—This baby needs a new nappy!
6. vacuum—You can use the hoover to clean this room.
7. freight—The goods train lumbered out of station.
8. truck—That crazy lorry is going 80 mph!
9. gasoline—We have got to stop for petrol; we are on empty.
10. vacation—We are going to Florida on holiday this year.

READING FOCUS

Sample Answer

I think that the author wanted to present the facts about the Loch Ness Monster and the people who study it in an unbiased, factual way so that readers could make up their own minds about whether or not the monster exists and what kind of creature it is.

ESL Activity

How many different names for money can students think of? Ask: What are names for money in the United States? What names for money from other countries can you think of?

THINK ABOUT EXPOSITION

Answers

1. The story begins by providing the setting of Loch Ness and the Expedition Headquarters. The reader feels like he is on a journey, suddenly reaches the top of a rise, and spies suspicious activity below.

2. Compares headquarters to other specific places; uses metaphors such as "cirrus wisps of show business and fine arts"; tells of a specific telephone call received that day; and sketches the character, Mary Piercy, who records the reported sighting.

3. Naming the books gives an air of authority to his writing; he appears to have investigated things thoroughly.

4. Because most of them do not think their jobs are nearly as important as tracking the monster and so do not talk much about their jobs.

5. That the Loch Ness Investigation is a group formed to preserve and identify a creature that some think is imaginary and others think is a monster.

SELECTION OBJECTIVES

After completing this selection, students will be able to

- understand the nuances of persuasion
- make a convincing argument
- evaluate reports of supernatural creatures
- write a persuasive text
- understand why opinions need supporting facts
- recognize the foreign roots of words
- make inferences about setting

Lesson Resources

The Great Amherst Mystery
- Selection Synopsis, Teacher's Edition, p. T107h
- Comprehension and Vocabulary Workbook, pp. 41–42
- Language Enrichment Workbook, p. 41
- Teacher's Resources
  Reinforcement, p. R21
  Test, pp. T39–T40

More About Persuasion

Did John McPhee's story convince students that the Loch Ness Monster exists? If it did, that was not really the author's intention: He did not set out to persuade the reader but rather, simply, to inform. A persuasive story, on the other hand, uses exposition as evidence to convince readers to accept a stated point of view: its purpose is intentional.

More About the Unit Theme

Have students recall the poem, "hist, whist," in which supernatural beings were treated lightheartedly. Ask: Is that what most people think of spirits from the unknown? Or, do they shudder just a little?

About the Author

Unlike most of the authors in this unit, Walter Hubbell is not a professional writer; he notes he is an actor

Learn About

PERSUASION

Is it possible that monsters, ghosts, and spirits really exist? In this selection, the author tells us about "poltergeists," or ghosts that create noisy disturbances. He did not believe in ghosts until he did some investigative work of his own. After his investigation, he was persuaded that poltergeists are real. He says he has seen what they can do.

"The Great Amherst Mystery" was written to persuade you, too. **Persuasion** is writing or speech that attempts to convince the reader or listener to adopt an opinion or course of action. The author tries to establish the truth of a proposition by presenting facts, testimony of reliable witnesses, and other evidence. He also uses other types of composition such as exposition, description, and narration. He wants to convince you to believe ghosts might exist.

As you read the next selection, ask yourself these questions:

1. How does the author try to persuade us that poltergeists exist?
2. Are the author's points convincing?

READING FOCUS

Make Inferences About Setting Sometimes an author will directly state where a story takes place. At other times, the reader must infer where the story takes place, or other details about the setting, by using clues that the author provides. As you read, look for clues that tell you more about the setting of this story.

WRITING CONNECTION

Try to persuade a friend to eat a certain kind of food he or she does not like. Write one paragraph arguing your case.

"by vocation," and "by avocation an investigator of the 'supernatural'." His style is straightforward, with few literary embellishments. Such a style can often be a real advantage: Candidness indicates the writer is sincere, and sincerity goes a long way in persuading people.

Cooperative Group Activity

Divide the class into groups of four or five. Ask each group to think of something—a TV program, the dentist's office, a particular neighborhood—that nearly everyone does not like. Then ask them to build a case for it. Suggest that they turn resistance to their advantage by mounting a persuasive

presentation of facts that are favorable. After each group presents its case to the class, take a poll to find out who was the most persuasive, and why. You may also, at this time, ask volunteers to present their individual arguments on food, which were developed in the Writing Connection activity.

The Great Amherst Mystery

by Walter Hubbell

It's a strange world, this one we live in. I don't believe in ghosts. That is, I didn't believe in ghosts before I investigated the mystery of Esther Cox. Now the only question is what to call them—ghosts, spirits, poltergeists, or what?

My name is Walter Hubbell. By vocation, I'm an actor. By avocation, I'm an investigator of the "supernatural." During the past few years, I've investigated many people who claimed they could talk to the spirits of the dead. They were all fakes, and I exposed them. As an actor, I know all the tricks that we use on the stage. I also know most of the tricks that magicians use to fool the public. I am, beyond doubt, able to judge whether or not deception was used in the case of Esther Cox. And it was not.

Truth is often stranger than fiction. What I have written here is truth—not fiction—and it is *very strange*.

I was acting in Canada when I first heard of Esther Cox. She was 19 years old at the time. She and her sister Jennie, age 22, lived in the home of an older married sister, Olive Teed. Daniel Teed, Olive's husband, was a foreman in a shoe factory. The Teeds had two small boys. Before the trouble started, all lived together in a rented house in the town of Amherst.

Then things started to happen. One night Esther thought she heard a mouse somewhere in her bed. She awakened her sister

---

poltergeist (POHL tur gyst) a noisy ghost
vocation (voh KAY shun) profession; career
avocation (av uh KAY shun) hobby
deception (dih SEP shun) trickery; action intended to fool another person

The Great Amherst Mystery ■ 201

Develop Vocabulary Skills
Almost most all the new vocabulary words end in suffixes, and four of them share the same suffix: -tion. Write on the chalkboard or overhead projector the new words. Point out the suffixes and their meanings. Have students identify the root of each word and determine its meaning.

ESL Activity
Have students work in pairs to develop arguments to persuade someone of another culture to try a food that is representative of their culture. Have them present their arguments to the class.

TEACHING PLAN

INTRODUCE

Motivation
Ask students, "How do you think you would feel if you walked into an old deserted house in an isolated part of the country? Even if you do not believe in ghosts, do you think you would feel like an intruder? Would you wonder if something bad might happen to you because you should not be there at all?"

Purpose-Setting Question
Can you be persuaded to believe that poltergeists exist?

READ

Literary Focus:
Persuasion
Encourage students to think about what makes an argument persuasive. Have them recall times in their own lives when they have been successful persuading someone to do something. Did they use facts to persuade someone? Examples from their own experience? As students read, have them make note of the ways that the author tries to persuade his readers to believe that poltergeists are real.

Reading Focus:
Make Inferences
About Setting
Ask students to note details about the setting of the story. As they read, tell them to ask themselves: Could the actions and personalities of so many closely related people living in the same house influence events in the house?

CLOSE

Have students complete Review the Selection on pages 206–207.

Jennie, who slept in the same room. They listened in silence, and soon went back to sleep. But the next night, both sisters heard the noise again, louder than ever. "It's in that box, under my bed," declared Esther. Together the two sisters pulled the green cardboard box out from under the bed. It jumped, and both girls screamed. Jennie slowly took hold of the box and placed it in the middle of the room. It jumped again, rising a foot in the air and falling back on its side. The girls' screams brought Daniel Teed hurrying into the room. He listened to their story. "You're both crazy," he announced, shaking his head as he kicked the box back under the bed. "Now go to sleep and don't disturb me again!"

This was just the beginning. A few nights later, another scream echoed through the house. It was Esther: "What's happening to me? I'm swelling up! I'm going to burst!" This time the whole family ran to the bedroom, and there was Esther, confused and worried, her whole body swollen beyond belief. What had happened? What could they do? Daniel Teed was about to call a doctor, when, quite suddenly, came a loud rapping noise, as if someone were pounding with a heavy hammer on the floor under Esther's bed. The swelling started to go down. The rapping continued, and Esther looked more comfortable. Soon she fell into a tired, troubled sleep.

The next morning Daniel Teed hurried to the family doctor. Dr. Thomas W. Carritte listened patiently, but he didn't believe a word. "I'll come this evening, and I'll stay through the night if I have to," he told Daniel. "But I guarantee you, none of this nonsense is going to happen while *I'm* in the house."

The doctor couldn't have been more wrong. After supper that evening, as he sat in Esther's room, he watched in wonder as an unseen hand seemed to slide the pillow out from under her head. A sheet and a light blanket were pulled from her bed. She began to swell up. Now the doctor had a job to do—but it was not he who cured Esther. It was, again, the loud rapping noises.

Dr. Carritte was as puzzled as everyone else. He knew the family, and he felt sure that no one was trying to fool him. As the rapping went on, he walked outside the house to see if he could discover what caused the noise. From outside the rapping sounded louder, like someone pounding on the roof. But there was no one—on the roof, in the yard, or anywhere.

Critical Thinking:
Summarize
Have students tell in a few sentences what happened to send Daniel Teed to the doctor.

Not long after, my acting job in Canada having ended, I arrived at the troubled house myself. At the time, I did not believe in ghosts, poltergeists, or spirits of any kind. I did believe that everything that happens has an explanation. From what I'd heard about Esther Cox, it didn't seem likely that she was playing tricks on people. But still, there had to be an explanation. Fortunately, I was able to rent a room from the Teeds, to be nearer the mystery I had come to investigate.

Esther Cox was a short, stout girl who could only be described as plain (her sister Jennie was the pretty one). Though far from dumb, she was not overly intelligent. She certainly didn't understand what was going on. Neither, I was soon persuaded, could she have planned it.

After I'd rented the room, I hadn't been in the house five minutes when my umbrella suddenly seemed to come to life. It flew across the living room. Soon after, Esther appeared in the kitchen doorway, carrying a plate. From behind her, something came flashing through the air—a large knife. It narrowly missed me. I rushed into the kitchen to see who had thrown it. That was my first introduction to ghosts. There was no one there.

"It looks like they don't like you," said Esther.

By "they," it turned out, Esther meant two poltergeists (or *ghosts*, as she called them). One she called "Maggie," the other "Bob." She claimed sometimes that she could see them. Once, as Olive Teed and I looked on in amazement, Esther stared at the thin air in the middle of the living room and told us that Maggie was standing there. Even more strange, the girl swore that Maggie was wearing a pair of black and white socks that belonged to Esther. Feeling a little foolish, I shouted, "Now Maggie, take off Esther's socks—and be quick about it!" A minute later, a pair of black and white socks appeared from out of nowhere. They dropped from the air in front of us to the floor.

After that I stopped looking for explanations. The only explanation was . . . the supernatural.

Whoever—or whatever—"Maggie" and "Bob" were, they seemed to be always in action. With my own eyes, I saw a heavy ash tray leave its place on a table and come whizzing at me, crashing into the wall as I ducked. Furniture constantly slid around the floors. As I entered the dining room one time, every chair fell over with a crash. Another time, needing a light for my pipe,

I remarked, "Bob, give me a few matches, if you please." Immediately, a lighted match fell out of the air.

But the poltergeists were not always so helpful. As the weeks passed, Esther's spells continued, and even grew worse. Sometimes she would lie on her bed as if dead, her body swelling up like a balloon, and then collapsing, over and over. Also, the poltergeists were ruining the furniture and damaging the walls. When they started lighting small fires, the Teeds were asked to move. The owner of the house had risked enough. The Teeds were good people, but they would have to go.

As an experiment, the Teeds decided to see what would happen if only Esther left. She was sent to live with a family named Van Amburgh on a farm in the country. And here the affair came to an end with the biggest mystery of all. With Esther out of the house, everything returned to normal. The rappings, the flying objects, the sliding furniture, the fires—all stopped at once.

And perhaps even more strangely, Esther's life in her new home was completely untroubled. Like all poltergeists, "Maggie" and "Bob" had departed as mysteriously as they had come.

It must be stated that the Teeds made no attempt to keep the strange events secret. Dr. Carritte and others were constantly in and out of the house. I have a statement signed by 16 persons who witnessed at least some of the happenings I've described. I have a letter from Olive Teed declaring that *all* I've written here is true. And Dr. Carritte writes:

"I take pen in hand to say that what Mr. Walter Hubbell has written about the mysterious Esther Cox is entirely correct. The young lady was a patient of mine both previous to and during those wonderful demonstrations. I tried various experiments, but with no satisfactory results. Honestly doubtful persons were on all occasions soon convinced that there was no fraud or deception in the case. Were I to publish the case in medical journals, as you suggest, I doubt it would be believed by doctors generally. I am certain I could not have believed such miracles had I not witnessed them."

Literary Focus: Persuasion
The last paragraph relies on the respect given medical doctors to establish credibility further. Ask students to discuss whether the letter is effective.

---

wonderful (WUN dur ful) curious; strange
demonstration (dem un STRAY shun) any happening that can be observed

The Great Amherst Mystery ■ 205

Mini Quiz

Write on the chalkboard or overhead projector the following questions and call on students to fill in the blanks. Discuss the answers with the class.

1. Walter Hubbell's profession is _____.

2. The first time Esther Cox heard a noise under her bed she thought it was a _____.

3. When Hubbell went to investigate the strange events, he rented a room from the _____.

4. Esther called the poltergeists _____ and _____.

5. The strange events in the house stopped when _____ left.

Answers
1. acting
2. mouse
3. Teeds
4. Maggie and Bob
5. Esther

UNDERSTAND THE
SELECTION

Answers

1. Esther thought that she heard a noise in a box under her bed; the next night, she and her sister Jennie heard the noise again, pulled the box out from under the bed, and watched as the box jumped.
2. Esther had swollen up terribly the night before and then fallen into a deep sleep. She seemed sick and the Teeds logically thought a doctor was needed.
3. The sock incident: Hubbell tells the poltergeist "Maggie" to take off Esther's socks, and they appear "out of nowhere."
4. As an actor, he knows how people can fake supernatural events; he knows what is real and what is not; he knows the tricks of stage magicians. These theatrical credentials add credibility to his views.
5. The doctor's professional status lends more credibility to the claims that poltergeists exist.
6. "Bob" provides a match for Hubbell when he wants to light his pipe.
7. The poltergeists were active only when Esther was present in the Teeds' house.
8. Sample answer: Esther Cox should have moved back into the Amherst house, if only briefly, just to see what might have happened.
9. Sample answer: Hubbell's opinions are usually backed up by facts, which make the opinions seem particularly strong.
10. Sample answer: Esther's swelling could have been caused by an allergic reaction to the food.

Respond to Literature

You might discuss the events before students make their choices. They may find Esther's swelling was most believable, "Bob's" providing a match the least believable. Students should give reasons for their answers.

Review the Selection

UNDERSTAND THE SELECTION

Recall

1. How did poltergeists first appear?
2. Why is Dr. Carritte called to the house?
3. What incident convinces Hubbell supernatural forces must be at work?

Infer

4. Why is it important that we know Hubbell's profession?
5. What effect does the doctor's presence in the story have?
6. Give an example of the poltergeists' being helpful.
7. Explain the significance of Esther's departure from the house to live in the country.

Apply

8. Would you have conducted the poltergeist investigation any differently?
9. Hubbell gives both opinions and facts. Which are more convincing?
10. Can you think of a rational, natural explanation for one of the incidents involving a poltergeist? Explain your answer.

Respond to Literature

What seemed to be the most believable events in the mysterious happenings that occurred? What seemed least believable?

---

206 ■ Unit 2

WRITE ABOUT THE SELECTION

Have you ever tried something you did not want to do at first, and ended up really liking it? Did you then try to convince others they should try it because they, too, might like it?

You were persuaded by that experience to change your mind. You now want to try to persuade others by relating your experience in writing.

Prewriting   You need a topic. Brainstorm for a few minutes to come up with some ideas. You could write about an experience involving food, music, a sport—anything. Once you have chosen a topic, make notes about what happened.

Writing   Refer to your notes when writing your story. Keep in mind your purpose, which is to persuade the reader to try what you are describing or to accept an opinion that you hold. Facts are needed to support your opinion that your experience is worthwhile.

Revising   Use specific language in your description. If a new kind of music sounded nice to you, for example, tell why. Did it have a driving beat? Which instruments were particularly good? Tell your reactions, but try to combine them with facts.

Proofreading   Reread your paper to check for errors in verb forms, particularly irregular verbs. Check also that you use the correct tense throughout the story. Use a dictionary to check any tense forms you are not sure of.

WRITE ABOUT THE SELECTION

Prewriting
Students could brainstorm cooperatively in groups. Then, discussion might help them focus their ideas.

Writing
As you circulate among students, stress the need for facts to support

opinion. Suggest that they avoid clichés, such as "Try it, you'll like it." The reader should be told *why* he or she will like it.

Revising
Have students exchange papers. Partners can provide feedback on whether the text is convincing. Remind students, however, that they are free to accept or reject

suggestions. As writers, decision making is their privilege!

Proofreading
Ask students to check that all verbs are in the correct form and tense.

T206

THINK ABOUT PERSUASION

The purpose of Hubbell's story is to persuade us that supernatural forces might exist. The author uses a large amount of exposition and description of events, to provide evidence supporting his view.

In the previous selection, John McPhee was like a detective collecting facts. In this selection, Hubbell is like a detective and lawyer together. He gathers facts and uses them to argue his case.

1. Is the first paragraph of the story fact or opinion?

2. Is the second paragraph fact or opinion?

3. The story shifts gears after the third paragraph. What happens?

4. What is the effect of the doctor's statement?

5. Read the first paragraph of the story again. Do you think a reader is more likely to accept Hubbell's statements after reading the whole story?

READING FOCUS

Make Inferences About Setting As you read, you were able to use clues to infer things about the setting of the story. In the beginning, it seems that the author is describing a typical "haunted house." Does this end up being the case? What can you infer about the house based on the ending of the story?

DEVELOP YOUR VOCABULARY

Many words that we use in English are actually borrowed from foreign languages. *Poltergeist* is a good example. It comes from these German words:

poltern: to make noise, rumble
geist: ghost

You can find information on the foreign roots of words in the dictionary. The information is given in brackets [ ] following the part-of-speech designation.

Find the foreign word in the following sentences. Use a dictionary to explain its roots.

1. The tall buildings shoot into the air like walls of a canyon.

2. My baby brother goes to kindergarten.

3. He likes buffet dinners because he can take exactly what he wants.

4. No anchovies on my pizza, please.

5. Old Faithful is a famous geyser out west.

6. Is her attitude a bit naive for her age?

Review the Selection ■ 207

THINK ABOUT PERSUASION

Answers

1. Opinion.
2. Both. Students should see that Hubbell now starts to present factual background to back up his opinions. Credibility is starting to be built.
3. Hubbell begins to describe specific incidents showing the presence of the poltergeists.
4. It gives credibility, both to the events Hubbell has described and to Hubbell himself.
5. Yes. Facts and quoted testimony (from the doctor) support Hubbell.

DEVELOP YOUR VOCABULARY

Answers

1. canyon: from the Spanish *cañón*; a pipe, tube, or deep gorge.
2. kindergarten: from the German *kinder* and *garten*; a children's garden.
3. buffet: from the French *buffet*; a sideboard or bench.
4. pizza: from the Italian *pizza*, which means an open pie made of rolled dough.
5. geyser: from the Icelandic *Geysir*; the name of a specific hot spring in Iceland.
6. naive: from the French *naif*; simple, natural, lacking skill or training.

READING FOCUS

Sample Answer

Even though it seems like the house is haunted by poltergeists at first, later it becomes evident that it is Esther who is causing the poltergeists to appear, not the house. When Esther leaves the house, so do the ghosts. Based on this information, I would infer that as long as Esther is not in the house, the house will be "normal."

WRITING APPLICATIONS

Write About Theme

Explain to students that this is their chance to be creative. A recording of the theme music for a science fiction show would help set the mood for this assignment.

Cooperative Group Activity

Prewriting: Have groups make a list and note any special characteristics that might affect a dialogue with a supernatural being; for example, poltergeists usually do not talk.

Writing: Circulate among students as they work individually. Offer help to students having difficulty.

Writer's Toolkit CD-ROM

Encourage students to use the Descriptive Word Bin: Exclamations in Dialogue (Writing Tools, Drafting) as they write.

Revising: Have students choose a partner to read their dialogue to them. Students should note if the partner stumbles or hesitates between speakers, it is an indication that the dialogue does not flow smoothly.

Proofreading: Have the same partner read the dialogue for correct punctuation. Ask the readers to pay close attention to all punctuation marks and that they do exactly what the marks indicate. The writer should listen for the appropriateness of the punctuation.

WRITING APPLICATIONS

Write About Theme

One summer day you are sitting in your backyard, and a strange-looking creature walks up to you.

"Hello," it says.

You realize you are facing an unknown being. You, for some unexplained reason, have been chosen to have the first human contact with this creature.

Write a dialogue of your encounter with this creature. What will you learn about the unknown?

Prewriting Decide first what the creature will be: perhaps an extraterrestrial being. For five minutes freewrite questions you would like to ask the creature. Then take another five minutes to freewrite possible answers.

Writing Put your questions in a logical order, and fill in the answers. Use this form for writing:

> **Me:**
> **Creature:**

Revising The best dialogues are those that flow logically from one question-and-answer to the next. This may be hard when you are talking with a strange being, but consider revising any sections that seem to "jump around" too much. Be sure you have the creature explain elements of the unknown with sharp detail.

Proofreading Although you have written a dialogue, you still need to punctuate correctly. Carefully use special punctuation marks, such as exclamations, for emphasis.

Write About Genre

You have learned in this unit that all short stories have four basic elements: plot, characters, setting, and theme. It helps in analyzing stories if you look very closely at these elements.

Choose one selection you particularly liked. Analyze how plot, characters, setting, and theme add to the story.

Prewriting Review any work you did for the "Think About . . . " sections that discuss the elements. How does the author of the story you have chosen develop a particular element? On the other hand, maybe he or she does not develop another element, and that interests you. Write the elements in the middle of a piece of paper, and make a cluster of your ideas around it.

Writing Use the cluster to write your analysis. Make sure you have a clear thesis statement, such as "Although all elements are present, plot is not important in John McPhee's nonfiction narrative 'The Loch Ness Monster.'" Develop your analysis from there.

Revising An analysis is similar to persuasion. You want to convince the reader that what you say is correct. Readers are more convinced by facts than opinions. Can you add more facts, or evidence, from the story to support your opinions?

Proofreading Reread your analysis carefully. Do you need new paragraphs when you discuss each element?

Write About Genre

Relate the four elements of a short story to points on a compass. Draw a horizontal and vertical axis, and at each of the four points write one of the four elements.

Cooperative Group Activity

Prewriting: Divide the class into groups, and have each group review one of the "Think About" sections in the Selection Reviews. Then ask each group to present a report.

Writing: Circulate among students as they work individually. Offer help to students having difficulty.

Writer's Toolkit CD-ROM

Encourage students to use the Cluster Diagram (Writing Tools, Narrowing a Topic) to complete the Prewriting activity.

Revising: Have students make a quick outline of the major points in their analysis. Under each point they should list at least one fact supporting that point.

Proofreading: Point out that having a separate paragraph for each element discussed is a logical way to organize the analysis. Suggest that students break the text according to major points.

BUILD LANGUAGE SKILLS

Vocabulary

Idioms are groups of words that have a special meaning all their own. You cannot add up the meanings of the individual words. You must know the new meaning of the entire group. An example is *over one's head.* The literal meaning is that something is positioned right over your head.

However, look at the phrase's meaning in this sentence: *Trigonometry is simply over my head.* Here, *over my head* means too difficult.

Each sentence below contains an idiom. Find it, and explain its meaning.

1. Please, put your best foot forward this time.

2. The forty-year-old man was getting gray above the ears.

3. The boy lit up when the teacher asked the question about computers.

4. I got a load of their shoulder holsters when they leaned over.

5. We rested on the stoop for awhile, getting our nerves back in shape.

6. "This particular problem," he said, "is only the tip of the iceberg."

7. The red leather basketball shoes in the wind caught Sam's eye.

8. Peggy's new haircut was cuter than a bug's ear.

Grammar, Usage and Mechanics

Three or more words linked in a series by the conjunctions *and* or *or* must be correctly punctuated as follows: I have ordinary abilities, looks, and thoughts. Note that a comma is used after all the words in a series except the last. One easy way to remember how many commas you need is to count the items in a series and then use one less comma. However, if there is a conjunction between every word in the series, you need no commas.

Correct the punctuation errors in the following sentences:

1. They were sitting kneeling or squatting in an easy way.

2. We have electricity washing machines vacuum cleaners modern bathrooms and modern medicine.

3. But there are no radios televisions telephones or cars.

4. They have dances card parties weddings birthdays block parties swimming and sports of all kinds.

5. Verna is a planet of air sun land and sea, like Earth.

6. Now the only question is what to call them—ghosts spirits poltergeists or what?

7. John McPhee used photographs testimony and legends as support for Nessie's existence.

Unit Review ■ 209

Grammar, Usage, and Mechanics

Answers

1. They were sitting, kneeling, or squatting in an easy way.
2. We have electricity, washing machines, vacuum cleaners, modern bathrooms, and modern medicine.
3. But there are no radios, televisions, telephones, or cars.
4. They have dances, card parties, weddings, birthdays, harvest parties, swimming, and sports of all kinds.
5. Verna is a planet of air, sun, land, and sea, like Earth.
6. Now the only question is what to call them—ghosts, spirits, poltergeists, or what?
7. John McPhee used photographs, testimony, and legends as support for Nessie's existence.

Some usage experts argue that a comma is unnecessary after the penultimate item in a series. Newspapers often use this style. Not inserting a comma could cause confusion, however, if the last two items in a series could be considered in apposition to the first item:

Example: With me on the trip were my sisters, Judy and Gaye. Are Judy and Gaye my sisters, or are they two friends who went with me in addition to my sisters? We can not tell. A comma would clear things up:

Example: With me on the trip were my sisters, Judy, and Gaye.

Cooperative Group Activity

Have students make up their own exercises, and then give them to others as a "test." Working in pairs, students look through the unit selections for five other examples of items in a series. They then write down the sentences, omitting the commas. Pairs exchange papers and insert correct punctuation.

BUILD LANGUAGE SKILLS

Vocabulary

Answers

1. best foot forward: do the best you can; show off your strong points

2. getting gray above the ears: your hair is turning gray because you are getting old

3. lit up: got excited, came to life

4. got a load of: saw, noticed

5. getting our nerves back in shape: calming down

6. tip of the iceberg: a small problem that is part of a much bigger one

7. caught Sam's eye: appealed to Sam

8. cuter than a bug's ear: very becoming, looking very good

More About Word Attack: Point out that idioms are a kind of language code. They often have interesting stories behind them.

Motivation

Relate an incident from your own experience to the class. As you speak, make sure you do not use slang, but do try to use at least one quotation, and do explain why the incident is memorable.

Teaching Strategy

Go through the directions with the students. Make sure that they understand all the steps. As homework, assign steps 2 and 3. In class have them work with a partner in organizing their paraphrase (step 4). Then suggest a practice run with their partner, followed by an evaluation to ensure that steps 5, 6, and 7 were covered. Students are then ready for the class presentations.

Evaluation Criteria

Have students first do a self-evaluation, using the seven steps and the final suggestion (on telling the title of the selection) as checkpoints. They can go over the self-evaluation with their partners. Partners should be encouraged to provide additional feedback.

It is human nature to want to share experiences with others. If you see a movie, you may want to talk about a scene that you particularly liked. If you hear a new song, you often want to tap the melody out for friends so they can get a feel for it, too. For this activity, you will be telling an incident you remember from a selection in this unit.

Before you share an incident from one of the selections in this unit, read over the following directions. They will help make your assignment clear.

1. You will have about two minutes to share your choice with the class. Remember to focus on one incident. Also, try to get to the point and keep to it.

2. In this assignment, the selection itself is not as important as the incident that you choose. Therefore, instead of thinking about a certain story, think about a single incident. It can be frightening, exciting, suspenseful, or just your favorite.

3. Go back to the selection, skim through it, find the incident, and reread it.

4. Now, paraphrase the incident in your mind. Think about how you would relate this incident to a friend. If necessary, take a few notes to help you focus on what you will say.

5. It is easy to get personally involved when you are talking about an incident that was your favorite. It is also easy to get caught using slang expressions. For this assignment, try to use vocabulary and expressions that are suitable for a literary discussion.

6. Do not be afraid to quote. Perhaps there was a particular way a character said something that added to the sheer excitement of this incident. Let the class in on it by sharing the exact words.

7. Be sure to tell why the incident was memorable to you. Think about the feelings you had after you read it, and express them to your audience.

By following the hints given above, you will find it easy to relate your favorite incident from this unit to your classmates. One last suggestion: Before you begin to talk about the incident, tell the title of the selection it came from; others might be interested in reading the entire story.

CRITICAL THINKING

Fact and Opinion This unit has contained selections about the unknown. It is a tricky subject to write about. The very word *unknown* presents a challenge. How can anyone write something about which he or she does not know much?

The writers of the nonfiction selections in this unit solved the problem through investigation. They went to the places where monsters or ghosts had supposedly been seen or felt, and gathered facts.

In the case of "The Great Amherst Mystery," the writer then used the facts to back up an opinion. Walter Hubbell said he believes that poltergeists and other such supernatural beings really do exist. If there had been no facts to back up his opinion, Hubbell would have looked very funny. However, he had fact after fact, supported by a number of people and their testimonies, to give his opinion credibility. It was far easier to accept his ideas on poltergeists after the facts had been presented.

When you write, support your opinions with facts. They are the things that convince readers. Remember Mr. Gradgrind's comment in Charles Dickens's *Hard Times:* "Now, what I want is, Facts . . . Facts alone are wanted in life."

Choose either "The Great Amherst Mystery" or "The Loch Ness Monster." List ten facts that the author used to tell his story.

EFFECTIVE STUDYING

Developing Study Habits Good study habits can help when you are working in any subject.

It helps to choose a study setting, one place you go regularly. If you associate that place just with studying, it is easier to work there. Ideally, the place would be quiet and away from distractions.

You should develop a study schedule. When will you work? Consider two things here. First, when can you study? If you play sports, obviously you cannot study after school. You need to find another time. Second, what times of day are you at your best? Some people cannot function after 8 P.M. Others are just getting going then. When you have a choice of study times, pick the time you are at peak power.

A third tip is to keep an assignment book. Write all of your assignments and when they are due.

Where and when do you study? Describe your special space and your study schedule.

Test Preparation

Try this memory game the next time you study for a test. Relate the facts you are studying to specific objects in your study area. Associating facts with familiar things may help you recall the facts later.

Unit Review ■ 211

 EFFECTIVE
STUDYING
Teaching Strategy
Discuss with students where and when they study, and if they keep an assignment book. Show them an appointment book or class outline schedule you might have.

Read the following questions to the class and have students answer them. Then discuss the answers.

1. Which is likely to be the worst study place?
   a. in front of the television
   b. the kitchen table
   c. a desk in your bedroom
2. What two things determine when you should study?
   a.
   b.
3. Name two advantages of keeping an assignment book.
   a.
   b.

Answers
1. c.
2. a. when it is possible for you to study
   b. when you are at your "peak"
3. a. you are organized
   b. you remember to turn assignments in on time

Career Connection

This unit focuses on the unknown, and how we can learn more about it. The role of the investigator is key to many of the stories. A writer is an investigator and the best examples are journalists. Becoming an investigative reporter requires many years of work and a desire to find information and make it both accessible and intelligible. Newspapers employ many kinds of reporters, many of whom start out as "stringers" or "freelancers"; that is they accept specific assignments from an editor rather than work full-time. Writing for a high school newspaper provides a taste of a reporter's work.

 CRITICAL
THINKING

Sample Answers
"The Loch Ness Monster:"
1. The creature swims 12 to 18 mph.
2. It is highly responsive and sensitive to sound.
3. There have been no reports of savagery on its part, with the exception of one report.
4. It keeps a wide margin between itself and mankind.
5. It feeds on fish and eels.
6. When they die, they settle onto the floor of the lake.
7. It prefers the warm waters of summer.
8. It is unattractive in appearance.
9. Its neck is about 6 feet long.
10. Its tail is long and pointed.

UNIT ACTIVITY

A Continuing Unit Project: Writing Newspaper Articles

Several of the stories in this unit involve the committing of a crime. Nearly all of the selections involve newsworthy events. Some of the stories would make front-page headlines; others might show up on features pages or in the obituary column.

Have students write a newspaper story about each selection they read. Let students decide what the focus of each story will be. Students can create additional details when they need to, but this information must always be in keeping with the selection.

Point out to students that a news story must always answer five basic questions: What happened? When did it happen? Where did it happen? Why did it happen? Who was involved? Ideally, these questions should be answered briefly within the first paragraph or two; the rest of the story should add supporting details.

A feature article may have a freer format, since features do not always focus on a specific event. Sometimes, for example, a feature will explore a certain subject, such as a science article about whales. Or a feature may consist of an interview with a famous person. A good feature will contain background information about the topic as well as any current developments in the field.

Another type of newspaper story that students might enjoy writing is the editorial. In this type of article, the writer is free to express an opinion about an event or situation. Remind students that opinions should always be presented logically and supported by facts.

Here are some general questions to help students get started as they write their newspaper articles:

What is the major event described in the selection?
What are the circumstances surrounding this event?
Who is the most important character in the selection?
What happens to this character?

How would you sum up in one sentence what the selection is about?

If students need more specific guidance, ask questions such as these about each selection.

■ "The Getaway"

How might a news story portray the counterman in the restaurant as a hero?

■ "Sherlock Holmes and the Speckled Band"

How would a newspaper reporter write about Dr. Roylott's death?

■ *Trifles*

How would a newspaper story describe Mrs. Wright?

■ "The Rattlesnake Hunt" from *Cross Creek*

How might this selection form the basis for a science feature in the newspaper?

■ "Earth"/"Earth"

What might a newspaper editor on another planet write about the destruction of Earth?

■ "The Lady or the Tiger?"

How would a newspaper describe the marriage of the young man to the lady behind the door? How would it describe the death of the young man when he is killed by a tiger?

■ "Displays of Skill: The Bat"/"The Bird of Night"

How would a science writer describe one or both of these animals?

■ "A Secret for Two"

How might Pierre's death be written up in a local newspaper?

Have students suggest photos, maps, or charts that might accompany their articles. When the articles are finished, create a booklet in which all the stories can be "published" for students to read on their own.

■ "The Getaway"
by John Savage (page 217)

SELECTION SYNOPSIS

While driving through western Texas, the narrator stops for coffee at an isolated diner. Soon two men appear, order coffee, and ask to see a map. The men are looking for a short way across the Rio Grande to Mexico. The counterman suggests that they head for a bridge at Hackett, a bridge too new to be shown on the map they are consulting. The men start to leave, then turn and pull guns on the counterman and the narrator. They disconnect the phone and empty the till. As they drive off, one of them deflates a tire on the narrator's car with a gun.

The counterman repairs the telephone quickly and calls the police. He learns that the holdup men have robbed a supermarket in nearby Wichita Falls. He informs the police that the men are headed for Hackett. When he hangs up, the narrator observes regretfully that the criminals will be across the border before the police can overtake them. The counterman smiles a knowing smile and says that the fugitives will not escape, for there is no bridge at Hackett.

SELECTION ACTIVITY

Have students write a play to dramatize the story, "The Getaway." Students can work in small groups to create their plays, or you can work with the class as a whole by using transparencies and an overhead projector.

Begin by discussing with students how to go about changing a story into a play. Point out some of the things they must do: choose a cast of characters, divide the story into scenes, decide on the setting for each scene, establish the plot, and write a script.

First, have students make a list of the characters in the story. The obvious and essential characters are the narrator, the counterman, and the two outlaws. The story could be dramatized effectively using just these people. Characters who are not essential but who could be added to the play include the policeman who answers the phone and the policemen who go after the outlaws.

Another character who could be added to the play is a narrator who stands outside the story—perhaps as the actual narrator who is now much older and telling this story as a flashback. If this technique is used, another character might be added to the play, a person to whom the narrator is speaking. For example, the narrator might be sitting in this very same restaurant 20 years later, reminiscing as he talks to a friend. He might start out by saying, "It was just about 20 years ago that I had a most incredible experience in this very restaurant. Let me tell you how it happened."

Next, have students decide how to divide the story into scenes. Usually in a play, a new scene indicates a change in location or a change in time, or both. If the action of a story is continuous in the same location, and if the story is short, it may be necessary to have only one scene unless a narrative technique such as the one described above is used. If this is the case, then the scene would shift back and forth between the conversation going on in the present and the narrator's memory of the events that happened in the restaurant many years ago.

Once the play has been divided (or not divided) into scenes, have students decide on the setting. In this story, the entire play could be set in the restaurant. Some additional settings that might be included are the highway before the narrator pulls into the restaurant, the police station when the counterman's phone call is received, and the interior of one of the patrol cars chasing the outlaws.

Tell students that their next task is to establish the plot. Have each student write a brief description of the plot of the short story. Have several students read their summaries aloud. Correct any misconceptions students might have. Then ask students if they wish to alter or extend the plot in any way. (Since this story is so well crafted, you will probably want to encourage students to keep the plot as it is.)

Finally, have students write a script. Most of the script for this play can be taken from the dialogue used in the story. Simply assign each quotation to the proper character. Have students add dialogue where they feel it is necessary or appropriate.

Once the play is complete, type it, or have it typed, and distribute copies to each student.

Discuss ways in which scenery, costumes, and props might enhance a performance of the play.

■ "Sherlock Holmes and the Speckled Band"
by Arthur Conan Doyle (page 225)

SELECTION SYNOPSIS

Sherlock Holmes and Dr. John Watson enter Holmes's Baker Street sitting room to find a frightened woman waiting for them. She says that she fears for her life, and Holmes promises to help her. The woman, whose name is Helen Stoner, tells Holmes that she and her twin sister Julia went to live in her stepfather's manor house upon the accidental death of their mother eight years before. The stepfather has little money, but the thousand pounds from the estate of his wife (Helen and Julia's mother) enabled the three to live comfortably. Helen explains that a substantial amount of the mother's estate was willed to each daughter when she marries. Helen goes on to say that a few years earlier, Julia became engaged. Then, two weeks before the wedding, Julia died mysteriously.

Through a flashback, the reader learns more details. On the night of Julia's death, Helen is awakened by a woman's scream. She also hears a low whistle and a clanging sound. She runs to the hallway, where she finds Julia about to collapse. All Julia can say before she dies is, "It was the band! The speckled band!"

Under Holmes's questioning, it is revealed that Julia managed to point toward her stepfather's room before dying, that Julia's room was locked and could not have been entered, and that the coroner was unable to determine the cause of death.

Helen reveals that she is now engaged. She has been obliged to move into Julia's room because of some repairs being done on the manor house. Holmes tells Helen that he must inspect Julia's room and the surrounding area and arranges to visit the manor house that afternoon, while Dr. Roylott, the stepfather, is away.

Helen has barely left the apartment when Dr. Roylott bursts in and angrily threatens Holmes for interfering in his affairs. Holmes remains unruffled during the encounter, and after a short time, Roylott leaves.

After doing some research, which reveals that Dr. Roylott would lose a great deal of income if a daughter marries, Holmes and Watson go to Stoke Moran, Dr. Roylott's manor.

Holmes, accompanied by Watson, visits Stoke Moran and inspects the murder scene. He notes especially a recently installed bellrope, which turns out to be a dummy, and nearby, a small, high vent, connecting Julia's room to her stepfather's. Holmes looks into Dr. Roylott's room, where he finds a large iron safe, a saucer of milk, and a small dog leash.

Holmes tells Helen that he and Watson will stay at the nearby inn until Roylott goes to bed. When Helen hears him retire, she is to signal Holmes and Watson, leave her window unlocked, and move into her old room for the night. Holmes and Watson will spend the night in Julia's room.

Holmes and Watson await Helen's signal at the inn and then hurry back to the manor. After waiting several hours, they hear a gentle hissing sound. Holmes strikes a match and then begins lashing at the bellrope with his cane. A low, clear whistle is heard. Then, a moment later, a horrible cry is heard in the next room.

Holmes and Watson hurry to Roylott's room, where they find his lifeless body slumped in a chair. A deadly swamp adder—the speckled band—is wound tightly around his brow. Holmes puts the snake back into the safe and locks the door. They leave the room to take Helen away from the house and get the police.

Back at the Baker Street apartment, Holmes sums up the mystery for Watson. Dr. Roylott, who made a hobby of keeping animals from India, used a deadly Indian snake to kill Julia, and then intended the same fate for Helen. When Holmes attacked the snake, the snake was driven back through the ventilator and turned on its master. Thus Roylott was destroyed by his own evil design.

SELECTION ACTIVITY

Have students do research to learn about Arthur Conan Doyle and his famous Sherlock Holmes stories. Then have students present their information in written or oral reports. Some of the information students can include in their reports is summarized below.

Doyle originally studied to be a doctor, but his practice was unsuccessful. He turned to writing as a means of supplementing his income. The character of Sherlock Holmes was patterned after one of Doyle's medical school professors, a man named Dr. Bell. Bell was noted for his uncanny reasoning ability and his habit of diagnosing his patients' characters, along with their ailments.

Sherlock Holmes is a famous fictional character. The first Holmes story was *Study in Scarlet*, written in 1887. Other books followed: *The Memoirs of Sherlock Holmes*, *The Hound of the Baskervilles*, *The Return of Sherlock Holmes*, *The Valley of Fear*, *His Last Bow*, and *The Case Book of Sherlock Holmes*.

Trifles
by *Susan Glaspell* (page 252)

SELECTION SYNOPSIS

Lewis Hale stopped by John Wright's farm to ask if his neighbor would be interested in joining him in a party telephone. At first no one answered the door; then a voice told him to come in. Hale found Mrs. Wright sitting in a rocking chair. When Hale asked to speak to John, Mrs. Wright told him that her husband was dead, that he died of "a rope around his neck" while he slept. Mrs. Wright claimed that she did not know who committed the crime.

When the play opens, Hale, Mrs. Hale, the county attorney, the sheriff, and the sheriff's wife have come to the Wright farmhouse to inspect the scene of the crime. Mrs. Wright has been taken to jail, for she is the prime suspect in the murder.

As the farmhouse is inspected for clues, it becomes apparent to the two women that Mrs. Wright has had a hard and unhappy life with her husband. These feelings are augmented when the women discover a strangled pet canary in Mrs. Wright's sewing box.

As the play progresses, the two women struggle with their feelings that perhaps the murder was justified—at least, they are in sympathy with Mrs. Wright. The play ends with no hint given about the outcome of Mrs. Wright's trial.

SELECTION ACTIVITY

Have students work in small groups to present the trial of Mrs. Wright. Discuss with students who the characters in the trial would be: Mrs. Wright and her lawyer, the prosecutor for the state, and witnesses such as Mr. and Mrs. Hale and Mrs. Peters. Instead of including a jury in each trial, have members of the class who view each group's trial act as a jury.

"The Rattlesnake Hunt" from *Cross Creek*
by *Marjorie Kinnan Rawlings* (page 273)

SELECTION SYNOPSIS

In this true story, the writer is invited to go on a rattlesnake hunt with a young herpetologist from Florida. At first, fear is the writer's dominant emotion, but as she learns more about the snakes, she becomes more courageous. By the end of the hunt, the writer joyfully states that she has won a victory over a great fear.

SELECTION ACTIVITY

Many facts about rattlesnakes can be learned from this selection. Some misconceptions about rattlesnakes are also discussed. In this activity, students will verify facts and gain additional information about rattlesnakes.

Have students begin by listing facts about rattlesnakes found in the article. Also have them list some of the misconceptions the writer had about snakes before she went on this trip. Students should verify all of the facts stated or implied in the story by checking encyclopedias and other reference books.

Then have students make a list of additional facts that they would like to know about rattlesnakes. Some possible questions include:

Where else besides the Everglades do rattlesnakes live?
Do rattlesnakes vary in size?
What should a person do if bitten by a rattlesnake?
What is a rattlesnake's main habitat?
What are the rattlesnake's sources of food?

Have students make notes of the information they gather. Have them prepare their notes in legible form to be handed in and graded. Then have students use their notes to participate in a class discussion about the characteristics of rattlesnakes.

"Earth"
by *John Hall Wheelock* (page 281)

"Earth"
by *Oliver Herford* (page 281)

SELECTION SYNOPSES

The subject matter of both poems is the end of the planet Earth. The poem by Wheelock implies that the earth is destroyed by human beings. In the poem by Herford, the earth burns up like a meteoroid and is seen from a distant planet as a shooting star.

Two issues very much on the minds of concerned citizens today are the threat of nuclear war and the destruction of the earth's environment. Groups concerned about both of these causes might choose to use Wheelock's poem as part of a propaganda campaign.

Have students work in small groups. Ask each group to choose one of these issues to represent. Then challenge them to use Wheelock's poem in a creative way to further their cause. For example, the poem might be printed on fliers the group could hand out. Also included on the fliers might be a commentary on the relevance of the poem and information about what concerned citizens can do. Another possibility would be to reproduce the poem on a poster. Yet a third possibility would be for a student to give an impassioned speech about the cause chosen, effectively using the poem and through well-placed quotations.

As students work on their projects, remind them of the irony expressed in this poem; the Martian decides that Earth creatures must have been intelligent in order to find a way to destroy themselves.

■ "The Lady or the Tiger?"
by Frank Stockton (page 285)

SELECTION SYNOPSIS

This is a famous story, and one of the elements that makes it famous is that it has no ending. The story tells the tale of a semi-barbaric king, who lived in olden times. When someone was accused of a crime that reached the king's attention, the accused person was thrown into an arena. There he had the choice of opening one of two doors. Behind one door was a tiger, which would devour him. Behind the other door was a beautiful lady who would marry him. The king reasoned that if the person were guilty, the Law of Chance would have him open the door with the tiger. If he were innocent, he would open the door with the lady.

This king had a beautiful daughter. A young man, a commoner, fell in love with her. The king was outraged, for the young man had no right to love his daughter. The young man was to be thrown into the arena to decide his fate. The king's daughter, who loved the young man, learned the secret of which door had the tiger and which had the lady. When the young man stepped into the arena, she signaled to him which door to open. Yet she knew that she would lose him either way; for if he lived, he would marry the lady behind the door. What happened when the young man opened the door? The writer never tells. He says that he will leave it up to the reader to decide which came out of the door: the lady, or the tiger.

SELECTION ACTIVITY

Have students work in small groups to dramatize a possible ending to the story. Students can choose various ways to present their endings. One possibility would be to write a monologue about the thoughts of the princess before she goes to the arena. The decision she makes, and the reasons for it, can infer the ending of the story. Another method would be to dramatize the actual opening of the door, and the young man's reaction.

■ "Displays of Skill: The Bat"
by Ruth Hershberger (page 295)

■ "The Bird of Night"
by Randall Jarrell (page 297)

SELECTION SYNOPSES

The first poem describes a bat, as told from the bat's point of view. The second poem is a third-person description of the owl.

SELECTION ACTIVITY

Have students choose one of the two animals, the bat or the owl, to research. Have students correlate their research with the poem and verify or refute any ideas about the animals that are presented. For example, they should verify facts about the bat presented in the first poem. Students who choose to research the owl should see if pictures of an owl match the description given in "The Bird of Night."

■ "A Secret for Two"
by Quentin Reynolds (page 301)

SELECTION SYNOPSIS

For half of the 30 years he has delivered milk, Pierre has been helped by his faithful horse, Joseph. The two have so much rapport that they appear to share a secret.

Joseph pulls the wagon from the dairy to Pierre's route without direction and stops by habit at each customer's house. Pierre cannot read or write, so customers call out any change in their regular orders when they hear his wagon. The dairy manager offers to let Pierre retire on full salary, but he declines.

One cold morning, Pierre comes to work to be told that Joseph is dead. He stumbles off down the street, tears streaming from his eyes. He is struck and killed instantly by a large truck. The ambulance doctor observes that the old man has been blind for years. With Joseph's help, Pierre has been able to keep his blindness a secret.

SELECTION ACTIVITY

Have students find out about the life and work of the author of this story, Quentin Reynolds. One fact that students might uncover is that Reynolds, who lived from 1902 to 1965, was best known as a war correspondent during World War II.

STUDENT READING LIST

Dahl, Roald. *Umbrella Man and other stories*. 1998. Viking.

Doyle, Arthur Conan. *Adventures of Sherlock Holmes*. 1992. Viking.

Livingston, Myra Cohn (ed.). *I Am Writing a Poem about a Game of Poetry*. 1997. Simon & Schuster/McElderry.

Read If You Dare: 12 twisted tales from the editors of READ Magazine. 1997. Millbrook, New Jersey.

from Globe Fearon Educational Publisher

Pacemaker Classics
  The Adventures of Sherlock Holmes
  by Sir Arthur Conan Doyle
The Bestsellers
  Night of Fire and Blood
  Star Gold

UNIT 3
Overview

UNIT OBJECTIVES
After completing this unit, students will be able to

- understand the basic elements of a drama: plot, characters, setting, theme, and conflict
- recognize aspects of a drama that distinguish it from a short story
- use a thesaurus to find synonyms
- use a dictionary to distinguish shades of meaning in synonyms
- recognize and understand vocabulary specific to professions or lifestyles
- analyze plot and write a conclusion or postscript to a story
- distinguish differences between first-person and third-person point of view presentations

UNIT SELECTIONS
The theme of this unit is suspense. The selections range from crime stories to stories with surprise endings. Also included are several poems having animals or extraterrestrial beings as characters.

- **"The Getaway"** (p. 217) A crime story told from an observer's unique perspective, the surprise ending shows that the observer is not as perceptive as he thinks.
  - LITERARY SKILL: setting
  - READING SKILL: make predictions
  - VOCABULARY: compound words
  - WRITING: add a postscript

- **"Sherlock Holmes and the Speckled Band"** (p. 225) One of the world's most famous fictional detectives solves a murder at an English manor. The story is presented as a drama.
  - LITERARY SKILL: characters
  - READING SKILL: evaluate the writer's craft
  - VOCABULARY: crime story vocabulary
  - WRITING: short television script

- **Trifles** (p. 252) A drama where the suspense lies partly in solving a murder but mainly in understanding the motive of the murderer. It is the model selection in this unit.
  - LITERARY SKILL: elements of drama
  - READING SKILL: draw conclusions
  - VOCABULARY: precise definitions
  - WRITING: a murder confession

- **"The Rattlesnake Hunt"** from **Cross Creek** (p. 273) This is a nonfiction narrative of a woman and a scientist who gather rattlesnakes in the Everglades.
  - LITERARY SKILL: narration
  - READING SKILL: identify problems and solutions
  - VOCABULARY: formation of nouns describing scientists
  - WRITING: explain process

- **"Earth"** and **"Earth"** (p. 281) These two poems which raise suspense beyond human comprehension by offering extraterrestrials' explanations of what happens when life on Earth ends.
  - LITERARY SKILL: tone
  - READING SKILL: evaluate the author's style
  - VOCABULARY: use a thesaurus
  - WRITING: news story

Suspense

I tell you a tale to-night
  Which a seaman told to me,
With eyes that gleamed in the lanthorn light
  And a voice as low as the sea.
                  —Alfred Noyes

The Whale Ship, Joseph Mallord William Turner. The Metropolitan Museum of Art,
Wolfe Fund, 1896. Catharine Lorillard Wolfe Collection

213

Introducing the Unit Theme

Ask students to examine the Alfred Noyes poem to determine setting. As a class, discuss this setting. Why does it seem particularly suited for telling tales of suspense? What would it be like to sit on the deck of a sailing vessel at sea and have "an old salt" "spin yarns" in the darkness? Ask students when they like to tell or read suspense stories. Make a list of the settings and determine common features.

Viewing Fine Art

Joseph Mallord William Turner (1775–1851) painted many seascapes. He was part of the Romantic movement that dominated European art in the late 18th and early 19th centuries. As with other Romantics, nature figures prominently in his works. His style was described by his famous contemporary John Constable as "airy visions, painted with tinted steam." Turner strived to convey emotion in his paintings. A sense of the vastness of the sea and the suspense of man's striving against the sea are evident in The Whale Ship. The colors and shading in this painting create a sensation of motion and activity. What might be about to happen?

- **"The Lady or the Tiger?"** (p. 285) This story challenges readers to finish where the author leaves off—and try to guess how the story ends.
  LITERARY SKILL: irony
  READING SKILL: make judgments
  VOCABULARY: identify root words
  WRITING: develop a conclusion

- **"Displays of Skill: The Bat"** (p.295) and **"The Bird of Night"** (p.297) Flying creatures of the night are the subject of these two poems. In the first poem, bats are made less mysterious, while in the second, the owl remains shrouded in mystery and suspense.
  LITERARY SKILL: word meaning
  READING SKILL: evaluate facts
  VOCABULARY: shades of meaning in synonyms
  WRITING: first person point of view

- **"A Secret for Two"** (p. 301) This is a story tion between a man horse who have a connection to ea
  LITERARY SKILL: r
  READING SKILL
  VOCABULARY
  WRITING

Suspense

Everyone loves the excitement of not knowing what is going to happen next. You think, you feel, you imagine a dozen different possibilities.

Suspense means waiting. In literature, a good author knows how to use that waiting period to get you more and more interested in the story. You see the setting and characters in your mind. You feel the plot and theme taking you on a roller coaster ride. A part of you seems to be with the characters as the suspense builds. Explore the world of suspense in this unit.

■ CRIMES

Crimes always make good suspense stories. The perpetrators must be found and their motives explained. Detectives piece together clues. They begin making sense out of what seems nonsense. A theory emerges, and it is proven true. The guilty are revealed!

Within this simple framework of the crime story, a writer can add twists and turns that are guaranteed to keep you guessing or to surprise you.

That is what John Savage does in "The Getaway." The story seems rather simple at first, but look for clues that will prepare you for the ending.

The master crime storyteller of all time is probably Arthur Conan Doyle. He created the greatest detective of all detectives, Sherlock Holmes, and his sidekick, Dr. Watson. Holmes and Watson try to solve a strange murder in a dramatized version of "Sherlock Holmes and the Speckled Band."

Trifles is a crime story that goes beyond the usual "whodunit" tale. It is important to know who killed John Wright, but this time understanding the reasons is essential to feeling the real suspense.

■ HAPPY AND NOT SO HAPPY ENDINGS

Suspense cannot go on forever. It must end sometime. How it ends in a story can make you feel happy or sad.

"The Rattlesnake Hunt" presents a different kind of suspense. Instead of people trying to outwit one another, a herpetologist teaches a writer how to outwit rattlesnakes.

Two poems, both titled "Earth," present not-so-happy endings to human existence on this planet. Even so, suspense is built into each.

■ PUZZLES

"The Lady or the Tiger?" is one of the most interesting suspense stories ever written. It ends in a rather puzzling fashion, and you will have to use all of your abilities to figure out the conclusion.

Think whether you could have named the flying animal described in "Displays of Skill: The Bat" if the poem had a different title. Even though "The Bird of Night" has no such giveaway in its title, you should be able to guess what the poet is describing before you reach the end.

Make doubly sure that you keep the title in mind when you read the last short story in the unit, "A Secret for Two." This story about a Montreal milk wagon driver is innocent enough, but there is real mystery behind it.

Now, explore the world of suspense—and hold your breath as the writers tell their tales!

Discussing the Unit Theme

Suspense can be created in a number of ways: through vivid description, through plot, and through conflict, for example. Yet there is one element that is basic to suspense: the withholding of information. Discuss with students the different kinds of writing they will find in this unit. Ask if any of the stories might relate to real events with which they are personally familiar. What kind of suspense exists in people's daily lives? Is there suspense only in personal affairs (such as not knowing if you've won an award), or does suspense also extend to broad fields such as international politics?

Cooperative Group Activity

Divide the class into groups and have each group develop a setting for a suspense story. Ask the groups to state the theme of the story; they must not give plot outlines, but they must be able to tell how the setting they've chosen is appropriate for a particular story.

SELECTION OBJECTIVES

After completing this selection, students will be able to

- understand setting
- explain the importance of a story's setting
- analyze the believability of a story
- write a postscript to a story's conclusion
- consider specific aspects of setting
- identify the root words that make up a compound word
- make predictions

Lesson Resources

The Getaway
- Selection Synopsis, Teacher's Edition, p. T217
- Comprehension and Vocabulary Workbook, pp. 43–44
- Language Enrichment Workbook, pp. 42–44
- Teacher's Resources Reinforcement, p. R22 Test, pp. T41–T42

More About Setting

The "where" of a setting can be more important than the "when." Point out to students that most great novelists—Gustave Flaubert, Leo Tolstoy, James Joyce, and more recently, Richard Wright and James Baldwin, reflect the times, or the "when," of their own lives.

Ask students: Why do you think great novels live from generation to generation? Lead students to understand that from their keen observations of the world around them, great writers draw universal truths. Ask students to name their favorite great novel, epic poem, or drama; suggest that they specify the setting—and its importance.

READING FOCUS

Make Predictions Authors do not always directly state what the outcome of a story will be. Instead, they give clues, using characters' actions and dialogue, to help the reader predict what will happen next in the story. As you read, pay attention to what characters say and do, and try to make predictions about what will happen next and how the problems in the story will be resolved.

SETTING

Setting is the "where" and "when" of a story. It includes the place and the time the story unfolds. Setting is always important to a story, but sometimes it is so important that you cannot imagine the story happening in any other place at any other time. The story requires that the action happen in this specific setting.

When that is the case, setting plays an important part in the story's plot. Somehow, where or when the story takes place will have a big impact on the action. In suspense stories, the answer to "when?" can keep you on the edge of your seat. The answer to "where?" can spell life or death for the characters.

As you read the next selection, ask yourself these questions:

1. Why is the "where" of the setting so important to this story?
2. Is the "when" of the setting also important to this story?

WRITING CONNECTION

Exotic foreign locales are sometimes the setting for stories or parts of stories. Think of a written story or a film where such a scene is important. In two or three sentences, explain why you think so.

More About the Unit Theme

How do students think suspense will be created in a story entitled "The Getaway"? Can they think of any other stories or films in which a "getaway" is an important part of the story? What happened in these other stories? Did the getaway succeed or fail?

Background Notes

You won't find the border town of Hackett on any map of Texas, but the author does accurately represent the difficulty of crossing the Rio Grande River from Texas to Mexico. The Rio Grande, which rises in New Mexico, runs the length of the border between Texas and Mexico. Few bridges cross it, particularly in the western section of the state.

Cooperative Group Activity

Divide the class into groups of four or five. Have them each relate an international incident—from TV or their own reading—and then choose one that the group can make into a skit for class presentation.

THE GETAWAY

by John Savage

Whenever I get sleepy at the wheel, I always stop for coffee. This time, I was going along in western Texas and I got sleepy. I saw a sign that said GAS EAT, so I pulled off. It was long after midnight. What I expected was a place like a bunch of others, where the coffee tastes like copper and the flies never sleep.

What I found was something else. The tables were painted wood, and they looked as if nobody ever spilled the ketchup. The counter was spick-and-span. Even the smell was OK, I swear it.

Nobody was there, as far as customers. There was just this one old boy—really only about forty, getting gray above the ears—behind the counter. I sat down at the counter and ordered coffee and apple pie. Right away he got me started feeling sad.

I have a habit: I divide people up. Winners and losers. This old boy behind the counter was the kind that they *mean* well; they can't do enough for you, but their eyes have this gentle, faraway look, and they can't win. You know? With their clean shirt and their little bow tie? It makes you feel sad just to look at them. Only take my tip: Don't feel too sad.

He brought the coffee steaming hot, and it tasted like coffee. "Care for cream and sugar?" he asked. I said, "Please," and the cream was fresh and cold and thick. The pie was good, too.

A car pulled up outside. The old boy glanced out to see if they wanted gas, but they didn't. They came right in. The tall one said, "Two coffees. Do you have a road map we could look at?"

"I think so," the old boy said. He got their coffee first, and then started rooting through a pile of papers by the telephone, looking for a map. It was easy to see he was the type nothing's too much trouble for. Tickled to be of service.

---

root (ROOT) dig or search around

The Getaway ■ 217

Background Note
The comment that "they were well-dressed, like a couple of feed merchants," is a clue to the dominant industry of the western part of Texas: ranching, an industry in which feed merchants prosper. In another part of the state, the narrator might have used "oil men" or "stock brokers."

Literary Focus:
Setting
Ask: What does the setting of this story tell you about the time it occurred?

I'm the same type myself, if you want to know. I watched the old boy hunting for his map, and I felt like I was looking in a mirror.

After a minute or two, he came up with the map. "This one's a little out of date, but . . ." He put it on the counter, beside their coffee.

The two men spread out the map and leaned over it. They were well dressed, like a couple of feed merchants. The tall one ran his finger along the Rio Grande and shook his head. "I guess there's no place to get across, this side of El Paso."

He said it to his pal, but the old boy behind the counter heard him and lit up like a light bulb. "You trying to find the best way south? I might be able to help you with that."

"How?"

"Just a minute." He spent a lot of time going through the papers by the telephone again. "Thought I might have a newer map," he said. "Anything recent would show the Hackett Bridge. Anyway, I can tell you how to find it."

"Here's a town called Hackett," the tall one said, still looking at the map. "It's on the river, just at the end of a road. Looks like a pretty small place."

"Not any more. It's just about doubled since they built the bridge."

"What happens on the other side?" The short one asked the question, but both of the feed-merchant types were paying close attention.

"Pretty fair road, clear to Chihuahua. It joins up there with the highway out of El Paso and Juarez."

The tall man finished his coffee, folded the map, put it in his pocket, and stood up. "We'll take your map with us," he said.

The old boy seemed startled, like a new kid at school when somebody pokes him in the nose to show him who's boss. However, he just shrugged and said, "Glad to let you have it."

---

feed merchant (FEED MUR chunt) person who buys and sells food for animals
Rio Grande (ree oh GRAND) river that separates the state of Texas from Mexico
El Paso (el PAS oh) a city in western Texas, near the border of Mexico
Chihuahua (chi WAH wah) city in northern Mexico
Juarez (HWAH res) Mexican city across the Rio Grande from El Paso

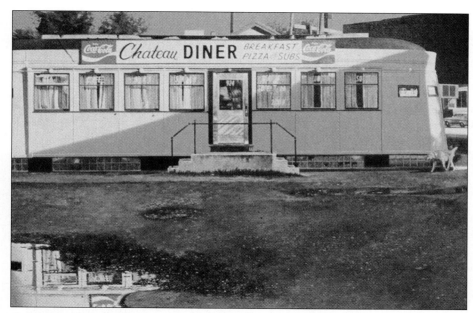

Chateau Diner, John Baeder. O.K. Harris Works of Art, New York

The feed merchants had a little conference on the way out, talking in whispers. Then they stopped in the middle of the floor, turned around, reached inside their jackets, and pulled guns on us. Automatic pistols, I think they were. "You sit where you are and don't move," the tall one said to me. "And *you*, get against the wall."

Both of us did exactly what they wanted. I told you we were a lot alike.

The short man walked over and pushed one of the keys of the cash register. "Every little bit helps," he said, and he scooped the money out of the drawer. The tall man set the telephone on the floor, put his foot on it, and jerked the wires out. Then they ran to their car and got in. The short man leaned out the window and shot out one of my tires. Then they took off fast.

I looked at the old boy behind the counter. He seemed a little pale, but he didn't waste any time. He took a screwdriver out of a drawer and squatted down beside the telephone. I said, "It doesn't always pay to be nice to people."

The Getaway ■ 219

T220

He laughed and said, "Well, it doesn't usually cost anything," and went on taking the base plate off the telephone. He was a fast worker, actually. His tongue was sticking out of the corner of his mouth. In about five minutes he had a dial tone coming out of the receiver. He dialed a number and told the rangers about the men and their car. "They did?" he said. "Well, well, well. . . . No, not El Paso. They took the Hackett turnoff." After he hung up, he said, "It turns out those guys robbed a supermarket in Wichita Falls."

I shook my head. "They sure had me fooled. I thought they looked perfectly all right."

The old boy got me another cup of coffee, and opened himself a bottle of pop. "They fooled me, too, at first." He wiped his mouth. "Then I got a load of their shoulder holsters when they leaned on the counter to look at the map. Anyway, they had mean eyes, I thought. Didn't you?"

"Well, I didn't at the time."

We drank without talking for a while, getting our nerves back in shape. A pair of patrol cars went roaring by outside and squealed their tires around the Hackett turnoff.

I got to thinking, and I thought of the saddest thing yet. "You *knew* there was something wrong with those guys, but you still couldn't keep from helping them on their way."

He laughed. "Well, the world's a tough sort of place at best, is how I look at it."

"I can understand showing them the map," I said, "but I'd never have told about the bridge. Now there's not a chance of catching them. If you'd kept your mouth shut, there'd at least be some hope."

"There isn't any—"

"Not a shred," I went on. "Not with a car as fast as they've got."

The way the old boy smiled made me feel better about him and me. "I don't mean there isn't any hope," he said. "I mean there isn't any bridge."

The Getaway ■ 221

Background Note
Wichita Falls is in north central Texas, about 500 miles from El Paso.

Critical Thinking:
Infer
The counterman may not be the "loser" that the narrator thought he was after all. What can students infer about the counterman based on his quick assessment of the robbers and their intentions?

Literary Focus:
Setting
The ending of the story reveals the important role that the setting plays in the story's resolution. Ask: How does the setting help to determine the robbers' fate?

Reading Focus:
Make Predictions
The final outcome of the story remains unclear until the last line when the counterman reveals that there is no bridge. Ask: What clues may have led you to predict this outcome or one similar to it?

Mini Quiz

Write the following sentences on the chalkboard or overhead projector and call on students to fill in the blanks. Discuss the answers with the class.

1. The narrator stopped for coffee because he _____ .

2. When they came into the restaurant, the two men asked to look at a _____ .

3. They were trying to get to _____ .

4. The first thing the counterman did after the robbery was _____ .

5. The two men carried their guns in _____ .

Answers
1. became tired while driving
2. road map
3. Mexico
4. fix the telephone
5. shoulder holsters

UNDERSTAND THE SELECTION

Answers

1. The story takes place in west Texas, near the Mexican border.
2. He thinks they are feed merchants.
3. When he saw their shoulder holsters as they leaned on the counter to look at the map, he thought they were criminals.
4. The narrator's first impression that he is a "loser" was wrong. He is a winner.
5. Probably, but he didn't want to give them anything that might have made them suspicious about the nonexistent Hackett Bridge.
6. to prevent the counterman and narrator from calling the police
7. In this sentence, nothing makes sense until we read the very last word. And then not only the sentence, but the whole story, takes on a new meaning.
8. Yes. We are quickly drawn into the story because the narrator is part of it. Also, he can use colloquial language, which adds a sense of realistic immediacy to the story.
9. Yes. In the fourth paragraph of the story, the narrator tells us not to feel "too sad" for the "losers" of the world. It's a hint the counterman is not a loser. However, the character of the counterman is so finely crafted that we have few hints from his actions that he knows exactly what he is doing when the criminals are planning their getaway.
10. Answers will vary.

Respond to Literature

One weakness in the story that could be pointed out is that it's hard to believe that criminals—on the run in unfamiliar territory—don't have a decent road map.

 ## WRITE ABOUT THE SELECTION

Prewriting

Have students read the relevant sections aloud. Ask for volunteers to be

---

UNDERSTAND THE SELECTION

Recall

1. Where does the story take place?
2. At first, who did the narrator think the two men were?
3. When did the counterman say he first thought that the men were criminals?

Infer

4. At the end of the story, is the counterman a "winner" or a "loser"?
5. Do you think the counterman had a newer map than the one he gave the men?
6. Why did the two men cut the telephone line?
7. How does the last sentence help maintain the story's suspense?

Apply

8. Does first-person point of view work well in this story?
9. Are there any hints about the surprise ending earlier in the story?
10. How might you have reacted if you had been the counterman?

> ### Respond to Literature
> Do you think that there are any weak points in this story? Is anything not believable? Explain your answer.

WRITE ABOUT THE SELECTION

What did the narrator of the story think when the counterman told him that there was no Hackett Bridge? Imagine that you are the narrator. How would this affect your opinion of the counterman? Imagine that you want to add a postscript describing what you felt and did after you learned that the bridge did not exist.

Prewriting Do a little reviewing before you begin writing. Reread the paragraphs that describe the narrator's feelings about the counterman, especially the third and fourth paragraphs at the beginning and the six paragraphs at the end of the story. How do you feel about those observations now that you know the ending of the story? Make a cluster of your feelings. Then imagine how each of those feelings might make you act. Add a phrase about each of those possible actions to your cluster.

Writing Use your cluster to write your postscript. Try to make a smooth transition from the story's current ending to your addition. Remember that you are telling the story from the narrator's point of view.

Revising Try to imitate the author's writing style. He uses short sentences, informal language, and figures of speech. Add some of these characteristics to your writing.

Proofreading Reread your description to check for errors. Authors often use incomplete sentences. You may, too, but make sure you know how to rewrite them so that they are complete sentences.

---

the narrator and the counterman and to "perform" the sections before the class.

Writing

As students work on their postscripts individually, circulate among them to observe their use of the clusters. If any student seems to be having difficulty, you might prompt some cluster additions.

Revising

Ask the class for a particularly distinctive passage from the story. Then write it on the chalkboard or overhead projector. Analyze what makes it distinctive by rewriting it in a neutral style, and then compare the passages.

Proofreading

Ask students to exchange papers and check that the postscripts have the same point of view as the story. Have them correct any errors in pencil before returning the paper.

THINK ABOUT SETTING

John Savage, the author of "The Getaway," blends the setting so skillfully into the plot of the story that it is easy to overlook the setting's importance. Consider both general and specific time and place when you think about setting.

For example, a story could take place in Los Angeles sometime in the 1980s. That would be the general "where" and "when." The specific setting might be in a house after dinnertime.

1. When do we learn the setting of "The Getaway"?

2. Why is the geographic location of the restaurant important?

3. Why is the restaurant itself important as a setting for the story?

4. Why is setting an important part of the plot of this story?

5. Is the time this story takes place important? Think both about the specific time and the general time.

READING FOCUS

Make Predictions As you read "The Getaway," you were able to use clues from the characters' thoughts, dialogue, and actions to predict what might happen next. What did you predict the ending would be? What clues helped you to make this prediction?

DEVELOP YOUR VOCABULARY

Compound words are made up of two or more root words. Sometimes they are hyphenated.

Often compound words are so common that you do not realize they are made from other words. A good example is the noun in the title of this selection: *getaway* = get + away.

Knowing the root words in a compound word can often help you find its meaning.

There are few strict rules on when a compound word is hyphenated. Check a dictionary if you are unsure which form is correct.

Tell the root words of the following compound words:

1. faraway
2. zigzag
3. screwdriver
4. mother-in-law
5. turnoff
6. newspaper

What compound words are made up of the following root words? Make sure you spell them correctly.

1. law, father, in
2. noble, man
3. way, rail
4. smith, black

Use each compound word from this exercise in an original sentence.

THINK ABOUT SETTING

Answers

1. in the first paragraph of the story
2. It's close to the Mexican border.
3. It is in a very lonely and desolate place, deserted except for the counterman. That's important as the story unfolds.
4. The counterman uses his familiarity with the area to outsmart the criminals. The criminals must rely on him for knowledge on how to reach Mexico.
5. The specific time is "long after midnight," which is important in creating a sense of emptiness and in making the timing of the getaway seem plausible. The general time is sometime in the automobile era.

DEVELOP YOUR VOCABULARY

Answers

Part 1

1. far + away
2. zig + zag
3. screw + driver
4. mother + in + law
5. turn + off
6. news + paper

Part 2

1. father-in-law
2. nobleman
3. railway
4. blacksmith

Sample Sentences:

1. He had a *faraway* look in his eyes.
2. The road *zigzags* over the mountain pass.
3. The *screwdriver* fell into the hole.
4. My *mother-in-law* recently retired as school principal.
5. The highway *turnoff* isn't hard to find.
6. The *newspaper's* slogan is: News you can use.
7. My *father-in-law* still works at the ice cream factory.
8. It was important to her mother that she marry a *nobleman*.
9. *Railway* lines are often in disrepair.
10. A *blacksmith* is as rare today as a buffalo nickel.

READING FOCUS

Sample Answer

I predicted that the counterman would have something to do with catching the robbers. He acts very calmly when he shows the robbers the map and when he fixes the phone and calls the rangers. He seems to know what he is doing. He also doesn't seem very upset that they got away, like he knew something that the narrator didn't know.

ESL Activity

Discuss in small groups or as a class. Is it important to judge a person on personal appearance? Is it possible to make a valid judgment about a person when you first meet him or her? Have students come to a consensus through their discussion.

SELECTION OBJECTIVES

After completing this selection, students will be able to

- understand the development of characters in a story
- recognize the protagonist and antagonist in a conflict
- analyze the appeal of certain characters
- write a short television script
- describe the conflict of a drama
- understand the special vocabulary in crime stories
- evaluate the writer's craft

Lesson Resources

Sherlock Holmes and the Speckled Band
- Selection Synopsis, Teacher's Edition, p. T211c
- Comprehension and Vocabulary Workbook, pp. 45–46
- Language Enrichment Workbook, pp. 45–47
- Teacher's Resources
  Reinforcement, p. R23
  Test, pp. T43–T44

More About Characters

Characters are often called either "flat" or "round." Flat characters are somewhat like the supporting players in a theatrical stock company, necessary to advance the plot but never in the lead. Round characters are distinct individuals whom the writer describes in detail. Because their actions are not predictable, they intrigue us. They are stars. So too was Sherlock Holmes. If Holmes has become a flat character over time, it is only because of the great popularity of the Conan Doyle stories; we tend now to see only the hat, the tweeds, the magnifying glass—not the man. Yet students should understand that Sherlock Holmes is the original master detective, the prototype for all the omniscient sleuths who would follow.

READING FOCUS

Evaluate the Writer's Craft The purpose of a mystery is to build suspense to keep the reader interested. An author may do this in several ways. One way is to provide some, but not all, details about key events. Instead, the reader has to look for clues and guess what will happen next. As you read this play, see how the author reveals details of plot and setting. Decide how this adds to the suspense and keeps you interested.

Learn About

CHARACTERS

Stories can have many **characters**. Some of them may not be human.

Usually, however, there is a main character. Likewise, there is usually a character who comes in conflict with the main character. The main character is called the **protagonist**. The character who comes in conflict with him or her is called the **antagonist**.

The conflict between the two characters is very important to the story. Usually, it must be resolved before the story concludes. How it is resolved often determines the ending. A skillful writer can use the conflict between the protagonist and antagonist to develop the story's characters and make them come alive.

As you read the next selection, ask yourself these questions:

1. Who are the protagonist and antagonist?
2. What is the conflict between them?

WRITING CONNECTION

Antagonize is a verb which means "to oppose" or "to provoke to action." A noun with the same root is *antagonist*, one who comes in conflict with or opposes the protagonist. Think of someone or something that antagonizes you. Write a paragraph or two about this.

More About the Unit Theme

Suspense is built into all murder cases. Holmes solves his cases intellectually, through "deduction." He's at least one step ahead of Watson and sometimes farther ahead of his readers. Other sleuths approach a case doggedly, tracking down clues almost from door to door. With all, however, suspense is the key ingredient.

About the Author

If Sherlock Holmes seems to approach a case like a scientist, it's no wonder. His creator, Sir Arthur Conan Doyle, was himself trained as a scientist—a doctor, to be exact. He was born in 1859 in Edinburgh, Scotland, and practiced medicine for about eight years before becoming a full-time writer.

Cooperative Group Activity

Have students organize, direct, and stage a one-act drama. They may write it themselves or adapt a one-act play that clearly portrays both protagonist and antagonist. The first step would be to organize the class into groups of four or five and then assign each a task. Possible audiences: school assembly, another class, or their parents.

SHERLOCK HOLMES AND THE SPECKLED BAND

by Arthur Conan Doyle   DRAMATIZED

CHARACTERS

SHERLOCK HOLMES, *the famous detective*
DR. WATSON, *his friend*
HELEN STONER, *the lady in danger*

JULIA STONER, *her sister*
DR. GRIMESBY ROYLOTT, *her stepfather*

SCENE 1

TIME: About 1900.

SETTING: The parlor in HOLMES'S *apartment on Baker Street, London, England.*

AT RISE[1]: A woman dressed in black and wearing a veil is seated on the window seat in the parlor. The room is comfortably filled with sofas, chairs, old furniture, and the usual belongings of the bachelor detective: books, newspapers, slippers, magnifying glass, pipe rack, various hats, and a violin among them. HOLMES *and* DR. WATSON *enter. The lady rises to greet them.*

HOLMES: Good morning, Madam. I'm Sherlock Holmes. (*Nodding toward* Watson) My close friend, Dr. Watson. You can speak freely in front of him. Please sit down by the fire. I'll order coffee, since I see that you're shivering.
HELEN (*changing her seat*): Not from cold.
HOLMES: What then?
HELEN: Fear, Mr. Holmes. Terror.

(*She raises her veil to reveal a face tired and gray. She looks about 30, but her hair already shows traces of gray. Her eyes are restless and frightened. She looks like a hunted animal.* HOLMES *studies her face.*)

---

[1]**at rise:** at the start of the scene; when the curtain rises

Sherlock Holmes and the Speckled Band ■ 225

Discussion

Ask: What is the picture of Holmes that has emerged so far? Does he seem almost too good to be true? Would you want him to be your private detective?

Literary Focus:
Character

Helen Stoner's fiancé seems suspect at this point; her characterization of him is suspicious. Ask: Could he be the antagonist in this play?

Reading Focus:
Evaluate the Writer's Craft

Point out to students that the writer lets the reader know how Holmes works and thinks by his comments. Ask: How do you know Holmes is very observant?

HOLMES: Don't be afraid. Just leave everything to me. Now . . . what sent you all this way by train? And so early in the morning, too.

HELEN: How did you know I . . . ?

HOLMES (*breaking in*): There's the second half of a return ticket in the palm of your left glove. Plain as day. Please relax. That drive in the dogcart must have been difficult.

(HELEN *gives a start of surprise. She stares at* HOLMES.)

HOLMES: It's no mystery, my dear madam. The left arm of your jacket has mud spots in seven places. The marks are fresh. Only a dogcart splashes mud in that way.

HELEN: Well, whatever your reasons, you're right. Mr. Holmes, I can't stand this strain any longer! I'll go mad. I have no one else to turn to, except . . . well, someone who cares for me, but can't help. I've heard of you, Mr. Holmes. Can you help me? I . . . right now, I can't pay you. But in a month or so, I'll be married, and then . . .

HOLMES (*breaking in*): Madam, my work is its own reward. I'll be happy to help you. Now, tell us everything. Everything.

HELEN: I'm afraid that . . . that's the horror of it. It's . . . so vague. My fears—they come from small things that might seem like nothing to you. Even my fiancé thinks it's all just nerves.

HOLMES: He says so?

HELEN: No, but it's in his soothing answers. And the way he turns his eyes from me. But you, Mr. Holmes—I've heard you can see all the evils that lie in the human heart. I'm surrounded by danger. Can you help me?

WATSON: Yes!

HOLMES: Thank you, Watson. Now, Madam—start with your name.

HELEN: It's Helen Stoner.

HOLMES: And you live . . . ?

HELEN: With my stepfather. He's the last member of one of the oldest families in England, the Roylotts of Stoke Moran.

HOLMES: Yes, I've heard the name.

---

vague (VAYG) not clear, hazy
fiancé (fee ahn SAY) husband-to-be
soothing (SOO*TH* ing) calming

226 ■ Unit 3

T226

HELEN: The family was once very rich. But they were ruined in the last century. Nothing's left but a few acres and the ancient house. And that's crushed under a mortgage. The last Roylott lived out his life there—a horrible life as a penniless nobleman. But his only son—that's my stepfather—he saw that things had to change. He borrowed some money. He got a medical degree and went out to India. He built a large practice there.

HOLMES: But he came back to England? Why?

---

mortgage (MAWR gij) loan given to purchase a house
practice (PRAK tis) the business of a doctor or lawyer

Sherlock Holmes and the Speckled Band ■ **227**

Literary Focus:
Hyperbole
Hyperbole is used to describe the financial woes facing the Roylott house: it's "crushed under a mortgage." Make sure students understand what a mortgage is. Then ask: What does this hyperbole add to your understanding of the size of the financial burden?

Background Note
India was a British colony at the time this story was written. Many young Englishmen went to India to make their fortunes in life.

Literary Focus:
Characters

Helen Stoner's description of her stepfather seems to raise Holmes's suspicions and move the story in a definite direction, with Dr. Roylott as the antagonist. Ask: Do you think Holmes may be correct in his suspicions?

Background Note

The symbol before the number 1000 is the symbol for the pound, £, which is the British currency unit. Exchange rates giving the current value of the pound can be found in the financial section of major newspapers.

HELEN: A string of robberies in his house in India. He got into a fit of anger about them and beat his native butler to death. They almost hanged him. He spent a long term in prison. Then he came back to England. A sad man. A very disappointed man.

HOLMES: And your mother, his wife?

HELEN: He married my mother in India. She was the widow of a Major-General Stoner. My sister Julia and I were twins. We were only two years old when my mother remarried.

HOLMES: Hm. Was she well-off at the time?

HELEN: Well, yes. She had quite a bit of money—at least £1000 a year. And she gave it all to Dr. Roylott while we lived with him. Julia and I were to each get a certain amount a year when we married.

HOLMES: Is your mother still living?

HELEN: She died soon after we came to England—eight years ago. A railway accident.

HOLMES: And you went on living with your stepfather?

HELEN: Yes, he gave up trying to practice medicine. He took us to live in the family house at Stoke Moran. The money my mother left was more than enough. We had all we needed to be happy.

HOLMES: But?

HELEN: It was my stepfather. A terrible change came over him. At first, the neighbors were so happy to see a Roylott back in the old family home. But instead of making friends, he shut himself up in the house. He hardly ever came out, except to get into fights with anyone who crossed his path. He has a terrible temper. As a matter of fact, some of his ancestors showed traces of . . . well, madness. In his case, it got worse because of those years in India.

HOLMES: What happened?

HELEN: A series of brawls. Two ended in the police court. He became the terror of the village. People would run when they saw him coming.

HOLMES: Is he dangerous?

HELEN: Well, he's a man of huge strength. And when he's angry, he's just out of control. Last week he threw the blacksmith over a bridge into a stream. I had to pay all the money I could get in a hurry to keep it quiet.

---

brawl (BRAWL) noisy fight

HOLMES: He has no friends, then?

HELEN: Only the gypsies. He lets them camp on his land. And they give him the hospitality of their tents. Sometimes for weeks on end. Oh, and he also has animals—Indian animals.

HOLMES: Really?

HELEN: Yes. They're sent over to him by a man in India. He's got a cheetah and a baboon. They just wander loose on the grounds. They scare people almost as much as he does! You can imagine what our life was like, Julia's and mine. No great pleasure. Julia was only 30 when she died, but her hair had already started to turn white. Like mine.

HOLMES: Your sister is dead, then?

HELEN: She died just two years ago. It's her death that I came to see you about.

HOLMES: Go on.

HELEN: Well, living the life we did, Julia and I met very few people our own age. But we had an Aunt Honoria, who lives near Harrow. We went to visit her sometimes. Julia was there at Christmas two years ago, and she met a major of the marines. They got engaged.

HOLMES: What did your stepfather think of that?

HELEN: He didn't object. But within two weeks of the date set for the wedding . . . (*She is very upset.*)

HOLMES: Please go on.

HELEN: The terrible event that . . .

HOLMES (*breaking in*): Please be precise. Details! I must have details.

HELEN: That's easy. It's all burned in my memory.
(*She appears about to cry.*)

HOLMES: Take it easy. Go ahead.

HELEN: The house, as I said, is very old. We use only one wing. The bedrooms are on the ground floor. The first is Dr. Roylott's, the second my sister's, and the third is mine. No connecting doors. But all three rooms open into the same hallway. Is that clear?

HOLMES: Perfectly.

HELEN: The windows of the three rooms open out on the lawn. That night—the night she died—Dr. Roylott had gone to his room early. But we knew he hadn't gone to bed.

---

cheetah (CHEET uh) wild cat with a spotted coat
precise (prih SYS) very exact

Sherlock Holmes and the Speckled Band ■ 229

Reading Focus:
Evaluate the Writer's Craft

Ask: Why does the writer suddenly shift back to an event from the past in Scene 2? Does this make Julia's experience more vivid and lend it more weight than if Helen had simply described it to Holmes?

HOLMES: How?

HELEN: Because my sister smelled the strong Indian cigars he smokes. So she left her room and came into mine. We sat for a while, talking about the wedding. Then we said goodnight. I remember it all so vividly. She got up to go. . . .

SCENE 2

SETTING: Helen's bedroom in the Roylott mansion.

AT RISE: JULIA *and* HELEN STONER *are seated on the bed. They kiss each other goodnight.* JULIA *walks to the door, then pauses, turning to look back at* HELEN.

JULIA: Helen, have you ever heard anyone whistle in the dead of the night?

HELEN: No! Why?

JULIA: You couldn't be whistling in your sleep, could you?

HELEN: No! What are you talking about?

---

vividly (VIV id lee) very clearly; as if lifelike

JULIA: It's just that the last few nights, I've heard a strange whistling. At about three o'clock in the morning! A low, clear whistle. I'm a light sleeper, and it wakes me up. I can't tell where the sound comes from—the next room, the lawn, I don't know.

HELEN: It must be the gypsies.

JULIA: I guess so. But if it's on the lawn, I wonder why you didn't hear it too.

HELEN: Oh, I sleep like a log.

JULIA: Well, it doesn't matter, anyway. Good night.

SCENE 3

SETTING: *The parlor in* HOLMES'S *apartment.*

AT RISE: HOLMES, WATSON *and* HELEN STONER *are sitting as before.* HELEN *goes on with her story.*

HELEN: She smiled at me and closed my door. I heard her key turn in the lock.

HOLMES: Her key? Did you usually lock yourselves in at night?

HELEN: Always.

HOLMES: Why?

HELEN: Remember—the cheetah and the baboon! We didn't feel safe unless our doors were locked at night.

HOLMES: Right. Go on.

HELEN: I couldn't sleep that night. It was wild weather, howling wind. The rain beat against the windows. Suddenly I heard a scream—a woman's scream. I knew it was my sister's voice. I rushed into the hall. Then I seemed to hear a low whistle— just as my sister had described it. Then there was a clanging sound, like metal falling. My sister's door was unlocked— and it started to open slowly. I stared at it. I didn't know what would come out! It was Julia. Her face was white with terror. Her hands were groping for help. She swayed as if she was drunk. I ran to her and threw my arms around her, but her knees gave way and she fell to the ground. She was twisting in terrible pain. I bent over her. Then suddenly, she shrieked— I'll never forget her voice! "Oh! Helen! It was the band! The speckled band!"

---

grope (GROHP) feel about blindly

Sherlock Holmes and the Speckled Band ■ 231

Literary Focus:
Setting
Point out to students that the flash-back in Scene 2 allowed the story to be told in the present tense— even though it was a past event. Discuss whether this is an effective use of setting.

Critical Thinking:
Analyze
Scene 3 brings the reader back to the present. Ask: What does Holmes know so far?

Reading Focus:
Evaluate the Writer's Craft
Ask how Holmes's questions to Helen about the night of her sister's death are clues themselves.

HOLMES: That's all? She didn't explain?

HELEN: She tried to say more. She stabbed her finger in the air towards the doctor's room. But then she choked and couldn't get the words out. I called out for my stepfather. But when he got to my sister's side, she was unconscious.

HOLMES: Didn't he do anything to bring her around?

HELEN: He sent for medical help from the village. But it was useless. She died without speaking again.

HOLMES: One moment. Are you sure about this whistle and this metallic sound? Could you swear to it?

HELEN: I don't know. I felt strongly that I heard it. But with the wind crashing, and the creaking of an old house—I don't know.

HOLMES: Was your sister dressed?

HELEN: No, she was in her nightgown. And she had a burnt match in one hand and a matchbox in the other.

HOLMES: So she struck a match and looked about her when it happened. That's important. And what did the coroner find was the cause of death?

HELEN: He was very careful because Dr. Roylott had caused so much trouble in the neighborhood. But he couldn't find the cause of death.

HOLMES: Could anyone have entered her room?

HELEN: The door was locked on the inside. The windows have old-fashioned shutters with broad iron bars, and they were locked every night. The walls are solid all around. So is the floor. The chimney's wide, but it's barred. My sister had to be alone when it happened. Besides, there were no marks of violence on her.

HOLMES: Poison?

HELEN: The doctors examined her for it. There wasn't any.

HOLMES: What do *you* think your sister died of, then?

HELEN: I think she died of pure fear and nervous shock. But what could have frightened her? I can't imagine.

HOLMES: The gypsies—were they on the grounds that night?

HELEN: Yes, there are nearly always some there.

---

coroner (CAWR uh nur) public officer who investigates deaths that may not be due to natural causes

HOLMES: Ah. And what did you think she meant by her last words about a band—a speckled band?

HELEN: I don't know. Sometimes I've thought it was just wild talk—she was dying. Or maybe it meant . . . some band of people. Perhaps the gypsies. Because of the spotted handkerchiefs they wear—she might have called them "the speckled band."

(HOLMES *shakes his head. Clearly, he is far from satisfied.*)

HOLMES: We're in deep waters here. Please tell us the rest.

HELEN: That was two years ago. My life became lonelier than ever—until lately. About a month ago, a friend—a dear friend I've known for years—asked me to marry him. My stepfather hasn't objected. So we're going to be married in the spring.

HOLMES: Then what brings you here?

HELEN: Two days ago, some repairs were started in the west wing of the house. My bedroom wall has been ripped up. So I've had to move into the room where my sister died. And sleep in the bed she slept in. It was terrifying. Last night, I lay awake thinking about her. Her terrible death. I suddenly heard—it was very quiet—I heard the low whistle. Just like the whistle on the night she died. I jumped up and lit the lamp, but there was nothing in the room. I was too shaken to go to bed again. So I got dressed. As soon as it was daylight, I came here.

HOLMES: Very wise. But have you told me everything?

HELEN: Yes. Everything.

HOLMES: You have not, Miss Roylott. You're protecting your stepfather.

HELEN: Why, what do you mean?

(HOLMES *leans toward* HELEN *and pushes back the bit of lace that covers her hand.*)

HOLMES: Ah. Five little black-and-blue spots. Just the sort of spots made by four fingers and a thumb. You've been treated cruelly.

HELEN (*embarrassed*): He's a hard man. Perhaps he doesn't really know his own strength.

(*A silence.* HOLMES *leans his chin on his hands and stares into the fire.*)

---

treat (TREET) deal with

Critical Thinking:
Infer
Point out that Helen's sister Julia was murdered before her wedding. Ask: What can the reader infer about Helen's safety now that she herself is engaged to be married?

Reading Focus:
Evaluate the Writer's Craft

Discuss how the writer is creating a sense of suspense and also sharing the direction of Holmes's suspicion. Ask: What is Holmes's hurry in Scene 3? Why must he and Watson go to Stoke Moran immediately? Why do they want to look over the rooms without Dr. Roylott's knowing?

Critical Thinking:
Analyze

In the same scene, Holmes put a few things together into a theory. Both he and Watson realize that there are some holes in this theory. Ask: What do you think Holmes's theory might be?

HOLMES: This is a very deep business. I have to know a thousand details before I decide what to do. But we haven't a moment to lose. If we come today to Stoke Moran, will we be able to look over these rooms? Without your stepfather knowing?

HELEN: Well, yes. As a matter of fact, he said he'd be going into town today. He'll probably be away all day.

HOLMES: Good. You wouldn't mind the trip, Watson?

WATSON: I'd love it.

HOLMES: Then we'll both come.

HELEN: Thank you. I feel better already. I'll be waiting for you this afternoon, then.

(HELEN *drops her veil back over her face and exits.*)

HOLMES: Well, what do you think of it all, Watson?

WATSON: Hm. Seems to be a dark, evil business.

HOLMES: Yes, it does.

WATSON: But the floor and the walls were all solid. The door, the windows, and the chimney were all blocked. If she's right about that, then her sister must have been alone when she fell ill.

HOLMES: Then what about those whistles? And what about the "speckled band"?

WATSON: I really couldn't say.

HOLMES: Well, let's put a few things together. First, the whistles at night. Second, the band of gypsies—very friendly with the old doctor. Third, the fact that the doctor has an interest in stopping his stepdaughter's marriage. And finally, the metallic clang. A sound that *might* have been caused by one of the metal bars on the shutters falling into place. I think we can wrap things up along those lines.

WATSON: But how could the gypsies have done it?

HOLMES: I haven't the faintest idea.

WATSON: Holmes, I can think of quite a few objections to this theory.

HOLMES: So can I. That's why we're going to Stoke Moran today. We'll see if the objections make sense. Or if they can be explained away.

---

deep (DEEP) hard to understand
theory (THEE uh ree) guess based on reasoning

(*The door has burst open. A huge man stands in the doorway. He wears a black top hat. He has on a long coat and carries a riding whip. He has a wrinkled, sun-burned face, which looks angrily at* HOLMES *and* WATSON *in turn.*)

ROYLOTT: Holmes?

HOLMES: Here. And you?

ROYLOTT: Dr. Grimesby Roylott, of Stoke Moran.

HOLMES (*very pleasant*): Have a seat, doctor.

ROYLOTT: I won't. My stepdaughter's been here. I've traced her. What's she been saying to you?

HOLMES: It's a little cold for this time of year, isn't it?

ROYLOTT (*yelling*): What has she been saying to you?

HOLMES (*still pleasant*): But I've heard the crocuses are doing well.

ROYLOTT: Hah! You put me off, do you? (*He takes a step forward and shakes his riding whip at* HOLMES.) I know you, you dog! I've heard of you before. Holmes, the meddler.

(HOLMES *smiles.*)

ROYLOTT: Holmes, the busybody!

(HOLMES *smiles even more broadly.*)

ROYLOTT: Holmes, the Scotland Yard[2] puppet!

HOLMES: Talking with you is very entertaining. When you go out, please close the door. There's a draft.

---

crocus (KROH kus) spring flower
meddler (MED lur) one who butts into other people's business
[2]**Scotland Yard:** detective department of the London police

Sherlock Holmes and the Speckled Band ■ **235**

Literary Focus:
Characters

The interchange between Holmes and Roylott at the end of Scene 3 is a good example of indirect character description. Ask: What is the difference between how Holmes reacts and Roylott reacts?

T235

ROYLOTT: I'll go when I've had my say. Don't you *dare* meddle with my business. I know she's been here. I traced her! I'm a dangerous man to go up against!

(*So saying,* ROYLOTT *picks up an iron poker and bends it over double.*)

ROYLOTT: See that you keep out of my grip.

(ROYLOTT *hurls the poker into the fireplace and stomps out.*)

HOLMES (*laughing*): He seems friendly. Larger than I am, of course. But still, too bad he didn't hang around. We could have matched grips.

(*So saying,* HOLMES *picks up the poker and straightens it out again.*)

HOLMES: He's rude, though. Imagine thinking I'm—I—a puppet of the police! But this little visit makes the job more interesting, though, doesn't it? I only hope Miss Stoner won't be hurt by her carelessness—letting this brute trace her here. Now, Watson, let's have some breakfast. Then I'll do a little detecting.

SCENE 4

SETTING: HOLMES'S *parlor, later that day.*

AT RISE: WATSON *is studying a medical book as* HOLMES *returns.*

HOLMES *holds in his hand a sheet of blue paper. On it are written a bunch of notes and numbers.*

WATSON: Find anything?
HOLMES: I've seen the will of the dead wife, Miss Stoner's mother.
WATSON: And?
HOLMES: Not an easy job! I had to work out the present prices of all these investments. But the result is—at the time she died, the total income was almost £1100 a year. Now, with the fall in farm prices, it's only about £750. Each daughter was to get about £250 if she married.
WATSON: What does that mean for Roylott?
HOLMES: It means that if both girls had married, the old hulk would have had very little for himself. Even one marriage would be a serious blow for him.

WATSON: So he has a strong motive for standing in the way of their marriages.

HOLMES: Right.

WATSON: What now?

HOLMES: Get your revolver. An Eley's Number 2[3] is an excellent argument with gentlemen who can twist steel pokers into knots. That and a toothbrush should be all you need. Then—let's go!

---

motive (MOHT iv) reason to act
[3]**Eley's Number 2:** old make of pistol

Sherlock Holmes and the Speckled Band ■ 237

Literary Focus:
Irony

At the end of Scene 4, Holmes uses irony to provide a bit of comic relief. Ask: What is unexpected about a detective who carries a pistol and a toothbrush?

Reading Focus:
Evaluate the Writer's Craft
At the end of Scene 5, Holmes describes himself as "someone more cunning" than Roylott. Ask: What does the fact that he refers to himself this way reveal about his personality? Are we meant to see him as more than just a humble detective? Explain.

Literary Focus:
Setting
The opening of Scene 6 is a good place to point out to students that a scene change is often a writer's device to change the setting. Now, the actors are outside rather than inside the house. Ask: How does this change in setting contribute to the plot?

SCENE 5

SETTING: A hallway in the mansion at Stoke Moran.

AT RISE: HOLMES *and* WATSON *are received by* HELEN STONER.

HELEN: I've been waiting. It's turned out very well. He's gone to town. And he's not likely to be back before dark.

HOLMES: Yes, we had the pleasure of meeting the doctor. He followed you to my office. Demanded to know what your business was. Then he threatened us with a poker.

HELEN: Good heavens! You weren't hurt?

HOLMES: Certainly not.

HELEN: He's so tricky. I never know when I'm safe from him. What will we do when he gets back?

HOLMES: Better ask what *he'll* do. He'll have to be on guard. Because now he's got someone more cunning than he is on his track. You must lock yourself in tonight. If he's violent, we'll take you to your aunt's at Harrow. Now, let's examine the outside and then the rooms.

SCENE 6

SETTING: Outside the house.

AT RISE: HOLMES *is walking slowly. He examines the outsides of the windows.*

HOLMES: This window belongs to the room where you used to sleep. The center one is your sister's room, and the one next to the main building is Dr. Roylott's. Correct?

HELEN: Exactly. But now I'm sleeping in the middle room.

HOLMES: Ah, the alterations. I notice there doesn't seem to be any urgent need for repairs there.

HELEN: There isn't. I think it was an excuse to move me from my room.

HOLMES: That's important. Now, on the other side of this narrow wing is the hallway. All three rooms open off it. There are windows in the hallway, of course?

HELEN: Yes, but very small ones. Too narrow for anyone to get through.

---

alteration (awl tuh RAY shun) change made to a building

238 ■ Unit 3

T238

HOLMES: Anyway, you both locked your doors at night. So your rooms couldn't have been entered from that side. Now, you've bolted these shutters?

HELEN: Yes, they're locked from the inside.

(HOLMES *examines the shutters very closely, trying every way to open them. He tests the hinges with a magnifying glass.*)

HOLMES: No one could pass these shutters—if they were bolted. Hm. This brings up a few problems with my theory.

SCENE 7

SETTING: A bedroom in the mansion.

AT RISE: The bedroom is furnished with fireplace, bed, chest of drawers, dresser, and two chairs. HOLMES *sits in one of them. He looks over every detail of the room.* HELEN *and* WATSON *stand watching him.*

WATSON: This is the room where your sister died?

HELEN: Yes. And where I'm sleeping now.

(HOLMES *points to a thick bell-rope that hangs down beside the bed. The end of the rope lies on the pillow.*)

HOLMES: This bell-rope[4]—where does the bell ring?

HELEN: In the housekeeper's room.

HOLMES: This rope looks newer than the other things.

HELEN: Yes, it was put there only a couple of years ago.

HOLMES: Your sister asked for it, I suppose.

HELEN: No, I never heard of her using it. We always used to get what we wanted ourselves.

HOLMES: Hm. Then why was such a nice bell-rope put in? Excuse me while I satisfy myself about this floor.

(HOLMES *throws himself face down on the floor. He has his magnifying glass in his hand. He crawls swiftly backward and forward. He examines the cracks between the boards. Then he jumps up and examines the woodwork on the walls. Then he stares at the bed closely. Finally, he takes the bell-rope and yanks it.*)

HOLMES: It's a dummy!

---

[4]**bell-rope:** rope that is attached to a bell that is used to call a servant

Sherlock Holmes and the Speckled Band ■ 239

Critical Thinking:
Analyze

At the end of Scene 6, when Holmes can't open the shutters from the outside, it upsets his working hypothesis. Ask: If the killer could not have broken in from outside, how else might the murder have taken place?

Reading Focus:
Evaluate the Writer's Craft
Through Holmes's discoveries, the author dispenses clues to the reader one at a time. Ask: How does the spacing of clues add to the suspense of the drama?

Critical Thinking:
Infer
Have students stop at the end of Scene 7 to brainstorm theories. Ask: What can you infer about the presence of the bell rope and ventilator in the bedroom?

WATSON: Won't it ring?

HOLMES: No. It's not even attached to a wire. Interesting. It's tied to a hook just above the little opening for the ventilator.

HELEN: How absurd! I never noticed that before.

HOLMES (*pulling the rope*): Very strange. There are one or two odd points about this room.

WATSON: What are they? I don't see anything odd.

HOLMES: Well, the builder must be a fool to open a vent into another room. With the same trouble, he could have opened it to the outside.

HELEN: The ventilator's quite recent, too.

HOLMES: Done about the same time as the bell-rope?

HELEN: Yes.

HOLMES: *Very* interesting. Dummy bell-ropes. Ventilators that don't ventilate.

WATSON: What does it mean?

HOLMES: Let's carry on in Dr. Roylott's room, please.

SCENE 8

SETTING: A slightly larger bedroom.

AT RISE: The room is plainly furnished. A cot, a shelf of books, an armchair beside the bed, a plain wooden chair, and a round table are the main pieces. There is also a large iron safe. HOLMES walks slowly around the room. He examines everything, HELEN and WATSON look on.

---

ventilator (VEN tuh lay ter) opening to allow fresh air into and stale air out of a room

HOLMES (*tapping the safe*): What's in here?

HELEN: My stepfather's business papers.

HOLMES: Oh. You've seen inside, then?

HELEN: Only once. Years ago. I remember a lot of papers in it.

HOLMES: There isn't a cat inside, for example?

HELEN: No! What a strange idea!

HOLMES: Well, look at this.

(HOLMES *lifts up a saucer of milk that stands on top of the safe.*)

HELEN: We don't keep a cat. But there's the cheetah. And the baboon.

HOLMES: Ah, yes, of course. Well, a cheetah is just a big cat. But a saucer of milk won't do much to satisfy its appetite. There's one thing. . . .

(HOLMES *squats down in front of the wooden chair and examines the seat.*)

HOLMES: Good. That's settled.

WATSON: What's settled? Holmes, what have you . . . ?

HOLMES (*breaking in*): Hello! Here's something interesting.

(HOLMES *picks up a small dog leash hanging on one corner of the bedpost. The leash is curled to make a loop, and tied.*)

HOLMES: What do you make of that, Watson?

WATSON: It's a common enough leash. But I don't know why it's tied that way.

HOLMES: That's not so common, is it? Oh, it's a wicked world. When a clever man turns his brains to crime, it's the worst of all. I think I've seen enough. (HOLMES'S *face is stern.*) Miss Stoner, you *must* follow my advice. In every way.

HELEN: Of course I will.

HOLMES: This is too serious for dilly-dallying. Your life may depend on it.

HELEN: Believe me—I'm in your hands.

HOLMES: Good. In the first place, both my friend and I must spend the night in Julia's room.

(WATSON *and* HELEN *look at* HOLMES *in amazement.*)

HOLMES: I'll explain. (*looking out the window*) Is that the village inn over there?

HELEN: Yes, the Crown.

Sherlock Holmes and the Speckled Band ■ 241

Literary Focus:
Plot
Near the beginning of Scene 8, Holmes says, "That's settled." Ask: What information is he referring to?

Literary Focus:
Plot

The author has skillfully built the suspense of the story to the climax that will occur in Scene 9. Ask: Do you know yet how the murder was committed? Why do you think as you do?

HOLMES: Good. Your windows could be seen from there?

HELEN: Yes.

HOLMES: All right, here's what you do. Stay in your room. When your stepfather comes back, say you've got a headache. Then when you hear him go to bed, open the shutters of your window. Undo the lock. Put your lamp there as a signal to us. Then take everything you need, and go back to your old room. Even with the repairs, you can manage there for one night, can't you?

HELEN: Oh, yes, easily.

HOLMES: Leave the rest to us.

HELEN: But what will you do?

WATSON: Yes, what *will* we do?

HOLMES: We'll spend the night in that room and find out what caused this whistling noise.

HELEN: I think you already know, Mr. Holmes.

HOLMES: Perhaps.

HELEN: Then please tell me. What caused my sister's death?

HOLMES: I'd rather have proof before I answer that.

HELEN: At least tell me if I'm right—did she die from some sudden shock?

HOLMES: No, I don't think so. I think there was something else. Something more. . . some *thing*. Now, Miss Stoner, we must leave. If Dr. Roylott came back and found us, our trip would have been useless. Be brave. If you do as I've said, we'll soon solve everything.

SCENE 9

SETTING: *A room at the Crown.*

AT RISE: HOLMES *is looking out a dark window.* WATSON *sits nervously.*

HOLMES: Here comes Roylott. Huge monster, isn't he? He's roaring at the poor driver. Look at him shaking his fists! (*turning to* Watson) You know, Watson, I don't know if I ought to take you tonight. It could be dangerous.

WATSON: Will I be any help?

HOLMES: Possibly a great deal.

WATSON: Then I'll come.

HOLMES: Very kind of you.

WATSON: You say danger. You must have seen more in those rooms than I did.

HOLMES: I didn't *see* more. I *deduced* more. I imagine you saw everything I did.

WATSON: I didn't see anything unusual. Except the bell-rope. And what could that be for? I can't imagine.

HOLMES: What about the ventilator?

WATSON: Well, yes, but I don't think that's so unusual—a small opening between two rooms. It was so small, a rat could hardly get through it.

HOLMES: Even before we got here, I knew there'd be a ventilator.

WATSON: What!

HOLMES: Oh, yes. Remember what she told us? Her sister could smell Dr. Roylott's cigar? So there had to be an opening between the two rooms. Nothing was said about it at the coroner's inquest. So it had to be small. Therefore—a ventilator.

WATSON: But what harm could that do?

HOLMES: Well, at the very least, it's an odd coincidence. A ventilator is made. A cord is hung. And a lady who sleeps in the bed dies. Doesn't that strike you?

WATSON: What's the connection? I can't see any.

HOLMES: Notice anything odd about that bed?

WATSON: No.

HOLMES: It was clamped to the floor. Ever see a bed bolted down like that before?

WATSON: Can't say I have.

HOLMES: She couldn't move her bed. It had to stay there right under the ventilator and the rope. We might as well call it a rope, since it was never meant to be used as a bell-rope.

WATSON: Holmes! I'm beginning to guess. If that's it, then . . . Why, we're just in time to prevent a horrible crime. A clever, horrible crime.

HOLMES: Clever enough. And horrible enough. Watson, when a doctor goes wrong, he makes a first-rate criminal. He has nerve, and he has knowledge. Don't *you* ever turn your mind to crime!

---

deduce (dih DOOS) figure out by reasoning
inquest (IN kwest) legal investigation into the cause of death
coincidence (koh IN suh duhns) two related events accidentally happening at the same time

Sherlock Holmes and the Speckled Band ■ 243

Reading Focus:
Evaluate the Writer's Craft

Ask: How does the writer use Watson's role to help the reader? Help students see that he is a trusted friend to Holmes, but he also acts as a foil for Holmes—someone for Holmes to explain things to and clarify things for. Watson asks the same sort of questions that the reader might be asking.

Critical Thinking:
Draw Conclusions

Ask: What does Holmes mean when he says, "I didn't see more. I *deduced* more"? Is this the main difference between him and Watson? Is this what makes him a good detective? Why do you think as you do?

Critical Thinking:
Analyze
At the end of Scene 9 Holmes says, "We'll have plenty of horror." Ask: Does Holmes mean this figuratively or literally? Are Watson and Holmes really in great danger?

Literary Focus:
Characters
Ask: What special expertise might a doctor have that would help in committing the crime? Does the fact that he is a doctor make Roylott a more dangerous antagonist?

WATSON: Never! What a horrible idea!

HOLMES: Believe me, we'll have plenty of horror before the night is over. Would you hand me my pipe, please? Might as well have a few cheerful hours first.

SCENE 10

SETTING: *The same, later.*

AT RISE: HOLMES, *looking out the window, sees a single light appear across the way.*

HOLMES: That's our signal!

(*The two hurry out.*)

SCENE 11

SETTING: JULIA'S *bedroom.*

AT RISE: *The room is dark.* HOLMES *and* WATSON, *their shoes off, enter.* HOLMES *carries a candle and a cane.*

HOLMES (*whispering*): The least sound would be fatal to the plan.

(WATSON *nods.*)

HOLMES (*whispering*): We have to sit without light. He'd see it through the ventilator.

(WATSON *nods again.* HOLMES *blows out the candle. Darkness.*)

HOLMES (*whispering*): Don't go to sleep. Your *life* may depend on it. Have your pistol ready.

(HOLMES *motions to* WATSON *to sit in the chair.* HOLMES *sits on the edge of the bed.* WATSON *takes out his pistol.* HOLMES *places his cane on the side of the bed. They wait. Total silence. Then a bird cries suddenly outside, and the two jump. Then they go back to waiting. A clock strikes twelve.*)

SCENE 12

SETTING: *The same.*

AT RISE: HOLMES *and* WATSON *are sitting in the same places.*

They are slumped over, showing signs of tiredness. WATSON *shakes his head to keep his eyes open. A clock strikes three. Suddenly, there is the sound of something moving. Then comes a gentle, soothing sound—like the sound of steam coming out of a kettle.* HOLMES *strikes a match. He springs from the bed. Then he begins lashing the bell-rope with his cane.*

HOLMES (*yelling*): You see it, Watson? You see it?

WATSON: What? What?

(*There is the sound of a low, clear whistle.* HOLMES *stops striking the bell-rope. He watches it closely. After a moment, a horrible cry is heard off-stage. It becomes louder and louder. It is a hoarse yell of pain and fear and anger.* WATSON *and* HOLMES *look at each other. The scream finally dies away.*)

WATSON: What does it mean?

HOLMES: It means it's all over. Probably for the best, too. Take your pistol, Watson. We'll go into Dr. Roylott's room.

SCENE 13

SETTING: DR. ROYLOTT'S *bedroom.*

AT RISE: HOLMES *and* WATSON, *with his pistol ready, enter the room. They see the iron safe, with its door ajar. Next to it, on a chair, sits* DR. ROYLOTT, *in his bathrobe. The dog leash is across his lap. Rigid, he stares at the ceiling. Around his brow is a yellow band, with brownish speckles. It seems to be bound tightly around his head.*

HOLMES: There's the speckled band!

(WATSON *takes a step forward. The speckled band begins to move! It lifts up a diamond-shaped head. It reveals the puffed neck of a deadly snake.*)

HOLMES: A swamp adder! The deadliest snake in India. Ten seconds after he was bitten—he died! It was obvious. The rope had to be there as a bridge for something passing through the hole and coming to the bed.

WATSON: But who'd think of a snake?

HOLMES: I thought of it right away. Remember, the doctor had pets from India. We knew that. A snake seemed just the sort of

Sherlock Holmes and the Speckled Band ■ 245

Reading Focus:
Evaluate the Writer's Craft

At the end of Scene 12, when the screaming stops, Holmes says, "It means it's all over." He seems to know exactly what has occurred, although the reader may still be confused. Ask: How does this fact sustain the suspense even past the climax of the story?

Background Note

The term "adder" in North America usually applies to nonpoisonous snakes; in Europe and India, an adder is a poisonous snake.

Literary Focus:
Plot

Ask students to reconstruct Julia Stoner's death. Then point out—if students haven't—that Roylott was killed the same way. In literature, this is called irony.

Critical Thinking:
Infer

Ask: What can you infer about the doctor from Holmes's and Watson's conversation?

weapon he'd choose. A kind of poison no test could discover. Then, too, it would take effect so quickly. A big advantage from his point of view.

WATSON: A wicked point of view, you mean.

HOLMES: Wickedly clever. Only a sharp-eyed coroner would find the two little punctures left by the fangs. Of course, there was also the whistle. That was a clue.

WATSON: I've been wondering about that. Snakes don't whistle, do they?

HOLMES: Don't be silly, Watson. The *doctor* whistled. The point is, he had to call back the snake before morning. He must have trained it—probably with milk—to return to him when he whistled. He'd put it through the ventilator. He knew it would crawl down the rope and land on the bed.

WATSON: But how could he be sure the snake would bite?

HOLMES: It might or it might not. She might escape every night for a week. But sooner or later . . .

WATSON: Horrible. Yes, I can see now how he must have done it.

HOLMES: Oh, I figured that out before I even went into his room. Then looking at his chair—that settled it.

WATSON: The chair?

HOLMES: Scuff marks. He'd been in the habit of standing on it. He'd have to in order to reach the ventilator. Then there was the speckled band. Let's put this thing back in its den. Then we can get Miss Stoner out of here and get the police in.

(HOLMES *picks up the dog leash and throws it around the snake's neck. He carries the deadly reptile at arm's length, throws it into the safe, and locks the door.*)

SCENE 14

SETTING: *The parlor in* HOLMES'S *apartment. The next day.*

AT RISE: HOLMES *and* WATSON *sit, having tea.*

HOLMES: I'm afraid I'd had the wrong idea about the case all along, Watson.

WATSON: You too?

HOLMES: That shows you how dangerous it is to reason without having *all* the facts.

WATSON: A natural mistake. After all, the gypsies, the word "band"—it was logical to suspect them.

HOLMES: Not at all. Sloppy thinking. There's only one thing *I* can say in my defense. That is, I instantly changed my mind when I saw the room couldn't be gotten at from outside.

WATSON: You were very clever to notice the ventilator and the bell-rope. I didn't. But even when you pointed them out, I was at sea.

HOLMES: Surely, Watson, after I showed you that the bell-rope was a dummy, you must have guessed . . . safe, the saucer of milk, the loop of cord for a leash. Elementary, my dear Watson.

WATSON: Wait a second. What about that metallic clang heard by Miss Stoner? What was that?

HOLMES: Her stepfather closing the safe, of course. And don't forget the softer noise—that was the snake's hiss. As soon as I heard it, I attacked the thing with my cane.

WATSON: To drive it back through the ventilator.

HOLMES: Exactly. And also, frankly, I had another purpose. My attack roused the snake's temper. Made it fly at the first person it saw.

WATSON: Dr. Grimesby Roylott!

HOLMES: Mmm. You might even say I sort of indirectly caused his death. Can't say it's likely to weigh very heavily on my mind. Will you pass me some toast, please, Watson?

Sherlock Holmes and the Speckled Band ■ 247

UNDERSTAND THE SELECTION

Recall

1. How much does Holmes charge Helen Stoner for his work?

2. What is the significance of the whistling that Helen's sister heard?

3. What was odd about Julia's bed?

Infer

4. Describe Helen Stoner's state of mind when she came to see Holmes.

5. The first meeting between Holmes and Dr. Roylott was stormy. How do you know that?

6. What was the real reason for the renovation in Helen's room?

7. Explain the meaning of, "Elementary, my dear Watson."

Apply

8. Why do you think Helen protects Dr. Roylott?

9. Give an example of "deduction," the type of reasoning for which Sherlock Holmes is famous.

10. Did Holmes have the right to cause the death of Dr. Roylott? Explain.

Respond to Literature

Why do you think the Sherlock Holmes mysteries have been popular for a century?

WRITE ABOUT THE SELECTION

Can you write the script for a 60-minute television crime show? Imagine the television producer has agreed to pick the best script submitted and produce it. You must follow the basic rule in crime stories: enough information must be given to allow the viewer to solve the crime. However, you must not make it too easy.

Prewriting First, think of a crime story. You can make up one, or use one you already know. Make a flow chart that shows the action of the story. Next to each box write the dialogue that will be needed for each character.

Writing Use the flow chart to help you write your script. You may use characters and stage directions; you may use a first-person narrator; or you may use third-person point of view. Indicate all stage directions and sound effects.

Revising Can the crime be solved with the information you have given? Check to make sure it can. Can the script be performed in 60 minutes? It will not be accepted for judging unless it can. Finally, make sure transitions between speakers or between thoughts are clear. The script must make sense to the reader.

Proofreading Reread your script and check that the dialogue for each speaker is marked as a new paragraph. Did you use correct punctuation? The script must be tight, with no loose ends.

UNDERSTAND THE SELECTION

Answers

1. Nothing; he tells her, "Madam, my work is its own reward."

2. It was Dr. Roylott calling the snake back.

3. It was clamped to the floor so it couldn't be moved.

4. Very upset; she said she was "surrounded by danger." She was afraid some evil existed that might cause her harm.

5. This is the only direct confrontation between protagonist and antagonist in the play. Roylott comes across as brutish, fearsome, and evil; Holmes comes across as cool, sophisticated, and unflappable.

6. to force her to move into Julia's room, which was next to the doctor's and had the vent through which the snake could crawl

7. Holmes is arrogantly implying to Watson that crimes can be solved easily through the process of deduction.

8. He is her stepfather and she is dependent on him.

9. In Scene 9, Holmes observes that there must be a ventilator shaft between the doctor's and Julia's room because Julia and Helen had smelled the doctor's cigars before they went to bed the night of Julia's death.

10. Sample answer: Holmes isn't really the one who caused Dr. Roylott's death because Roylott himself is the one who released the poisonous snake.

Respond to Literature

The Holmes mysteries present problem-solving conflicts that allow the reader to play detective along with Holmes.

WRITE ABOUT THE SELECTION

Prewriting

You may want to have students work in pairs for this entire assignment. Have them first brainstorm ideas, then write a sequential flow chart of the action.

Writing

Circulate as students work in pairs, giving help where needed. Make sure that point of view is consistent and that students divide the flow chart into separate writing assignments.

Revising

Have pairs exchange scripts. The script should be checked to make sure enough information is given to solve the crime. Then, have the partners combine their writing into a single script. Finally, have them time the script.

Proofreading

Ask students whether cuts must be made because of a time overrun. If so, advise them to go over the script together, deleting all unnecessary adjectives and adverbs.

THINK ABOUT CHARACTERS

Holmes notes at one point in the story, "We're in deep waters here." Indeed, in this episode of Holmes's adventures, he is pitted against an adversary he himself calls "cunning" and "clever." Do you agree? Explain the reasons for your answer.

1. Who is the protagonist and who is the antagonist in the story? Are they equally matched? Explain your answer.

2. Describe the conflict between them. What does each want to accomplish?

3. Do the protagonist and antagonist respect each other? What makes you think so?

4. The one direct confrontation between the protagonist and antagonist ends in a show of physical strength. Who won the confrontation?

5. How does the conflict between the protagonist and antagonist end?

READING FOCUS

Evaluate the Writer's Craft As you read the play, you were able to evaluate the writer's purpose for presenting specific details and information in certain ways. Choose one unusual or unexpected detail. Explain how this added to your enjoyment of the play.

DEVELOP YOUR VOCABULARY

Writing crime stories requires a special vocabulary. You must know terms associated with police work and the legal system.

An example is the word *coroner*. It means a "public officer who investigates deaths that may not be due to natural causes." A coroner can play a very important part in a murder mystery, so you should know the meaning of the word.

Below are some more words associated with crime stories. Make sure that you know how each one is pronounced and what it means. Use a dictionary if you are unsure. Then use each word in a sentence.

1. deduce	7. trial
2. felony	8. verdict
3. autopsy	9. sentence
4. will	10. forensic
5. inquest	11. defendant
6. plea	12. perpetrator

Review the Selection ■ 249

THINK ABOUT CHARACTERS

Answers
1. Holmes is the protagonist, Roylott the antagonist. No. Students may suggest that Holmes is more cunning.
2. Roylott is an angry and deliberate murderer; Holmes is a sharp detective. Roylott does not want to be found out; Holmes wants to solve the mystery.
3. Holmes respects Roylott's "cunning" and "cleverness"; Roylott despises Holmes. They reveal this in their dialogue.
4. No one, really. Holmes just shows he is as physically strong as Roylott. (Holmes might appear the winner because it's a surprise to learn that a sophisticated man can also bend a steel poker.)
5. with Roylott's death

DEVELOP YOUR VOCABULARY *continued*

9. *sentence*: the penalty of a court after guilt is pronounced.
10. *forensic*: pertaining to, or used in, courts of justice or public debate.
11. *defendant*: one who is sued or accused.
12. *perpetrator*: one who is named as the wrongdoer.

Sample sentences:
1. We can *deduce* a great deal from the clues.
2. He went to prison when he committed a *felony*.
3. They performed an *autopsy* to determine how she died.
4. She did not leave a *will*.
5. The suspicious detective ordered an *inquest*.
6. The woman's *plea* of innocence fell on deaf ears.
7. The *trial* dragged on for weeks.
8. The parents of the victim cried when the *verdict* was read.
9. The *sentence* handed down by the judge was harsh.
10. *Forensic* evidence was used during the trial.
11. The *defendant* pleaded guilty to the charges.
12. We did not know who the *perpetrator* of the crime was.

READING FOCUS
Sample Answer
The low whistle that is heard was an unusual detail which created suspense about what could cause that whistle.

DEVELOP YOUR VOCABULARY

Answers
1. *deduce*: to reason from known facts or general principles.
2. *felony*: a crime declared by law to be in the highest class of wrongdoing, such as murder, treason, or arson.
3. *autopsy*: an examination of a body to determine cause of death.
4. *will*: a legal document disposing of one's property at death.
5. *inquest*: an official investigation into someone's death.
6. *plea*: a defendant's response to a criminal charge.
7. *trial*: a judicial examination in court to decide a person's guilt or innocence.
8. *verdict*: the decision of a jury or judge in a trial.

T249

Use "Sherlock Holmes and the Speckled Band" to strengthen students' grasp of the elements of drama. You may want a volunteer to write these questions on the board.

- What is the plot? As students provide answers, map out the plot on the board.
- Who are the characters?
- What is the setting?
- What is the theme?
- What is the major conflict in the plot?

You might want to note, if students disagree with one another, that literature is not set fast in right or wrong answers but remains open to personal interpretation.

ELEMENTS OF DRAMA

Begin a class discussion on drama by first reviewing its main elements: **setting**, **characters**, **plot**, **theme**, **conflict**. Next, ask students to specify these elements in both *Romeo and Juliet* (Unit 1) and "Sorry, Wrong Number" (Unit 2). Then, call on volunteers to outline the elements of a favorite stage play, movie, or TV drama. Encourage students to choose a drama of superior quality, such as Lorraine Hansberry's *A Raisin in the Sun* or Alex Haley's *Roots*, which was adapted for a TV miniseries.

A drama is a play that tells a story that revolves around a conflict. Drama is made up of dialogue and action. When you go to the theater to see a play, you are not only hearing what the characters say, you are also seeing what they do.

When you read a drama, you are reading what the characters say, but you obviously do not see what they are doing. You must imagine this. Often notes called **stage directions**, in parentheses or brackets, indicate actions.

Since a drama tells a story, it shares the elements of all stories: plot, characters, setting, and theme. A part of the plot often stressed in drama is conflict. Conflict, usually between human characters, creates the action that keeps the play moving.

Plot   Since you have already studied the short story, you know that plot is the series of events, or actions, in a story. The plot of a story often begins with **exposition**, or background information. Then a **complication** develops. The **action rises**, leading to a **climax**. **Resolution** of any unanswered questions comes about after the climax, in **falling action**.

You should pay particular attention to plot clues when reading a drama because the events of the plot are presented differently than in a short story. Plot develops solely through the conversation of the characters. There is often no narrator so you must interpret the information the characters provide and piece it together.

Characters   It is the presentation of information through conversation that makes the characters an important element in any drama. You read exactly what the characters say, not what someone else reports them to have said.

The characters in a drama are, of course, the people in the story. You are introduced to them at the very beginning of the play, in the list of characters. This introduction is just that—a list. Unless you are already familiar with the drama, you have no idea which characters are the main ones and how they interact. You learn this through the dialogue.

To help your imagination, stage directions are sometimes given to describe characters' actions. Besides what we learn through these actions, any ideas or descriptions about the characters come indirectly, from what other characters say about them.

Setting   The setting of a drama is stated usually at the beginning of the play. If the setting changes during the play, the new setting is given at the opening of a scene or act.

When you see a drama performed on stage, you learn the "where" of the setting by looking at the stage set. You learn the "when" of the setting also by looking at the stage set and by seeing how the characters are dressed. The objects, or props, used in the setting, as well as the clothes, or costumes, of the characters, provide clues to the time that the drama takes place.

Theme   Theme is the message of the drama. It is the central idea behind the drama. As in short stories, there might be more than one theme in a drama. Sometimes there is no theme of real importance. Usually, however, from studying the conflict, a single, clear theme will emerge.

Conflict   Conflict is what keeps a drama moving. The need to resolve the conflict creates dramatic action that drives the plot to a climax. Conflict usually develops between characters, because characters and their actions are the basis of any play. In "Sherlock Holmes and the Speckled Band," the conflict is between a protagonist and an antagonist.

Conflict can also be within a character. If a character struggles to perform a difficult physical feat, for example, the conflict is between the character and his or her own fear.

As you read the next selection in this unit, look for the elements of drama. Ask yourself these questions:

1. How are the literary elements presented differently in a drama than they are in a short story?
2. What is the conflict in the drama?

Focus on Drama ■ 251

Real-Life Application

Many current television shows are dramas. Ask students for examples. Remind them that dramas tell a serious story (often with humor) and, therefore, "sitcoms" aren't appropriate examples. Then ask: Has television in general increased your awareness of good drama? Since TV is such a dominant influence in many people's lives, you might want to have a formal classroom debate on the subject.

SELECTION OVERVIEW

SELECTION OBJECTIVES

After completing this selection, students will be able to

- understand the elements of drama
- identify conflict in drama
- discuss circumstances that affect crimes
- write a persuasive statement from the point of view of a defendant
- analyze different kinds of conflict in drama
- become familiar with the idiom of midwestern, rural America
- draw conclusions

Lesson Resources

Trifles
- Selection Synopsis, Teacher's Edition, p. T211d
- Comprehension and Vocabulary Workbook, pp. 47–48
- Language Enrichment Workbook, pp. 48–50
- Teacher's Resources Reinforcement, p. R24 Test, pp. T45–T46 Literary Analysis, pp. L5–L6

More About the Unit Theme

Suspense in a crime story is usually created by the search for the perpetrator of the crime. Could understanding the motive of the perpetrator also create suspense? Isn't it sometimes interesting to read profiles of criminals?

About the Author

Susan Glaspell spent a good deal of her life in Greenwich Village in New York City, but she knew rural areas well. The daughter of a feed dealer, she had grown up and spent her early years as a writer in Iowa. Her short stories, novels, and plays focused on the individual, and many of her early works deal with individuals trapped by imprecise laws. Glaspell was one of the founders of the Provincetown Players, a group of actors, directors, and writers that included Eugene O'Neill.

Background Note

Omaha is a city in Nebraska, just across the Missouri River from Iowa. The setting of the play, therefore, is somewhere in that region of the Midwest. Glaspell was born in Davenport, in the eastern part of Iowa.

ESL Activity

Have students discuss in small groups or as a class how they would have handled the investigation of John Wright's death if they had been in charge. Would they have done something differently?

FOCUS ON DRAMA
STUDY HINTS

The characters are introduced at the opening of the drama. More information about them is given in the next section labeled "Scene." After these notes everything you learn about the characters will come from their conversations or the actions indicated in the stage directions.

This section, labeled "Scene," provides the setting of the drama. The action takes place in the kitchen of the now abandoned farmhouse of John Wright. The time period is not given, although there are clues in the play that indicate the play takes place sometime in the first half of the twentieth century.

The plot begins to develop here. Some exposition was given in the section labeled "Scene," but now we will find out more about what is going on.

TRIFLES

by Susan Glaspell

CHARACTERS

GEORGE HENDERSON, *county attorney*
HENRY PETERS, *sheriff*
LEWIS HALE, *a neighboring farmer*

MRS. PETERS
MRS. HALE

Scene: *The kitchen in the now abandoned farmhouse of* JOHN WRIGHT, *a gloomy kitchen, and left without having been put in order—unwashed pans under the sink, a loaf of bread outside the breadbox, a dish towel on the table—other signs of incompleted work. At the rear the outer door opens and the* SHERIFF *comes in followed by the* COUNTY ATTORNEY *and* HALE. *The* SHERIFF *and* HALE *are men in middle life, the* COUNTY ATTORNEY *is a young man; all are much bundled up and go at once to the stove. They are followed by the two women—the* SHERIFF'S *wife first, she is a slight wiry woman, a thin nervous face.* MRS. HALE *is larger and would ordinarily be called more comfortable looking, but she is disturbed now and looks fearfully about as she enters. The women have come in slowly, and stand close together near the door.*

COUNTY ATTORNEY (*rubbing his hands*): This feels good. Come up to the fire, ladies.

MRS. PETERS (*after taking a step forward*): I'm not—cold.

SHERIFF (*unbuttoning his overcoat and stepping away from the stove as if to mark the beginning of official business*): Now, Mr. Hale, before we move things about, you explain to Mr. Henderson just what you saw when you came here yesterday morning.

COUNTY ATTORNEY: By the way, has anything been moved? Are things just as you left them yesterday?

---

attorney (uh TUR nee) lawyer. A county attorney is a lawyer responsible for bringing criminal charges against someone.
wiry (WYR ee) lean and strong

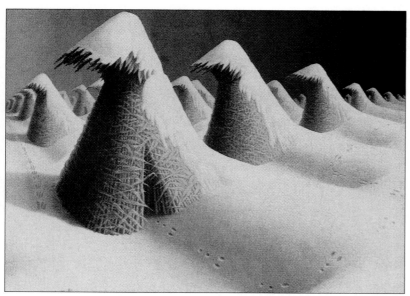

January, 1940, Grant Wood. Estate of Grant Wood/Licensed by VAGA, New York, NY

SHERIFF (*looking about*): It's just the same. When it dropped below zero last night I thought I'd better send Frank out this morning to make a fire for us—no use getting pneumonia with a big case on, but I told him not to touch anything except the stove—and you know Frank.

COUNTY ATTORNEY: Somebody should have been left here yesterday.

SHERIFF: Oh—yesterday. When I had to send Frank to Morris Center for that man who went crazy—I want you to know I had my hands full yesterday. I knew you could get back from Omaha by today and as long as I went over everything here myself—

COUNTY ATTORNEY: Well, Mr. Hale, tell just what happened when you came here yesterday morning.

HALE: Harry and I had started to town with a load of potatoes. We came along the road from my place and as I got here I said, "I'm going to see if I can't get John Wright to go in with me on

> Notice how the characters of the sheriff and the county attorney are developed through dialogue. The county attorney seems businesslike and thorough. The sheriff seems to be confronted with a great many problems. Still, he worries about things such as heat in the old farmhouse.

> Here is the main question of the plot: What happened at the Wright farmhouse yesterday morning? The plot develops as the characters search for an answer.

---

pneumonia (noo MOHN yuh) disease of the lungs; caused by an infection

Trifles ■ 253

Develop Vocabulary Skills

Have students work as groups to find the correct pronunciation and definition of the new vocabulary. Give each group the same number of words and have them report to the class as a whole.

Viewing Fine Art

Grant Wood (1892–1942) was a curious and unique combination of American regionalist painter and chronicler of the nation's farm belt. In this painting called *January, 1940*, he recalls the surrealist images of modern art. But he retained a realistic technique, so that the hayricks lined up in the snow (seen here) are recognizable but unbelievable. His view of the midwestern farm and its people was realistic and, at the same time, a humorous comment (note the tiny footprints). Ask: What details make this landscape seem surreal?

TEACHING PLAN

INTRODUCE

Motivation

Ask students if they think a crime is ever justified. You might choose a current and well-known case to initiate discussion. Then ask: Do you think a tyrant can drive good people to desperation? Keep an open mind as you read Susan Glaspell's drama.

Purpose-Setting Question

What alternatives are open to the person who finds life deadening and depressing?

READ

Literary Focus: *Elements of Drama*

The blue side notes in this annotated lesson provide a model for students to understand the literary elements introduced in Focus on Drama, pages 250–251. Because this is a play, students should pay careful attention to the characters' dialogue as they read. The dialogue is the author's main means of conveying characters' thoughts and feelings and reveals important information about their behavior. Encourage students to discuss what the dialogue reveals about the characters as they read.

Reading Focus: *Draw Conclusions*

An author does not always directly state information about characters or events in a story. It is up to the reader to draw conclusions about Mrs. Wright, since she never actually appears in the story. Encourage students to form their own opinions of her motivations and feelings as they read.

CLOSE

Have students complete Review the Selection on pages 270–271.

a party telephone." I spoke to Wright about it once before and he put me off, saying folks talked too much anyway, and all he asked was peace and quiet—I guess you know about how much he talked himself, but I thought maybe if I went to the house and talked about it before his wife, though I said to Harry that I didn't know as what his wife wanted made much difference to John—

COUNTY ATTORNEY: Let's talk about that later, Mr. Hale. I do want to talk about that, but tell now just what happened when you got to the house.

HALE: I didn't hear or see anything; I knocked at the door, and still it was all quiet inside. I knew they must be up, it was past eight o'clock. So I knocked again, and I thought I heard somebody say "Come in." I wasn't sure, I'm not sure yet, but I opened the door—this door (*indicating the door by which the two men are still standing*) and there in that rocker—(*pointing to it*) sat Mrs. Wright.

(*They all look at the rocker.*)

These notes in parentheses are stage directions. An actor would use them playing the part of Hale on the stage. However, they also help us to "see" the action and to understand what is happening.

COUNTY ATTORNEY: What—was she doing?

HALE: She was rockin' back and forth. She had her apron in her hand and was kind of—pleating it.

COUNTY ATTORNEY: And how did she—look?

HALE: Well, she looked queer.

COUNTY ATTORNEY: How do you mean—queer?

HALE: Well, as if she didn't know what she was going to do next. And kind of done up.

COUNTY ATTORNEY: How did she seem to feel about your coming?

This is a story within a story. It is a way for more background information to be introduced, even though the people mentioned are not characters in the play.

HALE: Why, I don't think she minded—one way or other. She didn't pay much attention. I said, "How do, Mrs. Wright, it's cold, ain't it?" And she said, "Is it?"—and went on kind of pleating at her apron. Well, I was surprised; she didn't ask me to come up to the stove, or to set down, but just sat there, not even looking at me, so I said, "I want to see John." And then she—laughed. I guess you would call it a laugh. I thought of Harry and the team outside, so I said a little sharp: "Can't I see John?" "No," she says, kind o' dull like. "Ain't he home?"

---

pleating (PLEET ing) pressing cloth together

says I. "Yes," says she, "he's home." "Then why can't I see him?" I asked her, out of patience. "'Cause he's dead," says she. *"Dead?"* says I. She just nodded her head, not getting a bit excited, but rockin' back and forth. "Why—where is he?" says I, not knowing what to say. She just pointed upstairs—like that (*himself pointing to the room above*). I got up, with the idea of going up there. I walked from there to here—then I says, "Why, what did he die of?" "He died of a rope round his neck," says she, and just went on pleatin' at her apron. Well, I went out and called Harry. I thought I might—need help. We went upstairs and there he was—lyin'—

COUNTY ATTORNEY: I think I'd rather have you go into that upstairs, where you can point it all out. Just go on now with the rest of the story.

HALE: Well, my first thought was to get that rope off. It looked—(*stops, his face twitches*)—but Harry, he went up to him, and he said, "No, he's dead all right, and we'd better not touch anything." So we went back down stairs. She was still sitting that same way. "Has anybody been notified?" I asked. "No," says she, unconcerned. "Who did this, Mrs. Wright?" said Harry. He said it businesslike—and she stopped pleatin' of her apron. "I don't know," she says. "You don't *know*?" says Harry. "No," says she. "Weren't you sleeping in the bed with him?" says Harry. "Yes," says she, "but I was on the inside." "Somebody slipped a rope round his neck and strangled him and you didn't wake up?" says Harry. "I didn't wake up," she said after him. We may have looked as if we didn't see how that could be, for after a minute she said, "I sleep sound." Harry was going to ask her more questions but I said maybe we ought to let her tell her story first to the coroner, or the sheriff, so Harry went fast as he could to Rivers' place, where there's a telephone.

COUNTY ATTORNEY: And what did Mrs. Wright do when she knew that you had gone for the coroner?

HALE: She moved from that chair to this one over here (*pointing to a small chair in the corner*) and just sat there with her hands held together and looking down. I got a feeling that I ought to

Here is the plot complication: Did Mrs. Wright kill her husband? A few lines further on the county attorney is already trying to determine a motive for the killing.

---

twitches (TWICH iz) pulls with a sudden jerk
notified (NOHT uh fyd) advised; informed
strangled (STRANG guld) choked; killed by squeezing

Trifles ■ 255

Critical Thinking:
Infer
The important aspect of Hale's long answers in response to the county attorney is the picture that emerges of Mrs. Wright. Ask: Why was Mrs. Wright acting so strangely when Hale entered the house?

The Judges c. 1907, Georges Rouault.
The Portland Museum of Art

make some conversation, so I said I had come in to see if John wanted to put in a telephone, and at that she started to laugh, and then she stopped and looked at me—scared. (*The* COUNTY ATTORNEY, *who has had his notebook out, makes a note.*) I dunno, maybe it wasn't scared. I wouldn't like to say it was. Soon Harry got back, and then Dr. Lloyd came, and you, Mr. Peters, and so I guess that's all I know that you don't.

COUNTY ATTORNEY (*looking around*): I guess we'll go upstairs first—and then out to the barn and around there. (*To the* SHERIFF) You're convinced that there was nothing important here—nothing that would point to any motive?

SHERIFF: Nothing here but kitchen things.

(*The* COUNTY ATTORNEY, *after again looking around the kitchen, opens the door of a cupboard closet. He gets up on a chair and looks on a shelf. Pulls his hand away, sticky.*)

---

cupboard (KUB urd) a closet fitted with shelves for holding cups

Literary Focus:
Foreshadowing

The sheriff says there is nothing of any importance downstairs in the house, just "kitchen things." Ask: How might these domestic objects foreshadow the discovery of events?

COUNTY ATTORNEY: Here's a nice mess.

(*The women draw nearer.*)

MRS. PETERS (*to the other woman*): Oh, her fruit; it did freeze. (*To the* COUNTY ATTORNEY.) She worried about that when it turned so cold. She said the fire'd go out and her jars would break.

SHERIFF: Well, can you beat the women! Held for murder and worrying about her preserves.

COUNTY ATTORNEY: I guess before we are through she may have something more serious than preserves to worry about.

HALE: Well, women are used to worrying over trifles.

(*The two women move a little closer together.*)

COUNTY ATTORNEY (*With the gallantry of a young politician*): And yet, for all their worries, what would we do without the ladies? (*The women do not unbend. He goes to the sink, takes a dipperful of water from the pail and pouring it into a basin, washes his hands. Starts to wipe them on the roller towel, turns it for a cleaner place*) Dirty towels! (*Kicks his foot against the pans under the sink*) Not much of a housekeeper, would you say, ladies?

MRS. HALE (*stiffly*): There's a great deal of work to be done on a farm.

COUNTY ATTORNEY: To be sure. And yet (*with a little bow to her*) I know there are some Dickson County farmhouses which do not have such roller towels.

(*He gives it a pull to expose its full length again.*)

MRS. HALE: Those towels get dirty awful quick. Men's hands aren't always as clean as they might be.

COUNTY ATTORNEY: Ah, loyal to your sex, I see. But you and Mrs. Wright were neighbors. I suppose you were friends, too.

MRS. HALE (*shaking her head*): I've not seen much of her of late years. I've not been in this house—it's more than a year.

COUNTY ATTORNEY: And why was that? You didn't like her?

MRS. HALE: I liked her all well enough. Farmers' wives have their hands full, Mr. Henderson. And then—

The word *"trifles"*, as used here, is important. "Trifles" is also the title of the play, but here it is a tip-off: Pay attention to small details such as broken jam jars. They might have something to do with the theme of the drama.

Here is an example of where you must piece together information from dialogue and stage directions to understand what is happening. What clues show that the county attorney really does not understand the harsh life of a farmer's wife?

---

preserves (prih ZURVZ) fruit kept from spoiling by special treatment
trifles (TRY fulz) anything of little value or importance
gallantry (GAL un tree) heroic courage; elaborate politeness to women
expose (ik SPOHZ) to lay open; uncover

Critical Thinking:
Infer

A small clue about Mrs. Wright's state of mind: "Well, women," says Hale, "are used to worrying over trifles." Ask: Was Mrs. Wright just worrying over trifles or something bigger?

Background Note

"Roller towels" refer to a piece of cloth whose ends are sewn together and then attached to a roller. The user turns to a clean place on the towel to dry his or her hands. The system works only as long as the towel is washed periodically.

Reading Focus:
Draw Conclusions

The county attorney pursues a new line of inquiry: questioning Mrs. Hale and Mrs. Peters. Ask: What does he learn from them? Does it seem important?

Critical Thinking:
Infer

Ask: In blaming "men"—not Mrs. Wright's cleaning habits—for a filthy roller towel, is Mrs. Hale starting to defend Mrs. Wright? Explain.

COUNTY ATTORNEY: Yes—?

MRS. HALE (*looking about*): It never seemed a very cheerful place.

COUNTY ATTORNEY: No—it's not cheerful. I shouldn't say she had the homemaking instinct.

MRS. HALE: Well, I don't know as Wright had, either.

COUNTY ATTORNEY: You mean that they didn't get on very well?

MRS. HALE: No, I don't mean anything. But I don't think a place'd be any cheerfuller for John Wright's being in it.

COUNTY ATTORNEY: I'd like to talk more of that a little later. I want to get the lay of things upstairs now.

(*He goes to the left, where three steps lead to a stair door.*)

SHERIFF: I suppose anything Mrs. Peters does'll be all right. She was to take in some clothes for her, you know, and a few little things. We left in such a hurry yesterday.

COUNTY ATTORNEY: Yes, but I would like to see what you take, Mrs. Peters, and keep an eye out for anything that might be of use to us.

MRS. PETERS: Yes, Mr. Henderson.

(*The women listen to the men's steps on the stairs, then look about the kitchen.*)

MRS. HALE: I'd hate to have men coming into my kitchen, snooping round and criticizing.

(*She arranges the pans under the sink which the* LAWYER *had shoved out of place.*)

MRS. PETERS: Of course it's no more than their duty.

MRS. HALE: Duty's all right, but I guess that deputy sheriff that came out to make the fire might have got a little of this on. (*Gives the roller towel a pull*) Wish I'd thought of that sooner. Seems mean to talk about her for not having things slicked up when she had to come away in such a hurry.

MRS. PETERS (*who has gone to a small table in the left rear corner of the room, and lifted one end of a towel that covers a pan*): She had bread set.

---

instinct (IN stingkt) a natural tendency; unconscious skill
snooping (SNOOP ing) searching or looking into other people's property or affairs without permission

(Stands still)

MRS. HALE (*Eyes fixed on a loaf of bread beside the breadbox, which is on a low shelf at the other side of the room. Moves slowly toward it.*): She was going to put this in there. (*Picks up loaf, then abruptly drops it, as though returning to familiar things.*) It's a shame about her fruit. I wonder if it's all gone. (*Gets up on the chair and looks*) I think there's some here that's all right, Mrs. Peters. Yes—here; (*holding it toward the window*) this is cherries, too. (*Looking again*) I declare I believe that's the only one. (*Gets down, bottle in her hand. Goes to the sink and wipes it off on the outside.*) She'll feel awful bad after all her hard work in the hot weather. I remember the afternoon I put up my cherries last summer.

(She puts the bottle on the big kitchen table, center of the room. With a sigh, is about to sit down in the rocking-chair. Before she is seated realizes what chair it is, with a slow look at it, steps back. The chair which she has touched rocks back and forth.)

MRS. PETERS: Well, I must get those things from the front room closet. (*She goes to the door at the right, but after looking into the other room, steps back.*) You coming with me, Mrs. Hale? You could help me carry them.

(They go in the other room; reappear, MRS. PETERS carrying a dress and a skirt, MRS. HALE following with a pair of shoes.)

MRS. PETERS: My, it's cold in there.

(She puts the clothes on the big table and hurries to the stove.)

MRS. HALE (*examining the skirt*): Wright was close. I think maybe that's why she kept so much to herself. She didn't even belong to the Ladies' Aid. I suppose she felt she couldn't do her part, and then you don't enjoy things when you feel shabby. She used to wear pretty clothes and be lively, when she was Minnie Foster, one of the town girls singing in the choir. But that was—oh, that was thirty years ago. This all you was to take in?

MRS. PETERS: She said she wanted an apron. Funny thing to want, for there isn't much to get you dirty in jail, goodness knows.

---

shabby (SHAB ee) seedy; poorly dressed

Trifles ■ 259

Mrs. Hale is a natural detective just because she understands "women's" work. Do you agree? Her character will now develop more fully, as will Mrs. Peters's. Pay attention to what they say and what they do.

There is no change in the setting, not even a minor one. The action continues to take place in the farmhouse kitchen.

Mrs. Hale gives us information that might be important. Minnie Foster seemed a different person from Mrs. John Wright.

Discussion

Discuss with students what life might have been like for women living in a rural area like this. Ask: How might life on the farm have affected their lives and made them more sympathetic towards each other?

Reading Focus:
Draw Conclusions

Mrs. Hale's description of Mrs. Wright reveals something new about her as a character. Ask: How has she changed over time? Encourage students to think about what might have brought about this change in Mrs. Wright.

Literary Focus:
Plot

The conversation between the two women reveals details about the crime that the men may have overlooked. Ask: What clues have the women seen that help them and the reader to better understand Mrs. Wright's behavior?

Reading Focus:
Draw Conclusions

Ask: What is meant when Mrs. Hale says, "I don't see any signs of anger around here"? It is a small but important aspect of the conflict that is unfolding between the women and the county attorney, who needs to find a motive.

But I suppose just to make her feel more natural. She said they was in the top drawer in this cupboard. Yes, here. And then her little shawl that always hung behind the door.

(*Opens stair door and looks*) Yes, here it is.

(*Quickly shuts door leading upstairs*)

The question the drama must answer is repeated. The dramatic action begins to rise, ever so slowly.

MRS. HALE (*abruptly moving toward her*): Mrs. Peters?

MRS. PETERS: Yes, Mrs. Hale?

MRS. HALE: Do you think she did it?

MRS. PETERS (*in a frightened voice*): Oh, I don't know.

MRS. HALE: Well, I don't think she did. Asking for an apron and her little shawl. Worrying about her fruit.

MRS. PETERS (*Starts to speak, glances up, where footsteps are heard in the room above. In a low voice*): Mr. Peters says it looks bad for her. Mr. Henderson is awful sarcastic in a speech and he'll make fun of her sayin' she didn't wake up.

MRS. HALE: Well, I guess John Wright didn't wake when they was slipping that rope under his neck.

MRS. PETERS: No, it's strange. It must have been done awful crafty and still. They say it was such a—funny way to kill a man, rigging it all up like that.

MRS. HALE: That's just what Mr. Hale said. There was a gun in the house. He says that's what he can't understand.

MRS. PETERS: Mr. Henderson said coming out that what was needed for the case was a motive; something to show anger, or—sudden feeling.

MRS. HALE (*who is standing by the table*): Well, I don't see any signs of anger around here, but (*She puts her hand on the dish towel which lies on the table, stands looking down at the table, one half of which is clean, the other half messy.*) It's wiped to here. (*Makes a move as if to finish the work, then turns and looks at loaf of bread outside the breadbox. Drops towel. Speaks in that voice of coming back to familiar things.*) Wonder how they are finding things upstairs. I hope she had it a little more red-up there.

---

shawl (SHAWL) a loose scarf used by women to cover the shoulders
abruptly (uh BRUPT lee) suddenly
sarcastic (sahr KAS tik) sneering or ironic, and meant to hurt feelings
crafty (KRAFT ee) shrewd; tricky
rigging (RIG ing) any gear or tackle

Ground Hog Day, Andrew Wyeth. Philadelphia Museum of Art

You know, it seems kind of *sneaking*. Locking her up in town and then coming out here and trying to get her own house to turn against her!

MRS. PETERS: But Mrs. Hale, the law is the law.

MRS. HALE: I s'pose 'tis. (*unbuttoning her coat*) Better loosen up your things, Mrs. Peters. You won't feel them when you go out.

(MRS. PETERS *takes off her fur tippet, goes to hang it on hook at back of room, stands looking at the under part of the small corner table.*)

MRS. PETERS: She was piecing a quilt.

Here sympathy is created for Mrs. Wright and the situation she is in. Mrs. Hale feels a kind of common bond with Mrs. Wright. Do you think so?

Critical Thinking:
Analyze

Mrs. Peters reminds Mrs. Hale that, "the law is the law." Ask: Was Mrs. Hale implying that somehow Mrs. Wright's actions may have been justified?

---

tippet (TIP it) garment like a scarf that covers the neck and shoulders
quilt (KWILT) a bed cover made by stitching a layer of cotton between
   two layers of fabric

Trifles ■ **261**

Again, the women show an understanding that the men lack of Mrs. Wright's work and life. Yet the men are the ones who are officially gathering the evidence.

(*She brings the large sewing basket and they look at the bright pieces.*)

MRS. HALE: It's log cabin pattern. Pretty, isn't it? I wonder if she was goin' to quilt it or just knot it?

(*Footsteps have been heard coming down the stairs. The* SHERIFF *enters followed by* HALE *and the* COUNTY ATTORNEY.)

SHERIFF: They wonder if she was going to quilt it or just knot it?

(*The men laugh, the women look abashed.*)

COUNTY ATTORNEY (*rubbing his hands over the stove*): Frank's fire didn't do much up there, did it? Well, let's go out to the barn and get that cleared up.

(*The men go outside.*)

MRS. HALE (*resentfully*): I don't know as there's anything so strange, our takin' up our time with little things while we're waiting for them to get the evidence. (*She sits down at the big table smoothing out a block with decision.*) I don't see as it's anything to laugh about.

MRS. PETERS (*apologetically*): Of course they've got awful important things on their minds.

(*Pulls up a chair and joins* MRS. HALE *at the table.*)

What is Mrs. Hale doing here? What do you think she is thinking?

MRS. HALE (*examining another block*): Mrs. Peters, look at this one. Here, this is the one she was working on, and look at the sewing! All the rest of it has been so nice and even. And look at this! It's all over the place! Why, it looks as if she didn't know what she was about!

(*After she has said this they look at each other, then start to glance back at the door. After an instant* MRS. HALE *has pulled at a knot and ripped the sewing.*)

MRS. PETERS: Oh, what are you doing, Mrs. Hale?

MRS. HALE (*mildly*): Just pulling out a stitch or two that's not sewed very good. (*Threading a needle*) Bad sewing always made me fidgety.

---

knot (NOT) tie a knoblike lacing
abashed (uh BASHT) embarrassed
resentfully (rih ZENT ful ee) angrily
apologetically (uh pol uh JET ik lee) defensively; spoken with excuses

MRS. PETERS (*nervously*): I don't think we ought to touch things.

MRS. HALE: I'll just finish up this end. (*Suddenly stopping and leaning forward*) Mrs. Peters?

MRS. PETERS: Yes, Mrs. Hale?

MRS. HALE: What do you suppose she was so nervous about?

MRS. PETERS: Oh—I don't know. I don't know as she was nervous. I sometimes sew awful queer when I'm just tired. (MRS. HALE *starts to say something, looks at* MRS. PETERS, *then goes on sewing.*) Well I must get these things wrapped up. They may be through sooner than we think. (*Putting apron and other things together.*) I wonder where I can find a piece of paper, and string.

MRS. HALE: In that cupboard, maybe.

MRS. PETERS (*looking in cupboard*): Why, here's a bird cage. (*Holds it up.*) Did she have a bird, Mrs. Hale?

MRS. HALE: Why, I don't know whether she did or not—I've not been here for so long. There was a man around last year selling canaries cheap, but I don't know as she took one; maybe she did. She used to sing real pretty herself.

MRS. PETERS (*glancing around*): Seems funny to think of a bird here. But she must have had one, or why would she have had a cage? I wonder what happened to it.

MRS. HALE: I s'pose maybe the cat got it.

MRS. PETERS: No, she didn't have a cat. She's got that feeling some people have about cats—being afraid of them. My cat got in her room and she was real upset and asked me to take it out.

MRS. HALE: My sister Bessie was like that. Queer, ain't it?

MRS. PETERS (*examining the cage*): Why, look at this door. It's broke. One hinge is pulled apart.

MRS. HALE (*looking, too*): Looks as if someone must have been rough with it.

MRS. PETERS: Why, yes.

(*She brings the cage forward and puts it on the table.*)

MRS. HALE: I wish if they're going to find any evidence they'd be about it. I don't like this place.

> It is Mrs. Peters's turn to play detective, although she might not be doing it consciously.

---

fidgety (FIJ it ee) nervous or uneasy

Trifles ■ 263

Reading Focus:
Draw Conclusions

In legal terms, Mrs. Hale is tampering with evidence by pulling out a knot and resewing part of the quilt. Ask: How is she hoping to help Mrs. Wright in some way by doing this?

Discussion

Mrs. Hale and Mrs. Peters have a slightly different attitude toward Mrs. Wright. Discuss with students how being the wife of the sheriff might be affecting Mrs. Peters's actions.

MRS. PETERS: But I'm awful glad you came with me, Mrs. Hale. It would be lonesome for me sitting here alone.

MRS. HALE: It would, wouldn't it? (*Dropping her sewing*) But I tell you what I do wish, Mrs. Peters. I wish I had come over sometimes when *she* was here. I—(*looking around the room*)—wish I had.

MRS. PETERS: But of course you were awful busy, Mrs. Hale—your house and your children.

MRS. HALE: I could've come. I stayed away because it weren't cheerful—and that's why I ought to have come. I—I've never liked this place. Maybe because it's down in a hollow and you don't see the road. I dunno what it is, but it's a lonesome place and always was. I wish I had come over to see Minnie Foster sometimes. I can see now—

(*Shakes her head.*)

MRS. PETERS: Well, you mustn't reproach yourself, Mrs. Hale. Somehow we just don't see how it is with other folks until—something comes up.

MRS. HALE: Not having children makes less work—but it makes a quiet house, and Wright out to work all day, and no company when he did come in. Did you know John Wright, Mrs. Peters?

MRS. PETERS: Not to know him; I've seen him in town. They say he was a good man.

MRS. HALE: Yes—good; he didn't drink, and kept his word as well as most, I guess, and paid his debts. But he was a hard man, Mrs. Peters. Just to pass the time of day with him—(*shivers*) Like a raw wind that gets to the bone. (*Pauses, her eye falling on the cage*) I should think she would'a wanted a bird. But what do you suppose went with it?

MRS. PETERS: I don't know, unless it got sick and died.

(*She reaches over and swings the broken door, swings it again, both women watch it.*)

MRS. HALE: You weren't raised round here, were you? (MRS. PETERS *shakes her head.*) You didn't know—her?

MRS. PETERS: Not till they brought her yesterday.

Here is some information about the setting tucked into the dialogue.

---

reproach (rih PROHCH) accuse and blame for a fault

Christina's World, Andrew Wyeth, 1948. Tempera on gessoed panel 32¼" × 47¾" (81.9 × 121.3 cm). The Museum of Modern Art, New York. Purchase. Photograph ©2000 The Museum of Modern Art, New York

Viewing Fine Art

Andrew Wyeth's painting *Christina's World* is probably his best known picture. (See Viewing Fine Art for pages 131 and 261.) In his typically precise style, Wyeth created a landscape that makes every blade of grass seem real. But the particular strength of the painting lies in its spaces. The isolation and perhaps desolation of the girl in the painting is poignantly clear. In his works of people, Wyeth sought a kind of psychological truth that he hoped would be revealed through his meticulous attention to design and detail. Ask: According to this painting, what does Christina's world consist of?

MRS. HALE: She—come to think of it, she was kind of like a bird herself—real sweet and pretty, but kind of timid and—fluttery. How—she—did—change. (*Silence; then as if struck by a happy thought and relieved to get back to everyday things.*) Tell you what, Mrs. Peters, why don't you take the quilt in with you? It might take up her mind.

MRS. PETERS: Why, I think that's a real nice idea, Mrs. Hale. There couldn't possibly be any objection to it, could there? Now, just what would I take? I wonder if her patches are in here—and her things.

(*They look in the sewing basket.*)

MRS. HALE: Here's some red. I expect this has got sewing things in it. (*Brings out a fancy box*) What a pretty box. Looks like

Literary Focus:
Plot
Point out that the playwright is very skillful in advancing the plot. A generous thought of Mrs. Hale's—taking the quilt to Mrs. Wright—leads to finding more crucial evidence. Ask: What is this evidence?

---

timid (TIM id) shy
fluttery (FLUT ur ee) moving rapidly and with uncertainty

Trifles ■ 265

The story nears its climax with the women's discovery of the dead bird. Ask: What sudden understanding does this give the women?

something somebody would give you. Maybe her scissors are in here. (*Opens box. Suddenly puts her hand to her nose.*) Why— (MRS. PETERS *bends nearer, then turns her face away*) There's something wrapped up in this piece of silk.

MRS. PETERS: Why, this isn't her scissors,

MRS. HALE (*lifting the silk*): Oh, Mrs. Peters—it's

A desire to give Mrs. Wright some "women's" work to pass the time in jail turns up what surely must be important evidence.

(MRS. PETERS *bends closer.*)

MRS. PETERS: It's the bird.

MRS. HALE (*jumping up*): But, Mrs. Peters—look at it! Its neck! Look at its neck! It's all—other side *to*.

MRS. PETERS: Somebody—wrung—its—neck.

The women are hiding something from the men. Why? Is everyone trying to solve the crime?

(*Their eyes meet. A look of growing comprehension, of horror. Steps are heard outside.* MRS. HALE *slips box under quilt pieces, and sinks into her chair. Enter* SHERIFF *and* COUNTY ATTORNEY. MRS. PETERS *rises.*)

COUNTY ATTORNEY (*as one turning from serious things to little pleasantries*): Well, ladies, have you decided whether she was going to quilt it or knot it?

MRS. PETERS: We think she was going to—knot it.

COUNTY ATTORNEY: Well, that's interesting, I am sure. (*Seeing the bird cage*) Has the bird flown?

MRS. HALE (*putting more quilt pieces over the box*): We think the— cat got it.

COUNTY ATTORNEY (*preoccupied*): Is there a cat?

(MRS. HALE *glances in a quick, covert way at* MRS. PETERS.)

MRS. PETERS: Well, not *now*. They're superstitious, you know. They leave.

We learn through dialogue that the men are looking for clues telling who could have entered the house to commit the murder. The women, suggest the stage directions, have a much greater understanding of what happened.

COUNTY ATTORNEY (*to* SHERIFF PETERS, *continuing an interrupted conversation*): No sign at all of anyone having come from the outside. Their own rope. Now let's go up again and go over it piece by piece. (*They start upstairs.*) It would have been some-one who knew just the—

---

comprehension (kom prih HEN shun) understanding or knowledge of something
pleasantries (PLEZ un treez) lively, agreeable talks
preoccupied (pree OK yuh pyd) thinking of something else
covert (KOH vurt) hidden or disguised
superstitious (soo pur STISH us) too much fear of the unknown

(MRS. PETERS *sits down. The two women sit there not looking at one another, but as if peering into something and at the same time holding back. When they talk now it is in the manner of feeling their way over strange ground, as if afraid of what they are saying, but as if they cannot help saying it.*)

MRS. HALE: She liked the bird. She was going to bury it in that pretty box.

MRS. PETERS (*in a whisper*): When I was a girl—my kitten—there was a boy took a hatchet, and before my eyes—and before I could get there—(*covers her face an instant*) If they hadn't held me back I would have—(*catches herself, looks upstairs where steps are heard, falters weakly*)—hurt him.

MRS. HALE (*with a slow look around her*): I wonder how it would seem never to have had any children around. (*Pause*) No, Wright wouldn't like the bird—a thing that sang. She used to sing. He killed that, too.

MRS. PETERS (*moving uneasily*): We don't know who killed the bird.

MRS. HALE: I knew John Wright.

MRS. PETERS: It was an awful thing was done in this house that night, Mrs. Hale. Killing a man while he slept, slipping a rope around his neck that choked the life out of him.

MRS. HALE: His neck. Choked the life out of him.

(*Her hand goes out and rests on the bird cage.*)

MRS. PETERS (*with rising voice*): We don't know who killed him. We don't *know.*

MRS. HALE (*her own feeling not interrupted*): If there'd been years and years of nothing, then a bird to sing to you, it would be awful—still, after the bird was still.

MRS. PETERS (*something within her speaking*): I know what stillness is. When we homesteaded in Dakota, and my first baby died—after he was two years old, and me with no other then—

The note, "with rising voice," suggests the action is rising faster and we are heading for the climax. The women seem to have a theory about what happened. What is their theory?

---

peering (PIR ing) looking closely
hatchet (HACH it) a tool for chopping; like an ax
falters (FAWL turz) walks unsteadily; stumbles
homesteaded (HOHM sted id) occupied land as a home

An unspoken understanding has grown between the two women regarding Mrs. Wright's actions. Ask: What are the women really discussing when they talk about the bird?

Reading Focus:
Draw Conclusions

The anecdote Mrs. Peters shares about her kitten is a subtle way for the playwright to suggest what might have happened to the bird. Ask: What likely drove Mrs. Wright to kill her husband, aside from the killing of the bird?

Reading Focus:
Draw Conclusions

Ask: How does Mrs. Peters' remembrance of her kitten indicate that she is moving towards Mrs. Hale's understanding of the crime?

Critical Thinking:
Analyze

Mrs. Peters has decided to join Mrs. Hale in withholding crucial evidence from the men. Ask students what they think made her decide to do this.

Mrs. Peters, the wife of the sheriff, sees the conflict clearly—crimes must be punished, but what if the crime is justifiable?

Here is the theme that has been hinted at before—life for farmers' wives is hard, and the suffering created a common bond among women.

MRS. HALE (*moving*): How soon do you suppose they'll be through, looking for the evidence?

MRS. PETERS: I know what stillness is. (*Pulling herself back*) The law has got to punish crime, Mrs. Hale.

MRS. HALE (*not as if answering that*): I wish you'd seen Minnie Foster when she wore a white dress with blue ribbons and stood up there in the choir and sang. (*A look around the room*) Oh, I wish I'd come over here once in a while! That was a crime! That was a crime! Who's going to punish that?

MRS. PETERS (*looking upstairs*): We mustn't—take on.

MRS. HALE: I might have known she needed help! I know how things can be—for women. I tell you, it's queer, Mrs. Peters. We live close together and we live far apart. We all go through the same things—it's all just a different kind of the same thing. (*Brushes her eyes, noticing the bottle of fruit, reaches out for it*) If I was you I wouldn't tell her her fruit was gone. Tell her it *ain't*, Tell her it's all right. Take this in to prove it to her. She—she may never know whether it was broke or not.

MRS. PETERS (*Takes the bottle, looks about for something to wrap it in; takes petticoat from the clothes brought from the other room, very nervously begins winding this around the bottle. In a false voice.*): My, it's a good thing the men couldn't hear us. Wouldn't they just laugh! Getting all stirred up over a little thing like a—dead canary. As if that could have anything to do with—with—wouldn't they *laugh*!

(*The men are heard coming down stairs.*)

MRS. HALE (*under her breath*): Maybe they would—maybe they wouldn't.

COUNTY ATTORNEY: No, Peters, it's all perfectly clear except a reason for doing it. But you know juries when it comes to women. If there was some definite thing. Something to show—something to make a story about—a thing that would connect up with this strange way of doing it—

(*The women's eyes meet for an instant. Enter* HALE *from outer door.*)

HALE: Well, I've got the team around. Pretty cold out there.

---

petticoat (PET ee koht) a loose underskirt

COUNTY ATTORNEY: I'm going to stay here a while by myself. (*To the* SHERIFF.) You can send Frank out for me, can't you? I want to go over everything. I'm not satisfied that we can't do better.

SHERIFF: Do you want to see what Mrs. Peters is going to take in?

(*The* LAWYER *goes to the table, picks up the apron, laughs.*)

COUNTY ATTORNEY: Oh, I guess they're not very dangerous things the ladies have picked out. (*Moves a few things about, disturbing the quilt pieces which cover the box. Steps back.*) No, Mrs. Peters doesn't need supervising. For that matter, a sheriff's wife is married to the law. Ever think of it that way, Mrs. Peters?

MRS. PETERS: Not—just that way.

SHERIFF (*chuckling*): Married to the law. (*Moves toward the other room.*) I just want you to come in here a minute, George. We ought to take a look at these windows.

COUNTY ATTORNEY (*scoffingly*): Oh, windows!

SHERIFF: We'll be right out, Mr. Hale.

(HALE *goes outside. The* SHERIFF *follows the* COUNTY ATTORNEY *into the other room. Then* MRS. HALE *rises, hands tight together, looking intensely at* MRS. PETERS, *whose eyes make a slow turn, finally meeting* MRS. HALE'S. *For a moment* MRS. HALE *holds her, then her own eyes point the way to where the box is concealed. Suddenly* MRS. PETERS *throws back quilt pieces and tries to put the box in the bag she is wearing. It is too big. She opens box, starts to take bird out, cannot touch it, goes to pieces, stands there helpless. Sound of a knob turning in the other room.* MRS. HALE *snatches the box and puts it in the pocket of her big coat. Enter* COUNTY ATTORNEY *and* SHERIFF.)

The bond among women will prevent Mrs. Peters and Mrs. Hale from telling the men what they know about John Wright's death.

COUNTY ATTORNEY (*facetiously*): Well, Henry, at least we found out that she was not going to quilt it. She was going to—what is it you call it, ladies?

MRS. HALE (*her hand against her pocket*): We call it—knot it, Mr. Henderson.

---

supervising (SOO pur vyz ing) inspecting with authority
scoffingly (SKOF ing lee) spoken with scorn or contempt
snatches (SNACH iz) grabs suddenly, rudely, or eagerly
facetiously (fuh SEE shus lee) jokingly, especially at an inappropriate time

Trifles ■ 269

Literary Focus: Plot

The county attorney refers jokingly to quilting. His attitude, no doubt, steels the will of Mrs. Peters to withhold evidence. Ask: How has his little joke quietly—and significantly—backfired?

Mini Quiz

Write the following sentences on the chalkboard or overhead projector and call on students to fill in the blanks. Discuss the answers with the class.

1. The county attorney wasn't immediately available because he was on a trip to _____.

2. The weather at the time the crime took place was _____.

3. The only jar of preserves left was a jar of _____.

4. Mrs. Wright's pet was a _____.

5. The article of clothing Mrs. Wright had asked to be brought to the jail was _____.

Answers
1. Omaha
2. cold
3. cherries
4. canary
5. an apron

UNDERSTAND THE SELECTION

Answers

1. he stopped to ask if John Wright would be interested in getting a party telephone line
2. because that's where the body of John Wright had been found
3. She was sewing a quilt.
4. She was once a very pretty, outgoing woman, now grown old, lonely, and sad with no life outside of her farmhouse. She's married to a hard, humorless man.
5. He was a loner who didn't want much to do with anyone.
6. She wanted to hurt the boy who killed the kitten—exactly what Mrs. Wright probably wanted to do to Mr. Wright after he killed the bird.
7. Even though inaction can't be punished, the things people neglect to do can perhaps cause as much suffering as a crime that is actually committed.
8. Answers will vary. Sample response: I would have paid more attention to the information that the women had about Mrs. Wright.
9. Answers will vary. Sample response: If the jury is sympathetic and a motive is not found, she may be found not guilty.
10. the desire to find out who killed John Wright, and why

Respond to Literature

Facts considered might be: state of disorder of house, Mrs. Wright sitting in rocker and not reporting her husband's death, not noticing much around her, acting strange about her husband's manner of death. Answers will vary.

WRITE ABOUT THE SELECTION

Prewriting

Go over the relevant sections as a class. Encourage students to make notes as you review the sections; these might help later when they freewrite the points they'll cover.

UNDERSTAND THE SELECTION

Recall

1. Why had Lewis Hale stopped at the Wright farmhouse?

2. Why did the sheriff and county attorney go upstairs in the farmhouse?

3. What was Mrs. Wright sewing at the time of John Wright's death?

Infer

4. Mrs. Wright is an absent character we learn much about. Describe her.

5. What does John Wright's not wanting a telephone tell you about him?

6. Why does Mrs. Peters tell about the kitten she had as a little girl?

7. Why does Mrs. Hale consider it a crime not to have visited at the Wrights?

Apply

8. How would you investigate John Wright's death differently?

9. Do you think Mrs. Wright will be found guilty of murder?

10. What keeps the story moving?

Respond to Literature

Investigating a crime is a difficult and challenging job. If you were in charge of investigating this crime, what facts would you consider important? Do you think the suspect's emotional state should be considered?

WRITE ABOUT THE SELECTION

Suppose that Mrs. Hale made a neighborly visit to the Wright Farm. Write a conversation that happens between Mrs. Hale and Mrs. Wright before the murder takes place. Include dialogue about how Mrs. Wright feels about her husband.

Prewriting Make a list of topics Mrs. Hale might talk about. Next to each topic on the list, jot down Mrs. Wright's response. Then make another list of things Mrs. Wright might want to discuss. Next to each item, jot down Mrs. Hale's response.

Writing Use your list of topics and responses to create an imaginary two-character scene for the play "Trifles." Your scene should take place before the murder actually happens. Use the play as a model to write the dialogue between Mrs. Hale and Mrs. Wright. Then add whatever stage directions you think are necessary.

Revising Read your scene aloud. Does your dialogue sound as if two women who are neighbors are actually talking to one another? Change any lines that do not sound real.

Proofreading Do not use quotation marks for dialogue in a play; instead, make sure each speech is preceded by the correct character's name followed by a colon. Also, check to see that you have inserted a parenthesis at the beginning and ending of all stage directions.

Writing

Circulate as students work individually. Check for effective openings and conclusions, and remind students that the most convincing arguments are those supported by evidence.

Revising

Have students work in pairs as they read their confessions aloud, asking partners for feedback on ways to improve their draft.

Proofreading

Review as a class what a run-on sentence is. You might also suggest that varying sentence length is important, especially when something is to be spoken.

THINK ABOUT DRAMA

Trifles is much more than a simple "who-dunit." In it, the elements of drama—plot, characters, setting, and theme—combine to make a suspenseful and meaningful play. The author has something important to tell us. She delivers her message through the play's conflicts. Who murdered John Wright quickly becomes secondary to why he was murdered.

1. The theme is closely related to the conflict presented in the play. What conflict exists between the five characters who actually appear in this play?

2. A second important conflict involves the play's absent characters. Explain this conflict.

3. Both of the conflicts involve a lack of understanding. Explain who is involved and what he or she did not understand.

4. Do the characters resolve the conflicts by the end of the play?

5. What do you think the author's message is?

DEVELOP YOUR VOCABULARY

Using specific words or phrases appropriate to a certain lifestyle makes a story seem more real. You must know exactly what the words mean, however, to understand fully what the author is talking about.

In *Trifles* many words associated with country or farm life are used. For example, at one point Hale mentions "Harry and the team outside." Harry is his companion outside, and the team is the horses they are using to haul potatoes to town. The dictionary gives this as a second definition for team: "Two or more horses or oxen harnessed to the same vehicle."

Make sure you know the precise definitions of the following words as they are used in *Trifles*. Consult a dictionary if you need help.

1. party telephone
2. stove
3. pleating
4. load of potatoes
5. put up food
6. dipperful
7. roller towel
8. quilt
9. preserves
10. a hollow

Choose five of the above words and use them in an original paragraph.

DEVELOP YOUR VOCABULARY

Sample Answers

1. *party telephone*: two or more telephones connected to the same line.
2. *stove*: a wood or coal stove used for heating and, possibly, baking (although it would then be called a cookstove).
3. *pleating*: to press cloth together.
4. *load of potatoes*: an imprecise amount of potatoes.
5. *preserves*: fruit preserved whole or in large pieces by cooking with sugar.
6. *dipper*: pumps often had dippers handing next to them so people could use the dipper as a glass to drink water.
7. *roller towel*: circular cloth towel on a roller that can be rotated to find a clean section.
8. *quilt*: a bedcover made by stitching a layer of soft cotton or wool between two layers of fabric.
9. *preserves*: canned fruits or vegetables.
10. *hollow*: a depression below the surrounding ground level.

THINK ABOUT DRAMA

Answers

1. The conflict was mainly one of the men's understanding versus the women's understanding. The women understood Mrs. Wright's motives, while the men wanted to prove her guilty.

2. The conflict between Mr. and Mrs. Wright, which must have been simmering for years, finally boiled over when he killed her canary.

3. The men in the play do not understand the women and the women's lives, just as Mr. Wright did not understand his wife.

4. No. The men will probably try Mrs. Wright in court, but there has been no increase in understanding about the hard life of a farm woman.

5. The author wants us to realize the hard conditions and unjust life that many women have been subjected to by the men they've married. Sometimes circumstances make criminal actions easier to understand.

SELECTION OBJECTIVES

After completing this selection, students will be able to

- understand narration
- describe the difficulties in telling a story
- discuss the symbolism of snakes
- explain a process
- analyze non-fiction narration
- define words used to describe different kinds of scientists
- identify problems and solutions

Lesson Resources

The Rattlesnake Hunt
- Selection Synopsis, Teacher's Edition, p. T211d
- Comprehension and Vocabulary Workbook, pp. 49–50
- Language Enrichment Workbook, pp. 51–52
- Teacher's Resources Reinforcement, p. R25 Test, pp. T47–T48

More About Narration

The ordering of events in a story is the most important part of narration, yet it is just the foundation for the story. A good storyteller, whether telling the story verbally or in writing, knows how to develop other aspects of the story. Try telling a story by simply listing the major points of the plot; it's not very appealing.

About the Author

Marjorie Kinnan Rawlings was born in Washington, D.C., but spent much of her adult life in Florida. She first moved there in 1928, when she and her first husband, Charles Rawlings, bought an orange grove in the back country of north central Florida. It was after the move to Florida that the budding writer began to have luck selling her stories to New York publishers. Rawlings found much material for her stories in the people, places, animals, and plants of her adopted

Learn About

NARRATION

The ability to tell a story has played an important part in human life as long as man has been able to communicate.

At first, stories were told orally. Then with the development of alphabets, stories began to be written down. Even today, however, the oral tradition remains strong in some cultures.

Whether stories are told orally or in writing, narration is the most common form of presenting them. **Narration** is simply the orderly telling of events.

The person doing the telling is the **narrator**. The narrator may be a character within the story. Sometimes the narrator does not take part in the events of the story but reports them from outside. Whether the narrator is inside or outside the action determines the point of view of the story.

As you read the next selection, ask yourself these questions:
1. Who is the narrator?
2. How does narration help organize the telling of the story?

WRITING CONNECTION

Did your parents tell stories to you when you were younger? Do you tell stories to a brother or sister? What is hard about telling a story? Write down three or four ideas.

READING FOCUS

Identify Problems and Solutions Often, a story revolves around one main conflict or problem. In order to solve this problem, characters may need to find solutions to a number of other, smaller problems that help them to overcome the main problem. These problems and solutions in a story are not always clearly defined. Use characters' words and actions to help you identify them.

state. She and Charles Rawlings divorced in 1933. She married again eight years later. Her second husband was a businessman from St. Augustine, Florida, and except for summers in an old farmhouse in New York state, she continued to live in Florida. She is buried near Cross Creek, Florida, not far from the orange grove she owned with her first husband.

More About the Unit Theme

Remind students that it's only natural to become tense when threatened—and most people look upon snakes as a threat; some even have difficulty watching them in zoos. Ask students how they feel about rattlesnakes or other poisonous snakes. Ask: Do we have any evidence that snakes benefit their environment?

Cooperative Group Activity

Divide the class into groups of four or five. Have each student in the group tell a favorite story for the Writing Connection activity. Then, ask the groups to choose one story to tell the whole class. After each story is told, the group members must tell the class why they chose that particular story. What did they find appealing about it?

The Rattlesnake Hunt
from Cross Creek

by Margorie Kinnan Rawlings

I discovered that for me rattlesnakes represented the last outpost of physical fear.

I discovered this when Ross Allen, a young Florida herpetologist, invited me to join him on a hunt in the upper Everglades—for rattlesnakes. . . . Ross and I drove to Arcadia in his coupe on a warm January day.

I said, "How will you bring back the rattlesnakes?"

"In the back of my car."

My courage was not adequate to inquire whether they were thrown in loose and might be expected to appear between our feet. Actually, a large portable box of heavy-meshed wire made a safe cage. Ross wanted me to write an article about his work and on our way to the unhappy hunting grounds I took notes on the mass of data that he had accumulated in his years of herpetological research. . . . As I had discovered with insects and varmints, it is difficult to be afraid of anything about which enough is known, and Ross' facts were fresh from the laboratory.

The hunting ground was Big Prairie, south of Arcadia and west of the northern tip of Lake Okeechobee. Big Prairie is a desolate cattle country, half marsh, half pasture, with islands of palm trees and cypress and oaks. At that time of year the cattlemen and Indians were burning the country, on the theory that the young fresh wire grass that springs up from the roots after a fire is the best cattle forage.

---

herpetologist (hur puh TOL uh jist) someone who studies reptiles and amphibians
everglade (EV ur glayd) a large region of swampland; the Everglades is a region of such land in southern Florida, about 100 miles long and 50 to 75 miles wide
coupe (KOOP) a small, two-door automobile
portable (PAWRT uh bul) capable of being easily carried
meshed (MESHT) made into a net
data (DAYT uh) collected facts
varmints (VAHR munts) animals regarded as troublesome
desolate (DES uh lit) having no people; in a state of ruin
cypress (SY prus) a cone-bearing tree of the pine family
forage (FOR ihj) food eaten by animals

The Rattlesnake Hunt ■ 273

Develop Vocabulary Skills

First, have students make flashcards of the new vocabulary; perhaps each student could make one card. Next, circulate the flashcards by having students pass theirs to a neighbor. They should then pronounce the new word and read the definition, asking their neighbor for help, if needed. Finally they should use the word in a sentence.

ESL Activity

Pair students to work on vocabulary that seems particularly troublesome. After they work together on pronunciation and meaning, have them write a short paragraph using the words to check comprehension.

TEACHING PLAN

INTRODUCE

Motivation
Ask: How do you handle a snake? If possible, have students visit a pet shop or zoo and interview personnel about dealing with snakes. They can also consult reference books. Set aside time for reports on their research. Then ask: Now that you know all about snakes, would you be willing to hunt them?

Purpose-Setting Question
Is there any way to overcome a specific fear?

READ

Literary Focus:
Narration
The narrator of "The Rattlesnake Hunt" is relating a story in which she is an active participant and not just an observer. Discuss with students as they read how this affects the narration of the story. Ask: Does it seem more vivid? More real? Encourage students to think about how the story might be different if the author were not participating in the action.

Reading Focus:
Identify Problems and Solutions
The narrator's fear of snakes presents a problem if she is to participate in the rattlesnake hunt. During the course of the event she is faced with other problems as well. Have students create a double-column chart with *Problem* and *Solution* as column headers. As they read, students can fill in the chart as they identify the problems the narrator faces over the course of the hunt and the solutions she comes up with.

CLOSE

Have students complete Review the Selection on pages 278–279.

Literary Focus:
Narration

Rawlings uses few embellishments in her narrative; when she does, they almost seem out of place. Ask: What effect is created by the repetition of the verb drop?

Ross planned to hunt his rattlers in the forefront of the fires. They lived in winter, he said, in gopher holes, coming out in the midday warmth to forage, and would move ahead of the flames and be easily taken. We joined forces with . . . Will, his snake-hunting companion of the territory, and set out in early morning, after a long rough drive over deep-rutted roads into the open wilds.

I hope never in my life to be so frightened as I was in those first few hours. I kept on Ross' footsteps, I moved when he moved, sometimes jolting into him when I thought he might leave me behind. He does not use the forked stick of conventional snake hunting but a steel prong, shaped like an L, at the end of a long stout stick. He hunted casually, calling my attention to the varying vegetation, to hawks overhead, to a pair of the rare whooping cranes that flapped over us. In mid-morning he stopped short, dropped his stick, and brought up a five-foot rattlesnake draped limply over the steel L. It seemed to me that I should drop in my tracks.

"They're not active at this season," he said quietly. "A snake takes on the temperature of its surroundings. They can't stand too much heat for that reason, and when the weather is cool, as now, they're sluggish."

The sun was bright overhead, the sky a translucent blue, and it seemed to me that it was warm enough for any snake to do as it willed. The sweat poured down my back. Ross dropped the rattler in a crocus sack and Will carried it. By noon, he had caught four. I felt faint and ill. We stopped by a pond and went swimming. The region was flat, the horizon limitless, and as I came out of the cool blue water, I expected to find myself surrounded by a ring of rattlers. There were only Ross and Will, opening the lunch basket. I could not eat. . . . Will went back and drove his truck closer, for Ross expected the hunting to be better in the afternoon. The hunting was much better. When we went back to the truck to deposit two more rattlers in the wire cage, there was a rattlesnake lying under the truck.

Ross said, "Whenever I leave my car or truck with snakes already in it, other rattlers always appear. I don't know whether this is because they scent or sense the presence of other snakes, or whether in this arid area they come to the car for shade in the heat of the day."

The problem was scientific, but I had no interest.

---

gopher (GOH fur) a rodent that digs into the ground
companion (kum PAN yun) a friend
jolting (JOHL ting) shaking from sudden jerks
prong (PRAWNG) a sharp-pointed instrument
vegetation (vej uh TAY shun) plant life
sluggish (SLUG ish) lacking energy; slow, inactive
translucent (tranz LOO suhnt) hazy or blurred
crocus sack (KROH kus SAK) a term used in the southern United States for a burlap bag

That night Ross and Will and I camped out in the vast spaces of the Everglades prairies. We got water from an abandoned well and cooked supper under buttonwood bushes by a flowing stream. The camp fire blazed cheerfully under the stars and a new moon lifted in the sky. Will told tall tales of the cattlemen and the Indians, and we were at peace.

Ross said, "We couldn't have a better night for catching water snakes."

After the rattlers, water snakes seemed innocuous enough. We worked along the edge of the stream and here Ross did not use his L-shaped steel. He reached under rocks and along the edge of the water and brought out harmless reptiles with his hands. I had said nothing to him of my fears, but he understood them. He brought a small dark snake from under a willow root.

"Wouldn't you like to hold it?" he asked. "People think snakes are cold and clammy, but they aren't. Take it in your hands. You'll see that it is warm."

Again, because I was ashamed, I took the snake in my hands. It was not cold, it was not clammy, and it lay trustingly in my hands, a thing that lived and breathed like the rest of us. I felt an upsurgence of spirit.

The next day was magnificent. The air was crystal, the sky was aquamarine, and the far horizon of palms and oaks lay against the sky. I felt a new boldness and followed Ross bravely. He was making the rounds of the gopher holes. The rattlers came out in the mid-morning warmth and were never far away. He could tell by their trails whether one had come out or was still in the hole. Sometimes the two men dug the snake out. At times it was down so long and winding a tunnel that the digging was hopeless. Then they blocked the entrance and went on to other holes. In an hour or so they made the original rounds, unblocking the holes. The rattler in every case came out hurriedly, as though anything were preferable to being shut in. All the time Ross talked to me, telling me the scientific facts he had discovered about the habits of the rattlers.

"They pay no attention to a man standing perfectly still," he said, and proved it by letting Will unblock a hole while he stood at the entrance as the snake came out. It was exciting to watch the snake crawl slowly beside and past the man's legs. When it was at a safe distance he walked within its range of vision, which he had proved to be no higher than a man's knee, and the snake whirled and drew back in an attitude of fighting defense. The rattler strikes only for paralyzing and killing its food, and for defense.

"It is a slow and heavy snake," Ross said. "It lies in wait on a small game trail and strikes the rat or rabbit passing by.

---

buttonwood (BUT un wuud) a small sycamore tree
innocuous (ih NAHK yoo uhs) harmless
upsurgence (uhp SER juhns) lifting
aquamarine (AH kwuh muh REEN) blue green
attitude (AT uh tood) in this case, a position or posture of the body
paralyzing (PAR uh lyz ing) losing of power or movement

The Rattlesnake Hunt ■ 275

Reading Focus:
Identify Problems and Solutions
When Ross gives Rawlings a snake to hold, it is the beginning of his lesson on how to overcome a fear of snakes. Have students pay attention to his methods. Ask: Is he a good teacher?

Critical Thinking:
Analyze
"The next day was magnificent" is the opening sentence in a long, descriptive paragraph. Ask: How does this description show Ross and his friend to be accomplished snake hunters?

Reading Focus:
*Identify Problems
and Solutions*

At this point in the story, the narrator finds that she has overcome her fear of snakes. Ask: How did she solve this problem?

It waits a few minutes, then follows along the trail, coming to the small animal, now dead or dying. It noses it from all sides, making sure that it is dead and ready for swallowing."

A rattler will lie quietly without revealing himself if a man passes by and it thinks it is not seen. It slips away without fighting if given the chance. Only Ross' sharp eyes sometimes picked out the gray and yellow diamond pattern, camouflaged among the grasses. In the cool of the morning, chilled by the January air, the snakes showed no fight. They could be looped up limply over the L and dropped in a sack or up into the wire cage on the back of Will's truck. . . . I went off hunting by myself, and though I found no snakes, I should have known what to do.

The sun was dropping low in the west. Masses of white cloud hung above the flat marshy plain and seemed to be tangled in the tops of distant palms and cypresses. The sky turned orange, then saffron. I walked leisurely back toward the truck. In the distance I could see Ross and Will making their way in too. The season was more advanced than at the Creek, two hundred miles to the north, and I noticed that spring flowers were blooming

---

saffron (SAF run) orange-yellow in color

among the lumpy hummocks. I leaned over to pick a white violet. There was a rattlesnake under the violet.

If this had happened the week before, if it had happened the *day* before, I think I should have lain down and died on top of the rattlesnake, with no need of being struck and poisoned. The snake did not coil, but lifted its head and whirred its rattles lightly. I stepped back slowly and put the violet in a buttonhole. I reached forward and laid the steel L across the snake's neck, just back of the blunt head. I called to Ross:

"I've got one."

He walked toward me.

"Well, pick it up," he said.

I released it and slipped the L under the middle of the thick body.

"Go put it in the box."

He went ahead of me and lifted the top of the wire cage. I made the truck with the rattler, but when I reached up the six feet to drop it in the cage, it slipped off the stick and dropped on Ross' feet. It made no effort to strike.

"Pick it up again," he said. "If you'll pin it down lightly and reach just back of its head with your hand, as you've seen me do, you can drop it in more easily."

I pinned it and leaned over.

"I'm awfully sorry," I said, "but you're pushing me a little too fast."

He grinned. I lifted the snake on the stick and again as I had it at head height, it slipped off, down Ross' boots and on top of his feet. He stood as still as a stump. I dropped the snake on his feet for the third time. It seemed to me that the most patient of rattlers might in time resent being hauled up and down, and for all man's quiet certainty that in standing motionless there was no danger, it would strike at whatever was nearest, and that would be Ross.

I said, "I'm just not man enough to keep this up any longer," and he laughed and reached down with his smooth quickness and lifted the snake back of the head and dropped it in the cage. It slid in among its mates and settled in a corner. The hunt was over and we drove back over the uneven trail to Will's village and left him and went on to Arcadia and home. Our catch for the two days was thirty-two rattlers.

I said to Ross, "I believe that tomorrow I could have picked up that snake."

Back at the Creek, I felt a new lightness. I had done battle with a great fear, and the victory was mine.

---

hummocks (HUM uks) areas of fertile, wooded land, higher than the surrounding swamp
whirred (WHERD) shook, making a buzzing sound
blunt (BLUNT) having a rounded point
resent (rih ZENT) to consider as an insult

The Rattlesnake Hunt ■ 277

Literary Focus: *Narration*

"I've got one," says Rawlings, as she describes in detail her first experience in catching a snake. Rawlings didn't have a tape recorder or video camera to record the event. Ask: How, then, was she able to reconstruct each vivid detail?

Discussion

Discuss how students feel about the ending. Was it too abrupt? Or did they like the direct simplicity of the last paragraph?

Mini Quiz

Write the following sentences on the chalkboard or overhead projector and call on students to fill in the blanks. Discuss the answers with the class.

1. The rattlesnake hunt occurs in the month of _____.

2. _____ are raised at Big Prairie.

3. Ross's companion was _____.

4. A snake's range of vision is no higher than _____.

5. Rawlings was leaning over to pick a _____ when she found her first rattlesnake.

Answers

1. January
2. Cattle
3. Will
4. a person's knee
5. violet

UNDERSTAND THE SELECTION

Answers

1. in the upper Everglades, at a place called Big Prairie
2. He uses an L-shaped steel prong attached to a long stick.
3. to paralyze and kill its food, and for defense
4. The cooler temperatures mean the snakes will be lethargic, especially early in the day, and easier to catch. Also, cattlemen and Indians are burning fires at this time of year; the snakes will be moving ahead of the fires, making their capture easier.
5. She was terrified. She couldn't even eat lunch.
6. He wanted to show Rawlings that snakes are not cold and clammy, but are warm, living, breathing animals. He succeeded in making her begin to overcome her fears of snakes.
7. The narrator, who is not a man, is hiding behind the false stereotype that women are weaker in strength and courage than men.
8. Sample answer: I might scream. I might want to touch it.
9. Sample answer: Yes, if for no other reason than all the information I learned about rattlesnakes.
10. Sample answer: No, I'm still scared of a tall building, even though I know it won't fall over.

Respond to Literature

She listened to and observed Ross as he handled snakes. She held a snake and practiced lifting one. Students may suggest overcoming fears of learning to swim or ride a bicycle when they were young.

WRITE ABOUT THE SELECTION

Prewriting

To accelerate this stage, students could work together in pairs. While one student reads the steps in catching a rattlesnake, the other jots them down in simple terms. Together they then map out the process.

UNDERSTAND THE SELECTION

Recall

1. In what general area of Florida did the rattlesnake hunt take place?
2. What sort of tool does Ross use?
3. Why does a rattler strike?

Infer

4. Why does Ross hunt in January?
5. Describe the narrator's feelings the first few hours of the hunt.
6. What motive does Ross have for hunting water snakes the first night?
7. Why does Ross laugh when, the narrator says, "I'm just not man enough to keep this up any longer"?

Apply

8. How might you react to seeing a snake?
9. The narrator was planning to write an article about Ross Allen's work. Do you think she succeeded in writing an interesting article? Why or why not?
10. The narrator says "it is difficult to be afraid of anything about which enough is known." Do you agree?

Respond to Literature

The narrator overcame her fear of snakes during the snake hunt. How did she do this? Give some examples of fears you have overcome.

WRITE ABOUT THE SELECTION

One of the best ways to practice clear, precise writing is to explain a process to someone. When the process is how to catch a snake, the danger of not explaining things well is real!

Since you are now an authority on rattlesnakes, you have been asked to explain to a scout troop how to catch a rattlesnake.

Prewriting Identify each step for catching a rattlesnake by scanning "Rattlesnake Hunt" for information. Note the steps explained in the story. As an example, you might write: Step 1, gather equipment and supplies, including a strong cage. Include all steps necessary for success and safety.

Writing Begin by making a general statement about the process you will describe. Then use your list of steps to write a detailed description of each step in the process.

Revising Review the information the author gives for hunting snakes, and check to be sure you have not omitted any of her steps. Read your description to someone else. Ask that person to comment about parts that seem unclear. Then revise those parts.

Proofreading Reread your description to check for errors. Make sure that you have used words correctly and precisely. Change any words that might confuse a reader who is unfamiliar with snake hunting.

Writing

The students could continue working together as a team, with each describing a different part of the process. Circulate as students work, offering assistance.

Revising

When their explanation is finished, have one student read it aloud while the other checks for accuracy against the map they laid out.

Proofreading

Remind students of their reading audience: a scout troop. Clear communication rather than a wordy, academic style is the keynote. Advise students, therefore, to delete all pretentious words and phrases.

THINK ABOUT NARRATION

You have been reading mostly mysteries and detective stories in this unit. "The Rattlesnake Hunt" is a little different. It is a nonfiction narration—reporting true events in their natural order.

1. Who is the narrator? For what purpose did he or she go on the rattlesnake hunt?

2. In what ways does the narrator help to organize the events of the story?

3. Since Ross Allen and his partner are old hands at catching rattlesnakes, the only suspense is created by the narrator's experiences. Which of her experiences provide suspense?

4. Does the narrator take part in the events of the story or report them from outside the action of the story?

5. How might the story have changed if another character had been the narrator?

READING FOCUS

Identify Problems and Solutions What was the main problem the narrator faced? Give two examples of smaller problems she described and the solutions she found.

DEVELOP YOUR VOCABULARY

Ross Allen, the snake hunter in the story, is a herpetologist, a person who studies reptiles and amphibians. The word *herpetologist* includes the suffix *-ist*. A suffix is an addition to the end of a word that forms another related word. The suffix *-ist* means "a person who studies, seeks, makes, or does." For example, an adventurist is a person who seeks adventure. Each word below includes the suffix *-ist*. Tell what each word means. Use a dictionary as needed.

1. scientist
2. geologist
3. phrenologist
4. botanist
5. chemist
6. alchemist
7. journalist
8. physicist
9. philatelist
10. numismatist
11. artist
12. ophthalmologist
13. dentist

Now, use the words in original sentences.

Review the Selection ■ 279

READING FOCUS

Sample Answer

In this story, the narrator has a fear of snakes, but she is going along on a rattlesnake hunt and needs to overcome her fear. She was afraid of being left behind and therefore moved when Ross moved. Ross asked her to hold a small snake and she agreed to hold it.

ESL Activity

Have students work in pairs to identify the root words for six of the Develop Your Vocabulary words. Offer assistance as needed.

THINK ABOUT NARRATION

Answers

1. the author, Marjorie Rawlings; to write an article about Ross Allen's work with snakes

2. The events are chronologically organized. Also, the author first describes the event and then relates her reaction to it.

3. the drive on the way to the snake hunt; the first few hours of the snake hunt; when she was picking the violet and discovered a snake

4. She is very actively involved.

5. Answers will vary. Students may suggest that another narrator might not be so fearful; another may be more scientific; another may be less insightful.

DEVELOP YOUR VOCABULARY

Answers

1. *scientist*: one whose profession is scientific research.

2. *geologist*: one who studies the history of the earth and its life, especially as recorded in rocks.

3. *phrenologist*: one who analyzes a person's character by studying the shape of the skull.

4. *botanist*: one who studies plants and plant life.

5. *chemist*: one who studies chemistry, which is the science dealing with the composition and properties of matter.

6. *alchemist*: one who practices alchemy, an early form of chemistry that had philosophical and magical associations.

7. *journalist*: a reporter or editor involved in news-gathering.

8. *physicist*: one who studies physics, the science of the relationship between matter and energy.

9. *philatelist*: one who collects and studies postage and imprinted stamps.

10. *numismatist*: one who collects and studies currency.

11. *artist*: one who practices any of the fine arts, such as painting, sculpture, music.

12. *ophthalmologist*: an eye doctor.

13. *dentist*: one who treats the teeth.

SELECTION OBJECTIVES

After completing these selections, students will be able to

- understand the element of tone
- analyze the relationship between tone and theme
- exercise the mental skill of speculation
- write a TV news account of a developing event
- analyze how tone deepens the meaning of a poem
- use a thesaurus to find synonyms
- evaluate the author's style

Lesson Resources

Earth/Earth
- Selection Synopses, Teacher's Edition, p. T211d
- Comprehension and Vocabulary Workbook, pp. 51–52
- Language Enrichment Workbook, p. 53
- Teacher's Resources Reinforcement, p. R26 Test, pp. T49–T50

More About Tone

Begin by emphasizing that tone exists in all writing. Next, ask students to think back on a previous selection, such as "The Rattlesnake Hunt." What was the tone? Compare its tone to that of *Trifles*. Then, point out that all literature—that is, the body of writing notable for beauty and force—has a distinctive, often subtle tone. It informs the reader of the writer's attitude toward his or her subject. Suggest that students consider the tone in each of the next selections.

More About the Unit Theme

Both poems end in catastrophe for Earth. But both treat the theme differently. From our limited knowledge about space, how do you view the world and your part in it?

READING FOCUS

Evaluate the Author's Style An author's writing style is the manner in which the author makes a point or delivers a message in a story. Often this style is as important as the point being made because it may make an impression on the reader. The style of a story or poem can add to its impact. As you read, pay close attention to the styles of both poems and determine how they add to the poems' message.

Learn About

TONE

When people talk, you often can determine how they really feel by listening to their tones. How a person's voice sounds—angry, excited, bored, tired—is sometimes as important as what the person says. What happens when you cannot listen to the person, but instead must read what he or she writes? Does tone still exist? It certainly does. However, you must pay closer attention to discover the tone.

Tone is the writer's attitude toward his or her subject as well as toward the reader. It is expressed indirectly, through the choice of words or the combining of words. Even the construction of a sentence, or punctuation, might hint at how the writer feels.

Look for answers to the following questions as you read the poems:
1. How is tone created?
2. What is the relationship between tone and the theme of the poem?

WRITING CONNECTION

Look in a newspaper or magazine for an advertisement with a catchy slogan. What is the tone of the slogan? How does it fit with the visual message? Report your findings in a paragraph.

About the Authors

John Hall Wheelock (1886–1978) was a lyric poet mostly writing about "lost love." In this poem, he is, however, showing that he has a sense of humor. He might be suggesting that he is aware of the possibility of an unexpected "blow-up" of anything, including the planet.

Oliver Herford (1863–1935) was an artist and humorist. This poem is written in a humorous vein. He does not speculate on the cause of the possible "fall through space" but only on the utterings of a child viewing this scene from another planet.

Cooperative Group Activity

Extend the Writing Connection activity by having students share their findings with the class. Ask: Does tone have anything to do with a slogan's appeal?

Develop Vocabulary Skills

Ask students what these words tell about the tone of Oliver Herford's poem: *shriveling*, *lice*, and *maggots*. Then ask why these are interspersed between such words as *philosophers* and *kings*?

EARTH *by John Hall Wheelock*

"A planet doesn't explode of itself," said drily
The Martian astronomer, gazing off into the air—
"That they were able to do it is proof that highly
Intelligent beings must have been living there."

EARTH *by Oliver Herford*

If this little world to-night
    Suddenly should fall through space
In a hissing, headlong flight,
    Shrivelling from off its face,
5   As it falls into the sun,
    In an instant every trace
Of the little crawling things—
    Ants, philosophers, and lice,
Cattle, cockroaches, and kings,
10   Beggars, millionaires, and mice,
Men and maggots all as one
As it falls into the sun—
Who can say but at the same
    Instant from some planet far
15 A child may watch us and exclaim:
    "See the pretty shooting star!"

Martian (MAHR shun) inhabitant of the planet Mars
shrivelling (SHRIV ul ing) shrinking; drying up
lice (LYS) plural of louse, a small insect that lives in the skin and hair of people
cockroaches (KOK rohch is) large black or brown insects that live everywhere
maggots (MAG uts) small wormlike animals that are the young form of flies or other insects

Earth/Earth ■ 281

Mini Quiz

Write on the chalkboard or overhead projector the following sentences and call on students to fill in the blanks. Discuss the answers with the class.

1. Both poems are entitled _____ .

2. The Martian astronomer thinks that _____ must have been living on Earth.

3. Oliver Herford suggests the world might fall _____ .

4. Herford calls all animal life on Earth _____ .

5. The observer in Herford's poem is watching from _____ .

Answers
1. "Earth"
2. highly intelligent beings
3. through space (into the sun)
4. little crawling things
5. some planet far away

TEACHING PLAN

INTRODUCE

Motivation
Show students a picture of the solar system, pointing out the location of the planet Earth. Ask them to suppose for a moment that there is life on another planet, such as Mars. What might Martians think of Earth as they look through a telescope?

Purpose-Setting Question
Are we alone in the universe?

READ

Literary Focus:
Tone
The tone of each of these poems reflects the writers' attitudes towards their subject—Earth and its people. The language and imagery used can help the reader to identify the common elements that establish the tone—the slightly distant, humorous attitude of the poets toward their subject.

Reading Focus:
Evaluate the Author's Style
Have students compare the ways that the authors of the two poems make their point. Both seem to be commenting on humanity's destructive nature and on its relative insignificance in the universe. But do they make their point in the same way? Discuss the language and imagery used, and which poem seems to have the greater impact and why.

CLOSE

Have students complete Review the Selection on pages 282–283.

Comparing Selections
Have students compare and discuss the form—or structure—of each poem.

UNDERSTAND THE SELECTION

Answers

1. A Martian astronomer observes the explosion.
2. It falls into the sun.
3. The child thinks Earth is actually a meteor, or a shooting star.
4. The Martian astronomer thinks it destroyed itself.
5. cold, scientific
6. When the end comes, we shall all be equals, the smallest maggots and the richest millionaires.
7. that life on this Earth might seem important to us but might be inconsequential in terms of the entire universe
8. end weight—We don't know the explanation for Earth's ending until the last line of each poem.
9. Sample answer: I think about someone on another planet peering through a telescope and looking at me.
10. Sample answer: probably nuclear war

Respond to Literature

Do students believe that UFOs exist? Has Earth already had visitors from other planets? There are some very persuasive accounts documenting UFOs. If they do exist, doesn't that mean there is intelligent life on other planets?

WRITE ABOUT THE SELECTION

Prewriting

Discuss as a class how news reporters decide on whom to call when they're covering a story. What gives a story credibility? What makes it complete? How can an in-depth story about a mysterious explosion in the sky be written in time for the next edition?

UNDERSTAND THE SELECTION

Recall

1. Who observes the explosion of Earth in John Hall Wheelock's poem?

2. How is Earth destroyed in Oliver Herford's poem?

3. What does a child on a distant planet think as Earth is being destroyed?

Infer

4. How is Earth destroyed in John Hall Wheelock's poem?

5. Explain the astronomer's attitude as he watches Earth explode.

6. Explain "Men and maggots all as one."

7. What is the theme of the Herford poem?

Apply

8. How is suspense achieved in each poem?

9. What do you think about when you see a shooting star?

10. Have you ever imagined how life on Earth could end? What do you think could be the most likely cause?

Respond to Literature

Both poems suggest that there is intelligent life on other planets. Do you think there is? Why do you think as you do?

WRITE ABOUT THE SELECTION

You are a television news reporter on a distant planet working the night news desk. Suddenly, there is a big explosion in the sky. How would you describe the explosion to your audience? How would you explain what caused it?

Prewriting You have no film footage, so you must do some quick interviews for your story. Make a list of people you might call for information, such as an astronomer, a military official or an astronaut. Also, you want to locate some eyewitnesses. Imagine what each of these people might tell you. List the information, keeping what each person says separate so you know what information came from what source.

Writing Organize your information into a news story. Remember, the most important information comes first in a news story, and you should answer the questions: who, what, where, when, and how. You may quote the people you interviewed.

Revising Since this is a broadcast news story, read your story aloud. Make sure all your information is stated clearly. Ask yourself which parts of your story will create pictures in the listeners' minds. Revise those parts that do not create word pictures. Think of a snappy way to end your story.

Proofreading Make sure that you correctly pronounce the names and titles of the people you interviewed.

Writing

Have students listen to and analyze a news broadcast before they begin their writing. You could assign this as homework or bring a tape of a broadcast to class. As they write, remind them of the "inverted pyramid" style of news stories: the most important news first, followed by more detailed information, such as eyewitness accounts.

Revising

Have students work in pairs, reading their news stories aloud to each other. How do the stories sound? Reading a story can help pinpoint transition problems.

Proofreading

Review with the class the correct way of writing a person's title. Rules on capitalization can be found in a stylebook.

THINK ABOUT TONE

Tone is the way a poet reveals attitudes and feelings. Everything in a poem helps to create tone. You must be a detective in order to discover clues to the way tone is created in a written work.

1. In the first line of Herford's poem, how does the poet indicate his attitude about the importance of the world?

2. How does Herford show his attitude toward living things, including people?

3. Alliteration is often a key to tone. It can be used to show humor, anger, or other feelings. Find an example of alliteration. Identify a feeling the poet is communicating.

4. The attitude of the Martian astronomer in Wheelock's poem could be the poet's attitude, too. What is the attitude about life on the planet in the poem?

5. What is the theme of Wheelock's poem? Does the tone reflect this?

READING FOCUS

Evaluate the Author's Style As you read each poem, you evaluated the style in which the authors delivered their messages. Which poem has a more effective style? How did the style help reveal the poem's message? Why?

DEVELOP YOUR VOCABULARY

A thesaurus can be a useful reference book. If you want to use alliteration, you will find many words with similar initial sounds. You will also find synonyms: words that have the same or similar meanings.

In some thesauruses, you look up the word for which you want a synonym, and the synonyms are listed. In other thesauruses, you look for the word in the index. Following the word is a page number. You then turn to that page to find the word and list of synonyms.

Now that you know how to use a thesaurus, find some synonyms for the word *beggar*. Choose the synonym beginning with *m*. Then find synonyms for the other words listed below. For each numbered word, choose a synonym that starts with the letter indicated.

1. beggar (**m**)
2. philosopher (**i**)
3. proof (**v**)
4. millionaire (**p**)
5. crawling (**c**)
6. exclaim (**s**)

Use each synonym in an original sentence.

Review the Selection ■ 283

THINK ABOUT TONE

Answers

1. He uses the word "little," which is a strange way to describe the world if you're living on it.
2. He views them as insignificant equals, introducing them as "little crawling things" and then listing examples, such as "ants," "philosophers," "cattle," and "kings."
3. "Men and maggots" in Herford's poem shows disdain for man's feeling of superiority in the world, if not the universe.
4. a humorous, detached analysis of how Earth's people caused their own destruction
5. Wheelock is suggesting we know too much for our own good. The cold, scientific tone of the Martian astronomer makes the theme seem very plausible.

DEVELOP YOUR VOCABULARY

Answers

1. mendicant
2. intellectual
3. verification
4. plutocrat
5. creeping
6. shout, scream

Sample sentences:

1. The *mendicant* was huddled over a fire on the street corner.
2. Talking with an *intellectual* can be frustrating.
3. "We need *verification* of compliance with the treaty!" the president thundered.
4. A *plutocrat* is someone who knows the value of a dollar.
5. I saw the boy *creeping* out from behind the bushes.
6. To *shout* when it's unnecessary is rude.

READING FOCUS

Sample Answer

Oliver Herford's poem was more effective because of the images that he used, such as "men and maggots all as one." He made humans seem no more important than ants or lice and the earth no more important than a shooting star. His rhyming, informal style adds to the sense of insignificance of life on the earth.

ESL Activity

Divide the class into small groups. Ask them to discuss whether an alien observing Earth would note cultural differences. Have groups share their conclusions with the class.

T283

SELECTION OVERVIEW

SELECTION OBJECTIVES

After completing this selection, students will be able to

- understand irony in literature
- recognize how irony is used to create humor
- analyze alternative endings to a story
- develop a conclusion to a story
- explain examples of irony
- identify root words
- make judgments

Lesson Resources

The Lady or the Tiger?
- Selection Synopsis, Teacher's Edition, p. T211e
- Comprehension and Vocabulary Workbook, pp. 53–54
- Language Enrichment Workbook, pp. 54–55
- Teacher's Resources Reinforcement, p. R27 Test, pp. T51–T52

More About Irony

Situational irony occurs when what a character expects to happen doesn't. Dramatic irony occurs when the reader knows something a character doesn't know. "The Lady or the Tiger?" turns dramatic irony around: A character knows something the reader doesn't know and doesn't find out. The unexpected reversal makes Stockton's story one of the best-known "trick" stories ever written.

About the Author

Imagine starting life as a wood engraver and ending it as a well-known writer and editor. That's what Frank Stockton did. His early stories were written for children's magazines, and then he turned to writing for adults. However, he never lost his sense of whimsy and imagination. "The Lady or the Tiger?" is perhaps his best-known work.

King Melchisedech in ceremonial robes, Flemish tapestry, late 15th century. Photograph Erich Lessing/Art Resource

READING FOCUS

Make Judgments You can make judgments about a story based on your opinion of the setting, plot, characters, style, or theme of the story. As you read, use the information you gather to make judgments and express opinions about the story. Always support your judgments with details from the story.

Learn About

IRONY

In Wheelock's poem about Earth exploding, he says, "Intelligent beings must have been living there." It seems like he is complimenting humans, but this is not so. He is really questioning how intelligent a species could be if it blows itself up.

When a writer means the opposite of what he or she actually says, the writer is using irony. **Irony** is a way to call attention to an idea by deliberately saying the opposite.

In literature, characters, settings, and plots can all have ironic features. The farmhouse setting in *Trifles* is in some ways ironic. Rural settings are usually considered peaceful. Farms are places for nurturing plant and animal life. The farmhouse setting in *Trifles* is instead a place of death.

As you read further ask yourself:
1. What is ironic about the king?
2. What is ironic about his justice?

WRITING CONNECTION

Irony is often used in jokes. What we expect to happen does not. Think of examples. Write them down. Then you and a partner create a short routine of ironic comedy to present to the class.

284 ■ Unit 3

Viewing Fine Art

This late 15th century Flemish tapestry shows King Melchisedech in ceremonial robes. Behind him is King Louis XII. With King Louis is the person who serves as both his barber and his surgeon. Ask: What details in the tapestry show how the king is regarded?

Cooperative Group Activity

To extend the Writing Connection activity, ask the class to think of a joke or epigram and analyze its humor. More often than not, the humor lies in irony. Example: It's so exhausting not to talk. Oscar Wilde, a famous wit and satirist, has turned the table with the word *not*; it's a reversal of the idea that listening is a bore.

THE LADY OR THE TIGER?

ADAPTED

by Frank R. Stockton

In the very olden time, there once lived a semi-barbaric king. His ideas, though somewhat polished and sharpened by the more civilized ways of distant neighbors, were still raw, savage and reckless, as became the half of him that was still barbaric. He was a man of wild imagination, and his word was law. Whenever he wished, his varied fancies became facts. He was greatly given to self-questioning, and when he and himself agreed upon anything, that thing was done. When everything in his kingdom moved smoothly, his manner was happy and genial; but whenever there was a little trouble, he was happier and more genial still. For nothing pleased him so much as to make the crooked straight, and crush down uneven places.

Among the borrowed ideas by which his barbarism had become softened was that of the public arena. In his arena, both men and beasts displayed their courage.

These displays, the king thought, uplifted the minds of his people.

But even here the wild imagination expressed itself. The arena of the king was not built to let his people watch men fight each other with sword and shield. It was not built to settle arguments between religious opinions and hungry jaws. No, its purpose was far better filled to uplifting the minds of the people. The huge arena, with its many rows of seats, its unseen passages, was a hall of justice. There crime was punished. There goodness was rewarded. There justice was decided by the completely fair and unprejudiced Law of Chance.

The system was simple. First a person had to be accused of a crime of enough importance to interest the king. Then public notice was given that on a certain day the accused man would appear in the king's arena. When the people of the city had gathered, the king entered.

---

semi- (SEM ih *or* SEM ee) prefix meaning half
barbaric (bahr BAR ik) wild and cruel; not yet civilized
fancies (FAN seez) notions or ideas, usually pleasant
genial (JEEN yul) pleasant; good-natured

The Lady or the Tiger? ■ 285

Literary Focus:
Irony

Point out to students the repetition of the words "fair," "perfect fairness," and "justice." Ask: How does this stress the irony of an obviously unjust situation?

Reading Focus:
Make Judgments

The plot of the story has not yet been defined but the reader can guess that the conflict will involve the Law of Chance in some way. Discuss with students whether the absence of any clearly defined characters or plot so far affects their opinions of the story.

Critical Thinking:
Infer

Clearly, under the Law of Chance innocent men could end up being devoured by the tiger. Ask: What can be inferred about some guilty men?

Surrounded by his family and servants, he sat on a throne high up on one side of the arena. Suddenly he gave a signal. A door far beneath him opened, and the accused person stepped out.

Right across from the man on trial were two doors, exactly alike and side by side. It was the duty and the privilege of the person on trial to walk straight to the doors and open one of them. He could open either door he pleased. He was given no help but that of the Law of Chance. If he opened the one, there came out of it a hungry tiger, the wildest and most cruel that could be found. The tiger immediately sprang upon him and tore him to pieces, as punishment for his guilt. The moment that the case of the criminal was so decided, doleful iron bells were rung. Great sighs went up, and the people left the arena with bowed heads and broken hearts. Why did one so young and handsome, or so old and well known, deserve so horrible an end?

But if the accused person opened the other door, there came out of it a lady, always well fitted to the man's age and place in life. In fact, she was always the most perfect wife that his majesty's servants could find among his fair subjects. And to this lady the man was immediately married, as a reward for his innocence. It mattered not that he might already have a wife and family, nor that he might be engaged to a woman of his own choice. The king allowed no such details to interfere with his grand ideas about punishment and reward. The wedding took place right away, and in the arena. Another door opened beneath the king, and a priest followed by dancing maidens and a group of singers, advanced to where the pair stood side by side. The wedding was short and joyful. Then the happy brass bells rang out, the people cheered and cheered, and the innocent man, following children throwing flowers in his path, led his bride to his home.

This was the king's semi-barbaric method of handing out justice. Its perfect fairness is clear. The criminal could not know out of which doorway would come the lady. He opened either door he pleased. He had not the slightest idea whether, in the next instant, he was to be devoured or married. Sometimes the tiger came out of one door, sometimes out of the other. The king's justice was not only fair, but also fast. The accused person was instantly punished if he found himself guilty. And if innocent, he was rewarded on the spot, whether he liked it or not. There was no escape from the judgments of the king's arena.

The system was a very popular one. The people never knew whether they were to witness a bloody slaughter or a joyous wedding. There was just no way they could know. This gave an interest to the event which it could not otherwise have had. Thus the masses were entertained and pleased. And even the thinking persons in the community could find no reason to say that the plan was unfair.

---

doleful (DOHL ful) sorrowful
fair (FAIR) nice looking
subject (SUB jehkt) person under authority of a king or government

286 ■ Unit 3

Tiger, Edward J. Detmold. The Metropolitan Museum of Art, The Elisha Whittelsey Collection

Edward J. Detmold (1883–1957) was an English painter and illustrator. A fine draftsman, Detmold managed in this picture to combine a realistically drawn tiger and feather with a complex, abstract pattern in the tiger's fur. This pattern is imitated by the delicately drawn feather with its "eye" and large white orb in the sky. Detmold's sophisticated design accents the tiger's ferocity by its placement on the diagonal, with its close up head apparently leaping into the picture from beyond the margin. Ask: What qualities that we associate with tigers are captured in this painting?

For did not the accused person have the whole matter in his own hands?

This semi-barbaric king had a daughter as blooming as his own lively imagination and with a soul as fiery and as proud as his own. As is usual in such cases, she was the apple of his eye, and was loved by him above all others. And her love? Well . . . among the king's servants was a handsome young man of that fineness of blood and lowness of station common to story-book heroes who love royal maidens.

This royal maiden was well satisfied with her lover. He was better looking and braver than anyone else in all the kingdom, and her love for him had enough of barbarism in it to make it very warm, and very, very strong. The love affair moved on happily for many months, until, one day, the king happened to learn of it. He did not waste an instant! He knew his duty in the matter at once. The youth was immediately put into prison, and a day was set for his trial in the king's arena.

This, of course, was an especially important happening in the kingdom. His majesty, as well as all the people, was greatly interested in the preparation for the trial. Never before had such a case occurred—never before had a subject dared to love the daughter of the king!

The tiger cages of the kingdom were searched for the most savage and relentless of beasts, from which the fiercest monster was to be chosen for the arena. And a search was also made among the ranks of maiden youth and beauty throughout the land. The young man was to have a fitting bride, if bride it was to be. Of course, everyone knew that the act of the accused man had, in fact, been done. He had loved the princess, and neither he, she, nor anyone in the kingdom thought of saying anything else. But the king would not think of letting any fact of this kind interfere with the tribunal, in which he took such great delight and satisfaction. No matter how it turned out, the youth's future would be decided. The king was especially interested in finding out whether the young man had done wrong in allowing himself to love the princess.

The day arrived. From far and near the people gathered, and they soon filled the great arena. Outside, more huge crowds, unable to get in, stood against the walls. The king was in his place, opposite the twin portals—so horrible in their likeness to each other!

All was ready. The signal was given. A door beneath the king opened, and the lover of the princess walked into the arena. Tall and handsome, he was greeted with a low hum of wonder and worry. Half the people had not known that such a youth had lived among them. No wonder the princess loved him! What a terrible thing for him to be there!

---

station (STAY shun) place in life
relentless (rih LENT lis) without pity; harsh and cruel
tribunal (try BYOO nul) court of justice
portals (PAWRT ulz) doors; entrances

288 ■ Unit 3

As the youth advanced into the arena, he stopped to turn, as the custom was, and bow to the king. But he did not think at all of that royal person. His eyes were fixed on the princess, who sat to the right of her father. Had it not been for the barbaric half of her soul, the lady probably would not have been there. But her strong spirit would not allow her to be absent from an event in which she was terribly interested. From the very moment of the king's order, she had thought of nothing else, night or day. She knew only that her lover's future was to be decided in the king's arena. Having more power and determination than anyone who had ever before been interested in such a case, she had done what no other person had done. She had learned the secret of the doors. She knew about the two little rooms across the arena from them. She knew in which stood the tiger, and in which waited the lady. Gold and power had brought that secret to the princess.

Not only did she know in which room stood the lady, ready to come out, all blushing and radiant, should her door be opened, but she also knew who the lady was. It was one of the most beautiful and lively maidens of the palace—and the princess hated her. Often she had seen, or imagined she had seen, things she didn't like. The lovely girl would throw glances of delight upon her lover, and sometimes, she thought, they had even been returned. Now and then she had seen them talking together. It was only for a moment or two,

but much can be said in a brief time. And what had they talked about? Something unimportant, probably. But how could she know that? The girl was lovely, but she had dared to raise her eyes to the loved one of the princess. With all the strength of the savage blood of her barbaric ancestors, the princess hated the woman who blushed and trembled behind that silent door.

And now, the man in the arena had turned to took at her. She sat there paler and whiter than anyone else in the sea of worried faces around her. His eye met hers. At once he saw, by that power of quick perception given only to those whose souls are one, that she knew! She knew behind which door waited the tiger, and behind which stood the lady. He had expected her to know it. He understood her perfectly. He knew that she would never rest until she had discovered this secret, hidden to all others, even to the king. The only sure hope for the youth was the success the princess had in solving this mystery, and the moment he looked upon her, he knew she had succeeded.

Then it was that his quick and anxious glance asked the question, "Which?" It was as plain to her as if he shouted it from where he stood. There was not an instant to be lost. The question was asked in a flash; it must be answered in another.

Her right arm lay on the cushioned wall before her. She raised her hand, and made a slight, quick movement to the right. No one but her lover saw it. Every eye but his was fixed on the man in the arena.

Critical Thinking:
Predict
"And now, the man in the arena had turned to look at her." This would be a good place to ask students what they think will happen. Ask: How would you predict the story's ending?

---

perception (pur SEP shun) awareness; understanding

The Lady or the Tiger? ■ 289

Literary Focus:
Narrative

This is where the story shifts gears. All of a sudden, the writer asks the reader to explore the situation with him, as though he doesn't know what will happen either. Ask: What is the effect of the shift in point of view, from the third person to the first person "we"?

Discussion

Ask students what they think the young maiden will decide to do and why.

He turned, and with a rapid step he walked across the empty space. Every heart stopped beating. Every breath was held. Every eye was fixed as if frozen upon that man. Without the slightest pause, he went to the door on the right, and opened it.

Now, the point of the story is this: Did the tiger come out of that door, or did the lady?

The more we reflect upon that question, the harder it is to answer. It involves a study of the human heart. It leads us into a wild jungle of love and hate, out of which it is difficult to find our way. Think of it, fair reader, not as a question that you yourself had to answer. No, the answer involves that hot-blooded, semi-barbaric princess. Think of her soul, at white heat in the combined fires of despair and jealousy. She had lost him, but who should have him?

How often, in her daylight hours and in her dreams, had she thought of her lover opening the door to find the cruel teeth of the tiger? How often had that thought made her tremble in horror and cover her face with her hands?

But how much oftener had she seen him at the other door! To think of his surprised delight as he opened the door of the lady! How her soul had burned! How she had torn her hair when she had seen him rush to meet that woman, with her flashing cheek and sparkling eye! When she had seen him lead her from the door! When she had heard the glad shouts from the crowd! When she had seen the priest, with his happy followers, advance to make them husband and wife! When she had seen them walk away upon their path of flowers, followed by the tremendous cheers of the people, in which her own shriek of despair was lost and drowned!

---

reflect (rih FLEKT) think

Would it not be better for him to die at once? Would it not be better to think of him waiting for her in some semi-barbaric heaven?

And yet, that awful tiger! Those shrieks! That blood!

The slight wave of her right hand had taken just an instant. But the motion had been made after days and nights of agonizing thought. She had known she would be asked, she had decided what she would answer, and without the slightest pause, she had moved her hand to the right.

The question of her decision is not one to be taken lightly, and it is not for me to set myself up as the one person who can answer it. So I leave it with all of you: Which came out of the opened door—the lady, or the tiger?

The Lady or the Tiger? ■ 291

Mini Quiz

Write on the chalkboard or overhead projector the following sentences and call on students to fill in the blanks. Discuss the answers with the class.

1. The story takes place in _____ .

2. The last person to enter the arena as a spectator was _____ .

3. The king thought his arena was _____ .

4. The princess learned _____ .

5. The question the young man asked of the princess with his eyes was _____ .

Answers

1. "the very olden time" (long ago)
2. the king
3. a hall of justice
4. the secret of the doors (what was behind the doors)
5. which door to choose

T291

UNDERSTAND THE SELECTION

Answers

1. The Law of Chance governed the proceedings.
2. The lady emerged, and the couple was married immediately.
3. the one on the right, as the princess had indicated
4. The king allowed the accused a choice which, to the king, was a very fair thing to do. The Law of Chance was the deciding factor.
5. The young man was of low station; also, the king was presumably jealous that anyone might take his daughter away from him.
6. No. He has made an informed choice based on the princess's inside information.
7. This is the question posed by the author at the end of the story. The reader must decide whether a lady or a tiger has been chosen.
8. No. The Law of Chance does not assure justice.
9. Sample answer: The tiger. The daughter can't bear to think of the young man with another woman.
10. It doesn't take into account whether the accused is guilty or innocent. Evidence is never looked at.

Respond to Literature

The king wins in both cases. He breaks up his daughter's relationship with the young man no matter who or what is behind the right door.

WRITE ABOUT THE SELECTION

Prewriting

Refer to discussion of Question 9 in Understand the Selection. Students could even debate informally which ending seems more appropriate. Points contradicting their view should be rebutted in their ending.

UNDERSTAND THE SELECTION

Recall

1. What law governed the proceedings in the arena?

2. What happened to a person who chose the door that revealed a lady?

3. Which door did the daughter's lover choose?

Infer

4. Explain how the king achieved justice.

5. Why did the king disapprove of the young man chosen by his daughter?

6. Is the Law of Chance being observed in the case of the daughter's lover?

7. Explain the significance of the title.

Apply

8. Is justice really being done in the king's "hall of justice"? Explain your answer.

9. Was the lady or the tiger behind the right door? Why do you think so?

10. What is a basic flaw with the king's system of justice?

> ### Respond to Literature
>
> Think about whether the king will achieve his goal in this story. What will happen if the open door reveals the tiger? What will happen if the open door reveals the lady?

WRITE ABOUT THE SELECTION

Which will it be: the lady or the tiger? Frank Stockton has given you a rather unusual opportunity. He has provided the setting, theme, and characters of a story, and most of the plot. He has left you hanging right before the climax. Now it is up to you to provide an ending.

Prewriting The last section of "The Lady or the Tiger?" has questions to help you decide what will be revealed behind the right door. Reread it. Then choose the lady or the tiger as the basis for an ending. Make an informal plot outline including what happens, as well as the reactions of the princess, the lover, the king, and the crowd.

Writing Use your informal outline to write a conclusion for the story. The length is up to you, but there must be resolution of the questions raised by the story. Imitate Frank Stockton's style as you write your narration.

Revising Reread parts of the story, and analyze what makes Frank Stockton's style distinctive. Revise or make additions to your conclusion to make your writing sound as though Stockton himself has written it. Use questions, as he does, for suspense.

Proofreading Reread your conclusion to check for errors. Pay close attention to end punctuation. Stockton uses many question marks and exclamation points, as well as periods. Make sure you know when to use each.

Writing

Circulate as students work individually. Help students to use their outline as they write.

Revising

As a class, reread a section of Stockton's story and analyze what makes the style distinctive. Ask students—perhaps working in groups—to look at specific points such as vocabulary, sentence length and construction, and use of figurative expressions. Have them report back to the class.

Proofreading

Review end punctuation rules with students. Illustrate your review with examples from Stockton's story.

THINK ABOUT IRONY

Answer the questions below about irony in "The Lady or the Tiger?".

1. What is ironic about this description of the king: ". . . his manner was happy and genial; but whenever there was a little trouble, he was happier and more genial still"?

2. Stockton says about the king's system of justice, "Its perfect fairness is clear." What is ironic about this?

3. "The king was especially interested in finding out whether the young man had done wrong in allowing himself to love the princess." Explain the irony in this statement.

4. "The king's justice was not only fair, but also fast." Given the way the story ends, what is ironic about this?

5. In some stories the reader knows something the characters do not. Is this true for "The Lady or the Tiger?"? Explain how this feature of the story is an example of irony.

READING FOCUS

Make Judgments As you read, you were able to make judgments about the characters, plot, setting, and theme of the story. Choose one of these story elements, and tell why you think it was especially interesting.

DEVELOP YOUR VOCABULARY

Prefixes and suffixes allow you to make additions to a root word to create new words with related meanings. Frank Stockton uses three related words from one base:

semi-barbaric   barbaric   barbarism

If you are familiar with the meaning of the base word and can identify and define the prefixes and suffixes, you can figure out the meaning of each of the following words.

Identify the bases and suffixes or prefixes of the following italicized words. Explain the meaning of the bases and the suffixes or prefixes. Use a dictionary as needed.

1. *Doleful* iron bells were rung.

2. The king was in his place, opposite the twin *portals*.

3. Gold and power had brought that secret to the *princess*.

4. The power of quick *perception* is only given to those whose souls are one.

5. Without the *slightest* pause, she moved her hand to the right.

Review the Selection ■ 293

THINK ABOUT IRONY

Answers

1. Usually people are unhappy when there's trouble, but not the king. It sets the ironic tone of the story, provides a description of the king, and is amusing.
2. It's not true. What Stockton really means is that the system is unfair.
3. The king's system of justice can in no way determine the morality of the young man's actions.
4. We never know what justice was meted out.
5. The princess knows something that we don't know and don't find out.

DEVELOP YOUR VOCABULARY

Answers

1. *doleful* = dole + ful. "Dole" means "sorrow"; "-ful" means "full of something." Hence, "full of sorrow."
2. *portal* = port + al. "Port" means "entrance"; "-al" means "like something." Hence, "like an entrance."
3. *princess* = prince + ess. A "prince" is a non-reigning male of a royal family; "-ess" is added to make the female form. Hence, "non-reigning female of a royal family."
4. *perception* = perceive + tion. "Perceive" is to recognize or realize; "-tion" means "the act" or "state of." Hence, "the act of recognizing."
5. *slightest* = slight + est. "Slight" means "small"; "-est" is used to form the superlative of an adjective or adverb. Hence, "smallest."

READING FOCUS

Sample Answer

The plot was basically interesting because the suspense of wondering what would happen when the young man opened the door held the reader's attention. The characters and setting were not very well developed, probably because the author was more concerned with emphasizing the plot. There was not real resolution at the end, which was a little disappointing.

ESL Activity

Have students work in small groups or pairs. Give each pair or group a list of root words. Tell them to see how many new words they can make by adding prefixes and/or suffixes. Have pairs or groups compare lists.

SELECTION OVERVIEW

SELECTION OBJECTIVES

After completing these selections, students will be able to

- understand connotation and denotation
- analyze shades of meaning
- discuss images created by connotation
- discover, through writing a poem, if point of view affects tone
- see how connotation works with other literary techniques
- explain connotations of specific words
- evaluate facts

Lesson Resources

Displays of Skill: The Bat/ The Bird of Night

- Selection Synopses, Teacher's Edition, p. T211e
- Comprehension and Vocabulary Workbook, pp. 55–56
- Language Enrichment Workbook, p. 56
- Teacher's Resources Reinforcement, p. R28 Test, pp. T53–T54

More About Word Meaning

Connotations are like prejudices: We make prejudgments about something, based on information that we've gathered haphazardly over the years. Understanding the connotations of words is not always easy. This is especially true for young readers who don't have the experience of years of reading behind them.

More About the Unit Theme

These two poems don't fit the mold of suspense forged by most of the other selections in this unit. Take the title away from "Displays of Skill: The Bat," though, and the poem is a jigsaw puzzle of pieces of information that would be hard to decipher as a description of a bat's habits. "The Bird of Night" is about an animal

READING FOCUS

Evaluate Facts Stories and poetry often contain factual information about their subjects. An author may use different sources to gather facts, depending upon the subject and purpose of the writing. As you read the two poems in this selection, look for facts. Think about how these facts enhance the poems.

WORD MEANING

When you look for a word in a dictionary you find a specific meaning. Words communicate feelings and attitudes as well as specific meanings. For example, you might describe something as *cheap*, meaning that it is low in price. However, some people have an attitude of contempt about things that are cheap. They look down upon them. Therefore, the word *cheap* also carries a feeling of being of lesser value.

The actual meaning of a word is called **denotation**. The feeling or attitude associated with a word is **connotation**.

Poets choose their words carefully. They use connotation as well as denotation to create tone and emotional impact.

Look for answers to the following questions as you read the poems:

1. What words suggest other meanings in addition to their literal definitions?
2. What feelings do you associate with each word you identified?

WRITING CONNECTION

Think of a word that provokes a strong feeling or attitude. Use a dictionary to find its specific meaning. Then write two sentences showing the denotation and connotation of the same word.

perceived as reserved and wise, the owl. Yet owls are predators, and an owl on the hunt is an animal whose principal asset is stealth.

Background Notes

What is it about flying creatures that might attract a poet? Herschberger might want to inform people about one of the more maligned members of the animal kingdom, the bat. Many people think bats are ugly and aggressive, but their flying abilities are a wonder to behold, and their appetite for insects surpasses that of any pesticide. Jarrell uses the owl to evoke a sense of mystery and pursuit. An introspective man, Jarrell might see the owl as a symbol of solitude.

Cooperative Group Activity

Use a theme approach for the Writing Connection activity. With students working in groups, give each group a theme (such as "cities" or "cars") and have them brainstorm specific words whose denotation and connotation differ. Students can then use these words in sentences and share them with the class.

Displays of Skill:
The Bat

by Ruth Herschberger

Being a mammal, I have less care than birds,
Being a flight-borne creature, need no home,
So while the beaver builds its dam, robin its nest,
I hook my hind feet into a wall or ceiling
5   And hang there looking at the world made silly
By being turned around and upside-down.
Sleep, sleep is my nourishment, I sleep
All day, all winter, and my young's but one.
At first I fly with it at my breast, even hunting,
10   But if it bores me I hang it on a wall
And go alone, enjoying insects frankly.
Tons, tons, I devour tons of insects, half
Of my weight is insects eaten within one night,
Yet cleverer than the swift or swallow, I deploy
15   Twist, turn, dodge, catch mosquitoes one by one.
And if the human family finds me odd,
No odder they, locked in their crazy yards.

---

mammal (MAM ul) a member of the highest class of vertebrate animals, including man
flight-borne (FLYT bawrn) able to fly
nourishment (NUR ish munt) food
swift (SWIFT) in this case, a bird of extreme speed in flight
deploy (dih PLOI) spread out systematically over an area

Displays of Skill: The Bat ■ 295

Develop Vocabulary Skills

Write the new vocabulary words on a chalkboard or transparency. Ask students if they know what the words mean. Write down any correct definitions; have students look up definitions for the words they don't know. After all the words have been defined on the board, ask students if the words mean exactly the same as in the poems. Ask: Are there slight differences in meaning that the stated definitions really don't explain?

Perhaps one of the most complex and interesting figures in art history, Francisco Goya (1746–1828) was simultaneously a brilliant court artist for the Spanish nobility and an incisive emotional critic of his times. Among his most extraordinary accomplishments were a series of etchings recording the brutalities of war and the inner torments of his people. Here, in one of his etchings, he comments on the typically 18th century struggle between reason and superstition; the reasonable man is shown sleeping. He dreams, nonetheless, of horrible animals and bats attacking him. Ask: How does the artist create an air of darkness and mystery in this picture?

Los Caprichos: El suena de la razon produce monstruos (The Sleep of Reason Produces Monsters), Francisco de Goya. National Gallery of Art, Washington, DC, Rosenwald Collection

The Bird of Night

by Randall Jarrell

A shadow is floating through the moonlight.
Its wings don't make a sound.
Its claws are long, its beak is bright.
Its eyes try all the corners of the night.

5   It calls and calls: all the air swells and heaves
And washes up and down like water.
The ear that listens to the owl believes
In death. The bat beneath the eaves,

The mouse beside the stone are still as death—
10   The owl's air washes them like water.
The owl goes back and forth inside the night,
And the night holds its breath.

---

swells (SWELZ) increases in size, volume, or force
heaves (HEEVZ) lifts up with effort
eaves (EEVZ) lower edges of a roof, especially that part sticking out over the walls of the building

The Bird of Night ■ 297

Critical Thinking:
Infer
In "The Bird of Night," the word *shadow* could mean a shadow of an owl or maybe an owl itself. Ask: Why does the author use the word *shadow*? Does this create a more mysterious image?

Literary Focus:
Word Meaning
Discuss how the words the author has chosen for this poem all seem to connote mystery and silence. Ask: What images used here are ones we might associate with night and death?

Reading Focus:
Evaluate Facts
Although this poem is clearly less dependent on facts than "Displays of Skill: The Bat," the author does display knowledge of owls and their habits. Discuss with students what factual information is included in this poem, such as the owl's hunting habits and prey.

Comparing Selections
Ask: Which of these two poems seems more "traditional" in form (or structure) to you? Why?

Mini Quiz

Write the following sentences on the chalkboard or overhead projector and call on students to fill in the blanks. Discuss the answers with the class.

1. The bat says that because it's a mammal it has less care than _____.

2. The world looks silly to the bat when _____.

3. Bats eat _____.

4. Owls eat _____.

5. The owl hunts at _____.

Answers
1. birds
2. it's hanging upside down
3. insects
4. bats and mice
5. night

UNDERSTAND THE SELECTION

Answers

1. A bat is a mammal.
2. She puts it hanging on a wall.
3. They fear death.
4. It's a "flight-borne" creature; when it needs rest, it hangs itself from a wall or ceiling.
5. It would fly quickly and erratically.
6. An owl flying is very quiet, with eyes roving from right to left in search of prey.
7. An owl preys on the bat and the mouse.
8. Answers will vary. Sample response: It isn't a bird, it eats a lot of insects, it carries its young on its breast.
9. It would eat about two ounces.
10. Because of their intent stare, they seem to be watching and thinking all the time.

Respond to Literature

Bats and owls are both creatures that hunt mainly at night, so they have come to be associated with the darkness and mystery of the night. They are also swift, silent hunters, which adds to their air of mystery and to the feeling of stillness, danger, and suspense.

WRITE ABOUT THE SELECTION

Prewriting

Remind students that writing in first person point of view means all information must come through you, the speaker. You must cause any action to happen. Point to "Displays of Skill: The Bat" to illustrate this.

Writing

Circulate as students work individually. Suggest specific reference books (for example, Peterson's *Field Guide to Birds*) for more information on owls.

Revising

Before having to consult a thesaurus, students might be able to help each other find words with appropriate connotations. Ask students for words for which they would like to find a more appropriate synonym and solicit suggestions from the class.

Proofreading

Review as a class the structure of "The Bird of Night." What is the rhyme pattern, where do lines break, and what punctuation is used?

UNDERSTAND THE SELECTION

Recall

1. What kind of an animal is a bat?
2. Where does a mother bat put her baby if she wants to go hunting alone?
3. What do animals listening to the owl believe or fear?

Infer

4. Why does the bat say it needs no home?
5. Describe what a bat hunting mosquitoes looks like.
6. Describe an owl flying.
7. What are some of the animals an owl preys upon?

Apply

8. "Displays of Skill: The Bat" contains a lot of information about this much-despised animal. What new things did you learn about bats?
9. If a bat weighs about 4 ounces, how many ounces of insects would it eat in one night?
10. Why do you think owls are thought to be wise?

Respond to Literature

In what ways do bats and owls help create suspense? Give examples.

WRITE ABOUT THE SELECTION

"Displays of Skill: The Bat" is written in a first-person point of view, but "The Bird of Night" is written in a third-person point of view.

The tone of each poem is very different. Could that be because of the different point of view in which each is written?

See if you can find out by writing in the first person about owls. Plan to write poetry. You may either adapt "The Bird of Night" to a poem written in the first person, or you may write a new poem.

Prewriting Decide if you will adapt Jarrell's poem or write your own. If you are adapting, circle all the words in Jarrell's poem you will have to change. If you are writing your own poem, make a cluster of words about the owl that you may want to use.

Writing Use either the circled poem or your cluster to write a first-person poem on owls. Remember that information must be presented from the owl's point of view. You may want to consult a reference book to learn more about the owl's habitat.

Revising When you revise your poem, think about adding words with connotations that fit the meaning and feeling you want. Use a thesaurus as needed.

Proofreading Reread your poem to check for errors. Decide where to break lines, where to indent, and whether you want to use end-of-line punctuation. Mark your copy accordingly.

ESL Activity

Have students brainstorm in small groups what they learned about how a bat lives. They should take notes on what they learned and discuss any misconceptions they may have had about bats.

THINK ABOUT WORD MEANING

Poets rely on connotations of words when they use figurative language in their poems. Below are examples from the previous poems.

1. In "The Bird of Night," a simile is used in the second stanza. What is being compared to water? How is the word *swells* connected to water? What feeling or image does the word *swells* connote?

2. What other words in the poem also have a connection to or a connotation involving water?

3. Another simile is used to describe the bat and mouse as the owl floats through the night. What is it?

4. Hyperbole is used in "Displays of Skill: The Bat." Where? What feelings or connotations are associated with this exaggeration?

5. What word fits particularly well with the hyperbole?

6. List five other words with connotations that add to both poems' effectiveness.

> ### *READING FOCUS*
>
> **Evaluate Facts** What facts did the author of "Displays of Skill: The Bat" include in her poem? What facts did the author of "The Bird of Night" use? How do these facts enhance the poems?

DEVELOP YOUR VOCABULARY

Knowing the connotation of a certain word requires that you know the denotations of the word as well.

Examine the word *swells*, for example, from "The Bird of Night." Why did the poet use *swells* instead of *expands*? They both mean "to increase in size."

Swell is often used to describe waves at sea. The connotation of *swell* is appropriate for comparing air to water.

Below are other words used in the two poems. Each is paired with a synonym the way *swells* was paired with *expands*. Decide why the poet chose to use the word he did. Write the denotation for each. Then identify the connotation of each word. Be ready to explain why the connotation is appropriate for the poem in which the word is used.

1. floating/flying
2. bright/colorful
3. heaves/moves
4. hook/attach
5. devour/eat
6. deploy/move

Review the Selection ■ 299

---

3. They are "still as death."
4. "Tons, Tons, I devour tons of insects." One connotation that might be associated with devouring is the negative connotation of violence or the aggressive consuming of something.
5. "Devours"
6. Answers will vary. Sample response: *shadow, deploy, dodge, locked, still*

DEVELOP YOUR VOCABULARY

Answers

1. *float*: to be suspended in air or water
   fly: to move through the air, as though suspended
   "Float" connotes movement through both air and water, which fits with the simile of the air like water.
2. *bright*: giving off or reflecting much light
   colorful: having many colors
   "Bright" connotes contrast between light and dark, not just a different color.
3. *heaves*: to rise and fall rhythmically
   moves: to change position
   "Heaves" and "moves" both connote movement or activity.
4. *hook*: to seize or make fast with a hook
   attach: to connect
   "Hook" connotes a much stronger connection than "attach" and is more appropriate to the way a bat fits its claws around an object.
5. *devour*: to eat greedily and completely
   eat: to consume food
   "Devour" connotes hunger and the ability to eat a lot, which is appropriate for an animal that eats half its weight in one night.
6. *deploy*: spread out
   move: change position
   "Deploy" connotes an orderly, systematic approach which would be appropriate for an animal that needs to eat half its weight in insects each night.

READING FOCUS

Sample Answer

"Displays of Skill: The Bat" included information about where bats live, how they sleep and care for their young, what they eat, and how and when they hunt. "The Birds of Night" described the claws, beak, and eyes of an owl. It also said when the owl flies, how quiet the wings are, and what is the owl's prey. The facts about bats and owls help to create the tone in each poem—for example, the bat hangs upside-down "looking at the world made silly," and the owl's "wings don't make a sound."

THINK ABOUT WORD MEANING

Answers

1. The air the owl moves about is like water. Both ocean waves and rivers swell. A sense of grandness and washing over
2. Water words: "floating," "heaves," " washes"

SELECTION OVERVIEW

SELECTION OBJECTIVES

After completing this selection, students will be able to

- understand plot
- write a plot summary
- describe advantages of using foreign settings
- write a eulogy
- analyze character, setting, and theme in relation to plot
- use context clues to understand foreign words and expressions
- make inferences

Lesson Resources

A Secret for Two
- Selection Synopsis, Teacher's Edition, pp. T211e–T211f
- Comprehension and Vocabulary Workbook, pp. 57–58
- Language Enrichment Workbook, pp. 57–58
- Teacher's Resources Reinforcement, p. R29 Test, pp. T55–T56

More About Plot

"Plot" as a verb means "to chart a course." A pilot or a ship captain plots his or her course before starting off on a journey. In the same way, a writer plots the course of a story. A writer might start with the theme of the story, think of the characters, and establish setting before working out the plot itself. The plot, though, is usually what weaves the elements of a story together. The action of the plot enables development of characters, setting, and theme.

More About the Unit Theme

Attachments between people, or between people and their pets, are often puzzles. Others can't understand what they see in each other. Mystery seems to surround the bond between them: the chance to penetrate the mystery provides suspense.

T300

READING FOCUS

Make Inferences An author does not always directly state information about characters, setting, or plot. Usually, the author is more indirect, using dialogue and descriptive detail to give information. It is up to the reader to infer or guess about characters and events in the story. As you read, try to make inferences about the plot and characters using clues from the story.

Learn About

PLOT

The most important element of many stories, dramas included, is **plot**. Such stories depend upon action for their developments. Characters and settings are important, and so are the themes, but the energy of the plot moves the story forward.

You should be familiar with the basic pattern of plots. First, there is **exposition**, or background information. Then a **complication** develops, raising a question or several questions that must be answered during the remainder of the story. The **action rises**, and the **climax** is reached. The **action falls**, and any questions not answered in the climax are answered in the **resolution**.

As you read the selection, ask yourself these questions:

1. What are the main complications or questions in the plot?
2. How is each complication resolved or question answered?

WRITING CONNECTION

In a few sentences explain the plot of any story you have read in this unit. Describe the major points of the plot, identifying necessary background information, all important complications, the climax, and the resolution.

Background Notes

Montreal—named for Mont-Royal, a 763-foot hill that rises above the city—is the second most populous city in Canada. It maintains the air of a European city with many distinctive neighborhoods. It was originally an Indian settlement called "Hochelaga," but the French took it over. The British gained possession of it and all of Canada during the French and Indian War (1754–1763). Montreal's location on the St. Lawrence River has assured it an economic importance that has made it the cultural center of the country. Although it was once the political capital of Canada, Ottawa, 130 miles to the west, is Canada's seat of government. Montreal is about 400 miles north of New York City.

Cooperative Group Activity

To extend the Writing Connection activity, choose the plot of a story from this unit or a previous unit to describe as a class. Write the story title on a chalkboard or transparency and list the major points of the plot. Turn the points into sentences to produce a plot summary.

A SECRET FOR TWO

ADAPTED   *by Quentin Reynolds*

Montreal is a very large city. But, like all large cities, it has some very small streets. Streets, for instance, like Prince Edward Street, which is only four blocks long. No one knew Prince Edward Street as well as did Pierre Dupin. For Pierre had delivered milk to the families on the street for thirty years now.

During the past fifteen years, the horse that drew the milk wagon used by Pierre was a large white horse named Joseph. In Montreal, especially in that part of Montreal that is very French, the animals, like children, are often given the names of saints. When the big white horse first came to the Provincale Milk Company, he didn't have a name. They told Pierre that he could use the white horse. Pierre stroked the softness of the horse's neck. He stroked the sheen of its splendid belly, and he looked into the eyes of the horse.

"This is a kind horse, a gentle and faithful horse," Pierre said. "I can see a beautiful spirit shining out of the eyes of the horse. I will name him after good St. Joseph, who was also kind and gentle and faithful and a beautiful spirit."

Within a year, Joseph knew the milk route as well as Pierre. Pierre used to boast that he didn't need reins—he never touched them. Each morning Pierre arrived at the stables of the Provincale Milk Company at five o'clock. The wagon would be loaded and Joseph hitched to it. Pierre would call, *"Bonjour, vieil ami,"* as he climbed into his seat. Joseph would turn his head, and the other drivers would smile and say that the horse would smile at Pierre. Then Jacques, the foreman, would say, "All right, Pierre, go on."

Montreal (mon tree AWL) city in eastern Canada that has French as its official language
sheen (SHEEN) brightness; shininess

TEACHING PLAN

INTRODUCE

Motivation
Deliverymen were once common fixtures in American cities and towns, but they are fast disappearing. Do you have any personal anecdotes concerning deliverymen that you can tell the class? If not, ask older teachers or local residents. Talk with students about the various roles of the deliveryman (food seller, bearer of gossip, dispenser of treats to children) and how shopping patterns have changed.

Purpose-Setting Question
Can a person become dependent on an animal?

READ

Literary Focus:
Plot
As students read, have them identify the events that define the pattern of the plot. Discuss the fact that these events may not always be directly stated; they may be inferred. Also, discuss plot resolution and whether the complication in this story is resolved satisfactorily.

Reading Focus:
Make Inferences
The author of "A Secret for Two" conveys information about Pierre and Joseph in subtle ways. We learn about their relationship through descriptions of their routine and their behavior towards one another. Even the complications in the plot are inferred rather than stated. Have students pay careful attention to Pierre's behavior in order to understand the problem he faces.

CLOSE

Have students complete Review the Selection on pages 306–307.

Develop Vocabulary Skills
Write the new vocabulary words on a chalkboard or transparency. Read the definitions to students, and ask them to choose what they think is the correct word. Erase the definitions when the matching has been completed, and ask the students to give definitions for the words.

ESL Activity

Pierre and Jacques are French names. Ask students to relate common names in their countries. Ask whether the names mean something special in their languages. Chart the different countries, names, and special meanings, if any.

T301

Pierre would call softly to Joseph, *"Avance, mon ami."* And this splendid combination would stalk proudly down the street.

The wagon, without any direction from Pierre, would roll three blocks down St. Catherine Street, then turn right two blocks along Roslyn Avenue; then left, for that was Prince Edward Street. The horse would stop at the first house, allow Pierre perhaps

---

stalk (STAWK) walk in a stiff, proud way

302 ■ **Unit 3**

Discussion

Ask: How well does the author convey the relationship between Pierre and his horse? Tell why you think as you do.

thirty seconds to get down from his seat and put a bottle of milk at the front door, and would then go on, skipping two houses and stopping at the third. So down the length of the street. Then Joseph, still without any direction from Pierre, would turn around and come back along the other side. Yes, Joseph was a smart horse.

Pierre would boast, at the stable, of Joseph's skill. "I never touch the reins. He knows just where to stop. Why, a blind man could handle my route with Joseph pulling the wagon."

So it went on for years—always the same. Pierre and Joseph both grew old together, but gradually, not suddenly. Pierre's huge walrus mustache was pure white now. Joseph didn't lift his knees so high, or raise his head quite as much. Jacques, the foreman of the stables, never noticed that they were both getting old until Pierre appeared one morning carrying a heavy walking stick.

"Hey, Pierre," Jacques laughed. "Maybe you got the gout, hey?"

"*Mais oui, Jacques,*" Pierre said a bit uncertainly. "One grows old. One's legs get tired."

"You should teach that horse to carry the milk to the front door for you," Jacques told him. "He does everything else."

He knew every one of the forty families he served on Prince Edward Street. The cooks knew that Pierre could neither read nor write. So instead of following the usual custom of leaving a note in an empty bottle if an additional quart of milk was needed, they would sing out when they heard the rumble of his wagon wheels over the cobbled street, "Bring an extra quart this morning, Pierre."

"So you have company for dinner tonight," he would call back gaily.

Pierre had a remarkable memory. When he arrived at the stable, he'd always remember to tell Jacques, "The Paquins took an extra quart this morning. The Lemoines bought a pint of cream."

Jacques would note these things in a little book he always carried. Most of the drivers had to make out the weekly bills and

---

gout (GOUT) painful disease of the joints, usually of the feet and the hands
cobbled (KOB uld) paved with stones, usually referring to a street (when used as an adjective)

A Secret for Two ■ 303

Literary Focus:
Plot
The change from exposition to the development of a complication is subtle. Ask: Does it seem that Joseph and Pierre will continue to work happily together forever?

Critical Thinking:
Infer
Pierre boasts about Joseph's ability to know just where to go and when to stop along the route. Ask: Why do you think this fact is particularly important to Pierre as he ages? What might it infer about his future?

Reading Focus:
Make Inferences
Important details about Pierre are sprinkled throughout the story. Remind students that this story is a puzzle and they should be on the lookout for important information. Ask: What details have you noticed so far? What do they lead you to believe about the outcome?

Reading Focus:
Make Inferences

"You know I think those two share a secret." This comment must be important. The title of the story derives from it. Ask: What secret might Pierre and Joseph share? What can you infer from the clues you have been gathering?

collect the money. But Jacques, liking Pierre, had always excused him from this task. All Pierre had to do was to arrive at five in the morning, walk to his wagon, which was always in the same spot at the curb, and deliver his milk. He returned some two hours later, got down stiffly from his seat, called a cheery "*Au'voir*" to Jacques, and then limped slowly down the street.

One morning the president of the Provincale Milk Company came to inspect the early morning deliveries. Jacques pointed Pierre out to him and said, "Watch how he talks to that horse. See how the horse listens and how he turns his head toward Pierre? See the look in that horse's eyes? You know, I think those two share a secret. I have often noticed it. It is as though they both sometimes chuckle at us as they go off on their route. Pierre is a good man, Monsieur Président, but he gets old. Would it be too bold of me to suggest that he be retired and be given perhaps a small pension?" he added anxiously.

"But of course," the president laughed. "I know his record. He has been on this route now for thirty years and never once has there been a complaint. Tell him it is time he rested. His salary will go on just the same."

But Pierre refused to retire. He was panic-stricken at the thought of not driving Joseph every day. "We are two old men," he said to Jacques. "Let us wear out together. When Joseph is ready to retire—then I, too, will quit."

Jacques, who was a kind man, understood. There was something about Pierre and Joseph that made a man smile tenderly. It was as though each drew some hidden strength from the other. When Pierre was sitting in his seat, and when Joseph was hitched to the wagon, neither seemed old. But when they finished their work, then Pierre would limp down the street slowly, seeming very old indeed. The horse's head would drop, and he would walk very wearily to his stall.

Then one morning Jacques had dreadful news for Pierre when he arrived. It was a cold morning and still pitch-dark. The air was iced that morning. And the snow that had fallen during the night glistened like a million diamonds piled together.

Monsieur (muh SYUR) French for Mister
pension (PEN shun) retirement pay

Literary Focus:
Plot

Call attention to how the action of the plot continues to rise when Jacques tells Pierre the "dreadful news." Ask: What feeling does this give the reader?

Jacques said, "Pierre, your horse, Joseph, did not wake up this morning. He was very old, Pierre. He was twenty-five, and that is like being seventy-five for a man."

"Yes," Pierre said, slowly. "Yes. I am seventy-five. And I cannot see Joseph again."

"Of course you can," Jacques soothed. "He is over in his stall, looking very peaceful. Go over and see him."

Pierre took one step forward, then turned. "No . . . no . . . you don't understand, Jacques."

Jacques clapped him on the shoulder. "We'll find another horse just as good as Joseph. Why, in a month you'll teach him to know your route as well as Joseph did. We'll . . ."

The look in Pierre's eyes stopped him. For years Pierre had worn a heavy cap. The peak came low over his eyes, keeping the bitter morning wind out of them. Now Jacques looked into Pierre's eyes, and saw something that startled him. He saw a dead, lifeless look in them. The eyes were mirroring the grief that was in Pierre's heart and his soul. It was as though his heart and soul had died.

"Take today off, Pierre," Jacques said. But already Pierre was hobbling off down the street; and had one been near, one would have seen tears streaming down his cheeks and have heard half-smothered sobs. There was a warning yell from the driver of a huge truck that was coming fast. There was the scream of brakes. But Pierre apparently heard neither.

Five minutes later an ambulance driver said, "He's dead. Was killed instantly."

"I couldn't help it," the driver of the truck protested. "He walked right into my truck. He never saw it, I guess. Why, he walked into it as though he were blind."

The ambulance doctor bent down. "Blind? Of course the man was blind. See those cataracts? This man has been blind for five years." He turned to Jacques. "You say he worked for you? Didn't you know he was blind?"

"No . . . no . . . " Jacques said softly. "None of us knew. Only one knew—a friend of his named Joseph. . . . It was a secret, I think, just between those two."

---

peak (PEEK) front part of a cap
cataract (KAT uh rakt) clouding of the eye's lens that can cause blindness

A Secret for Two ■ 305

Reading Focus:
Make Inferences
Explain that an important clue to the secret between Pierre and Joseph appears when Pierre says he can't see Joseph again. Ask: What might he mean by this?

Critical Thinking:
Analyze
Jacques deduces that the dead, lifeless look in Pierre's eyes is caused by grief. Ask: Is his deduction sound?

Literary Focus:
Plot
The climax of the story occurs when Pierre is killed. Ask: What secret does the reader learn in the last two paragraphs?

Discussion
Ask: What details of the story make sense now that the reader knows Pierre was blind? Ask students to think back and piece the puzzle together.

Mini Quiz

Write the following sentences on the chalkboard or overhead projector and call on students to fill in the blanks. Discuss the answers with the class.

1. Pierre's milk route was along _____ Street.

2. Pierre's horse was named for _____ .

3. The president of the milk company offered Pierre a _____, but he refused it.

4. The season during which Joseph died was _____.

5. _____ caused Pierre's blindness.

Answers
1. Prince Edward
2. St. Joseph
3. pension
4. winter
5. Cataracts

UNDERSTAND THE SELECTION

Answers

1. It is set in Montreal, Canada.
2. They sing out when they hear his wagon coming.
3. He worked there for 30 years.
4. He is able to look at Joseph and "see a beautiful spirit shining out of the eyes of the horse."
5. Jacques doesn't make Pierre write out weekly bills. Also, Jacques asks the company president for a pension for Pierre.
6. Pierre says that "a blind man could handle my route with Joseph pulling the wagon." Later, Jacques tells the milk company president, "You know, I think those two share a secret." Even the title—"A Secret for Two"—is foreshadowing.
7. He understands the bond that Pierre and Joseph had.
8. Probably so; he seemed to enjoy his work. He stayed with it without complaining.
9. Answers will vary. Sample: It's possible but highly unlikely in this day and age. We depend on eyesight for too many things.
10. This story gives you a subtle feeling of suspense; it really doesn't hit until the end. Determining the nature of the relationship between Pierre and Joseph is the mystery of the story and that creates suspense.

Respond to Literature

Students should see that romance associated with anything foreign presents an opportunity that a good writer can explore in depth.

WRITE ABOUT THE SELECTION

Prewriting

Have the class work cooperatively to collect sample epitaphs. Ask students to visit a cemetery and copy some from headstones or do research in the library. Point out that some epitaphs are autobiographical; that is, the person wrote his or her own epitaph before he/she died.

Writing

Circulate as students work individually. Check their epitaphs to see if enough information is provided to make a brief outline for the eulogy.

Revising

Reread sections of the story as a class. Students themselves might be able to suggest what sections are appropriate.

Proofreading

Review with the class subject-verb agreement rules. Mention particularly troublesome situations, such as when "neither" is used.

UNDERSTAND THE SELECTION

Recall

1. In what city is "A Secret for Two" set?
2. How do Pierre's customers order extra milk?
3. How long had Pierre worked for the Provincale Milk Company?

Infer

4. How do you know that Pierre is not blind at the beginning of the story?
5. Give an example showing that Pierre has a good relationship with his boss.
6. Find an example of foreshadowing.
7. What was Jacques's reaction when he learned that Pierre had been blind for five years?

Apply

8. Do you think Pierre was happy with his life? Why or why not?
9. Do you think it is possible for someone to be blind without others knowing about it?
10. This unit has as its theme "suspense." Is "A Secret for Two" a suspense story? Explain your answer.

Respond to Literature

Why do foreign cities make especially good settings for stories?

WRITE ABOUT THE SELECTION

A **eulogy** is a speech or piece of writing praising someone who has died. What might be said to eulogize Pierre Dupin? On the surface, he was a simple man. He could not read or write. However, inside, he must have been patient, strong, and trusting, as well as dedicated.

Imagine you are speaking at Pierre Dupin's funeral delivering the eulogy.

Prewriting   Start by thinking of an epitaph you could write for Pierre's tombstone. (An epitaph is an inscription on a headstone in memory of the person buried there.) The epitaph will serve as an outline for writing a longer, more complete eulogy. List qualities that you admire which were exhibited by Pierre Dupin in the story.

Writing   Write the eulogy based on the epitaph you wrote and the list of qualities you compiled. Expand on any ideas you have mentioned, and add new ones.

Revising   As you revise the eulogy, think back on the information about Pierre given in the story. Are there any traits or characteristics you have neglected to mention? Add them. Make sure you have provided examples from the story for each of the traits mentioned.

Proofreading   Reread your eulogy and check for errors. Make sure that all verbs agree with their subjects. Check to see that verb tenses are consistent. If you begin speaking of Pierre in past tense, make sure all verbs are past tense.

THINK ABOUT PLOT

The **plot**, or the action of a story, is based on conflicting human motivations and responses. To develop a plot successfully, the sequence of events must include human motivations. For instance, some motivations in "The Lady or the Tiger?" are jealousy, protectiveness, and love. In the story "A Secret for Two," human motivations are a major element of the plot. However, other literary elements also affect the plot.

1. The plot of this story requires a certain kind of character. What kind of person is Pierre? What does he value? What motivates his behavior?

2. The plot also requires a certain kind of setting. What characteristics of the neighborhood in Montreal where Pierre works are important to the plot?

3. What complications develop in the story?

4. What is the climax of the story?

5. How does Pierre's boss, Jacques, affect the plot of "A Secret for Two"?

6. What is the conflict in the story? How does this conflict affect the plot?

READING FOCUS

Make Inferences As you read, you were able to make inferences about the characters and plot in the story. What clues allowed you to infer that Pierre was losing his sight?

DEVELOP YOUR VOCABULARY

Using context clues can sometimes help in understanding the meaning of foreign words and expressions. Follow these steps to use context clues:

a. Reread the sentence in which the foreign word or phrase appears; also reread the sentences before and after.

b. Substitute words that you think are similar to the English words.

c. If the English words make sense, your choice of meaning is probably accurate.

Use context clues to discover the meaning of the French phrases from "A Secret for Two." Copy the sentences substituting an English meaning for each French phrase.

1. Pierre would call, "*Bonjour, vieil ami,*" as he climbed into his seat.

2. Pierre would call softly to Joseph, "*Avance, mon ami.*"

3. "*Mais oui, Jacques,*" Pierre said a bit uncertainly.

4. He returned some two hours later, got down stiffly from his seat, and called a cheery "*Au'voir*" to Jacques.

5. Pierre is a good man, *Monsieur* President, but he gets old.

Review the Selection ■ 307

WRITING APPLICATIONS

Write About Theme

Divide the class into groups. Ask the students in each group to choose a section from one of the stories they've read that they think would make an interesting "playlet." Only dialogue can be used, so they might have to adapt the section. Ask the groups to perform their playlets.

Prewriting: Remind students of any selections not represented in the "playlets" and review the characters and plot.

 Writer's Toolkit CD-ROM
Encourage students to use the Chain of Events (Writing Tools, organizing details) to complete the Prewriting activity.

Writing: Work with students to make sure they each have a list of characters and that they have mapped a plot. Remind them they can change scenes if they want different settings.

Revising: Have students work in pairs. The writer reads his or her drama aloud, while the partner listens. After the reading, the listener "critiques" the drama, paying particular attention to plot development.

Proofreading: Have students choose new partners to read the drama, checking for errors and providing general feedback.

WRITING APPLICATIONS

Write About Theme

In this unit, you have been introduced to some interesting characters who have been involved in some exciting situations. Two stories were dramas, so you have studied the elements of drama. Why not put your knowledge of drama to work?

Write an original play, using any of the characters from any of the selections in this unit. Make the play suspenseful. After all, suspense is what these characters are accustomed to!

Prewriting Choose the characters you would like to use in your play. List them. Then think of a plot. Map the plot, with each major development in a box. Write some ideas on the map about how the dialogue or the stage directions will advance the plot.

Writing Use the plot map, your list of characters, and your notes about the dialogue and stage directions to write the play.

Revising Make sure you have paced the action of the play. Review the steps in plot development, and check to see that you have followed them.

Proofreading Reread your play to check for errors. Make any changes you feel are necessary.

Write About Genre

The elements of drama are the same as those for all stories, with added emphasis on the conflict. Conflicts in dramas are usually between human characters. The conflict is caused by a clash between their personalities, traits, or beliefs. How the characters struggle with one another is a very important part of the drama.

Take a closer look at the conflict in one of the dramas you have read.

Prewriting Review the work you did for the "Thinking About" sections. Then choose the drama that most interests you. Make a chart, listing the conflict and the characters involved. Under each character's name, write all of the traits important to the conflict.

Writing Use the chart to write a description of the conflict. Then analyze the role of the conflict in the drama. How does it relate to other elements, particularly theme?

Revising When you are revising, think of ways to use material from the drama itself to illustrate what you are saying. For example, can you quote something a character says to illustrate a point?

Proofreading Reread what you have written as a check for errors. Try to vary the structure of sentences. If too many sentences are constructed in the same way, the reader could become bored.

Write About Genre

Remind the students that in the last unit the elements of a short story were shown as points on a compass. Draw the four-pointed compass again with plot, characters, setting, and theme labeled. Add a fifth line and label it "conflict." Ask: In what genre of literature is conflict the central element?

Prewriting: Have students work in pairs to discuss dramas they've read and the conflicts in each.

Writing: Circulate among students as they work individually. Check the charts they've made for accuracy and completeness.

Revising: Students might reread portions of the dramas together in order to find material.

Proofreading: Ask students to analyze the structure of their sentences. Is a similar pattern used in many of them? Show how sentences can be rewritten to vary structure.

 Writer's Toolkit CD-ROM
Encourage students to use the Sentence Openers Variety Checker (Writing Tools, revising/editing) to complete the Proofreading activity.

Vocabulary

Characters are developed through description. The words the author chooses for the description are important. Pay attention not only to the **denotations**, or "dictionary definitions," of the words, but also to their **connotations**, or "emotional meanings."

Many words used to describe people have negative or positive connotations. These connotations help the reader form an impression of the character.

Below are some words used in the selections in this unit to describe characters. Make a "+" after positive words, and a "−" after negative words. Then use each in a sentence.

1. kind
2. gentle
3. faithful
4. smart
5. reckless
6. raw
7. wildly imaginative
8. genial
9. fiery
10. proud
11. brave
12. cunning
13. clever
14. rude

Grammar, Usage, and Mechanics

Verbs must agree with their subjects. If the subject is singular, the verb must be singular. If the subject is plural, the verb must be plural. Make sure you match the verb correctly with the subject.

In the sentences below, what is the correct form of the verbs in parentheses? Write the verb, and tell whether it is singular or plural.

1. This old boy behind the counter was the kind that (mean) well.

2. Both of the feed-merchant types (were) paying close attention.

3. It (lead) us into a wild jungle of love and hate.

4. (Do) the tiger come out of the door, or (do) the lady?

5. There (was) only Ross and Will opening the lunch basket.

Unit Review ■ 309

Grammar, Usage, and Mechanics

Answers
1. means; singular
2. were; plural
3. leads; singular
4. does, does; singular
5. were; plural

The key to solving subject-verb agreement is finding the subject. Encourage students to underline the subject of each sentence before they determine verb number.

Cooperative Group Activity

Divide the class into two teams. Give the teams 20 minutes to come up with 20 sentences testing subject-verb agreement. Verbs should be in present tense. Gather their sentences and have the two teams sit on opposite sides of the room. Read one of Team A's sentences to Team B, leaving out the verb; supply the infinitive form at the end. Correct responses receive 1 point. The team with the highest point total wins.

 BUILD LANGUAGE SKILLS

Vocabulary

Answers
1. kind +
2. gentle +
3. faithful +
4. smart +
5. reckless −
6. raw −
7. wildly imaginative +
8. genial +
9. fiery − or +
10. proud +
11. brave +
12. cunning −
13. clever − or +
14. rude −

Sample Sentences:
1. My grandmother is very kind.
2. The horse was gentle.
3. The mail carrier was faithful.
4. My smart brother gets good grades.
5. To act reckless is to ask for trouble.
6. The wind was raw and cold.
7. The girl was wildly imaginative.
8. Our genial host invited us to be seated.
9. His fiery temper often caused him difficulty.
10. Father said he was proud of my accomplishments.
11. The brave soldier won a medal.
12. The criminal was cunning.
13. The clever student figured out the puzzle.
14. Rude remarks are never appreciated.

T309

SPEAKING AND LISTENING

A theme is the meaning or message of a piece of literature. Some stories and poems have more than one theme, and others have a theme of only minor importance.

Sometimes plot and theme are confused. A plot is the "what happens" in a poem or story. For example, the plot of a story might concern a young soldier during his first battle. The events of the plot might include the man's thoughts, the battle itself, and the outcome of the battle. However, the theme of the story might be the idea that fighting solves nothing.

Understanding the plot and theme of a story is sometimes easier if you share your ideas with classmates and talk about how the events of a story help illustrate the theme.

Before you begin a discussion of the plot and theme of a selection in this unit, consider the following:

1. Read the selection carefully. Try to identify the author's message. Since a story or play can contain more than one idea, it is possible to have several themes. Be aware that although there may be several, only one is the main theme.

2. Think about the events in the story. As you become familiar with what happens, you will be able to see how these events point toward a theme.

3. Study the characters until you know them well. Notice how personality traits or important characteristics they have make a statement about their outlooks on life.

4. Consider the different points of view of the characters. Decide whether others share their outlooks. Think about general ideas the different characters might represent.

5. Remember that an author may or may not state his theme somewhere in the story. He or she may merely suggest a theme through the events of the plot and the attitudes of the characters. If this is the case in the selection you choose to discuss, be sure to examine the events in the plot, the dialogue of the characters, and the setting for clues to the theme of the story.

Now, as a class or in small groups, choose a poem, play, or story from this unit that you believe has a strong theme: one that seems to be written to get a certain idea across to the reader. First, discuss what you believe the main theme to be. Then talk about how the events and characters in the selection illustrate the theme. Discuss elements of the setting that contribute to the theme. Keep the steps and suggestions above in mind as you and your classmates discuss the selection.

310 ■ Unit 3

Career Connection

Many stories in this unit involve police officers and detectives. Students might like to know about the law enforcement field. Police officers are required to have a high school education, and many departments prefer college graduates. Police officers are often in dangerous situations. A concern for people is necessary, as well as a sense of fairness and justice. Most departments offer on-the-job training. Police officers who show a special interest and skill in investigating and solving crimes can be assigned to a department's investigation unit.

CRITICAL THINKING

Deductions   Sherlock Holmes's detecting skills are based on deduction. "You must have seen more in those rooms than I did," states Watson in "Sherlock Holmes and the Speckled Band." The master detective replies, "I didn't see more. I *deduced* more. I imagine you saw everything I did."

Actually, Holmes's first deductions about who killed Julia Stoner were wrong. He had reached an unsound conclusion. Why? Holmes himself explains: It is dangerous "to reason without having *all* the facts."

There are three parts to deductive reasoning. They are called a **syllogism**: a major premise, a minor premise, and a conclusion. You must be sure the two premises are correct before making a deduction. If any facts are missing or incorrect, your conclusion will be wrong, or unsound.

> *Example:*
> Policemen wear blue uniforms.
> Mr. Kahil wears a blue uniform.
> Mr. Kahil is, therefore, a policeman.

Sound logical? Well, maybe. However, what if you find out that Mr. Kahil is a bus driver? The deduction does not seem very sound, does it? The problem with this syllogism is that the premises may be true, but other important facts are ignored. Many people besides policemen wear blue uniforms.

Rewrite the examples. Make a correct deduction.

EFFECTIVE STUDYING

Using Dictionaries   Reading and writing are not always easy. You might not know the definition of a word. You might want to use a certain synonym that you are sure exists, but that you cannot think of. What if you encounter a foreign word or phrase?

A **dictionary** lists words alphabetically. It also provides information about definitions of words, pronunciations of words, origins of words, and different forms of words, such as noun, verb, adjective and adverb forms.

Two-language dictionaries translate foreign words into English. They are useful if you read stories with foreign phrases.

A **thesaurus** lists synonyms for words, and sometimes antonyms as well. Some thesauruses list words alphabetically, as in a dictionary. Others have indexes that refer you to numbered sections.

Many word-processing programs include **spell-checkers** and thesauruses. These features can be a great help, although a spell-checker is certainly no substitute for a dictionary.

What reference books would you use to find the meaning of *adios*, find a substitute for the word *afraid*, and check the spelling of a difficult word?

> ### Test Preparation
> Although you might not have a dictionary with you when you take a test, you should always reread your work to check for spelling. Also check that you have used every word the way you meant to use it.

Unit Review ■ 311

UNIT ACTIVITY

A Continuing Unit Project:
Literary Magazines

The theme of this unit is discoveries. The word "discoveries" might also be an appropriate title for a series of literary reviews.

Tell students that during their study of this unit they are to suppose they are writers for a literary magazine. The magazine, a quarterly, is about to publish its winter (or spring, or summer) edition. The title of this edition is to be "Discoveries." Students will write for the magazine a review of each selection they read in this unit.

Take a few minutes to discuss with students the elements a literary review might include. One obvious item would be a discussion of the particular genre that a selection represents: fiction, nonfiction, drama, poetry. Another important item would be an analysis of how the writer handles certain elements of storytelling: theme, setting, plot, character, use of sound, imagery, symbolism, tone, or point of view. In some cases, for example, a writer will be very masterful in developing the psychology and personality of a particular character. In other cases, a writer may paint a vivid picture of a particular setting. In still others, a writer may make a unique and powerful statement about a particular theme.

Students may find it helpful to read articles from literary magazines, such as the *New York Times Book Review*, or reviews published in local newspapers. Some general questions to help students get started include

What is the genre of this selection?

How does this particular genre work well for the subject matter?

What literary element in this selection stands out? Why?

What is your overall impression of the selection? Did you find it interesting or moving? Did you feel that you could not put it down? Did you find yourself becoming bored or confused as you read?

Would you recommend the selection to a friend? Why or why not?

If your class needs more structure, try creating questions for each selection such as those listed below.

■ **"Chee's Daughter"/"Navaho Chant"**
How does the writer use symbolism to make this story more meaningful?

■ **"The Gold Medal"**
How does the writer create a contrast between flat and round characters?

■ **"Four Skinny Trees"**
How does the unusual form of this poem add to your enjoyment and understanding of it?

■ **"Ta-Na-E-Ka"**
How is the autobiographical aspect of this story effective?

■ **"Dead at Seventeen"**
What unusual literary techniques are used in this selection?

■ **"Thank You, M'am"**
How does the writer create the characters of Luella Bates Washington Jones and the boy?

■ **Four Haiku/"A bee thumps"**
Why is the haiku form especially suited to the subject matter of these poems?

■ **"Starvation Wilderness"**
Do you feel that the writer's narrative of this real-life adventure story is effective?

■ **"Dreams"/Untitled/"Sympathy"**
Which poet, Hughes or Dunbar, comes across as more optimistic and hopeful about life? Why?

Have students place their finished reviews in a loose-leaf binder or folder. Then have students exchange reviews with a partner to read and evaluate.

■ "Chee's Daughter"
by Juanita Platero and Siyowin Miller (page 317)

■ "Navaho Chant"
Traditional Navaho Song (page 333)

SELECTION SYNOPSES

In "Chee's Daughter" a young Navaho named Chee loses his wife in a battle against tuberculosis. When Chee returns home to the family compound, he discovers that his precious little daughter is gone. Chee's parents tell him that his in-laws, with whom he has never gotten along, have taken his daughter to live with them. They have done this according to the Navaho custom in which a dead woman's children go to live with her parents.

The loss of the little girl is more than Chee can bear. He goes to talk to his father-in-law, Old Man Fat. Old Man Fat is not willing to part with the child, however. Chee does not know what to do. At first he thinks he might escape his grief by leaving the area and getting a job in a distant place. Then he hears news of a new road that might take a lot of business away from Old Man Fat's trading post. In Chee's mind a plan forms. Chee works night and day for many months, farming his land; only he knows why.

Finally, the day comes when Chee has an abundance of food from his land. He rides out to see Old Man Fat and Fat's wife. Much as Chee had suspected, his in-laws have become impoverished. The little girl has become a burden, another mouth to feed. Chee dumps the food that he has brought at their feet. They see that it is just enough food for two people to get through the winter. They keep the food and hand Chee his little girl.

"Navaho Chant" is a poem that is part of a traditional Navaho song. It speaks of the "White Corn Boy" and the beauty of the land.

SELECTION ACTIVITY

Have students research various aspects of Navaho history and culture. Students may wish to research in depth one topic that particularly interests them, such as Navaho art or the history of the Navahos in the United States.

■ "The Gold Medal"
by Nan Gilbert (page 337)

SELECTION SYNOPSIS

Amanda, a young African American girl, is tired of being seen as a type by everyone around her. Her mother is concerned that she be a good example in the mainly white community into which they have just moved. A neighbor lady and the candy store owner see her, and all teenagers, as potential troublemakers. Even her sympathetic and friendly science teacher seems to stereotype her as a promising African American student whom he wants to help fit into the mostly white school.

One day, Amanda becomes upset during science class and runs from the school. Her awkwardness and unhappiness disappear as she runs. By accident she runs across a pasture and falls into a huge hole. An old man comes over to see if she is hurt. It turns out that the man has dug the hole as a grave for his dying dog, Chief. The man invites Amanda to meet his dog. He also compliments Amanda by calling her a runner. The old man shows Amanda medals the dog has won. He also shows her a gold medal that he bought for the dog himself, because he believed the dog would be a true winner. At the end of the story, the man gives Amanda the gold medal to keep. He expresses his belief in her and encourages her to believe in herself.

SELECTION ACTIVITY

A person who would have had something in common with Amanda is Jesse Owens (1913–1980), the African American track star who won four Olympic gold medals. Owens's achievement was especially significant in that he won his medals in the 1936 Olympics in Berlin, Germany. At that time Hitler was in power, and he was declaring that African Americans and other races were physically and mentally inferior to Aryans. Owens's victory was a blow to Hitler's propaganda campaign.

Have students go to the library and gather information about Jesse Owens's life and accomplishments. Have them write short biographies of Owens. Then encourage students to learn about other African Americans who have been outstanding in sports.

"Four Skinny Trees"
by Sandra Cisneros (page 349)

SELECTION SYNOPSIS

The speaker of this poem identifies with the four trees growing on the street outside her home. The trees manage to survive in spite of the hostile environment in which they exist. The speaker knows that if the trees did not continue to strive—to put down their roots and hang on—they would die. When the speaker grows discouraged, she gets the courage to "keep" by looking at the trees.

SELECTION ACTIVITY

Point out to students that some critics consider this Cisneros work a short story rather than a poem. Tell students that they are to take a position for or against this opinion. Group them according to their opinions. Have them work together to write a brief persuasive essay in which they defend their opinions. Remind students that in persuasive writing the author tries to establish the truth of a proposition by presenting facts and other evidence. Put these questions on the board for the groups to consider as they prepare their essays:

What elements of poetry does this selection contain?

What elements of a short story does the selection contain? You may want to suggest that each group assign different tasks to members such as researching the elements of poetry and/or short story, preparing an outline, writing the essay, revising the essay according to members' suggestions, and, finally, proofreading the essay.

When essays are completed have groups share theirs with the class.

"Ta-Na-E-Ka"
by Mary Whitebird (page 353)

SELECTION SYNOPSIS

Mary Whitebird and her cousin Roger are nearly 11 years old, the age at which Kaw Indians must undergo an initiation into adulthood, called Ta-Na-E-Ka. In this ritual, Kaw boys and girls are sent into the woods for five days to survive on their own. During this time they must sleep outdoors and eat insects and anything else they can find.

Mary and Roger both dread the ordeal, but Mary comes up with a plan. Secretly, she borrows five dollars from her teacher, Mrs. Richardson. Mary's intention is to buy food at a restaurant near the edge of the woods. Ernie, the kind restaurant owner, befriends Mary and lets her sleep as well as eat at the restaurant. Mary helps Ernie cook and set tables and picks wildflowers in the woods. When Mary returns home after the initiation, Roger is bruised and exhausted, but Mary is obviously rested and well fed. Mary confessed her survival tactics to her grandfather, who trained her and Roger for the Ta-Na-E-Ka. Her traditional yet understanding grandfather admits that she was clever and courageous in her own way, and did indeed prove that she is a survivor.

SELECTION ACTIVITY

In this activity, students will gather information and write reports about coming-of-age rituals that take place in various cultures. Students might choose to write about rituals such as the bar mitzvah or confirmation ceremony, which are both related to religion, or any other ritual from a specific culture, familiar or unfamiliar, that marks the transition from childhood to adulthood. Students can research a ritual that is still practiced today, or they can learn about one that has been practiced in the past.

Tell the students to include in their papers a description of the ritual and its purpose. Also ask them to compare the ritual to the Ta-Na-E-Ka.

"Dead at Seventeen"
from Ann Landers (page 364)

SELECTION SYNOPSIS

This Ann Landers column contains a message that Bear Bryant, the famous football coach, used to read regularly to freshmen at the University of Alabama. The message is in the form of an imaginary plea written in the first person. It expresses the feelings of a 17-year-old boy who has just been killed in an auto accident as a result of his careless driving. The boy bemoans the fact that he is a traffic fatality. His life has been cut short, and he has brought grief to his parents and friends. The teenager asks for just one more chance and promises, all too late, to be the most careful driver in the world.

Two organizations that have been formed for the purpose of reducing traffic fatalities are MADD (Mothers Against Drunk Driving) and SADD (Students Against Driving Drunk). Although both organizations focus on the consequences of reckless driving related to the use of alcohol, they still have much in common with the message of "Dead at Seventeen."

Have students learn about these organizations and what they do. Also ask them to find out if either organization has a chapter in their city or town. If so, you may want to arrange for a member of the organization to speak to your class.

■ "Thank You, M'am"
by Langston Hughes (page 369)

SELECTION SYNOPSIS

Roger, a teenage boy, fails in an attempt to snatch the purse of Mrs. Jones. She refuses to release the boy and drags him to her apartment. She orders him to wash up and later makes a meal for both of them. Roger tells Mrs. Jones that he wanted money to buy a pair of blue suede shoes. After they eat, she gives him ten dollars to buy the shoes and tells him to behave himself from now on. Roger is at a loss for words. He wants to say more to her than, "Thank you, m'am," but he doesn't manage to say even that.

SELECTION ACTIVITY

Arrange for students to read the short story "Where Love Is, There God Is Also" by Tolstoy (available in Globe *World Anthology*). In this story, an incident is described in which the old cobbler, Martin, catches a boy stealing an apple from a woman's basket. The way he handles the incident is similar in certain ways to the way Mrs. Jones treats Roger in "Thank You, M'am." Have students write short papers in which they compare and contrast the two stories.

■ Four Haiku
by Buson, Anonymous, Richard Wright, Issa (page 377)

■ "A bee thumps"
by Richard Sund (page 377)

SELECTION SYNOPSES

The four haiku paint images from nature that have parallels in human life. The short poem about the bee is in a style similar to that of haiku.

SELECTION ACTIVITY

Japanese art has much in common with Japanese haiku, particularly in its use of nature as subject. Have students go to the library or a museum and find examples of Japanese painting. Have them describe in their own words the characteristics of pictures they find. Then challenge them to find a picture that could be used to illustrate or complement one of the poems in this selection.

■ "Starvation Wilderness"
by Olive A. Fredrickson (page 381)

SELECTION SYNOPSIS

At the beginning of this true adventure, the narrator, her husband, Walter, and their 6-month-old daughter, Olive, set out to trap muskrats and other animals in northern Canada. The area in which they camp is rich in fur-bearing animals but lacking in game. Their food supply dwindles dangerously low; thus they call the area Starvation Wilderness. They set out in bitterly cold weather to find more supplies, and after a difficult journey—made more so by the fact that the narrator is pregnant—they come upon Bennett, another trapper, who sells them food.

They return to their original camp but find game and animals for trapping scarce. They travel farther west, camping in a tent. Trapping is better there, but many hardships follow, not the least being a disastrous fire in their tent. Finally the ice breaks up on the river, and the small family makes a difficult journey by boat back to Bennett's cabin. The riverboat picks them up there, and the narrator returns to civilization in time to have her baby, another daughter, named Vala. Walter resumes trapping in the fall, but the narrator has had enough of the far north. She resolves to remain behind with her children.

SELECTION ACTIVITY

Have students use encyclopedias and other reference books to learn about the fur-trapping industry in North America. Have them relate the information that they find to the story "Starvation Wilderness."

- **"Dreams"**
  by Langston Hughes (page 395)

- **Untitled**
  Anonymous (page 396)

- **"Sympathy"**
  by Paul Laurence Dunbar (page 396)

SELECTION SYNOPSES

The theme of the first poem is the importance of having dreams and goals in one's life. The theme of the second poem is that many selves may exist in one person. The theme of the last poem is the parallel between a caged bird and a person who yearns to be free.

SELECTION ACTIVITY

The message of the untitled poem in this selection is both humorous and profound. Have students work in small groups to create skits that dramatize the poem. Students can act out the poem in silence, using only pantomime; they can act out the poem as it is read or recited; or they can extend the poem by creating dialogue or a more definite plot.

STUDENT READING LIST

Gallo, Donald R. (ed.) *No Easy Answers: Short Stories About Teenagers Making Tough Choices*. Delacorte, 1997.

Peck, Richard. *Lost in Cyberspace*. Dial, 1995.

Weiss, M. Jerry and Helen S. *From One Experience to Another: Stories About Turning Points*. Forge, 1997.

Meltzer, Milton. *Langston Hughes: An Illustrated Edition*. Millbrook, 1997.

From Globe Fearon Educational Publisher

Latino Poetry
African American Poetry
Multicultural Literature Collection
　　Plains Native American Literature
　　African American Literature
Tapestry: A Multicultural Anthology
The Globe Reader's Collection
　　Stories of Adventure and Survival
Adapted Classic
　　Treasure Island by Robert Louis Stevenson
Amazing Adventures Series
　　The Inner Voice
Uptown, Downtown Series
　　The Longest Night

UNIT 4
Overview

UNIT OBJECTIVES

After completing this unit, students will be able to

- understand the four basic elements of nonfiction: plot, point of view, tone, and theme
- distinguish fact from opinion
- use the skill of note-taking effectively
- build on knowledge of literary elements in order to write both creatively and analytically
- use context clues to determine meanings of words
- use new words in sentences

UNIT SELECTIONS

The theme of the unit is discoveries: learning new things about oneself, others, the world, and life itself.

- **"Chee's Daughter"** (p. 317) features a main character who discovers that his values and choices in life have been right after all.

  LITERARY SKILL: symbols/symbolism

  READING SKILL: make inferences

  VOCABULARY: adjectives and adverbs

  WRITING: write about the characters

- **"Navaho Chant"** (p. 333) emphasizes the discovery of beauty in a symbol of nature.

  LITERARY SKILL: symbols/symbolism

  READING SKILL: identify fact and opinion

  VOCABULARY: prepositions

  WRITING: writing from a different point of view

- **"The Gold Medal"** (p. 337) illustrates how others can help a person discover him- or herself.

  LITERARY SKILL: character traits

  READING SKILL: use connotations

  VOCABULARY: adverbs ending in -ly

  WRITING: story extension

- **"Four Skinny Trees"** (p. 349) shows how trees lead the speaker to discover their aspects and draw strength and inspiration from them.

  LITERARY SKILL: speaker

  READING SKILL: identify main idea

VOCABULARY: pronunciation

WRITING: a descriptive paragraph

- **"Ta-Na-E-Ka"** (p. 353) describes the author's discoveries as she undergoes a traditional ritual of the Kaw Indians.

  LITERARY SKILL: autobiography

  READING SKILL: recognize facts that support opinions

  VOCABULARY: contractions

  WRITING: story extension

- **"Dead at Seventeen"** (p. 364), the model selection, tells the poignant story of a discovery made too late.

  LITERARY SKILL: elements of nonfiction

  READING SKILL: recognize valid opinions

  VOCABULARY: slang

  WRITING: expressing a personal reaction

- **"Thank You, M'am"** (p. 369) involves a young boy and an older woman he tries to rob and the important discoveries they make about each other.

  LITERARY SKILL: theme

  READING SKILL: make predictions

  VOCABULARY: synonyms

  WRITING: story extension

Introducing the Unit Theme
Arrange a display of some of these items: a light bulb, empty containers of antibiotics, a computer, a telephone, a piece of synthetic fabric, a radio or TV, a camera. Ask students to imagine life without each of the items. Then ask how the item has changed their lives. Encourage students to include broad economic and social changes in their discussion. Point out that each item represents a discovery and those discoveries bring about changes, both good and bad.

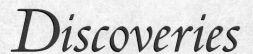

Discoveries

It is well to observe the force and
virtue and consequence of discoveries. . .
—Francis Bacon

Girl on the Bridge, Edvard Munch. Three Lions/Superstock

313

Viewing Fine Art

Edvard Munch (1863–1944) was a Norwegian painter and printmaker. His emotionally charged paintings often express themes of isolation, fear, death, and anxiety. How does the depiction of the girl sugge Munch's themes of isolatio and anxiety? What kind of covery do you think might h brought on this mood?

- **Four Haiku and "A bee thumps"** (p. 377) emphasize discoveries about nature that relate to human experience.
  LITERARY SKILL: haiku
  READING SKILL: identify fact and opinion
  VOCABULARY: use a thesaurus
  WRITING: create a haiku poem

- **"Starvation Wilderness"** (p. 381) features an author who discovers important things about herself during a life-or-death struggle.
  LITERARY SKILL: conflict
  READING SKILL: summarize
  VOCABULARY: use a dictionary
  WRITING: record a personal plan

- **"Dream," Untitled, and "Sympathy"** (p. 395) are poems that emphasize discoveries about life.
  LITERARY SKILL: rhyme
  READING SKILL: analyze figurative language
  VOCABULARY: words with multiple meanings
  WRITING: record a personal experience

Discoveries

What do you think of when you hear the word *discovery*? Perhaps you think of a great scientific discovery, like the automobile engine. Perhaps you think of discovering something valuable, such as diamonds or gold. You may even think of discovering something new, like a cheap source of energy.

Francis Bacon, the English essayist, wrote about the importance of looking at the effects of discoveries. Think of the changes television, frozen food, and computers have made in the 20th century. Discoveries have the power to change the world, either for better or for worse. Do you see the discovery of nuclear energy as beneficial or destructive? This idea of change also applies to your own discoveries. Once you make a discovery, your world—and your own inner reality—are forever changed. Life is never quite the same again.

The selections in this unit will focus on discoveries that people make about themselves, others, the world around them, and life. The selections will help you think about the discoveries that you have made.

■ DISCOVERIES ABOUT YOURSELF

In the short story "Chee's Daughter," a Navaho man doubts the wisdom of his values when his wife dies and he loses his daughter. A bold plan to win back his daughter succeeds, and Chee discovers that his values were right for him after all. Have you ever experienced self-doubt when faced with difficult circumstances? What did you discover about yourself? The speaker of "Four Skinny Trees" discovers reasons for encouragement and inspiration.

Sometimes a person needs the help of another to find out who he or she really is. In the short story "The Gold Medal," a young African American girl discovers an aspect of her true self through a chance encounter with a wise and kindly old man.

Have you ever taken part in a ritual that is part of your religion or community, such as a bar mitzvah, baptism, or initiation? What did you discover about yourself as a result of this experience?

In the true story "Ta-Na-E-Ka," a young Native American girl describes her participation in the coming-of-age ritual that is part of the tradition of the Kaw Indians. Sent out to spend five days and nights alone in the wilderness, the girl comes up with a clever plan. She discovers that she can survive in the most unusual circumstances.

■ **ABOUT OTHERS**

People discover things about themselves and one another in relationships. What things have you discovered recently about the people in your life? Did some of these things surprise you? In the short story "Thank You, M'am," a boy is *very* surprised by some things he discovers about a woman whom he meets in an unusual way. "Navaho Chant" helps you recognize how some Native Americans view nature. Nature is beautiful and the crops think like human beings. Why do you think the Navahos see nature in such a positive way?

■ **ABOUT THE WORLD**

City streets can be very dangerous, but you can make discoveries—good and bad—there. Is nature dangerous, too? Sometimes, nature can be a harsh teacher. In the true story "Starvation Wilderness," a young couple learns that the far north country is no place for two people and a small baby in winter. Yet the story has a positive side, too, as characters discover their own courage and endurance. Poems can also help you make discoveries about the world. The haiku offers insights into nature and human nature. Discover what "Sympathy," "Dreams," and an untitled poem have to say about self-awareness, freedom, and dreams. These poems offer discoveries about a world inside everyone.

Discoveries are a part of everyday living. Most discoveries come about as a result of analysis, disclosure, and exploration. Sometimes, however, discoveries are made purely by accident. What important discoveries have you made? What changes have these discoveries made in your life?

Discussing the Unit Theme

Write on the chalkboard the headings *self*, *others*, *the world*, and *life*. As you guide students through the opening section of the discussion, ask them to write down discoveries they have made that fit into each of the four categories. Then ask for volunteers to share their lists with the class.

Read through the rest of the material on discoveries with the students, allowing time for discussion of each question. Ask students to share their thoughts about which selections in the unit they are most eager to read, and why.

Cooperative Group Activity

Divide the class into small groups. Assign each group one of the following topics: the classroom, people in their classroom, the school building, the school grounds. Challenge each group to discover at least five things about its topic; for example, the group assigned to people in their classroom might conduct a survey to discover opinions, tastes, or vital statistics. Alternatively, the groups might observe people in the class to discover mannerisms, appearances, or behavior. Remind the groups to observe and share only positive discoveries with the class.

SELECTION OVERVIEW

SELECTION OBJECTIVES

After completing this selection, students will be able to

- understand symbols and symbolism
- identify some common symbols
- identify characters' discoveries
- respond to characters
- identify specific symbols in the story
- use adjectives and adverbs
- make inferences

Lesson Resources

Chee's Daughter
- Selection Synopsis, Teacher's Edition, p. T311c
- Comprehension and Vocabulary Workbook, pp. 59–60
- Language Enrichment Workbook, pp. 60–62
- Teacher's Resources Reinforcement, p. R30 Test, pp. T57–T58

More About Symbols and Symbolism

Have students think of other examples of common symbols. You might start them off by suggesting that they think of symbols connected with certain holidays: Valentine's Day hearts, St. Patrick's Day shamrocks, Halloween pumpkins, Christmas trees. Write student responses on the chalkboard. Then have them discuss the meaning and significance of each symbol.

Background Notes

The Navajos are the second largest Native American group in the United States. In 1990, the U.S. Navajo population was estimated to be about 225,000.

READING FOCUS

Make Inferences Sometimes a writer tells you directly what is happening. In other cases, the writer gives certain details, and you infer, or draw a conclusion, by putting together the pieces of information that are given.

Consider this description: "No one spoke to me at the party. No one smiled. When I tried to chat with several people, they all turned away." From these details, you can infer that the guest was not welcome at the party. Look for details that can help you make inferences about both the action and characters in "Chee's Daughter."

SYMBOLISM IN FICTION

A **symbol** is something that stands for something else. For example, a heart is often used as a symbol of love.

Literature is full of symbolism, or the use of symbols. Often in a story, a symbol stands for an idea, a feeling, or a quality. Sometimes a certain symbol is used several times throughout a story. When a symbol is used in this way, you know that it emphasizes an important idea. This type of symbol may appear at the beginning or end of a story, as well as at critical points in the plot.

In the story "Chee's Daughter," symbols convey important ideas about Chee and his values. As you read "Chee's Daughter," ask yourself:

1. What symbol in the story represents Chee's faith in the land?
2. At what points in the story is this symbol used?

WRITING CONNECTION

Writers use symbols to convey important ideas about characters. Think of something you own that is especially important to you. Then write a paragraph explaining how this object could be used as a symbol to describe the kind of person you are.

316 ■ Unit 4

ESL Activity

Show students photographs of various things that can function as symbols, such as a lamb, a state flag, a dove, a crown, and a sports team mascot. Ask students to provide facts about each thing shown. For example, a lamb is a farm animal that eats grass and provides meat and wool. Then ask what that same thing might symbolize. For example, a lamb is often a symbol of innocence or peacefulness. After students have discussed each symbol, have them give other examples of symbols they have encountered.

Cooperative Group Activity

Have students work in pairs to complete the Writing Connection activity. Ask each student to draw and color a picture of a symbol—a car, a tree, a catcher's mitt, a castle—that tells something important about him- or herself. Next, have students exchange papers. Ask each student to decide what the symbol tells about his or her partner.

Chee's Daughter

by Juanita Platero and Siyowin Miller

The hat told the story, the big, black, drooping Stetson. It was not at the proper angle, the proper rakish angle for so young a Navaho. There was no song, and that was not in keeping either. There should have been at least a humming, a faint, all-to-himself "he he he heya," for it was a good horse he was riding, a slender-legged, high-stepping buckskin that would race the wind with light knee-urging. This was a day for singing, a warm winter day, when the touch of the sun upon the back belied the snow high on distant mountains.

Wind warmed by the sun touched his high-boned cheeks like flicker feathers, and still he rode on silently, deeper into Little Canyon, until the red rock walls rose straight upward from the streambed and only a narrow piece of blue sky hung above. Abruptly the sky widened where the canyon walls were pushed back to make a wide place, as though in ancient times an angry stream had tried to go all ways at once.

This was home—this wide place in the canyon—levels of jagged rock and levels of rich red earth. This was home to Chee, the rider of the buckskin, as it had been to many generations before him.

He stopped his horse at the stream and sat looking across the narrow ribbon of water to the bare-branched peach trees. He was seeing them each springtime with their age-gnarled limbs transfigured beneath veils of blossom pink; he was seeing them in autumn laden with their yellow fruit, small and sweet. Then his eyes searched out the indistinct furrows of the fields beside the stream, where each year the corn and beans and squash drank thirstily of the overflow from summer rains. Chee was trying to outweigh today's bitter betrayal of hope by gathering to himself these reminders of the integrity of the land. Land did not cheat! His mind lingered deliberately on all the days spent here in the sun caring for the young plants, his songs to the earth and to the life springing from it: ". . . In the middle of the wide field . . . Yellow Corn Boy . . . He has started both ways . . .," then the harvest and repayment in full measure. Here was the old

rakish (RAYK ish) stylish
transfigured (trans FIG yurd) changed in form or appearance

Chee's Daughter ■ 317

Literary Focus:
Symbolism
Ask students what a hogan is and what it is made from, based on the description in the story. Do they think all modern Navajo live in hogans? In what way could the hogan be considered a symbol of the way of life Chee has chosen?

Reading Focus:
Make Inferences
Ask: How do the characters' actions and words indirectly reveal that Chee's wife has recently died?

feeling of wholeness and of oneness with the sun and earth and growing things.

Chee urged the buckskin toward the family compound where, secure in a recess of overhanging rock, was his mother's dome-shaped hogan, red rock and red adobe like the ground on which it nestled. Not far from the hogan was the half-circle of brush like a dark shadow against the canyon wall—corral for sheep and goats. Farther from the hogan, in full circle, stood the horse corral made of heavy cedar branches sternly interlocked. Chee's long thin lips curved into a smile as he passed his daughter's tiny hogan squatted like a round Pueblo oven, beside the corral. He remembered the summer day when together they sat back on their heels and plastered wet adobe all about the circling wall of rock and the woven dome of piñon twigs. How his family laughed when the Little One herded the bewildered chickens into her tiny hogan as the first snow fell.

Then the smile faded from Chee's lips and his eyes darkened as he tied his horse to a corral post and turned to the strangely empty compound. "Someone has told them," he thought, "and they are inside weeping." He passed his mother's deserted loom on the south side of the hogan and pulled the rude wooden door toward him, bowing his head, hunching his shoulders to get inside.

His mother sat sideways by the center fire, her feet drawn up under her full skirts. Her hands were busy kneading dough in the chipped white basin. With her head down, her voice was muffled when she said, "The meal will soon be ready, son."

Chee passed his father sitting against the wall, hat over his eyes as though asleep. He passed his older sister who sat turning mutton ribs on a crude wire grill over the coals, noticed tears dropping on her hands. "She cared more for my wife than I realized," he thought.

Then, because something must be said sometime, he tossed the black Stetson upon a bulging sack of wool and said, "You have heard, then." He could not shut from his mind how confidently he had set the handsome new hat on his head that very morning, slanting the wide brim over one eye: he was going to see his wife and today he would ask the doctors about bringing her home; last week she had looked so much better.

His sister nodded but did not speak. His mother sniffed and passed her velveteen sleeve beneath her nose. Chee sat down, leaning against the wall. "I suppose I was a fool for hoping all the time. I should have expected this. Few of our people get well from the coughing sickness. But *she* seemed to be getting better."

His mother was crying aloud now and blowing her nose noisily on her skirt. His father sat up, speaking gently to her.

Chee shifted his position and started a cigarette. His mind turned back to the Little One. At least she was too small to understand what had happened, the Little One who had been born three years

---

compound (KAHM pound) group of buildings

Passing By, E. Martin Hennings. The Museum of Fine Arts, Houston, TX. Gift of the Ranger Fund, National Academy of Design

before in the sanitarium where his wife was being treated for the coughing sickness, the Little One he had brought home to his mother's hogan to be nursed by his sister whose baby was a few months older. As she grew fat-cheeked and sturdy-legged, she followed him about like a shadow. Somehow her baby mind had grasped that of all those at the hogan who cared for her and played with her, he—Chee—belonged most to her. She sat cross-legged at his elbow when he worked silver at the forge; she rode before him in the saddle when he drove the horses to water; often she lay wakeful on her sheep pelts until he stretched out for the night in the darkened hogan and she could snuggle warm against him.

Chee blew smoke slowly and some of the sadness left his dark eyes as he said,

Chee's Daughter ■ 319

Literary Focus:
Symbolism and Setting
The setting of the trading post contrasts sharply with Chee's home in Little Canyon. Have students discuss these contrasts. You may wish to direct their attention to the four paragraphs on pages 320 and 321 beginning with "Several cars were parked . . ." for details. Ask: What way of life does the trading post represent?

"It is not as bad as it might be. It is not as though we are left with nothing."

Chee's sister arose, sobs catching in her throat, and rushed past him out the doorway. Chee sat upright, a terrible fear possessing him. For a moment his mouth could make no sound. Then: "The Little One! Mother, where is she?"

His mother turned her stricken face to him. "Your wife's people came after her this morning. They heard yesterday of their daughter's death through the trader at Red Sands."

Chee started to protest but his mother shook her head slowly. "I didn't expect they would want the Little One either. But there is nothing you can do. She is a girl child and belongs to her mother's people; it is custom."

Frowning, Chee got to his feet, grinding his cigarette into the dirt floor. "Custom! When did my wife's parents begin thinking about custom? Why, the hogan where they live doesn't even face the East!" He started toward the door. "Perhaps I can overtake them. Perhaps they don't realize how much we want her here with us. I'll ask them to give my daughter back to me. Surely, they won't refuse."

His mother stopped him gently with her outstretched hand. "You couldn't overtake them now. They were in the trader's car. Eat and rest, and think more about this."

"Have you forgotten how things have always been between you and your wife's people?" his father said.

That night, Chee's thoughts were troubled—half-forgotten incidents became disturbingly vivid—but early the next morning, he saddled the buckskin and set out for the settlement of Red Sands. Even though his father-in-law, Old Man Fat, might laugh, Chee knew that he must talk to him. There were some things to which Old Man Fat might listen.

Chee rode the first part of the fifteen miles to Red Sands expectantly. The sight of sandstone buttes near Cottonwood Spring reddening in the morning sun brought a song almost to his lips. He twirled his reins in salute to the small boy herding sheep toward many-colored Butterfly Mountain, watched with pleasure the feathers of smoke rising against tree-darkened western mesas from the hogans sheltered there. But as he approached the familiar settlement sprawled in mushroom growth along the highway, he began to feel as though a scene from a bad dream was becoming real.

Several cars were parked around the trading store which was built like two log hogans side by side, with red gas pumps in front and a sign across the tarpaper roofs: *Red Sands Trading Post—Groceries · Gasoline · Cold Drinks · Sandwiches · Indian Curios.* Back of the trading post, an unpainted frame house and outbuildings squatted on the drab, treeless land. Chee and the Little One's mother had lived there when they stayed with his wife's people. That was according to custom—living with one's wife's people—but

---

buttes (BYOOTS) small mountains with steep sides

Chee had never been convinced that it was custom alone which prompted Old Man Fat and his wife to insist that their daughter bring her husband to live at the trading post.

Beside the Post was a large hogan of logs, with brightly painted pseudo-Navaho designs on the roof—a hogan with smoke-smudged windows and a garish blue door which faced north to the highway. Old Man Fat had offered Chee a hogan like this one. The trader would build it if he and his wife would live there and Chee would work at his forge making silver jewelry where tourists could watch him. But Chee had asked instead for a piece of land for a cornfield and help in building a hogan far back from the highway and a corral for the sheep he had brought to this marriage.

A cold wind blowing down from the mountains began to whistle about Chee's ears. It flapped the gaudy Navaho rugs which were hung in one long bright line to attract tourists. It swayed the sign *Navaho Weaver at Work* beside the loom where Old Man Fat's wife sat hunched in her striped blanket patting the colored thread of a design into place with a wooden comb. Tourists stood watching the weaver. More tourists stood in a knot before the hogan where the sign said: *See Inside a Real Navaho Home 25¢.*

Then the knot seemed to unravel as a few people returned to their cars; some had cameras; and there against the blue door Chee saw the Little One standing uncertainly. The wind was plucking at her new purple blouse and wide green skirt; it freed truant strands of soft dark hair from the meager queue into which it had been tied with white yarn.

"Isn't she cunning!" one of the women tourists was saying as she turned away.

Chee's lips tightened as he began to look around for Old Man Fat. Finally he saw him passing among the tourists collecting coins.

Then the Little One saw Chee. The uncertainty left her face and she darted through the crowd as her father swung down from his horse. Chee lifted her in his arms, hugging her tight. While he listened to her breathless chatter, he watched Old Man Fat bearing down on them, scowling.

As his father-in-law walked heavily across the graveled lot, Chee was reminded of a statement his mother sometimes made: "When you see a fat Navaho, you see one who hasn't worked for what he has."

Old Man Fat was fattest in the middle. There was indolence in his walk even though he seemed to hurry, indolence in his cheeks so plump they made his eyes squint, eyes now smoldering with anger.

Some of the tourists were getting into their cars and driving away. The old man said belligerently to Chee, "Why do you come here? To spoil our business? To drive people away?"

---

gawdy (GAWD ee) showy; bright-colored
queue (KYOO) a braid of hair worn at the back of the neck
cunning (KUHN ing) cute
indolence (IN duh lens) laziness

Chee's Daughter ■ 321

"I came to talk with you," Chee answered, trying to keep his voice steady as he faced the old man.

"We have nothing to talk about," Old Man Fat blustered and did not offer to touch Chee's extended hand.

"It's about the Little One." Chee settled his daughter more comfortably against his hip as he weighed carefully all the words he had planned to say. "We are going to miss her very much. It wouldn't be so bad if we knew that *part* of each year she could be with us. That might help you too. You and your wife are no longer young people and you have no young ones here to depend upon." Chee chose his next words remembering the thriftlessness of his wife's parents, and their greed. "Perhaps we could share the care of this little one. Things are good with us. So much snow this year will make lots of grass for the sheep. We have good land for corn and melons."

Chee's words did not have the expected effect. Old Man Fat was enraged. "Farmers, all of you! Longhaired farmers! Do you think everyone must bend his back over the short-handled hoe in order

Familia India, Amado M. Pena, Jr. El Taller, Inc.

322 ■ **Unit 4**

to have food to eat?" His tone changed as he began to brag a little. "We not only have all the things from cans at the trader's, but when the Pueblos come past here on their way to town we buy their salty jerked mutton, young corn for roasting, dried sweet peaches."

Chee's dark eyes surveyed the land along the highway as the old man continued to brag about being "progressive." *He no longer was tied to the land.* He and his wife made money easily and could *buy* all the things they wanted. Chee realized too late that he had stumbled into the old argument between himself and his wife's parents. They had never understood his feeling about the land—that a man took care of his land and it in turn took care of him. Old Man Fat and his wife scoffed at him, called him a Pueblo farmer, all during that summer when he planted and weeded and harvested. Yet they ate the green corn in their mutton stews, and the chili paste from the fresh ripe chilis, and the tortillas from the cornmeal his wife ground. None of this working and sweating in the sun for Old Man Fat, who talked proudly of his easy way of living—collecting money from the trader who rented this strip of land beside the highway, collecting money from the tourists.

Yet Chee had once won that argument. His wife had shared his belief in the integrity of the earth, that jobs and people might fail one but the earth never would. After that first year she had turned from her own people and gone with Chee to Little Canyon.

Old Man Fat was reaching for the Little One. "Don't be coming here with plans for my daughter's daughter," he warned. "If you try to make trouble, I'll take the case to the government man in town."

The impulse was strong in Chee to turn and ride off while he still had the Little One in his arms. But he knew his time of victory would be short. His own family would uphold the old custom of children, especially girl children, belonging to the mother's people. He would have to give his daughter up if the case were brought before the Headman of Little Canyon, and certainly he would have no better chance before a strange white man in town.

He handed the bewildered Little One to her grandfather who stood watching every movement suspiciously. Chee asked, "If I brought you a few things for the Little One, would that be making trouble? Some velvet for a blouse, or some of the jerky she likes . . . this summer's melon?"

Old Man Fat backed away from him. "Well," he hesitated, as some of the anger disappeared from his face and beads of greed shone in his eyes. "Well," he said again. Then as the Little One began to squirm in his arms and cry, he said, "No! No! Stay away from here, you and all your family."

The sense of his failure deepened as Chee rode back to Little Canyon. But it was not until he sat with his family that evening in the hogan, while the familiar

---

jerky (JUR kee) beef strips that have been dried in the sun

Chee's Daughter ■ 323

Discussion
Ask students if Old Man Fat's idea of being progressive is really better than being a "long-haired farmer."

Literary Focus:
Minor Character
Ask: Did Chee's wife share his feelings about the land? Explain.

Reading Focus:
Make Inferences
Ask: How does Chee approach his father-in-law on the subject of his daughter? How does Old Man Fat respond? What traits of the two characters can you infer from their actions and words?

T323

Reading Focus:
Make Inferences

Chee asks himself several questions in this part of the story. Ask: What is the conflict these questions represent? What sort of decision must Chee make?

bustle of meal preparing went on about him, that he began to doubt the wisdom of the things he'd always believed. He smelled the coffee boiling and the oily fragrance of chili powder dusted into the bubbling pot of stew; he watched his mother turning round crusty fried bread in the small black skillet. All around him was plenty—a half of mutton hanging near the door, bright strings of chili drying, corn hanging by the braided husks, cloth bags of dried peaches. Yet in his heart was nothing.

He heard the familiar sounds of the sheep outside the hogan, the splash of water as his father filled the long drinking trough from the water barrel. When his father came in, Chee could not bring himself to tell a second time of the day's happenings. He watched his wiry, soft-spoken father while his mother told the story, saw his father's queue of graying hair quiver as he nodded his head with sympathetic exclamations.

Chee's doubting, acrid thoughts kept forming: Was it wisdom his father had passed on to him or was his inheritance only the stubbornness of a longhaired Navaho resisting change? Take care of the land and it will take care of you. True, the land had always given him food, but now food was not enough. Perhaps if he had gone to school he would have learned a different kind of wisdom, something to help him now. A schoolboy might even be able to speak convincingly to this government man whom Old Man Fat threatened to call, instead of sitting here

like a clod of earth itself—Pueblo farmer indeed. What had the land to give that would restore his daughter?

In the days that followed, Chee herded sheep. He got up in the half light, drank the hot coffee his mother had ready, then started the flock moving. It was necessary to drive the sheep a long way from the hogan to find good winter forage. Sometimes Chee met friends or relatives who were on their way to town or to the road camp where they hoped to get work; then there was friendly banter and an exchange of news. But most of the days seemed endless; he could not walk far enough or fast enough from his memories of the Little One or from his bitter thoughts. Sometimes it seemed his daughter trudged beside him, so real he could almost hear her footsteps—the muffled pad-pad of little feet clad in deerhide. In the glare of a snow bank he would see her vivid face, brown eyes sparkling. Mingling with the tinkle of sheep bells he heard her laughter.

When, weary of following the small sharp hoof marks that crossed and re-crossed in the snow, he sat down in the shelter of a rock, it was only to be reminded that in his thoughts he had forsaken his brotherhood with the earth and sun and growing things. If he remembered times when he had flung himself against the earth to rest, to lie there in the sun until he could no longer feel where he left off and the earth began, it was to remember also that now he sat

---

acrid (AK rid) bitter to the tongue
forage (FAWR ij) food for animals
banter (BAN tur) good-natured teasing

like an alien against the same earth; the belonging-together was gone. The earth was one thing and he was another.

It was during the days when he herded sheep that Chee decided he must leave Little Canyon. Perhaps he would take a job silversmithing for one of the traders in town. Perhaps, even though he spoke little English, he could get a job at the road camp with his cousins; he would ask them about it.

Springtime transformed the mesas. The peach trees in the canyon were shedding fragrance and pink blossoms on the gentled wind. The sheep no longer foraged for the yellow seeds of chamiso but ranged near the hogan with the long-legged new lambs, eating tender young grass.

Chee was near the hogan on the day his cousins rode up with the message for which he waited. He had been watching with mixed emotions while his father and his sister's husband cleared the fields beside the stream.

"The boss at the camp says he needs an extra hand, but he wants to know if you'll be willing to go with the camp when they move it to the other side of the town." The tall cousin shifted his weight in the saddle.

The other cousin took up the explanation. "The work near here will last only until the new cutoff beyond Red Sands is finished. After that, the work will be too far away for you to get back here often."

That was what Chee had wanted—to get away from Little Canyon—yet he found himself not so interested in the job beyond town as in this new cutoff which was almost finished. He pulled a blade of grass, split it thoughtfully down the center as he asked questions of his cousins. Finally he said: "I need to think more about this. If I decide on this job, I'll ride over."

Before his cousins were out of sight down the canyon Chee was walking toward the fields, a bold plan shaping in his mind. As the plan began to flourish, wild and hardy as young tumbleweed, Chee added his own voice softly to the song his father was singing: ". . . In the middle of the wide field . . . Yellow Corn Boy . . . I wish to put in."

Chee walked slowly around the field, the rich red earth yielding to his footsteps. His plan depended upon this land and upon the things he remembered most about his wife's people.

Through planting time Chee worked zealously and tirelessly. He spoke little of the large new field he was planting because he felt so strongly that just now this was something between himself and the land. The first days he was ever stooping, piercing the ground with the pointed stick, placing the corn kernels there, walking around the field and through it, singing, ". . . His track leads into the ground . . . Yellow Corn Boy . . . his track leads into the ground." After that,

---

alien (AYL yun) or (AYL ee yun) foreigner; stranger
zealously (ZEHL uhs lee) eagerly; fanatically

Chee's Daughter ■ 325

The traditional designs of Native American weaving from the southwestern United States provide the pattern for this contemporary painting by Amado Pena. By dividing his painting into stark areas of black and gray and strips of colored design, the artist almost completely disguises the two women he is picturing. He thus fuses the Native American theme with a kind of modern formalism. Ask: What colorful article of clothing is depicted in the painting? How does the art shown on this page symbolize what Chee is feeling?

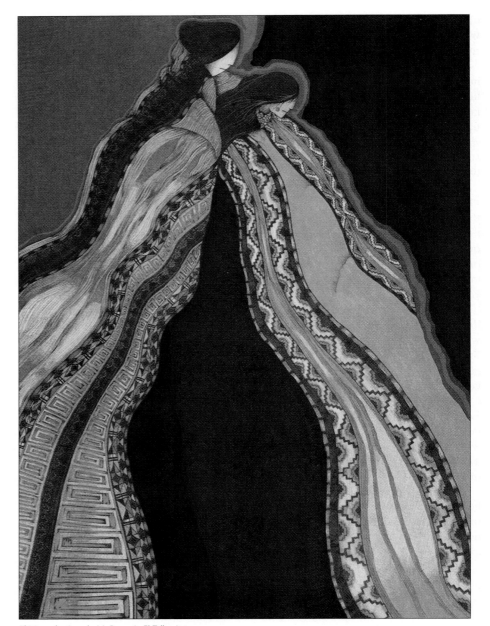

El Mercado, Amado M. Pena, Jr. El Taller, Inc.

each day Chee walked through his field watching for the tips of green to break through; first a few spikes in the center and then more and more until the corn in all parts of the field was above ground. Surely, Chee thought, if he sang the proper songs, if he cared for this land faithfully, it would not forsake him now, even though through the lonely days of winter he had betrayed the goodness of the earth in his thoughts.

Through the summer Chee worked long days, the sun hot upon his back, pulling weeds from around young corn plants; he planted squash and pumpkin; he terraced a small piece of land near his mother's hogan and planted carrots and onions and the moisture-loving chili. He was increasingly restless. Finally he told his family what he hoped the harvest from this land would bring him. Then the whole family waited with him, watching the corn: the slender graceful plants that waved green arms and bent to embrace each other as young winds wandered through the field, the maturing plants flaunting their pollen-laden tassels in the sun, the tall and sturdy parent corn with new-formed ears and a froth of purple, red, and yellow cornbeards against the dusty emerald of broad leaves.

Summer was almost over when Chee slung the bulging packs across two pack ponies. His mother helped him tie the heavy rolled pack behind the saddle of the buckskin. Chee knotted the new yellow kerchief about his neck a little tighter, gave the broad black hat brim an extra tug, but these were only gestures of assurance and he knew it. The land had not failed him. That part was done. But this he was riding into? Who could tell?

When Chee arrived at Red Sands, it was as he had expected to find it—no cars on the highway. His cousins had told him that even the Pueblo farmers were using the new cutoff to town. The barren gravel around the Red Sands Trading Post was deserted. A sign banged against the dismantled gas pumps: *Closed until further notice.*

Old Man Fat came from the crude summer shelter built beside the log hogan from a few branches of scrub cedar and the sides of wooden crates. He seemed almost friendly when he saw Chee.

"Get down, my son," he said, eyeing the bulging packs. There was no bluster in his voice today and his face sagged, looking somewhat saddened; perhaps because his cheeks were no longer quite full enough to push his eyes upward at the corners. "You are going on a journey?"

Chee shook his head. "Our fields gave us so much this year, I thought to sell or trade this to the trader. I didn't know he was no longer here."

Old Man Fat sighed, his voice dropping to an injured tone. "He says he and his wife are going to rest this winter; then he'll after that build a place up on the new highway."

Chee moved as though to be traveling on, then jerked his head toward the pack ponies. "Anything you need?"

flaunting (FLAWNT ing) showing off

Chee's Daughter ■ 327

Literary Focus:
Symbolism
Have students skim page 327 to identify the passage that best expresses Chee's continuing faith in the land.

Reading Focus:
Make Inferences
Ask: What details describing the trading post differ from those on pages 320 and 321? What has caused these changes? How have these changes affected Old Man Fat and his wife?

Discussion
Why does Chee pretend not to know that the trader is gone when he has been planning all summer to give supplies to his in-laws in exchange for his daughter?

"I'll ask my wife," Old Man Fat said as he led the way to the shelter. "Maybe she has a little money. Things have not been too good with us since the trader closed. Only a few tourists come this way." He shrugged his shoulders. "And with the trader gone—no credit."

Chee was not deceived by his father-in-law's unexpected confidences. He recognized them as a hopeful bid for sympathy and, if possible, something for nothing. Chee made no answer. He was thinking that so far he had been right about his wife's parents: their thriftlessness had left them with no resources to last until Old Man Fat found another easy way of making a living.

Old Man Fat's wife was in the shelter working at her loom. She turned rather wearily when her husband asked with a noticeable deference if she would give him money to buy supplies. Chee surmised that the only income here was from his mother-in-law's weaving.

She peered around the corner of the shelter at the laden ponies, and then she looked at Chee. "What do you have there, my son?"

Chee smiled to himself as he turned to pull the pack from one of the ponies, dragged it to the shelter where he untied the ropes. Pumpkins and hardshelled squash tumbled out, and the ears of corn—pale yellow husks fitting firmly over plump ripe kernels, blue corn, red corn, yellow corn, many-colored corn, ears and ears of it—tumbled into every corner of the shelter.

"Yooooh," Old Man Fat's wife exclaimed as she took some of the ears in her hands. Then she glanced up at her son-in-law. "But we have no money for all this. We have sold almost everything we own—even the brass bed that stood in the hogan."

Old Man Fat's brass bed. Chee concealed his amusement as he started back for another pack. That must have been a hard parting. Then he stopped, for coming from the cool darkness of the hogan was the Little One, rubbing her eyes as though she had been asleep. She stood for a moment in the doorway and Chee saw that she was dirty, barefoot, her hair uncombed, her little blouse shorn of all its silver buttons. Then she ran toward Chee, her arms outstretched. Heedless of Old Man Fat and his wife, her father caught her in his arms, her hair falling in a dark cloud across his face, the sweetness of her laughter warm against his shoulder.

It was the haste within him to get this slow waiting game played through to the finish that made Chee speak unwisely. It was the desire to swing her before him in the saddle and ride fast to Little Canyon that prompted his words. "The money doesn't matter. You still have something. . . ."

Chee knew immediately that he had overspoken. The old woman looked from him to the corn spread before her. Unfriendliness began to harden in his father-in-law's face. All the old arguments between himself and his wife's

---

surmised (sur MYZD) supposed; made a guess

people came pushing and crowding in between them now.

Old Man Fat began kicking the ears of corn back onto the canvas as he eyed Chee angrily. "And you rode all the way over here thinking that for a little food we would give up our daughter's daughter?"

Chee did not wait for the old man to reach for the Little One. He walked dazedly to the shelter, rubbing his cheek against her soft dark hair and put her gently into her grandmother's lap. Then he turned back to the horses. He had failed. By his own haste he had failed. He swung into the saddle, his hand touching the roll behind it. Should he ride on into town?

Then he dismounted, scarcely glancing at Old Man Fat, who stood uncertainly at the corner of the shelter, listening to his wife. "Give me a hand with this other pack of corn, Grandfather," Chee said, carefully keeping the small bit of hope from his voice.

Puzzled, but willing, Old Man Fat helped carry the other pack to the shelter, opening it to find more corn as well as carrots and round, pale yellow onions. Chee went back for the roll behind the buckskin's saddle and carried it to the entrance of the shelter where he cut the ropes and gave the canvas a nudge with his toe. Tins of coffee rolled out, small plump cloth bags; jerked meat from several butcherings spilled from a flour sack, and bright red chilis splashed like flames against the dust.

"I will leave all this anyhow," Chee told them. "I would not want my daughter nor even you old people to go hungry."

Old Man Fat picked up a shiny tin of coffee, then put it down. With trembling hands he began to untie one of the cloth bags—dried sweet peaches.

The Little One had wriggled from her grandmother's lap, unheeded, and was on her knees, digging her hands into the jerked meat.

"There is almost enough food here to last all winter," Old Man Fat's wife sought the eyes of her husband.

Chee said, "I meant it to be enough. But that was when I thought you might send the Little One back with me." He looked down at his daughter noisily sucking jerky. Her mouth and both fists were full of it. "I am sorry that you feel you cannot bear to part with her."

Old Man Fat's wife brushed a straggly wisp of gray hair from her forehead as she turned to look at the Little One. Old Man Fat was looking too. And it was not a thing to see. For in that moment the Little One ceased to be their daughter's daughter and became just another mouth to feed.

"And why not?" the old woman asked wearily.

Chee was settled in the saddle, the barefooted Little One before him. He urged the buckskin faster, and his daughter clutched his shirtfront. The purpling mesas flung back the echo: ". . . My corn embrace each other. In the middle of the wide field . . . Yellow Corn Boy embrace each other."

---

straggly (STRAG lee) wandering off course

Chee's Daughter ■ 329

Literary Focus:
Symbolism
Help students to see that Chee sings different parts of the corn song at different points in the story, and that the lines relate to what is happening in the story. For example, on page 325 the lines of the song reflect Chee's planting activities. Ask students how the lines Chee sings in the last paragraph on page 329 reflect what happens at the end of the story.

Critical Thinking:
Apply
Chee's song about the Corn Boy is the story's central symbol. Ask: Are there other symbols or symbolic characters in this story? If so, describe them. Do you think Chee's daughter is a symbolic character? If so, what might she symbolize?

Mini Quiz

Write on the chalkboard or overhead projector the following sentences and call on students to fill in the blanks. Discuss the answers with the class.

1. At the beginning of the story, Chee's _____ has just died.

2. Chee's daughter has been taken from him by _____, according to the Navajo custom.

3. Chee goes to the Red Sands Trading Post in order to see _____.

4. For a short time Chee thinks he should leave _____.

5. Finally, Chee decides to win back his daughter by _____.

Answers
1. wife
2. his wife's parents
3. his father-in-law
4. his home, Little Canyon
5. growing food to bring his in-laws

Review the Selection

UNDERSTAND THE SELECTION

Recall

1. What event has just taken place in Chee's life?

2. What does Chee find out at home after his wife's death?

3. What does Chee decide to do about it?

Infer

4. Why did Old Man Fat think he was superior to Chee?

5. What trait in his father-in-law did Chee hope would work to his advantage?

6. Why did Chee suspect that his father-in-law's fortunes would worsen?

7. Why did Chee empty all the bundles of food on the floor before he left?

Apply

8. Select details in the story that show how Chee's in-laws have gone from prosperity to poverty.

9. Do you agree with Chee that "jobs and people might fail one, but the earth never would"?

10. What might have happened if Chee had taken the job offered by his cousins?

Respond to Literature

What discoveries did Chee make in the course of the story? What did he finally discover about his own values?

330 ■ Unit 4

WRITE ABOUT THE SELECTION

In the short story "Chee's Daughter," several characters are important to the story's development. There is Chee himself, the Little One, Old Man Fat, and Old Man Fat's wife. How do you feel about each of these characters? Do you admire Chee? Do you agree with Old Man Fat's values and actions? Do you feel sorry for the Little One? Do you like or dislike Old Man Fat's wife? Explain why.

Prewriting Make a chart of the four characters. List your feelings about each character, both positive and negative. Then decide which character you feel most strongly about. That will be the subject of your paragraph.

Writing Use the ideas in your list to write a paragraph that describes your reaction to a character in "Chee's Daughter."

Revising To revise your paragraph, think of adding a sentence that reflects an opinion different from yours. For example, if you disliked Old Man Fat, you might add the sentence: "I did not like Old Man Fat, but some people might admire him because he did what was most practical in the situation." Be sure to use evidence from the story to support your opinion and the opposing opinion.

Proofreading Check your paper for mistakes in spelling, usage, and mechanics. Be sure you have used commas before the conjunctions in compound sentences.

THINK ABOUT SYMBOLISM

A symbol links a specific thing with a certain idea, value, people, or way of life. A symbol points to something beyond itself, to a greater meaning.

1. What object is used as a symbol in the opening of "Chee's Daughter"?

2. What does this symbol tell you about Chee's mood?

3. What symbol do the authors use to represent the land?

4. In what way is this symbol woven into the story?

5. Explain why the authors end the story with this symbol.

READING FOCUS

Make Inferences To understand the characters' feelings and actions in "Chee's Daughter," you often had to make inferences from statements by and about the characters. What can you infer about Chee's mood at the beginning of the story? at the end of the story? On what details are your inferences based?

DEVELOP YOUR VOCABULARY

An **adjective** is a word that modifies or describes a noun. For example, the word *fat* is an adjective because it can describe nouns such as *man*, *dog*, *baby*, or *face*: fat man, fat dog, fat baby, fat face.

An **adverb** is a word that modifies or describes a verb. An adverb tells how an action takes place. For example, the word *fast* is an adverb. *Fast* can be used to describe the way a person runs (he runs fast), thinks (she thinks fast), or talks (the teacher talks fast).

Review the meaning of each of these words from "Chee's Daughter." Decide whether each word is an adjective or an adverb. Then use each word in an original sentence. In your sentences, underline the noun or verb that the adjective or adverb modifies.

1. rakish
2. zealously
3. straggly
4. gaudy
5. acrid

THINK ABOUT SYMBOLISM

Answers

1. Stetson hat
2. Something is wrong with Chee; he is downcast.
3. the corn
4. Parts of a song about the Corn Boy appear throughout the story.
5. It is Chee's faith in the land that wins back his daughter. The song about the corn at the end of the story is like a hymn of celebration.

DEVELOP YOUR VOCABULARY

Sample Answers

1. Adjective. The hat was worn at a rakish <u>angle</u>.
2. Adverb. He <u>worked</u> zealously.
3. Adjective. She had several pieces of straggly <u>hair</u>.
4. Adjective. She was wearing a gaudy <u>dress</u>.
5. Adjective. The food left an acidic <u>taste</u> in his mouth.

READING FOCUS

Sample Answer

Chee is sad and bitter at the beginning of the story. His wife had died and he had hoped that she would live. By the end of the story, Chee is happy. He sings the song of the Corn Boy as he did before when he was contentedly tending the land he loves.

ESL Activity

Ask students to think about what they value most in life. Encourage them to consider relationships, rewarding activities, their ideas about right and wrong, and favorite activities. Discuss how knowing what they value can help them make important decisions in life.

SELECTION OVERVIEW

SELECTION OBJECTIVES

After completing this selection, students will be able to

- understand the use of symbolism
- create symbols from nature
- relate the theme of the poem to discoveries
- write from a different point of view
- analyze the use of figurative language
- use prepositions
- identify fact and opinion

Lesson Resources

Navaho Chant
- Selection Synopsis, Teacher's Edition, p. T311c
- Comprehension and Vocabulary Workbook, pp. 60–61
- Language Enrichment Workbook, pp. 63–64
- Teacher's Resources
  Reinforcement, p. R30
  Test, pp. T57–T58

More About Symbolism

Although a symbol is usually a tangible object, it can be something less concrete, such as a song, a color, or lines from a story or poem. It also can be something quite vast, such as the land, the sky, the earth or space. Have a student read the lines about the Corn Boy that appear in the story "Chee's Daughter." Guide students to recognize the connection between these lines and "Navaho Chant."

Background Notes

Hanging a colorful rug in the doorway of a home is a tradition of the Navajo culture. The image in the poem "beautiful goods curtain which hangs at the doorway" is drawn from this tradition.

READING FOCUS

Identify Fact and Opinion A fact is a statement that can be measured or proven. An opinion is a statement that tells what a person believes. "This poem has sixteen lines" is a fact. "This chant is very interesting to me" is an opinion. Facts and opinions can occur side by side in any type of writing.

As you read "Navaho Chant," note the statements you think are opinions of the speaker and which you think are facts.

332 ■ Unit 4

SYMBOLISM IN POETRY

A **symbol** is an object that represents a larger idea. Symbolism is often used in poetry because it can express a great deal of meaning in the space of a few words.

In the story "Chee's Daughter," the land is very important to Chee. Throughout the story, fragments of a Navaho song about the Corn Boy run through Chee's mind. This song—and the corn itself—are symbols of Chee's deep connection to the land. The Navaho Chant that you are about to read is part of the song that Chee sings,

In the poem "Navaho Chant," there are many symbols. As you read the poem, ask yourself:

1. Who is speaking in the poem?
2. What does the symbol "home" represent?

WRITING CONNECTION

Native American writers and others often use objects from nature as symbols. Think of something in nature that is meaningful to you. For example, perhaps you find special meaning in sunsets, the ocean, clouds, snow, or a certain kind of tree. Write a short poem or paragraph in which this object from nature is used as a symbol of a larger idea.

Develop Vocabulary Skills

The vocabulary in this selection is relatively simple. You may wish to point out to students that the word "goods" means fabric or material, and that "pollen" is the powdery substance that is transferred in plant production.

ESL Activity

Invite students to read the chant aloud in unison. You may wish to "line out" the chant by reading each line first and then having students repeat it.

Cooperative Group Activity

Have students work in pairs to complete the Writing Connection activity. Ask each pair to create a single poem in which something from nature is used as a symbol of a larger idea. Have students read the poem aloud together.

T332

Corn Ceremony, Narciso Abeyta (Ha-So-De), Navaho, Courtesy, Alice G. Howland

NAVAHO CHANT

Traditional Navaho Song

I am the White Corn Boy.
I walk in sight of my home.
I walk in plain sight of my home.
I walk on the straight path which is towards my home.
5   I walk to the entrance of my home.
I arrive at the beautiful goods curtain which hangs at the doorway.
I arrive at the entrance of my home.
I am in the middle of my home.
I am at the back of my home.
10 I am on top of the pollen seed footprint.
I am like the Most High Power Whose Ways Are Beautiful.
Before me it is beautiful,
Behind me it is beautiful,
Under me it is beautiful,
15 Above me it is beautiful,
All around me it is beautiful.

Navaho Chant ■ 333

UNDERSTAND THE SELECTION

Answers

1. the White Corn Boy
2. home
3. the Great High Power Whose Ways Are Beautiful
4. Home is the land or the earth; it also refers to the actual home, or house, of the Navaho.
5. a straight row of corn in a field
6. the pollen that falls onto the earth from the seeds of a plant
7. one of great beauty, peace, and fulfillment
8. similar, in that a great journey has successfully ended and a feeling of beauty and fulfillment is the result
9. Answers may vary. An example: Home. The word is repeated to emphasize the continual movement toward that goal; home is the destination, the place of fulfillment.
10. Sample answer: Movement of the growing corn plant upward toward and through the surface of the earth, then taller and taller.

Respond to Literature

Have students draw diagrams to represent a journey in their own lives or the lives of one of the characters in this unit. Emphasize that a journey need not be a physical one; it can also be a journey toward a personal goal, or an inward journey of changing thoughts, ideas, and feelings.

WRITE ABOUT THE SELECTION

Prewriting

Make a list on the chalkboard or on an overhead transparency of possible points of view. Have students discuss the various aspects of each one.

Writing

Have students work on this section individually. Go around the classroom, helping any student who is having difficulty. Ask students to consider the vantage point of the viewer: Is the viewer above the corn, below it, or around it? Is the viewer larger, smaller, shorter, taller, or about the same size as the corn?

UNDERSTAND THE SELECTION

Recall

1. Who is speaking in the poem?
2. Where is the speaker going?
3. To whom does the speaker liken himself?

Infer

4. What is the meaning of the word "home" in the poem?
5. What might the "straight path" refer to?
6. What is the "pollen seed footprint"?
7. What is the speaker's feeling at the end of the poem?

Apply

8. Compare the feeling of the poem to Chee's feeling at the end of "Chee's Daughter."
9. Select a word that is used repeatedly throughout the poem. Explain the importance of the word.
10. Explain how this poem might be dramatized in movement.

Respond to Literature

The speaker in the poem completes a kind of journey and, as a result, discovers certain feelings. What feelings have you discovered in yourself after completing a journey or reaching a goal?

WRITE ABOUT THE SELECTION

The poem "Navaho Chant" is written from the Corn Boy's point of view. How might the same poem be written from another point of view? Your task is to write a paragraph in which a person, animal, or object in nature views the Corn Boy.

Prewriting Make a list of possible points of view. For example, the corn could be seen by a bird, an old person, a child, an insect, or the earth itself. Decide which viewpoint you find most interesting; then let this be the point of view of your paragraph. Jot down as many ideas as you can think of about how the corn would look from the viewpoint you have chosen.

Writing Use the ideas from your notes to write a paragraph that describes the corn from another point of view. Your paragraph should make it clear who or what is viewing the corn. Do you want to use first person (*I*) or third person (*he, she, it, they*)?

Revising Try writing all or part of your paragraph in a chant style similar to the poem itself. It is often helpful to read aloud what you have written to see if it really has the sound of a chant or song.

Consider adding or eliminating details to make your paragraph more descriptive.

Proofreading Check for errors in spelling, usage, and mechanics. Remember to capitalize the first word in each line if you wrote your paragraph as a chant.

ESL Activity

Have students think of a song they know that uses repetition effectively. They may wish to consider children's songs as well as current popular songs by favorite groups. Invite students to sing or recite a portion of the song. You may wish to have them do additional research to confirm or discover all the words of the song before reciting.

THINK ABOUT SYMBOLISM

Symbolism is a form of figurative language. **Figurative language** expresses meaning that is more than just the dictionary definition of the words themselves. A symbol is something that has meaning in itself but also stands for something else. The special meaning of a symbol depends on the poem or story in which it appears.

1. What is the special meaning of the word *home* in "Navaho Chant"?

2. Why do you think the author of the poem chose to use this word?

3. What choice of words describes the movement of the corn as it grows?

4. How does the poem make the corn seem like a person?

5. What is the Most High Power Whose Ways Are Beautiful?

READING FOCUS

Identify Fact and Opinion Create a fact and opinion chart for "Navaho Chant." Divide a sheet of paper in half. On the left, write the lines of the poem that state opinions. On the right, write the lines that state facts. Then write a paragraph about your impression of the poem. Use supporting details from your chart.

DEVELOP YOUR VOCABULARY

A **preposition** can be used to describe the relationship between two words or phrases. For example, in the sentence, "The ground is under the corn," the preposition *under* describes the relationship between the corn and the ground.

In "Navaho Chant," prepositions are important to the meaning of the poem. Explain how each of the prepositions listed below is used in the poem to describe a relationship. Then use each preposition in an original sentence.

1. on	5. behind
2. to	6. under
3. at	7. above
4. before	8. around

Review the Selection ■ 335

THINK ABOUT SYMBOLISM

Answers
1. It means the earth, the land itself.
2. The earth is where the corn lives.
3. the idea of "walking to my home"
4. The corn has a name—White Corn Boy; it speaks, it walks; it lives in a home.
5. the Navaho concept of God; perhaps the earth itself since tribal cultures often worship nature

DEVELOP YOUR VOCABULARY

Sample Answers
The prepositions below show the relationships between:
1. on-me and the pollen seed footprints
2. to-me and the entrance door
3. at-me and the beautiful goods curtain
4. before-me and nature
5. behind-me and nature
6. under-me and nature
7. above-me and nature
8. around-me and nature

Sample sentences:
1. We balanced on the railing.
2. I approached the entrance to the tunnel.
3. We should arrive at about the same time.
4. Before us the sea stretched for miles.
5. I heard a loud noise behind me.
6. She keeps the box under her bed.
7. The sun shone brightly above us.
8. Seagulls filled the air all around us.

READING FOCUS

Sample Answer
Opinions: I am like the Most High . . . Beautiful. Above me it is beautiful. All around me it is beautiful. Facts: I am the White Corn Boy. I walk in sight of my home. I arrive at the entrance of my home.

To me, this poem shows the importance of nature to the Navaho. The ground nurtures the corn, and the corn nurtures the Navaho. Everything above, below, and around the corn is beautiful.

SELECTION OVERVIEW

SELECTION OBJECTIVES

After completing this selection, students will be able to

- identify character traits
- write a description of a character
- identify the main character's self-discovery
- create a new episode for a story
- identify flat and round characters
- use adverbs ending in -ly
- use connotations

Lesson Resources

The Gold Medal

- Selection Synopsis, Teacher's Edition, p. T311c
- Comprehension and Vocabulary Workbook, pp. 63–64
- Language Enrichment Workbook, pp. 65–67
- Teacher's Resources Reinforcement, p. R31 Test, pp. T59–T60

More About Character Traits

Have students recall the story "Chee's Daughter." Ask: Is Chee a flat or round character? Also ask about the other characters in the story. Point out that round characters are much more interesting to read about than flat characters. They are easier to identify with because they are three-dimensional and therefore fuller representations of real people.

Background Notes

Amanda, the main character in "The Gold Medal," may have admired a person like Jesse Owens. Owens was an African American athlete who won four gold medals in the 1936 Olympics and set the world record for the running long jump. Owens's performance at the 1936 Olympics in Berlin, Germany, upset Hitler's attempt to use the games to prove Aryan superiority.

READING FOCUS

Use Connotations Many words have connotations; that is, they suggest certain feelings. These feelings may be positive or negative. For example, the word *skinny* has a negative connotation, while the word *slender* has a more positive connotation. Writers pay close attention to the connotations of the words they use. By noticing these connotations, you can make inferences about the characters' attitudes and opinions.

Learn About

CHARACTER TRAITS

In literature, a character is a person who the author invents through words. An author creates a character by describing the character and by having the character say and do certain things. An author also creates a character by commenting on the character's thoughts and feelings.

Characters in stories can usually be classified as either flat or round. **Flat characters** are stereotypes: the crazy teenager, the greedy businessman, the crabby old lady. **Round characters** come across as real people. They have many facets, or parts, to their personalities.

The story "The Gold Medal" contains both flat and round characters. As you read the story, ask yourself:

1. Is Amanda a flat or a round character?
2. What stereotypes exist among the other characters?

WRITING CONNECTION

Think of a person you meet almost every day. If you were writing a story about yourself, would this person appear as a flat or a round character? Write a paragraph in which you describe this person.

Cooperative Group Activity

Have students work in groups of three or four to extend the Writing Connection activity. Ask students to jot down at least one trait or characteristic of each member of their group; for example, Jeff has red hair; Alicia is a good dancer. Then have students pool their notes and work together to write a brief character sketch of each group member. Ask the students to evaluate among themselves which sketch had the most round character; then have the groups present that sketch to the rest of the class.

THE
GOLD
MEDAL

by Nan Gilbert

The day had been too much for Amanda. It had started out bad and got no better, one thing piling on another all day long.

"That skirt is too short," her mother had frowned during this morning's last minute inspection. "Did you scrub your teeth? Are your fingernails clean?"

"Mom, I'm not a *baby*!" Amanda had let out a hopeless squawk and fled. It was no use. When her mother looked at her, she didn't see Amanda—not really. She saw an Example to help show their new neighbors that the Dawsons were as clean and quiet and well-mannered as any family on the block.

"I'm not an Example!" grumbled Amanda rebelliously. "I'm *me*!"

Amanda Dawson—tall for her years, a little thin, leggy as a newborn colt. Flopping short black ponytail, jutting elbows, springy knees. Long feet that could trip her up—and frequently did. Face plain and unremarkable except for large, liquid, chocolate-brown eyes, just one shade darker than her scrubbed, shining skin.

What did her mother see, if she didn't see Amanda? Amanda's quick imagination leaped to present her with the picture of a Proper Example: a spotlessly clean, tidy creature who kept her elbows in and her knees hidden . . . whose hair never worked loose from its tight rubberband . . . who didn't run or shout or use slang . . . whose name was always on the honor roll. . . .

"You there—shoo! Don't trespass! Keep to the sidewalk!"

Absorbed in her picture-making, Amanda had unthinkingly taken the shortcut across Mrs. Hawthorne's corner

---

rebelliously (rih BEL yus lee) resisting authority
jutting (JUHT ing) sticking out sharply
absorbed (ab SAWRBD) deeply interested

The Gold Medal ■ 337

lot. Now the old lady had popped from her house like a cuckoo from a clock.

"Oh, woe!" muttered Amanda, retreating quickly. "Here we go again!"

The first time this had happened, Amanda had felt bewildered. The short-cut was worn bare by years of school-children's feet, and others seemed to be using it freely.

"I'm not hurting anything," she had said.

Her protest roused the old lady to a flurry of shrill bird-like cries. "This is private property—I have my rights!"

Now, loping back to the sidewalk, pursued by indignant chirps, Amanda told herself resignedly, "Mrs. Hawthorne doesn't see me either." When the old lady looked at Amanda, it was as though she saw not just one girl, but a whole regiment of Amandas, marching across her lot, crushing flowers and shrubs!

Amanda sighed. How did you make someone really *see* you? So they'd know you were *you*? Not a Regiment. Not an Example.

Not a Gang of Hoodlums, either! That's what Mr. Grogan always saw when he looked at her, Amanda decided. By the time Amanda entered Mr. Grogan's store to buy a candy bar, her imagination was growing livelier by the minute.

Mr. Grogan was all smiles and jokes— "Well, well, what's it going to be this time? A nice big box of chocolates, maybe?" he asked.

But he watched Amanda carefully as she lingered over the candy display. When she brought her purchase to the counter, he made an excuse to peek into her lunch sack—"My, my, won't get any fatter on a diet like that!"

No need to look—I didn't steal anything! For a second, Amanda was afraid she had said the words out loud. Mom would split a seam if she even suspected Amanda of speaking up like that, pert and sassy! Hastily, Amanda grabbed her sack and ducked out of the store. Until she had her imagination under control, she'd better keep a close guard on her tongue!

Head down, Amanda scuffed slowly toward school. The day had hardly begun and already it rested heavily on her shoulders. Nor did she expect anything inside the walls of Jefferson School to lighten the load.

School was Amanda's greatest trial this fall. Instead of a familiar building filled with old friends, her family's move to a new home had made Amanda a stranger among strangers. As yet she had made no real friends to replace those she had lost.

---

bewildered (bih WIL durd) confused; puzzled
flurry (FLUR ee) noisy confusion
indignant (in DIG nunt) angry
resignedly (rih ZYN id lee) without a struggle
regiment (REJ uh ment) a military unit
pert (PURT) bold speech or behavior

The Gold Medal ■ 339

Discussion
How does Amanda's imagination make people and places seem worse than they really are? Ask students if they ever feel like they are being picked on by adults in their lives the way Amanda does.

Reading Focus:
Use Connotations
Make a quick word web on the chalkboard for *hoodlums*. Ask students what feelings or other associations are suggested by this word. Record their responses in the web. Also ask them to list synonyms for this word that have a similarly negative connotation.

Literary Focus:
Flat Characters
Point out that flat characters are usually minor characters that appear briefly in a story or remain in the background. Ask students to give an example of a flat character in the story so far.

Literary Focus:
Flat and Round Characters

Help students to see that the character of Mr. Moore, Amanda's science teacher, is not quite as flat as Mr. Grogan or Mrs. Hawthorne. Although his main trait is kindness, he seems a bit more complex and real to the reader because he is capable of "hurt surprise." Ask: Why does Amanda think Mr. Moore is kind to her?

Reading Focus:
Use Connotations

Tell students that the basic meaning of a word, or its dictionary definition, is its *denotation*. Point out that two words can have the same denotation but very different connotations. For example, *stupid* and *uneducated* both denote "lacking knowledge," but *stupid* has a much more negative connotation. Ask: Can you think of two words that have the same denotation but opposite connotations?

Critical Thinking:
Infer

When Amanda asserts that she has as much right as anyone to be stupid, she is expressing her right to be judged as a human being and not by race. How does the author imply that Amanda is feeling stress from racial tensions?

Though some of the girls were cordial and kind, nobody asked her home after school or stopped at Amanda's house for cookies and pop. And she knew there were others—or maybe it was their parents—who didn't like her being at Jefferson at all. This thought added to the day's accumulating weight of gloom.

During the noon break, Amanda avoided the lunchroom. She took her sack-lunch outside to a sheltered corner of the building. For some reason, today the sunny nook seemed lonely. Each bite Amanda swallowed had to fight its way past a great lump that unexpectedly blocked her throat.

When the bell summoned her back to class, Amanda reluctantly joined the hurrying, chattering crowds in the hall. Her next class was science, taught by Mr. Moore. Amanda thought Mr. Moore the nicest of all the teachers; for him she tried extra hard to do good work. Her first lonely, awkward day in Jefferson, Mr. Moore had welcomed her with genuine warmth. And he was always generous with his after-school time, ready to help her if there was something she didn't understand.

But now, slumped low in her backrow seat, with the lump still big in her throat and a growing heaviness in her heart, Amanda thought, "He doesn't see me either. He'd treat *any* black kid the same way." Because he's kindhearted. Because he truly wants to help a black child fit into a white world. For him, she was the symbol of a cause he believed in. She wasn't herself at all.

Mr. Moore had to call her name twice before she realized he had asked her a question. Amanda stared at him somberly.

"I don't know," she said.

"Oh, come now, Amanda, of course you do. Remember, it's what we talked about yesterday—"

"I don't know!" The lump in Amanda's throat broke suddenly into a loud, dismaying sob. "Why is it so awful if *I* don't know? Lots of times *they* don't know, and you never look so—so—" It was Mr. Moore's look of hurt surprise that sent her dashing out of the room, that and the new and louder sob rising in her throat.

From the doorway she turned to face him. "I don't care—it's true!—I've got as much right to be st-stupid as anybody!" The second sob got away from her before she could slam the door. Humiliated, she pelted down the hall and out of the building.

The day was too lovely for gloom— an Indian summer afternoon, with rich

---

cordial (KAWR jul) warm, friendly
reluctantly (rih LUK tunt lee) unwillingly; slowly
genuine (JEN yoo in) real, authentic
somberly (SOM bur lee) sadly; unhappily
dismaying (dis MAY ing) losing courage or confidence
pelt (PELT) to hurry or rush

golden warmth spread over the fields and hills like an eiderdown quilt. In spite of herself, her bowed shoulders lifted, her heart lightened. . . .

And she began to run. Running, to Amanda, was like flying. There was special joy in the clean rush of air against her upraised face, the pounding blood in her veins. When Amanda ran, she left all her coltish awkwardness behind. Her stride lengthened; her arms pumped; her long feet—that could trip her up when she walked—barely skimmed the ground.

Down the road she flew, and across a pasture where horses pricked their ears at her in mild amazement. She had to stop for breath—panting, laughing, giddy with this supercharge of oxygen—then she was off again. Up and over a gentle slope where a giant cottonwood offered an oasis of cool green shade she flew.

Too late Amanda saw the high heap of overturned earth below the tree. The springs in her tiring legs coiled and propelled her upward. Arms and legs stretched wide in a split. Thin body bent flat over her forward knee, Amanda cleared the pile of dirt—

But not the excavation behind it. Arms flailing, legs treading the air, she lunged for the far side, then fell back ingloriously into the hole.

"You hurt?" a voice asked with quavery concern.

Amanda sat up, dazed, and brushed dirt from her hands and skirt. Her startled brown eyes, almost level with the rim of hollowed-out earth, saw for the first time the bent figure of an old man under the tree.

"N-no," she said.

"That was mighty pretty running," the old man said with approval, "and as nice a hurdle as ever I've seen. I'm glad you didn't hurt yourself." After a moment, he added, "That's a grave you're settin' in."

Amanda squeaked and scrambled out onto the grass. "A—a *grave?*"

"Yep, for Chief. Chief's my dog."

"Oh—" Amanda cast about for words. "I—I'm sorry he's dead."

"He isn't. Not yet anyway." The old man struggled to his feet. He leaned heavily on his spade as he surveyed his handiwork. "Just about ready. Yep, a few more days and it'll be done. Wouldn't want anyone else to dig it—not for Chief. But if I was to do it, I figured I'd better get started. Can't turn more'n a few spadefuls a day."

Amanda looked at the excavation

---

eiderdown quilt (EYE dur doun KWILT) a comforter filled with soft duck feathers
giddy (GID ee) dizzy, lightheaded
cottonwood (KOT un wuud) kind of wide-spreading tree
propel (pruh PEL) to drive forward
excavation (eks kuh VAY shun) hole made by digging
flailing (FLAYL ing) waving wildly
treading (TRED ing) stepping on
ingloriously (in GLAWR ee us lee) disgracefully
quavery (KWAY vur ee) trembling; shaking

342 ■ Unit 4

over which the old man was now pulling a piece of tarpaulin. "He—must be a big dog."

"He's that, all right. Used to be, anyway." The old man weighted the tarpaulin with a rock at each corner, then straightened slowly. "Kinda thin now, poor old boy. You want to come meet him? Chief was a runner, too, in his day—and his day lasted a lot longer than most."

Taking her consent for granted, he started down the other side of the slope toward a small house almost hidden behind a tangle of vines and shrubbery. Amanda looked a little wildly toward town, but an emotion much stronger than her alarm tugged her in the opposite direction. A runner, the old man had said—just like that. Here was someone who had looked at her and seen—not a Black Child or an Example or a Black Regiment, but Amanda herself—a runner. Wordless with upswelling gratitude, she followed the old man through a door. When Amanda's eyes adjusted to the dim light inside, she made out the form of a big black dog sprawled near the window in a dappling of green-filtered sunlight. Except for a single thump of tail, he didn't move. The old man stooped low, patted the black head and scratched gently behind long velvety ears.

Cautiously, Amanda went nearer. She didn't know much about dogs; she was uncertain how to treat one that seemed so barely alive. "Is he—uh—pretty old?"

"Sixteen," the old man said. "Yep, that's pretty old for a dog. 'Specially a hunter like Chief . . . we've had some high times together, haven't we, old boy?"

The tail thumped once again. Amanda knelt gingerly and stroked the black coat; it was silky soft, but there seemed nothing between it and the bones beneath. To cover her dismay, she said hurriedly, "I guess a dog is a pretty good friend, isn't he?"

"The right kind of dog—yep, no better."

"You mean, like a hunter maybe?"

The old man snorted, "Breed's the least of it! Line up a hundred Labradors and, chances are, you wouldn't find another like Chief. Wasn't another in his own litter like him. I know—I had the pick of the litter."

Grunting a little with the effort, he straightened and moved to a chair by an ancient roll-top desk. "My friend couldn't figure why I took the pup I did. 'Sam,' he says, 'that's the runt of the lot! Look here—see how lively this one is!' But I held to my choice—yes siree, I knew I had a winner."

"How?" asked Amanda, fascinated.

---

tarpaulin (tahr PAW lin) a waterproof sheet used to protect
dappling (DAP ling) group, or bunch of spots
gingerly (JIN jur lee) very carefully
Labradors (LAB ruh dawrz) breed of big dogs
litter (LIT ur) young animals born at one time

The Gold Medal ■ 343

"By the look in his eyes. There he sat, all paws and floppy head, as forlorn a pup as you'd see by any ash can, but those eyes were watching me. 'Believe in me,' they said, 'and I can do anything.'" The old man laughed. "Guess you think I'm a little foolish—well, maybe so. But I wasn't wrong about Chief, no sir! This proves it."

The old desk creaked as he rolled up the cover. In every pigeonhole within there was a ribbon—red ribbons, blue ribbons, purple ribbons, and a single gold medal. "Won 'em all, Chief did," the old man said proudly. He touched one after another. "Best working dog . . . best in class . . . best of show . . ."

Out of curiosity, Amanda reached for the gold medal. "Why, it's a *runner's* medal!" she cried.

The old man took the medal from her and studied it fondly. "Yep, this was his first—bought it myself. Chief cried his heart out that day, wanted to do miracles for me but he just didn't have the know-how yet. 'Never you mind,' I told him. 'I know you're a champion.' Next time I went to town, I bought him a medal to wear till he'd proved himself to everyone else."

As if he had followed their conversation, the black dog thumped his tail once more, and fleetingly raised his head. The old man nodded. "Yep, you're right, Chief. You showed 'em. Don't need this one anymore."

Unexpectedly, he extended it to Amanda. "*You* wear it, Sis. You got the look—just like Chief had. Wear it till you win your own."

Amanda gulped. She sniffed back tears and had to rub her nose childishly. "They look at me—" she sobbed, "but they don't *see* me!"

"You see yourself, don't you?" the old man asked mildly. "Well, then, what more do you need? A dream, and the ambition to work for it—enough for anybody." Gently he closed her fingers over the medal.

forlorn (fur LAWRN) miserable
pigeonhole (PIJ un hohl) small compartment in a desk

The Gold Medal ■ 345

UNDERSTAND THE SELECTION

Answers

1. frustrated; nothing has gone right
2. She runs out of the class because she is so frustrated at not being seen as herself.
3. She begins to run.
4. She wants to prove that her family is as good as any other family on the block.
5. He wants to help African American children fit into a white world.
6. mostly white
7. Both are runners, and both have the ability to do great things, even though others may not see it.
8. Sample answer: Amanda will feel better about herself and not mind so much the way she is treated by her mother and others.
9. Sample answer: She would have felt guilty about leaving school and more upset with herself than ever.
10. Sample answer: Hurt that she did not appreciate all that he had done for her.

Respond to Literature

Have students work individually to write a journal entry about an adult who has been a positive influence in their lives. Ask for volunteers to read their journal entries to the class.

WRITE ABOUT THE SELECTION

Prewriting

Show students how to make a diagram to help them in brainstorming ideas for their paragraphs. Draw a circle on the chalkboard or overhead transparency. Then write in a word or phrase that describes the topic of the paragraph: for example, "next day at school." Next draw lines around the circle, like the spokes of a wheel. On each line, write a phrase or sentence that describes something that could happen the next day: for example, "Amanda calls the principal's office; Amanda apologizes to Mr. Moore; other students ask Amanda where she went."

UNDERSTAND THE SELECTION

Recall

1. What is Amanda's mood at first?
2. What happens to Amanda in class?
3. What does Amanda do after she leaves school?

Infer

4. Why is Amanda's mother so eager for her to be an example?
5. According to Amanda, why is Mr. Moore always nice to her?
6. Would you guess that Amanda's school and neighborhood are racially mixed, mostly African American, or mostly white?
7. In what ways does the old man think that Amanda and Chief are alike?

Apply

8. How do you think receiving the gold medal will affect Amanda?
9. What do you think would have happened to Amanda that day if she had not met the old man?
10. You are Mr. Moore. How did you feel when Amanda left class?

Respond to Literature

How did the old man help Amanda discover herself? In what ways was he different from the other adults in Amanda's life?

WRITE ABOUT THE SELECTION

At the end of the story, Amanda is still with the old man. What do you think will happen to Amanda when she reenters her everyday world of home and school? Write a paragraph that describes something that happens to Amanda within the next 24 hours after the story ends.

Prewriting Make a list of the situations that Amanda will probably have to face. For example, how will Amanda explain her muddy clothes to her mother? Will she get in trouble for leaving school early? What will she say to Mr. Moore? Choose the situation that most interests you and let this be the subject of your paragraph. Then jot down some of the details that you wish to include.

Writing As you write your paragraph, ask yourself these questions: Which characters are involved in this situation? What do they say and do? How does Amanda feel about this situation? Has her experience with the gold medal changed her feelings and attitudes? What is the outcome of the situation?

Revising Rewrite your paragraph so that it flows easily after the last paragraph of the story. See if you can make the tone and style of your paragraph similar to that of the author.

Proofreading Check your paragraph for mistakes in spelling, usage, and mechanics. Be sure to use question marks if you use questions in your paper.

Writing

As students work on this section individually, circulate to help those who are having difficulty. As students develop their episodes, encourage them to keep asking themselves questions such as "What might happen next?" or "What if . . ."

Revising

Have students work in small groups. Encourage them to read their paragraphs aloud to each other and to consider the comments of the group before they revise.

Proofreading

Have students trade papers with a partner. Then have the pair check each other's papers for errors.

THINK ABOUT CHARACTER

Round characters tend to develop and change as a story progresses. Flat characters, on the other hand, tend to stay the same. Often the flat characters form a kind of background for the main character's story.

1. Explain why you think Amanda is a flat or a round character.

2. How do other characters in the story see Amanda—as flat or round?

3. Identify three flat characters in the story and their stereotypes.

4. Based on what you know about Amanda's mother, how do you think she would react if Amanda were to pursue running as a sport or career?

5. Would you say that the animal character in the story is flat or round?

READING FOCUS

Use Connotations On your own, choose a word (an adjective) that sums up your opinion of "The Gold Medal." Avoid the words *good* or *bad*. Then, as a class, draw a long horizontal line on the chalkboard to represent a scale. Mark the center of the scale with a zero. Label one end of the scale "very positive" and the other "very negative." Take turns recording the words you chose on the scale. Write your word at the appropriate place on the scale depending on its connotation and how strong it is.

DEVELOP YOUR VOCABULARY

Many adverbs are formed by adding *-ly* to an adjective. For example, the adverb *quickly* is formed by adding *-ly* to the adjective *quick*. If you are not sure of the meaning of an adverb that ends in *-ly*, try to figure out the meaning of the adjective from which it has been formed. The adverb should have a similar meaning. For example, a quick (adjective) runner will run quickly (adverb).

Review the meanings of these adverbs from "The Gold Medal." Underline the adjective from which each is formed. Then use each adverb in an original sentence.

1. rebelliously
2. frequently
3. unthinkingly
4. resignedly
5. reluctantly
6. unexpectedly
7. somberly
8. childishly
9. mildly
10. fleetingly

Review the Selection ■ 347

THINK ABOUT CHARACTER

Answers

1. She is a round character because she seems like a real person who has many aspects to her personality.

2. All see her as flat except for the old man.

3. Mother—typical of the type who wants her children to make a good impression; neighbor—crabby old lady; Mr. Moore—liberal who tries to help African Americans; storekeeper—adult who distrusts teenagers.

4. Answers will vary. Some may think that she would like the status if Amanda becomes a champ; others may think that she would not think this occupation was acceptable for her respectable daughter.

5. Round in the sense that the dog developed in many ways; the old man compares the dog to Amanda.

DEVELOP YOUR VOCABULARY

Answers

Sample sentences are given.

1. *rebellious*—She walked away from the school *rebelliously*.
2. *frequent*—Amanda used the short-cut f*requently*.
3. *unthinking*—Amanda walked across the lawn *unthinkingly*.
4. *resigned*—She looked *resignedly* at the test score.
5. *reluctant*—She accepted the criticism *reluctantly*.
6. *unexpected*—Amanda met the old man *unexpectedly*.
7. *somber*—Her mother looked at her *somberly* when she saw the dirty dress.
8. *childish*—The grocer disliked teenagers who behaved *childishly*.
9. *mild*—Mr. Moore looked at her *mildly*.
10. *fleeting*—She thought *fleetingly* of her mother's comments.

READING FOCUS

Sample Answer

An adjective such as "inspiring" would be placed very close to the "very positive" end of the scale. A word such as "enjoyable" might fall halfway between the positive end and the zero, or neutral, mark.

T347

SELECTION OBJECTIVES

After completing this selection, students will be able to

- identify the speaker in a poem
- choose a speaker to express an idea
- identify aspects of a character's personality
- write to describe a view
- analyze the speaker in a poem
- use a dictionary to determine pronunciation
- identify main idea

Lesson Resources

Four Skinny Trees

- Selection Synopsis, Teacher's Edition, p. T311c
- Comprehension and Vocabulary Workbook, pp. 65–66
- Language Enrichment Workbook, p. 68
- Teacher's Resources Reinforcement, pp. R32 Test, pp. T61–T62

More About the Speaker

Have students create statements in which they relate to an object or something in nature. For example, "I hear the wind in the trees whispering to me." Write some of the statements on the board. Discuss how these could be changed to second-person speaker.

About the Author

Sandra Cisneros (1954–) writes in a unique style that combines the forms of prose and poetry. She has said, "I wanted stories like poems, compact and lyrical and ending with reverberation." Some critics refer to her works like the one in this selection as short stories, but most refer to them as prose poems or "intrinsically narrative" poems.

READING FOCUS

Identify Main Idea Poets usually express the main idea of a poem indirectly. One way to find the main idea in a poem is to first think about what the different parts of the poem mean. Try pausing briefly after each paragraph of "Four Skinny Trees." Then restate each paragraph in your own words. What is the main idea the poet is trying to express?

348 ■ Unit 4

Learn About

SPEAKER

The **speaker** in a poem is a person, animal, or object that relates what is happening. A speaker is another term for the narrator. Sometimes the poet and the speaker are the same. Sometimes they are not. For example, in "Navaho Chant," you may remember that the speaker is the corn.

A poem can be written in the first, second, or third person. A poem written in the **first person** uses the pronouns *I* and *me*. A poem written in the **second person** speaks directly to the reader or to some real or imaginary person or object. This type of poem uses the pronoun *you*. A poem written in the **third person** uses the pronouns *he*, *she*, or *it*.

As you read the poem, ask yourself:

1. Who is the speaker?
2. In what person is the poem written? How can you tell?

WRITING CONNECTION

Think of an idea or feeling about a day's event that you would like to communicate. Write a short poem or paragraph in which you create a speaker to voice your idea. For example, write a poem about students from a locker's point of view.

More About the Unit Theme

The speaker in "Four Skinny Trees" discovers aspects of herself in the trees outside her room and also discovers that she can draw strength and inspiration from them. What other discoveries in nature have inspired people?

ESL Activity

Have students work in pairs to create a poem or paragraph in which two objects in the classroom voice their thoughts or ideas. For example, the clock and the door might tell each other how some students watch the clock and cannot wait to rush out the door.

Cooperative Group Activity

After students have completed their Writing Connection assignment, ask volunteers to read their works to the large group. Have group members then guess who the speaker is or try to describe the speaker.

Four Skinny Trees

by Sandra Cisneros

They are the only ones who understand me. I am the only one who understands them. Four skinny trees with skinny necks and pointy elbows like mine. Four who do not belong here but are here. Four raggedy excuses planted by the city. From our room we can hear them, but Nenny just sleeps and doesn't appreciate things.

Their strength is secret. They send ferocious roots beneath the ground. They grow up and they grow down and grab the earth between their hairy toes and bite the sky with violent teeth and never quit their anger. This is how they keep.

Let one forget his reason for being, they'd all droop like tulips in a glass, each with their arms around the other. Keep, keep, keep, trees say when I sleep. They teach.

When I am too sad and too skinny to keep keeping, when I am a tiny thing against so many bricks, then it is I look at the trees. When there is nothing left to look at on this street. Four who grew despite concrete. Four who reach and do not forget to reach. Four whose only reason is to be and be.

---

raggedy (RAG ih dee) tattered, frayed, or torn like a rag
ferocious (fuh ROH shus) very cruel; savage
despite (dih SPYT) in spite of

Four Skinny Trees ■ 349

UNDERSTAND THE SELECTION

Answers

1. They all have skinny necks and pointy elbows. They don't belong there.
2. a person named Nenny
3. ferocious roots, height
4. Sample answer: She doesn't like the city because she lives in one room with another person in a place where there are lots of bricks and concrete.
5. Sample answer: No, she is sad and feels like she doesn't belong and can't go on.
6. Sample answer: Nenny is probably her grandmother and is probably old, because she sleeps a lot.
7. Sample answer: She feels small and unimportant and doesn't like the city.
8. It gives her the inspiration to keep trying.
9. Sample answer: I would think about my good friends and family.
10. Sample answer: I would compare myself to a racecar because we are both always trying to stay ahead of the crowd.

Respond to Literature

Discuss with students how they perceive the speaker's situation. How will she be able to better her life? Organize students into small groups and challenge each group to write a brief scenario showing the speaker's situation in ten years. Have each group include an explanation of how the speaker got to that point.

WRITE ABOUT THE SELECTION

Prewriting

Use the board or overhead projector to make a rough sketch of a view from the classroom. Make a brief list of what is seen, and add a few words to describe each item on the list. Then, allow students to work individually to visualize, sketch, and make their own lists.

Review the Selection

UNDERSTAND THE SELECTION

Recall

1. How are the trees like the speaker?
2. Who shares a room with the speaker?
3. What physical traits do the trees have that keep them alive?

Infer

4. How does the speaker feel about the city?
5. Is the speaker a happy person? Explain.
6. What can you infer about Nenny from the poem?
7. Why does the speaker feel like giving up sometimes?

Apply

8. When the speaker sees that the trees grow "despite concrete" and they "do not forget to reach," how does this help her?
9. If you were sad, what would you think about for encouragement?
10. What object, other than a tree, could you compare yourself to? What features of the object are similar to your features or behaviors?

Respond to Literature

If you could see the speaker of "Four Skinny Trees" in ten years, would you expect her to have succeeded? Explain.

---

350 ■ Unit 4

WRITE ABOUT THE SELECTION

The speaker in "Four Skinny Trees" was inspired by the view from her room. Write a paragraph or short poem that describes what you can see from the window of a room where you live.

Prewriting Visualize yourself looking out the window. What would you see? Make a rough sketch of the view, and then use your sketch as a guide to list what you will describe. Jot down some details about each part of the view, such as its size, shape, color, or purpose.

Writing Describe the images in your sketch from left to right or right to left. Remember to give as many details as you can to help the reader picture your description.

Revising You might ask a partner to read and respond to your description. Ask if you should use more descriptive words or details and whether the reader can imagine the scene. Use your partner's comments to revise and clarify your description.

Proofreading Check for errors in spelling, usage, and mechanics. Remove any unnecessary commas and make sure that all your sentences have ending marks.

Writing

As students write their descriptions, let them know it is all right to include their feelings about the view, as the speaker did in "Four Skinny Trees."

Revising

Allow time for both partners to read and comment on one another's descriptions.

Proofreading

Create a proofreading team of 3–5 students in which one student checks each paper for spelling, another for correct grammar, another for complete sentences, and so on.

ESL Activity

Encourage students to participate on a proofreading team so they can observe the process. Students who are not yet proficient in English spelling and grammar could check for correct capitalization and punctuation.

THINK ABOUT THE SPEAKER

The **speaker** in a poem is like the narrator in a story. The speaker in a poem can be a real or imaginary person, animal, or object. Sometimes a poem will have more than one speaker. However, the poem is usually told from one main point of view.

1. Do you think the poet is the speaker? Explain.

2. From what point of view is the poem told?

3. What characteristics do the trees and the speaker share?

4. The speaker says that she can "hear" the trees from her room. What does this show about her feelings for the trees?

READING FOCUS

Identify Main Idea As you read the poem, you analyzed each paragraph to determine its main idea. Now state the main idea of the entire poem in a sentence.

DEVELOP YOUR VOCABULARY

In English, many words do not sound the way they are spelled. For example, in the word *often*, the *t* is silent.

You can find out how to pronounce a word by looking it up in the dictionary. Following the entry word, you will find the pronunciation of the word in parenthesis. The symbols and letters that tell you how to pronounce the word are called **diacritical marks**. For example, the diacritical marks that show the pronunciation for the word *often* are (ôf´ən). The key to these marks can be found at the bottom of the dictionary page.

Look in the dictionary for each of these words from "Four Skinny Trees." Write the diacritical marks for each word and practice saying the word aloud. Then read the entire poem aloud.

1. excuses
2. appreciate
3. ferocious
4. concrete

SELECTION OVERVIEW

SELECTION OBJECTIVES

After completing this selection, students will be able to

- understand autobiography
- write an autobiographical episode
- identify characters' discoveries
- write a story extension
- appreciate historical and cultural aspects of autobiography
- use contractions
- recognize facts that support opinions

Lesson Resources

Ta-Na-E-Ka
- Selection Synopsis, Teacher's Edition, p. T311d
- Comprehension and Vocabulary Workbook, pp. 67–68
- Language Enrichment Workbook, pp. 69–70
- Teacher's Resources Reinforcement, p. R33 Test, pp. T63–T64

More About Autobiography

Point out to students that although an autobiography usually is written in the first person, as in "Ta-Na-E-Ka," it does not have to be. An autobiography might be told in the third person and read like a novel.

Background Notes

The Kaw, or Kansa, were a small tribe of Plains Indians who spoke Siouan and lived in eastern Kansas. In 1846, the Kaw ceded their reservation lands along the Kansas River to the government and moved to a smaller reservation near the Neosho River. The Kaw were removed from this reservation in 1873 and moved to the Oklahoma Territory, opening up the Neosho River Valley for white settlement.

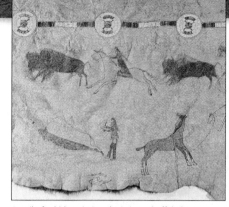

Detail of a hide painting depicting a buffalo hunt, Plains Indian, Shoshoni, c.1875. Werner Forman Archive, H.W. Read Collection, Plains Indian Museum, Buffalo Bill Historical Center, Cody, Wyoming

READING FOCUS

Recognize Facts That Support Opinions

Opinions carry more weight when they are backed up with facts. Opinions occur in many kinds of writing, from ads and newspaper editorials to short stories and poems.

When a writer gives facts to support an opinion, you should examine them closely. Ask yourself: Do they really relate to the writer's point? Likewise, when you express an opinion about a character or story, you should select facts from the story or from your experience to support your opinion.

Learn About

AUTOBIOGRAPHY

An **autobiography** is the story of a person's life written by that person. Because the author is writing about himself or herself, an autobiography is usually written in the first person.

An autobiography may tell about a person's entire life, or it may focus on just part of it. Short stories that are autobiographical usually tell about a particular event or incident in the author's life.

From an autobiography you learn about the author as a person. You also learn about the circumstances of the author's life. As you read "Ta-Na-E-Ka," ask yourself:

1. What situation in Mary Whitebird's life is described in the story?
2. What do you learn about the author from the way she handles the situation?

WRITING CONNECTION

Choose an interesting or amusing incident that has happened to you during the past several weeks. Write a paragraph in which you recount the incident as if you were writing your autobiography. Be sure to include not only the facts, but also your feelings about the incident.

352 ■ Unit 4

Viewing Fine Art

Native Americans painted geometric patterns and symbolic representations on material that was readily available. Hide painting, like what is shown here, typically served as a record of tribal history. Ask: What event has been recorded?

Cooperative Group Activity

Have students work in pairs to complete the Writing Connection activity. Have the students ask each other questions that would provide useful material for an autobiography. Students may find it helpful to quiz each other about the incident that they plan to write about in their paragraphs. If students have a tape recorder, they may want to use it during the interviews.

TA-NA-E-KA

ADAPTED

by Mary Whitebird

As my birthday drew closer, I had awful nightmares about it. I was reaching the age at which all Kaw Indians had to take part in Ta-Na-E-Ka. Well, not all Kaws. Many of the younger families on the reservation were beginning to give up the old customs. But my grandfather, Amos Deer Leg, stood by the old traditions. He still wore handmade beaded moccasins instead of shoes. He kept his iron-gray hair in tight braids. He could speak English, but he spoke it only with white men. With his family he used a Sioux dialect.

Grandfather was one of the last living Indians who actually fought against the U.S. Cavalry. Not only did he fight, he was wounded in a skirmish at Rosebud Creek. This was the famous battle in which the well-known Kaw chief Flat Nose lost his life. At the time, my grandfather was only eleven years old.

Eleven was a magic word among the Kaws. It was the time of Ta-Na-E-Ka, which means "flowering of adulthood."

My grandfather had told us about it hundreds of times. It was the age, he said, "when a boy could prove himself to be a warrior. And a girl can take the first steps to womanhood."

"I don't want to be a warrior," my cousin, Roger Deer Leg, confided to me. "I'm going to become an accountant."

"None of the other tribes make girls go through the survival ritual," I complained to my mother.

"It won't be as bad as you think, Mary," my mother said. "Once you've gone through it, you'll never forget it. You'll be proud."

I even complained to my teacher, Mrs. Richardson. I felt that, as a white woman, she would side with me.

She didn't. "All of us have rituals of one kind or another," Mrs. Richardson said. "And look at it this way: How many girls have the chance to compete on equal terms with boys? Don't look down on your heritage."

---

dialect (DY uh lekt) local manner of speaking
skirmish (SKUR mish) minor battle in a war
confide (kun FYD) tell as a secret
ritual (RICH oo ul) ceremony; tradition
heritage (HER ih tij) what is handed down to a person from ancestors

Ta-Na-E-Ka ■ 353

Reading Focus:
Recognize Facts That Support Opinions

Roger says he would give anything to get out of Ta-Na-E-Ka, but Mary says, "I don't see how we have any choice." Ask: What facts might she use to support this opinion?

Critical Thinking:
Analyze

Have students discuss the hardships that many Native Americans would have had to endure before modern conveniences existed. Why is physical endurance less important than it used to be?

Heritage, indeed! I didn't plan to live on a reservation for the rest of my life. I was a good student. I loved school. My favorite stories were about knights in armor and fair ladies and dragons. I had never once thought that being Indian was exciting.

But I've always thought that equal rights for women started with the Kaw. No other Indian tribe treated women more "equally" than the Kaw. Unlike most other Sioux tribes, the Kaw allowed men and women to eat together. And hundreds of years ago, a Kaw woman had the right to reject a man chosen for her—even if her father had arranged a marriage.

The wisest women (usually the old ones) often sat in tribal councils. Furthermore, most Kaw legends are about "Good Woman," a kind of super person. Good Woman led Kaw warriors into battle after battle, which they always seemed to win.

And girls as well as boys were required to go through Ta-Na-E-Ka.

The actual ceremony varied from tribe to tribe. But since the Indians' life on the plains depended on survival, Ta-Na-E-Ka was a test of survival.

"Endurance is the highest virtue of the Indian," my grandfather explained. "To survive, we must endure. When I was a boy, Ta-Na-E-Ka was more than just the symbol it is now. We were painted white with the juice of a sacred herb. Then we were sent naked into the wilderness, without so much as a knife. We couldn't return until the white had worn off. It wouldn't wash off. It took almost eighteen days.

"During that time," he went on, "we had to stay alive. We did it by trapping food, eating insects and roots and berries, and watching out for enemies. And we did have enemies—both the white soldiers and the Omaha warriors. They were always trying to capture Kaw boys and girls going through their endurance tests. It was an exciting time."

"What happened if you couldn't make it?" Roger asked. He was born only three days after I was, and we were being trained for Ta-Na-E-Ka together. I was happy to know he was frightened, too.

"Many didn't return," Grandfather said. "Only the strongest and shrewdest. Mothers were not allowed to weep over those who didn't return. If a Kaw couldn't survive, he or she wasn't worth weeping over. It was our way."

"What a lot of hooey," Roger whispered. "I'd give anything to get out of it."

"I don't see how we have any choice," I replied.

Roger gave my arm a little squeeze. "Well, it's only five days."

Five days! Maybe it was better than being painted white and sent out naked for eighteen days. But not much better.

We were to be sent, barefoot and in bathing suits, into the woods. Even our very traditional parents put their foot

---

endurance (en DUUR uns) ability to withstand hardship; survival
virtue (VUR choo) good quality
shrewdest (SHROOD ist) cleverest
traditional (truh DISH uh nul) following old customs

354 ■ Unit 4

T.C. and Me: Revisited, Amado M. Pena, Jr. El Taller, Inc.

Indian artist Amado Pena has made many paintings that explore his Native American identity. Here he shows himself (in the framed center picture) dressed in Indian clothing but seated in an American Victorian chair on an Indian rug. The larger, but less precisely identified Native American (T.C.), surrounds him, perhaps as a memory or a vision. With his long hair and traditional blanket he represents the past, but he also symbolizes a dignified heritage. Ask: How do the settings of the center picture and the surrounding picture differ?

down when Grandfather suggested we go naked. For five days we'd have to live off the land. We'd have to keep warm as best we could and get food where we could. It was May. But on the northernmost shores of the Missouri River, the days were still chilly and the nights fiercely cold.

Grandfather was in charge of the month's training for Ta-Na-E-Ka. One day he caught a grasshopper. Then he showed us how to pull its legs and wings off in one flick of the fingers. And how to swallow it.

I felt sick, and Roger turned green. "It's a darn good thing it's 1947," I told Roger teasingly. "You'd make a terrible warrior." Roger just made a face.

I knew one thing. This was one Kaw Indian girl who wasn't going to swallow a grasshopper—no matter how hungry she got. And then I had an idea. Why hadn't I thought of it before? It would have saved nights of bad dreams about squooshy grasshoppers.

Ta-Na-E-Ka ■ 355

Literary Focus:
Autobiography

Point out that the reader does not discover the precise time period of the story until page 355. Guide students in summarizing the circumstances of the author's life at the time of the story. Ask: To what Native American group does Mary belong? Where does she live? How do the young people's attitudes toward the event she is facing differ from those of the older people in the story?

Discussion

After students have read through the section in which Mary borrows the five dollars from Mrs. Richardson, pause for discussion. Ask students to speculate as to why Mary has borrowed the money and how they think she will use it.

Reading Focus:
Recognize Facts That Support Opinions

Mary's cousin, Roger, seems to be truly fearful about going through Ta-Na-E-Ka. Ask: What facts from the story support this opinion of him? What feelings does Mary seem to have as she anticipates the ritual?

I headed straight for my teacher's house. "Mrs. Richardson," I said, "would you lend me five dollars?"

"Five dollars!" she exclaimed. "What for?"

"You remember the ceremony I talked about?"

"Ta-Na-E-Ka. Of course. Your parents have written and asked me to excuse you from school so you can take part in it."

"Well, I need some things for the ceremony," I said, in a half-truth. "I don't want to ask my parents for the money."

"It's not a crime to borrow money, Mary. But how can you pay it back?"

"I'll baby-sit for you ten times."

"That's more than fair," she said. She went to her purse and handed me a crisp, new five-dollar bill. I'd never had that much money at once.

"I'm happy to know the money's going to be put to a good use," Mrs. Richardson said.

A few days later, Ta-Na-E-Ka began. First came a long speech from my grandfather. It was all about how we had reached the age of decision, how we now had to take care of ourselves. We had to prove that we could survive the most horrendous of ordeals.

All the friends and relatives gathered at our house for dinner and made jokes about their own Ta-Na-E-Kas. They all advised us to fill up now, since for the next five days we'd be eating crickets. Neither Roger nor I was very hungry.

"I'll probably laugh about this when I'm an accountant," Roger said, trembling.

"Are you trembling?" I asked.

"What do you think?"

"I'm happy to know boys tremble, too," I said.

At six the next morning, we kissed our parents and went off to the woods. "Which side do you want?" Roger asked. According to the rules, Roger and I would stake out "territories" in separate areas of the woods. We weren't to communicate during the whole ordeal.

"I'll go toward the river, if it's okay with you," I said.

"Sure," Roger answered. "What difference does it make?"

To me, it made a lot of difference. There was a marina a few miles up the river, and there were boats anchored there. At least I hoped so. I figured that a boat was a better place to sleep than under a pile of leaves.

"Why do you keep holding your head?" Roger asked.

"Oh, nothing. Just nervous," I told him. Actually, I was afraid I'd lose the five-dollar bill, which I had tucked into my hair with a bobby pin. As we came to a fork in the trail, Roger shook my hand. "Good luck, Mary."

"N'ko-n'ta," I said. It was the Kaw word for *courage*.

---

horrendous (haw REN dus) horrible; awful
ordeal (awr DEEL) severe test; harsh experience
stake out (STAYK out) mark the limits of
marina (muh REE nuh) large area set up for docking boats

The sun was shining and it was warm. But my bare feet began to hurt right away. I saw one of the berry bushes Grandfather had told us about. "You're lucky," he had said. "The berries are ripe in the spring, and they are delicious and nourishing." They were orange and fat and I popped one into my mouth.

Argh! I spat it out. It was awful and bitter. Even grasshoppers were probably better tasting. However, I never intended to find out.

I sat down to rest my feet. A rabbit hopped out from under the berry bush. He nuzzled the berry I'd spat out and ate it. He picked another one and ate that, too. He liked them. He looked at me, twitching his nose. Then I watched a red-headed woodpecker tap on an elm tree. I caught a glimpse of a skunk waddling through some twigs. All of a sudden, I realized I was no longer frightened. Ta-Na-E-Ka might be more fun than I'd expected. I got up and headed toward the marina.

"Not one boat," I said to myself, depressed. But the restaurant on the shore, "Ernie's Riverside," was open. I walked in, feeling silly in my bathing suit. The man at the counter was big and tough-looking. He wore a sweat-shirt with the words "Fort Sheridan, 1944," and he had only three fingers on one of his hands. He asked me what I wanted.

"A hamburger and a milk shake," I said. I held the five-dollar bill in my hand so he'd know I had money.

"That's a pretty heavy breakfast, honey," he said.

"That's what I always have for breakfast," I lied.

"Forty-five cents," he said, bringing me the food. (Back in 1947, hamburgers were twenty-five cents and milk shakes were twenty cents.) "Delicious," I thought. "Better'n grasshoppers. And Grandfather never once said that I couldn't eat hamburgers."

While I was eating, I had a grand idea. Why not sleep in the restaurant? I went to the ladies' room and made sure the window was unlocked. Then I went back outside and played along the riverbank. I watched the water birds, trying to identify each one. I planned to look for a beaver dam the next day.

The restaurant closed at sunset, and I watched the three-fingered man drive away. Then I climbed in the unlocked window. There was a night light on, so I didn't turn on any lights. But there was a radio on the counter. I turned it on to a music program.

It was warm in the restaurant, and I was hungry. I helped myself to a glass of milk and a piece of pie. But I meant to keep a list of what I'd eaten, so I could leave money. I also meant to get up early. Then I could sneak out through the window and head for the woods before the three-fingered man returned. I turned off the radio. I wrapped myself in the man's apron. And, in spite of the hardness of the floor, I fell asleep.

---

nuzzle (NUZ ul) nudge with the nose

Critical Thinking:
Apply
Mary borrowed $5 from her teacher, chose the marina area of the woods as her territory, and planned to sleep on a boat. Ask: What do these actions tell you about Mary's attitude towards the Ta-Na-E-Ka tradition?

Literary Focus:
Character
After students have read to the end of p. 357, ask if they were surprised that Mary decided to go to the restaurant to eat and sleep during her survival ritual. What opinion do they have of Mary at this point in the story? Why?

"What the heck are you doing here, kid?"

It was the man's voice.

It was morning. I'd overslept. I was scared.

"Hold it, kid. I just wanna know what you're doing here. You lost? You must be from the reservation. Your folks must be worried sick about you. Do they have a phone?"

"Yes, yes," I answered. "But don't call them."

I was shivering. The man, who told me his name was Ernie, made me a cup of hot chocolate. Meanwhile, I explained about Ta-Na-E-Ka.

"Darndest thing I ever heard," he said, when I was through. "Lived next to the reservation all my life, and this is the first I've heard of Ta-Na whatever-you-call-it." He looked at me, all goose bumps in my bathing suit. "Pretty silly thing to do to a kid," he muttered.

That was just what I'd been thinking for months. But when Ernie said it, I became angry. "No, it isn't silly. It's a custom of the Kaw. We've been doing this for hundreds of years. My mother and my grandfather and everybody in my family went through this ceremony. It's why the Kaw are great warriors."

"Okay, great warrior," Ernie chuckled, "suit yourself. And if you want to stick around, it's okay with me." Ernie went to the broom closet and tossed me a bundle. "That's the lost-and-found closet," he said. "Stuff people left on boats. Maybe there's something to keep you warm."

The sweater fitted loosely, but it felt good. I felt good. And I'd found a new friend. Most important, I was surviving Ta-Na-E-Ka.

My grandfather had said Ta-Na-E-Ka would be filled with adventure. I was certainly having my fill. And Grandfather had never said we couldn't accept hospitality.

I stayed at Ernie's Riverside for the whole five days. In the mornings, I went into the woods. There I watched the animals and picked flowers for each of the tables in Ernie's. I had never felt better. I was up early enough to watch the sun rise on the Missouri, and I went to bed after it set. I ate everything I wanted—insisting that Ernie take all my money for the food.

"I'll keep this in trust for you, Mary," Ernie promised. "In case you are ever desperate for five dollars."

I was sorry when the five days were over. I'd enjoyed every minute with Ernie. He taught me how to make western omelets and Chili Ernie Style. (That's still one of my favorite dishes.) And I told Ernie all about the legends of the Kaw. I hadn't realized I knew so much about my people.

But Ta-Na-E-Ka was over. As I neared my house, at about nine-thirty in the evening, I became nervous all over again. What if Grandfather asked me about the berries and the grasshoppers? And my feet were hardly cut. I hadn't lost a pound, and my hair was combed.

---

omelet (OM lut) eggs beaten up, fried, and folded in half when done

"They'll be so happy to see me," I told myself hopefully, "that they won't ask too many questions."

I opened the door. My grandfather was in the front room. He was wearing the ceremonial beaded deerskin shirt which had belonged to *his* grandfather.

"N'g'da'ma," he said. "Welcome back."

I hugged my parents warmly. Then I let go when I saw my cousin Roger sprawled on the couch. His eyes were red and swollen. He'd lost weight. His feet were an unsightly mass of blood and blisters. And he was moaning: "I made it, see, I made it. I'm a warrior. A warrior."

My grandfather looked at me strangely. I looked clean, well fed, and radiantly healthy. My parents got the message. My uncle and aunt gazed at me with hostility.

Finally my grandfather asked, "What did you eat to keep you so well?"

I sucked in my breath and blurted out the truth: "Hamburgers and milk shakes."

"Hamburgers!" my grandfather growled.

"Milk shakes!" Roger moaned.

"You didn't say we *had* to eat grasshoppers," I said meekly.

"Tell us about your Ta-Na-E-Ka," my grandfather commanded.

I told them everything, from borrowing the five dollars, to Ernie's kindness, to watching the beaver.

"That's not what I trained you for," my grandfather said sadly.

I stood up. "Grandfather, I learned that Ta-Na-E-Ka *is* important. I didn't think so during training. I was scared stiff of it.

I handled it my way. And I learned I had nothing to be afraid of. There's no reason in 1947 to eat grasshoppers when you can eat a hamburger."

Inside, I was shocked at my own boldness. But I liked it. "Grandfather, I'll bet you never ate one of those rotten berries yourself."

Grandfather laughed! He laughed aloud! My mother and father and aunt and uncle were all dumbfounded. Grandfather never laughed. Never.

"Those berries—they are terrible," Grandfather admitted. "I could never swallow them. On the first day of my Ta-Na-E-Ka, I found a dead deer—shot by a soldier, probably. It kept my belly full for the entire period of the test!"

Grandfather stopped laughing. "We should send you out again," he said.

I looked at Roger. "You're pretty smart, Mary," Roger groaned. "I'd never have thought of what you did."

"Accountants just have to be good at arithmetic," I said comfortingly. "I'm terrible at arithmetic."

Roger tried to smile, but couldn't. My grandfather called me to him. "You should have done what your cousin did. But I think you are more aware of what is happening to our people today than we are. I think you would have passed the test under any circumstances, in any time. Somehow, you know how to live in a world that wasn't made for Indians. I don't think you're going to have any trouble surviving."

Grandfather wasn't entirely right. But I'll tell about that another time.

Literary Focus:
Autobiography
Remind students that an autobiography reveals something important about the character or personality of the author. Ask: What do readers learn about Mary Whitebird from the way she handles her experiences during Ta-Na-E-Ka? What words would you use to describe Mary? Also, encourage students to reflect on the differences in personality between Mary and Roger based on their responses to same event.

Mini Quiz

Write on the chalkboard or overhead projector the following sentences and call on students to fill in the blanks. Discuss the answers with the class.

1. The Ta-Na-E-Ka is a _____ .

2. Ta-Na-E-Ka takes place when a person is _____ years old.

3. During Ta-Na-E-Ka a person has to spend _____ days in _____ .

4. Mary spent her Ta-Na-E-Ka in _____ .

5. Robert spent his Ta-Na-E-Ka in _____ .

Answers

1. survival ritual
2. eleven
3. five, the woods
4. Ernie's restaurant
5. the woods

Prev
Using
a list of

UNDERSTAND THE SELECTION

Answers

1. Kaw survival ritual that symbol-izes the passage of 11-year-olds into adulthood
2. her cousin Roger
3. at Ernie's restaurant by the river
4. Many Kaws are giving up the old customs to live like modern Americans rather than tradi-tional Native Americans.
5. Because he plans to be an accountant, he does not think that the Kaw traditions are going to help him much in life.
6. They treated them as equals, even in tests of physical endu-rance such as the Ta-Na-E-Ka.
7. Sample answer: They realized that she had had a much easier time of it than Roger did.
8. Sample answers: She felt sorry for him but not unhappy about what she had done; she felt a lit-tle ashamed of what she had done; she admired Roger for doing what was expected of him; she thought Roger was a little foolish for doing things the "old" way.
9. Answers will vary. Some may think she would have succeeded, others may think she would have gone hungry or been scared.
10. In today's world, the author's grandfather sees that Ta-Na-E-Ka is not necessary for survival; he understands his granddaughter's adaptability, just as he under-stands, and is saddened by, the relegating of Ta-Na-E-Ka to mere symbol.

Respond to Literature

Ask students what they think Mary might have discovered if, like Roger, she had stayed in the woods. Encourage students to speculate as to whether she would have been resourceful in this environment and how.

WRITE ABOUT THE SELECTION

Writing

students' suggestions, create events, on the chalkboard

Review the Selection

UNDERSTAND THE SELECTION

Recall

1. What is Ta-Na-E-Ka?

2. Who else goes through Ta-Na-E-Ka with Mary?

3. Where does Mary spend Ta-Na-E-Ka?

Infer

4. What can you infer about what is happening in the Kaw culture?

5. Why does Roger object to Ta-Na-E-Ka?

6. What was unusual about the way Kaws treated women?

7. Why were Mary's relatives hostile toward her when she returned?

Apply

8. How do you think Mary Whitebird felt when she saw Roger after Ta-Na-E-Ka?

9. Predict what would have happened if Mary Whitebird had stayed in the woods the way her cousin did.

10. Why does Grandfather say that Ta-Na-E-Ka is just a symbol today?

Respond to Literature

Do you agree or disagree with the fol-lowing statement? Why?

"Mary Whitebird made some impor-tant discoveries during the Ta-Na-E-Ka, but not the ones her grandfather expected her to make."

WRITE ABOUT THE SELECTION

At the conclusion of the story, Mary Whitebird's grandfather says, "Somehow, you know how to live in a world that wasn't made for Indians. I don't think you're going to have any trouble surviv-ing." Then the author comments, "Grand-father wasn't entirely right. But I'll tell about that another time."

What do you think may have hap-pened to Mary later in life to cause her to make this comment? Write a paragraph in which you describe an event in Mary's life that happens after Ta-Na-E-Ka.

Prewriting Make a list of possible situa-tions that could challenge Mary's ability to survive. Write what the outcome might be.

Writing Choose a situation from your list and let this be the subject of your para-graph. Make it clear in your paragraph how much time has elapsed since the end of "Ta-Na-E-Ka." For example, you might be writing about the day that Mary Whitebird enters college. This event would take place about nine years after the Ta-Na-E-Ka ritual.

Revising Read your paragraph and note any sentences that seem too long or too choppy. Make run-ons into separate sentences. Combine short sentences to make more sophisticated compound or complex ones. Rewrite these sentences.

Proofreading Check your paper for errors in spelling, usage, and mechanics. Be sure you have used abbreviations correctly.

---

or overhead transparency, that might have challenged Mary's sur-vival in later life.

Writing

Have students work on this section individually. As students write, remind them to consider the charac-ter and personality of Mary White-bird as it is revealed in "Ta-Na-E-Ka." Point out that their paragraphs

should be consistent with what they already know about Mary.

Revising

Have students work in small groups to revise their paragraphs. Ask the members of each group to think of themselves as literary critics or book editors who must decide if a partic-ular example would fit in with the original story.

Proofreading

Ask for volunteers to have their papers displayed on an overhead projector. Proofread these papers as a class exercise.

THINK ABOUT AUTOBIOGRAPHY

When you read an autobiography, you see the author's world through his or her eyes. You learn how the author views the times, the social conditions, and the geographic location in which he or she lives. In this way, autobiographies provide valuable historical information.

1. What is the setting for "Ta-Na-E-Ka"?

2. How old is Mary when "Ta-Na-E-Ka" takes place? Why is this age important?

3. If Mary Whitebird's autobiography were cataloged in the library as a social studies book, under what subject might it be classified?

4. Why is Grandfather a significant character in this story?

5. What do Mrs. Richardson's comments about Ta-Na-E-Ka add to the story?

READING FOCUS

Recognize Facts That Support Opinions
Respond to this opinion: Roger benefited as much from his experience as Mary did from hers during Ta-Na-E-Ka. Cite several facts to support this opinion. These facts should come from the story, as well as from challenging experiences you have had.

DEVELOP YOUR VOCABULARY

A **contraction** is a shortened form of two words. The two words are joined together by leaving out one or more letters. An apostrophe takes the place of the missing letter or letters. For example, the contraction *isn't* is a combination of the words *is not*. In the story "Ta-Na-E-Ka," the author uses many contractions. She does this in order to give the story a natural, informal tone.

Write the two words that have been combined to form each contraction.

1. I don't want to be a warrior.

2. Once you've gone through it, you'll never forget it.

3. Many didn't return.

4. We couldn't return until the white had worn off.

5. You'd make a terrible warrior.

Review the Selection ■ 361

THINK ABOUT AUTOBIOGRAPHY

Answers

1. Kaw Indian reservation; 1947
2. 11; the age at which a Kaw must go through the Ta-Na-E-Ka survival ritual
3. Kaw Indians or Native Americans
4. He is the one who has kept his family following the Kaw traditions. He also lived during a time when Native American life was much different from the way it was in 1947.
5. As a white person who teaches Native American children, she respects and values the Kaw tradition. She sees the fact that Kaws treat women as equals as significant.

DEVELOP YOUR VOCABULARY

Answers

1. do not
2. you have, you will
3. did not
4. could not
5. you would

READING FOCUS

Sample Answer
Roger did benefit from Ta-Na-E-Ka as much as Mary did. He may have learned that he had more capacity for physical endurance than he had thought or that he could survive in spite of having fears and doubts. His eyes were red, probably from lack of sleep. His feet were bloody and blistered, and he had become thin from lack of food. However, he felt victorious when he said, "I'm a warrior."

Nonfiction literature can include biographies, autobiographies, articles and essays, and diaries. A biography is an account of a person's life; an autobiography is an account written about one's own life; an article or essay is a short piece about a specific topic; and a diary is a daily record of a writer's experiences, observations, or feelings. Some types of nonfiction writing are usually not considered literature. These include straight news reporting, instruction manuals, and recipes.

ELEMENTS OF NONFICTION

Have students tell the **plot** of "Ta-Na-E-Ka." Ask them to cite the conflict or major problem the main character must overcome. From that starting point, find out from students what other lesser problems Mary had to face.

Have students relate the idea of plot and conflict to the events of "Chee's Daughter." Ask them to state in the form of a question the problem that faces Chee.

Ask students to compare the **points of view** of the selections they have read so far in this unit. Elicit that "Chee's Daughter" is told in the third person, but "The Gold Medal" and "Ta-Na-E-Ka" are told in the first person. Encourage students to comment on whether they feel these points of view are effective, or whether they would like to read any of these selections told from a different point of view.

Ask students what similarity in **tone** exists in "The Gold Medal" and "Ta-Na-E-Ka." Guide them to recognize that the similarity is due to the similar ages of the main characters.

Nonfiction is literature that tells about real life, real people, and events that actually happened. Autobiographies, biographies, and essays are all nonfictional accounts. Autobiographies and biographies tell stories, or narratives, about real people. Essays express writers' thoughts and opinions on a topic. You can better understand these narratives by thinking about the four main parts, or elements, of nonfiction: plot, point of view, tone, and theme.

Plot   The plot is a series of events that make up a narrative, such as a nonfictional account. In nonfiction, the plot describes both the things that happen to the characters and the things that the characters do. As the plot unfolds, you learn what happens and why it happens. An important part of the plot is **conflict**. Usually the central character is presented with a set of problems that he or she must overcome. These problems will force the main character to struggle with another character or group of characters, an object, or nature. Sometimes the struggle is within the main character's own self.

As you read a nonfictional account, you can identify three main parts: introduction, body, and conclusion. The **introduction** sets the stage and draws you into the world of the characters. A good introduction will spark your curiosity and make you ask questions such as: "What is this account about? Who is telling it? What has happened? What is going to happen?" In the **body**, the plot unfolds. You follow the main character's struggles and conflicts until you reach the outcome or climax. When the entire account has been told, the author brings it to a **conclusion**. The conclusion may sum up the events or it may offer a comment on the value or importance of the account. In some cases, the author may hint at what happens next in the characters' lives. For example, in "Ta-Na-E-Ka," Mary Whitebird indicates that, later in life, she did not always cope so well with the world as she did during her Ta-Na-E-Ka.

Point of View Every narrative must be written from a certain point of view. That is, someone must tell what is happening. Usually a nonfictional account is told from either a first-person or a third-person point of view.

When a narrative is told in the **first person**, the narrator is usually a character in the story. You can tell when a narrative is told in the first person because the narrator refers to himself or herself as *I* and *me*. A first-person narrator can be a major character or a minor character. An important point to remember in first-person narration is that the information given is limited to what the narrator can see, hear, think, know, and feel. Most autobiographies are written in the first person.

A **third-person** narrator stands outside the story. The narrator refers to each character as *he* or *she*. A third-person narrator is not limited by what one person can see, hear, or know, but is free to comment on any aspect of the narrative. Biographies usually have a third-person point of view.

Tone The tone communicates the author's feelings about the subject of his or her account. The tone can be serious or humorous, personal or detached, lighthearted or somber, casual, formal, or any combination of these. For example, in "Ta-Na-E-Ka," Mary Whitebird's narration is serious but also somewhat lighthearted, reflecting an 11-year-old girl's thinking.

Theme A person writes a nonfictional account because he or she has something to say. The message the writer wants to send to the reader is the theme, or main idea of the account. Some nonfiction accounts state the theme clearly, while others ask you to figure it out for yourself.

As you read "Dead at Seventeen," discover the elements of nonfiction that are present. Ask yourself these questions:
1. What is the point of view?
2. How is this point of view unusual?

Real-Life Application

Have students discuss examples of nonfiction movies and historical dramas on TV. You may wish to obtain a video of a popular nonfiction movie or a TV broadcast to show the class. After the viewing discuss with students how the various elements of nonfiction are used.

SELECTION OVERVIEW

SELECTION OBJECTIVES

After completing this selection, students will be able to

- identify elements of nonfiction
- write a personal response
- understand a discovery made too late
- understand the use of slang in literature
- recognize valid opinions

Lesson Resources

Dead at Seventeen
- Selection Synopsis, Teacher's Edition, p. T311d
- Comprehension and Vocabulary Workbook, pp. 69–70
- Language Enrichment Workbook, pp. 71–72
- Teacher's Resources Reinforcement, p. R34 Test, pp. T65–T66 Literary Analysis, pp. L7–L8

Background Notes

Syndicated columnist Ann Landers published this story that Coach Bryant used to read to every freshman class at the University of Alabama. Landers hoped that Bryant's successor would carry on the tradition after Bryant's death.

Tombstones, Jacob Lawrence. Collection of the Whitney Museum of American Art

Dead at Seventeen

from Ann Landers

FOCUS ON
NONFICTION
STUDY HINTS

The introduction sets the tone for the selection. How does the introduction draw you into the account?

Dear Readers: Today's column is dedicated to that beautiful guy, Paul "Bear" Bryant, the "winningest coach" from the University of Alabama. The Bear, who died last Jan. 26, used to read this column to every freshman class on opening day.

It would be lovely if Ray Perkins, the Bear's successor, carried on the tradition. Bryant loved his kids and he wanted them to stay alive.

Agony claws my mind. I am a statistic. When I first got here I felt very much alone. I was overwhelmed with grief, and I expected to find sympathy.

I found no sympathy. I saw only thousands of others whose bodies were as badly mangled as mine. I was given a number and

364 ■ Unit 4

Viewing Fine Art

Jacob Lawrence (1917–2000) has devoted his career to depicting the life of African Americans. Strong political and social comments characterize Lawrence's work. In *Tombstones*, one of his most famous paintings, Lawrence's pessimistic view is suggested by the slumped postures of the apartment dwellers and the presence of a basement shop that sells tombstones. At the same time, the bright color accents and the white cross sound a more positive note. Ask: Why might Lawrence have included a mother holding a baby in a composition that includes symbols of death?

Develop Vocabulary Skills

Begin by noting that some of the words in the selection are slang, either because they are standard words that have assumed a new meaning—as in *cool, dense, ripped*—or are newly coined. As an oral exercise ask students for other examples of words that are currently in with young people. Have students use the words in sentences that show their meaning.

ESL Activity

Point out that funeral customs vary from culture to culture. Ask students to describe different rituals associated with the death of an individual. For example, funeral rituals may focus on celebrating the person's life as well as grieving for the loss of that person.

placed in a category. The category was called "Traffic Fatalities."

The day I died was an ordinary school day. How I wish I had taken the bus! But I was too cool for the bus. I remember how I wheedled the car out of Mom. "Special favor," I pleaded. "All the kids drive." When the 2:50 bell rang, I threw my books in the locker . . . free until tomorrow morning! I ran to the parking lot, excited at the thought of driving a car and being my own boss.

It doesn't matter how the accident happened. I was goofing off—going too fast, taking crazy chances. But I was enjoying my freedom and having fun. The last thing I remember was passing an old lady who seemed to be going awfully slow. I heard a crash and felt a terrific jolt. Glass and steel flew everywhere. My whole body seemed to be turning inside out. I heard myself scream.

Suddenly, I awakened. It was very quiet. A police officer was standing over me. I saw a doctor. My body was mangled. I was saturated with blood. Pieces of jagged glass were sticking out all over. Strange that I couldn't feel anything. Hey, don't pull that sheet over my head. I can't be dead. I'm only 17. I've got a date tonight. I'm supposed to have a wonderful life ahead of me. I haven't lived yet. I can't be dead.

Later I was placed in a drawer. My folks came to identify me. Why did they have to see me like this? Why did I have to look at Mom's eyes when she faced the most terrible ordeal of her life? Dad suddenly looked very old. He told the man in charge, "Yes, he's our son."

The funeral was weird. I saw all my relatives and friends walk toward the casket. They looked at me with the saddest eyes I've ever seen. Some of my buddies were crying. A few of the girls touched my hand and sobbed as they walked by.

Please somebody—wake me up! Get me out of here. I can't bear to see Mom and Dad in such pain. My grandparents are so weak from grief they can barely walk. My brother and sister are like zombies. They move like robots. In a daze. Everybody. No one can believe this. I can't believe it, either.

Please, don't bury me! I'm not dead! I have a lot of living to do! I want to laugh and run again. I want to sing and dance. Please don't put me in the ground! I promise if you give me just one more chance, God, I'll be the most careful driver in the whole world. All I want is one more chance. Please, God, I'm only 17.

Paul "Bear" Bryant

Notice the point of view. How is this point of view effective?

The body text in the next five paragraphs contains the plot of the account. You learn what happened to the narrator and how he felt.

As the conclusion begins, notice that you are back to where the narrator is now.

The author's purpose for writing the story is clear. This is the theme of the account.

Dead at Seventeen ■ 365

INTRODUCE

Motivation

Ask students how they feel about driving a car. Do they view it as something they can't wait to do? Does it represent freedom to them? Is driving a privilege and a responsibility or just something that everybody does? Relate students' responses to the theme of "Dead at Seventeen."

Purpose-Setting Question

Why would a person take chances in a car?

READ

Literary Focus: *Elements of Nonfiction*

The blue side notes in this selection provide a model for students to understand the literary elements introduced on pages 362–363. Encourage students to watch for these elements as they read the selection.

Reading Focus: *Recognize Valid Opinions*

Ask students which of the opinions about the speaker is valid based on the facts in the selection.

- People who do foolish and dangerous things usually regret them later.
- People who do foolish and dangerous things usually get away with them.
- People who do foolish and dangerous things usually tell others about them.

CLOSE

Have students complete Review the Selection on pages 366–367.

Critical Thinking: *Infer*

Ask students how they think the boy's mother may have felt about lending him the car. Have students relate their answers to times when they think their parents might have been too permissive or too strict.

Mini Quiz

1. "Dead at Seventeen" is about a boy who _____.
2. In the account he is speaking after _____.
3. At his _____ he sees all his friends and relatives.
4. Before the accident happened, the boy was enjoying _____.
5. The boy wishes now that he could have _____.

Answers

1. died in a car accident
2. death
3. funeral
4. his freedom
5. another chance

UNDERSTAND THE SELECTION

Answers

1. a 17-year-old boy who has died in a car crash
2. dead and buried
3. He was killed in a car accident.
4. excited to be free and have a car to drive
5. He was dead.
6. put in a compartment at the morgue
7. sorry, because they are upset about his death
8. If he could have another chance to live, he would be the most careful driver in the world.
9. Sample answer: She felt guilty and responsible for his death.
10. Sample answers: I would be very angry that he took the chances he did. I would want to tell the story to others so that they will drive carefully. I would wonder why I had survived.

Respond to Literature

Have students work in small groups. Ask each group to discuss among themselves other discoveries made too late. For example, a student might learn that he or she should have studied more for a test or saved money for a special event. Have each group make a list of their discoveries to share with the class.

WRITE ABOUT THE SELECTION

Prewriting

You may want to have students work in small groups to find out whether anyone in the group has ever been in an accident. If so, ask the student to summarize the experience for the group as a warm-up before students begin writing.

Review the Selection

UNDERSTAND THE SELECTION

Recall

1. Who is telling this account?
2. Where is the narrator?
3. What has happened to him?

Infer

4. Describe the narrator's mood as he leaves school at the end of the day.
5. In what state was the narrator when he "awakened"?
6. Explain the meaning of the phrase "placed in a drawer."
7. How does the narrator feel about his parents, relatives, and friends?

Apply

8. What kind of bargain does the narrator wish to make with God?
9. How do you think this boy's mother felt after loaning him the car?
10. Suppose you had been a passenger in the narrator's car. How would you feel if you had lived?

Respond to Literature

How is this boy's discovery different from or similar to discoveries you have made in your own life? Have you ever discovered something too late?

WRITE ABOUT THE SELECTION

The selection "Dead at Seventeen" originally appeared in an Ann Landers column. Landers wrote that there was a coach at the University of Alabama who used to read this story to every freshman class on opening day. She said that he loved his kids and wanted them to stay alive.

Write a paragraph in which you express your reaction to this selection. Is it one that you will remember? How might it influence you in the future?

Prewriting Read the selection again and write down any thoughts and feelings that come to mind. Try to relate the selection to your own life and experience. Have you ever been involved in a car accident? Have you ever known anyone who was killed in an accident? Have you ever ridden with someone who was driving carelessly? How did you feel?

Writing Use your notes to write a response to "Dead at Seventeen." Include in your paragraph your overall feeling about the selection.

Revising Imagine that you are writing this paragraph in a letter to a friend. Add a sentence about why you think your friend should read the selection.

Proofreading Check your paragraph for errors in spelling, usage, and mechanics. Correct any sentence fragments by making them into complete sentences.

366 ■ Unit 4

Writing

As students work on this section individually, go around the classroom and help those who are having trouble. Remind students that an effective way to back up their opinions is to include quotations from the selection.

Revising

Have students work with a partner to revise their selections. Students can imagine that they are writing letters to each other about their ideas.

Proofreading

Select one or two student papers to display on an overhead projector. Have the class point out any errors that need correction.

THINK ABOUT NONFICTION

A nonfiction story tells about real people and events. The four main parts of a nonfictional account are plot, point of view, tone, and theme. A narrative also has a recognizable introduction, body, and conclusion.

1. What is the tone of "Dead at Seventeen"?

2. What is the account's point of view? Is the narrator the person to whom the events actually happened? Why or why not?

3. How does the introduction draw you into the account?

4. Briefly summarize the series of events that take place.

5. What is the message of the account? Why do you think the author wrote it?

DEVELOP YOUR VOCABULARY

Slang is nonstandard language that is used in casual speech. Slang expressions are often popular with teenagers. For example, the author of "Dead at Seventeen" uses slang expressions in order to make the voice of the seventeen-year-old story-teller seem more real and believable.

Slang tends to change with time. For example, teenagers in the 1950s referred to something really great as "keen." When slang expressions are used over a period of time by a large number of people, they often become entry words in the dictionary.

Identify the slang expression in each of the following sentences. Then rewrite each sentence using standard language to express the same idea.

1. I was too cool to take the bus.

2. That's a sharp dress you have on.

3. You're so dense.

4. I blew it.

5. Somebody ripped off my pen.

Review the Selection ■ 367

SELECTION OVERVIEW

SELECTION OBJECTIVES

After completing this selection, students will be able to

- understand the theme
- write about a theme of personal importance
- identify characters' discoveries
- write a story extension
- analyze theme in fiction
- use synonyms
- make predictions

Lesson Resources

Thank You, M'am
- Selection Synopsis, Teacher's Edition, p. T311d–311e
- Comprehension and Vocabulary Workbook, pp. 71–72
- Language Enrichment Workbook, pp. 73–75
- Teacher's Resources Reinforcement, p. R34 Test, pp. T67–T68

More About Theme

One of the themes in "Thank You, M'am" is that important discoveries can be made when two persons, who do not know each other, meet. Ask students what other story in this unit also has this as one of its themes. ("The Gold Medal")

About the Author

The principal subject of Langston Hughes's work is the experience of African Americans in the United States—their pleasures, joys, and sorrows. Hughes has written in almost every literary form: poems, novels, plays, songs, biographies, histories, and essays.

Learn About

READING FOCUS

Make Predictions When you make predictions, you try to guess what will happen in a story before it actually happens. Confirming your predictions is one way to measure how well you understand the story. Revising predictions helps you summarize what has happened so far and adds to your enjoyment. Your own experience can help you make predictions about a story. Jot down your predictions. Compare them to what happens in the story. Then make new predictions based on what you have read.

THEME

A **theme** is an idea or message in a story, play, or poem. It is possible for a piece of literature to have several themes. Only one of these, however, will be the main theme. For example, in the story "The Gold Medal," the main theme is Amanda's discovery of her true self apart from the roles people tried to impose on her. A less important theme, or **subtheme**, is the dilemma of an African American girl in a society that is made up mostly of white people.

You can often recognize the theme of a story by thinking, "Why did the author write this story, play, or poem?" As you read "Thank You, M'am," ask yourself:

1. What message does Langston Hughes wish to convey?
2. How does the story communicate this message?

WRITING CONNECTION

Imagine that you are a short-story writer. What kind of a theme might you choose? Write a paragraph in which you describe a theme that is meaningful to you. (For example, you might want to write about standing up for someone who is being teased.) Discuss how you would handle the theme and the message you would communicate.

Cooperative Group Activity

Divide the class into groups of four or five to complete the Writing Connection activity. Ask each group to choose a theme about which its members wish to write. The theme should be on an issue that is important to them. Next, have each group member contribute one or two sentences about the theme. Then have the groups use the sentences to write a single paragraph that they can share with the class.

THANK YOU, M'AM

by Langston Hughes

She was a large woman with a large purse that had everything in it but hammer and nails. It had a long strap, and she carried it slung across her shoulder. It was about eleven o'clock at night, and she was walking alone, when a boy ran up behind her and tried to snatch her purse. The strap broke with the sudden single tug the boy gave it from behind. But the boy's weight and the weight of the purse combined caused him to lose his balance.

---

slung (SLUNG) hung; made to swing loosely

INTRODUCE

Motivation
Ask students if they have ever had a chance encounter with a stranger that proved to be unusual. Relate their responses to the encounter between the boy and Luella Bates Washington Jones.

Purpose-Setting Question
How would you react if someone younger than you tried to take your purse or wallet?

READ

Literary Focus:
Theme
Encourage students to consider how the characters feel about and act toward each other as the story progresses. Ask: What do the characters discover about and learn from each other? Help students use their responses to identify the theme of the selection.

Reading Focus:
Make Predictions
Tell students that writers give clues that can help them predict. Look at the title. Ask: Is there a clue in the title to what might happen in the story? Think about dialogue or behavior that surprises you. Ask: Does it change any of your previous predictions? Think about surprising plot developments. Ask: Why did this happen? What will happen next?

CLOSE

Have students complete Review the Selection on pages 330–331.

Develop Vocabulary Skills

Write on the chalkboard sentences that use the vocabulary words footnoted in the story. Ask students to determine from the context what they think each word means. Discuss the meanings of the words in preparation for the students' reading of the selection.

ESL Activity

Invite pairs of students to read the story aloud as a dialogue. You may wish to have them photocopy the story twice and highlight one character's lines on each copy. Remind them that they should read only the words and sentences that appear in quotation marks. Encourage them to read through their own lines once alone. As they do, they should think about what the character is feeling and put appropriate expression into their spoken lines. After the pairs have read together, ask two volunteers to read the dialogue to the entire class.

Instead of taking off full blast as he had hoped, the boy fell on his back on the sidewalk, and his legs flew up. The large woman simply turned around and kicked him right square in his blue-jeaned sitter. Then she reached down, picked the boy up by his shirt front, and shook him until his teeth rattled.

After that the woman said, "Pick up my pocketbook, boy, and give it here."

She still held him tightly. But she bent down enough to permit him to stoop and pick up her purse. Then she said, "Now ain't you ashamed of yourself?"

Firmly gripped by his shirt front, the boy said, "Yes'm."

The woman said, "What did you want to do it for?"

The boy said, "I didn't aim to."

She said, "You a lie!"

By that time two or three people passed, stopped, turned to look, and some stood watching.

"If I turn you loose, will you run?" asked the woman.

"Yes'm," said the boy.

"Then I won't turn you loose," said the woman. She did not release him.

"Lady, I'm sorry," whispered the boy.

"Um-hum! Your face is dirty. I got a great mind to wash your face for you. Ain't you got nobody home to tell you to wash your face?"

"No'm," said the boy.

"Then it will get washed this evening," said the large woman, starting up the street, dragging the frightened boy behind her.

He looked as if he were fourteen or fifteen, frail and willow-wild, in tennis shoes and blue jeans.

The woman said, "You ought to be my son. I would teach you right from wrong. Least I can do right now is to wash your face. Are you hungry?"

"No'm," said the being-dragged boy. "I just want you to turn me loose."

"Was I bothering *you* when I turned that corner?" asked the woman.

"No'm."

"But you put yourself in contact with *me*," said the woman.

---

frail (FRAYL) weak

"If you think that that contact is not going to last awhile, you got another thought coming. When I get through with you, sir, you are going to remember Mrs. Luella Bates Washington Jones."

Sweat popped out on the boy's face and he began to struggle. Mrs. Jones stopped, jerked him around in front of her, put a half nelson about his neck, and continued to drag him up the street. When she got to her door, she dragged the boy inside, down a hall, and into a large kitchenette-furnished room at the rear of the house. She switched on the light and left the door open. The boy could hear other roomers laughing and talking in the large house. Some of their doors were open, too, so he knew he and the woman were not alone. The woman still had him by the neck in the middle of her room.

She said, "What is your name?"

"Roger," answered the boy.

"Then, Roger, you go to that sink and wash your face," said the woman, whereupon she turned him loose—at last. Roger looked at the door—looked at the woman—looked at the door— *and went to the sink.*

"Let the water run until it gets warm," she said. "Here's a clean towel."

"You gonna take me to jail?" asked the boy, bending over the sink.

"Not with that face, I would not take you nowhere," said the woman. "Here I am trying to get home to cook me a bite to eat, and you snatch my pocketbook! Maybe you ain't been to your supper either, late as it be. Have you?"

"There's nobody home at my house," said the boy.

"Then we'll eat," said the woman. "I believe you're hungry—or been hungry—to try to snatch my pocketbook!"

"I want a pair of blue suede shoes," said the boy.

"Well, you didn't have to snatch *my* pocketbook to get some suede shoes," said Mrs. Luella Bates Washington Jones. "You could of asked me."

"M'am? "

The water dripping from his face, the boy looked at her. There

---

half nelson (HAF NEL sun) wrestling hold on back of neck
whereupon (HWAIR uh pon) after which
suede (SWAYD) soft leather with a velvet-like surface

Thank You, M'am ■ 371

Literary Focus:
Theme and Character
Mrs. Jones says to Roger (on page 370), "You ought to be my son. I would teach you right from wrong." Ask: Does Mrs. Jones treat Roger as if he were her own child? Have them give examples to support their answer. Ask them if they are surprised by her response to Roger and why.

Discussion
Roger doesn't try to escape when Mrs. Jones releases her grip. Why not? Is he beginning to trust her? Is he just afraid? Ask students if they would try to escape if they were in a similar circumstance.

Discussion
Ask students whether they think that Luella Bates Washington Jones may have snatched some purses in her day, and why.

Reading Focus:
Make Predictions
Ask: Which of your predictions about the characters were confirmed? What new predictions do you have about what will happen?

was a long pause. A very long pause. After he had dried his face, and not knowing what else to do, dried it again, the boy turned around, wondering what next. The door was open. He could make a dash for it down the hall. He could run, run, run, *run*!

The woman was sitting on the daybed. After a while she said, "I were young once and I wanted things I could not get."

There was another long pause. The boy's mouth opened. Then he frowned, not knowing he frowned.

The woman said, "Um-hum! You thought I was going to say *but*, didn't you? You thought I was going to say, *but I didn't snatch people's pocketbooks*. Well, I wasn't going to say that." Pause. Silence. "I have done things, too, which I would not tell you, son—neither tell God, if He didn't already know. Everybody's got something in common. So you set down while I fix us something to eat. You might run that comb through your hair so you will look presentable."

In another corner of the room behind a screen was a gas plate and an icebox. Mrs. Jones got up and went behind the screen. The woman did not watch the boy to see if he was going to run now, nor did she watch her purse, which she left behind her on the daybed. But the boy took care to sit on the far side of the room, away from the purse, where he thought she could easily see him out of the corner of her eye if she wanted to. He did not trust the woman *not* to trust him. And he did not want to be mistrusted now.

"Do you need somebody to go to the store," asked the boy, "maybe to get some milk or something?"

"Don't believe I do," said the woman, "unless you just want sweet milk yourself. I was going to make cocoa out of this canned milk I got here."

"That will be fine," said the boy.

She heated some lima beans and ham she had in the icebox, made the cocoa, and set the table. The woman did not ask the boy anything about where he lived, or his folks, or anything else that would embarrass him. Instead, as they ate, she told him about her job in a hotel beauty shop that stayed open late, what the work was like, and how all kinds of women came in and out, blondes, redheads, and Spanish. Then she cut him a half of her ten-cent cake.

---

plate (PLAYT) small burner for cooking

Critical Thinking:
Synthesize
Ask students how they think the boy feels about the woman by the end of the story.

Literary Focus:
Character
Have students discuss how the author creates the character of Luella Bates Washington Jones. Begin by asking students to consider what the character says, what she does, and how she reacts. Guide students to recognize that she is definitely a round character, as is the boy. Then have them list four or five words that describe the character.

"Eat some more, son," she said.

When they were finished eating, she got up and said, "Now here, take this ten dollars and buy yourself some blue suede shoes. And next time, do not make the mistake of latching onto *my* pocketbook *nor nobody else's*—because shoes got by devilish ways will burn your feet. I got to get my rest now. But from here on in, son, I hope you will behave yourself."

She led him down the hall to the front door and opened it. "Good night! Behave yourself, boy!" she said, looking out into the street as he went down the steps.

The boy wanted to say something else other than, "Thank you, m'am," to Mrs. Luella Bates Washington Jones, but although his lips moved, he couldn't even say that as he turned at the foot of the barren stoop and looked up at the large woman in the door. Then she shut the door.

---

barren (BAR un) dull; uninteresting
stoop (STOOP) front step

Thank You, M'am ■ 373

Reading Focus:
Make Predictions
Ask: Which of your predictions were confirmed? Which were not? What surprised you?

Mini Quiz

Write on the chalkboard or overhead projector the following sentences and call on students to fill in the blanks. Discuss the answers with the class.

1. As the story opens, a boy tries to _____.

2. The attempt fails because _____.

3. The woman involved takes the boy _____.

4. She learns that the boy wants _____.

5. At the end of the story, she gives him _____.

Answers

1. snatch a woman's purse

2. the boy loses his balance and falls

3. home with her

4. blue suede shoes

5. ten dollars to buy the shoes

UNDERSTAND THE SELECTION

Answers

1. a boy snatches Mrs. Jones's purse
2. to her home
3. ten dollars
4. He either has no parents or they do not spend much time at home.
5. She reminds him that it was he who put himself in contact with her, not the other way around.
6. a rooming house
7. She says that she did things about which she would not tell.
8. Sample answer: He is curious about what is going to happen next.
9. Some may think he buys the suede shoes; some may have other ideas.
10. Answers will vary. Encourage students to explain why they think he will or will not behave from now on.

Respond to Literature

Point out to students that although certain things about Luella Jones and the boy are revealed in the story, much about them remains a mystery. Have students make a chart of what is known about each character. Then have students discuss things they do not know but, if they had the opportunity, would like to discover about each character.

WRITE ABOUT THE SELECTION

Prewriting

On the chalkboard or overhead transparency, create some sample brainstorming notes based on students' suggestions. An outline such as the following may be helpful:

Roger's age: 14 or 15

Occupation: petty criminal

Where he is: jail

Why: caught shoplifting

Memories: does not remember Luella Jones

UNDERSTAND THE SELECTION

Recall

1. What is the opening incident?
2. Where does Mrs. Jones take the boy?
3. What does Mrs. Jones give the boy at the end of the story?

Infer

4. What can you infer about the boy's parents?
5. What argument does Mrs. Jones use when the boy begs her to turn him loose?
6. In what kind of house does Mrs. Jones live?
7. What hint in the story tells you that Mrs. Jones did not always behave herself when she was young?

Apply

8. Why do you think the boy does not run from Mrs. Jones's house when he has the chance?
9. What will the boy do with the money?
10. Predict whether or not you think the boy will behave himself from now on.

Respond to Literature

What do Mrs. Jones and the boy discover about each other? Do you think discoveries like this can happen in real life?

WRITE ABOUT THE SELECTION

Suppose that many years have passed and that the boy in "Thank You, M'am" is an adult. How do you think he would remember his encounter with Luella Bates Washington Jones? Write a paragraph in which the boy (now grown up) tells about Mrs. Jones.

Prewriting Take a few minutes to brainstorm about the details you want to include in your paragraph. Decide how old you want the boy to be and what the circumstances of his life are (such as rich, poor, successful, in jail).

Writing Use the ideas from your brainstorming session to write a paragraph from the adult boy's point of view. Be sure to make clear the boy's feelings about Mrs. Jones and the incident with the purse. Also, make clear what effect, if any, the incident had on the boy as he grew older. Base your paragraph on Langston Hughes's message to the readers in the story.

Revising You can make your paragraph more effective by adding specific details from the story as seen from the boy's point of view. Rearrange phrases and eliminate boring words to make your story come alive.

Proofreading Check your paragraph for errors in spelling, usage, and mechanics. Add periods or other end marks to correct run on sentences. Make sure that every sentence ends with a period, question mark, or exclamation mark.

Writing
As students write their paragraphs, ask them to think about how they might feel if they had been the boy in the story and are now grown up.

Revising
Have students work in pairs. Students should suggest to each other ways to make their paragraphs more effective.

Proofreading
Have students proofread their own papers as you proofread a sample paper on an overhead projector.

THINK ABOUT THEME

When thinking about the theme of a story, it is important not to confuse theme with plot. The **plot** of a story is what happens in the story, while the **theme** is the message or main idea of the story. Stories with different plots might have the same theme.

1. What is the theme of "Thank You, M'am"?

2. Do you agree with the message of the story?

3. Why do you think Mrs. Jones treated the boy the way she did?

4. What did Mrs. Jones hope her encounter with the boy would accomplish?

5. In general, do you think that people like Mrs. Jones tend to make other people better or that others just take advantage of them?

READING FOCUS

Make Predictions As you read "Thank You, M'am," you were able to make, confirm, and revise predictions. How were your predictions about the title and the characters confirmed? Did you have to revise any of your other predictions? If so, how?

DEVELOP YOUR VOCABULARY

A **synonym** is a word that has the same or almost the same meaning as another word. For example, the boy in "Thank You, M'am" tries to *snatch* Mrs. Jones's purse. Two words that are synonyms for *snatch* are the words *take* and *grab*.

Review these words from "Thank You, M'am" and other stories in this unit. Write at least one synonym for each word. Then write an original paragraph that uses the words from the list.

1. slung
2. frail
3. barren
4. gingerly
5. quaver
6. zealously
7. surmised
8. acrid
9. shrewdest
10. horrendous

Review the Selection ■ 375

SELECTION OBJECTIVES

After completing this selection, students will be able to

- understand haiku
- create their own haiku
- discover relationships between images from nature and life
- analyze the imagery in haiku
- use a thesaurus to locate new words
- identify fact and opinion

Lesson Resources

Four Haiku/A bee thumps
- Selection Synopses, Teacher's Edition, p. T311e
- Comprehension and Vocabulary Workbook, pp. 73–74
- Language Enrichment Workbook, p. 76
- Teacher's Resources Reinforcement, p. R35 Test, pp. T69–T70

More About Haiku

A haiku usually communicates a single image. Several of the poems on page 377 use images from nature to describe characteristics of people. To summarize each characteristic, have students complete the phrase "A person who . . . ." For example, the frog may represent a person who talks a lot but has little substance.

Background Notes

Haiku originated in the first three lines of the traditional 31-syllable tanka. During the Tokugawa period (1603–1867), the haiku became more popular as poets welcomed the opportunity to describe everyday things in a simple form.

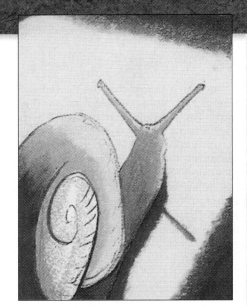

Learn About

HAIKU

Haiku is a form of poetry that has been popular in Japan for over 300 years. A **haiku** consists of 17 syllables arranged in three lines. Haiku often has a 5-7-5 pattern of syllables (the first line has five syllables, the second line has seven, and the third line has five). Sometimes, when haiku are translated into English, they do not follow this pattern. All haiku strives to say much in as few words as possible.

Usually a haiku refers to or describes something in nature. A haiku may also have some symbolic meaning. You will also notice that the last selection about a bee is too long to be a haiku. But, like haiku, it uses the world of nature as a symbol for something else.

As you read the four haiku that follow, ask yourself:

1. What do these poems say about the objects they are describing?
2. What do these poems say about people and life?

WRITING CONNECTION

Think of an object in nature that interests you: perhaps an animal, insect, flower, or tree. Write a description of the object in haiku form, using three lines in a 5-7-5 pattern of syllables.

READING FOCUS

Identify Fact and Opinion Haiku and many others forms of poetry are descriptive. The speaker makes factual observations about the world. However, the overall tone of the poem may express an opinion, or point of view, about the thing that the speaker observes. As you read the poems, notice how each speaker conveys an opinion by the way he or she states facts.

ESL Activity

Have students working in a small group take turns reading the five poems aloud. Then ask the students to select the poem that appealed to them the most. Have students explain, one at a time, what was striking to them about the poem.

Viewing Fine Art

Rockwell Kent (1882–1971) was an American artist who was best known for his illustrations. Kent's eloquent landscape illustrations, like the one on page 377, often accompanied text he had written himself. Ask: What details in this painting would make good subjects for haiku?

Cooperative Group Activity

In ancient Japan the haiku was originally a long poem, with 5-7-5 patterns alternating with 7-7 patterns. Have students work in pairs to create a haiku. The first student will write a 5-7-5 verse; the second student will write a 7-7 verse. The first student will then write another 5-7-5 verse, and so on, until they finish their haiku.

Shadows of Evening, Rockwell Kent. Collection of the Whitney Museum of American Art

Four Haiku

1

Here . . . there. . .
the sound of waterfall is heard—
young leaves, everywhere.   —*Buson*

2

Friend, that open mouth
reveals your whole interior. . .
Silly hollow frog!   —*Anonymous*

3

Make up your mind snail!
You are half inside your house
and halfway out!   —*Richard Wright*

4

Insects, why cry?
We all go
that way.   —*Issa*

A bee thumps

5

A bee thumps against the dusty window
falls to the sill,
climbs back up, buzzing;
falls again;

and does this over and over.
If only he would climb higher!
The top half of the window is
open.   —*Robert Sund*

Four Haiku/A bee thumps ■ 377

TEACHING PLAN

INTRODUCE

Motivation
Create a visual display of the images presented by several of the haiku in this selection. The display can be in the form of photographs, drawings, or other graphics. For example, you might include a picture of a frog and a snail. Encourage students to talk about what these pictures make them think of. Relate the discussion to the haiku they are about to read.

Purpose-Setting Question
What do you think of when you see a frog? a snail? an insect?

READ

Literary Focus:
Haiku
Every haiku contains a discovery. The style of the poem is such that one tends to say, "Oh, I never saw it that way!" The discovery in a haiku is often an image from nature that provides an interesting commentary on some aspect of human life.

Reading Focus:
Identify Fact and Opinion
Ask: In the fourth haiku, what fact(s) does the speaker include? What opinion does the speaker express? Have students answer these questions for each poem on the page.

CLOSE

Have students complete Review the Selection on pages 378–379.

Comparing Selections
Ask: What is the common subject used as symbols in all of these poems?

Develop Vocabulary Skills
The words used in this selection are fairly simple. Some words that you may wish to discuss before students read the selection include *interior* and *thumps*.

Mini Quiz

Write on the board or overhead projector the following sentences and call on students to fill in the blanks. Discuss the answers with the class.

1. In the second haiku the frog is a metaphor for _____.

2. Poet Richard Wright tells the snail to _____.

3. The haiku by Issa is about _____.

4. The first haiku talks about the sound of a _____.

5. In the poem about the bee, the open window symbolizes _____.

Answers
1. empty-headed people
2. make up its mind
3. insects
4. waterfall
5. freedom

T377

UNDERSTAND THE SELECTION

Answers

1. outdoors, near trees and a waterfall
2. a frog
3. trying to get out a window
4. spring
5. someone who talks too much
6. It describes something in nature that also symbolizes an aspect of human life.
7. person trying to solve a problem by doing the same thing over and over again, rather than trying a new way
8. The snail looks as if it does not know whether it wants to be in or out of its shell.
9. Sample answer: We all die eventually.
10. It refers to the snail's shell.

Respond to Literature

As a class project, have students create a mural of the images presented by the five poems. Students can choose to recreate the images from nature, or they can create images that reflect the human meaning of each poem. For example, a person who cannot decide between two paths would be a fitting representation of the snail.

WRITE ABOUT THE SELECTION

Prewriting

Use the chalkboard or an overhead transparency to create a list of possible titles based on suggestions from the class.

Writing

For students who have chosen to write haiku, provide guidance where needed on how to use the 5-7-5 syllable form.

Revising

Have students read their poems out loud to a partner. Ask the partners to comment on whether the image produced is clear and vivid. Have students suggest adjectives that would improve their partners' poem.

Proofreading

Punctuation in poetry can be tricky because there are no strict rules. Display several students' poems on an overhead projector and ask the class if they agree with the punctuation.

UNDERSTAND THE SELECTION

Recall

1. What is the setting for the first haiku?
2. What animal is described in the second haiku?
3. What is the bee doing in the last poem?

Infer

4. What time of year does the first haiku describe?
5. What human quality might be symbolized by the animal in the second haiku?
6. In what ways is the last poem similar to a haiku?
7. What human predicament might the bee symbolize?

Apply

8. How might the title "Indecision" apply to the haiku about the snail?
9. What is the meaning of the haiku about insects?
10. What is the meaning of the word "house" in the poem about the snail?

> ### *Respond to Literature*
> What images do these five poems bring to mind? Do the images relate only to nature, or do they relate to human life as well?

378 ■ Unit 4

WRITE ABOUT THE SELECTION

Several of the poems in this selection symbolize human qualities that are represented by animals. Think of a person you know (it might be you!) who has a characteristic that might be presented in a haiku about an animal. Then write a haiku or poem describing this person.

Prewriting Make a chart of several animals that lend themselves to this assignment. (For convenience, you can use the animals in the haiku you studied, such as "Frog" or "Snail.") Under each title you list, write down the human characteristic that is symbolized. Then write down the names of people you know who have this characteristic.

Writing Decide which name on your list would make the best subject for your haiku or poem. Then describe this person with words that you could use in the poem. Try to include a specific incident involving the person that illustrates the characteristic you are writing about.

Revising The use of adjectives is important in a description. Reread your poem and add or substitute at least three adjectives that make the picture of the person you are writing about more vivid.

Proofreading Check for mistakes in spelling, usage, and mechanics. Be sure to use apostrophes to make nouns possessive.

ESL Activity

Have students illustrate each haiku. ESL students may benefit from working in pairs with proficient speakers of English. Encourage pairs to alternate roles: one student reads a poem aloud while the other student sketches.

THINK ABOUT HAIKU

A **haiku** paints a picture in words. The subject of the haiku is usually an object in nature. Very often, the meaning of a haiku goes beyond its subject. The subject becomes a symbol of a human characteristic or an aspect of human life.

1. In the second poem, how is the interior of the frog described?

2. How does this description comment on a person who is like the frog?

3. In the poem about the bee, what does the bee not realize?

4. How does this poem apply to someone who keeps making the same mistake over and over?

5. Describe the picture that is painted in the first haiku.

READING FOCUS

Identify Fact and Opinion Tell what is being described in each poem. Then write the opinion that the words or tone convey. Tell how the speaker feels or what the **speaker** believes about the thing he or she is describing.

DEVELOP YOUR VOCABULARY

A **thesaurus** is a dictionary of synonyms. When you look up a word in a thesaurus, you will find a list of words that have meanings that are similar to the meaning of that word.

The words in a thesaurus can be very helpful when writing a poem, story, or essay. Suppose you are writing a haiku and you need a one-syllable word that means ocean. If you look up the word *ocean* in a thesaurus, you will find the word *sea* which has the same meaning.

Look up the following words in a thesaurus, and find at least two synonyms for each word. Then use each word in an original sentence.

1. interior   4. sound
2. hollow   5. fall
3. house   6. window

Review the Selection ■ 379

READING FOCUS

Sample Answers

1. waterfall and leaves; 2. frog; 3. snail; 4. insects; 5. a bee.
1. The sound of falling leaves and the waterfall is everywhere. 2. The frog's mouth is so big, it reveals the frog's insides. 3. The snail is partially exposed. 4. Insects should appreciate their short life. 5. A bee thumps: A bee cannot see his way out of the window.
1. serenity; 2. amusement; 3. poet feels the snail is indecisive; 4. impatience; 5. poet may feel the bee is rather stupid.

T379

THINK ABOUT HAIKU

Answers

1. as hollow
2. a person whose mouth is always open is empty inside—in other words, a superficial person
3. that the top half of the window is open
4. If the person tries a different approach, he or she will find success.
5. Answers will vary. Students should get a sense of a forest or other natural area with many trees; the season is spring and there is a waterfall.

DEVELOP YOUR VOCABULARY

Sample Answers

1. inside, contents—Joe wants to be an interior decorator.
2. empty, unfilled—The tree trunk was hollow.
3. home, abode—They built a house.
4. noise, clamor—The sound of the jet was deafening.
5. descend, topple—The children fall down at the end of the game.
6. portal, casement—The window was open.

SELECTION OBJECTIVES

After completing this selection, students will be able to

- understand the use of conflict
- describe a conflict
- evaluate characters' discoveries
- apply the theme of a story
- analyze conflict in a story
- use a dictionary to find additional information about words
- summarize

Lesson Resources

Starvation Wilderness
- Selection Synopsis, Teacher's Edition, pp. T311e
- Comprehension and Vocabulary Workbook, pp. 75–76
- Language Enrichment Workbook, pp. 77–79
- Teacher's Resources
    Reinforcement, p. R36
    Test, pp. T71–T72

More About Conflict

The conflict in a story sets up the problem or series of problems that the main character will have to overcome. The unknown outcome of the conflict provides suspense—will the character succeed or fail?

More About the Unit Theme

The hero and heroine in the selection are somewhat naïve about what life will be like in northern Canada in winter. As the plot unfolds, the couple find themselves in increasingly precarious circumstances, and they make many harsh discoveries about the realities of nature in the far north.

Portage in the Hoarfrost River, Canada, Sir George Back. Royal Geographical Society, London, UK/Bridgeman Art Library

READING FOCUS

Summarize When you summarize a piece of writing, you state only the main ideas or events that are presented. Stories can usually be divided into a beginning, middle, and end. When you read a longer story, try pausing at the end of each part to summarize what has happened. Summarizing the action in your own words can help you remember and understand the story. A summary should always be simpler and shorter than the piece you are summarizing.

380 ■ Unit 4

CONFLICT

An important ingredient in the plot of a story is **conflict**. A conflict is a meeting of two opposing forces. Often the central character in a story is involved in a struggle with another character. In some stories, however, the struggle is between the main character and nature, or between the main character and some other thing. It is also possible for the conflict to be within a person.

A story begins to develop once a conflict is established. As you read "Starvation Wilderness," ask yourself:

1. What is the conflict in this story?
2. What is the outcome of the conflict?

WRITING CONNECTION

Think of a conflict that you have been involved in recently. It may have been a confrontation with another person, or it may have been a difficult set of circumstances or a conflict within your own mind. Write a short paragraph in which you describe the nature of the conflict and the way it was handled. Also, indicate the outcome of the conflict.

Viewing Fine Art

Sir George Back (1796–1878) was a British admiral and arctic navigator who painted as well as published accounts of his voyages. One of Back's longer expeditions was from 1819–1822 when his group traced part of North America's continental limit. For 675 miles, they traveled by canoe, carefully mapping the Northern coastline of what is now Canada's Northwest Territories. Ask students what sorts of conflicts might have occurred about 200 years ago in an area like the one in the painting.

Cooperative Group Activity

Have students work in small groups. Challenge each group to dramatize a conflict. Groups may choose one of their members' completed Writing Connection activities. Each dramatization should show clearly both the conflict and the outcome of the conflict. Have groups share their dramatizations with the class.

STARVATION WILDERNESS

ADAPTED

by Olive A. Fredrickson

Our scow was heavy. It was an old 30-footer that we had bought at Fort Fitzgerald. But with only two grown-ups, a baby, and a pair of sled dogs on board, it rode high. The steady current of the Slave River pushed us north far faster than anyone could have walked on shore.

We had oars, and now and then my young husband, Walter, used them for a short distance. But there was no need for it. Mostly he just steered. We watched the early-fall scenery slip past or played with our six-month-old daughter, Olive. When we weren't cuddling her, she slept as contented as a kitten in the small cardboard box that was her crib.

Muskrat sign was plentiful along the river. Wherever there was green grass along the shore, snow geese pastured by the hundreds. We were rarely out of hearing of their wild voices. We had come to a land of plenty, Walter and I agreed. It was a dream country for a young trapper and his wife.

The time was late August of 1922. The trip had come about when Walter met two trappers, Nels Nelson and Pete Anderson, at Fort Fitzgerald. They had trapped the fall before down the Slave in Northwest Territories. They had come out before Christmas, they said, with 1,600 muskrat skins that brought $1.50 apiece. There were lakes all over the country, they told Walter, and every one of those lakes crawled with marsh rats.

My husband was a trapper at heart, above everything else. For him stories of that kind were like wild tales of gold to other men. He gave up then and there all thought of going to Fort McMurray, where I had been looking forward to the presence of other women, a few comforts, and a doctor in case the baby or I needed one. The three of us, Walter decided, would spend the winter trapping on those rich fur grounds.

We bought the scow and 34 single-spring traps. We also bought 400 pounds of flour, 50 pounds of white sugar, and four 50-pound sacks of potatoes. I remember that we paid $12 for each of those sacks. Coal oil[1] was $2 a gallon at Fitzgerald. We completed our grub list with beans, rice, salt pork, oatmeal,

---

scow (SKOU) barge; tub-like boat for carrying cargo
cuddling (KUD ling) holding and petting
muskrat (MUSK rat) brown animal that lives in and near water, about two feet long; also called *marsh rat* and *rat* in the selection
presence (PREZ uns) nearness; being there
[1]coal oil: kerosene, sometimes made from coal

Starvation Wilderness ■ 381

Discussion

At various points in the story, pause and ask students to discuss alternatives to the plight of the characters. Probably, more students will agree that the author and her husband did not always make the wisest choices. Perhaps there were times when they should have turned back or sought help; certainly, they might have learned more beforehand about where they were going.

Literary Focus:
Plot

Point out that writers sometimes give clues that can help readers predict what will happen in the story. Ask: On page 382, what clues suggest that the young couple may encounter problems in the wilderness?

baking powder, salt, and tea—and cornmeal for the dogs.

We loaded the scow and shoved off on August 23 for the trip down the Slave to our trapping grounds. We were in completely unfamiliar country. It was the first time either of us had been that far north. We were on our way into what Walter had been told was good fur country. He was completely happy. I'll confess that I wasn't quite so cheerful as he was about wintering with a child not yet a year old hundreds of miles from the nearest doctor.

Nels and Pete had told us to look for an old sawdust pile on the west shore of the river. We should settle down around there, they had said. We passed the sawdust pile on our fourth day of floating. We tied up the scow, let our two dogs loose for a run, got the tent up, and carried our supplies up the bank. It was close to midnight when we finished. We tied the dogs to trees and turned in.

After we had gotten to sleep, I was awakened by some animal gnawing on the salt pork[2] we had brought into the tent. At first I thought one of the dogs had gotten loose. But as my eyes grew accustomed to the dim light in the tent I made out a large skunk.

The tent was only 9 × 12 feet. That skunk was working on the pork within three feet of my face. I shook Walter awake. We tried to drive the skunk off, but it wouldn't budge.

"I'll have to shoot it or we won't have any pork," Walter finally said. We knew it wasn't a very good idea, but we had no choice.

Shooting a skunk inside a tent is a big mistake. Whoever invented tear gas[3] simply copied something that skunks have used for thousands of years. It wouldn't be truthful to say the air turned blue, but it certainly turned something. Our eyes started to water. We were almost blinded. We began to gag. I grabbed the baby and fumbled my way outside. After a minute or so, Walter stumbled out behind me, dragging the dead skunk. He threw it over the riverbank. We hauled our bedding outside and spent the rest of the night in the open. We were tired enough to sleep anywhere. The next morning I told Walter that his way of saving our salt pork was no good. The pork smelled almost as bad as the tent.

Next we started work on a cabin for our winter home. We planned to live in it only until November, when the lakes would freeze and we'd have to quit trapping. So we threw it up hurriedly. It was built of small green logs. It was soon finished, and about October 1 we put our traps out.

As it happened, we stayed on in that rough cabin until spring. For one thing, there was a lot of fur, mink as well as muskrat. There was also firewood handy. The cabin stood in a thick grove of spruces, where it was sheltered from the wind.

---

[2]**salt pork:** fat pork cured with salt to keep fresh
[3]**tear gas:** kind of gas that burns the eyes, sometimes use to control riots
gag (GAG) cough with a sick feeling

We had torn our scow apart to make doors and windows. I suggested to Walter that he build a boat. It was a clumsy boat, for we had no way to bend the heavy boards of the scow.

The trapping looked good, but now we faced another problem. Wild meat was so scarce that we got worried. There wasn't a moose or deer track anywhere. Before winter closed in on us, we had named that belt of timber and swampy lakes Starvation Wilderness. Snow came to stay on October 10. After that the whole country was white and lifeless.

Trapping was good. We were looking at our traps twice a day. We'd hike out to the lakes together. Then I'd take Olive and the dog team with a small toboggan and cover half the line. Walter would go over the other half. We'd meet at midday. On the way back to camp, he covered my end of the line and I took his.

We both trapped until the first of November. Then the lakes were frozen. The temperature had dropped too low for us to be out in the wind and cold. From December until the end of March, the temperature rarely climbed as high as 10° below zero. There were days when it went to 65° below. The wind cut like a knife. We huddled in our shack and tried to keep warm.

Spruce pitch dripped from the roof poles and matted my long curls that Walter liked so much. In desperation I finally took the scissors one day when he was out looking at fox traps and cut my hair as short as I could. He was so upset when he came home that his face turned gray.

We got through that bitter winter until February. By then we knew we'd run out of food long before June, when we had planned to catch the first steamboat coming up the Slave. We had known since October that I was pregnant. Our second baby would be born in July. We didn't dare to wait for the boat, knowing that before the end of winter we'd have nothing to eat.

We were in no shape for the 60-mile trip out to Fort Smith. Our two dogs were old and not strong enough to pull Olive and me on the sled. The baby could ride, but I'd have to walk. We didn't have suitable clothing for cold of 40° and 50° below zero. What we lacked were fur parkas and fur-lined moccasins. But as our food dwindled, we made ready for the trip. Walter would leave Olive and me at Fort Smith and come back in time to trap again as soon as the lakes opened.

We put hot water in the water bottle, and we heated stones. We wrapped the baby in our whole bedroll of four blankets with the stones and water bottle beside her, and struck out up the Slave. The empty toboggan with Olive aboard was all our dogs could pull.

It was bitterly cold, probably around

---

belt (BELT) area; region
toboggan (tuh BOG un) large, flat sled
parka (PAHR kuh) fur jacket with a hood
dwindle (DWIN dul) become less and less
bedroll (BED rohl) roll of blankets or other bedding

Starvation Wilderness ■ 383

Reading Focus:
Summarize
Have students summarize the situation that causes the couple to leave their cabin for Fort Smith.

40° below. The going was hard. We made poor time. The dogs pulled willingly enough for a while. But the heavy going was too much for them. We had traveled about 15 miles when they began to give out. They stopped frequently. More than once they lay down in the snow. Walter urged them on and pushed all he could on the toboggan handles to help them. But we both knew we weren't going to go much farther.

The winter days are very short there in the North. By 3:30 in the afternoon, dusk was beginning to come down. Across the river there was a little cabin with smoke curling out of the chimney. I can't remember that I was ever gladder to see a human habitation.

Critical Thinking:
Analyze
Up to this point in the narrative, the Fredricksons show many skills and admirable qualities. Ask: What are these skills and qualities? The couple also made many mistakes in both actions and judgment. Ask: What mistakes did the couple make? Ask: What motivation prompted them to make these mistakes, even when they should have known better? What was their main reason for their journey into the wilderness?

Winter, George Gardner Symons. Scripps College, Claremont

habitation (hab ih TAY shun) a building to live in

384 ■ Unit 4

Viewing Fine Art

George Gardner Symons (1863–1930) was an American landscape painter. Born in Chicago, he became a student at the Chicago Art Institute and also studied art in Europe. Symons is best known for his snow scenes in the Berkshire Mountains of Massachusetts. Though he spent most of his career on the east coast, in 1896 he moved to California with a friend where he spent the latter half of his life. Ask students to describe their responses to the scene. Would they like to visit the spot? Why or why not?

The cabin belonged to two young trappers. We pulled in thinking we could stay the night. But there wasn't room to walk between the stove, beds, and table. It was plain that they couldn't put us up. They told us that four miles farther up the Slave another trapper, Bert Bennett, had a comfortable cabin. We rested a little while, and started for Bennett's place with the early dark thickening over the frozen snowy wilderness. I didn't feel as if I could go 500 feet, much less four miles.

That was one of the worst hikes I've ever had. Each mile of the four seemed like 10. The dogs stopped every few yards to lie down. Walter went ahead to break trail and pull them along with a short length of rope. I pushed on the toboggan handles for a change. It was too dark for Walter to see where he was putting his snowshoes, and he must have fallen 100 times. I had pain in every inch of the legs, my back, and all through my body. I finally realized I was leaning on the toboggan handles more than I was pushing, It seemed to me that the easiest thing to do would be to walk off into the snow and lie down and sleep forever.

But there was Olive to think of, I reminded myself. I could hear her whimper now and then and I wondered if she was freezing. There was nothing I could do about it if she was. I didn't dare open the bedroll she was wrapped in to look at her. I just kept putting one foot ahead of the other, stumbling and staggering along, terribly cold, until I lost all track of time and place.

A shout from Walter brought me out of my stupor. "Hello, there!" he yelled. I looked ahead and could see a square of light shining out of a window. Oh, what a welcome sight!

I don't remember Bennett opening the door, or Olive and me being carried into the warmth of the cabin. The first thing I recall was Walter pulling off my coat. Then somebody set a bowl of hot soup in front of me and shook me and told me to eat.

In a daze I watched Bennett take off Olive's rabbit-skin coat and start to feed her. They told me afterward that I cried out, "No, don't take her coat off. She'll freeze!" But I have no memory of that. I did not even realize that we were safe and warm inside four walls. The next thing I remember, Walter was telling me to get up for breakfast.

I was too stiff and sore to make it. But he pulled me out of bed and made me move my legs and body. It's surprising how much power of recovery you have at 21. I was four months pregnant, and I had run and walked 23 miles the day before in deep snow. When Bennett looked at his thermometer that morning it was 61° below. The wonder was that the three of us had not frozen to death on the trail.

We realized then that we could not make it to Fort Smith. It was dangerous and foolhardy to try. Luckily, Bennett had

---

stupor (STOO pur) dazed or dull state; loss of feeling
foolhardy (FOOL hahr dee) foolishly risky; much too bold

Starvation Wilderness ■ 385

Literary Focus:
Conflict
Ask students to describe the specific problems the wife and husband have encountered so far. List these on the chalkboard. Then, have students review the list to make sure they see that most of the problems relate to the harsh environment in which the couple live. Ask them to use the list to state the basic conflict in the story.

Reading Focus:
Summarize
You may wish to have students reread page 385. Ask: How would you summarize the family's trek from the first trapper's cabin to the Bennett place?

extra supplies that he could spare. He sold us flour and beans enough to see us through, and even lent Walter 24 good muskrat traps.

We stayed three days with Bennett. I regained my strength. At the end of the three days I was as good as new. The dogs were in better shape than when we'd begun our terrible trip up-river. We were ready to go back to our cabin and see the winter out. With muskrat at $1.50 each, there was more good money to be made as soon as the lakes started to open. When the first boat came up the Slave, we would be waiting for it.

We started out on a clear morning with the sun shining. Wind had drifted and packed the snow solidly enough that we seldom broke through. The dogs and Walter and I all had easy going. We pulled up in front of our lonely little cabin just as it was coming full dark.

We did not see or hear a living thing except each other, the dogs, and three foxes that Walter trapped, until the end of March. It seemed as if all the game, even rabbits, had died off or left the country. Neither of us had ever seen a winter wilderness so lifeless and still.

We fed the three fox carcasses to the dogs. They were starved enough to gulp them down. The beans and flour Bert Bennett had sold us were running low, and we were eating less than half of what we wanted.

Toward the first of April, we decided to start our mink and muskrat trapping,

even though the lakes were still covered with three feet of ice. It wasn't so much that we wanted fur. We needed the muskrats as food for ourselves and the dogs. Things had reached a point where I hated to eat because we had almost nothing for the dogs. None of us would last much longer without meat.

We made a trip to the nearest lake where we had trapped before freeze-up. We found the shallow lake frozen solid. Not a muskrat was left. When we turned the dogs back toward camp that afternoon, Walter and I were about as worried as two people could get.

A few days after that we packed up the little food we had left. We took our tent, bedding, and traps, and went eight miles west to some bigger lakes that Walter had found earlier.

We put up the tent at the first lake. We found water under the ice, cut into muskrat houses, and caught a few muskrat. They eased the pinch of our hunger, but we were not taking enough for ourselves and the dogs.

At last Walter made the unhappy announcement that the dogs would have to be destroyed. I realized that was kinder than letting them starve. But the idea of it almost broke my heart. It had to be done, but I cried until I was sick.

Less than a week after that the weather broke in our favor. The sun came out warm and bright. The snow started to melt, and the lakes opened up around the shores. We began trapping muskrats by

---

carcass (KAHR kus) body of dead animal

Trapper in the Wilderness, Sydney Laurence. Shelburne Museum, Shelburne, VT

the dozens. If the night was cold and ice formed, our luck fell off. Some days we took only five or six pelts, but one day we took 70. We were living on muskrat meat, and for the first time that winter we had enough to eat. I boiled it and gave Olive the broth in her bottle. She thrived on it.

When spring comes to the North it comes with a rush. Suddenly it is sunny day after day. The days are long and warm. But the short dark hours of the spring nights are often cold. It was hard to keep warm in our tent, even with a fire in the tiny stove. That stove was to cause the worst disaster of all.

We continued trapping while the snow melted and the creeks rose and became little rivers. Walter and I agreed that we'd stay camped at the lake until May 10. Then we'd hike back to our cabin. We'd go up the Slave to Bert Bennett's place in our rowboat, and there

---

thrive (THRYV) grow healthy and strong

Starvation Wilderness ■ 387

Reading Focus:
Summarize
Remind students that fictional stories can contain interesting factual information. Have students summarize what trapping animals is like in the far north in the late winter and early spring. Have them refer to pages 386 and 387.

Viewing Fine Art

Sydney Laurence (1865–1940) was an American Realist painter who studied at the National Academy in Paris and led an extremely adventurous life. The scene in this painting is the wilderness of Alaska, where he traveled to in 1906 in search for gold. While in Alaska, he took a four-month trip with a dog sled and a team of dogs. He also built a cabin there. He returned to his cabin many times and there he painted frequently. Supposedly, as a young boy, he ran away to sea, became the first mate of a boat and saved the captain's life when the boat capsized. As an adult, he was a war correspondent and traveled extensively in China and Africa. American Realists were known for their landscapes and their concern with detail and accuracy. Ask students how they would like to live in the cabin pictured.

catch the first steamer of the season to Fort Smith. But things don't always go as people plan them.

On the morning of May 2, I was in the tent baking bannock in the little stovepipe oven. I stepped outside to look for Walter and saw him coming a quarter-mile up the lake. I took Olive by the hand and walked to meet him. She was toddling all over by then. When we met, I took part of his load of fresh pelts and the three of us started back.

All of a sudden we heard ammunition exploding at a terrible rate. Then smoke and flames rolled up around the tent. Walter dropped his sack of fur and ran. I grabbed Olive and hurried after him as fast as I could. When I got to the tent my husband was dragging out charred food and burning pieces of blankets. I grabbed the things as he pulled them out and doused them in the lake.

It was all over in 10 minutes. A tent burns fast.

What we had saved would have made a very small bundle. There were two or three half-burned pieces of blanket. There were the few matches in our pockets and in a waterproof container. Walter's .22 was safe. There were four shells in it, and Walter had a box in his pocket. The rest of our ammunition was gone. Most of the rat pelts had been hanging in a tree outside the tent and were safe.

Of our food, we had about four cups of flour, wet and mixed with cinders, and a pound or so of beans. For Olive, luckily, there were a few undamaged cans of milk.

With muskrat meat, that handful of supplies would have to see us through until we could reach Bennett's cabin. That meant a hard hike of 8 or 10 miles through difficult country, and then 23 miles by rowboat against the spring current of the mighty Slave. Worst of all, we knew we could not make the trip up-river until the Slave broke up. We had no idea when that would happen.

Things looked pretty grim. I was expecting a second baby in less than two months, and we knew we had a very rough time ahead. But there was no use sitting beside the ruins of our tent and worrying. The thing was to get started.

We hung our traps in trees where we would be able to find them the following fall. We ate our bannock and a good meal of muskrat we had roasted earlier, rolled Olive in the patches of bedding, and lay down under a tree to rest for a few hours. We did not dare to use a match for a fire. We had to hoard them for times of need.

When we awoke we made up our loads and were ready to start. I wrapped Olive in the blanket pieces. I'd carry her on my back. She was so thin she wasn't very heavy. I rolled one cooking pot, knives, forks, spoons, a cup, and the baby bottle in a scrap of blanket and tied it all on my back behind her. Walter's load consisted of the dry muskrat pelts,

---

bannock (BAN uk) kind of flat bread
charred (CHAHRD) partly burned
douse (DOUS) soak with water
hoard (HAWRD) store away; save

Ask: What accident intensifies the main conflict in the story? The author is expecting a second baby. Have students predict how this fact will intensify the conflict in the story.

about 250 in all, our stove—it weighed only about 10 pounds—and three lengths of stovepipe.

We left the burned-out camp with me carrying all I could handle and Walter packing a load of about 110 pounds. Every creek was roaring full and was two or three times as wide as usual. Many times Walter had to make three trips through the swollen and icy creeks, one with his pack, one with Olive and my load, and a third to help me across.

It took two days of the hardest kind of travel to get back to our cabin. At the end of the first day we stopped and made a camp under a clump of spruces. We roasted a muskrat we had brought along. We went without breakfast and our noon meal the second day. But in the middle of the afternoon, I shot a small muskrat. It wasn't big enough to make a good meal for one hungry person, let alone three. But we stopped and cooked it on the spot and divided it up.

It was midnight when we trudged up to our cabin. We were tired, discouraged, and hungry. But at least we had a roof over our heads again and four walls to keep out the cold at night. We didn't mind too much going to bed without supper.

When daylight came, I got up and scraped each empty flour sack for the little flour that remained in it. One look at the Slave that morning confirmed our worst fears. Water was running between the ice and shore. We couldn't get out on the river. We wouldn't have dared. There was no hope of following the shore up to Bennett's place either, because of the many large creeks that flowed into the river. We had no choice but to wait for the ice to go out.

The 11 days between May 10 and the time when the ice finally went out of the Slave were a nightmare of hunger and worry—mostly hunger.

Because we were so short of matches, we kept plenty of wood on hand and fed the fire. We never let it go out.

I found a roll of wire and set snares for ducks, rabbits, muskrats—anything. In all, I snared two red squirrels and a blackbird. We pulled up dead grass along the edge of the water and ate the tender yellow shoots below. One day I saw a fool hen— a spruce grouse—perched on a low branch of a tree. I hurried to rig a snare on a pole. I reached up and dropped it over her head and jerked her to the ground. That was the best meat we had all that time. For once poor little Olive got all the broth she wanted.

Hunger cramps kept us awake at night, and when we slept we dreamed troubled dreams of food. In my own case, being seven months pregnant didn't make things any better. Right then I needed to eat for two. Each night we slept less. Each day we got weaker. The

---

confirm (kun FURM) prove true
snare (SNAIR) loop or noose for catching small animals or birds
shoot (SHOOT) first part of growing plant to appear
grouse (GROUS) kind of wild bird, a little smaller then a chicken

Starvation Wilderness ■ 389

Reading Focus:
Summarize

Ask: How does the author summarize the 11 days between May 10 and the time when the river ice breaks up? What does the break-up allow the family to do?

Discussion

Ask students to think about how hungry they would get living on grass and bark. What do they think is the longest time a person could live without food?

baby's whimpering for food tore us apart. Walter cursed himself over and over for bringing Olive and me down the Slave.

If we had brought a few traps back from our tent camp, we could have caught muskrats or ducks. But we'd left all the traps behind. For three days our only food was what we called spruce tea. I stripped green needles off and boiled them. We drank a few spoonfuls every couple of hours. It eased the hunger cramps and seemed to give us some strength.

Olive was no longer running around the cabin. She sat quiet and played with whatever was at hand. There was no color in her lips and cheeks. Her eyes looked hollow and dull. I can't put into words how worried and afraid Walter and I were.

We made crude hooks by bending safety pins and tried fishing in the open water along the shore of the river, using pieces of red yarn for bait. Our catch totaled one very small jackfish. I tapped a small birch tree (they were few and far between in that area) for sap. It tasted good, but we had only half a cup to divide among the three of us.

At last, at 10 o'clock on the morning of May 21, the ice in the Slave began to move. By midnight it was gone, and the water was rolling past our door. At 3:00 in the morning of the 22nd we shoved our little boat into the river and were on our way to Bennett's.

It was dangerous to try traveling so soon after the ice went out. Chunks of ice weighing many tons kept sliding off the banks and drifting down with the current, but we had no choice.

Walter rowed, and I sat in the stern and paddled and steered us away from floating ice. It was killing work. Our closest call came that first day. Rowing close to shore, we saw a huge block of ice come sliding off a pile 40 feet high. It crashed into the water almost alongside us. The force of it lifted our rowboat into the air and sent it flying. We wound up 150 feet out in the swiftest part of the current, right side up only because we had happened to be pointed in the right direction when the ice thundered down.

Walter and I drank spruce tea and gathered and ate grass roots. We also drank water often because it seemed to ease our hunger. We just kept rowing until we gave out. Then we'd rest, and then we'd row some more.

It took us six days to make the 23-mile trip up the Slave to Bert Bennett's cabin. They were as dreadful as any days I can remember. We pulled up to shore at his place at midnight on May 27—dirty, ragged, starving, and so burned by wind and sun that we hardly knew our own reflections when we looked in a mirror. In those six days we had eaten nothing but spruce tea, grass roots, and the inner bark of trees.

A Mr. and Mrs. King from Fort Smith were at Bennett's. They had come down on the ice in March. She gave us each half a biscuit and a couple of spoonfuls of stewed apricots, but the food was too much for our stomachs. We awakened three hours later with dreadful cramps and were miserably sick for the next 12 hours.

Reading Focus:
Summarize

Ask students to summarize the family's trip on the Slave River as they travel back to the Bennett cabin. What detail indicates the extreme starvation of the family?

It was four days before I was well enough to be out of bed. Mrs. King fed me a few spoonfuls of canned soup and cream every hour, and at the end of that time I felt fine. By then Walter and Olive had bounced back too.

Bennett and the Kings fixed us up with some clothing. We waited out a comfortable and happy month until the *Miss Mackenzie* came up the Slave on her first trip of the year. We boarded her near the end of June, and the trip to Fort Smith was lovely.

We sold our furs in Fort Smith. We had 560 muskrat pelts, 27 mink, three red foxes, four skunks, and a few weasels. The fox pelts brought $25 each, the mink $10.

We paid off our debts and had $1,060 left in cash. We had never had money that came harder.

Our second daughter, Vala, was born on July 18. Vala was a scrawny, blue-gray baby, weighing only $3\frac{1}{2}$ pounds. For three weeks my doctor did not think either she or her mother would live. But we made it, and Vala grew to be a healthy, pretty girl.

Walter went back to his trapline in the fall, but I'd had enough of the North. It's a place of great beauty, and the winter stillness is spellbinding, but it can also be terribly cruel. I knew I would never winter in a trapper's shack with my two little girls if I could help it. I stayed behind.

Starvation Wilderness ■ 391

Critical Thinking:
Apply
Ask students to list the pros and cons of a wilderness experience such as the author and her family had.

Literary Focus:
Conflict
Ask: How is the conflict in the story resolved? What decision about the future does the author make at the end of the story? Why do you think she makes this decision?

Mini Quiz

Write on the chalkboard or overhead projector the following sentences and call on students to fill in the blanks. Discuss the answers with the class.

1. The author and her husband spent the winter in _____ .

2. They were there because they hoped to _____ .

3. They had to kill their dogs because _____ .

4. They lost many of their belongings when _____ .

5. The author and her husband were not able to travel the Slave in the spring because _____ .

Answers

1. the wilderness of northern Canada

2. trap animals for fur

3. they did not have enough food for them

4. their tent caught fire

5. the river was frozen

UNDERSTAND THE SELECTION

Answers

1. in far northern Canada
2. from late August until the end of June
3. fur trapper
4. The author admits that she was worried about spending the winter in this area, despite her husband's cheerfulness.
5. finding enough to eat
6. They had only a few matches left.
7. A skunk gets into their tent and begins to eat their salt pork.
8. The author had not been able to eat enough while she was pregnant.
9. There was not enough food to feed the dogs.
10. Answers will vary. The traps may have been heavy and awkward to carry.

Respond to Literature

Have students recount the major events of the story in diary form, as if they are one of the characters on the journey. Encourage them to write under each entry the discoveries that they make. For example, "May 3: Could not go to Fort Smith because river was frozen. Discovered that traveling the Slave is restricted because of ice even in late spring."

WRITE ABOUT THE SELECTION

Prewriting

On the chalkboard or overhead transparency, make a sample outline using students' suggestions.

Writing

As students work on this section independently, go around the room and help those who are having trouble. Some students may enjoy writing their paragraphs in the style of a handbook or guidebook for outdoor enthusiasts.

Revising

Have students work in pairs. Ask students to read each other's papers and make suggestions for revising.

Proofreading

Have students choose different partners to exchange papers for proofreading. Encourage students to use editorial proofreading symbols when correcting one another's papers.

Review the Selection

UNDERSTAND THE SELECTION

Recall

1. Where does this story take place?

2. During what time of year does this story take place?

3. What is the occupation of the author's husband?

Infer

4. What hint is given fairly early in the story that this adventure may not turn out as well as planned?

5. What was the greatest problem that the author and her husband faced in the wilderness?

6. Why did the author and her husband never let their fire go out after their tent was destroyed?

7. What is the first thing to go wrong?

Apply

8. Why do you think the author's baby was so tiny when it was born?

9. Why did the couple kill their dogs?

10. Why do you think the couple left their traps behind when they returned to their cabin in May?

Respond to Literature

What did the author learn from her discoveries in "Starvation Wilderness"?

392 ■ Unit 4

WRITE ABOUT THE SELECTION

One of the problems faced by the author and her husband in "Starvation Wilderness" was that they were inexperienced in dealing with such rugged country and climate. Suppose that you are planning a camping trip in the wilderness. What can you learn from the events of this story? Write a paragraph in which you discuss several things that you would do or not do on your trip, based on Olive A. Fredrickson's experiences.

Prewriting Reread the story and make notes as you think of ideas for your paragraph. Be especially aware of things that go wrong during the couple's adventure—you will want to learn from their mistakes.

Writing Use your notes to write a paragraph about the way you would undertake a trip in the wilderness. Be sure to give reasons for your actions, based on the story.

Revising Sometimes a paragraph reads more smoothly when ideas are expressed in a different order. Try changing the order in which you discuss your ideas and decide if this makes a better paragraph. Consider adding or subtracting sentences. You may want to substitute sentences or phrases also.

Proofreading Check your paragraph for mistakes in spelling, usage, and mechanics. Be sure to capitalize proper nouns you may have used.

ESL Activity

Have students share survival stories from the news, books, movies, or personal experience. If some of the stories have wilderness settings, have students compare and contrast the person's experiences with those of Olive A. Fredrickson. For example, was lack of food the main problem or was it something else? For each story students describe, help them to identify the main conflict that is reflected in the person's struggles.

T392

THINK ABOUT CONFLICT

The conflict in a story provides a set of problems for the main character or characters to overcome. How successfully the characters meet these problems determines the outcome of the story. Very often the conflict in a story provides suspense—you find yourself asking questions such as "What will happen next?" or "Will this character survive?"

1. What is the conflict in "Starvation Wilderness"?

2. What was the outcome of the conflict?

3. What kinds of problems did the young couple have to overcome?

4. Do you think that some of these problems could have been avoided?

5. At what points in the story were you uncertain about the young couple's ability to survive?

READING FOCUS

Summarize Write a short paragraph about Olive A. Fredrickson's experiences living as a trapper in far northern Canada. In the first sentence, summarize the main conflict that she and her husband face. Then write two to four sentences that highlight their worst hardships.

DEVELOP YOUR VOCABULARY

You are probably used to looking in a dictionary to find the meanings of unfamiliar words. From the dictionary you can also learn the correct spelling and pronunciation of a word. You can learn the part of speech and origin of the word too. Some dictionaries include a phrase to show you how a word is used correctly in a sentence. Studying all the information in a dictionary entry will help you master a word, and make it a part of your working vocabulary.

Review the meanings of these words from "Starvation Wilderness" in your dictionary. Be sure to read all parts of the dictionary entry. Then use each word in an original sentence.

1. scow
2. presence
3. dwindle
4. douse
5. habitation
6. stupor
7. carcass
8. thrive
9. hoard
10. confirm

Review the Selection ■ 393

SELECTION OVERVIEW

SELECTION OBJECTIVES

After completing this selection, students will be able to

- understand rhyme
- identify a rhyme scheme
- identify discoveries about life
- relate a poem to their own experience
- analyze rhyme and repetition in a poem
- use words with multiple meanings
- analyze figurative language

Lesson Resources

Dreams/Untitled/Sympathy
- Selection Synopses, Teacher's Edition, pp. T311e–311f
- Comprehension and Vocabulary Workbook, pp. 77–78
- Language Enrichment Workbook, pp. 80–81
- Teacher's Resources Reinforcement, p. R37 Test, pp. T73–T74

More About Rhyme

Sometimes poems have words within the same line that rhyme. For example: "How sad and bad and mad it was!" (Browning) or "…O fleet sweet swallow" (Swinburne).

About the Authors

Langston Hughes, one of the foremost African American poets of the 20th century, is noted for his hopeful outlook on life and people. It is fitting that he would write about the importance of keeping dreams alive in one's life.

Dunbar, on the other hand, often wrote about the sorrows and difficulties African American people faced. His parents were former slaves, so he had first-hand knowledge of these difficulties. Certainly the poem "Sympathy" might well reflect the feelings of an African American person, especially in the early 20th century.

T394

READING FOCUS

Analyze Figurative Language Figurative language refers to the imaginative use of words, especially in comparisons. For example, a poet might write, "My love is a rose." This kind of figurative language, which makes a direct comparison between two things, is called a metaphor. In another kind of figurative language, personification, the poet describes a thing, animal, or idea as if it were a person. A poet might write, for example, "The roses hung their heads." As you read the poems, identify the kind of figurative language that is used in each.

Learn About

RHYME

Two words rhyme when they have a similar sound. For example, *wait* and *date* rhyme, as do *sell* and *bell*. Many poems include words that rhyme, especially at the ends of lines.

As you read a poem, you can often recognize a **rhyme scheme,** or pattern of similar sounds. You can describe the rhyme scheme with letters. For example:

> Jack and Jill
> Went up the hill
> To fetch a pail of water.
> Jack fell down
> And broke his crown
> And Jill came tumbling after.

In this nursery rhyme, the rhyme scheme is aa b cc d. Lines 1 and 2 rhyme; lines 4 and 5 rhyme with a different sound. Lines 3 and 6 do not rhyme with any other lines.

Rhyme can make a poem enjoyable to read. As you read the poems in this selection, ask yourself:

1. What is the rhyme scheme of each poem?
2. Which sounds are rhymed in each poem?

WRITING CONNECTION

Write a simple poem that has the rhyme scheme aa b cc d.

ESL Activity

Ask students to think of an example of an individual who has realized an important dream. Encourage them to consider people they know personally as well as well-known people. Point out that dreams may be small or large, near-term or long-term.

Cooperative Group Activity

Divide the class into small groups. Assign each group a rhyme scheme. Then ask each group to write a single poem that uses the scheme. Students in the group can compose the entire poem together, or each member of the group can contribute one or two lines.

Harriet Tubman, Series No. 10, Jacob Lawrence.
Hampton University Museum

DREAMS

by Langston Hughes

Hold fast to dreams
For if dreams die
Life is a broken-winged bird
That cannot fly.

Hold fast to dreams
For when dreams go
Life is a barren field
Frozen with snow.

---

barren (BAR un) bare, sterile

Dreams ■ 395

Viewing Fine Art

Jacob Lawrence (see Viewing Fine Arts for page 364) is a leading African American artist. Here he chronicles the story of Harriet Tubman, who made some 15 dangerous trips from the South to free slaves. Lawrence portrays the frightening nighttime escapes using dark, ominous shapes but emphasizes the bright stars that Tubman used to plot her direction. Tubman's yellow coat seems to reflect the starlight and contrasts with the massive black chain at her feet. Ask: What do the chains in the picture represent?

T395

There were three girls walked down the road,
As down the road walked she:
    The girl she was,
    The girl they saw,
    The girl she wanted to be.

SYMPATHY

by Paul Laurence Dunbar

I know why the caged bird sings, ah me,
    When his wing is bruised and his bosom sore—
When he beats his bars and he would be free;
It is not a carol of joy or glee,
    But a prayer that he sends from his heart's deep core,
But a plea, that upward to Heaven, he flings—
I know why the caged bird sings!

---

plea (PLEE) appeal; request

396 ■ Unit 4

Paul Laurence Dunbar (1872–1906)

After Paul Laurence Dunbar graduated from high school, the best job that he could find was that of an elevator operator in a local hotel. His life took a decided turn for the better when his poetry was discovered by William Dean Howells, an outstanding American literary critic. Dunbar soon became well-known in literary circles around the country.

Paul Laurence Dunbar was the son of former slaves. He grew up in Dayton, Ohio, where he was the only African American in his high school class. Dunbar's literary ability was obvious during high school, where he wrote poetry and served as editor of the high school newspaper and yearbook. Dunbar also published an African American newsletter, which was printed by his high school classmate Orville Wright, one of the famous Wright brothers.

Dunbar's poetry often captured the humor and gentleness of the lives of African American people in the rural South. He became most famous for his poems written in dialect, although he also wrote poems in standard English.

Many of Dunbar's poems seem old-fashioned today, partly because of their style, and partly because they reflect racial attitudes that have become outdated in late-20th-century America. Yet many of his writings, such as the selection in this unit, have stood the test of time.

In addition to books of poetry, Paul Laurence Dunbar also wrote short stories and novels. He died when he was only 33 years old, having produced nearly all of his work in just ten years.

Author Biography ■ 397

MORE ABOUT THE AUTHOR

Although Dunbar grew up in a poor household, he was exposed to poetry at an early age through his mother. A former slave, who became a washerwoman, she developed a love of poetry after hearing it read aloud by the family she had earlier worked for. She passed on this love of poetry to Paul, who was reciting and even writing poetry by the age of 6.

Unknown and African American, Paul Laurence Dunbar had to publish his first volume of poetry at his own expense. By the time he was 25, however, his poetry had attracted national attention. Dunbar frequently gave public readings, and his work appeared in newspapers and popular magazines of the day. At a reading at the World's Fair, when he was only 21, Dunbar met the famed abolitionist Frederick Douglass, who called him "the most promising young colored man in America."

Additional Works
BY PAUL LAURENCE DUNBAR

You may wish to suggest these works by Paul Laurence Dunbar for additional reading.

Lyrics of a Lonely Life. Citadel, 1984. A selection of Dunbar's early poems. (poetry)

Poems of Cabin and Field. AMS, 1997. (poetry)

Selected Poems. Dover, 1997. (poetry)

Best Stories of Paul Laurence Dunbar. Reprint Services, 1938. (fiction)

The Sport of the Gods. Signet, 1999. In Dunbar's last novel, an African American family moves to a northern city. (fiction)

UNDERSTAND THE SELECTION

Answers

1. goals in life
2. a girl walking down the road
3. a bird in a cage
4. Without them, life becomes bleak and empty.
5. Life is empty, and cold, with no growth.
6. No, but the poet sees three girls in the one person.
7. a person who is restricted in some way
8. flying free
9. The bird might symbolize a person who does not feel free to do as he or she wishes in life.
10. Sample answer: In "The Gold Medal," Amanda feels that people do not see her as she really is; by the end of the story she has a better idea of who she really is and a dream of what she hopes to become.

Respond to Literature

Encourage students to consider the different views of life represented by these three poems. The first poem is very positive, encouraging the reader to hold onto dreams. The second poem contains a paradox, that is, the notion that a single person is really many different people, at least at different times and in different situations. The third poem is less positive, for it deals with restrictions in life that may or may not be lifted.

WRITE ABOUT THE SELECTION

Prewriting

As students make their prewriting notes, ask for volunteers to share some of their thoughts with the class. This may help students who are having trouble identifying their responses to the poems.

UNDERSTAND THE SELECTION

Recall

1. What is the meaning of the word "dreams" in the first poem?

2. What is the subject of "Untitled"?

3. In the poem "Sympathy," what is the poet observing?

Infer

4. Why does the author of "Dreams" feel that dreams are important?

5. What is the meaning of "Life is a barren field/Frozen with snow"?

6. In the untitled poem are there really three girls walking down the road? Explain your answer.

7. What might the caged bird symbolize in "Sympathy"?

Apply

8. In "Sympathy," what might the caged bird rather be doing than singing?

9. Dunbar was an African American whose parents were slaves. How does this fact fit in with the meaning of his poem?

10. Can you apply the meaning of the untitled poem to any of the stories or plays you have read in this unit?

Respond to Literature

What discoveries about life are reflected in these three poems?

WRITE ABOUT THE SELECTION

Each of the three poems in this selection expresses something that the poet has learned about life. Which poem do you agree with most or feel most strongly about? Which poem expresses something that you have also discovered? Write a paragraph in which you relate the theme of one of the poems to your own life experience.

Cluster all the details and feeling you have that relate to the poem that you chose. Write down everything that comes to mind. You can decide what to use later.

Prewriting   Read each of the poems several times. As you read, ask yourself, "Have I ever felt this way? When?" Jot down your ideas on a piece of paper. Decide which poem you will use as the subject of your paragraph.

Writing   Use the ideas from your notes to write your response to one of the poems. Try to include specific events or examples from your life that relate to the poem you have chosen.

Revising   Add vivid words to make your ideas come alive. Substitute specific verbs for ordinary ones. For example, "My mind raced" is more exciting than "I thought."

Proofreading   Make sure that all the words you have used are spelled correctly. Look up in the dictionary any words that you are unsure of and correct the spelling if necessary.

Writing

As students work on this section individually, go around the classroom and help those who are having trouble. Ask students specific questions about the event or feeling they are trying to describe in order to help them clarify their ideas.

Revising

Have students work in groups of three or four. Within the group each member should read his or her paragraph aloud, and then ask for comments from other group members.

Proofreading

Have a group of students form a spell-check team. Ask members of the class to submit their papers to the team, whose members will then look for spelling errors. Have the team members check one another's papers by using a dictionary.

T398

THINK ABOUT RHYME

The **rhyme scheme** is the pattern of similar sounds in a poem. Usually words rhyme at the ends of lines, although sometimes words rhyme within lines. Rhyme makes a poem pleasing to read.

Another technique that adds to the enjoyment and meaning of a poem is **repetition**. A poet will often repeat certain words or sounds in order to create an effect.

1. What is the rhyme scheme in "Dreams"?

2. What phrase is repeated in the poem? Why do you think it is repeated?

3. What is the rhyme scheme in the untitled poem?

4. What word is repeated in the untitled poem? What effect does this repetition create?

5. What is the rhyme scheme in "Sympathy"?

READING FOCUS

Analyze Figurative Language Which poem that you read used personification? Which used metaphors? Which poem did you like best? Explain how the poet's use of figurative language influenced your choice.

DEVELOP YOUR VOCABULARY

Many words in English have more than one meaning. For example, the word *bore* can mean to make a hole in something, or it can mean something or someone who is boring. When you read a word such as *bore*, you can often tell from the context what the word means. If you are uncertain of the meaning of a word with multiple meanings, you should look up the word in the dictionary.

Study these words from this selection. Tell which meaning of each word is used in the poems. Then write an original sentence to show how to use each meaning of each word.

1. dreams
2. fast
3. fly
4. field
5. core
6. saw
7. beats
8. free
9. wing
10. flings

Review the Selection ■ 399

THINK ABOUT RHYME

Answers
1. abcb
2. "Hold fast to dreams." It is the essential message of the poem.
3. abcdb
4. girl; it emphasizes the concept of three girls in one, because the word is repeated three times.
5. abaabcc

DEVELOP YOUR VOCABULARY

Answers
Sample sentences:
1. goals in life—She had *dreams* about becoming an actress. He had many *dreams* while he slept.
2. tight—Hold *fast* to what you know is right. The car can go quite *fast*.
3. soar in the sky—Planes *fly* at an altitude of several thousand feet. The *fly* managed to get through the screen.
4. open land—The farmer plowed the *field*. She wants to work in the *field* of medicine.
5. innermost part—We heard a rumble coming from the *core* of the volcano. The *core* of the apple is filled with seeds.
6. looked at—I *saw* the three girls. I will *saw* the log into two pieces.
7. bangs or hits—The boy *beats* against the door with his fist. If Sam *beats* Jenny at tennis, it will be his first victory.
8. without restriction—The prisoner was allowed to go *free*. The movie is *free* for senior citizens.
9. an appendage used for flying—The bat's *wing* is webbed. The gym is in the west *wing* of the school.
10. throw hard—She could really *fling* the ball. We're going out tonight for a wild *fling*.

READING FOCUS

Sample Answer

I liked "Dreams" the best because I felt the metaphors were more dramatic than the personification in "Sympathy."

WRITING APPLICATIONS

Write About Theme

On slips of paper, write the name of each selection in this unit. Put the slips of paper in a bag or basket. Have a volunteer pick a slip at random and read the name of the selection. Challenge students to write down in three minutes as many aspects of discovery in the selection as they can remember. After several selections have been chosen, have various students share their notes with the class.

Cooperative Group Activity

Writing: Have students who have chosen the same selection get together in a group. Ask each group to work together to write a paper that reflects the feelings of all group members about the selection. If students in the group have differing or contrasting viewpoints, this should be brought out in the writing. Have each group select one of its members to read its paper to the class.

Write About Genre

Make a chart to review the four elements of nonfiction: plot and story, point of view, tone, and theme. Under each heading have students add notes that review what they have learned. For example, under Plot and Story, students might add, "events in a story; makes reader wonder what will happen next; may use flashback; includes conflict."

WRITING APPLICATIONS

Write About Theme

All of the characters in this unit have made discoveries. They have made discoveries about themselves, others, the world around them, and life. As you have read their stories, you have made discoveries also. Perhaps you discovered something about a real person, place, or event. Perhaps you discovered a new way of looking at an issue based on the message of a selection. Choose four selections from this unit and tell what you have discovered as a result of reading them.

Prewriting Before you begin to write, decide which four of the selections had the greatest impact on you. Think for a few moments about each one and ask yourself, "What did I discover as a result of reading this selection? What new ideas, thoughts, and feelings do I have now that I did not have before?"

Writing Use the notes from your prewriting to write about the discoveries you have made. Include how you think these discoveries will make a difference in your life.

Revising Read your paper to make sure that it is well-organized. Does each paragraph contain one main idea? Does each paragraph have a clear topic sentence? Add or remove details to make the paragraph better organized.

Proofreading Correct any mistakes in spelling, usage, and mechanics.

Write About Genre

In this unit you have studied the elements of nonfiction in two of the selections. Now you can use these elements to analyze those selections.

First, decide which selection you feel most strongly about, either in a positive or negative way. Then compare and contrast it with the other two selections in terms of plot and story development, point of view, tone, and theme.

Prewriting Review briefly the work that you did for the "Think About . . ." for the nonfiction sections. Then make a chart in which you write the names of the two selections across the top. List the four literary elements down the side of the chart. Fill in your chart with details about each element from the selections.

Writing Use your chart to write a comparison of the two selections. If you feel that one selection used a particular element more effectively than the other, say so—but be sure to back up your opinion with evidence from the selection.

Revising Add to your paper any transitional phrases that will make your ideas flow more smoothly. The following are examples of transitional phrases: *first, most important, finally, next.*

Proofreading Correct any mistakes in spelling, usage, and mechanics. Use quotation marks around titles of short selections.

Cooperative Group Activity
Prewriting: Have students work in pairs to create their charts. Students should pair with others who have chosen the same selections, then make one chart between them.

Writer's Toolkit CD-ROM
Encourage students to use the Cluster Diagram (Writing Tools, Narrowing a Topic) or the Idea Web (Writing Tools, Gathering Details) to complete the prewriting activity.

Vocabulary

A helpful way to find the meaning of a word you do not know is to use context clues. Context clues help you figure out what a word means by the way it is used in a sentence.

Example: "I'm not an Example!" grumbled Amanda *rebelliously*. "I'm me!"

If you did not know the meaning of the word *rebelliously*, you could guess the meaning by the context clues. You know that Amanda is unhappy, and that she disagrees with her mother. You also can see that *rebelliously* must go with the word *grumbled*. Therefore, you could recognize that *rebelliously* means resisting authority or control.

Use context clues to determine the meaning of each italicized word, and then write out its meaning.

1. A rabbit hopped out from under the berry bush. He *nuzzled* the berry I'd spat out and ate it.

2. Why did they have to see me like this? Why did I have to look at Mom's eyes when she faced the most terrible *ordeal* of her life?

3. Across the river there was a little cabin with smoke curling out of the chimney. I can't remember that I was ever gladder to see a human *habitation*.

4. Mrs. Jones stopped, jerked him around in front of her, put a *half nelson* about his neck, and continued to drag him up the street.

Grammar, Usage, and Mechanics

When you write a sentence, it is important that the subject and the verb agree. The basic rule for subject-verb agreement is:

A **singular subject** must use a **singular verb**.

Chee *guesses* that his in-laws have become poor.

A **plural subject** must use a **plural verb**.

Chee's in-laws *guess* that Chee wants his daughter back.

The subject of a sentence is usually a noun or a pronoun. Pronouns can cause problems when they function as subjects of sentences. The pronouns *he*, *she*, and *it* always use a singular verb. *We* and *they* always use a plural verb. The pronoun *I* usually uses a plural verb:

> I go to school.
> *not*
> I goes to school.

The pronoun *you* always uses a plural verb.

Correct any errors in subject-verb agreement in the following sentences. (Not all of the sentences have errors.)

1. You takes the food I brought.

2. The old man gives Amanda the gold medal.

3. The old man and Amanda talks to each other.

4. "This is private property—I has my rights!"

5. My grandfather look at me strangely.

Grammar, Usage, and Mechanics

Answers

1. You take the food I brought.
2. correct
3. The old man and Amanda talk to each other.
4. "This is my private property—I have my rights."
5. My grandfather looked at me strangely.

Review with students the subject/verb agreement for forms of the verb *to be*. Write these sentences on the chalkboard.

1. I will be home early. Dad will be home after six.
2. Hal was late for school. You were also late.
3. I am five feet, four inches tall. You are shorter than I. Jim is taller than I.

Point out that the future tense is the same for all subjects: I will, you will, he will, we will, you will, they will. In the past tense, the first and third person use *was* (I was, he was); the second person and all plural forms use *were* (you were, we were, they were). In the present tense *I* is paired with *am* (I am); *are* is used with singular and plural forms of *you*, as well as with the plural first person and the plural third person (you are, we are, they are); and the singular third-person subjects use *is* (he is).

Cooperative Group Activity

Have students work with a partner or in small groups to write sentences that have errors in subject-verb agreement. Encourage students to use pronouns as well as nouns as subjects. Have each group trade sentences with another group to make corrections. Then return the papers to the original group to check.

BUILD LANGUAGE SKILLS

Vocabulary

Sample Answers

1. pushed with the nose
2. a difficult or trying experience
3. place where people live
4. a hold on the neck

More About Word Attack: Point out that sometimes a context clue is in the form of an in-text definition, that is, the word actually is defined in the story, if one reads carefully. Write this example from "The Gold Medal" on the chalkboard:

Up and over a gentle slope where a giant *cottonwood* offered an oasis of cool green shade she flew. Too late Amanda saw the high heap of overturned earth below the tree.

Guide students to realize that the words "cool green shade" and "tree" provide a definition of "cottonwood" as a shade tree.

Cooperative Group Activity

Have students work in small groups to determine the answers to the three questions in the text. Then ask each group to write a similar, original question of their own. Have groups trade questions to answer with each other.

After reading "Dead at Seventeen" students might be interested in a career as a journalist. A journalist is a person who gathers, writes, and edits news. Journalists can choose from a variety of media through which to work, including newspapers, magazines, and even radio and television. A journalist works most often on location, or "in the field," to gather information. A television anchorperson, on the other hand, primarily reports on news already gathered. A journalist must have a college degree in an appropriate field, such as English, journalism, or communications. High school students interested in this career should gain experience by working on their high school newspapers and by developing the habit of keeping a daily journal.

SPEAKING AND LISTENING

When you make a speech about literature in your English class, you usually have some kind of script to follow. You decide what topic or selection you are going to discuss, and then you follow certain guidelines to help in the discussion. Sometimes it's fun to build a lesson around a more spontaneous activity. Speaking extemporaneously doesn't mean speaking without preparation. It does mean, however, that you don't have to write anything out and you don't have to memorize. It is an example of impromptu speaking.

Although this type of speaking may be new to you, you will have a bit of fun in this lesson. Read the following strategy so you'll be a well-informed participant.

1. Think about all the various selections in this unit. Focus on the characters or people to whom you've been introduced. Along with others in your class, name as many as you can. If necessary, glance back at the selections.

2. Now, choose two people or characters you have read about. Go back to the selections where they can be found.

Read sections of the selection that describe or give information about the character. Become familiar with things the characters say, do, feel, and how they look and act. Think of adjectives to describe the characters.

3. Finally, imagine each character as an animal. What animal would he or she be? To help you decide, go back to the ideas you came up with in step two. Compare the character's traits to those of an animal. Decide what animal, in your opinion, is most like that character.

That's basically it! The next part is the most fun and really the easiest. As a class, or in small groups, take turns speaking about "Characters or People as Animals." Limit your speaking time to a minute or less so that everyone has a chance to speak. In your talk tell about the character's traits, the animal you've compared him to, and why you feel it is an appropriate comparison. Other students may talk about the same person or character; if so, don't worry. It will be fun to hear another classmate's interpretation.

CRITICAL THINKING

Fact and Opinion When reading nonfiction, it is important to be able to tell the difference between fact and opinion. A **fact** is something that can be proven or verified. For example, it is a fact that Kaw Indians go through the Ta-Na-E-Ka ritual at age 11.

An **opinion**, on the other hand, cannot be proven. An opinion is what a person thinks or believes about something. Opinions are usually based on a combination of emotions and facts. An example of an opinion is that the Ta-Na-E-Ka ritual is not very important.

In a true story, facts include such information as time, place, details of events, general data about characters, and so on. Opinions tend to be expressed by the characters in the story or by the author's comments about the events and characters. Opinions may also be suggested by the theme or message of the story. Choose one nonfiction selection from the unit and answer the following questions.

1. What seems to be the author's opinion about the events of the story and the outcome of the story? How can you tell? Do any characters in the story voice opinions that differ from the author's opinion?

2. If you were writing a newspaper report of the events of this story, what facts would you include? How would the story in a newspaper differ from the same story written as a piece of literature?

EFFECTIVE STUDYING

Note Taking An important skill that will help you do better in school is note taking. Note taking in class is important because you need to remember the information and explanations that the teacher gives. To take notes in class, use a spiral or loose-leaf notebook with enough blank pages to ensure that you will not run out of paper in the middle of class. Use the same notebook every day, so that your notes for that subject will be all together and in the right order.

As you take notes in class, try to write an outline of the lesson. Some teachers write an outline on the board, which is very helpful. Even if there is no written outline, you can tell how a teacher has organized the lesson if you listen carefully.

Sometimes as you are taking notes, the teacher will say something that you do not understand or cannot hear clearly. Write down what you hear as best you can. Then circle what you wrote. After class or during a time when you can ask questions, ask the teacher to explain it to you.

Many students find it helpful to copy over the notes that they take in class. You can do this each night or before a test.

Test Preparation
When you take a test, rewrite the directions in your own words. This way, you will understand exactly what you have been asked to do.

A Continuing Unit Project:
Writing Biographies

The selections in this unit are about heroes. Some of the heroes are real people; many are imaginary. Some of the heroes would be famous in the time and place in which they lived; others would be heroes only to a few people close to them. Some of the heroes might be remembered in history; others might be forgotten. Yet all these heroes have something in common—a particular quality that sets them a little bit apart from other people, that makes their lives significant in some way.

In this activity, students will write biographical sketches of the heroes they read about. For actual people, students will research the person's life and present a factual biography. For imaginary characters, students will use information contained in the selections, plus any additional details they wish to create. The only restriction is that the imagined information cannot contradict the information or inferences provided in the text.

Discuss with students some of the necessary elements in a good biography. One thing that should be clear in a biography is why the person is important enough to write about. A biography should also do more than just list the events and facts of a person's life; it should give a good impression of the person's character and personality.

Students may find it helpful to study the writers' biographies in this text as a guide to writing biographical sketches. Point out that these biographies focus on each person's contribution as a writer, while the students' biographies will focus on each character as a hero.

Have students write a biography after reading each selection in the unit. Some general questions that will help them get started include:

Who is the hero in this selection?
What makes this person special?
What facts do you know about this person's life?

What do you know about this person's character and personality?
What do you know about this person's appearance?
About how old is the hero in the selection?

If students need additional guidance, pose questions such as the following for each selection.

■ **"Amigo Brothers"**
How might Felix or Antonio be a role model for other kids growing up on the Lower East Side of New York City?

■ **"On the Ledge"**
Which person would you rather write about, Sergeant Gray or Walter?

■ **"Terror in the North"**
Would other teenagers be interested in reading your biography of Stina?

■ **"The Secret Life of Walter Mitty"**
How might you write a biography of someone who is really an antihero?

■ **from *I Have a Dream***
What additional facts would you like to know about Martin Luther King, Jr.?

■ **Warrior Song I/Warrior Song II/Song of Failure/ War Song**
How might one of these soldiers be written about in a Native American history book?

■ **"Ulysses and the Trojan Horse" and "Ulysses Meets the Cyclops"**
What does this selection tell you about the personality of Ulysses?

When students have completed all their biographies for the unit, select several from each selection to be read aloud. Discuss with the class the different interpretations that may have been given to the lives of various heroes.

■ "Amigo Brothers"
by Piri Thomas (page 409)

SELECTION SYNOPSIS

Antonio Cruz and Felix Varga, best friends who have grown up together on New York's Lower East Side, are pitted against each other in a boxing match to determine who will represent their Boys Club in a championship tournament. The boys realize that the competition is putting a strain on their friendship, yet each is determined to fight as hard as possible to become the winner. Although they promise each other they will come out of the fight able to pick up their friendship where they left off, both have misgivings. While they are in training, Felix moves to stay with his aunt in the Bronx, and the boys agree not to see each other until the day of the fight.

During the fight, the two compete so savagely that the referee and trainers must pull them apart. Yet at the end of the fight, the boys leave the ring arm in arm—before the winner is announced. The reader is left to decide who became the champion.

SELECTION ACTIVITY

Have students use books and magazines about sports, as well as almanacs and other reference sources to learn about the sport of boxing. Have students work in pairs or groups to find the answers to one or more of the following questions:
1. What are the rules and regulations that govern a boxing match?
2. What are the different weight classifications?
3. Who are some famous boxing champions? Do any have backgrounds similar to Felix and Antonio?
4. What is the history of boxing?
5. Who are the current boxing champions of the world?
6. How much money do professional boxers make?
7. How does a boxer train for a fight?

■ "On the Ledge"
by Thompson Clayton (page 425)

SELECTION SYNOPSIS

When the story opens, young Walter Whitfield in on the ledge of a building six stories up. As the story progresses, Sergeant Gray of the police department is able to rescue Walter, both emotionally and physically. First, however, Gray must overcome his own fear of heights before he can attempt to rescue the young man. In the end, the story takes a surprising twist, and Walter ends up saving Gray from a serious slip on the ledge. Ultimately, the two make their way back to safety inside the building.

SELECTION ACTIVITY

A growing problem in the United States today is teenagers committing suicide. Have students work in groups or pairs to learn more about this problem and what is being done to remedy it. Some sources of information that students can use include newspaper and magazine articles, recently published books on the topic, local mental health centers, teen help lines, halfway houses and drug rehabilitation centers for teenagers, mental health centers at colleges and universities, doctors in private practice, and hospital mental health outpatient services.

■ "Terror in the North"
by Eloise Engle (page 433)

SELECTION SYNOPSIS

Stina, a teenaged girl from Seattle, Washington, goes to Seward, Alaska, to live with her aunt and uncle after her mother dies. At the beginning of the story, Stina feels that she can never measure up to the rugged, "gutsy" Alaskans. She believes she is a coward and not an Alaskan in any sense of the word. Because of this, she declines to participate in a clean-up campaign to ready the town of Seward to receive the All-American Cities Award. Instead, she goes to the home of the Stetson family to baby-sit for their three-month-old son.

The story combines fact with fiction by introducing events related to the severe earthquake that actually occurred in the area on March 27, 1964. A young Alaskan, Dan Darby, happens to drop by to see Stina at the Stetson home. Shortly thereafter, an earthquake and tidal wave force them to flee from the house. When faced with this natural disaster, Stina proves her heroism and bravery by returning to the house to rescue the infant at the risk of her own life. As the three of them—Dan, Stina, and the baby—are about to be rescued, Stina feels ready at last to call herself an Alaskan.

Although earthquakes cannot be prevented, scientists are attempting to predict them far enough in advance so that people can be evacuated. Scientists are also hoping that major quakes can be predicted years in advance so that the growth of cities can be planned around potential disasters.

Have students find out what progress is being made in this new field of study. A great deal of attention is being given to earthquake prediction in Tokyo, Japan. Many newspaper articles have been written about the Earthquake Prediction Center in Tokyo. A considerable amount of research is also being carried out in the United States.

■ "The Secret Life of Walter Mitty"
by James Thurber (page 443)

SELECTION SYNOPSIS

Walter Mitty is a timid, henpecked man who leads a boring and frustrated life. In his imagination, however, he is a hero. In this humorous selection, James Thurber has Mitty move in and out of fantasy as he goes through a typical day. In his daydreams, Mitty sees himself as a famous surgeon, the pilot of a hydroplane, and the defendant in a murder trial. The story ends with his ultimate fantasy: Mitty imagines himself fearlessly facing a firing squad.

SELECTION ACTIVITY

Have students research the life and work of James Thurber (1894–1961). Thurber is well known as a writer, humorist, and artist. He strenghtened his career as a journalist when he joined *The New Yorker* magazine in 1927. Thurber did much to establish the tone and style of this popular magazine as both a writer and editor. One of Thurber's more famous stories is "The Secret Life of Walter Mitty," which was later made into a movie.

■ from *I Have a Dream*
by Martin Luther King, Jr. (page 453)

SELECTION SYNOPSIS

This selection is an excerpt from a well-known speech of Martin Luther King, Jr. It was given on a hot August afternoon in Washington, D.C., in 1963 on the steps of the Lincoln Memorial.

Much has happened in the Civil Rights movement since Martin Luther King, Jr., made his famous speech in 1963. Among the more significant developments was the passage of important civil rights legislation during the Johnson Administration.

Have students find out how laws governing civil rights have changed over the last 25 years. Encourage them to find out in particular which laws may have been enacted in their own state during this period of time. Also have students find out how civil rights laws may differ from one state to another.

■ Warrior Song I/Warrior Song II
by the Omaha (page 459)

■ Song of Failure/War Song
by Teton Sioux (page 461)

SELECTION SYNOPSES

These short poems are by Teton Sioux and Omaha Indians. They poignantly describe the bravery and heroism of men who must face failure, defeat, and death.

SELECTION ACTIVITY

Although the four Native American poems are very short, they paint vivid pictures with words. Challenge students to create drawings to illustrate each poem. The drawings could be in the style of Native American art, or they could be in the students' own style. Display the finished drawings around the classroom, along with copies of the related poems.

■ "Ulysses and the Trojan Horse"
by Homer (page 465)

■ "Ulysses Meets the Cyclops"
by Homer (page 474)

SELECTION SYNOPSES

In this version of the well-known classical tale of the Greeks' trickery in building the Trojan horse, great detail and drama are used to engage the reader's interest.

After ten years of struggle, the Trojans assume that the Greeks have given up the battle and sailed away. The Trojans view the horse that they find among the reeds by the shore as a peace offering. Despite Laocoön's warning, they bring the horse into the city to ensure Trojan prosperity. Shortly thereafter, they are overcome by the Greek soldiers hidden inside.

The story of Ulysses and the Cyclops is told in the first person. The story opens with the curious Ulysses on the island of the Cyclops. Against the advice of his soldiers, Ulysses enters the giant's cave. He and his men are sealed in, and two of the men are eaten by the giant. Ulysses, however, manages to get the Cyclops drunk and then wounds him in the eye. The crafty Ulysses then manages to get himself and his remaining men out of the cave, camouflaged as sheep. Ulysses, however, lives to regret the fact that his curiosity about the Cyclops resulted in the loss of some of his friends.

SELECTION ACTIVITY

Ask: What if Ulysses was greeted by a team of news reporters upon his arrival back in Greece? What kind of interview might Ulysses give to the media, to be broadcast on the Ancient Greek Nightly News?

Have students work in pairs or small groups to stage interviews with the hero Ulysses. To gain additional information about Ulysses, students may wish to consult Homer's epic poems, the *Odyssey* and the *Illiad* (or a synopsis of the poems).

STUDENT READING LIST

Rice, Tanya. *Mother Teresa*. 1998. Chelsea House.

Rosenberg, Liz (ed.) *Earth-shattering Poems*. 1997. Holt/Edge.

Masters, Anthony. *True Stories: Survival*. 1997. Sterling.

Mankiller. Wilma and Wallis. *Mankiller: A Chief and Her People*. 1993. SMP.

From Globe Fearon Educational Publisher

Latino Poetry
African American Poetry
World Myths and Legends: Native American
Freedom Fighters
     Martin Luther King, Jr.
Multicultural Literature Collection
     African American Literature
     Plains Native American Literature

UNIT 5
Overview

UNIT OBJECTIVES

After completing this unit, students will be able to

- understand additional elements of the short story: point of view, tone, symbolism, and writing techniques
- conduct an imaginary interview
- distinguish between valid and invalid inferences
- use an effective strategy for taking objective tests
- build on knowledge of literary elements in order to write both creatively and analytically
- use root words to figure out word meanings
- use new words in sentences

UNIT SELECTIONS

The theme of the unit is heroes: likely heroes and unlikely heroes, real heroes and imaginary heroes.

- **"Amigo Brothers"** (p. 409) presents two boys who struggle with the difference between being a public hero and a private hero.

  LITERARY SKILL: plot elements

  READING SKILL: recognize changes in relationships

  VOCABULARY: Spanish words

  WRITING: story extension

- **"On the Ledge"** (p. 425) the model selection, has two heroes, one of whom is very unlikely.

  LITERARY SKILL: elements of fiction

  READING SKILL: infer cause and effect

  VOCABULARY: parts of speech

  WRITING: character development

- **"Terror in the North"** (p. 433) features a girl who surprises herself and others during an earthquake.

  LITERARY SKILL: foreshadowing

  READING SKILL: understand the sequence of events

  VOCABULARY: synonyms

  WRITING: human interest stories

- **"The Secret Life of Walter Mitty"** (p. 443) tells the sad but humorous story of a man who is a hero only in his own imagination.

  LITERARY SKILL: story techniques

  READING SKILL: identify cause and effect

  VOCABULARY: figurative phrases

  WRITING: personal fantasies

- **from *I Have a Dream*** (p. 453) introduces a real 20th century hero through an excerpt from the famous speech made by civil rights leader Dr. Martin Luther King, Jr.

  LITERARY SKILL: persuasive speech

  READING SKILL: identify main idea and supporting details

  VOCABULARY: multiple-meaning words

  WRITING: one's own ideas

- **"Warrior Song I," "Warrior Song II," "Song of Failure," "War Song"** (p. 459) depict heroes of the Teton Sioux and Omaha Indians.

  LITERARY SKILL: open form poetry

  READING SKILL: recognize similarities in poetry

Heroes

The Hero can be Poet, Prophet, King, Priest or what you will, according to the kind of world he finds himself born into.

—Thomas Carlyle

Aspects of Negro Life: An Idyll of the Deep South, Aaron Douglas.
The Schomburg Center/New York Public Library

405

Introducing the Unit Theme

Arrange a display of books, magazines and newspaper articles which describe various types of heroes. Include both historical and contemporary heroes who represent many walks of life: astronauts, famous scientists and explorers, political figures, sports stars, media personalities, and local heroes. Also, include some human interest stories that describe an ordinary person taking part in a heroic action such as rescuing a person from a burning building. After students have viewed the display, ask them which, if any, are heroes to them. Point out that their responses are based in part on their own ideas about what constitutes a hero.

Viewing Fine Art

In the 1930s, Aaron Douglas (1898–1979) painted murals under the sponsorship of the WPA, or Works Progress Administration. The WPA was formed by the Roosevelt administration during the Depression to create jobs for all kinds of workers, including artists. Douglas created a series of four murals focusing on the history and national contributions of African Americans. "Song of the Towers," the last mural in the series, depicts the movement of African Americans to northern cities. Ask: What parts of the painting suggest an urban setting? In what way could the lives of ordinary workers be considered heroic?

VOCABULARY: homophones
WRITING: personal responses

■ **"Ulysses and the Trojan Horse" and "Ulysses Meets the Cyclops"** (p. 465) are two tales about a legendary Greek hero.
LITERARY SKILL: epic poetry
READING SKILL: understand character relationships

VOCABULARY: nouns and verbs
WRITING: a monster story

Heroes

Who are your heroes? Do you look up to famous athletes such as Jackie Joyner-Kersee and Michael Jordan? Is your idea of a hero an astronaut or a rock star? Perhaps you most admire a courageous person in your own school or neighborhood.

The dictionary defines a hero as someone known for great strength, courage, and daring. A hero can also be a person honored for special achievements and attributes. As Thomas Carlyle points out, heroes are shaped, in part, by the times and the circumstances in which they find themselves. For example, Martin Luther King, Jr., became a hero in a world that was ready to hear his message about civil rights. However, in the end, could it have been personal courage in the face of hostility that actually shaped the circumstances—and the times? The true nature of heroism has always aroused great interest, even debate, among people everywhere.

The selections in this unit focus on heroes. You will meet likely heroes and unlikely heroes, real heroes and imaginary heroes.

■ LIKELY HEROES

Sometimes literature presents a situation in which a person has to choose between being a public hero and a private hero. This is the kind of situation in which two Puerto Rican boys find themselves in the short story "Amigo Brothers." In order to win a championship boxing match, each boy must beat his best friend. What would you do in a situation like this? Although the story ends with only one champion, both boys become heroes.

■ UNLIKELY HEROES

There are certain actions that make a person a hero in any time and any place. One is risking one's life for another. In the short story

"Terror in the North," a high school girl finds the strength to rescue a baby boy during an earthquake. In the story "On the Ledge," a police officer risks his life to prevent a suicide. This story has a surprise ending as the police officer finds himself in need of a rescue—and a very unlikely hero emerges.

Have you ever thought about being a hero? Have you ever day-dreamed about doing something daring or courageous? In his short story "The Secret Life of Walter Mitty," James Thurber paints a humorous and somewhat sad picture of a man whose heroism exists only in his own fantasies.

■ REAL HEROES

"I Have a Dream" is a famous speech by Martin Luther King, Jr. King was a special kind of hero who was assassinated because of his passionate devotion to the cause of racial equality. Is there a cause that you believe in so deeply that you would rather die than give it up?

■ MYTHICAL HEROES

In literature, as in life, many people become heroes during war. One of the most famous heroes in literature is a mythological figure named Ulysses, whom the poet Homer created as a great warrior in ancient Greece. You will read about two of the hero's adventures in "Ulysses and the Trojan Horse" and "Ulysses Meets the Cyclops." You may discover similarities between Ulysses and your own personal heroes.

Who your heroes are tells a lot about you—the person you are and the person you hope to become. Perhaps you will find a hero of your own in these pages. As you read each selection, you might ask yourself, What is a hero? What do my heroes have in common with the hero in this selection?

Heroes ■ 407

Discussing the Unit Theme

Guide students through the opening discussion on heroes. Then pause to have students view the display material that you set up for Introducing the Unit Theme. Ask them to write down the names of three people whom they consider to be heroes. The people may or may not be those represented in the display. Have students put their lists aside for the time being.

Return again to the theme discussion. As you read through the rest of the material, discuss with the class each question that is raised. When you are finished, have students look again at the names of their three heroes. Ask: How does the material that we have just read pertain to your three heroes? Call on volunteers to relate their choices to the concepts of heroism as set forth in the theme discussion.

Cooperative Group Activity

Divide the class into small groups. Challenge each group to conduct a survey in which they find out who people's heroes are. Encourage each group to survey a different population. For example, one group might survey students in their own grade, a second group might survey students in another grade, and a third might choose to survey senior citizens. Other populations that might be polled include children in elementary school and people chosen at random at a shopping mall or street corner. Have each group report their findings to the class.

SELECTION OVERVIEW

SELECTION OBJECTIVES

After completing this selection, students will be able to

- understand plot elements
- create a plot sequence
- decide who in the story is a hero
- create a new episode for a story
- analyze plot development
- appreciate the use of Spanish words
- recognize changes in relationships

More About Plot Elements

It is the development of the plot that holds the reader's interest in a story. Encourage students to think about the stories in this book that they especially liked. Then ask them to describe how the unfolding of the plot captured their interest.

About the Author

Piri Thomas knows what he is talking about when he refers to "street negatives." Thomas grew up in New York City and spent seven years in prison. It was in prison that he began to write. After his release, Thomas began to help young people who seemed likely to get into trouble. The story "Amigo Brothers" describes the kind of alternative to crime that Thomas might recommend.

READING FOCUS

Recognize Changes in Relationships The relationship between two story characters often involves conflict, or the meeting of two opposing forces. How the conflict is resolved often involves changes in the relationship of the characters. Try to recognize such changes as you pay attention to the characters' actions and words in this story.

PLOT ELEMENTS

Early in a story, an important plot problem is introduced. This is the first of a series of problems the character must solve. In a good story each problem is more interesting than the one before it. This is called **rising action**. The rising action in a story eventually leads to a climax. The **climax** is the most exciting part of the story. It is the part where the conflict comes to a head.

Some short stories end with the climax, but most do not. These stories continue beyond the climax with an element called the **resolution**. The resolution answers any remaining questions that the reader might have and gives the story a sense of completion.

As you read "Amigo Brothers," ask yourself:

1. What is the climax of the story?
2. What plot question remains unanswered?

WRITING CONNECTION

Think of a recent situation in your own life that could be the basis of a short story. List the events of the plot, then indicate which of these events would be the climax of the story. Write a few sentences to describe what you might add to the story as a resolution.

ESL Activity

Have students work in pairs to create a simple plot diagram on a sheet of paper. First, have them draw a diagonal line that slants upward and spans most of the page width. Then have them draw a short downward diagonal that connects to the end of the first line. The drawing should look like a not-too-steep mountain peak with the peak shifted to the far right. As students read, have them write the events that mark the opening problem, the rising action, and the climax on their diagram.

Cooperative Group Activity

Have students work in pairs to complete the Writing Connection activity. Have each pair present their description for class discussion. As an added challenge, you might ask students to describe the rising action in a famous story—a nursery tale, for instance—without revealing characters' names. Then have the class guess the title of the story.

ΛMIGO BROTHERS

ADAPTED

by Piri Thomas

Antonio Cruz and Felix Vargas were both seventeen years old. They were so together in friendship that they felt themselves to be brothers. They had known each other since childhood, growing up on the lower east side of Manhattan in the same tenement building on Fifth Street between Avenue A and Avenue B.

Antonio was fair, lean, and lanky, while Felix was dark, short, and husky. Antonio's hair was always falling over his eyes, while Felix wore his black hair in a natural Afro style.

Each youngster had a dream of someday becoming lightweight champion of the world. Every chance they had the boys worked out, sometimes at the Boys Club on 10th Street and Avenue A and sometimes at the pro's gym on 14th Street. Early morning sunrises would find them running along the East River Drive, wrapped in sweat shirts, short towels around their necks, and handkerchiefs Apache style around their foreheads.

While some youngsters were into street negatives, Antonio and Felix slept, ate, rapped, and dreamt positive. Between them, they had a collection of *Fight* magazines second to none, plus a scrapbook filled with torn tickets to every boxing match they had ever attended, and some clippings of their own. If asked a question about any given fighter, they would immediately zip out from their memory banks divisions, weights, records of fights, knockouts, technical knockouts, and draws or losses.

Each had fought many bouts representing their community and had won two gold-plated medals plus a silver and bronze medallion. The difference was in their style: Antonio's lean form and long reach made him the better boxer, while

---

amigo (uh MEE goh) A Spanish word meaning *friend*. Other Spanish words in the story add flavor to the text but will not be defined.
tenement (TEN uh munt) low-grade housing
Apache (uh PACH ee) Native American group of the southwest
negative (NEG uh tiv) bad habit or behavior
bout (BOUT) fight
medallion (muh DAL yun) large medal

Amigo Brothers ■ 409

T409

Literary Focus:
Plot Elements
Ask: What plot question needs to be answered by the end of the story?

Felix's short and muscular frame made him the better slugger. Whenever they had met in the ring for sparring sessions, it had always been hot and heavy.

Now, after a series of elimination bouts, they had been informed that they were to meet each other in the division finals that were scheduled for the seventh of August, two weeks away—the winner to represent the Boys Club in the Golden Gloves Championship Tournament.

The two boys continued to run together along the East River Drive. But even when joking with each other, they both sensed a wall rising between them.

One morning less than a week before their bout, they met as usual for their daily workout. They fooled around with a few jabs at the air, slapped skin, and then took off, running lightly along the dirty East River's edge.

Antonio glanced at Felix who kept his eyes purposely straight ahead, pausing from time to time to do some fancy leg work while throwing one-twos followed by upper cuts to an imaginary jaw. Antonio then beat the air with a barrage of body blows and short devastating lefts with an overhand jaw-breaking right.

After a mile or so, Felix puffed and said, "Let's stop a while, bro. I think we both got something to say to each other."

Antonio nodded. It was not natural to be acting as though nothing unusual was happening when two ace-boon buddies were going to be blasting each other within a few short days.

They rested their elbows on the railing separating them from the river. Antonio wiped his face with his short towel. The sunrise was now creating day.

Felix leaned heavily on the river's railing and stared across to the shores of Brooklyn. Finally, he broke the silence.

"Gee, man. I don't know how to come out with it."

Antonio helped. "It's about our fight, right?"

"Yeah, right." Felix's eyes squinted at the rising orange sun.

"I've been thinking about it too, *panin*. In fact, since we found out it was going to be me and you, I've been awake at night, pulling punches on you, trying not to hurt you."

"Same here. It ain't natural not to think about the fight. I mean, we both are *cheverote* fighters and we both want to win. But only one of us can win. There ain't no draws in the eliminations."

Felix tapped Antonio gently on the shoulder. "I don't mean to sound like I'm bragging, bro. But I wanna win, fair and square."

Antonio nodded quietly. "Yeah. We both know that in the ring the better man wins. Friend or no friend, brother or no . . ."

Felix finished it for him. "Brother. Tony, let's promise something right here. Okay?"

---

sparring (SPAHR ing) practice boxing with another
elimination (ih lim uh NAY shun) in a tournament, dropped after one loss
barrage (buh RAHJ) huge number, as of bombs or blows
devastating (DEV uh stayt ing) carrying destruction

410 ■ **Unit 5**

"If it's fair, *hermano*, I'm for it." Antonio admired the courage of a tug boat pulling a barge five times its welterweight size.

"It's fair, Tony. When we get into the ring, it's gotta be like we never met. We gotta be like two heavy strangers that want the same thing and only one can have it. You understand, don'tcha?"

"*Si*, I know." Tony smiled. "No pulling punches. We go all the way."

"Yeah, that's right. Listen, Tony. Don't you think it's a good idea if we don't see each other until the day of the fight? I'm going to stay with my Aunt Lucy in the Bronx. I can use Gleason's Gym for working out. My manager says he got some sparring partners with more or less your style."

Tony scratched his nose pensively. "Yeah, it would be better for our heads." He held out his hand, palm upward. "Deal?"

"Deal." Felix lightly slapped open skin.

"Ready for some more running?" Tony asked lamely.

"Naw, bro. Let's cut it here. You go on. I kinda like to get things together in my head."

"You ain't worried, are you?" Tony asked.

"No way, man." Felix laughed out loud. "I got too much smarts for that. I just think it's cooler if we split right here. After the fight, we can get it together again like nothing ever happened."

The *amigo* brothers were not ashamed to hug each other tightly.

"Guess you're right. Watch yourself, Felix. I hear there's some pretty heavy dudes up in the Bronx. *Sauvecito*, okay?"

"Okay. You watch yourself too, *sabes*."

Tony jogged away. Felix watched his friend disappear from view, throwing rights and lefts. Both fighters had a lot of psyching up to do before the big fight.

The days in training passed much too slowly. Although they kept out of each other's way, they were aware of each other's progress via the ghetto grapevine.

The evening before the big fight, Tony made his way to the roof of his tenement. In the quiet early dark, he peered over the ledge. Six stories below the lights of the city blinked and the sounds of cars mingled with the curses and the laughter of children in the street. He tried not to think of Felix, feeling he had succeeded in psyching his mind. But only in the ring would he really know. To spare Felix hurt, he would have to knock him out, early and quick.

Up in the South Bronx, Felix decided to take in a movie in an effort to keep Antonio's face away from his fists. The flick was *The Champion* with Kirk Douglas, the third time Felix was seeing it.

---

welterweight (WEL tur wayt) boxer in a weight division between lightweight and middleweight
pensively (PEN siv lee) thoughtfully
psyching (SYK ing) getting into shape mentally (slang)
mingle (MING gul) mix

Amigo Brothers ■ 411

Reading Focus:
Recognize Changes in Relationships

Ask: How does the movie affect Felix's perception of Tony?

Literary Focus:
Conflict

Each fighter experiences an inner conflict as well as the outer conflict about the actual fight. Have students discuss the different conflicts presented so far in the story and predict how they might be resolved.

Critical Thinking:
Evaluate

Ask: What do you think of Felix's method of "psyching" himself for the fight? Will it work? Why do you think as you do?

The champion was getting beat, his face being pounded into raw wet hamburger. His eyes were cut, jagged, bleeding, one eye swollen, the other almost shut. He was saved only by the sound of the bell.

Felix became the champ and Tony the challenger.

The movie audience was going out of its head, roaring in blood lust at the butchery going on. The champ hunched his shoulders grunting and sniffing red blood back into his broken nose. The challenger, confident that he had the championship in the bag, threw a left. The champ countered with a dynamite right that exploded into the challenger's brains.

Felix's right arm felt the shock. Antonio's face, superimposed on the screen, was shattered and split apart by the awesome force of the killer blow. Felix saw himself in the ring, blasting Antonio against the ropes. The champ had to be forcibly restrained. The challenger was allowed to crumble slowly to the canvas, a broken bloody mess.

When Felix finally left the theater, he had figured out how to psyche himself for tomorrow's fight. It was Felix the Champion vs. Antonio the Challenger.

He walked up some dark streets, deserted except for small pockets of wary-looking kids wearing gang colors. Despite the fact that he was Puerto Rican like them, they eyed him as a stranger to their turf. Felix did a fast shuffle, bobbing and weaving, while letting loose a torrent of blows that would demolish whatever got in its way. It seemed to impress the brothers, who went about their own business.

Finding no takers, Felix decided to split to his aunt's. Walking the streets had not relaxed him, neither had the fight flick. All it had done was to stir him up. He let himself quietly into his Aunt Lucy's apartment and went straight to bed, falling into a fitful sleep with sounds of the gong for Round One.

Antonio was passing some heavy time on his rooftop. How would the fight tomorrow affect his relationship with Felix? After all, fighting was like any other profession. Friendship had nothing to do with it. A gnawing doubt crept in. He cut negative thinking real quick by doing some speedy fancy dance steps, bobbing and weaving like mercury. The night air was blurred with perpetual motions of left hooks and right crosses. Felix, his *amigo* brother, was not going to be Felix at all in the ring. Just an opponent with another face. Antonio went to sleep,

---

lust (LUST) powerful desire
superimposed (soo pur im POHZD) placed on top of
awesome (AW sum) causing fear and wonder
restrained (rih STRAYND) held back
wary (WAIR ee) on guard; watchful
torrent (TAWR unt) rushing stream or downpour
demolish (dih MOL ish) reduce to ruins
fitful (FIT ful) uneasy; very restless
perpetual (pur PECH oo ul) never stopping; without pause

Literary Focus:
Rising Action

As the action rises, the conflict in the story becomes more intense. Have students describe the neighborhood's reaction to the upcoming fight and the events leading up to the fight itself (on pages 414–415). Ask: How do these events add to the excitement of the story? How might they affect what the two main characters are feeling?

hearing the opening bell for the first round. Like his friend in the South Bronx, he prayed for victory, via a quick clean knockout in the first round.

Large posters plastered all over the walls of local shops announced the fight between Antonio Cruz and Felix Vargas as the main bout.

The fight had created great interest in the neighborhood. Antonio and Felix were well liked and respected. Each had his own loyal following. Betting fever was high and ranged from a bottle of soda to cold hard cash on the line.

Antonio's fans bet with unbridled faith in his boxing skills. On the other side, Felix's admirers bet on his dynamite-packed fists.

Felix had returned to his apartment early in the morning of August 7th and stayed there, hoping to avoid seeing Antonio. He turned the radio on to *salsa* music sounds and then tried to read while waiting for word from his manager.

The fight was scheduled to take place in Tompkins Square Park. It had been decided that the gymnasium of the Boys Club was not large enough to hold all the people who were sure to attend. In Tompkins Square Park, everyone who wanted could view the fight, whether from ringside or window fire escapes or tenement rooftops.

The morning of the fight Tompkins Square was a beehive of activity with numerous workers setting up the ring, the seats, and the guest speakers' stand. The scheduled bouts began shortly after noon and the park had begun filling up even earlier.

The local junior high school across from Tompkins Square Park served as the dressing room for all the fighters. Each was given a separate classroom with desk tops, covered with mats, serving as resting tables. Antonio thought he caught a glimpse of Felix waving to him from a room at the far end of the corridor. He waved back just in case it had been him.

The fighters changed from their street clothes into fighting gear. Antonio wore white trunks, black socks, and black shoes. Felix wore green trunks, white socks, and white boxing shoes. Each had dressing gowns to match their fighting trunks with their names neatly stitched on the back.

The loudspeakers blared into the open windows of the school. There were speeches by dignitaries, community leaders, and great boxers of yesteryear. Some were well prepared, some improvised on the spot. They all carried the same message of great pleasure and honor at being part of such a historic event. This great day was in the tradition of champions emerging from the streets of the lower east side.

Interwoven with the speeches were the

---

unbridled (un BRYD uld) uncontrolled
blare (BLAIR) make a loud noise
dignitary (DIG nuh ter ee) important person
improvised (IM pruh vyzd) made up quickly, without planning
emerging (ih MURJ ing) coming out of
interwoven (in tur WOH vun) mixed with

414 ■ **Unit 5**

sounds of the other boxing events. After the sixth bout, Felix was much relieved when his trainer Charlie said, "Time change. Quick knockout. This is it. We're on."

Waiting time was over. Felix was escorted from the classroom by a dozen fans in white T-shirts with the word FELIX across their fronts.

Antonio was escorted down a different stairwell and guided through a roped-off path.

As the two climbed into the ring, the crowd exploded with a roar. Antonio and Felix both bowed gracefully and then raised their arms in acknowledgment.

Antonio tried to be cool, but even as the roar was in its first birth, he turned slowly to meet Felix's eyes looking directly into his. Felix nodded his head and Antonio responded. And both as one, just as quickly, turned away to face his own corner.

Bong—bong—bong. The roar turned to stillness.

"Ladies and Gentlemen, *Señores y Señoras.*"

The announcer spoke slowly, pleased at his bilingual efforts.

"Now the moment we have all been waiting for—the main event between two fine young Puerto Rican fighters, products of our lower east side."

"Loisaida," called out a member of the audience.

"In this corner, weighing 134 pounds, Felix Vargas. And in this corner, weighing 133 pounds, Antonio Cruz. The winner will represent the Boys Club in the Tournament of Champions, the Golden Gloves. There will be no draw. May the best man win."

The cheering of the crowd shook the window panes of the old buildings surrounding Tompkins Square Park. At the center of the ring, the referee was giving instructions to the youngsters.

"Keep your punches up. No low blows. No punching on the back of the head. Keep your heads up. Understand? Let's have a clean fight. Now shake hands and come out fighting."

Both youngsters touched gloves and nodded. They turned and danced quickly to their corners. Their head towels and dressing gowns were lifted neatly from their shoulders by their trainers' nimble fingers. Antonio crossed himself. Felix did the same.

BONG! BONG! ROUND ONE. Felix and Antonio turned and faced each other squarely in a fighting pose. Felix wasted no time. He came in fast, head low, half hunched toward his right shoulder, and lashed out with a straight left. He missed a right cross as Antonio slipped the punch and countered with one-two-three lefts that snapped Felix's head back, sending a mild shock coursing through him. If Felix had any small doubt about

Reading Focus:
Recognize Changes in Relationships
Ask: What thoughts might have gone through each fighter's mind at the moment their eyes met? Do you think Felix and Tony will follow through on their plan?

---

acknowledgment (ak NOL ij munt) recognition; thanks
bilingual (by LING gwul) able to use two languages
nimble (NIM bul) quick and accurate
pose (POHZ) position; way of standing
countered (KOUNT urd) returned a blow with another blow
coursing (KAWR sing) running or flowing

Amigo Brothers ■ 415

T415

their friendship affecting their fight, it was being neatly dispelled.

Antonio danced, a joy to behold. His left hand was like a piston, pumping jabs one right after another with seeming ease. Felix bobbed and weaved and never stopped boring in. He knew that at long range he was at a disadvantage. Antonio had too much reach on him. Only by coming in close could Felix hope to achieve the dreamed-of knockout.

Antonio knew the dynamite that was stored in his *amigo* brother's fist. He ducked a short right and missed a left hook. Felix trapped him against the ropes just long enough to pour some punishing rights and lefts to Antonio's hard midsection. Antonio slipped away from Felix, crashing two lefts to his head, which set Felix's right ear to ringing.

Bong! Both *amigos* froze a punch well on its way, sending up a roar of approval for good sportsmanship.

Felix walked briskly back to his corner. His right ear had not stopped ringing. Antonio gracefully danced his way toward his stool none the worse, except for glowing glove burns, showing angry red against the whiteness of his midribs.

"Watch that right, Tony." His trainer talked into his ear. "Remember Felix always goes to the body. He'll want you to drop your hands for his overhand left or right. Got it?"

Antonio nodded, sprayed water out between his teeth. He felt better as his sore midsection was being firmly rubbed.

Felix's corner was also busy.

"You gotta get in there, fella." Felix's trainer poured water over his curly Afro locks. "Get in there or he's gonna chop you up from way back."

Bong! Bong! Round two. Felix was off his stool and rushed Antonio like a bull, sending a hard right to his head. Beads of water exploded from Antonio's long hair.

Antonio, hurt, sent back a blurring barrage of lefts and rights that only meant pain to Felix, who returned with a short left to the head followed by a looping right to the body. Antonio countered with his own flurry, forcing Felix to give ground. But not for long.

Felix bobbed and weaved, bobbed and weaved, occasionally punching his two gloves together.

Antonio waited for the rush that was sure to come. Felix closed in and feinted with his left shoulder and threw his right instead. Lights suddenly exploded inside Felix's head as Antonio slipped the blow and hit him with a pistonlike left, catching him flush on the point of his chin.

Bedlam broke loose as Felix's legs momentarily buckled. He fought off a series of rights and lefts and came back with a strong right that taught Antonio respect.

Antonio danced in carefully. He knew

---

dispelled (dih SPELD) driven away; ended
feinted (FAYNT id) pretended to attack one place while really attacking another
flush (FLUSH) straight; even with
bedlam (BED lum) confusion
momentarily (moh mun TER uh lee) for an instant

Felix had the habit of playing possum when hurt, to sucker an opponent within reach of the powerful bombs he carried in each fist.

A right to the head slowed Antonio's pretty dancing. He answered with his own left at Felix's right eye which began puffing up within three seconds.

Antonio, a bit too eager, moved in too close and Felix had him entangled into a rip-roaring, punching toe-to-toe slugfest that brought the whole Tompkins Square Park screaming to its feet.

Rights to the body. Lefts to the head. Neither fighter was giving an inch. Suddenly a short right caught Antonio squarely on the chin. His long legs turned to jelly and his arms flailed out desperately. Felix, grunting like a bull, threw wild punches from every direction. Antonio, groggy, bobbed and weaved, evading most of the blows. Suddenly his head cleared. His left flashed out hard and straight catching Felix on the bridge of his nose.

Felix lashed back with a haymaker, right off the ghetto streets. At the same instant, his eye caught another left hook from Antonio. Felix swung out trying to clear the pain. Only the frenzied screaming of those along ringside let him know that he had dropped Antonio. Fighting off the growing haze, Antonio struggled to his feet, got up, ducked, and threw a smashing right that dropped Felix flat on his back.

Felix got up as fast as he could in his

---

flailed (FLAYLD) waved or beat aimlessly
evading (ih VAYD ing) avoiding
frenzied (FREN zeed) very excited; raving

Critical Thinking:
Infer
Ask students to describe how playing possum draws in the opponent.

Literary Focus:
Rising Action
Ask students which boy they think will win the boxing match. Why? Do they find themselves rooting for a particular boxer? If so, why?

own corner, groggy but still game. He didn't even hear the count. In a fog, he heard the roaring of the crowd, who seemed to have gone insane. His head cleared to hear the bell sound at the end of the round. He was glad. His trainer sat him down on the stool.

In his corner, Antonio was doing what all fighters do when they are hurt. They sit and smile at everyone.

The referee signaled the ring doctor to check the fighters out. He did so and then gave his okay. The cold water sponges brought clarity to both *amigo* brothers. They were rubbed until their circulation ran free.

Bong! Round three—the final round. Up to now it had been tic-tac-toe, pretty much even. But everyone knew there could be no draw and that this round would decide the winner.

This time, to Felix's surprise, it was Antonio who came out fast, charging across the ring. Felix braced himself but couldn't ward off the barrage of punches. Antonio drove Felix hard against the ropes.

The crowd ate it up. Thus far the two had fought with *mucho corazón*. Felix tapped his gloves and commenced his attack anew. Antonio, throwing boxer's caution to the winds, jumped in to meet him.

Both pounded away. Neither gave an inch and neither fell to the canvas. Felix's left eye was tightly closed. Claret red blood poured from Antonio's nose. They fought toe-to-toe.

The sounds of their blows were loud in contrast to the silence of a crowd gone completely mute. The referee was stunned by their savagery.

Bong! Bong! Bong! The bell sounded over and over again. Felix and Antonio were past hearing. Their blows continued to pound on each other like hailstones.

Finally the referee and the two trainers pried Felix and Antonio apart. Cold water was poured over them to bring them back to their senses.

They looked around and then rushed toward each other. A cry of alarm surged through Tompkins Square Park. Was this a fight to the death instead of a boxing match?

The fear soon gave way to wave upon wave of cheering as the two *amigos* embraced.

No matter what the decision, they knew they would always be champions to each other.

BONG! BONG! BONG! "Ladies and Gentlemen. *Señores* and *Señoras*. The winner and representative to the Golden Gloves Tournament of Champions is . . ."

The announcer turned to point to the winner and found himself alone. Arm in arm the champions had already left the ring.

---

game (GAYM) ready and willing
clarity (KLAR uh tee) clearness
claret red (KLAR it RED) deep purplish red
mute (MYOOT) unable to talk; quiet

418 ■ Unit 5

Literary Focus:
Climax and Resolution

Have students reread and then discuss the last two paragraphs of the story. Have them identify the climax of the story. Ask: Was this the climax you expected? Then ask them if they think the story contains a resolution. Focus their thinking by asking: At the end of the story, is it clear that the boys will remain friends? Explain. Help students to see that there are two main questions that drive the plot: Who will win the fight? Will the boys remain friends after the ordeal? The first question is not answered but the second question is.

Reading Focus:
Recognize Changes in Relationships

Have students speculate on whether the friendship of the two boys will be stronger or weaker in the future.

Discussion

Have students discuss whether they think the ending of the story is realistic or not. Encourage them to give reasons for their opinions.

Background Notes

If the last round of a boxing match ends without a knockout, the judges may declare a winner by decision. The boxer who has accumulated the largest number of points for solid blows struck is declared the winner.

Amigo Brothers ■ 419

Mini Quiz

Write on the chalkboard or overhead projector the following questions and call on students to fill in the blanks. Discuss the answers with the class.

1. Tony and Felix think of themselves as brothers because _____.

2. Both boys want to become _____.

3. The boys are informed that they must _____ each other in the championship tournament.

4. They decide not to _____ until the tournament.

5. When it comes time to announce the winner, the boys _____.

Answers

1. they had been such close friends for so many years
2. the lightweight boxing champion of the world
3. fight against
4. see each other
5. had already left the ring together

UNDERSTAND THE SELECTION

Answers

1. on the Lower East Side of New York City
2. the lightweight boxing champion of the world
3. not to see each other until the fight
4. They knew that they would be fighting against each other in less than a week.
5. pull punches; that is, not really fight
6. to try not to think about Antonio
7. Felix would pretend to be more hurt than he was so that his opponent would come in close; then Felix would strike him.
8. Sample answer: Who won the fight is not the most important part of the story.
9. the importance of true friendship; that true friendship can withstand even the test of two friends having to fight against each other in the ring
10. Answers will vary.

Respond to Literature

Have students discuss the idea of public heroes and private heroes. Point out that people often do things in their private lives that make them heroes to themselves or the people close to them. For example, a man might choose to spend more time at home with his children rather than run for public office or become president of a local organization. Have students think of people they know who have had to make these types of choices.

WRITE ABOUT THE SELECTION

Prewriting

Write on an overhead transparency or the chalkboard a sample story outcome.

For example:
"The winner is—Felix Varga!"
As the announcer says his name, the two boys turn around.
Tony lifts Felix's arm in the air as a sign of victory.

The crowd cheers; they see that both boys are winners.

Writing

As students work on this section independently, check to see that each student has a clear idea of what the outcome is to be in his or her episode.

Revising

Have students work in pairs. Ask each student to suggest at least one line of dialogue for his or her partner's paper. Students then can decide whether or not their partner's dialogue will add to or detract from their ending of the story.

Proofreading

Review with students some of the uses of italics. For example, foreign words are usually italicized, as are words that are to be given special emphasis.

UNDERSTAND THE SELECTION

Recall

1. Where did Antonio and Felix live?

2. What did each boy hope to become?

3. What big decision do the boys make before the fight?

Infer

4. Why did the boys feel a wall rising between them?

5. When the boys first learned that they were going to fight against each other, what were they tempted to do?

6. Why does Felix see the movie?

7. What does the author mean when he says that Felix "had a habit of playing possum when hurt"?

Apply

8. Why do you think that the author does not tell who is the winner of the fight?

9. What is the message, or theme, of this story?

10. Imagine yourself in Felix's or Antonio's place. Would you have been able to fight your best friend? Why or why not?

Respond to Literature

Were Felix and Antonio heroes? Explain why you do or do not think so.

WRITE ABOUT THE SELECTION

At the end of "Amigo Brothers," the announcer is about to point to the winner of the fight. Who do you think the winner is? How do you think each boy reacts when notified who the winner is? Do you think they care who won? Write an episode to add to "Amigo Brothers" that tells what happened after the fight.

Prewriting Make an informal outline of what you think happened after the fighters left the ring. You might want to include details about the reaction of the crowd and any further statements by the announcer. You might want to limit your ending to the reactions of the two boys on learning the identity of the winner.

Writing Use your informal outline as a guide to help you to write the last episode to the story. You might also want to reread a few paragraphs of the original story to make a smooth connection between the author's and your writing style.

Revising When you revise your paragraph, consider adding dialogue where appropriate.

Proofreading Before you correct your final handwritten paragraph, decide whether you will use any Spanish words. All Spanish words should be written in *italics*. You can indicate italics by underlining the word on your paper. Also correct any errors in spelling, punctuation and mechanics.

THINK ABOUT PLOT ELEMENTS

The plot of any story has certain elements. The action of a story that leads to the climax is called **rising action**. In rising action, you learn about the main characters and everything that is going to be important in the story. The rising action leads to the climax or most exciting part of the story. Then the story moves to its conclusion. The set of actions bringing the story to an end after the climax is called the **falling action**. With falling action, the story winds down to the resolution.

1. What is the climax of "Amigo Brothers"?

2. Does the story have a resolution? Explain.

3. In what way is this story similar to "The Lady or the Tiger?" which you read in Unit 3?

4. What plot questions are introduced in "Amigo Brothers"?

5. Which plot question remains unanswered?

READING FOCUS

Recognize Changes in Relationships
As you read, you discovered the conflict between the two characters and how that conflict affected their relationship. How did their relationship change? Give three specific examples from the story.

DEVELOP YOUR VOCABULARY

Many words in the English language are derived from Spanish. For example, the Spanish word *pueblo* means "village." In English, the word refers to only one type of dwelling in a Native American village in the southwestern United States. Another Spanish word that has found its way into English is *amigo*, which means "friend." If you like Mexican food, you are probably familiar with a flatbread called *tortilla*. Tortilla is a variation of the word *torta*, which means "cake."

In the short story, "Amigo Brothers," a number of Spanish words appear in the text. The author uses these words to add flavor to the story. Use a Spanish-English dictionary to find the meanings of the following words from "Amigo Brothers." Then write a definition for each word.

1. panin
2. cheverote
3. hermano
4. sabe
5. salsa

THINK ABOUT PLOT ELEMENTS

Answers
1. the moment when the announcer is about to tell the winner of the fight
2. Yes; the boys do remain friends at the end of the fight, as shown by the fact that they embrace each other and leave the ring before an official winner is declared.
3. "The Lady, or the Tiger?" has a similar climax. In both stories, the reader must decide the outcome of the story (or part of it in the case of "The Amigo Brothers").
4. What will the boys decide to do about the upcoming fight? Will they remain friends? Who will win the fight?
5. who won the fight

DEVELOP YOUR VOCABULARY

Answers
1. partner, buddy (slang)
2. really great
3. brother, companion
4. you know
5. a popular kind of Latin American dance music

READING FOCUS

Sample Answer

Their upcoming bout caused them to distance themselves from each other. One example is when "they both sensed a wall rising between them." (p. 410) Another is when Felix went to stay with his aunt. A third is when both prayed for a quick knockout.

ESL Activity

Have the students reread pages 416–418 as a class to make notes on the actions of the two boxers. Then have ESL students and proficient English speakers pair up. Ask the partners to work together to write an account of the fight in the manner of a sports announcer. Have pairs of students read their account of the fight aloud to the class.

Guide students through the elements of a short story that are featured in the text: point of view, tone, symbolism, and writing technique. Remind students that they have encountered these elements in "Amigo Brothers."

ELEMENTS OF FICTION

In discussing point of view, ask students what the advantages are to different points of view. For example, the first-person point of view has the advantage of telling a story through the eyes of someone who is actually in the story. The third-person point of view can be broader; that is, seeing and knowing what all the characters are doing, thinking and feeling.

Next, ask students what factors influence the tone of a story. One factor is the author's intention in writing the story: Does he or she want to be humorous? serious? persuasive? Another factor is the characteristics of the storyteller. For example, if a story is told in the first person by a young person, it might be casual in tone. Yet another factor is subject matter. A story such as "Dead at Seventeen" (Unit 4) has a very serious tone because it is about a fatal auto accident.

Have students discuss the use of symbolism in "Amigo Brothers." Help them to see that, in many ways, the fight is a symbol: It represents the thing (boxing) that both boys want to do most in life, yet it also represents a threat to their friendship.

As students read "On the Ledge," have them think about the use of dialogue. Ask them to notice how dialogue is used to develop characters and to add tension and suspense to the story.

You can increase your enjoyment and understanding of fiction by remembering its four major elements. To review, they are setting, characters, plot, and theme. Now you can add to your understanding by learning about four additional elements: **point of view**, **tone**, **symbolism**, and **writing technique**.

Point of View   Every story must be written from a certain point of view. Someone, a character or speaker, must tell the story.

Most stories are written from either a first-person or third-person point of view. When **first-person** point of view is used, the narrator is a participant in the story. He or she may be either a major or minor character. Throughout the story, this character refers to himself or herself as "I" and "me." Since everything in the story is told from this character's point of view, the action and narration are limited to what only this character can see, hear, think, know, or feel.

In a **third-person** narrative, the narrator is not a participant in the story. The narrator must refer to each character in the story as "he" or "she." In some third-person stories, the narrator is **omniscient**, or all-knowing. The narrator stands outside the story and knows what goes on in the minds of all the characters. In other stories, the narrator takes a **limited** point of view and knows the thoughts and feelings of only a single character. A third-person narrative is less personal than a story told from first-person point of view.

Tone   The author's attitude toward his or her subject as well as toward his or her reader is called the tone. It may be funny, sad, light-hearted, or sarcastic. The choice of tone can even be ironic. You will recognize this tone in "The Secret Life of Walter Mitty."

Symbolism In literature, a symbol is something that stands for something else. Usually a symbol stands for something that you cannot see or touch; it may be a feeling, quality, or idea. For example, in the short story "Amigo Brothers," the boys' scrapbook symbolizes the way they feel about boxing and each other.

Sometimes a symbol is an action rather than an object. In "Amigo Brothers," the two boys hug each other tightly after agreeing not to see each other until the championship fight. The hug can be seen as a symbolic gesture that tells the way the two boys feel about each other.

Writing Technique Authors use many special techniques to enhance a short story. These include dialogue, flashback, foreshadowing, description, narration, and commentary.

Dialogue helps an author to create a character. You know from your own experience that you can tell many things about a person by the way he or she talks. In a story, dialogue tells the reader what a character says and how he or she says it.

Often, events in a story are told in chronological order. Sometimes, however, an author makes use of flashback. In **flashback**, a scene from an earlier time is inserted into the story.

As you read "On the Ledge," look to see what elements of the short story are present. Ask yourself these questions:

1. What is the point of view of the story? Is the narrator's point of view omniscient or limited?
2. What writing techniques does the author use? How do these techniques enhance the story?

SELECTION OVERVIEW

SELECTION OBJECTIVES

After completing this selection, students will be able to

- identify elements of the short story
- identify the heroes in a story
- extend character development
- identify various parts of speech
- infer cause and effect

Lesson Resources

On the Ledge
- Selection Synopsis, Teacher's Edition, p. T403b
- Comprehension and Vocabulary Workbook, pp. 81–82
- Language Enrichment Workbook, pp. 84–86
- Teacher's Resources
  Reinforcement, p. R39
  Test, pp. T77–T78
  Literary Analysis, pp. L9–L10

More About Character Development

Point out that authors may reveal their characters in several ways, through (1) dialogue, (2) statements about the character by the narrator or other characters, and (3) descriptions of the characters' actions. Ask students to find examples of these three techniques as they read this story.

Cooperative Group Activity

Ask students to brainstorm ideas for other stories that could have the title "On the Ledge." Tell them the only requirement is that the story include a teenager who becomes stranded on a ledge of some kind. As they brainstorm, have them consider questions such as these: Where is the ledge located? Why does the teenager go out onto the ledge? What is his or her attitude or state of mind? What action will take place? What will happen to resolve this situation? What is the tone of the story and who is narrating it? Have students summarize their stories for the class.

T424

Radiator Building - Night, Georgia O'Keeffe, Alfred Stieglitz Collection

424 ■ Unit 5

Viewing Fine Art

Georgia O'Keeffe (1887–1986) was one of America's pioneer abstractionist painters. As the wife of Alfred Stieglitz, a well-known photographer and champion of modernist styles, O'Keeffe experimented with close-ups and dramatically lighted images that were influenced by the art of photography. In this painting she used the formal composition of modern geometric art with its sharply focused edges to express the city at night. Ask: What does the drama of night in the city depicted here help you infer about the story that follows?

ON THE LEDGE

by Thompson Clayton

Sergeant Gray leaned out a sixth-floor window. Eight feet to his left, on a narrow ledge, stood a young man with frightened eyes. The young man's back was flat against the building. His arms were spread wide. His fingers gripped the edges of the rough bricks.

Gray looked down and swallowed hard. Six floors below, a crowd had gathered. Somewhere down on the street a siren screamed.

If I go out there, Gray thought, *I'll fall for sure.* High places had always scared Gray. He looked over at the young man. The youth's open shirt was wet with sweat. A strong wind blew his pants tight against his legs.

"Take it easy, fella," Gray said. The youth was about the size of his own 17-year-old son. "There's a lot of people down there you could hurt if you fall."

The young man looked down. His eyes seemed to be completely white. He said nothing.

"What's your name, pal?" asked Gray.

The boy swallowed and answered. "Walt," he said. "Walter Whitfield."

"Walt, you've got a lot of guts to go out there. More than I have. You must have a big problem. You want to talk about it?"

"You a cop?" asked Walter.

"I try to be," said Gray.

"Then I don't want to talk to you," said Walter.

> *FOCUS* ON FICTION
> STUDY HINTS
>
> As the story opens, the boy's position on the ledge is symbolic of his position in life.

> Notice that the point of view of the story is the third person. But the reader sees things primarily from Gray's point of view. This is called limited third person.

> By now you can tell that the tone of the story is one of extreme urgency; time has all but run out for Walter Whitfield.

On the Ledge ■ 425

Develop Vocabulary Skills

Most of the words used in this story will be familiar to students. Based on the reading level of your particular class, you may wish to choose several words from the story to preteach.

ESL Activity

Ask students to discuss what qualities make a person a hero. Then discuss who the heroes are in this story and what qualities make them heroes.

Background Notes

In recent years the suicide rate among adolescents in the United States and other Western nations has increased significantly. Each year in the United States, almost 5,000 young people between the ages of 15 and 24 kill themselves.

TEACHING PLAN

INTRODUCE

Motivation

Ask students to think about what they would do if they saw someone about to jump out of a high window or harm himself or herself in some other way. Relate students' responses to Sergeant Gray's dilemma in "On the Ledge."

Purpose-Setting Question

Why would someone only 17 years old be stranded on the ledge of a tall building?

READ

Literary Focus:
Elements of Fiction

Explain to students that although the story is told in the third person, the point of view is still primarily that of Sergeant Gray. Help them to see that the narrator does not describe anything that is seen, heard, or felt outside of Sergeant Gray's mind. The actions of other characters are described but not their thoughts, feelings, or motives. Ask: What is this point of view called?

Reading Focus:
Infer Cause and Effect

Although the author does not come right out and say that the young man is about to commit suicide, readers can infer this. Ask what students can infer about the relationship between Sergeant Gray and Walter when the sergeant says, "You've got a lot of guts to go out there." Ask: How might this cause Walter to feel?

CLOSE

Have students complete Review the Selection on pages 430–431.

Gray took off his cap and mopped his forehead. His head was wet and sticky. His damp shirt stuck to his back.

"Would you talk to someone else, Walter?" Gray asked.

"Maybe."

"Who, Walter? Your mother?"

"My mother's dead," Walter said. His voice shook.

"I'm sorry, Walter. Would you talk to your girlfriend then?"

"No!" Walter said angrily.

"Your brother?"

Once again Walter swallowed hard. "I might," he answered.

"What's his name?" asked Gray.

"John—John Whitfield."

"Does he live in town?"

"He has an office on Belton Street."

"Know his phone number?" Gray asked.

"No, it's in the book."

"Get it," Gray said over his shoulder to a policeman named Morely.

Morely reached for a phone book. "I'll have it in a minute," he said.

"We're calling him, Walter," Gray said with a smile. He looked down at the street. A long silver-and-red fire truck was backing into a space cleared by the police.

"I'll jump," said the boy. His teeth showed white against his tanned face. "If they raise a ladder, I'll jump."

Gray leaned out and signaled the firefighters below. They stopped and looked up. Gray waved his arms to show the firefighters they were to stop.

"All right, Walter. They won't raise it," Gray said.

"I've got Walt's brother on the phone," said Morely. "He says he's on his way."

"Your brother's coming," said Gray. "Think you can hold on?"

"I can make it." The burning noonday sun was now full on the youth's face. He licked his lips.

"Can I get you a drink?" asked Gray.

"No!"

"Anything else?"

"Only my brother," Walter replied.

Gray watched the boy's face. In the last minute the color had drained away. "You feeling OK, Walter?"

City Night, Georgia O'Keeffe. The Minneapolis Institute of Arts

Viewing Fine Art

In *City Night*, the painting shown here, Georgia O'Keeffe (1887–1986) experimented further with abstracting forms from the city scene. These early paintings are dramatically different from her later paintings of the American Southwest with their animal bones, flowers, and rocks. Here the towering geometric shapes of New York's tall buildings and crevices of light between them create a sharp-edged abstraction. O'Keeffe once remarked that she fell under "a camera's eye vision of life." She was encouraged in her early work by the American photographer Alfred Stieglitz, whom she married in 1924. The influence of black-and-white photography is clearly seen in this stark painting. Ask: Why is the painting a good illustration for this story?

The author gives a hint of what Gray will have to do as no one comes forward to help.

"Dizzy," Walter answered.

Gray swung around to Morely. "You think you could go out there?"

"Just thinking about it scares me half to death," said Morely.

Gray's eyes looked over the small group in the room. "Any of you done any high climbing? We need somebody to go out to help that kid. He might faint."

The men looked away. Two or three young office girls looked at him with wide eyes. There were no takers. Gray turned to the window again.

Looking at the youth, Gray was surprised at the sudden change. Walter's face now looked gray. His knees were shaking.

"Hang in there, Walter," Gray said. He tried to keep his voice calm. He wished now that they had put up the ladder. Maybe Walter wouldn't have jumped.

Down in the street the crowd had grown. Besides the fire truck, there were three police cars and an ambulance.

Gray looked over at Walter again. The boy started to lean outward—away from the building. For a moment he seemed about to fall. But then he caught himself, grabbing at the brick wall. His fingers showed white under the strain.

Gray could see that Walter was about to give up. "Morely," he called, "that boy's not going to make it!"

"What are we going to do?" Morely asked, fear in his voice.

"If you'll hold on to me, I'll try to reach him," Gray answered.

Slowly, carefully, he climbed over the windowsill and out onto the ledge.

"Walter, I'm coming to help you," he said softly. Walter's mouth opened, but no sound came out.

Morely reached out the window and grabbed Gray's left leg. Gray knelt on a ledge just six inches wide. He did not look down. He began inching his way toward Walter.

Gray could see that Walter was shaking with fear. Gray had to calm him somehow.

The author uses both dialogue and tone to reveal more about the kind of person Gray is.

"Walter, can you move a little closer . . . so I can reach your hand?" Gray said softly. "Take it easy . . . a little at a time."

Walter said nothing. But he was slowly trying to slide his foot toward Gray. He stretched out his hand, trying to touch Gray's. They were still two feet apart.

"I can't," Walter said, his voice shaking.

"Hold on," said Gray. His mouth felt dry. "I'm coming." He moved closer to Walter. Morely could no longer hold him.

Making a quick move, Gray reached for Walter's shaking hand. Then suddenly Gray's knee slipped. Six floors below the watching crowd gasped. Gray tried to regain his balance. He wavered back and forth. He was going over—

Suddenly he felt a hard hand. Somehow, in that terrible moment, Walter had found the strength and courage to save him.

Slowly the two made their way back to the window. Inside, they lay on the floor, drained of all strength.

"Sergeant," Walter said softly.

"Yeah, kid," Gray answered.

"I'm sorry," Walter said. Gray smiled.

It was then that he knew Walter Whitfield was going to make it.

Notice that Gray and Walter say few words to each other here, but they have reached a mutual understanding and respect.

Critical Thinking:
Draw Conclusions
Ask: Why does Gray think that Walter is going to make it?

---

waver (WAY vur) move in an unsteady way

Mini Quiz

Write on the chalkboard or overhead projector the following questions and call on students to fill in the blanks. Discuss the answers with the class.

1. Sergeant Gray sees _____ outside his window.

2. The one person that Walter is willing to see is _____.

3. Sergeant Gray is afraid that Walter will _____ before help arrives.

4. _____ goes out on the ledge to rescue Walter.

5. When Gray's knee slips, _____ rescues him.

Answers

1. a boy on a ledge

2. his brother

3. faint and/or fall

4. Sergeant Gray

5. Walter

T429

UNDERSTAND THE SELECTION

Answers

1. on a ledge outside a sixth-floor window
2. He is out on a ledge and in danger of falling or jumping.
3. go out onto the ledge to help Walter
4. commit suicide by jumping off the ledge
5. Sample answer: They must be somewhat close since the brother is the only person Walter is willing to talk to.
6. He does not want to talk to Gray when he learns that Gray is a cop.
7. His attitude is one of concern and compassion.
8. Answers will vary. Most students will probably feel that he did, because he won Walter's trust and made Walter care enough to save him and come in off the ledge.
9. Sample answer: Walter might have fainted and fallen to the ground.
10. Sample answer: Walter was beginning to care about somebody besides himself and to take responsibility for his actions.

Respond to Literature

Have students compare and contrast the heroic actions of Sergeant Gray and Walter. Both Gray and Walter attempt to save another's life. In Gray's case, however, the deed is enhanced by his willingness to put aside his fear of heights, when no one else would go out to help Walter, and to risk his life for someone he does not know. Gray's action came after a great deal of thought; Walter's action was spontaneous.

WRITE ABOUT THE SELECTION

Prewriting

Ask several volunteers to read aloud some of the questions they have about Walter. Then ask the class to respond with possible answers.

UNDERSTAND THE SELECTION

Recall

1. Where does the story take place?
2. What is Walter's predicament?
3. What does Sergeant Gray try to do?

Infer

4. What do you think Walter is planning to do?
5. What can you infer about Walter's relationship with his brother?
6. What clue makes you suspect that Walter may have been in trouble with the law in his past?
7. How would you describe Sergeant Gray's attitude toward Walter?

Apply

8. Do you feel that Sergeant Gray said and did the right things in this situation? Why or why not?
9. Predict what might have happened if Sergeant Gray had not gone out after Walter.
10. How do Walter's actions at the end of the story indicate a change in him?

Respond to Literature

Do you think that this story has one or two heroes? Explain your answer.

WRITE ABOUT THE SELECTION

As you read "On the Ledge," you learned a little about Walter from his conversations with Sergeant Gray. Do you think that knowing more of Walter's background might help to explain why he is on the ledge? Try to flesh out Walter's character by writing a paragraph in which you give some additional information about him, such as what he is thinking and feeling as he awaits his brother's arrival.

Prewriting Begin by making a list of questions about Walter, such as, why is he angry when Sergeant Gray mentions his girlfriend? After each question, jot down what you think might be a possible answer.

Writing Use your list of questions and answers to develop a character sketch of Walter Whitfield. Let the paragraph reflect your idea of the kind of person you think Walter is. You must base your sketch on information from the story, but keep in mind that the purpose of your paragraph is to provide information about Walter that goes beyond the story.

Revising Make sure that all of the details in your paragraph are consistent with the story. Eliminate or change any details that are not consistent.

Proofreading Whenever a story uses dialogue, be sure to insert quotation marks correctly. Reread your sketch again to ensure that you have made a paragraph indention each time a different character speaks.

Writing

Have students work on this section independently. Help those who are having trouble by asking questions such as these: If you met Walter at a party, what do you think he would be like? Do you think you would like to have Walter as a friend?

Revising

Have students trade papers with a partner. Ask each student to check his or her partner's paper for consistency with the story.

Proofreading

Display on a overhead projector several examples of dialogue from familiar stories. Point out to students the correct use of indention and punctuation. Leave the examples on display as students proofread their papers.

THINK ABOUT STORY ELEMENTS

Four additional elements of the short story are point of view, tone, symbolism, and writing techniques. **Point of view** is the position from which the story is told. **Tone** is the author's attitude toward the subject matter and toward the reader. **Symbolism** is using a concrete object or action to stand for something. **Writing techniques** include dialogue and flashback. Dialogue, conversation between characters in a story, can reveal aspects of each speaker's personality, provide background information, or advance the plot. Flashbacks allow writers to give you important information that occurred before the events of the story.

1. Describe the point of view of "On the Ledge."

2. What is the symbolic meaning of Gray's mopping his forehead?

3. What is the tone of the story?

4. What do you learn about Gray through dialogue?

5. What do you learn about Walter through dialogue?

DEVELOP YOUR VOCABULARY

You can improve your understanding of a word and its meaning by knowing the part of speech it belongs to. For example, in the sentence "His damp shirt stuck to his back," the word *damp* is an adjective. By knowing that *damp* is an adjective and by knowing that it means wet or moist, you can use the word effectively in other sentences.

Each of the words in italics is a noun, verb, or adjective. Use the dictionary to identify the part of speech of each italicized word. Then use each word in an original sentence.

1. His fingers *gripped* the edges of the rough bricks.

2. Walter had found the *strength* to save him.

3. Somewhere down the street a *siren* screamed.

4. On a *narrow* ledge stood a young man.

5. He began *inching* his way toward Walter.

6. He *wavered* back and forth.

Review the Selection ■ 431

SELECTION OVERVIEW

SELECTION OBJECTIVES

After completing this selection, students will be able to

- understand foreshadowing
- write an episode that uses foreshadowing
- identify characters' heroic actions
- write a human-interest news story
- analyze foreshadowing techniques
- use synonyms
- understand the sequence of events

Lesson Resources

Terror in the North
- Selection Synopsis, Teacher's Edition, pp. T403b–T403c
- Comprehension and Vocabulary Workbook, pp. 83–84
- Language Enrichment Workbook, pp. 87–89
- Teacher's Resources Reinforcement, p. R40 Test, pp. T79–T80

More About Foreshadowing

Ask students to think about times when they have had a premonition or an intuitive feeling about something that was about to happen. For example, someone might have had a feeling upon receiving a letter—and before it was opened—that it contained bad news. Explain that an author often tries to give the reader a similar kind of feeling in a story by using foreshadowing.

More About the Unit Theme

In "Terror in the North," a teenaged girl is caught in a serious earthquake while babysitting. Her decision to go back into the house to rescue the infant brings out qualities of heroism that she did not know she had.

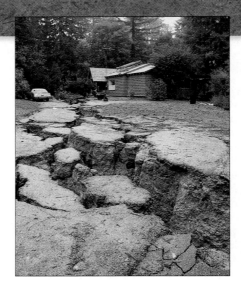

READING FOCUS

Understand the Sequence of Events
To understand the plot of a story, you need to be able to tell the sequence of events. Writers do not always relate the events of a story in the order in which they occurred. For example, the author might describe certain present events at the beginning of a story. Then, he or she might describe a series of events from the past, as background. As you read, notice words and phrases that refer to time, such as "three days ago" or "when she was a child," to understand the sequence of events.

FORESHADOWING

Writers use **foreshadowing** to give the reader hints about what is going to happen in a story. You can think of foreshadowing as a clue that encourages you to make predictions as you read. For example, in the story "On the Ledge," the author gives you several clues that Sergeant Gray may eventually go out on the ledge to help Walter. One clue is that Gray is thinking about how scared he is of high places and about what might happen *if* he went out.

The story you are about to read is filled with foreshadowing. As you read "Terror in the North," ask yourself:

1. How does the opening sentence by Stina's history teacher foreshadow the events of the story?
2. How do Stina's reactions to her teacher's speech foreshadow trouble ahead?

WRITING CONNECTION

Write an opening sentence for a story that has one or more details that could foreshadow the events of the plot. For example, you might write, "My sister, who is usually very talkative, is sitting silently by the window."

Background Notes

The great wave that is described in "Terror in the North" is a tidal wave, or tsunami. Tidal waves are usually the result of earthquakes that occur under the ocean floor. A tidal wave may cause coastal waters to rise as high as 30 meters.

Cooperative Group Activity

Extend the Writing Connection activity by having students work in pairs. Ask each pair to write about a single episode that involves foreshadowing. The episode may be something that actually happened, or it may be made up. When one student (from each pair) reads the episode aloud, have the student stop after the foreshadowing and ask the class, "What do you think is going to happen?" Encourage the class to respond before the student continues to the conclusion.

TERROR IN THE NORTH

ADAPTED

by Eloise Engle

"*S*ometime during our lives," said the history teacher, "we all face our moment of truth."

Stina Olson sat up straight in her seat. How did he know that a problem like this had been troubling her? Could he tell just by looking at her that she was questioning what kind of person she really was?

"As history shows," he continued, "few people really know how they will behave under extreme stress. Heroism often appears in wartime. Or sometimes we find heroic deeds in peacetime, when the enemy is fire, flood, hurricane, or earthquake."

Stina Olson relaxed again. He's certainly not talking about me, she thought. I'm the world's greatest coward.

About four o'clock on the afternoon of March 27, 1964, Stina decided she would *not* go along with the others from school. They were going to help clean and paint their town, Seward, Alaska. Seward was scheduled to receive the All-American Cities Award in just one week. There were plenty of last-minute jobs to be done before tourists from all over flocked in. But this was not her concern. She was not an Alaskan in any sense of the word. She had, in fact, arrived only a few months before, to live with her aunt and uncle after her mother had died. Living in Seattle, she had always felt close to the 49th state. But now things were different. Being an Alaskan, she had learned, meant far more than just living here. Oh, it was all mixed-up. But it had something to do with a pioneer spirit, a love for the wilderness, and a little thing called "guts." No matter how hard she tried, she could not find these things within herself. So lately she had simply given up the idea of ever fitting in.

It wasn't that the people of Seward hadn't been friendly when she first arrived—the adults, that is. But the kids had a kind of "show me" attitude. At least it seemed that way to Stina. She had

---

extreme (ik STREEM) very great
stress (STRES) pressure; uncomfortable strain
Seattle (see AT ul) city in the state of Washington, the most northwestern of the "lower 48" states and the closest to Alaska

Terror in the North ■ 433

always been self-conscious about being shorter and more slender than other girls her age. This, along with her blonde hair, blue eyes, and fair skin, took at least two years off her 16. Not being very good at sports was another mark against her.

There was the time when Dan Darby had asked her to go along with the gang on a hiking trip. She had packed a lunch and climbed into her heaviest jeans and boots. Then she started out, only nearly to collapse from fright when they reached the top of a cliff that dropped straight down into Resurrection Bay. Dan, who was almost six feet tall and just about the best-looking boy in town, just shook his head in wonder. "Boy, they sure grow 'em frail in the 'Lower 48' these days."

She forced herself to sneak another look. The city below jutted out into the turquoise-blue water. Colorful fishing boats sailed in and out of the bay. The sun shone down on the sparkling water, and Stina had to agree to the country's beauty. But that didn't help that little cowardly streak running up her spine.

"I . . . I'm going to start back down," she murmured.

"Okay, okay." Dan took her arm and guided her along the dangerous mountainside. He was quiet for quite a while. Then he said, "You'll get used to it . . . eventually . . . I think."

But she didn't. She went fishing for silver salmon and wound up seasick.

Now, at five o'clock, she headed for the Stetson house. She was to baby-sit for their three-month-old infant. She thought that she was at least freeing two adults for the clean-up job. *I'm the one behind the gun,* she told herself grimly. *Even if I don't fit in here, I can do something calm and simple like babysitting.*

The Stetsons' house had been built only two years before. It was one of the nicest in town. Stina truly enjoyed being there because of the wide view of the harbor from the living-room window.

"The baby has been fed and he's just about ready to fall asleep," Mrs. Stetson told Stina. "There are sodas in the refrigerator, and . . . oh yes, some delicious roast moose. Help yourself."

After they left, Stina settled down in an easy chair by the window. She began looking through a magazine. For some strange reason she couldn't concentrate, not even on the pictures. Her whole body felt tense. She didn't know why. Was it because twilight was now creeping over the bay? Or was it simply because she was alone and mad at herself? No, there was something more.

She shuddered and tried to think of something pleasant. But it was no use. She pushed up her sweater sleeves and saw the goosebumps on her arms. *Now,*

---

self-conscious (SELF KON shus) very aware of oneself; embarrassed or shy
frail (FRAYL) weak
jutted (JUT id) stuck out
eventually (ih VEN choo uhl ee) in the end; at some time
grimly (GRIM lee) harshly; sternly
concentrate (KON sun trayt) pay close attention

why do I feel this way? She glanced at her watch. Five thirty. *Something is happening somewhere . . . I know it!*

Something *was* happening somewhere. About 150 miles southeast, and about 12 miles beneath the icy green waters of Prince William Sound, powerful forces were at work on the earth's crust. Twisting, straining layers of rock began to move. The raging forces beneath the thin, rocky crust would not be stilled. The tremendous power, held back for centuries, could no longer be kept in harness. The largest single catastrophe ever to hit any state in the union began a rampage that would affect one million square miles. . . .

"Who's there?" Stina called out in answer to a pounding at the door.

"It's me. Dan." He hurried into the room carrying a large paper sack. "I can only stay a minute. I brought you some of the gang's leftover hot dogs." He looked through the bag. "And here are some potato chips and cake."

Stina was more ashamed than ever. She forced herself to laugh. "You're great, Dan. Now I won't have to eat moose for supper."

He started toward the door. "I'll try to stop in later. That is . . . if you want me to."

"Oh, I do," she blurted out. "I . . . I really don't mean to seem unfriendly. I honestly like it here but . . ." *There was*

that strange feeling again! "Dan, don't go. Please stay and have a soda."

She hurriedly poured some soda over ice. Then she set the glasses on the coffee table. But they did not stay put. The ice tinkled as the fizzing soda danced over the rims of the glasses. Stina frowned. She looked in puzzlement at Dan. Then she looked past him at the china figurines on the bookcase. These, too, were bouncing up and down. Suddenly, there was a strange and terrible sound, a sort of "Vroooooo." It came from far away or under the earth. Stina's whole body stiffened. "What . . . what was that?" she gasped.

Dan shrugged his shoulders and laughed lightly. "Oh, probably just a little earthquake. We have 'em all the time. Alaskans get used to 'em. Sit tight, and don't be afraid."

The whole house began to shake violently. Furniture fell over and slid around the room. The chimney on the roof crumbled, and now Stina began to feel seasick. "Oh, no . . . no!" she screamed, as she almost fell to the floor.

Dan wasn't laughing anymore. "It's a good strong one, I'll say that for it," he said. He grabbed her arm and pushed her toward the doorway where there would be support from overhead. "Don't panic now."

Now the pictures on the wall began to crash to the floor. Lamps sailed across the room. The floor beneath them cracked

---

catastrophe (kuh TAS truh fee) a sudden, horrible disaster
rampage (RAM payj) wild outbreak
blurted (BLURT id) said suddenly
figurine (fig yuh REEN) small statue

Terror in the North ■ 435

Literary Focus:
Foreshadowing
Have students relate the feeling of uneasiness that Stina had to what is now occurring.

Softly, Vivian Caldwell

and groaned. The kitchen cupboard doors swung open, emptying dishes, silverware, canned foods, pots, and pans onto the floor. Flour, sugar, milk, syrup all crashed into a huge heap. The shattering glass and splintering house joints roared in her ears as she jerked free from Dan.

"Let go of me!" she screamed. "I've got to get out of here." This must be a nightmare. It couldn't be real. But even as she tried to get to the front door, her feet flew from under her.

It was probably less than a minute since the horrible shaking began, but it seemed as if it would never end. "Please stop," she cried. "Please!" Looking out the window she could see trees crashing down. Huge cracks ripped open the earth and horrible black mud squirted up. The ground itself was rolling in waves. In the distance she could see the dock area. "Look, Dan!" she gasped.

They stared, horror-stricken. The entire waterfront north of Washington Street slid into the bay. With it went the dock, warehouse, and huge fuel-storage tanks of an oil company. And then the other waterfront buildings north to San Juan dock, the small boat harbor—everything in sight—slipped away in underwater slides. Almost immediately, the lid blew off in another oil-storage tank area. Orange flames leaped into the air as eight tanks exploded. And in back of the flames, speeding down the bay at hundreds of miles an hour, was a huge tidal wave of sea water.

Dan grabbed Stina's arm. "We've got to get out of here. That wave is coming inland!" Somehow Stina managed to follow Dan out of the house. They scrambled up on top of some oil barrels and from there onto a neighbor's garage. "This will never hold," Dan yelled. "Here, we'll have to jump over to the housetop."

He went first, then braced himself to catch Stina. "Hurry!" he called.

She bent down to leap—and then she remembered! Oh no! Oh no! "Dan, I forgot about the baby. I've got to go back for him!"

"You can't, Stina! There isn't time! You'll be killed!"

But she could hear nothing except the pounding of her own heart. It was as if suddenly tons of strength had been pumped into her trembling body. She did not look back to the safety of the rooftop. Nor did she glance outward to the Bay, with the wall of water racing nearer and nearer. She thought only of the helpless infant whose life would be gone if she could not reach him in time. As she struggled up the broken steps of the house, she remembered the words of the history teacher. . . . Something about a "moment of truth." Yes, this was her moment of truth. She was terrified. But she was not running from her responsibility in order to save her own skin. This discovery about herself seemed to pour into her even more strength. Stumbling past broken furniture, upturned chairs, and falling plaster, she reached the bedroom. Then she snatched up the baby, wrapped him in a blanket, and ran out of the house again.

"Over here, Stina. Hurry!" Dan yelled.

Stina's throat was hot and dry. But her legs could still move, and that was what counted. She handed Dan the baby and began to climb up onto the rooftop. She saw the towering wall of water bearing down on them. Two minutes later it struck the Stetsons' house, tearing it to pieces. The garage they had been on top of, only minutes before, went next.

Beneath her, she felt the porch of the house being torn away. The bedrooms, splintering and swirling, went next. The baby, now in Stina's arms, was crying. As long as he was crying, there was strength and life in his tiny form. Stina was grateful that he could not know of his nearness to death.

"Hang on tight," Dan ordered. Suddenly the rooftop raft sailed dizzily away in the swirling water. There was nothing left of the house but the living room beneath them. As they sped on through the muddy water, she saw a raging fire in the distance. She dimly wondered if its fiery fingers would reach as far inland as

---

tidal wave (TYD ul WAYV) huge, destructive, ocean wave
bearing (BAIR ing) pressing; advancing rapidly

Terror in the North ■ **437**

Critical Thinking:
Analyze
Ask students if they think that the story is believable. Make sure that students back up their answers. Some students may feel that all or parts of the story are far-fetched. For example, why were Dan and Stina not at all concerned about their own families while the earthquake was occurring?

Literary Focus:
Foreshadowing
Ask: What specific event at the waterfront foreshadows extreme danger for Stina and Dan at the Stetson house?

Reading Focus:
Understand the Sequence of Events
To make sure students understand the sequence of events in this part of the story, ask: Why do Dan and Stina scramble onto the top of the neighbor's garage? Why does Stina go back to the Stetsons' house? What happens after Stina rescues the baby?

Reading Focus:
*Understand the Sequence
of Events*

Have students locate the phrase
that lets them know that the sixth
wave is the final wave. Ask: After
the sixth and last tidal wave sub-
sides, what does Stina observe
around her from her rooftop raft?

their rooftop perch.

They bumped into trees, parts of
houses, and buildings. It seemed certain
their raft would split wide open.
Unbelievable minutes, that seemed like
an entire lifetime, went by. At last
they found themselves caught between
trees. Dan leaped into action. He tied
the roof to the trees with the television
wires. Now, at least, they were anchored
to something. But the waves reached
as high as the attic and lapped at the
roof itself.

The sixth and last of the tidal waves
finally fell back. Only then did Dan risk
lowering himself into the house. Stina,
holding the baby, sat tight. "Be careful,
Dan," she yelled.

As she waited, darkness fell. She could
still see familiar objects sailing by. The
moonlight reflected on a car. As it floated
by like a toy, it flipped over on its side.
Minutes later, the bodies of two dogs came
near. She almost cried out because she
thought she recognized one of them as her
family's pet.

It seemed as if Dan had been gone
forever. What could he be doing? "Dan,

La Vague, Gustave Courbet. The Brooklyn Museum, Gift of Mrs. Horace Havemeyer

438 ■ Unit 5

Viewing Fine Art

Gustave Courbet (1819–1877)
was a French painter who held
revolutionary views about both
art and politics. He maintained
that the artist should paint what
he sees, rather than seeking
noble or romantic subjects. He
pictured common people in their
daily lives and scenes of nature
that were bold and realistic. For
his political activities Courbet was
sentenced to death. He escaped
but spent the rest of his life in
exile. Ask: What might it feel like
to have this wave crash near you
or around you? How does the
painting help you to understand
Stina's situation?

are you all right?" she called out.

"I'm coming," he answered, and swung himself onto the rooftop again. "We're in luck . . . two candles, a lighter, and a can of juice for Junior."

Stina was grateful for them. But as the heavy chill in the air grew sharper, she shivered more and more.

"Do you suppose there's some kind of insulation in the roof?" she asked. "If we could get at it, it might help to keep us warm."

"Good idea," Dan said. He began pulling up shingles and tearing out insulation with which they could wrap themselves for warmth. Then there was nothing to do except . . . wait.

"Somebody will rescue us," he comforted Stina. "Our best bet is to stay put."

"I know. I'm not afraid anymore."

"So I noticed," Dan said, smiling. "And I take back any kidding I ever did about you. Just wait till word gets around."

Down at the waterfront, the raging fires had been carried back to sea by the returning waves. Dock pilings that had been snapped off were floating upright. Coated with tar, their top sections were aflame. They looked like candles floating in the night all over the bay.

What seemed hours dragged by. Then Stina's heart leaped as she saw the beautiful gleam of approaching flashlights. There were sounds of human voices calling. "You up there. Are you all right?"

Dan cupped his hands to his mouth and shouted, "We're fine."

He peeked inside the blanket to look at the baby. Then he put his arm around Stina. "All three of us are okay," he said huskily, "thanks to you, Stina."

Stina managed a smile. Then she bent forward to yell as loudly as she could, "There are three wet, cold Alaskans up here. Come and get us!"

Literary Focus:
Foreshadowing
What actions taken by the characters foreshadowed a safe outcome for Dan and Stina?

Discussion
Have the students compare Stina's feelings about "fitting in" at the beginning of the story and now. Ask: What do you think made Stina feel differently?

---

pilings (PYL ingz) wooden poles driven into the ground to form part of a wall or a foundation

Terror in the North ■ 439

Mini Quiz

Write on the chalkboard or overhead projector the following sentences and call on students to fill in the blanks. Discuss the answers with the class.

1. The story takes place in _____.

2. Stina is babysitting when _____ occurs.

3. Visiting Stina is _____.

4. Stina decides to go back into the house in order to _____.

5. At the end of the story, Stina and Dan are _____.

Answers
1. Seward, Alaska
2. an earthquake
3. Dan
4. rescue the baby
5. reached by rescuers

UNDERSTAND THE SELECTION

Answers

1. Seward, Alaska
2. 16
3. A severe earthquake occurs.
4. Compared to other young Alaskans, she found herself lacking in courage and "pioneer spirit."
5. He seemed to like her but was perplexed by her frailty.
6. She felt that she should have been working with the others on the town project.
7. She was probably afraid that if she looked back, her fear would stop her from rescuing the baby.
8. her feeling that something was wrong
9. the realization that she was not shirking her responsibility to save her own skin
10. For the first time Stina considers herself an Alaskan.

Respond to Literature

The speech by Stina's history teacher focuses on acts of courage during war or natural disasters. Ask students to think of other situations that might bring out heroic qualities in a person. You can begin by asking them to consider risks that are not physical. For example, a teenager might be a hero for standing up to his friend and convincing him not to drink or take drugs.

WRITE ABOUT THE SELECTION

Prewriting

Obtain examples from newspapers and magazines of well-written human interest stories. Read aloud or have students read several of the stories. Then discuss the elements that make up a good human interest story.

Writing

As students work on this section independently, circulate to help those who are having trouble. Ask questions that will help students focus on information that they may be omitting.

Revising

Students may enjoy working in small groups to role-play interviews with Stina and Dan. The interviews can help students think of quotes to use as they revise.

Proofreading

Write on the chalkboard or overhead transparency a list of proper names that appear in the story. Have students use the list to check their own spellings of these names.

UNDERSTAND THE SELECTION

Recall

1. Where does this story take place?
2. How old is Stina?
3. What happens while Stina is babysitting for the Stetsons?

Infer

4. Why was Stina questioning the kind of person she was?
5. What can you infer about Dan's feelings toward Stina at the beginning of the story?
6. Why was Stina embarrassed when Dan brought her leftover food?
7. Why did Stina not look back when she went to rescue the baby?

Apply

8. What caused Stina to ask Dan to stay with her at the Stetsons' house?
9. What realization about herself gives Stina the greatest strength?
10. At the end of the story, what is the significance of the phrase "three wet, cold Alaskans"?

Respond to Literature

What action of Stina's illustrates the history teacher's opening statement? How realistic do you think this action is?

440 ■ Unit 5

WRITE ABOUT THE SELECTION

Stina's rescue of the baby would make a wonderful human interest story for the news media. Suppose that you are a news reporter asked to cover the Alaskan earthquake. You interview Stina and Dan; then write a feature story for a newspaper or a TV news broadcast.

Prewriting   Begin by clustering the facts that must always be present in a news story: who, what, when, where, why. Use your cluster to write interview questions. Then write down what you think Stina and Dan might say in an interview.

Writing   Use your cluster and notes to write a feature story about Stina's rescue of the baby. Remember that a good news story must capture the reader's interest. Also keep in mind that when writing a news story, it is important *not* to include your own opinion, but to let the story speak for itself.

Revising   You can improve the effectiveness of your story by adding direct quotes from Stina and Dan. Make sure that you use proper punctuation when using direct quotations.

Proofreading   As you reread your story for errors in spelling, pay careful attention that recurring names are spelled the *same* way throughout the story. The name Olson, for instance, could be misspelled very easily as Olsen. Concern for small proofreading details will lend credibility to your story.

ESL Activity

Have students work in small groups to create a timeline of events that occur in the story on March 27, 1964. If needed, explain the parts of a timeline. Encourage students to review the story for time clues that will help them place the events in order.

T440

THINK ABOUT FORESHADOWING

Foreshadowing prepares the reader for a surprise by giving hints about what might happen later in the story.

Foreshadowing also involves the reader in a kind of predicting game. Part of the fun of reading the story is seeing if your predictions are correct. Answer these questions about foreshadowing.

1. How does the opening speech in "Terror in the North" clearly foreshadow Stina's immediate future?

2. What specific situations does the history teacher mention that relate to the events of the story?

3. How does Stina's reaction to the speech foreshadow what will happen to her?

4. What definite clues about the upcoming disaster are present while Stina is babysitting?

5. What change in Dan's behavior signals the severity of the earthquake?

READING FOCUS

Understand the Sequence of Events
Use your understanding of the sequence of events to answer this question: Which events took place *before* March 27, 1964?
An earthquake occurs.
Stina moves to Alaska.
Stina goes hiking with other kids and becomes scared.
Stina looks after the Stetsons' baby.
Stina rescues a baby.

DEVELOP YOUR VOCABULARY

Synonyms are words that have the same, or almost the same, meaning. For example, in the sentence "Stina's action was very courageous," the word *courageous* could be replaced by the word *brave*. *Brave* is a synonym for *courageous*. The basic purpose of a thesaurus is to provide lists of synonyms for the words you look up. Some dictionaries provide synonyms after the definitions.

Consult a thesaurus or a dictionary to find synonyms for the italicized words in the sentences below. Decide which word could replace the italicized word in each sentence. Try to choose words that are new to you. Then use each new word in an original sentence.

1. The rescue required *extreme* strength.

2. The police officer knew how to work under *stress*.

3. Stina felt *self-conscious* around the other young people.

4. The teacher spoke *grimly* to the students.

5. Compared to the others, Stina was considered *frail*.

Review the Selection ■ 441

SELECTION OBJECTIVES

After completing this selection, students wil be able to

- identify story techniques
- use several story techniques to recount an incident
- evaulate a character's concept of heroism
- write a personal fantasy
- analyze the use of story techniques
- use figurative expressions
- identify cause and effect

Lesson Resources

The Secret Life of Walter Mitty
- Selection Synopsis, Teacher's Edition, p. T403c
- Comprehension and Vocabulary Workbook, pp. 85–86
- Language Enrichment Workbook, pp. 90–92
- Teacher's Resources Reinforcement, p. R41 Test, pp. T81–T82

More About Story Techniques

Writers use various techniques to develop a character's internal life. One such technique is called stream of consciousness. Stream of consciousness is writing a character's thoughts as he or she has them in whatever order and syntax occur. A similar technique is to present a character's daydream or fantasy as if it were an event that is actually happening. This is the technique James Thurber uses in his story about Walter Mitty.

More About the Unit Theme

Unlike the other stories in this unit, this selection is about someone who is not a hero but who imagines that he is. An important element in the story is that the main character never does anything to make his dreams come true. His drab life is directly in contrast to his fantastic daydreams.

Learn About

STORY TECHNIQUES

A writer may choose to use special techniques in order to tell a story. The main technique of a fiction writer is **narration**. This is reporting the events of the story in chronological order. The purpose is to make the story clear. **Description** is another technique that brings scenes and feelings alive for the reader. Another technique is **flashback**. In flashback, an episode from an earlier time is inserted into the story. Writers also use **dialogue**. Dialogue is two or more characters talking to each other. **Repetition** of an idea or phrase can be used to make a point clear to the reader.

As you read "The Secret Life of Walter Mitty," ask yourself these questions:

1. What special techniques does the writer use to enhance the story?
2. How do these techniques help make the story believable?

WRITING CONNECTION

Choose two of these techniques to tell about an important event in your life. Although you are writing about a real event, you can use another writer's tool—imagination—to create appropriate effects even if they did not really happen.

READING FOCUS

Identify Cause and Effect Many of the events in a story are linked by cause and effect. A cause is something that brings about a certain result. The result is called an effect. To determine the cause of an event in a story, ask yourself, Why did it happen? The cause might be some other event in the story. In other cases, the cause may be a certain feeling or attitude a character has.

About the Author

James Thurber (1894–1961) was born in Columbus, Ohio. He began his career as a newspaper reporter and then became well-known as a writer, editor, and cartoonist for the *New Yorker* magazine. Later in life, Thurber lost his eyesight but continued to write. "The Secret Life of Walter Mitty," which is probably Thurber's most famous story, is characteristic of his work in its mix of sadness and humor.

Cooperative Group Activity

Have several students work together to create a single piece of writing about an event that has happened to one member of the group. Students can use their completed Writing Connection activity as background. Students may find it helpful if each member of the group contributes the use of a particular technique. For example, one student might write dialogue, while another writes an episode that is a flashback.

THE SECRET LIFE OF WALTER MITTY

by James Thurber

"**W**e're going through!" The Commander's voice was like thin ice breaking. He wore his full-dress uniform, with the heavily braided white cap pulled down rakishly over one cold gray eye. "We can't make it, sir. It's spoiling for a hurricane, if you ask me." "I'm not asking you, Lieutenant Berg," said the Commander. "Throw on the power lights! Rev her up to 8,500! We're going through!" The pounding of the cylinders increased: ta-pocketa-pocketa-pocketa-*pocketa-pocketa*. The Commander stared at the ice forming on the pilot window. He walked over and twisted a row of complicated dials. "Switch on No. 8 auxiliary!" he shouted. "Switch on No. 8 auxiliary!" repeated Lieutenant Berg.

"Full strength in No. 3 turret!" shouted the Commander. "Full strength in No. 3 turret!" The crew, bending to their various tasks in the huge, hurtling eight-engined Navy hydroplane looked at each other and grinned. "The Old Man'll get us through," they said to one another. "The Old Man ain't afraid of Hell!" . . .

"Not so fast! You're driving too fast!" said Mrs. Mitty. "What are you driving so fast for?"

"Hmm?" said Walter Mitty. He looked at his wife, in the seat beside him, with shocked astonishment. She seemed grossly unfamiliar, like a strange woman who had yelled at him in a crowd. "You were up to fifty-five," she said. "You know I don't like to go more than forty.

---

hydroplane (HY droh playn) a seaplane

The Secret Life of Walter Mitty ■ 443

Motivation
Ask students to think about their favorite fantasies. Do they ever think of themselves as heroes or superstars in dramatic situations? Ask for volunteers to share some of their fantasies, as a lead-in to the fantasy life of Walter Mitty.

Purpose-Setting Question
Why would someone spend most of his life daydreaming about being a hero?

READ

Literary Focus:
Story Techniques
Remind students that most writers use special techniques to tell a story. Ask volunteers to give a definition as you mention each of the following: narration, description, flashback, dialogue, repetition. Then discuss the purpose of each technique. Urge students to look for these techniques as they read.

Reading Focus:
Identify Cause and Effect
Tell students that a cause and effect relationship exists when one event (the cause) results in another event (the effect). Have students note the cause and effect of each of Mitty's daydreams as they read the story.

CLOSE

Have students complete Review the Selection on pages 450–451.

Develop Vocabulary Skills
Point out to students that many of the vocabulary words and phrases footnoted in the story are of a particular time: World War II. Some phrases are Thurber's own invention. You may want to write each word and phrase on the chalkboard and then ask students to pronounce them.

ESL Activity
Invite students to act out each of the five fantasies that Walter Mitty has, along with the gesture or event that snaps him out of his daydream. Encourage them to emphasize the drama in each daydream episode and the contrast between the imaginary Mitty and the everyday Mitty.

Reading Focus:
Identify Cause and Effect

From reading the first two pages of the story, students should be able to get an idea of the kind of person Mrs. Mitty is. Have students give their opinions of what Mrs. Mitty is like and how her personality might contribute to Mitty's need to escape the realities of his life.

Literary Focus:
Story Techniques

Make sure students are aware of when the narrative shifts from Mitty's everyday life to his fantasies and back. Ask: What technique does Thurber use to quickly sketch Mitty's imaginary dramas?

You were up to fifty-five." Walter Mitty drove on toward Waterbury in silence, the roaring of the SN202 through the worst storm in twenty years of Navy flying fading in the remote, intimate airways of his mind. "You're tensed up again," said Mrs. Mitty. "It's one of your days. I wish you'd let Dr. Renshaw look you over."

Walter Mitty stopped the car in front of the building where his wife went to have her hair done. "Remember to get those overshoes while I'm having my hair done," she said. "I don't need overshoes," said Mitty. She put her mirror back into her bag. "We've been all through that," she said, getting out of the car. "You're not a young man any longer." He raced the engine a little. "Why don't you wear your gloves? Have you lost your gloves?" Walter Mitty reached in a pocket and brought out the gloves. He put them on, but after she had turned and gone into the building and he had driven on to a red light, he took them off again. "Pick it up, brother!" snapped a cop as the light changed, and Mitty hastily pulled on his gloves and lurched ahead. He drove around the streets aimlessly for a time, and then he drove past the hospital on his way to the parking lot.

. . ."It's the millionaire banker, Wellington McMillan," said the pretty nurse. "Yes?" said Walter Mitty, removing his gloves slowly. "Who has the case?"

"Dr. Renshaw and Dr. Benbow, but there are two specialists here. Dr. Remington from New York and Mr. Pritchard-Mitford from London. He flew over." A door opened down a long, cool corridor and Dr. Renshaw came out. He looked distraught and haggard. "Hello, Mitty," he said. "We're having the devil's own time with McMillan, the millionaire banker and close personal friend of Roosevelt. Obstreosis of the ductal tract.[1] Tertiary. Wish you'd take a look at him." "Glad to," said Mitty.

In the operating room there were whispered introductions: "Dr. Remington, Dr. Mitty. Mr. Pritchard-Mitford, Dr. Mitty." "I've read your book on streptothricosis," said Pritchard-Mitford, shaking hands. "A brilliant performance, sir." "Thank you," said Walter Mitty. "Didn't know you were in the States, Mitty," grumbled Remington. "Coals to Newcastle,[2] bringing Mitford and me up here for tertiary." "You are very kind," said Mitty. A huge, complicated machine, connected to the operating table, with many tubes and wires, began at this moment to go pocketa-pocketa-pocketa. "The new anesthetizer is giving way!" shouted an intern. "There is no one in the East who knows how to fix it!" "Quiet, man!" said Mitty, in a low, cool voice. He sprang to the machine, which was now going pocketa-pocketa-queep-pocketa-queep. He began fingering delicately a row of

---

[1] **obstreosis of the ductal tract:** Thurber has invented this and other medical terms
[2] **coals to Newcastle:** The proverb, "bringing coals to Newcastle," means bringing things to a place unnecessarily—Newcastle, England, was a coal center and so did not need coal brought to it.

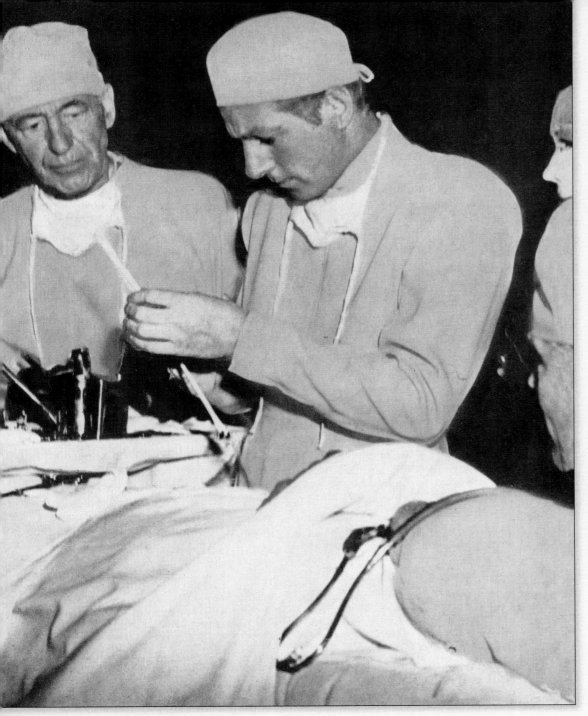

Critical Thinking:
Compare and Contrast
Have students contrast Mitty's real personality with his imagined version of himself. Ask: What connections might there be between them?

glistening dials. "Give me a fountain pen!" he snapped. Someone handed him a fountain pen. He pulled a faulty piston out of the machine and inserted the pen in its place. "That will hold for ten minutes," he said. "Get on with the operation." A nurse hurried over and whispered to Renshaw, and Mitty saw the man turn pale. "Coreopsis has set in," said Renshaw nervously. "If you would take over, Mitty?" Mitty looked at him and at the craven figure of Benbow, who drank, and at the grave, uncertain faces of the two great specialists. "If you wish," he said. They slipped a white gown on him; he adjusted a mask and drew on thin gloves; nurses handed him shining . . .

"Back it up, Mac! Look out for that Buick!" Walter Mitty jammed on the brakes. "Wrong lane, Mac," said the parking-lot attendant, looking at Mitty closely. "Gee. Yeh," muttered Mitty. He began cautiously to back out of the lane marked "Exit Only." "Leave her sit there," said the attendant. "I'll put her away." Mitty got out of the car. "Hey, better leave the key." "Oh," said Mitty, handing the man the ignition key. The attendant vaulted into the car, backed it up with insolent skill, and put it where it belonged.

They're so cocky, thought Walter Mitty, walking along Main Street; they think they know everything. Once he had tried to take his chains off, outside New Milford, and he had got them wound around the axles. A man had had to come out in a wrecking car and unwind them, a young, grinning garage-man. Since then Mrs. Mitty always made him drive to a garage to have the chains taken off. The next time, he thought, I'll wear my right arm in a sling; they won't grin at me then. I'll have my right arm in a sling and they'll see I couldn't possibly take the chains off myself. He kicked at the slush on the sidewalk. "Overshoes," he said to himself, and he began looking for a shoe store.

When he came out into the street again, with the overshoes in a box under his arm, Walter Mitty began to wonder what the other thing was his wife had told him to get. She had told him twice, before they set out from their house for Waterbury. In a way he hated these weekly trips to town—he was always getting something wrong. Kleenex, he thought. Squibb's, razor blades? No. Toothpaste, toothbrush, bicarbonate, carborundum, initiative and referendum?[3] He gave it up. But she would remember it. "Where's the what's-its-name?" she would ask. "Don't tell me you forgot the what's-its-name." A newsboy went by shouting something about the Waterbury trial.

---

[3] **carborundum** (kahr buh RUN dum), **initiative** (ih NISH uh tiv) and **referendum** (ref uh REN dum): Thurber is purposely making a nonsense list: carborundum is a hard substance used for scraping, initiative is the right of citizens to introduce ideas for laws, and referendum is the right of citizens to vote on laws.

Literary Focus:
Flashback

Discuss with students the adept way in which Thurber moves from reality to fantasy and back again. Point out that each daydream is triggered by a real-life situation. The daydream begins where the real-life incident ends—but there is always a connection. For example, as Mitty drives past the hospital, the story switches to an operating room where Mitty imagines himself to be a famous surgeon. Also point out that it is always a disagreeable encounter with reality that brings Mitty out of his daydream. For example, the daydream about the surgeon ends when the parking lot attendant yells at Mitty for being in the wrong lane. Ask: What story technique is the author employing in these situations?

. . ."Perhaps this will refresh your memory." The District Attorney suddenly thrust a heavy automatic at the quiet figure on the witness stand. "Have you ever seen this before?" Walter Mitty took the gun and examined it expertly. "This is my Webley-Vickers 50.80," he said calmly. An excited buzz ran around the courtroom. The judge rapped for order. "You are a crack shot with any sort of firearms, I believe?" said the District Attorney, insinuatingly. "Objection!" shouted Mitty's attorney. "We have shown that the defendant could not have fired the shot. We have shown that he wore his right arm in a sling on the night of the fourteenth of July." Walter Mitty raised his hand briefly and the bickering attorneys were stilled. "With any known make of gun," he said evenly, "I could have killed Gregory Fitzhurst at three hundred feet *with my left hand*." Pandemonium broke loose in the courtroom. A woman's scream rose above the bedlam and suddenly a lovely, dark-haired girl was in Walter Mitty's arms. The District Attorney struck at her savagely. Without rising from his chair, Mitty let the man have it on the point of the chin. "You miserable cur!"

"Puppy biscuit," said Walter Mitty. He stopped walking and the buildings of Waterbury rose up out of the misty courtroom and surrounded him again. A woman who was passing laughed. "He said 'Puppy biscuit,'" she said to her companion. "That man said 'Puppy biscuit' to himself." Walter Mitty hurried on. He went into an A&P, not the first one he came to but a smaller one farther up the street.

Critical Thinking:
Infer
Have students look at the photographs of Mitty included in this story. Ask: What can you infer about Walter Mitty from the details in the photographs and the expressions on his face?

Reading Focus:
Identify Cause and Effect
Ask: What real-life incident causes Mitty to drift into a fantasy about being questioned in a murder trial? What fantasy incident causes Mitty to suddenly remember the thing his wife told him to get?

Critical Thinking:
Analyze

Ask: In the daydream sequences
what makes Mitty seem heroic? Do
such heroes exist in real life? Why
do you think as you do?

"I want some biscuit for small, young dogs," he said to the clerk. "Any special brand, sir?" The greatest pistol shot in the world thought a moment. "It says 'Puppies Bark for It' on the box," said Walter Mitty.

His wife would be through at the hairdresser's in fifteen minutes, Mitty saw in looking at his watch, unless they had trouble drying it; sometimes they had trouble drying it. She didn't like to get to the hotel first; she would want him to be there waiting for her as usual. He found a big leather chair in the lobby, facing a window, and he put the over-shoes and the puppy biscuit on the floor beside it. He picked up an old copy of *Liberty* and sank down into the chair. "Can Germany Conquer the World Through the Air?" Walter Mitty looked at the pictures of bombing planes and of ruined streets.

. . . "The cannonading has got the wind up in young Raleigh,[4] sir," said the sergeant. Captain Mitty looked up at him through tousled hair. "Get him to bed," he said wearily. "With the others I'll fly alone." "But you can't, sir," said the sergeant anxiously. "It takes two men to handle that bomber and the Archies[5] are pounding hell out of the air. Von Richtman's circus[6] is between here and Saulier." "Somebody's got to get that ammunition dump," said Mitty. "I'm going over. Spot of brandy?" He poured a drink for the sergeant and one for himself. War thundered and whined around the dugout and battered at the door. There was a rending of wood and splinters flew through the room. "A bit of a near thing," said Captain Mitty carelessly. "The box barrage is closing in," said the sergeant. "We only live once, Sergeant," said Mitty, with his faint, fleeting smile. "Or do we?" He poured another brandy and tossed it off. "I never see a man could hold his brandy like you, sir," said the sergeant. "Begging your pardon, sir." Captain Mitty stood up and strapped on his huge Webley-Vickers automatic. "It's forty kilometers through hell, sir," said the sergeant. Mitty finished one last brandy. "After all," he said softly, "what isn't?" The pounding of the cannon increased; there was the rat-tat-tatting of machine guns, and from somewhere came the menacing pocketa-pocketa-pocketa of the new flame-throwers. Walter Mitty walked to the door of the dugout humming "Auprès de Ma Blonde."[7] He turned and waved to the sergeant. "Cheerio!" he said. . . .

Something struck his shoulder. "I've been looking all over this hotel for you," said Mrs. Mitty. "Why do you have to hide in this old chair? How did you expect me to find you?" "Things close in," said

---

[4]**has got the wind up in young Raleigh:** Has made young Raleigh nervous.
[5]**Archies:** a slang term for anti-aircraft guns
[6]**Von Richtman's circus:** a German airplane squadron
[7]**"Auprès de Ma Blonde"** (Oh preh duh mah BLON duh): "Next to My Blonde,"
  a popular French song.

Walter Mitty vaguely. "What?" Mrs. Mitty said. "Did you get the what's-its-name? The puppy biscuit? What's in that box?" "Overshoes," said Mitty. "Couldn't you have put them on in the store?" "I was thinking," said Walter Mitty. "Does it ever occur to you that I am sometimes thinking?" She looked at him. "I'm going to take your temperature when I get you home," she said.

They went out through the revolving doors that made a faintly derisive whistling sound when you pushed them. It was two blocks to the parking lot. At the drugstore on the corner she said,

"Wait here for me. I forgot something, I won't be a minute." She was more than a minute. Walter Mitty lighted a cigarette. It began to rain, rain with sleet in it. He stood up against the wall of the drugstore, smoking. . . . He put his shoulders back and his heels together. "To hell with the handkerchief," said Walter Mitty scornfully. He took one last drag on his cigarette and snapped it away. Then, with that faint, fleeting smile playing about his lips, he faced the firing squad; erect and motionless, proud and disdainful, Walter Mitty the Undefeated, inscrutable to the last.

The Secret Life of Walter Mitty ■ 449

Reading Focus:
Identify Cause and Effect
Ask: What attitude does Mrs. Mitty seem to have toward her husband? Why might her comments to him on this page have triggered Mitty's fantasy about facing a firing squad? How does the image of "Walter Mitty the Undefeated" contrast with Mitty's real-life behavior toward his wife?

Literary Focus:
Repetition
Ask: How does Thurber use repetition in the story to make his point about Mitty more clear to the reader? What is his point?

Mini Quiz

Write on the chalkboard or overhead projector the following questions and call on students to fill in the blanks. Discuss the answers with the class.

1. In his first daydream Mitty is a _____ .

2. He is brought out of it when _____ speaks to him.

3. When Mitty drives past a hospital, he dreams that he is a _____ .

4. A newsboy shouting about a trial leads Mitty to dream about being _____ .

5. At the end of the story, Mitty daydreams that he is _____ .

Answers
1. hydroplane commander
2. his wife
3. world-famous surgeon
4. a defendant in a murder trial
5. facing a firing squad

UNDERSTAND THE SELECTION

Answers

1. His secret life is daydreaming. He lives this life in his head.
2. a hydroplane commander, a famous surgeon, a defendant in a murder trial, a World War II flying ace, and a man facing a firing squad
3. They are cool, competent, and courageous.
4. dull and humdrum
5. bossy; she tells him what to do.
6. like a child (when she reminds him to put on his gloves); like someone who is mentally ill (she wants the doctor to look him over)
7. not very respectfully; like someone who is bumbling or not very smart
8. They are highly skilled and respected; they are fearless; they stand apart from the crowd.
9. No. He cannot stand up to his wife very well. If he were willing to take real risks, he would not need so much fantasy.
10. Sample answer: Mitty's life is so pitiful that a heroic death is the only escape.

Respond to Literature

Have students compare and contrast this story with "Amigo Brothers." Guide students to recognize that Tony and Felix dream about becoming heroes as boxing champions, but, unlike Mitty, they work toward their goal. Also, their dream is realistic in that they both seem to possess the talent and potential for becoming champion boxers. Continue the discussion by pointing out that when used constructively, fantasies and daydreams actually can help a person achieve a goal, but for Mitty, fantasy is an escape from the challenges of life.

WRITE ABOUT THE SELECTION

Prewriting

Have students meet in small groups to brainstorm about fantasy ideas. Ask one member of each group to

---

Review the Selection

UNDERSTAND THE SELECTION

Recall

1. What is Walter Mitty's secret life? Where does he live it?

2. What characters does Mitty imagine himself as?

3. How do these characters behave under pressure?

Infer

4. What is Walter Mitty's life really like?

5. What kind of a person is Mrs. Mitty? How do you know?

6. How does she treat her husband? Give some examples.

7. How do other people treat Walter Mitty?

Apply

8. What do all of Mitty's imagined characters have in common?

9. Do you think that Mitty is a risk-taker? Explain your answer.

10. Why do you think the author ends the story with Mitty facing a firing squad? Is it an appropriate way to end the story?

Respond to Literature

Walter Mitty is certainly not a heroic figure. Why does "The Secret Life of Walter Mitty" appear in a unit about heroes?

WRITE ABOUT THE SELECTION

Do you have a secret life the way Walter Mitty does? Do you sometimes think of yourself as a hero? Your assignment is to write a fantasy episode about yourself in the style of Walter Mitty.

Prewriting Take a few minutes to brainstorm about some of your favorite fantasies. What kind of person do you dream about being? Do you see yourself as a famous athlete or movie star? Do you picture yourself as President of the United States? Do you see yourself as the most popular person in school? Perhaps you see yourself doing something brave, like rescuing a baby from a burning building. Decide which of your fantasies fits you best. Then brainstorm the details you want to include in your fantasy.

Writing Use your prewriting outline to create a fantasy in the style of Walter Mitty. Begin your paragraph with the incident that touches off the fantasy. Then end your paragraph with the incident that brings you back to reality; invent a character like Mrs. Mitty if you need to.

Revising Walter Mitty's fantasies are written in the third person with a fair amount of dialogue. They read like miniature short stories. Revise your paragraph so that your fantasy fits this same style.

Proofreading Be sure that your reader knows when you shift from reality to fantasy and back again by clearly marking new paragraphs.

---

jot down notes of the fantasies that are discussed.

Writing

As students work on this section independently, write on the chalkboard these phrases:

1. reality into fantasy
2. the fantasy
3. back to reality

Have students refer to the phrases as a reminder that their paragraphs should include the real incident that triggers the fantasy, the fantasy itself, and a real incident that ends the fantasy.

Revising

Have students meet in the same groups as in the prewriting activity. Ask the members of each group to

evaluate one another's papers and suggest ways that dialogue can be added or improved to enhance the fantasy. You may want to reinforce the idea that in any creative literary effort, the writer has the ultimate say-so and may reject suggestions that do not improve the quality of the work under discussion.

THINK ABOUT STORY TECHNIQUES

Authors use special techniques to make fiction come alive. **Flashbacks** tell about episodes that happened before the story takes place. **Narration** moves the story forward in chronological order. **Description** adds details that appeal to your senses. **Dialogue**, conversation between characters, gives you, the reader information about characters, setting, and plot. **Repetition** emphasizes ideas and important points. James Thurber uses some of these special techniques in "The Secret Life of Walter Mitty. "

1. What special techniques does Thurber use in this story?

2. How do these techniques enhance the story?

3. What type of dialogue is used in the story?

4. How does this technique make the story more enjoyable?

5. How do these special techniques enable the author to develop the character of Walter Mitty?

READING FOCUS

Identify Cause and Effect As you read this story, you found the cause that brought about each event. Describe one example of cause and effect in "The Secret Life of Walter Mitty."

DEVELOP YOUR VOCABULARY

A **figurative expression** is a group of words with a meaning that goes beyond its literal meaning. Figurative expressions are part of everyday speech as well as literature. You probably hear or use several figurative expressions every day. An example is "falling head over heels in love." Of course this expression does not mean that the person really does a somersault; it means the person is deeply and uncontrollably in love.

Identify the figurative expression in each sentence from the story. Then write the meaning of each expression.

1. "Pick it up, brother!" snapped a cop as the light changed.

2. An excited buzz ran through the courtroom.

3. War thundered and whined around the dugout.

Review the Selection ■ 451

THINK ABOUT STORY TECHNIQUES

Answers
1. Every so often, he has the main character lapse into a daydream.
2. It illustrates how Mitty constantly is moving between fantasy and reality.
3. Each daydream contains dialogue as if it were a little short story. Also, dialogue is usually what brings Mitty back to reality at the end of a daydream.
4. The daydreams themselves come alive and seem very real; then Mitty is brought back to reality with a jolt.
5. They give the reader an accurate picture of Mitty's thought patterns and somewhat predictable behavior.

DEVELOP YOUR VOCABULARY

Answers
1. pick it up; hurry, move faster
2. excited buzz; people talking excitedly created a buzzing sound
3. war thundered and whined; the sounds of battle outside could be heard in the dugout

READING FOCUS

Sample Answer
The pictures of bombing planes in a magazine prompt Walter Mitty to imagine himself as a World War II flying ace.

ESL Activity

Encourage students to read Thurber's story aloud in a small group, taking turns every page or every few paragraphs. Have them comment on remarks or passages that strike them as humorous.

SELECTION OVERVIEW

SELECTION OBJECTIVES

After completing this selection, students will be able to

- understand persuasive speech
- assess heroic qualities
- write a speech intended to persuade
- identify with the speaker's ideals
- analyze techniques of persuasive speech
- use words with multiple meanings
- identify main idea and supporting details

Lesson Resources

from *I Have a Dream*
- Selection Synopsis, Teacher's Edition, p. T403c
- Comprehension and Vocabulary Workbook, pp. 87–88
- Language Enrichment Workbook, pp. 93–94
- Teacher's Resources Reinforcement, p. R42 Test, pp. T83–T84

More About Persuasive Speech

Although persuasive speech must be backed up with examples, reasons, and facts, it should also appeal to the emotions. A good persuasive speaker makes people want to do or believe in what he or she is proposing. Sometimes a speaker does this by appealing to certain ideals, such as patriotism or brotherhood. Sometimes a speaker appeals to a need or desire of the listener. (Advertisers do this all the time.) A speaker may also be persuasive simply because his or her own enthusiasm and conviction are contagious.

Learn About

PERSUASIVE SPEECH

When was the last time that somebody talked you into something? Did that person take a stand on an issue and defend it in a logical way? Did the individual urge you to take action? If so, that person was using **persuasive speech**. The purpose of persuasive speech is to convince the listener to believe in a certain idea or take a certain action. Strong evidence—examples, reasons, and facts—is an important part of a persuasive speech. A good persuader doesn't offend by name calling but is calm, objective, and reasonable.

Writers use certain words and techniques when they want to be persuasive. Look for repetition, parallel structure, and quotes. As you read "I Have a Dream," ask yourself these questions:

1. What techniques does Martin Luther King, Jr., use to persuade his audience to believe in his ideas?
2. How does the first line of his speech capture the listeners' attention and make them want to hear more?

WRITING CONNECTION

Suppose that you are running for an elected office, either in your school or in your community. Write a short speech in which you persuade people to vote for you.

READING FOCUS

Identify Main Idea and Supporting Details A piece of writing contains a main idea, which is the central point the author wishes to make. The main idea is developed by related sentences referred to as supporting details. The main idea may be expressed directly or may have to be inferred. As you read, try to locate the main idea of this selection and the details that support the main idea.

452 ■ Unit 5

More About the Unit Theme

Dr. Martin Luther King, Jr., is a real 20th century hero. He gave his life for what he believed, and brought about significant change. The extent of King's influence on American civil liberties is illustrated by the fact that his birthday is now celebrated as a national holiday.

Background Notes

This speech was given by Dr. Martin Luther King, Jr., on a hot August afternoon in 1963. The speech was a part of the march for equal justice for all citizens to the steps of the Lincoln Memorial in Washington, DC. About 200,000 marchers heard Dr. King deliver what has become one of the best-known speeches of the last half-century.

Cooperative Group Activity

For the Writing Connection activity, divide students into groups of five. Assign each student the task of convincing the group to do something. Then ask the groups to rate each presentation on the basis of how convincing it was. The winners could then repeat their speeches for the entire class.

from

I HAVE A DREAM

by Martin Luther King, Jr.

I say to you today, my friends, that in spite of the difficulties and frustrations of the moment, I still have a dream. It is a dream deeply rooted in the American dream.

I have a dream that one day this nation will rise up and live out the true meaning of its creed:

---

frustrations (frus TRAY shuns) unhappy feelings that come from not being able to reach one's goals
creed (KREED) formal statement of belief

from I Have a Dream ■ 453

Develop Vocabulary Skills

Write on the chalkboard the vocabulary words footnoted in the story. Use each word in an original sentence, then ask student volunteers to do the same, orally.

ESL Activity

Play a recording of King's speech, or a portion of it. As students listen, have them jot down statements or ideas that were difficult to understand. Allow students to listen to these passages again and work through the challenging concepts and vocabulary with a student who is proficient in English.

Reading Focus:
Identify Main Idea and Supporting Details

Make sure students see that one of the main ideas in King's speech is that African Americans did not enjoy equality with whites at the time of the speech. Have them identify details in the speech that support this implied main idea.

Background Notes

Dr. King's main concern was equality for African Americans. He also refers in this speech to unity among Protestants and Catholics, Jews and Gentiles. The president of the college that Martin Luther King, Jr., attended once said that King had become a symbol of hope for oppressed people everywhere.

"We hold these truths to be self-evident: that all men are created equal." . . .

I have a dream today. . . .

This is our hope. . . . With this faith we will be able to work together, pray together, struggle together, go to jail together, stand up for freedom together, knowing that we will be free one day.

This will be the day when all of God's children will be able to sing with a new meaning "My country, 'tis of thee, sweet land of liberty, of thee I sing. Land where my fathers died, land of the pilgrims' pride, from every mountainside, let freedom ring." And if America is to be a great nation this must become true. So let freedom ring from the prodigious hilltops of New Hampshire. Let freedom ring from the mighty mountains of New York. . . .

But not only that; let freedom ring from Stone Mountain of Georgia.

Let freedom ring from Lookout Mountain of Tennessee! . . . From every mountainside, let freedom ring.

When we let freedom ring, when we let it ring from every village and every hamlet, from every state and every city, we will be able to speed up that day when all of God's children, black men and white men, Jews and Gentiles, Protestants and Catholics, will be able to join hands and sing in the words of the old Negro spiritual, "Free at last! Free at last! Thank God almighty, we are free at last!"

---

self-evident (SELF EV ih dunt) needing no proof; obviously true
prodigious (pruh DIJ us) great; huge
hamlet (HAM lit) very small village
Gentiles (JEN tylz) originally, people who are not Jewish

Mini Quiz

Write on the chalkboard or overhead projector the following sentences and call on students to fill in the blanks. Discuss the answers with the class.

1. The theme of Dr. King's speech is _____.

2. Dr. King says that he dreams of the day when _____.

3. Dr. King indicates that at the present time [of his speech] there are many _____ and _____.

4. King refers to New Hampshire, New York, Georgia, and Tennessee as places where _____.

5. King quotes the African American spiritual, _____.

Answers

1. equality, especially racial equality
2. all people will be treated as equal
3. difficulties; frustrations
4. freedom should ring
5. "Free at Last"

Martin Luther King, Jr. (1929–1968)

"You are living a faith that most men preach about but never experience. . . . Your name has become a symbol of courage and hope for oppressed people everywhere." These were the words that the President of Morehouse College used to describe one of the school's most famous students, Dr. Martin Luther King, Jr.

Born in Atlanta, Georgia, as Michael Luther King, Dr. King adopted the name of the great Protestant reformer Martin Luther. After attending the local high school, King received his B.A. degree from Morehouse College, then trained for the ministry at Crozer Theological Seminary. Later he earned a Ph.D. from Boston University.

Martin Luther King's public career began in 1955, when a small group of civil-rights advocates in Montgomery, Alabama, protested racial segregation on the city's bus system. An African American woman named Rosa Parks refused to give up her seat on a bus to a white male and was quickly arrested. In response to the incident, local African Americans founded the Montgomery Improvement Association (MIA) and chose Martin Luther King, Jr., as their leader.

King went on to head the Southern Christian Leadership Conference (SCLC), which fought against racism in both the North and South. As he continued the fight against racial injustice, Dr. King went to jail more than 30 times, was attacked at his home with bombs and shotguns, and was slugged, stabbed, and stoned. Although King was a continual victim of violence, he refused to use or advocate violence himself.

Martin Luther King, Jr., died when he was only 39 years old. He was killed by an assassin's bullet one evening in Memphis, Tennessee. He had gone to Memphis to support a strike by the city's sanitation workers.

Author Biography ■ 455

MORE ABOUT THE AUTHOR

The eloquent writing and speaking style of Martin Luther King, Jr., was influenced by the tradition of the Southern African American ministry. Both his father and maternal grandfather were ministers. When King entered Morehouse College in Atlanta, Georgia, he was at first interested in a career in law or medicine. By his senior year, however, he had decided to become a minister.

King was a pastor at a Baptist church in Montgomery, Alabama, when he was asked to lead the bus boycott launched by Rosa Parks. Trained in the nonviolent philosophy of Gandhi, King justified the civil-rights protest this way:

> "For many years we have shown an amazing patience. . . . But we have come here tonight to be saved from that patience that makes us patient with anything less than freedom and justice."

Additional Works
BY MARTIN LUTHER KING, JR.

You may wish to suggest these works by Martin Luther King, Jr., for additional reading.

Why We Can't Wait. New American Library, 1991. (nonfiction)

A Testament of Hope: The Essential Writings and Speeches of Martin Luther King, Jr. Harper, 1991. (an anthology)

The Autobiography of Martin Luther King, Jr. Warner, 1998. (nonfiction)

UNDERSTAND THE SELECTION

Answers

1. equality and freedom for all people
2. that someday in the United States all people will be treated as equals
3. participants in a freedom march at the nation's capital
4. There have been setbacks and difficulties.
5. The idea of equality goes as far back as the founding of America.
6. African Americans must be treated as equals to whites.
7. He names different states as examples of where this dream must come true.
8. belief in the American dream and in human brotherhood
9. Sample answer: They might become more involved in fighting or voting for laws to bring about equal rights.
10. Sample answer: Yes. At the end of the speech he says, "we will be able to speed up that day when all of God's children . . . will be able to join hands and sing . . . we are free at last!"

Respond to Literature

Have students discuss how Martin Luther King, Jr.'s role as a hero was shaped by the times and circumstances in which he lived. Remind students of the Carlyle quotation that opened this unit. Also, discuss with students the idea that King had certain personal qualitites that might make him a hero in any time and place.

WRITE ABOUT THE SELECTION

Prewriting

You can help students think of ideas for their paragraphs by displaying newspaper and magazine articles that deal with current problems in the United States.

UNDERSTAND THE SELECTION

Recall

1. What is the subject of King's speech?
2. What is King's dream?
3. To what audience is King speaking?

Infer

4. What can you infer about the circumstances surrounding the cause that King believes in?
5. What is the meaning of the phrase "a dream deeply rooted in the American dream"?
6. What does King imply must happen if America is to be a great nation?
7. How does King make it clear that his dream is not just for one geographic location?

Apply

8. To what feelings of his listeners was King appealing?
9. Predict what type of action people might take after hearing this speech.
10. Would you say King expects his dream to come true? Explain your answer.

Respond to Literature

In what way was King a hero to the people who heard this speech?

WRITE ABOUT THE SELECTION

Martin Luther King, Jr., expressed his hope for the United States in his famous "I Have a Dream" speech. Suppose that you were asked to give a speech with the same title. Do you have a dream for the United States? Is it similar to or very different from Dr. King's dream? Write a paragraph beginning with the words, "I have a dream. . . ." Let your paragraph reflect something that you would like to see happen in the United States.

Prewriting   Take a few minutes to brainstorm about some of the causes about which you feel strongly. Perhaps you dream of the day when illegal drugs are no longer a problem. Perhaps you dream of crime-free cities. Maybe you dream of a day when no one in America is homeless. Make a list of your ideas. Then choose the one that you feel is most important to you.

Writing   Use your prewriting idea to compose a paragraph about your dream for America. Remember that your goal is to persuade your readers to agree with you and to fight for the cause you believe in.

Revising   Read your paragraph aloud as if you were giving a speech. Rewrite any parts of your paragraph that sound awkward or wordy. Then reread the paragraph aloud.

Proofreading   Be on the alert to insert a word or words that have been omitted, or delete a word that is written twice. You want your final speech to be letter perfect for ease of delivery.

Writing

As students work on this section independently, help them make their arguments more convincing by challenging some of their ideas. This approach also can help point out areas where students might need to add facts or concrete examples.

Revising

Have students read their paragraphs aloud in small groups. Group members can rate one another's speeches according to content and overall effectiveness.

Proofreading

Have students trade papers with a partner to proofread.

T456

THINK ABOUT PERSUASIVE SPEECH

A persuasive writer knows how to capture the reader's attention and appeal to the reader's feelings. Effective persuasive writing includes examples, reasons, and facts as evidence to convince the reader to accept an opinion or to take action. A persuasive writer also knows how to use techniques such as repetition and quotations to enhance his or her persuasive piece.

1. How does the first line of King's speech capture your attention and make you want to read more?

2. What words or phrases does King repeat throughout his speech?

3. What quotations does King use?

4. Why are these quotations effective?

5. How persuasive is King's speech? Explain why you think so.

READING FOCUS

Identify Main Idea and Supporting Details As you read "I Have a Dream," you were able to identify the main idea of the speech and the supporting details. How would you summarize the main idea of the selection? What is one detail that supports this main idea?

DEVELOP YOUR VOCABULARY

Many English words have more than one meaning. For example, the word *meet* can mean "to meet someone" or it can mean "a contest, such as a track meet." You can tell which meaning of a word is being used by noting the meaning of the entire sentence in which the word appears.

Write the correct meaning of each italicized word. Then write an original sentence in which you use another meaning of the same word. Use the dictionary if you need help.

1. We let the bell *ring* for five minutes.

2. John is from the *state* of Alabama.

3. He allowed the bird to go *free*.

4. It is my *dream* to become a professional baseball player.

5. Juan is the *head* of his family since his father died.

Review the Selection ■ 457

ESL Activity

Work with students to develop a list of causes they feel are important enough to take a stand on. Ask: What would you be willing to do to advance these causes? Would you give money, make speeches, write letters to decision makers, protest in public? Which techniques do they feel are most effective and why? Have pairs of students choose a cause from the list. Ask the partners to work together to write a short persuasive paragraph soliciting support for their cause.

T457

SELECTION OVERVIEW

SELECTION OBJECTIVES

After completing these selections, students will be able to

- understand the form of a poem
- identify and write open and closed verse
- discuss an aspect of heroism
- relate poems to personal experience
- use homophones
- recognize similarities in poetry

Lesson Resources

Warrior Song I, Warrior Song II, Song of Failure, War Song
- Selection Synopses, Teacher's Edition, p. T403c
- Comprehension Workbook, pp. 89–90
- Language Enrichment Workbook, p. 95
- Teacher's Resources Reinforcement, p. R43 Test, pp. T85–T86

More About Form

The most obvious clue to the form of a poem is its rhythm. If a rhythmic pattern can be recognized in a poem, then the poem has a closed form. If there is an obviously irregular rhythm, then the form is open.

Background Notes

The Omaha are North American Plains Indians who speak a Siouan language. The name Omaha means "upstream people." A small number still live on reservations in Nebraska. About half of the Teton, or Lakota, Sioux live on reservations in the northern plains. The other half live throughout the United States in urban areas.

Return to Minute Man, National Park Service

READING FOCUS

Recognize Similarities in Poetry Making comparisons between poems is one way to increase your enjoyment and understanding of poetry. Poems can be similar in their outward form, such as length and use of rhyme. They can also be similar in tone, point of view, or theme. As you read the four poems here, look for similarities between two or more of the poems.

OPEN AND CLOSED FORM

The **form** of a poem is the outward arrangement of the poem, as opposed to the content or subject matter. Form includes such things as rhythm, rhyme, and arrangement of stanzas. In other words, form is how a poem looks as well as the techniques the poet uses to write.

The form of a poem can be closed or open. **Closed form** refers to poetry that has a recognizable pattern. Probably when you think of poetry, you think of a poem written in closed form. Most major types of poetry are closed, including sonnets, ballads, blank verse, and couplets. **Open form** poetry has no recognizable pattern. An example of open form is free verse, which is poetry written with an obviously irregular rhythm.

As you read the four Native American poems, ask yourself these questions:
1. Which poems have a closed form? What patterns are present?
2. Which poems have an open form?

WRITING CONNECTION

Write a simple four-line poem about a subject that interests you. First, write the poem in a regular rhythm and pattern of rhyme. Then try writing about the same subject using four lines of free verse.

ESL Activity

To help students understand the difference between closed and open forms of poetry, have them turn to the two poems on page 31 of the text. Point out some of the structural differences between the poems. Coastworth's poem has a rhyme scheme, two four-line parts (although they are not separated into stanzas), and lines of similar length. Point out that these regularities make it an example of closed form. Contrast this to the irregular rhythm of Clemmons's poem, which reads almost like everyday speech.

Cooperative Group Activity

To help students complete the Writing Connection activity, choose a subject that evokes strong emotions such as success or failure. Pair students and have them write a single poem about this strong feeling. The poem can be open or closed; the students should be able to explain what the form is and why.

Young Omaha, War Eagle, Little Missouri, and *Pawnees,* Charles Bird King.
The Granger Collection

Warrior Song I

by the Omaha

No one has found a way to avoid death,
To pass around it;
Those old men who have met it,
Who have reached the place where death stands waiting,
Have not pointed out a way to circumvent it.
Death is difficult to face.

Warrior Song II

by the Omaha

I shall vanish and be no more,
But the land over which I now roam
Shall remain
And change not.

Warrior Song I/Warrior Song II ■ 459

Develop Vocabulary Skills

The words used in these poems will probably be familiar to most students. You might ask students to look over the poems before reading them and have them ask about any words that they do not understand.

Viewing Fine Art

Charles Bird King (1785–1862) was an American artist who specialized in portraits of Native Americans. King made many of the paintings in the National Indian Portrait Gallery in Washington. King's Native American portraits emphasize decorative warpaint, feathers, and costume details. Since King never saw the subjects in their own surroundings, his portraits are somewhat less revealing than those of explorer-artists who traveled to Native American territory or lived among them. Ask: What might the two objects in the foreground represent?

INTRODUCE

Motivation
Ask students to name the bravest person they know. Have them explain why they feel as they do. Then ask: Do you think this person is ever afraid? Do you think this person ever worries about failing? Do you think this person ever thinks about dying? Suggest that the students look for ways these Native American poems deal with the issues of fear, failure, and death.

Purpose-Setting Question
Is it a victory to have tried and failed, rather than never to have tried at all? Explain.

READ

Literary Focus:
Open Form Poetry
Ask students how they decide whether a poem's form is open or closed. They should understand that the most obvious clue is a poem's rhythm. If a rhythmic pattern cannot be recognized, and there is an obvious irregular rhythm, the form is open. Tell students to decide how effective the open form is in the Native American poems as they read them.

Reading Focus:
Recognize Similarities in Poetry
Remind students that similarities exist in poetry in a number of ways. These similarities include form, subject matter, point of view, and theme. Ask students to identify at least two similarities among the four poems and to provide details from the poems as support.

CLOSE

Have students complete Review the Selection on pages 462–463.

Buffalo Hunter, Unknown American. Gift of Harriett Cowles Hammett Grahm in Memory of Buell Hammett

Viewing Fine Art

The life of the different Native American groups was a subject of great fascination to European Americans. Some artists made imaginary pictures, while others traveled with explorers or government expeditions, and a few actually joined Native American encampments. The anonymous artist of this graceful painting probably used a good deal of imagination, but the deep colors, rhythmic composition, and spectacular lighting make it a dramatic and successful picture. Notice, for example, the contrasting straight lines (horse's legs and shadows) and curving lines (bow, horse's flank, cloud lines), which both contrast with the strong horizontals of the background. Ask: Do you think the scene shown is realistic. Why or why not?

Song of Failure

by the Teton Sioux

A wolf
I considered myself,
But the owls are hooting
And the night
I fear.

War Song

by the Teton Sioux

Soldiers,
You fled.
Even the eagle dies.

Literary Focus:
Open Form Poetry
Ask: How can you tell that both poems are open in form?

Reading Focus:
Recognize Similarities in Poetry
Have two volunteers read the poems on this page aloud. Ask: In addition to form, do you notice any other similarities between the two poems?

Critical Thinking:
Infer
Ask: What is the poet of "War Song" saying about the soldiers by saying that "even the eagle dies"?

Comparing Selections
Ask students if they think that the land is unchanging, as described in "Warrior Song II." Guide them to understand that compared to the life of a person the land is more permanent, yet even land can change in response to natural forces or human activities. Then have students compare the themes of the first two poems with the themes of the last two poems and discuss. Guide students to understand that the most important theme that these poems share is the fleeting nature of human existence.

Mini Quiz

Write on the chalkboard or overhead projector the following sentences and call on students to fill in the blanks. Discuss the answers with the class.

1. "Warrior Song I" talks about meeting _____.

2. "Warrior Song II" compares the life of a man to _____.

3. According to "War Song," the soldiers _____ from battle.

4. The speaker in "Song of Failure" compares himself to a _____.

5. He says that he is afraid of _____.

Answers
1. death
2. the land
3. ran away
4. wolf
5. night

UNDERSTAND THE SELECTION

Answers

1. fear
2. defeat in battle
3. death
4. Soldiers have retreated.
5. as fearless as a wolf
6. he finds that he can feel fear
7. Death comes to all and cannot be avoided.
8. He points out that even the bravest bird, the eagle, must die some time.
9. "Warrior Song II," because the poet speaks of his own death in the first person
10. Answers will vary depending on students' views and experiences with death.

Respond to Literature

Have students compare the four poems to the story of Walter Mitty that they read earlier in this unit. Help them to see that both the story and poems deal with failure but that the messages are very different. Mitty is a pathetic character because he never attempts anything. He dreams of being a hero but in reality is not a hero. The poems, on the other hand, describe men who did try to do something herioic. They may have encountered fear, death, failure, but, unlike Mitty, they did make an honest attempt.

WRITE ABOUT THE SELECTION

Prewriting

Have students get together in small groups to discuss their prewriting ideas on failure, fear, and defeat. Have one member of each group report back to the class with a summary of the group's discussion.

Writing

As students work on this section individually, circulate to help those who are having trouble. Help students to recall the details of their experiences, or feelings, by asking them to describe the setting, the time of year, how old they were. Ask students which poem they have chosen, and why.

UNDERSTAND THE SELECTION

Recall

1. What is the subject of "Song of Failure"?

2. What is the subject of "War Song"?

3. What is the subject of "Warrior Song I" and "Warrior Song II"?

Infer

4. What has happened on the battlefield in "War Song"?

5. How did the speaker in "Song of Failure" see himself at first?

6. How did his view of himself change?

7. What universal truth is expressed in "Warrior Song I"?

Apply

8. How does the speaker in "War Song" make defeat seem less painful?

9. Does "Warrior Song I" or "Warrior Song II" give a more personal view of the subject matter? Why?

10. Explain which poem expresses your own thoughts most closely.

Respond to Literature

What aspects of heroism are described in these four poems?

WRITE ABOUT THE SELECTION

The four Native American poems deal with four aspects of human experience—fear, failure, defeat, and death. In one way or another, these experiences are common to everyone. You have probably experienced some if not all of them at some time in your life. Which of the poems is most meaningful to you? Choose one of the poems, and write about how it relates to a feeling or experience that you have had.

Prewriting Take a few minutes to think about times when you have failed, have been afraid, or have been defeated in some way. Also, think about times when you have thought about death or perhaps have been touched by the death of someone you know. Then read the poems over several times, and make notes of the experiences that come to mind as you read each one.

Writing Choose the poem that most strongly appeals to you. Use your prewriting notes to write a paragraph in which you relate the poem to an experience or feeling that you have had. Be sure you connect your experience to the poem. You might compare and/or contrast your feelings with those of the Native American poets.

Revising If you are recounting an incident in the past tense, make sure that you use correct verb forms. Change any verb forms that are incorrect.

Proofreading See that there are no errors in spelling, usage, or mechanics.

Revising

Review some common verb forms with students. Encourage students to ask about any verb forms they are not sure of as they revise.

Proofreading

Put on an overhead projector several students' papers. Proofread the papers as a class exercise.

ESL Activity

Have the students choose one of the themes of the four poems—fear, defeat, or death—and create a collage to illustrate the theme.

T462

THINK ABOUT FORM

A poem with closed form has a recognizable rhythm, rhyme and stanza pattern; an open form poem does not. If you are uncertain about the form of a poem, it may help to read the poem out loud. If there is a regular pattern of rhythm or rhyme, you should be able to hear it. If you still have trouble, try beating or clapping the long and short sounds of each line as you say it.

1. Would you describe the form of the four Native American poems as open or closed?

2. What features of these poems is your conclusion based on?

3. Do any of the poems have lines that rhyme?

4. How does the form of "War Song" enhance the meaning of the poem?

5. Describe the form of "Warrior Song I."

READING FOCUS

Recognize Similarities in Poetry Choose two of the poems you just read. Explain how they are similar in form, tone, point of view, and theme.

DEVELOP YOUR VOCABULARY

Homophones are words that sound alike but have different spellings and different meanings. For example, *weak* and *week* are homophones.

Choose the correct homophone to complete each sentence. Then use the other homophone in an original sentence.

1. You are (*so*, *sew*) lucky to have an older brother.

2. I don't know (*weather*, *whether*) I should go to the store or not.

3. A vegetarian is someone who does not eat (*meet*, *meat*).

4. I'd like a piece of apple pie, (*to*, *too*).

5. Do you (*need*, *knead*) a job?

THINK ABOUT FORM

Answers
1. All have an open form.
2. They do not have a regular rhythm or pattern of rhyme.
3. no, although the first poem has three lines that end with "it"
4. The very terse form of the first two lines makes the flight of the soldiers more dramatic.
5. free verse

DEVELOP YOUR VOCABULARY

Sample Answers
1. so—I will *sew* the button on the shirt.
2. whether—The *weather* is pleasant today.
3. meat—I will *meet* you at three o'clock.
4. too—I will go *to* the store.
5. need—*Knead* the bread a little harder.

READING FOCUS

Sample Answer
Two similar poems are "Warrior Song II" and "Song of Failure." Both are written in open form and focus on the insignificance of the individual. They are both written in first-person point of view and emphasize the superiority of nature over mankind.

SELECTION OBJECTIVES

After completing these selections, students will be able to

- understand epic poetry
- create an epic incident
- discuss the qualities of an epic hero
- create a monster story
- analyze an epic poem
- use nouns and verbs
- understand character relationships

Lesson Resources

Ulysses and the Trojan Horse
Ulysses Meets the Cyclops
- Selection Synopses, Teacher's Edition, pp. T403c–403d
- Comprehension and Vocabulary Workbook, pp. 91–94
- Language Enrichment Workbook, pp. 96–99
- Teacher's Resources
  Reinforcement, pp. R44–R45
  Tests, pp. T87–T88

More About Epic Poetry

An epic is an adventure story that centers around one main character. This character is the hero of the story, and will show qualities such as strength, daring, cleverness, courage, and wisdom. The adventures in an epic are presented as a series of episodes. Early epics, such as the *Odyssey*, came from an oral tradition and are known as folk epics. Later epics that were written down by a single author, such as Dante's *Divine Comedy*, are known as classical or art epics.

More About the Unit Theme

The stories in this selection center around the larger-than-life mythological hero, Ulysses. The quality that sets Ulysses apart from his followers is not physical strength or

Learn About

EPIC POETRY

An **epic** is a long narrative poem that tells about the adventures of heroes and gods. The style of an epic is usually formal and dramatic. Ancient epics were often orally passed down from one generation to the next. The central character of an epic is called an **epic hero**. This hero may be a character from history or from legend. The epic hero is often a great, larger-than-life figure.

The basis for the two selections you are about to read is the *Odyssey*, the great epic by Greek poet Homer. In the *Odyssey*, the epic hero is named Odysseus. However, in many versions of the epic adventures, he is often referred to as Ulysses.

As you read "Ulysses and the Trojan Horse" and "Ulysses Meets the Cyclops," ask yourself these questions:

1. How do the selections fit the definition of an epic?
2. What qualities does Ulysses have that make him an epic hero?

WRITING CONNECTION

Think of a recent event in your life or in the news. Write a brief account of the event as if it were an epic adventure. Be sure to include an epic hero.

READING FOCUS

Understand Character Relationships
The relationships between characters are an important part of a story. To understand the relationship between any two characters, examine their actions as well as what they say to and about each other. Pay attention to how the relationships between the characters affect the plot.

courage in battle (although he possesses these things), but cleverness of mind. Ulysses also demonstrates great tenderness in his love for his wife and son and his tremendous sorrow over the loss of some of his men to the monster Cyclops.

About the Author

Nothing certain is known about Homer's life and personality. One of the characteristics of his poetry is that he never mentions his name or gives any biographical information about himself. Scholars generally agree that he lived in the 8th or 7th century B.C. in Ionia along the coast of Asia Minor.

Cooperative Group Activity

Extend the Writing Connection activity by having students work in groups of four or five. Challenge each group to write a short epic incident in which all group members are involved as characters in the story. Students may enjoy using contemporary or futuristic subject matter—such as a trip on a space shuttle—as the topic of their epic.

ULYSSES
AND THE
TROJAN HORSE

ADAPTED

by Homer

Across the sea from Greece, in what is now Turkey, there was once a fair, rich city, the most famous in the world. This city was called Ilium by its own people. In story and song, it is known as Troy. It stood on a sloping plain some distance back from the shore. Around the city were high, strong walls that no enemy could climb or batter down.

Inside the gates were the homes of the people. There was also a fine stone palace for the king and his sons, and a beautiful temple of Athena. Athena was the goddess who watched over the city. Outside the walls were gardens and farms and woodlands. Far in the distance rose the rocky heights of Mount Ida.

Troy was a very old city. For hundreds of years it had been growing in power and pride. "Ilium will last forever," the Trojans used to say as they looked at its solid walls and noble buildings. They were wrong. Sad changes began to take place, and cruel war cut down the pride of Troy.

The Greek armies came across the sea. They came to conquer the city. The reason was this: one of the princes of Troy, Paris by name, had done a grave wrong to Greece. He had stolen and carried away the most beautiful of all Greek women, Helen, the wife of Menelaus of Sparta. The Greeks cried for revenge. Heroes and warriors from every Greek city and town joined hands against Troy.

Of all the Greek heroes, the wisest and shrewdest was Ulysses, the young king of Ithaca. Yet he did not go willingly to war. No, he would rather have remained at home with his good wife, Penelope, and his son, Telemachus. He was far happier pruning his grapevines and plowing his fields than he could ever be in the turmoil of battle. But the princes of Greece demanded his help. Rather than be thought a coward, he agreed.

Trojan (TROH jun) of Troy; also a person of Troy
shrewdest (SHROOD ist) cleverest, often in a tricky way
turmoil (TUR moil) disorder; unrest

Ulysses and the Trojan Horse ■ 465

Develop Vocabulary Skills

Have students work in small groups. Assign each group several of the vocabulary words footnoted in the selection to look up in the dictionary. Then ask each group to share the definitions with the class.

TEACHING PLAN

INTRODUCE

Motivation

Ask students to think about how they would feel if they had to carry on a battle or struggle for ten years. Would they keep on going or give up? Encourage students to talk about their feelings. Relate the discussion to the long battle between the Greeks and the Trojans, followed by the long journey home of a band of Greek warriors.

Purpose-Setting Question

How might a nation be tricked into thinking a war is over when it is not?

READ

Literary Focus:
Epic Poetry

Point out that a characteristic of the *Odyssey* that later writers copied is beginning the story in the middle of the action. Also point out that although the *Odyssey* is an epic poem, it has been referred to by some experts as literature's first novel because of its exciting narrative and effective use of flashbacks.

Reading Focus:
Understand Character Relationships

Paris and Helen are minor characters in this story about Ulysses. However, their relationship is important in setting the stage for the story. Have students identify Paris and Helen and explain how their actions set in motion the story of "Ulysses and the Trojan Horse." Then ask them to identify the most important character relationship in "Ulysses Meets the Cyclops." Ask: How do you think this relationship will contribute to the rising action of the story?

CLOSE

Have students complete Review the Selection on pages 478–479.

Reading Focus:
Understand Character Relationships

Ask: What can you infer about Ulysses's character by analyzing his relationship with his wife Penelope?

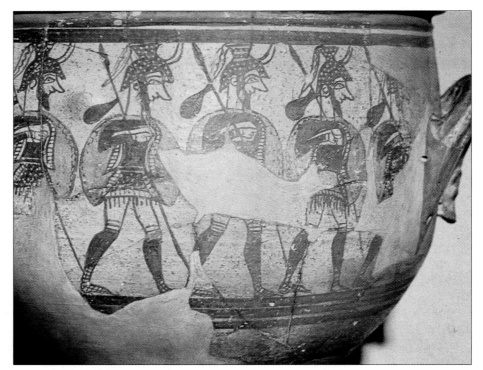

The Warrior Vase from Mycenae, Greece, Scala/Art Resource

"Go, Ulysses," said Penelope. "I'll keep your home and kingdom safe until you return."

And so he sailed away. Forgetting the quiet delights of home, he turned all his thoughts to war.

Ulysses and his Greek warriors came to Troy in a thousand little ships with sails and oars. They landed on the beach at the foot of the plain. They built huts and tents along the shore. They kindled fires.

Around their camp, they threw up a wall of earth and stones. Then they dared the warriors of Troy to come out and meet them in battle.

So the siege began. For more than nine years, the city was surrounded by determined foes. But the walls were strong, and the Trojans were brave. Fierce battles were fought outside the gates. Some were won by the Greeks, some by the Trojans. But neither side could gain a final victory.

---

siege (SEEJ) continued military attack; blockade

466 ■ Unit 5

The Trojans could not drive the invaders from their shores. And the Greeks could not force their way into the city.

"Athena protects us," said the hopeful people of Troy. "While the Palladium is with us, our city can't be taken."

The Palladium was a beautiful statue that stood in the temple of Athena. The Trojans believed that it had a strange power to protect its friends.

"It's useless for us to fight longer," said some of the Greeks. "We can never win while the Palladium is in Troy."

"We've already stayed too long," said others. "Let's abandon this hopeless siege and go home."

But Ulysses wouldn't give up. On a dark and stormy night, he stole into the city. He got past the guards unseen. He crept into the temple of Athena while all the watchers were asleep. There he seized the Palladium and carried it in triumph to the Greek camp.

"Now we'll surely win," said the Greeks.

But still the Trojans persevered. Their gates were well guarded, and the siege went on.

One morning in the early summer, all Troy was awakened at daybreak. The guards on the walls were shouting: "They're gone! The Greeks are gone!"

Soon a hundred eager men, women, and children were standing on the wall. They strained their eyes in the gray light of dawn, trying to make out the hated tents by the beach and the dark ships along the shore.

"They're not there," said a guard. "There's no sign of the Greeks. Thanks to Athena, they've left us at last." Suddenly the guard pointed toward the shore and cried, "Look! There's a strange, dark object among the reeds. It's by the inlet where the boys used to go swimming. What is it?"

Everyone looked. Sure enough, there was something among the reeds. It was smaller than a ship and larger than a man. In the dim light of morning, it looked like a sea monster lately emerged from the waves.

Just then the sun rose above Mount Ida, casting a rosy golden light on sea and shore. It made every object on the beach plainly visible. There was no longer any doubt about the strange thing in the reeds.

"It's a horse!" shouted one and all.

"But not a real horse," said the guard. "It's much too large. It's a huge, ill-made image that the Greeks have left behind—perhaps to frighten us. And now I remember! For several days, there was something unusual going on behind the reeds and bushes there—workmen hurrying back and forth, and much noise of hammering. They were building this thing."

Just then Laocoön, a prince of Troy, joined them. He was an old man, wrinkled and gray—a priest of Apollo, wiser

persevered (pur suh VIRD) kept going by not giving up
reeds (REEDZ) tall grass that grows in a marsh
emerged (ih MURJD) came out
image (IM ij) copy; likeness

Ulysses and the Trojan Horse ■ 467

than most of his fellows. After looking long and carefully at the strange image, he turned to the crowd. "It's a trick," he said. "My children, beware of the cunning Greeks. They've made this image to fool you. I warn you to have nothing to do with it."

About the middle of the morning, Priam, the old king of Troy, issued an order. It was announced in all the streets. "Our enemies have gone," it said. "Peace and safety are ours once again. At noon the gates of the city shall be opened. At that time, our people may return to their peaceful occupations."

Then there was great joy in every corner of the city. It was as though day had dawned after a long and fearful night. How sweet it was to feel free from dread! How good to go about one's business in peace!

The women talked and sang as they began to clean their houses. The shopkeepers brought out their goods and offered fine bargains to the first buyers. The blacksmiths lighted fires in their forges, and began to hammer old spears into peacetime tools. The fishermen mended their nets. The farmers counted their rakes and hoes and plows. Everyone talked about the fine crops they would have on lands that had been idle so long.

But not all the people were so busy. Long before noon, a great crowd had gathered before the gate on the seaward side of town. They were anxious to get out of the long-surrounded city. No sooner was the gate opened than there was a wild rush across the plain toward the shore. Men as well as boys were eager to see whether the Greeks had left anything valuable behind.

They wandered along the beach, looking in every corner of the old camp. But all they found were a few bits of pottery, a broken sword or two, and a few cheap trinkets.

They kept well away from the inlet where the reeds grew. Even the boldest wouldn't go near the huge wooden horse. For Laocoön, the priest, had warned them again to beware of it. So they just stood at a distance and gazed at the strange, unshapely thing. What evil trick, they wondered, were the Greeks plotting?

Suddenly on the other side of the camp a great shouting was heard. Some Trojans who had been hunting in the marshes were seen approaching with a prisoner.

"A Greek! A Greek!" was the shout. Men and boys ran forward to see the captive and join in cursing him. The poor fellow was led by a leather thong twisted around his neck. As he stumbled along over the sand, the crowd jeered. They hit him with sticks and sand and anything they could lay hold of. The blood was trickling down his face. His eyes were

---

cunning (KUN ing) clever in a tricky way; sly
forges (FAWRJ iz) furnaces used to heat metal
idle (YD ul) unused; not busy
thong (THAWNG) strip of leather
jeered (JIRD) made fun of in a nasty way

swollen. But his persecutors, as they saw his wounds, only shouted louder. "A Greek! A Greek! Get rid of him!"

Then all at once the uproar stopped. Silence fell upon the crowd. For standing in his chariot nearby was one of the officers of the king.

"What prisoner is this? Why are you abusing him?" he asked.

"We think he's a Greek," answered the hunters. "We found him in the tall grass by the marshes. He was already wounded and half-blind. So it was easy for us to take him."

"Already wounded!" said the officer.

"That's strange." Then turning to the prisoner, he asked, "How is this? Tell me whether you're a Greek or a friend of Troy. What's your name, and your country?"

"My name," said the prisoner, "is Sinon. By birth I'm a Greek, yet I have no country. Until ten days ago, I called myself a friend of Greece. I fought bravely alongside her heroes. But see these wounds. Can I remain friendly to those who maimed me and would have taken my life, too?"

"Tell us about it," said the officer. "And tell us truly. Have the Greeks

Reading Focus:
Recognize Character Relationships

Have students predict whether Sinon is really friend or foe to the Trojans. Ask: What details in the story led you to your prediction?

Wooden Horse of Troy on 7th century B.C. vase found on Mykonos, Greece, Archaeological Museum, Mykonos, Greece/Erich Lessing/Art Resource

maimed (MAYMD) injured badly; crippled

Ulysses and the Trojan Horse ■ **469**

Viewing Fine Art

The epics of Homer were a major subject of vase art in ancient Greece. The story of the wooden horse of Troy was the theme of many such pictures. Here in an early (7th century B.C.) Greek vase, the horse appears in typical geometric style. Later Greek art turned to more naturalistic and realistic representations. Some critics have suggested that the strong, spare style of this early period of art was similar to Homer's poetic style. Ask: What figures are carved on the vase all around the horse? How does this vase compare to the one pictured on page 466?

Reading Focus:
Understand Character Relationships

Laocoön is an old man, a prince of Troy, and a priest of Apollo. Ask: What does the Trojans' reaction to Laocoön's warnings tell you about his relationship with them? How does it contribute to plot development?

Discussion

What is significant about Laocoön hurling his spear at the Trojan horse?

sailed home for good?" He told the hunters to loosen the thong about the prisoner's neck.

"Yes, I'll tell you," answered Sinon. "And I'll be brief. When Ulysses stole the Palladium from your temple, the Greeks felt sure the city was about to fall. Then day after day passed, and they didn't win a single fight. So they began to despair. A council was held. It was decided to give up the siege and sail for home. But great storms arose on the sea. The south wind never let up. No ship could put to sea."

"But what about the horse?" cried the Trojans. "The horse!"

"The horse," said Sinon, "was built on the advice of the soothsayer, Calchas. He told the Greeks, 'Athena is angry because her statue, the Palladium, was stolen from her temple. That's why the storms rage so fiercely. And they'll go on raging until you make a statue of a horse and leave it on this shore as a sign of your shame and repentance. Never can your ships return to Greece until that is done."

"So the statue was built. The soothsayer said it would carry prosperity and peace wherever it went. But the Greeks didn't want it to be a benefit to Troy. That's why they built it so wide and high that it can't be taken through your gates. They placed it among the reeds by the shore. They hoped the waves might carry it out to sea."

"Ah, so that's their plan, is it?" cried the excited Trojans. "Well, we'll see

about that!" And, forgetting about Sinon, the whole company and the king's officer rushed madly to the great horse.

"Beware, my countrymen, beware!" cried the voice of old Laocoön. He struggled through the crowd. "This is a trick of the Greeks. The horse won't bring you happiness and prosperity, but misery and ruin. Throw it into the sea, or burn it to ashes. But don't receive it into the city."

With these words, he hurled his spear at the huge image. The weapon struck it full in the chest. Those who stood nearest swore that they heard deep, hollow groans and a sound like the rattle of shields coming from the monster's throat.

"To the sea with it! The sea!" cried a few who believed in the old priest.

But most shouted, "To the city with it! The city! We'll outwit the Greeks yet!"

Some ran to the city for ropes and wheels. Others hurried to make a breach in the wall large enough for the monster to pass through. Ropes were tied to its neck and forelegs. Wooden rollers were put under the platform on which it stood.

Men with axes and hoes ran forward to clear a path across the plain. Then the strongest and most willing seized hold of the long ropes and began to pull. Others pushed from behind. Still others prayed to Athena.

So they tugged and sweated, and finally the huge image began to move.

---

soothsayer (SOOTH say ur) one who foretells the future
repentance (rih PEN tuns) feeling of sorrow about one's bad deeds; regret
prosperity (pro SPER ih tee) wealth; success

The Burning of Troy, Della Borla. The Uffizi, Scala/Art Resource

The wheels creaked and groaned. The shouts of the Trojans were so loud that the sound was heard far out to sea.

Slowly but steadily, the crowd advanced, dragging the wonderful horse that they believed would bless the city. The sun had set before they passed through the breach in the wall. Darkness was beginning to fall when the groaning wheels stopped. The great horse came to a standstill in a quiet corner close by the temple of Athena.

"My friends," said the king's officer, "we've done a fine day's work. Athena's horse rests near the place where it will stay. Now the happiness of Troy is certain. Go home. Tonight, for the first time in ten years, we can sleep secure."

With joyful shouts and friendly good nights, the crowd broke up. Every man went quietly to his own house. Soon the city was dark. The streets were silent and empty. And Athena's horse stood huge and wooden beside the temple wall.

About midnight, a man started to sneak out of the temple. He crept to the breach in the wall. In one hand he carried a basket of tar. In the other was a small torch that he had lighted at the temple fire. Carefully, he climbed to the top of the wall. Then he sat still and waited. Soon the sky began to grow lighter and the shadows in the city less dark. The moon rose, bright and round. The rooftops, the city wall, the plains, and the sea—all were silvered over with soft moonbeams.

---

breach (BREECH) broken place; gap

Ulysses and the Trojan Horse ■ 471

The man on the wall looked eagerly toward the sea. What were those dark objects moving swiftly over the water toward the shore? A thousand ships. The cunning Greeks had not started for home, as the Trojans had thought. They had gone only to the island of Tenedos. There they had lain all day, hidden in coves and inlets. Soon their vessels would again be beached in their old places by the empty camp.

The man on the wall was ready. He lifted his torch and dropped it carefully into the basket of tar. A bright flame rose up. It lit up the plain and the wall and the man's face. His eyes were red, his face wounded and swollen. It was Sinon.

Lights were soon seen on the ships. Then Sinon hurried down to the spot where the great horse was standing. With the flat edge of his sword, he struck its foreleg three times. There was a noise like the rattling of armor. Then a panel in the horse's chest slid aside. A man's head, in a gleaming helmet, appeared.

"Is all well, Sinon?" asked a deep voice.

"All's well, Ulysses. Our ships have landed, and our friends are marching across the plain. The foolish Trojans lie sleeping in their homes, little dreaming of what awaits them."

A rope ladder was let down, and Ulysses descended to the ground. Then fifty other heroes followed him, glad to be in the open air again. All was going the way Ulysses had imagined it would when he had planned the Trojan Horse.

"Sinon," said Ulysses, "what are those scars on your face? Did the Trojans abuse you?"

"They abused me, but they didn't make these wounds," answered Sinon. "I made them myself, so I could persuade the Trojans to fall into our trap."

"I understand, Sinon," said Ulysses. "People call me the man of wiles! But now that title must be yours. And now, for the ending of the whole business! Follow me, my men. Let fire and sword do their worst!"

The Trojans awoke from their dreams of peace to see their homes in flames. They heard the shouts of the triumphant Greeks. They knew that nothing was left for them but captivity or death. So the long siege came to an end, and the fair rich city beyond the sea was overthrown.

Ten years had passed since the siege began. When the city lay in ashes, the Greeks set out in their ships. All sought to return to their native lands. Fondly, then, the thoughts of Ulysses turned to his beloved wife, Penelope, and his child, and the rugged hills and shores of Ithaca.

"Spread the sails, my men, and row hard," he said. "For Penelope waits at home for my return, and keeps my kingdom for me."

But scarcely were his little ships well out to sea when fearful storms arose. The vessels were tossed now this way, now that. They were at the mercy of winds and waves that drove them far, far off course. Soon they were sailing by savage shores and strange lands where wild men lived.

---

coves (KOHVS) small inlets or bays
wiles (WYLS) tricks meant to trap or deceive

Reading Focus:
Understand Character Relationships

Have students describe the relationship between Sinon, who helped trick the Trojans into accepting the wooden horse, and his commander, Ulysses. Ask: What clues in the story did you use to discover the relationship? Why is the relationship important to the story?

Critical Thinking:
Predict

After students have read "Ulysses and the Trojan Horse," pause and have them predict what they think will happen to Ulysses and his men on their trip home. To heighten the suspense, you may wish to have a student read the last paragraph of the story aloud. Guide students to recognize the foreshadowing technique that is used in the phrase "where wild men lived" to set the stage for an encounter with the Cyclops.

Homer (8th Century B.C.)

MORE ABOUT THE AUTHOR

Scholars have no direct proof that Homer is the author of the *Iliad* and the *Odyssey*. Their belief that Homer authored these works is based on the fact that the ancient Greeks themselves always attached his name to the two epics.

Homer's epics had a wide influence on Greek culture. They were valued not just as works of literature but as a symbol of their culture. The youth of ancient Greece looked to the heroes in these works as role models and often learned whole portions of the poems by heart. The ancient Romans also considered knowledge of Homer's great epics essential to a good education. So did the scholars of the Renaissance, who rediscovered the works of the ancient Greeks. The *Iliad* and the *Odyssey* influenced later European literature as well, and in new translations they are still widely read and enjoyed today.

Additional Works BY HOMER

You may wish to suggest these works by Homer for additional reading.

The Iliad, translated by Robert Fagles. Penguin, 1997. Homer tells the story of the Trojan War. (poetry)

The Odyssey, translated by Robert Fagles. Homer relates Ulysses's adventures on his wanderings after the Trojan War. (poetry)

The person who is believed to be the author of these two selections is called Homer. Most scholars believe that Homer lived nearly 3,000 years ago in Greece. We know very little about Homer's life. Legends say that he was a blind poet. His friends are supposed to have led him from city to city.

In those days, stories were listened to, not read. Long stories were often put into rhyme, or poetry form, to make them easier to remember. Traveling poets like Homer told tales that had been handed down for generations. Homer learned many of the familiar rhymes and plots for his poems from those who came before him. He changed and improved the old tales and made up new ones, too. At some point in history, someone, maybe one of Homer's listeners, wrote down two long poems as Homer had told them.

These works are called the *Iliad* and the *Odyssey*. They are considered to be the basis for much Western literature. The *Odyssey* tells of the adventures of the Greek hero Odysseus (also called Ulysses) in the Trojan War, around the 12th or 13th century, and his long journey home after the war. These two selections, in story form rather than poetry, are based on a translation of the *Odyssey*.

Homer probably kept his audiences spellbound for hours. Sit back and suppose that a traveling poet is telling you of amazing deeds that were done long, long ago.

ULYSSES MEETS THE CYCLOPS

ADAPTED
by Homer

Literary Focus:
Epic Poetry
Make sure students notice the shift to first-person point of view in this story. Ask: Who is the narrator of the story? How does the first-person point of view change the way you think about Ulysses?

They were giants, oafs. Living on a large island of their own, they knew no law. They went by the name of Cyclops—it means "eye like a wheel." Each of the monsters had only one—a huge, round eye in the middle of its forehead.

The mouth of a cave gaped above the water. This was the home of one Cyclops. As we rowed nearer to land, we saw him, taking his sheep out to graze. He seemed no man at all. No, he looked like a hairy mountain, rising up all alone on a plain.

We beached our ship. "Stay here and be on the lookout," I told the crew. Taking my twelve best fighters, I went ahead. With me, I brought food and wine. This was no common wine. It was a ruby-red brandy given me by the gods.

---

oafs (OHFS) stupid, awkward persons
gaped (GAYPT) opened wide; yawned

I thought we might need a powerful drink like this. In fact, I knew it in my bones. We were setting foot in the lair of a beast—a wild man, all power and no law.

We scampered up to the cave. The Cyclops was still out with his sheep. So inside we went and feasted our eyes on his treasure—cheese, lambs and goats, bowls of milk.

My men crowded around me. They begged me, "Let's make off with the goats and the cheese. We ought to get back on the open seas while we can!"

Now I know they were right, but I didn't listen at that time. I wanted to see the caveman—and find out what gifts he might have for a guest like me. So we saw him. For some of my friends, it was an awful sight.

But we built a fire, ate some cheese, and waited. Towards evening, the Cyclops came back. A load of firewood was on his shoulder. He dumped it with a crash that echoed off the walls of the cave. In an instant, we all scurried to the far corner.

Next, he brought in the sheep he was going to milk. Then he picked up a huge rock and jammed it in the mouth of the cave. Two dozen wagons pulled by sweating horses could not have budged that rock.

He did his chores and fed the fire. As flames lit up the cave, his eye saw us. "Strangers," he said, "who are you? Are you good trading men? Or are you pirates?" His deep voice thundered against our hearts.

I answered, "We are soldiers on our way home. We ask your help. Our gods teach us to honor strangers. We beg you, great sir—do the same. Take care to please the gods, or Zeus will be angry."

From his savage chest came the answer. "You are a nitwit, trying to scare me with your gods," he said. "A Cyclops doesn't give a fig for any of them. We're more powerful. I'd never let you go for fear of Zeus—unless I felt like it. Tell me now, where did you leave your ship? Nearby?"

That was what he wanted to know! But I was too clever for him, and I lied boldly. "My ship?" I said. "It broke against the rocks of your shore. We are the only men left."

We got no pity from him. He grabbed at us. His hands caught two of my friends like squealing puppies. He beat their brains out and cut them up for his supper. He gobbled the meat like a hungry lion. We cried out to Zeus. But the Cyclops went on filling his giant belly.

Finally, having eaten enough, he lay down to sleep. Now I had the chance to act! Drawing my sword, I crept up close to him. I picked out the spot where I'd stab him. But I was stopped by a sudden thought. If I killed him, we'd all die. We could never push aside the huge rock that blocked the door. No, all we could do was moan and twiddle our thumbs till morning.

---

lair (LAIR) resting place of a wild animal; den
scurried (SKUR eed) moved quickly
Zeus (ZOOS) chief of the Greek gods

Ulysses Meets the Cyclops ■ 475

Background Notes
Greek laws of hospitality mandated an exchange of gifts. A host was expected to welcome his guests and give them gifts.

Critical Thinking:
Infer
Ask: What clue do you find that Ulysses might outwit the Cyclops?

Reading Focus:
Recognize Character Relationships
Ask: What kind of welcome does the Cyclops give Ulysses and his men?

Soon after dawn, he did his chores. He snatched up another two men for breakfast. Then, gathering the sheep, he flicked aside the rock and went out. But in an instant, he had popped the rock back in again. He did it as easily as you'd stick the stopper in a bottle. We could hear him whistle as he climbed with his flock. Then there was silence.

What could we do? I looked around. Inside the cave lay the trunk of a fallen tree. The log was as long and thick as the mast of my ship. I chopped off a six-foot section and let my men scrape it smooth.

Next, I carved one end into a pointed spear. This my men and I plunged deep in the fire till it was as tough as iron. Finally, we dragged the weapon well back in the cave. Under one of the dung piles that lay everywhere, we hid it.

Just before evening, the Cyclops came back with his flock. Once inside, he wedged his stony door into place. He milked the sheep. He did his evening chores, caught two more men, and ate dinner.

Now was the time. I stepped forward, holding out a bowl. In it was the wine I'd brought with me.

"Here, Cyclops," I said, "have a little wine. You'll see what fine things we had in the hold of our ship."

He grabbed the bowl and drank. The drink pleased him so much that he had to have more.

"Give me another, please," he said. "And tell me your name. I'll give you a gift that will make you happy. Even a Cyclops knows grape juice from a heavenly drink like this!"

Three times I filled the bowl, and three times he emptied it. When he had gotten slow and silly, I called out to him. I spoke in friendly tones.

"Cyclops, you ask my name? My name is NOBODY. That's what my mother, my father, and all my friends call me."

"Then I'll eat NOBODY last—his friends come first. That's my gift to you."

Even as he spoke, he stumbled. He fell back and lay there with his giant head leaning to one side. Sleep captured him like any of us. Drunk, he lay there. He hiccupped. Wine dribbled from his lip, and bits of human meat stuck to his chin.

Now we drew out the rough-hewn spear. Again we thrust it in the fire. I whispered brave words to my men, urging them to get up their courage. As we pulled the spear out of the flames, it glowed red-hot. We dashed forward, raised the spear, and rammed it into the Cyclops's eye. Leaning on the spear, I twirled it till it was spinning like a drill. The eyeball sizzled. The veins popped. And the eye rolled down the giant's cheek.

Now the Cyclops roared so wildly that the cave walls shook. Full of fear, we scattered to the corners of the cave. The Cyclops yanked out the bloody spear and flung it to the ground. Then he began to roar, calling for the other Cyclops, who lived in caves nearby. Hearing him,

---

plunged (PLUNJD) pushed something quickly into something else
rough-hewn (RUF HYOON) roughly made; not polished
thrust (THRUST) shoved

they came and crowded round outside the cave door.

"What's wrong?" they called to him. "Why such a loud cry on this starry night? We can't get any sleep. Is someone stealing your flock? Has someone tricked you or hurt you?"

From inside the cave, the giant bellowed, "NOBODY! NOBODY'S tricked me! NOBODY'S hurt me!"

"Oh, well," they answered. "If nobody's hurt you, then we can't help." And they all went back to bed.

I was almost bursting with laughter. The name had fooled them! But now the Cyclops, groaning with pain, staggered to the door. He groped blindly and clawed away the boulder. Then he sat down in the doorway. His arms were spread wide to catch any fool who tried to escape. He was hoping I might try it. I wasn't going to. Instead, I plotted and planned. How could I outwit death?

Here's the plan I liked best: The giant's sheep were big and fat, with heavy wool. The Cyclops could see nothing. So I took some cords of willow from his bed. Standing the sheep three abreast, I tied them together. Under each three, I tied a man. Tucked up below the middle sheep, he was protected on both sides.

Last of all, I took the fattest ram, the finest of the whole flock. Myself I hid under his belly, snuggling up to his woolly curls. With the fleece wound around my fingers, I hung on. So we all breathed hard and waited for dawn.

When dawn rose, the sheep began to bustle and bleat. Their cries echoed round the cave. They moved toward the doorway, with us under them. The Cyclops, weak with pain, wouldn't let them pass. His fingers felt over the fleece of each ram. But he never found the men, hiding underneath. So he let each sheep out in turn.

Last of all came my ram, weighed down by his thick fleece—and me. The Cyclops felt him, then bent his face down. "Old thing," he said, "why are you the last to go? You never linger this way. Why now? Can you be sad about your master's eye? This NOBODY won't get out of here alive! I wish you had brain and voice to tell me where he is now. If only I knew where he hid from my anger! I'd smash him against the floor until his brains splashed all over the walls!"

Then, with a sigh, he stood aside and let us go. Once outdoors, I wriggled loose from the ram's belly. I dropped onto the soft grass. Then, going here and there, I set my men free. With many looks back, we herded the giant's fat sheep before us. We loaded them onto the ship and sailed away. But our sadness was as large as the ocean. Our sorrow was as endless as the future. We had our lives, but we'd lost our friends.

---

groped (GROHPT) felt about with the hands
ram (RAM) male sheep
bustle (BUS ul) move about busily
bleat (BLEET) make the natural cry of a sheep

Ulysses Meets the Cyclops ■ 477

Critical Thinking:
Analyze
Ask the students if they think that Ulysses showed shrewdness when he told the Cyclops his name. Ask: What evidence do you have of this?

Reading Focus:
Understand Character Relationships
Ask: What can you infer about Ulysses's relationship to his men from his comment in the last paragraph of the story?

Background Notes
In the complete *Odyssey* the adventures of Ulysses have a happy ending. Many more things happen to him after he leaves the Cyclops, but he finally returns to Ithaca, is reunited with his wife and re-establishes himself as king.

Mini Quiz

Write on the chalkboard or overhead projector the following sentences and call on students to fill in the blanks. Discuss the answers with the class.

1. "Ulysses and the Trojan Horse" is about a war between _____ and _____.

2. The story takes place in _____.

3. Ulysses and his men sneak into the city inside a _____.

4. Ulysses lands on the island of the Cyclops because _____.

5. The Cyclops is a giant who _____.

Answers

1. Greece; Troy
2. Troy
3. wooden horse
4. storms blew his ship off course
5. has one eye

UNDERSTAND THE SELECTION

Answers

1. They wanted revenge because a Trojan prince named Paris had stolen the most beautiful Greek woman, Helen, wife of Menelaus.
2. more than nine years
3. Their ship had been blown off course by storms as they sailed home from Troy.
4. The Greeks had left Troy.
5. The Trojans believed that it had a strange power to protect its friends.
6. to convince the Trojans that he had turned against the Greeks
7. When Cyclops cried out, he would say "Nobody is hurting me" and those who heard would think nothing was wrong.
8. his cleverness
9. They thought the war was over when the Greeks left the shores of Troy; they brought the wooden horse into the city; they trusted Sinon.
10. He did not want to leave his wife and son to go to war; at the end of the Cyclops tale, he mourns the loss of his friends.

Respond to Literature

Have students list the heroic qualities of Ulysses; then make a chart as a study aid. Point to the chart as you ask students if these qualities would be admired today. Compare Ulysses to some real-life heroes, such as Martin Luther King, Jr. For example, one thing that these two heroes had in common is their devotion to family and their hesitancy to leave home or to cause their wives discomfort. However, devotion to a cause greater than themselves led both men to sacrifice domestic comforts.

WRITE ABOUT THE SELECTION

Prewriting

On the chalkboard or on an overhead transparency, write down some possible monster characteristics, based on students' suggestions.

UNDERSTAND THE SELECTION

Recall

1. Why did the Greeks attack Troy?
2. How long did the war between the Greeks and the Trojans last?
3. Why did the Greeks land on the island of the Cyclops?

Infer

4. Why did the Trojans think the war was over?
5. Why did Ulysses steal the statue of Athena?
6. Why did Sinon wound himself?
7. Why did Ulysses tell the Cyclops that his name was "Nobody"?

Apply

8. What quality of Ulysses gave him victory over his enemies?
9. What mistakes did the Trojans make in their war with the Greeks?
10. What factors in the stories indicate that Ulysses is a warm and human person?

Respond to Literature

To the Greeks, Ulysses was the perfect hero because he was not only brave but also intelligent. Do you think that Ulysses would be a great hero today? Explain your answer.

---

478 ■ Unit 5

WRITE ABOUT THE SELECTION

The Cyclops is one of the first monsters to appear in literature. Your challenge in this section is to write a paragraph in which you create a monster that would scare even the Cyclops.

Prewriting Think of all the monsters you have seen in movies or read about. Brainstorm some of the characteristics of these monsters. Then think about the specific attributes you want to describe: appearance; where the monster lives; what the monster eats; who the monster is most likely to scare. Now add a version or two about why your monster would frighten the Cyclops.

Writing Use your brainstorming to create a description of a very scary monster. You can write your description in the third person, or, like Ulysses, you can describe your monster from a first-person point of view.

Revising Look at the adjectives and adverbs that you have used in your paragraph. Are these the best words you can think of to describe your monster? Add any adjectives or adverbs that you feel will make your description more vivid.

Proofreading Because monsters naturally lend themselves to descriptive exaggeration, you may have been tempted to punctuate your writing with numerous exclamation marks. As you proofread, however, practice restraint in using exclamation marks. Your writing will be more effective.

Writing

As students work on this section independently, go around the classroom and help those who are having trouble. Ask questions similar to those asked in the Prewriting section to help students formulate their descriptions of a monster.

Revising

Pair off students. Have them describe to their partners the special characteristics of their monsters. Encourage the partners to ask questions that stimulate the use of colorful adjectives and adverbs.

Proofreading

Have students work with a partner to check for correct punctuation.

ESL Activity

Have students work in pairs to create a visual of a monster. Then have them brainstorm adjectives that describe their monster. Encourage them to use these adjectives in their paragraphs.

THINK ABOUT EPIC POETRY

An **epic** is a long poem or prose piece that tells a heroic story. Ancient epics were often recited orally or sung. In some cultures, in Africa and in Ireland, as well as in other cultures, the oral tradition continues to this day.

Point of view is the position from which a story is told. In the first-person point of view, the storyteller is one of the characters in the story; action and commentary are limited to what that one character can see, hear, know, think, and feel. Although the impersonal third-person point of view is more common, both points of view are found in epic works.

1. How does the selection "Ulysses and the Trojan Horse" fit the definition of an epic?

2. From what point of view is this story told?

3. From what point of view is "Ulysses Meets the Cyclops" told?

4. How do the two different points of view affect the way you think about Ulysses, the epic hero?

READING FOCUS

Understand Character Relationships As you read the selections, you were able to understand relationships between story characters. Choose one of the stories and describe what you feel is the most important relationship. Explain how this relationship affects the plot of the story.

DEVELOP YOUR VOCABULARY

A **noun** is a word that names a person, place, or thing. For example, in the sentence, "They hid inside a wooden horse," *horse* is a noun. A **verb** is a word that expresses action or a state of being. For example, in the sentence, "The Greeks attacked the Trojans," the word *attacked* is a verb.

Review the meanings of these words from "Ulysses and the Trojan Horse" and "Ulysses Meets the Cyclops." Decide whether each word is used as a noun or a verb in the stories. Then write an original sentence that uses each word in the same form, noun or verb, as in the story.

1. turmoil
2. siege
3. persevered
4. reeds
5. emerged
6. image
7. forges
8. thong
9. jeered
10. prosperity
11. breach
12. cove
13. wiles
14. oafs
15. gaped
16. lair
17. scurried
18. plunged

Review the Selection ■ 479

Unit Review Resources

TEACHER'S RESOURCES
- Writing Process, pp. W49–W60
- Grammar, Usage, and Mechanics, pp. G49–G60
- Speaking and Listening, pp. S25–S30
- Critical Thinking, pp. C25–C30
- Choose from Reading in the Content Areas, pp. RCA1–RCA72
- **Standardized Test Preparation**
  Unit 5 Test, pp. UT9–UT10

WRITING APPLICATIONS

Write About Theme
Make a list on the chalkboard of the main characters in this unit. Then tell students that they are a panel of judges who must select four characters to be placed in a Heroes Hall of Fame. Have the class vote for the four heroes they think should be awarded places. Tally the results to see which characters win.

Writer's Toolkit CD-ROM
Encourage students to use the Descriptive Word Bin (Writing Tools, Drafting, Setting, Descriptions) to complete the Writing Activity.

Cooperative Group Activity
Have students form proofreading teams in which one student checks papers for spelling, another checks for grammar, and so on. Have students submit their papers to the team for a thorough proofing.

Write About Genre
Write the words *tone, symbolism, point of view,* and *techniques* on slips of paper or index cards. Place the cards face down on a desk or table. Have a student volunteer draw a card at random. Challenge the student to make a correct statement about the element of the short story that he or she has drawn. The statement can be part

of a definition, or it can be an example. Let the class decide if the statement is correct or incorrect. Repeat the process with another student, and so on, until all four elements have been discussed adequately.

WRITING APPLICATIONS

Write About Theme
In this unit, you have read about many different kinds of heroes. You have thought about the qualities that make up a hero. Now is your chance to write about the heroes you liked best. Choose four characters from this unit for a "Heroes Hall of Fame." Write about the Heroes Hall of Fame in whatever way will describe your heroes best. For example, you may want to narrate a guided tour of the Hall of Fame, or you may want to have the heroes step from their places and tell their own stories.

Prewriting Begin by choosing the four characters from this unit that you want included in the Heroes Hall of Fame. Then review each character's story. Cluster the details of each character's story that best illustrate why the character is a hero.

Writing Use your prewriting cluster to develop a story entitled "The Heroes Hall of Fame." Be sure to describe the setting of the Hall of Fame.

Revising As you revise your paper, keep in mind the point of view that you have chosen. For example, if you are writing a guided tour, then the entire story should be written in the third person. Eliminate or rewrite anything that is not consistent with the point of view that you have chosen.

Proofreading If you have used dialogue or direct quotations, be sure you have used quotation marks and indented with each change of speaker.

Write About Genre
You have studied point of view, tone, symbolism, and techniques. These are all important elements of the short story. Choose two selections from this unit, one that you especially liked and one you disliked. Compare and contrast these works in terms of the literary elements that you have studied to explain why, in your opinion, one short story is better than the other.

Prewriting Review the work that you did for the "Think About" sections in this unit. Then make a chart that has the name of the two selections you have chosen at the top and the four literary elements down the side. Fill in the spaces on the chart with details about each element from the stories. Include everything you can think of on your chart. You can decide later if you want to use all your facts and ideas.

Writing Use your chart to prepare a paper in which you compare and contrast the two selections you have chosen. Be sure to organize your paper so that you move logically from one point to the next, and remember to prove your favorite is the superior story. You will need to do more than just point out the differences.

Revising Transitional phrases can make your writing smoother. If you did not use such phrases as *first, next, most important,* and *finally,* add them when you revise.

Proofreading Be sure to set off an introductory prepositional phrase that has more than three words with a comma.

Cooperative Group Activity
Prewriting: Have students pair with others who have chosen the same selections. Ask them to create a single chart in which they both express their ideas. If their ideas are in disagreement, they each may wish to write in a different color pen or pencil.

Writer's Toolkit CD-ROM
Encourage students to use the Venn Diagram (Writing Tools, Prewriting) to help them compare and contrast the two selections.

BUILD LANGUAGE SKILLS

Vocabulary

Since roots carry the basic meaning of the word, they are the foundation of developing your vocabulary. If you learn to figure out roots, you will improve your vocabulary and your reading comprehension. A **root** is a word or word part that is used to form other words. For example, the root in the word *excitement* is *excite*, which means to stir up strong feeling. Sometimes you can use the root word to find the meaning of a larger word.

Write the root in each of the following words. Use the root to find the meaning of the larger word. Check the meanings in a dictionary, then use each word in an original sentence.

1. dignitary	16. embattled
2. emerging	17. seaward
3. acknowledgment	18. prosperity
4. dispelled	19. repentance
5. momentarily	20. irresistible
6. frenzied	21. picturesque
7. evading	22. mythical
8. elimination	23. awesome
9. devastating	24. fitful
10. pensively	25. courageous
11. waver	26. monstrous
12. eventually	27. relationship
13. figurine	28. uncontrolled
14. frustration	29. historic
15. circumvent	30. gracefully

Grammar, Usage, and Mechanics

Using direct quotations can add to your writing. When you use a person's or a character's exact words, you must enclose the words in quotation marks. If there is an introductory expression, you must follow it with a comma. An interrupting expression must have commas before and after. A quotation that is followed by a concluding expression should end with a comma, question mark, or exclamation point.

Examples:

Introductory expression: Annie said, "The way I plan to do it is better."

Interrupting expression: "It angers me," he said, "that no one can do this right."

Concluding expression: "Get lost!" the young man bellowed.

Add quotation marks, commas, and end punctuation marks to these quotations.

1. Watch that right Tony said the trainer

2. Stina replied You're great, Dan

3. Let go of me she screamed

4. Hang on tight Dan ordered or we'll surely drown

5. The cop snapped Pick it up brother

Unit Review ■ 481

BUILD LANGUAGE SKILLS

Vocabulary

Answers

1. dignity	7. evade	13. figure	22. myth
2. emerge	8. eliminate	14. frustrate	23. awe
3. knowledge	9. devastate	15. circle	24. fit
4. dispel	10. pensive	16. battle	25. courage
5. moment	11. wave	17. sea	26. monster
6. frenzy	12. event	18. prosper	27. relate
		19. penance	28. control
		20. resist	29. history
		21. picture	30. grace

More About Word Attack: Point out that although the root is often found at the beginning of a word (for example, the root in *excitement* is *excite*), this is not always the case. Sometimes the root is found in the middle or end of a word. Write this example on the board:

embattled

Explain that the root of this word is battle, and that *em-* is a prefix which means "in the midst of."

Grammar, Usage, and Mechanics

Answers

1. "Watch that right, Tony," said the trainer.
2. Stina replied, "You're great, Dan."
3. "Let go of me!" she screamed.
4. "Hang on tight," Dan ordered, "or we'll surely drown."
5. The cop snapped, "Pick it up, brother!"

Point out that a direct quotation must end with a punctuation mark inside the quotes. Write on the chalkboard the following incorrect examples.

John said, "Let's go swimming".
"I cannot see the road" shouted Dan.
"Yes"! she cried, "Now I know what to do"!
"Which way," asked Dennis, "should I go to get to Philadelphia"?

Point out that in the first example, the period should be inside the quotation marks. In the second example a comma or exclamation point must be added inside quotation marks after the word *road*. In the third example the exclamation points must be placed inside, not outside, the quotation marks. In the fourth example the question mark should be inside, not outside, the quotation marks.

Cooperative Group Activity

After students have completed exercises 1–5 in the text, have them work in small groups to create their own sentences that need quotation marks, commas, and end punctuation marks. Have groups trade papers with one another, then write answers for the exercises.

SPEAKING AND LISTENING

Motivation

Ask students to recall interviews that they have seen or listened to on TV and radio talk shows. Discuss the characteristics of the interviews: the ways in which the interviewer and the person being interviewed related to one another; how the interview brought out (or failed to bring out) the personality of the person being interviewed.

Teaching Strategy

Emphasize to students the need to prepare for their roles as interviewers. Point out that a good interviewer does considerable research on a person before interviewing him or her. Go on to explain that those students acting as the people being interviewed are like actors and actresses—they must assume the role of a particular character, then stay in character as they answer questions.

Evaluation Criteria

Does the interview reveal the character's personality and ideas? Has the interviewer prepared questions based on knowledge of the character? Does the student being interviewed stay in character and sound spontaneous?

One way to share vicariously in a character's adventures, trials, and triumphs is to do an imaginary interview with that character.

Part of the fun of an imaginary interview is the opportunity to identify with one of your favorite characters and to bring that character to life. Also, you have the opportunity to work with a partner.

In this unit you have met a variety of heroes. It's likely that one is someone you found to be interesting. To prepare yourself for this assignment, think about selections you've read in this unit, and recall the characters in them. Then, follow these guidelines to help you prepare your imaginary interview.

1. Pair up with another student. Glance over the selections in the unit and choose a character who would be a good candidate for an interview. Although the character doesn't have to be particularly likable, it should be someone you find memorable. The more diverse and complex the character is, the more interesting the interview.

2. Decide who will be the interviewer and who will be the character being interviewed. You could change roles midway if you like, or, if you choose, you could play both parts!

3. Talk about and decide with your partner whether you want to do a supportive kind of interview or if you prefer a more confrontational style.

4. Next, develop at least five questions that an interviewer might ask the character. The answers to the questions should reveal the character's opinions and his or her personality.

5. Make some notes on possible answers to the questions. Your job is to try to use words the character might use. Try to emulate the character in your answers.

6. As the interviewer, practice asking the questions. Use the appropriate tone and expressions in asking the questions. As the person being interviewed, practice the answers until they seem perfect. You want to sound spontaneous, so just consult your notes; don't read directly from them.

After you've practiced with your partner and feel confident, take your show to a larger audience. Try to keep your interview to three minutes. Following the steps above will help you to be adequately prepared.

482 ■ Unit 5

Career Connection

After reading the story "Terror in the North," students might be interested in a career as a seismologist. Seismologists are earthquake scientists who study the areas where earthquakes are most likely to occur. They study data obtained by a seismograph, an instrument that measures and records seismic vibrations. They also study how the Earth's crust moves along fault lines. People who are interested in becoming seismologists should obtain a bachelor's degree in geophysics or seismology. For field work, assistants with less formal education might be used and given on-the-job training.

CRITICAL THINKING

Inferences An **inference** is an understanding of something that has not been stated directly. It is based on a suggestion that the author makes indirectly. For example, in the story "On the Ledge," it can be inferred that Walter has a decent relationship with his brother.

When trying to infer an author's meaning, it is important not to jump to conclusions. For example, suppose that you are trying to infer something about the home life of the boys in "Amigo Brothers." It would be an invalid inference to say that Felix and Antonio are from broken homes, because there is no evidence to support this idea. It would be a valid inference, however, to say that the boys live in modest economic circumstances.

Good stories, poems, and plays always ask the reader to make inferences. Choose one selection from this unit that you feel contains important inferences, and answer the following questions.

1. Consider an inference that is central to the meaning of the story. What is it? What evidence can you find to back up the inference?

2. What invalid inferences might a reader be tempted to make when reading this story? How would these invalid inferences confuse the meaning of the story?

3. How does making inferences make a story more interesting?

EFFECTIVE STUDYING

Taking Tests In order to do well in school, it is important to know how to take objective tests. An **objective test** is one that requires you to recall factual information. It may consist of short answer questions, multiple choice questions, or true and false questions. An objective test may also include matching exercises.

These suggestions will provide a good strategy for taking an objective test.

1. Write your name on each page.

2. Skim through the test. Decide how much time to give each question. Notice if some questions are worth more points than others.

3. Jot down any information you want to remember in the margins of the test or on scrap paper, if this is allowed.

4. Answer the easy questions first. Circle the numbers of any questions you are not sure of.

5. Go with your first answer unless you have a very good reason to change it.

6. Go back over your test to make sure you have followed directions correctly and answered all of the questions.

Test Preparation
When taking an essay test, think before you write. Jot down your important points and work them into an outline. Do this on the back of your test paper or on scrap paper.

Unit Review ■ 483

UNIT ACTIVITY

A Continuing Unit Project: Illustrated Reading Log

A reading log is a learning strategy that gives students a chance to explore and express their own responses to literature. In addition, logs serve as a source of prewriting notes for other activities in the unit.

Have students create illustrated reading logs as they read this unit. After reading each selection, ask students to write in their logs. Emphasize to students that they are to write what they think and feel, not just describe the story.

Take time to discuss with the students the kinds of things they might write about. For example, they might jot down thoughts or questions that come to mind as they read; the relationship of the selection to the unit theme, generations; or the way the selection relates to their own experiences. Allow students about ten minutes for each entry. The entries need not be more then half a page in length.

Here are some general questions you can ask students to help get them started:

What did you learn as you read this selection?

What questions do you have?

What was the main message of the selection?

How did you feel after reading the selection?

If you find that your class needs more structure, create questions such as these for the selection.

■ "Andre"/"Family Album"

Which family would you rather be a member of, Andre's or the one in the "Family Album"? Why?

■ "Bread"

Have you ever done something wrong for a good reason? What happened?

■ "Somebody's Son"

How do you think David's father felt about his son?

■ "The Medicine Bag"

What do you think Martin will tell his son about the medicine bag?

■ "Medicine"/"Grandfather"

How did reading these poems make you feel?

■ "Some People"/"My People"

Is there a group of people with whom you are proud to belong? What kind of people do you avoid?

■ "Otto"/"Christmas morning i"

In what way does the "i" in the title of the second poem tell you something about the main character?

■ "Whale Hunting"/"Luther Leavitt"

Is the second poem really about Luther Leavitt? Explain.

Have students create covers and tables of contents for their logs, as well as illustrations. (Students who do not like to draw can cut pictures from magazines.) Have students share their logs with one another in small groups. Then collect and evaluate the logs.

■ "Andre"
by Gwendolyn Brooks (page 489)

■ "Family Album"
by Diane Stevenson (page 490)

SELECTION SYNOPSES

Andre is the speaker in the first poem; he dreams that he has the opportunity to choose his own parents. The speaker in the "Family Album" takes the reader on a tour of the pictures in her family photograph album.

SELECTION ACTIVITY

Each section in the "Family Album" represents a picture in the narrator's family photograph album. Have the students choose a section from the poem and illustrate the photograph being described in that section. Ask students to read the section carefully to get a true feeling for the setting of the photograph and the mood and posture of the family member(s) in the photograph. Students should then try and capture that feeling in their illustrations. After the students have drawn their photographs, have each student display what he or she has drawn. The rest of the class may guess which section that student illustrated.

■ "Bread"
by Amado V. Hernandez (page 497)

SELECTION SYNOPSIS

The speaker in this poem is a poor man who committed robbery, then murder, while trying to steal food to feed his sick child. Now that he is in prison he receives the bread every day that could have saved his child's life.

SELECTION ACTIVITY

Have students compare the theme of "Bread" to the theme of the play, "Trifles," which they read in Unit 3. Discuss with students how both selections describe crimes that some people may feel were justified.

Divide the class into teams and have students take sides in a debate about the guilt or innocence of the characters in the two selections—Mrs. Wright who is accused of her husband's murder in "Trifles," and the man in "Bread," who stole and killed to get food for his daughter.

■ "Somebody's Son"
by Richard Pindell (page 501)

SELECTION SYNOPSIS

A young man, named David, has left home to "find himself" and avoid his father's insistence that he go to college. After many months of traveling across the country, David writes a letter to his mother, asking her to ask his father if he can come home. He asks his mother to have his father tie a white cloth to the apple tree if the answer is yes. David promises that he will be passing by the farm, which is near Baltimore, soon.

David hitches a ride from a kind-hearted man on the highway, then rides the train into Baltimore County.

As the train approaches the apple tree on his father's farm, David cannot stand the strain of wondering whether there will be a white cloth tied to the tree. He begs the person next to him on the train to look and see if it is there. The man in the next seat answers with the astonished reply, "I see a white cloth tied on almost every twig."

SELECTION ACTIVITY

Ask students to imagine they are a close friend of David, the boy in "Somebody's Son." While David is away from home, he sends postcards from each place he passes through. On the postcards, he describes where he is, what he is doing, and what his thoughts and feelings are.

Have students draw and write the postcards that they think David might have sent. They can use the information in the story as a starting point, but they will have to use their own imaginations to create additional information. Also encourage students to show through their postcards, which should be dated, the process by which David comes to the conclusion that he is ready to come home.

■ "The Medicine Bag"
by Virginia Driving Hawk Sneve (page 511)

SELECTION SYNOPSIS

Martin, a teenage boy who is part Native American, comes home from school one day to find that his Sioux great-grandfather has come from South Dakota for a surprise visit. The old man senses that he is dying, and Martin's mother, his granddaughter, is the closest living relative.

At first, Martin is fearful that his friends will make fun of his grandpa, but soon he realizes that they are in awe of the colorful old man. A more serious concern develops, however, when it becomes apparent that Grandpa plans to give Martin the medicine bag—a sacred leather pouch that has been passed from one male to another for many generations. Martin is afraid that he will have to wear the pouch and endure the ridicule of his peers.

The day comes for Martin to receive the bag. Grandpa tells Martin the history of the bag and what it means to him. Then, much to Martin's surprise, Grandpa gives him the bag, but tells him not to wear it "in this time and place where no one will understand."

Instead, he tells Martin to keep it until he is on the reservation. A few days later, Grandpa dies, and Martin goes to the reservation to put sacred sage in the bag as Grandpa directed.

SELECTION ACTIVITY

From the library, obtain a copy of Virginia Driving Hawk Sneve's nonfiction book, *They Led a Nation*. This book is a collection of biographical sketches of Sioux chiefs who have led their people throughout history. Each sketch is about a page long, with a drawing. Make a copy of enough biographies so that a different biographical sketch can be given to each student.

Have each student read a biographical sketch aloud. Also read, or have a student read, Sneve's introduction to the book. Then discuss with the class the picture of Sioux life and history that Sneve's portrait provides.

■ "Medicine"
by Alice Walker (page 525)

■ "Grandfather"
by Shirley Crawford (page 527)

SELECTION SYNOPSES

The subject matter of these poems is a child's view of grandparents. In the first poem, a child remembers the companionship of her grandfather, who is now dead. In "Medicine," a child goes into her grandparents' bedroom, where the grandmother is taking care of the sick grandfather.

SELECTION ACTIVITY

Both of these poems paint pictures with words. The poems also lend themselves well to dramatization as well as dance. The first poem would be especially suitable to a dance interpretation.

Have students work alone or in groups to present a visual interpretation of each poem. The interpretation can be in the form of a drawing, a painting, a clay sculpture, a dance or dramatization. The important thing is that the visual interpretation enables viewers to "see" the poem come alive.

Have students present their interpretations to the class. Students who have created art works can display them around the room, and students who have chosen dance or drama can perform their interpretations.

■ "Some People"
by Rachel Field (page 531)

■ "My People"
by Bernice George (page 531)

SELECTION SYNOPSES

The theme of "Some People" describes two different kinds of people. "My People" describes how the speaker views being Navajo.

SELECTION ACTIVITY

In this activity, students will work in groups to create skits in which these two speakers of each poem turn up at a party.

Remind students that they must decide on a setting for the party. Then challenge them to create dialogue that is clearly in character for each speaker. Also encourage students to be imaginative in creating situations that will bring out the humor and the message of each poem.

■ "Otto"
by Gwendolyn Brooks (page 535)

■ "Christmas morning i"
by Carol Freeman (page 535)

SELECTION SYNOPSES

The subject matter of both poems is Christmas and the gifts that children hope to receive, but do not. Otto covers his feelings for the sake of his father, while the speaker in the second poem focuses on her own disappointment.

SELECTION ACTIVITY

Have students assemble a picture that illustrates the characters, events, and themes of these two poems. For example, students might draw pictures of Otto and his father, and of the grandmother sewing the rag doll. After students have finished their albums, have them display them in the classroom.

- **"Whale Hunting"**
  by Sally Nashook Puk (page 539)

- **"Luther Leavitt"**
  by Alfred Brower (page 539)

SELECTION SYNOPSES

Set in Alaska, these two poems describe some of the community activity that goes along with whale hunting.

SELECTION ACTIVITY

Have students work in pairs or in groups to research the whaling industry in North America. Some topics that students should consider include:

The history of the industry and how it has changed

The technology of the industry today

The problem of many types of whales being endangered species

The products obtained from whales

Areas in the world were whaling is still a viable industry (this information can be presented using a map)

STUDENT READING LIST

Paulsen, Gary, *Sarney: A Life Remembered*, 1997. Doubleday

Yolen, Jane, *Gray Heroes: Elder Tales from Around the World*. 1999. Penguin Books

Bolden, Tonya, *And Not Afraid to Dare: Stories of 10 African-American Women*. 1998. Scholastic.

Straub, Deborah G. (ed.) *Native North American Voices*. 1997. UXL

Sneve, Virginia D. H. *The Trickster and the Troll*. 1997. University of Nebraska Press.

From Globe Fearon Educational Publisher

Multicultural Literature Collection
African American Literature
Plains Native American Literature
Tapestry: A Multicultural Collection of American Literature

UNIT 6
Overview

UNIT OBJECTIVES

After completing this unit, students will be able to

- understand five elements of poetry: denotation and connotation, rhythm, sound, form, and symbolism
- talk about real people and imaginary characters from notes
- understand how generalizations are made
- use an effective strategy in matching, multiple-choice, and true false tests
- build on a knowledge of literary elements to strengthen creative and analytic writing
- understand how negative prefixes reverse the meaning of root words
- increase the use of new words in sentences

UNIT SELECTIONS

The theme of the unit is generations: the succession of families, the passing on of one's heritage, and the on-going traditions within a group.

- **"Andre"** and **"Family Album"** (p. 489) express how children view their parents and other family members.

  LITERARY SKILL: rhythm

  READING SKILL: compare and contrast poetry elements

  VOCABULARY: synonyms

  WRITING: extending characterization

- **"Bread"** (p. 497), the model selection, is a poem about a father who is in jail for stealing food for his hungry child.

  LITERARY SKILL: symbolism

  READING SKILL: identify setting and mood

  VOCABULARY: homophones

  WRITING: express a personal opinion

- **"Somebody's Son"** (p. 501) describes the enduring bond between a runaway teenager and his family.

  LITERARY SKILL: tone

  READING SKILL: understand character relationships

  VOCABULARY: silent letters

  WRITING: extend a story

- **"The Medicine Bag"** (p. 511) describes the relationship between a teenage boy and his Native American great-grandfather.

  LITERARY SKILL: plot

  READING SKILL: compare and contrast character traits

  VOCABULARY: words from other cultures

  WRITING: express a personal viewpoint on a theme

- **"Medicine"** and **"Grandfather"** (p. 525) both express a child's view of grandparents.

  LITERARY SKILL: form

  READING SKILL: identify theme

  VOCABULARY: adjectives

  WRITING: tell a story from a different point of view

Introducing Unit Theme
Draw a family apple tree on the chalkboard. On one of the lowest branches write "your name" inside an apple; complete the other lowest row of branches with apples for brothers or sisters. On the branches above, draw more apples, and write "mother," "father," "grandmother," "grandfather," and so on, in each. Ask students to copy the tree, then fill the apples with names of the people in their family. Point out that the tree represents several generations.

Generations

My grandmothers were strong.
They followed plows and bent to toil.
They moved through fields sowing seed.
They touched earth and grain grew.
They were full of sturdiness and singing.
My grandmothers were strong.

—Margaret Walker

The Family. Marisol, 1962. Painted wood and other materials, 6'10⅝" × 65½"
Collection, The Museum of Modern Art, New York

Viewing Fine Art

Marisol, a contemporary artist of Venezuelan descent, was born in Paris in 1930. The artist creates distinctive standing sculptures using painted wood and a variety of found objects. Although Marisol does not consider herself to be a political artist, her often humorous and incisive works comment on a variety of social issues. Her art is a mix of folk art and contemporary pop art. Ask: How many generations of a family are shown in the sculpture? How can you tell?

485

- **"Some People"** and **"My People"** (p. 531) focus on groups of people. One poem describes two kinds of people; the other is about the Navajo people.
  LITERARY SKILL: figures of speech
  READING SKILL: make inferences
  VOCABULARY: figurative expressions
  WRITING: describe two kinds of people

- **"Otto"** and **"Christmas morning i"** (p. 535) describe disappointed reactions of children on Christmas Day.
  LITERARY SKILL: theme in poetry
  READING SKILL: compare and contrast poems
  VOCABULARY: nouns and verbs
  WRITING: tell a story from a different point of view

- **"Whale Hunting"** and **"Luther Leavitt"** (p. 539) describe the whaling activities of families in Alaska.
  LITERARY SKILL: tone in poetry
  READING SKILL: identify cause and effect
  VOCABULARY: antonyms
  WRITING: revive personal memories

Generations

Can you picture yourself as a grandmother or grandfather? What kind of grandparent do you think you would be? Would you, as a grandparent, in any way resemble the grandmothers whom Margaret Walker describes in her poem "Generations"? In the poem that opens this unit, Margaret Walker talks about the qualities in her grandmothers that she admires. What qualities do you think your future grandchildren will admire in you?

Grandparents, parents, and children make up three generations in a family. The word *generation* comes from the Latin word *genus*, meaning "birth." The span of time that exists between the birth of parents and the birth of their children is equal to one generation.

The poems and stories in this unit are about generations—parents and children, grandchildren and grandparents. Some of the selections also touch on a larger meaning of the word *generation*—the idea of cultural heritage or tradition. Tradition is the handing down from one generation to the next of a body of customs, beliefs, proverbs, stories, and long established practices and teachings. The average period between the birth of one generation and the next is roughly 30 years. People are a product of their cultural heritage such as African American, Native American, European, or Asian. Reading these selections will help you become more aware of your own place in the generations of your family and within your cultural group.

■ PARENT AND CHILD

The generation outside of your own that you probably know best is your parents'. Have you ever wondered what life would be like if you could have chosen your parents? In the poem "Andre," the speaker realizes that, given that chance, he would choose his own parents from the many different parents in the world.

Sometimes being a parent can be painful, as two poems in this unit illustrate. In the poem "Bread," a man is sent to jail because he tries to steal food for his hungry child. In the poem "Otto," a father cannot give his children the gifts that they want for Christmas.

You may have heard the expression "generation gap." A generation gap exists when parents and children have trouble understanding one another's needs, feelings, and ideas because of the difference in their ages. One short story in this unit offers hope that the generation gap can, at least in part, be overcome. In the story "Somebody's Son," a boy runs away from home to find out more about life and himself. As you read the story, you will find out what happens when the boy decides that he is ready to go back home again. Perhaps the story will give you insight into what people of two different generations might feel about each other. How true do you find the relationship between generations in this story?

■ GRANDPARENTS AND GRANDCHILDREN

For many children and young adults, grandparents are special people. In the short story "The Medicine Bag," a teenaged boy and his family receive a surprise visit from the boy's 86-year-old Sioux great-grandfather. An important part of the story is the way the man passes on to his great-grandson a tradition of the Sioux Indians.

In the poem "Grandfather," Shirley Crawford writes about her grandfather's life and death and wonders who her own grandchildren will be. In the poem "Medicine," Alice Walker considers the realities of illness and old age as she watches her grandparents.

■ IMPORTANT OTHERS

Perhaps you have had other people in your life who have been as important to you as family. In the humorous poem "Some People," Rachel Field explains why she prefers the company of some people and not others. The two short poems "Whale Hunting" and "Luther Leavitt" describe important people in the lives of two young poets.

With your family and with your cultural heritage, you are a link between the past and the future. How has your life been shaped by the generations that have come before you?

Discussing the Unit Theme

Guide students through the opening three paragraphs of discussion on generations. Then ask them to jot down some characteristics of their own family members who are of different generations. Read through the rest of the unit theme discussion with students, allowing students to discuss the question that is raised in the last paragraph. Then ask students if they can relate anything they have read to the notes they wrote about their own relatives.

Cooperative Group Activity

Divide the class into small groups. Ask each group to create a family tree showing at least three generations of an imaginary set of characters. (It might help students to imagine that they are writing a short story or a novel about the characters.) Each group's tree should include such information as the name of each family member, when he or she lived, and, at the bottom of the page, a short narrative about what their lives were like. For example, a group might create a family from early American history in which the grandmother and grandfather were brought over on a slave ship, their son was born in Massachusetts, and his son fought in the Civil War.

SELECTION OVERVIEW

SELECTION OBJECTIVES

After completing these selections, students will be able to

- understand rhythm
- identify the viewpoint of the speaker in a poem
- extend characterization in a poem
- analyze rhythmic patters in a poem
- use synonyms
- compare and contrast poetry elements

Lesson Resources

Andre/Family Album
- Selection Synopses, Teacher's Edition, pp. T483a–T483b
- Comprehension and Vocabulary Workbook, pp. 93–94
- Language Enrichment Workbook, p. 100
- Teacher's Resources
  Reinforcement, p. R46
  Test pp. T89–T90

More About Rhythm

Encourage students to think about why rhythm is so appealing in a poem or song. Point out that one reason is that rhythm creates a repeated pattern. Once a person picks up a rhythmic pattern, the mind begins to anticipate hearing the same pattern again. This anticipation or expectation is part of the pleasure of listening or reading.

About the Author

Gwendolyn Brooks has written several poems about families in which the title of the poem is the name of the speaker. In this poem, the speaker is a boy named Andre. Later in the unit students will read a poem in which a boy named Otto is the speaker.

READING FOCUS

Compare and Contrast Poetry Elements
When you compare two things, you note similarities. When you contrast two things, you note differences. When you read poetry, there are several elements you can compare and contrast. These include topic, point of view, and style. For example, two poems might have the same point of view but different styles. As you read, pay attention to the elements of each poem that are similar and different.

488 ■ Unit 6

RHYTHM

Rhythm is a regular recurrence of units of sound. It is rhythm that makes you tap your feet when you are listening to music. It is also rhythm that makes you feel like dancing to music.

Poems, like music, often have distinct rhythmic patterns. You can discover the rhythm of a poem by reading the poem aloud and clapping the sound of each syllable in a word as you read. You will find that accents automatically fall on certain words, as well as on certain syllables within a word.

Some poetry does not have a recognizable and consistent rhythmic pattern. This type of poetry is called **free verse**. You can still clap out the rhythm of each line, but each line in the poem will have a different rhythm.

As you read the two poems, ask:

1. Do both poems have recognizable rhythmic patterns?
2. What are the rhythmic patterns?

WRITING CONNECTION

Choose a familiar nursery rhyme such as "Jack and Jill" or "Humpty Dumpty." Clap out the rhythm of the nursery rhyme as you say it aloud. Then see if you can fit words of your own to the rhythmic pattern of each nursery rhyme.

ESL Activity

Locate several poems with distinct patterns of rhythm and several in free verse. For patterns of rhythm, choose a variety of poems with both obvious and less obvious rhythms; also choose some without rhyme. Read one or more lines from the poems. Pause after each reading to discuss the rhythm. Invite students to say the lines aloud to increase their understanding of rhythm.

Cooperative Group Activity

For the Writing Connection activity, choose a verse with a familiar rhythmic pattern, such as a nursery rhyme. Pair students and have each write a poem that fits the rhythm. Then have pairs decide how to present their poems to the class—as a song, a reading in unison, or each taking alternate lines.

ANDRE

by Gwendolyn Brooks

I had a dream last night. I dreamed
I had to pick a Mother out.
I had to choose a Father too.
At first, I wondered what to do,
There were so many there, it seemed,
Short and tall and thin and stout.

But just before I sprang awake,
I knew what parents I would take.

And *this* surprised and made me glad:
They were the ones I always had!

---

stout (STOWT) having a heavy-set body
sprang (SPRANG) past tense of the verb *spring*; arose suddenly

Andre ■ **489**

Develop Vocabulary Skills
Familiarize students with the vocabulary words footnoted in the selection by asking volunteers to use the words in the original sentences.

Critical Thinking:
Infer
Ask: Who is the "I" in this poem?

TEACHING PLAN

INTRODUCE

Motivation
Ask students to think about how they view the members of their immediate families. How would they paint pictures of their family members with words? Where would they place themselves in the picture and what would be its setting?

Purpose-Setting Question
What would happen if children could choose their parents?

READ

Literary Focus:
Rhythm
To illustrate the rhythm in "Andre," have students clap the accented syllables in the first two lines as they say the words aloud with you. Point out that this exercise exaggerates the pattern of rhythm. Then read the same lines aloud in a more natural speaking rhythm. Point out that even when a pattern of accented syllables is subtle, it helps to hold the poem together and make it pleasing to listen to.

Reading Focus:
Compare and Contrast Poetry Elements
Have students make a three-column chart with *topic*, *point of view*, and *style* as the headers. Tell them to use the chart to note the similarities and differences between these aspects of the poems.

CLOSE

Have students complete Review the Selection on pages 492–493.

Reading Focus:
Compare and Contrast Poetry Elements

Have students compare and contrast the time period covered in each poem. Ask: What device does Stevenson use to describe scenes from her early life and even before she was born? What does the speaker in "Andre" describe?

Literary Focus:
Free Verse

Read part 1 of the poem aloud to students. Then read it a second time as you lightly clap the accented syllables. Guide students to see that each line has a different rhythm. Point out that the poem as a whole has an irregular rhythm similar to that of everyday speech. Ask: What do we call this type of poetry?

Critical Thinking:
Analyze

Ask: What does Part 4 of the poem emphasize about the speaker's family?

Comparing Selections

Ask: In each poem, which generation(s) is the speaker thinking about?

FAMILY ALBUM

by Diane Stevenson

1

A child with only the sun
in her eyes, my sister shields her face,
hand palm out, as if to say no.

2

Alone, the garden behind her fragments
5   of color, my mother seems to listen.
July, 1947: I am here, too, inside,
as yet invisible, though the sun
must filter through, like blood, to me.
I must be hearing her heart.

3

10   At two, I sit in the grass,
legs forward, facing the sun.
On the lawn in front of me,
a dark figure approaches,
almost touching my feet.
15   I look up, blink, and my father
records himself, a shadow,
just out of range.

4

Florida, 1960. My sister and I kneel,
behind us three generations of women.
20   No son's been born for a hundred years.
Even the palms are graceful women,
and hibiscus opens its wide, red mouth.

---

shields (SHEELDZ) defends; protects
fragments (FRAG muhnts) parts or pieces
range (RAYNJ) the area in which an object can be seen
hibiscus (hy BIS kus) a garden plant or shrub bearing large, showy flowers

490 ■ Unit 6

Mini Quiz

Write the following sentences on the chalkboard or overhead projector and call on students to fill in the blanks. Discuss the answers with the class.

1. Andre dreams that he must choose _____.

2. He decides to choose _____.

3. The speaker in the second poem is looking at pictures in _____.

4. The first picture she sees is of _____.

5. The third picture shows the speaker and _____.

Answers
1. a mother and father
2. the parents he has
3. a family photograph album
4. her older sister
5. her father

Gwendolyn Brooks (1917–   )

As a young girl, Gwendolyn Brooks was an avid reader. She was also shy, which may explain why she chose to express herself through writing. She published her first poem at age 14.

After college, Brooks worked as a maid and office worker. Eventually, she became publicity director for a youth organization of the National Association for the Advancement of Colored People in Chicago. While working, Brooks continued to write poetry. By her mid-twenties, her poems were appearing in magazines and literary journals. She was 28 when her first book of poems was published.

Critics have praised her poetry for recording "the neglected miracles of everyday existence." A down-to-earth and inspiring speaker, Gwendolyn Brooks frequently gives public readings of her poetry.

Gwendolyn Brooks is one of the leading poets of the United States and was the first African American poet to win a Pulitzer Prize. Her keen interest in people is expressed in her writing.

Born in Topeka, Kansas, Gwendolyn Brooks has spent most of her life in Chicago. The sights, sounds, and people of Chicago's South Side are the subject of many of her poems, which create a vibrant picture of African American urban life.

Numerous honors and awards have come to Brooks throughout her career. Her first published collection of poems, *A Street in Bronzeville* (1945), won her critical acclaim and *Mademoiselle* magazine's Merit Award as the outstanding woman of the year. Brooks has received two Guggenheim Foundation fellowships, the American Academy of Arts and Letters award, the Frost Medal, and a National Endowment for the Arts award. In 1968, she was named Poet Laureate of the State of Illinois. From 1985 to 1986, she was consultant in poetry to the Library of Congress.

Although Gwendolyn Brooks's formal education ended with junior college, she has through her own efforts continued her education. In addition to being a poet, she is an expert in modern literature, a writer of book reviews, and a frequent lecturer at colleges and universities. In 1990, she became a professor of English at Chicago State University.

Author Biography ■ 491

Additional Works
BY GWENDOLYN BROOKS

You may wish to suggest these works by Gwendolyn Brooks for additional reading:

Family Pictures. Broadside, 1971. (poetry)

The Near Johannesburg Boy and Other Poems. Third World Press, 1991. A collection of poems about South Africa. (poetry)

Selected Poems. HarperCollins, 1999. (poetry)

Report from Part One. Broadside, 1972. A collection of memoirs, interviews, and letters. (autobiography)

UNDERSTAND THE SELECTION

Answers

1. having to choose a mother and father
2. He chooses the same parents he has.
3. herself, her sister, her mother and father, her grandmother and great-grandmother
4. Sample answer: He realizes that he is lucky to have the parents that he has.
5. He probably learned that he really likes his parents after all—something many children think they do not.
6. inside her mother's womb
7. He was probably somewhat distant and remote—"just out of range."
8. Sample answer: I chose my parents because I could tell they really loved me.
9. Answers will vary. Students should specify their relationship to each person they name.
10. the poet's mother, grandmother, and great-grandmother

Respond to Literature

In addition to their individual responses, you may want to extend students' thinking by having students work in groups of four on this related activity. Ask each group to create a series of four sketches to represent the four time periods described in "Family Album." Allow students to change the setting from a garden to one of their choice but have them stay within the structure of the poem. When the sketches are finished, ask each group: What do your sketches tell about the characters in the poem? If some groups have interpreted the poem differently, discuss the reasons for their interpretations.

WRITE ABOUT THE SELECTION

Prewriting

Have students write in pairs or small groups to make their charts. In this way, the ideas of several students will be represented, and students will have more prewriting material to choose from.

UNDERSTAND THE SELECTION

Recall

1. About what does the speaker of "Andre" dream?

2. What choice does he make?

3. About what family members is the author of "Family Album" writing?

Infer

4. Why do you think that Andre is glad about his choices?

5. Do you think Andre learned something about himself through this experience?

6. Where is the author of "Family Album" in July of 1947?

7. What can you infer about the importance of her father in the poet's life?

Apply

8. Suppose that you picked out your own parents. Why did you choose them?

9. If you were to write a poem called "Family Album," who would be the characters in your poem?

10. Who are the three generations of women that the poet refers to in Part 4 of "Family Album"?

Respond to Literature

Which of these poems more accurately reflects your feelings about members of other generations in your family? Explain.

WRITE ABOUT THE SELECTION

Each section of the poem "Family Album" is like the description of a photograph in a picture album. Based on what the poet has written, can you imagine what each member of the family is like? Write a paragraph in which you provide additional information about one or several of the characters described in the poem.

Prewriting Across the top of a sheet of paper, write the names of the generations —grandmother, mother, etc.—that are represented in this poem. Under each name, write down your ideas of what that person might be like.

Writing Use your prewriting list to decide which character or characters you wish to write about. You may find that your description will be more interesting if you include information about the character's relationships with other family members.

Revising You may be able to improve your paragraph by adding a direct quote or reference from the poem. Feel free to place the quote where it will be the most effective—at the beginning, middle, or end of your paragraph.

Proofreading If you have used a direct quotation or reference from the poem, be sure you have inserted quotation marks. The quote or reference may be so closely woven into your writing that you do not need to begin it with a capital letter. You decide. Be sure all your sentences end with periods, question marks, or exclamation marks.

Writing

Remind students that their descriptions should stay true to the way each person is presented in the poem.

Revising

Have students trade papers with a partner. Ask each student to write on a slip of paper a quote from the poem that would go well with his or her partner's paragraph.

Proofreading

Before students proofread their papers, review with them the correct use of punctuation inside and outside the quotation marks.

ESL Activity

Have students work in pairs and choose at least two close relatives and list the things they like about each. Then have them use a thesaurus to more accurately describe their subjects.

THINK ABOUT RHYTHM

Rhythm refers to the regular rise and fall in the flow of sound in a poem. Rhythm can be thought of as a pattern of long and short sounds. In a poem, long sounds occur when a word or syllable is accented. Poets often select words for the sounds they create. Rhythm is the music of poetry.

1. Does the poem "Andre" have a regular rhythmic pattern?

2. If so, can you describe the pattern in terms of long and short syllables?

3. One line in "Andre" has a different pattern from all the rest. Which line is it? What is its rhythmic pattern?

4. Why do you think the author made one line different from the rest?

5. Does the poem "Family Album" have a regular rhythmic pattern? What does this tell about the type of poetry it is?

READING FOCUS

Compare and Contrast Poetry Elements
Compare and contrast the point of view in "Andre" and "Family Album." Who is the speaker? Is the speaker talking about the present or the past? Provide details from the poems as examples.

DEVELOP YOUR VOCABULARY

Synonyms are words that have the same or nearly the same meaning. The words *large* and *big* are synonyms; so are the words *small* and *little*.

In each of the following groups of words, all of the words are synonyms except one. On a separate sheet of paper, write the word in each group that does not belong with the others. Then choose one synonym in each group to use in an original sentence.

1. short, stout, heavy, bulky

2. covers, shields, opens, hides

3. fragments, pieces, colors, parts

4. invisible, hidden, unseen, alone

5. look, choose, pick, select

6. glad, uncertain, happy, joyful

7. thin, stout, frail, wiry

8. under, beneath, below, after

9. take, capture, approach, seize

10. remote, near, distant, far

 THINK ABOUT RHYTHM

Answers
1. yes
2. short-long, short-long
3. "Short and tall and thin and stout"—long, short-long, short-long, short-long
4. Answers will vary. Sample: The poet wanted to emphasize the line.
5. No. It is free verse.

 DEVELOP YOUR VOCABULARY

Answers
Sample sentences are given.
1. *short*—The *bulky* package was too big for the mailbox.
2. *opens*—A dark curtain *covers* the windows.
3. *colors*—He swept up the *fragments* of broken glass.
4. *alone*—She found the key in a *hidden* compartment.
5. *look*—Please *select* a dessert from the menu.
6. *uncertain*—Marie was *glad* the ordeal was over.
7. *stout*—The stray kitten was *frail* from hunger.
8. *after*—The water flowed *under* the bridge.
9. *approach*—The troops attempted to *seize* the fort.
10. *near*—We hiked to a *remote* cabin in the mountains.

READING FOCUS

Sample Answer
Both poems are written in the first-person point of view. In "Andre," the speaker describes a recent experience. In "Family Album," the speaker describes scenes from her own and her family's past.

Another use of sound that is similar to assonance is **consonance**. Consonance is a form of rhyme in which the consonants in stressed syllables agree but the words do not, as in *dogged* and *dagger* or *wide* and *wade*. Partial consonance is also possible, such as in *shadow* and *meadow*.

ELEMENTS OF POETRY

When discussing *denotation* and *connotation*, use "Family Album" as an example.

Ask: At the end of the poem, what is the denotation of the word *palms*?

Have a volunteer read "Family Album" aloud. Ask students if the poem has a rhythmic pattern.

Ask students to find two more examples of alliteration in "Family Album."

In the poem "Bread," make sure that students understand that bread is both a *universal symbol* and a *contextual symbol*.

*A*s with many other skills, reading poetry takes practice. Your ability to understand and enjoy poetry will increase as you learn more about the various elements of poetry, including denotation and connotation, rhythm, sounds, form, and symbolism.

Denotation and Connotation Good poets choose their words carefully, for they know that a word can often have more than one meaning. One kind of meaning is the dictionary definition of the word; that is called the word's **denotation**. Another meaning is what a certain word suggests or brings to mind; this is called the word's **connotation**.

A good example of denotation and connotation is the words *house* and *home*. Both words have nearly the same definition in the dictionary (denotation), but what the words suggest (connotation) is quite different. The word *house* suggests a building in which people live. The word *home* suggests not just a physical structure, but the emotional center of a family.

Rhythm **Rhythm** is a regular pattern of strong and weak units of sound. Another word for strong is **accented**. In the normal flow of speech, certain syllables and words are accented. For example, in the sentence, "Father and Mother are home," the first syllables of *father* and *mother* are accented, and the word *home* is accented. The rhythmic pattern of the sentence is: strong-weak-weak/strong-weak-weak/strong.

Rhythm is part of what makes poetry enjoyable to read and to listen to. Many poems have distinct rhythmic patterns. For example, in the poem "Andre," most of the lines have a rhythmic pattern of weak-strong/weak-strong. You can discover the rhythm of a poem by reading the poem aloud and clapping each sound as you read. This will help you identify the accented and unaccented sounds.

Some poetry does not have a recognizable rhythmic pattern. This type of poetry is called **free verse**. You can still clap out the rhythm of each line, but each line in the poem may have a different rhythm.

Sounds   Some ways poets use pleasing sounds are assonance, onomatopoeia, and alliteration.

Assonance is a type of rhyme in which the vowels but not the consonants sound alike. For example, the vowel *e* has the same sound in the words *met* and *neck*.

Onomatopoeia is the use of words that sound like the thing to which they refer. Some words that can be used this way include *bubbly, hiss, pop, tick-tock*. In the poem "Family Album," the use of the word *blink* can be considered onomatopoeia.

Alliteration is the repetition of the same sound at the beginning of words that are next to or near each other. The tongue twister "Peter Piper picked a peck of pickled peppers" is an example of alliteration. In the poem "Family Album," the last line of the second section contains alliteration: "I must be hearing her heart."

Form   The **form** of a poem is the way the poem is constructed. Form can be closed or open. **Closed poetry** includes the couplet, ballad, and epigram. **Open poetry** has no recognizable pattern. One kind of open poetry is free verse.

Symbolism   A **symbol** is something that stands for something else. Symbols are very important in poetry since poets must often use compact language.

There are many different kinds of symbols that a poet can use. Some are called **universal** or **general symbols** because they tend to mean the same thing to most people. Some symbols, called **contextual symbols**, have meanings just within the context of a particular poem.

As you read "Bread," ask yourself these questions:

1. What is the form of the poem?
2. What universal and contextual symbols are present?

Real-Life Application

Rhythm is an essential part of popular music. Ask students what songs are currently popular. Then have them analyze the rhythmic pattern in the lyrics of several of those songs.

SELECTION OVERVIEW

SELECTION OBJECTIVES
After completing this selection, students will be able to

- understand elements of poetry
- analyze the use of specific elements in a poem
- evaluate the effect of social problems on generations
- express a personal opinion
- use homophones
- identify setting and mood

Lesson Resources

Bread
- Selection Synopsis, Teacher's Edition, p. T483b
- Comprehension and Vocabulary Workbook, pp. 95–96
- Language Enrichment Workbook, p. 101
- Teacher's Resources Reinforcement, p. R47 Test, pp. T91–T92 Literary Analysis, pp. L13–L14

Background Notes
Since the poem is a translation, the reader can infer that the author of the poem is probably from a country other than the United States. The setting also suggests another country. However, the specific setting is not critical to understanding the poem or its theme.

496 ■ Unit 6

ESL Activity

Have students work in small groups to discuss situations that could start out as fun or mischievous but then turn into a serious problem. Then have each group report the results of their discussion to the class. As they report, compile of list of the situations.

BREAD

by Amado V. Hernandez

He had been imprisoned
for so many years,
time was a chain around his neck
knotted up in the windings of his life.

5   A piece of bread
and a can of broth
are left at the door by the guard,
he grabs them with dirty hands.

When the wretched man
10   is about to swallow,
the tear-soaked bread drops,
rubbing against the bruise in his heart.

He remembers why
he was imprisoned:
15   he stole a box of crackers
because his sick child was groaning with hunger.

Trying to get away
from the fist of the law,
he killed his pursuer—
20   and never saw his little girl again!

Now life wears away
wearily, though now every day
he is given the bread that might have saved
his child, who died of hunger.

---

windings (WYND ingz) course of events
broth (BRAWTH) clear soup
wretched (RETCH id) miserable
pursuer (pur SOO er) one who chases another

Bread ■ 497

FOCUS ON POETRY
STUDY HINTS

Bread is a universal symbol. What is its meaning?

Note the rhythmic pattern of each line. What form of poetry is this?

Note the alliteration of *bread* and *broth* at the end of lines 5 and 6.

What is the connotation of the word *grabs*?

Bread and *bruise* are an example of alliteration within two lines.

The words *wears* and *wearily* are an example of alliteration. *Saved* and *day* are an example of assonance. How is bread an important contextual symbol in this poem?

UNDERSTAND THE SELECTION

Answers

1. a prison
2. a piece of bread and a can of broth
3. He killed the person chasing him for stealing a box of crackers.
4. Time weighed heavily on the man since he would spend the rest of his life in jail.
5. Sample answer: He is very hungry; this is all that he receives to eat.
6. He thinks of his little girl and how hungry she was.
7. for life
8. Sample answer: The police might have been sympathetic to his plight and let him go.
9. Sample answer: He may have been so desperate to get food to his daughter that he did not think clearly.
10. Sample answers: He might have begged; he might have asked a storekeeper to give him food in exchange for chores or other work.

Respond to Literature

Ask students to discuss their thoughts about prison conditions and how they are related in this poem. Ask: How does the crime he committed influence your degree of sympathy? Have students give examples from the poem that elicit certain feelings regarding how they feel about the man.

WRITE ABOUT THE SELECTION

Prewriting

Have students get together in small groups to discuss their reactions to the poem. Ask one member of each group to summarize the discussion for the class.

UNDERSTAND THE SELECTION

Recall

1. What is the setting of the poem?

2. What did the guard leave outside the door each day?

3. What crime did the central character commit?

Infer

4. What is the meaning of the metaphor "time was a chain around his neck"?

5. Why do you think the prisoner grabs at the bread and broth?

6. Why do you think he cannot swallow the bread?

7. For how long do you assume the man will be in prison?

Apply

8. What do you think might have happened if the man had not killed his pursuer?

9. Do you think that the man in the poem acted wisely? Why do you think he acted as he did?

10. How else might he have handled his problem?

Respond to Literature

Do you feel sympathy for the man in prison? Explain your response.

WRITE ABOUT THE SELECTION

There is an unexpected twist to the poem "Bread," which is expressed in the last stanza. The prisoner stole bread to try and save his child's life. Now in prison, when it is too late, he receives bread every day. What is your reaction to this turn of events? Write a paragraph in which you express your opinion about the series of events described in the poem.

Prewriting Read the poem several times. As you read, make notes about your feelings and reactions. Do not hold back; your emotions may be very strong.

Writing Use your notes to write a paragraph in which you react to the plight of the prisoner. As you write, you may find it helpful to imagine first that you are the man stealing the crackers—how would you feel? Then imagine that you are the storekeeper whose crackers are stolen. Finally, imagine that you are the police or the prison guard. To add realism to your writing, you might want to include a few slang terms that you use every day.

Revising The final sentence of your paragraph should sum up your opinion. Try writing your final sentence several different ways, then choose the sentence that provides the strongest conclusion.

Proofreading Make sure that your paragraph is correct in subject/verb agreement. If you chose to use any slang terms, do not enclose them in quotation marks. It will only distract the reader.

Writing

Before students begin writing, discuss the meaning of irony. Point out that this poem has an ironic twist, because the bread that the man receives in jail could have saved the life of his child. Encourage students to refer to this irony in their writing.

Revising

Have students trade papers with one or two students to see which concluding sentence they like best.

Proofreading

Put several students' papers on the overhead projector. Proofread the papers as a class exercise.

THINK ABOUT THE ELEMENTS

Some important elements of poetry include denotation and connotation, symbolism, sounds, rhythm, and form. **Denotation** is the literal meaning of a word, while **connotation** is the meaning or feeling that a word evokes. When **symbolism** is used, a concrete thing stands for a more abstract idea. The symbolic meaning of a word may be **universal** or **contextual**. Sometimes, poets choose words according to their sounds, using such devices as **alliteration**, **assonance**, and **onomatopoeia**. **Rhythm** is the pattern of accented and unaccented sounds. **Form** is the way that a poem is constructed.

1. What is a universal symbol for food in the poem? What is a contextual symbol of the man's loss and regret?

2. What form is the poem written in?

3. Give two examples of alliteration.

4. Give an example of assonance.

5. What is the connotation of the word *grabs*?

DEVELOP YOUR VOCABULARY

Homophones are words that sound alike but have different spellings and meanings. The words *beet* and *beat* are examples of homophones. If you can recognize that homophones have different spellings for different meanings, you will make fewer errors in usage.

Give a homophone for each of the italicized words in the sentences below. Then use both words in one sentence.

1. He took a *piece* of apple pie.

2. He *ate* the pie quickly.

3. The *bread* was on the table.

4. He had been imprisoned *there* for many years.

5. It took *so* long to get home.

6. Can I get something *for* you?

7. The *time* passed slowly.

8. He tried *to* get away.

 THINK ABOUT THE ELEMENTS

Answers

1. bread; bread
2. Free verse: each line has a different rhythmic pattern.
3. *bread* and *broth*; *bread* and *bruise*; *wears* and *wearily*
4. *day* and *saved*
5. desperation

DEVELOP YOUR VOCABULARY

Answers
Sample sentences are given.
1. *peace*—He took a *piece* of his mother's pie just to keep *peace* at the dinner table.
2. *eight*—He *ate eight* brownies.
3. *bred*—Scientists have *bred* a new kind of wheat plant that can produce better *bread*.
4. *their, there, they're*—They're unhappy about *their* jobs shoveling coal over *there*.
5. *sew*—It took *so* long to *sew* that dress.
6. *four*—I need *four* more people *for* my baseball team.
7. *thyme*—It is *time* to buy another jar of *thyme*.
8. *two, too*—We will be willing *to* go, *too*, if you can get *two* more tickets.

SELECTION OBJECTIVES

After completing this selection, students will be able to

- understand tone
- use tone to describe an incident
- evaluate differences in a written discussion of a particular subject
- create a new episode for a story
- analyze the tone of a short story
- identify silent letters in words
- understand character relationships

Lesson Resources

Somebody's Son
- Selection Synopsis, Teacher's Edition, p. T483b
- Comprehension and Vocabulary Workbook, pp. 97–98
- Language Enrichment Workbook, pp. 102–103
- Teacher's Resources Reinforcement, p. R48 Tests, pp. T93–T94

More About Tone

Encourage students to think about the tone of the poems that they have read so far in this unit. Point out that the tone of a poem or story is often influenced by the subject matter, as in "Bread"; it can also be influenced by the age and personality of the speaker, as in "Andre."

More About the Unit Theme

In many ways, this story illustrates the classic conflict between the generations. A young man disagrees with his father about going to college (and probably about other things) and runs away from home. By the end of the story, however, both want to see each other again, even though the disagreement may still be there.

READING FOCUS

Understand Character Relationships
You can better understand the characters in a story by noticing their relationships with other people. A character might be friends with one person but have a less positive relationship with another person. Each relationship brings out a different side of the character. To note similarities and differences in relationships, look at how the characters behave toward each other and what they say to each other.

Learn About

TONE

The **tone** of a piece of literature is the author's attitude toward the subject of his or her writing. Tone can also include the author's attitude toward the reader.

The tone of a story or poem can be funny, serious, lighthearted, sarcastic, or sad. An author may write in a friendly, personal way, or in a formal, impersonal way. From the tone of a story or poem, you may think that the author has an emotional feeling for the subject, or you may get the opposite impression.

As you read "Somebody's Son," ask yourself:

1. What is the author's attitude toward David?
2. How does the author address the reader?

WRITING CONNECTION

Think of an incident that happened to you recently. Write two descriptions of that incident, using a different tone for each version. For example, suppose that you decide to write about a fight that you had with a brother or sister. You might try writing the first version of the incident with a humorous tone, then write the second version of the incident with a sad tone.

Background Notes

Explain that a yellow ribbon tied around an oak tree is a sign that a love relationship still exists after a long separation. Students might enjoy hearing the lyrics of the once popular song "Tie a Yellow Ribbon 'Round the Old Oak Tree." The theme of the song is similar to that of *Somebody's Son*.

Cooperative Group Activity

Have students work in pairs, for the Writing Connection activity. Ask each pair to write two versions of the same incident, having one member write in one tone, and the partner in another. They should decide together what tone each will use. Call on several pairs to read their two versions to the class.

SOMEBODY'S SON

by Richard Pindell

He sat, washed up on the side of the highway, a slim, sun-beaten driftwood of a youth. He was hunched on his strapped-together suitcase, chin on hands, elbows on knees, staring down the road. Not a car was in sight. But for him, the dead, still Dakota plains were empty.

Now he was eager to write that letter he had kept putting off. Somehow, writing it would be almost like having company.

He unstrapped his suitcase and fished out of the pocket on the underside of the lid a small, unopened package of stationery. Sitting down in the gravel of the roadside, he closed the suitcase and used it as a desk.

Dear Mom,

If Dad will permit it, I would like to come home. I know there's little chance he will. I'm not going to kid myself. I remember he said once, if I ever ran off, I might as well keep on going.

All I can say is that I felt leaving home was something I had to do. Before even considering college, I wanted to find out more about life and about me and the best way for us (life and me) to live with each other. Please tell Dad—and I guess this'll make him sore all over again—I'm still not certain that college is the answer for me. I think I'd like to work for a time and think it over.

You won't be able to reach me by mail, because I'm not sure where I'll be next. But in a few days I hope to be passing by our place. If there's any chance Dad will have me back, please ask him to tie a white cloth to the apple tree in the south pasture—you know the one, the Grimes Golden beside the tracks. I'll be

---

hunched (HUNCHT) bent over

Somebody's Son ■ 501

TEACHING PLAN

INTRODUCE

Motivation
Ask students to think about how it feels to doubt whether someone loves you. Also ask them to think about what it would be like to leave a person or place and then decide that you want to go back. Relate the discussion to David's situation.

Purpose-Setting Question
Why might a young man who has run away from home decide to go back?

READ

Literary Focus:
Tone
Tell students to consider the words the author chose to use to convey the story. Word choice often reveals the author's attitude. Reading aloud can help students identify tone, as well.

Reading Focus:
Understand Character Relationships
Have students take notes on the relationships that David has with the other characters in the story as they read. Ask: What do these relationships reveal about David's personality? What do they reveal about the personalities of the other characters?

CLOSE

Have students complete Review the Selection on pages 508–509.

Develop Vocabulary Skills
Discuss with students the meanings of the words footnoted in the selection. Ask volunteers to use the words in original sentences. Point out that *denouement* is a French word.

ESL Activity

Note that many children think about running away from home at some time. Have students make a list of the things that children seldom consider when they think about running away. Have students consider how running away would affect them and others.

going by on the train. If there's no cloth on the tree I'll just quietly, and without any hard feelings toward Dad—I mean that— keep on going.

Love, David

The sunset that evening was a violent one. Jagged clouds, trapped in cross-currents, rammed each other like primitive men-of-war and burst into flames, burning one by one into deep purple ash.

It made the boy sad to see the sun go down. He had learned that always at the moment when darkness prevails, loneliness draws closer.

A series of headlights made a domino of the highway. High beams flickered over him curiously. He put out his thumb almost hesitantly, wishing he didn't have to emerge so suddenly, so menacingly. One by one, the cars passed him, their back draft slapping him softly, insultingly, on the cheek.

Much later, turning woodenly to gaze after a car, he saw the glow of taillights intensify. Brakes squealed. The car careened wildly to a stop, and he was running down the road to capture it, his breath rushing against his upturned collar and the taillights glowing nearer as in a dream.

A door was flung open like a friendly arm reaching out to a tired swimmer. "Hop in, boy."

It was a gruff, outdoors voice. "I pret' near missed you. You ain't easy to see out there."

"Thanks, mister."

"Forget it. Used the thumb a lot myself when I was a kid."

"How far are you going?" asked David.

The man named a small place in Iowa about two hundred miles away. David settled back in anticipation of a good ride.

"Where you headin'?" the man asked him.

David glanced at him. His nose was big and jutting; his mouth, wide and gentle. His was a face formed without beauty—and without hesitation. He had a tough-friendly way of accepting David as a man, something which David was still young enough to appreciate as a fine luxury.

---

prevails (prih VAYLZ) gains power over
careened (kuh REEND) turned on one side

Somebody's Son ■ 503

The boy looked out on the highway with affection. It would be a good ride with a good companion. "Home," he said with a grin. "I'm heading home."

The man heard the smile in the boy's voice and chuckled. "That's a good feelin', ain't it? Where 'bouts?"

"Maryland. We have a farm about thirty miles outside of Baltimore."

"Where you been?"

"West Coast, Canada, a little of Mexico."

"And now you're hightailin' for home, huh?" There was a note in the man's voice as if this were a pattern he understood intimately.

"Yes, sir."

David smiled wryly to himself, remembering another day. It was in the San Joaquin Valley. He was picking grapes. As usual, the sun ruled mercilessly. Grape leaves drooped. Pickers were humped in varying attitudes of defense, some with bandannas covering the backs of their necks. Even the dirt had sagged beneath the blazing heat, crumbling into limp, heavy powder.

David looked down at his feet plowing through the grayish stuff. For four hours now it seemed he had not raised his eyes from his feet. He stopped abruptly and looked back down the row, measuring his progress. He had gone maybe fifty yards.

The faint clink of scissors landing in his half-filled basket came to him and then the foreman was bawling at him, "Hey! Where do you think you're going? It ain't lunchtime yet!" David stared at his feet and the dust; and his feet were stretching out as far as they could reach, his fist was tight around the handle of his suitcase, and the dust swirling madly behind him. He didn't even stop to pick up his money.

When he reached the highway and the cars kept passing him, it was all he could do to keep from jumping out in front of them to make them stop.

"Yeah," the driver was saying now, "I know how it is." The comers of his eyes crinkled as if he were going to smile, but he didn't. "I was out on that same old road when I was a kid. Bummin' around. Lettin' no grass grow under me. Sometimes wishin' it would."

---

wryly (RY lee) humorously; twisted to one side

"And then, afterward," David asked, "did you go back home?"

"Nope. I didn't have no home to go back to, like you do. The road was my only home. Lost my ma and pa when I was a little shaver. Killed in a car wreck."

"That's rough," David said with such feeling the man glanced at him sharply.

The boy was staring into the night. The man shifted his grip on the wheel, deftly straddling a dead jack rabbit. He spoke softly to the boy as if he were aware he was interrupting important thoughts. "Bet you could do with some sleep."

"You sure you won't be needing me later to help keep you awake?" David asked.

"Don't worry 'bout me none. I like drivin' at night. You just lean back there and help yourself."

"Well, okay," David said. "Thanks."

Sometime later, he was awakened by a sharp decrease in speed. They were entering a town. He sat up and jerked the letter out of his jacket pocket. He had almost forgotten.

"Excuse me, sir, but would you mind stopping at a mailbox so I can mail this? I want to make sure that it gets home before I do."

"Course not," the man said. "Here's one comin' up now." He pulled over to the curb and stopped.

When the boy got back in, the man smiled kindly. "Bet your folks'll be tickled to hear from you."

"I hope so, sir." David tilted his head back and closed his eyes.

The next day, rides were slow. They were what David called "farmer rides," a few miles here, a couple of miles there, with long waits in between.

Toward nightfall, he forsook the unfriendly asphalt and swung onto a panting, slow-moving freight aimed stolidly east. As the train trundled laboriously over the Mississippi, a few drops of rain slapped the metal floor of his gondola car, and then, suddenly, he was surrounded by water, the river beneath him, and everywhere else, walls of rain. He crawled into a corner and huddled under some scraps of heavy paper that had been used to wrap freight.

---

deftly (DEFT lee) cleverly
asphalt (AS fawlt) road pavement
stolidly (STOL id lee) dully; unemotionally
trundled (TRUN duld) rolled along; moved on wheels

Somebody's Son ■ 505

Literary Focus:
Tone
Ask: In a word, how would you describe the driver's attitude toward David? How does his attitude toward David contribute to the tone of the story?

Discussion
Have students discuss the difference between David and the man who picks him up on the highway.

For thirty miles, the rain pounded him, slashing his paper hut to tatters and turning his clothes into puddles of mush.

As, cold and wet, he swayed with the motion of the car, his last seven months haunted him. A spinning constellation of faces, flaring up and dying away, careened toward him. Faces of truck drivers, waitresses, salesmen, cops, employment agents, winos, tramps, cowboys, bartenders. Faces of people who had been kind to him; faces of people who had used him. They went on and on.

Well, he would never see them again. He had experienced them quickly, dazedly, as they had experienced him. He had no idea where they were now, and they did not know where he was.

Finally the rain stopped. He lunged erect, inviting the warm, night air to dry him. He looked out over the top of his racketing steel box. He faced east—toward home. They didn't have any idea where he was, either.

The train was hammering along beside a highway. He stared at the houses on the other side. How would it be at home? Would his house be like that one, the one with the porch light burning? Or would it be like that one, where the porch was dark and where over each of the lighted windows a yellow shade was pulled down firmly to the sill?

A couple of days later, in the middle of Maryland, maddeningly close to home, the flow of rides narrowed to a trickle and then ceased altogether. When cars weren't in sight, he walked. After a while, he didn't even bother to stop and hold out his thumb. Furiously, he walked.

Later, seated on the passenger train—the only freights around here ran at night—he wished with slow, frightened heartbeats that he were back on the road, headed the other way.

Three inches from his nose was the dust-stained window through which in a few minutes he would look out across his father's fields. Two different pictures tortured him—the tree with the white cloth and the tree without it. His throat closed and he could hardly breathe.

He tried to fortify himself with the idea that whether or not he still was welcome, at least he would see the place again.

The field was sliding closer, one familiar landmark at a time. He couldn't stop the train. The frenzied wheels were stamping out

Reading Focus:
Understand Character Relationships

Ask: Why does David feel "tortured" as the train takes him closer to his home? What does this feeling tell you about David's hope for his relationship with his father?

T506

the end of the crescendo that had begun with the clink of the scissors in his half-filled basket of grapes. Nothing could postpone the denouement now. The tree was around the next bend.

He couldn't look. He was too afraid the cloth would not be there—too afraid he would find, staring back at him, just another tree, just another field, just another somebody else's strange place, the way it always is on the long, long road, the nameless staring back at the nameless. He jerked away from the window.

Desperately, he nudged the passenger beside him. "Mister, will you do me a favor? Around this bend on the right, you'll see an apple tree. I wonder if you'll tell me if you see a white cloth tied to one of its branches?"

As they passed the field, the boy stared straight ahead. "Is it there?" he asked with an uncontrollable quaver.

"Son," the man said in a voice slow with wonder, "I see a white cloth tied on almost every twig."

---

crescendo (krih SHEN doh) increasing in loudness
denouement (day noo MAHN) the final outcome
quaver (KWAY vur) shake, tremble

Somebody's Son ■ 507

T507

UNDERSTAND THE SELECTION

Answers

1. the highways and rails between the Dakotas and Maryland
2. his mother
3. to find out if his father will let him come back home
4. Having graduated high school about seven months ago, David is about 18 or 19 years old.
5. He thinks that college is important and that David should go.
6. They have a good relationship. David is able to confide in her.
7. His parents want him back home more than he ever imagined.
8. Sample answer: David's father realized how much he missed David in his absence.
9. Sample answer: He recognized David as an adult for being out on his own.
10. Answers will vary but many students would feel great joy.

Respond to Literature

Have students make a chart of the contrasts and similarities that exist between the man on the highway and David's father. Encourage students to make comparisons that are based on inferences rather than on what is spelled out in the story. Then ask students to speculate on the kind of father the man on the highway might have been.

WRITE ABOUT THE SELECTION

Prewriting

Encourage students to freewrite the dialogue between parents and son.

Writing

As students work on this section, walk around the classroom. To help those who are having trouble, draw them out by asking how they would feel in David's place.

UNDERSTAND THE SELECTION

Recall

1. What is the setting of the story?
2. To whom does David write a letter?
3. What is the purpose of the letter?

Infer

4. About how old is David? How do you know?
5. What can you infer about David's father's attitude toward college?
6. What can you infer about David's relationship with his mother?
7. What message was given to David at the end of the story?

Apply

8. Do you think that David's father might have changed during the time David was away? Explain your answer.
9. Why do you think that the man David rode with accepted David as a man?
10. Suppose that you are David. How would you feel as the train passed the apple tree?

Respond to Literature

How do the man on the highway and David's parents show different qualities of the same generation? How do they show similar qualities?

WRITE ABOUT THE SELECTION

At the end of "Somebody's Son," David realizes that he can go home again. What do you think happens when David finally gets home? What conversations might he have with his father? His mother? His friends? Add an episode to "Somebody's Son" that tells what happens after David returns home.

Prewriting Create an informal outline of what might happen the day David arrives home. Include details of conversations David might have with his parents and others. Look for clues in the details of the story.

Writing Use your prewriting outline to write a paragraph that adds an episode to "Somebody's Son." Be sure to tell about David's feelings as he walks into his house for the first time after his absence.

Revising When you revise your paragraph, add dialogue that makes the feelings of David and his parents clear as well as specific details that make the setting clear.

Proofreading Read over your paragraph to check for errors. Make sure that you have used correct punctuation when writing dialogue. Remember that periods, commas, question marks, and exclamation points all fall inside the quotation marks when they are part of a character's speech. Be sure that all your sentences end with periods, question marks, or exclamation marks.

Revising

Have students work in threes to go over their dialogue. Suggest that for greater realism, they role-play David, his father, and his mother.

Proofreading

Show some examples on the chalkboard or overhead projector of correctly punctuated dialogue. Then have students correct their own papers.

ESL Activity

Have students work in pairs to write a letter to a friend who is considering running away. How can they convince the friend to stay home and work things out? Tell them to decide what the tone of the letter should be, and to read the letter aloud to see if they accomplished their goals.

THINK ABOUT TONE

The **tone** of a literary work communicates the author's attitude toward his or her subject. The tone may be humorous or serious, sarcastic or sad. Tone can also include the author's attitude toward the reader. Some literary works have a friendly, informal tone, while others have a more detached, formal tone.

1. What is the tone of "Somebody's Son"?

2. What does the tone tell you about the author's attitude toward his subject?

3. What do you feel is the author's attitude toward you, the reader?

4. In the story, David writes a letter. What is the tone of that letter?

5. What does the tone tell you about David's attitude toward his home and his parents?

READING FOCUS

Understand Character Relationships
As you read "Somebody's Son," you were able to understand the relationships between the characters. Describe the relationship between David and the driver. What did this relationship tell you about the driver's personality?

DEVELOP YOUR VOCABULARY

Some English words have silent letters. For example, in the word *knife*, the *k* is silent. Words with silent letters can be tricky to spell and pronounce. Another group of words that can be difficult to spell and pronounce are words with letter combinations that sound like other letters; for example, the *ph* in *pharmacy* sounds like *f*.

Identify the silent letters, or the letter combinations that sound like other letters, in each word below. Then use the word in an original sentence.

1. asphalt
2. denouement
3. knight
4. knowledge
5. wryly
6. gourmet
7. write
8. whisker
9. photograph
10. physics
11. thyme
12. wreck

Review the Selection ■ 509

THINK ABOUT TONE

Answers
1. serious yet warm
2. He has compassion and understanding for David.
3. Answers will vary. The author's attitude toward the reader might be described as unbiased, since he presents the information objectively and lets readers form their own opinions.
4. serious
5. He has a genuine desire to come home and improve his relationship with his father.

DEVELOP YOUR VOCABULARY

Answers
Sample sentences are given.
1. *ph*—The road was paved with *asphalt*.
2. *oue*—The *denouement* was what he had hoped for.
3. *k, gh*—Sir Lancelot was a famous *knight*.
4. *k, w*—He has a great deal of *knowledge* about science.
5. *w*—David smiled *wryly* after his sarcastic remark.
6. *et*—The deli sold only *gourmet* food.
7. *w, e*—*Write* the answers on the board.
8. *h*—The cat's *whisker* was long and white.
9. *ph*—She handed me a *photograph* of her mother.
10. *ph*—*Physics* is a difficult subject.
11. *h, e*—The recipe called for a dash of *thyme*.
12. *w*—My aunt Millie is a nervous *wreck*.

READING FOCUS

Sample Answer

The driver respects David as a young man getting along on his own, as he once did. David feels comfortable with the driver, who may even remind him of his own father. The driver may be a father himself or want to be one. His personality traits include caring, good listener, and intuitive.

T509

SELECTION OVERVIEW

SELECTION OBJECTIVES

After completing this selection, students will be able to

- understand the elements of plot
- identify those elements in a short story
- discuss a relationship between different generations
- write from personal experience
- appreciate words from other cultures
- compare and contrast character traits

Lesson Resources

The Medicine Bag
- Selection Synopsis, Teacher's Edition, pp. 483b–483c
- Comprehension and Vocabulary Workbook, pp. 99–100
- Language Enrichment Workbook, p. 104
- Teacher's Resources Reinforcement, p. R49 Test, pp. T95–T96

More About Plot

Some stories have a very definite plot in which the four or five elements can be seen clearly. Other stories have a less distinct plot or no real plot at all. An example of a story that does not have a real distinct plot is "The Secret Life of Walter Mitty," which students read in the last unit. The appeal of this story lies not in the unfolding of the plot, but the unfolding of Mitty's inner life through a series of episodes.

More About the Unit Theme

This selection spans three generations when a teenaged boy is surprised by a visit from his great-grandfather. The boy discovers that it is his great-grandfather's wish to pass on to him something valuable from his Native American heritage.

Iowa Medicine Man, See-Non-ty, George Catlin. Corbis Bettmann

READING FOCUS

Compare and Contrast Character Traits
When you compare and contrast the traits of characters, you note similarities and differences. Two characters in a story may have contrasting traits. For example, they might have different attitudes toward the same thing. Even a single character can have contrasting traits. He or she might change during the story or have mixed feelings about another character, for example. As you read, ask yourself questions such as: Do the characters feel the same way about what happens? Do the characters change by the end of the story?

Learn About

PLOT

The plot is the plan or pattern of events that unfolds in a story. The five important elements of plot are exposition, complication, crisis, climax, and resolution.

The **exposition** is the introduction of the plot. In the exposition, you learn who the main character is and the kind of problems he or she will face in the story. Then comes the **complication**—a setback encountered by the main character in attempting to overcome the problem. The decisive moment is called the **crisis**. During the crisis, the main character either wins or loses the struggle to overcome the problem. The outcome of the crisis is called the **climax**, the most exciting part of the story, usually at or near the end. Many stories end with the climax, but some do not. These stories are followed by a **resolution**, a kind of wrap-up of the story in which further questions are answered.

As you read "The Medicine Bag," ask yourself:
1. What is the plot of the story?
2. What problem is presented for the main character to overcome?

WRITING CONNECTION

Choose a story in this book that you have read. Then make a list of the five plot elements as they appear in the story.

Viewing Fine Art

George Catlin (1796–1872) was one of America's best-known artist-explorers. Many expeditions into unexplored country took along an artist to record the sights and make portraits of the Native Americans. Catlin was an official government artist who eventually became the nation's leading artist of Native Americans and a defender of their rights. Catlin sought to be the historian for natives of North America which he achieved. Ask: How does this portrait compare to other portraits of Native Americans you have seen?

Cooperative Group Activity

Have students work in small groups for the Writing Connection activity. Ask each group to create a plot outline for the story it choses. The outline should include the five plot elements.

The Medicine Bag

by Virginia Driving Hawk Sneve

My kid sister Cheryl and I always bragged about our Sioux grandpa, Joe Iron Shell. Our friends, who had always lived in the city and only knew about Indians from movies and TV, were impressed by our stories. Maybe we exaggerated and made Grandpa and the reservation sound glamorous, but when we'd return home to Iowa after our yearly summer visit to Grandpa, we always had some exciting tale to tell.

We always had some authentic Sioux article to show our listeners. One year Cheryl had new moccasins that Grandpa had made. On another visit he gave me a small, round, flat, rawhide drum that was decorated with a painting of a warrior riding a horse. He taught me a real Sioux chant to sing while I beat the drum with a leather-covered stick that had a feather on the end. Man, that really made an impression.

We never showed our friends Grandpa's picture. Not that we were ashamed of him, but because we knew that the glamorous tales we told didn't go with the real thing. Our friends would have laughed at the picture because Grandpa wasn't tall and stately like TV Indians. His hair wasn't in braids but hung in stringy, gray strands on his neck, and he was old. He was our great-grandfather, and he didn't live in a tepee, but all by himself in a part log, part tar-paper shack on the Rosebud Reservation in South Dakota. So when Grandpa came to visit us, I was so ashamed and embarrassed I could've died.

There are a lot of yippy poodles and other fancy little dogs in our neighborhood,

---

Sioux (SOO) Native American tribes of the northern plains of the United States and nearby southern Canada
moccasins (MOK uh sunz) heelless slippers of soft flexible leather, originally worn by Native Americans
tepee (TEE pee) a cone-shaped tent of animal skins, used by the Plains Indians
Rosebud Reservation: a small Indian reservation in south-central South Dakota

The Medicine Bag ■ 511

Develop Vocabulary Skills
When preteaching the vocabulary words footnoted in the story, you may want to ask volunteers to draw some of the Native American items on the chalkboard; for example; tepee, bolo, thong, moccasins.

Critical Thinking:
Infer

Ask students what they can infer about Grandpa's age, lifestyle, and physical condition from the author's descriptions.

Literary Focus:
Plot

Point out that the central problem in a story involves a conflict—a struggle between the main character and something else. If the character struggles against an outside force—another character or the forces of nature, for example—the plot involves an external conflict. If the struggle takes place within the character, it is called an internal conflict. Ask: So far, does the conflict in the story seem to be an internal conflict or an external conflict?

but they usually barked singly at the mailman from the safety of their own yards. Now it sounded as if a whole pack of mutts were barking together in one place.

I got up and walked to the curb to see what the commotion was. About a block away I saw a crowd of little kids yelling, with the dogs yipping and growling around someone who was walking down the middle of the street.

I watched the group as it slowly came closer and saw that in the center of the strange procession was a man wearing a tall black hat. He'd pause now and then to peer at something in his hand and then at the houses on either side of the street. I felt cold and hot at the same time as I recognized the man. "Oh, no!" I whispered. "It's Grandpa!"

I stood on the curb, unable to move even though I wanted to run and hide. Then I got mad when I saw how the yippy dogs were growling and nipping at the old man's baggy pant legs and how wearily he poked them away with his cane. "Stupid mutts," I said as I ran to rescue Grandpa.

When I kicked and hollered at the dogs to get away, they put their tails between their legs and scattered. The kids ran to the curb where they watched me and the old man.

"Grandpa," I said and felt pretty dumb when my voice cracked. I reached for his beat-up old tin suitcase, which was tied shut with a rope. But he set it down right in the street and shook my hand.

"*Hau. Takoza.* Grandchild," he greeted me formally in Sioux.

All I could do was stand there with the whole neighborhood watching and shake the hand of the leather-brown old man. I saw how his gray hair straggled from under his big black hat, which had a drooping feather in its crown. His rumpled black suit hung like a sack over his stooped frame. As he shook my hand, his coat fell open to expose a bright red satin shirt with a beaded bolo tie under the collar. His get-up wasn't out of place on the reservation, but it sure was here, and I wanted to sink right through the pavement.

"Hi," I muttered with my head down. I tried to pull my hand away when I felt his bony hand trembling, and looked up to see fatigue in his face. I felt like crying. I couldn't think of anything to say so I picked up Grandpa's suitcase, took his arm, and guided him up the driveway to our house.

Mom was standing on the steps. I don't know how long she'd been watching, but her hand was over her mouth and she looked as if she couldn't believe what she saw. Then she ran to us.

"Grandpa," she gasped. "How in the world did you get here?"

She checked her move to embrace Grandpa and I remembered that such a display of affection is unseemly to the Sioux and would embarrass him.

---

bolo tie (BOH loh TY) a man's string tie, held together with a decorated sliding device

"*Hau*, Marie," he said as he shook Mom's hand. She smiled and took his other arm.

As we supported him up the steps, the door banged open and Cheryl came bursting out of the house. She was all smiles and was so obviously glad to see Grandpa that I was ashamed of how I felt.

"Grandpa!" she yelled happily. "You came to see us!"

Grandpa smiled, and Mom and I let go of him as he stretched out his arms to my ten-year-old sister, who was still young enough to be hugged.

"*Wicincala*, little girl," he greeted her and then collapsed.

He had fainted. Mom and I carried him into her sewing room, where we had a spare bed.

After we had Grandpa on the bed, Mom stood there helplessly patting his shoulder.

"Shouldn't we call the doctor, Mom?" I suggested, since she didn't seem to know what to do.

"Yes," she agreed with a sigh. "You make Grandpa comfortable, Martin."

I reluctantly moved to the bed. I knew Grandpa wouldn't want to have Mom undress him, but I didn't want to, either. He was so skinny and frail that his coat slipped off easily. When I loosened his tie

Reading Focus:
Compare and Contrast Character Traits
Ask: What contrasting, or mixed, feelings does the main character have toward his great-grandfather? Which statements, thoughts, or actions by the main character demonstrate these mixed feelings?

Viewing Fine Art

This painting by Amado Peña examines the current state of the Native American in the Southwest. Here two Native American men are seated in Victorian chairs in a modern room. Both wear a combination of contemporary and traditional clothing. On the wall next to them are portraits of similarly seated figures, perhaps of relatives. One figure appears to be an old, frail man, and the other has a darkened face. The painting is a commentary on the changing lifestyle and identity of Native Americans. Ask: What details suggest that the figure on the right is an old man? What might he represent to the younger figure on the left? Do you think these figures would be familiar to Martin's great-grandfather?

Memories, Amado M. Peña, Jr. El Taller, Inc.

The Medicine Bag ■ 513

and opened his shirt collar, I felt a small leather pouch that hung from a thong around his neck. I left it alone and moved to remove his boots. The scuffed old cowboy boots were tight, and he moaned as I put pressure on his legs to jerk them off.

I put the boots on the floor and saw why they fit so tight. Each one was stuffed with money. I looked at the bills that lined the boots and started to ask about them, but Grandpa's eyes were closed again.

Mom came back with a basin of water. "The doctor thinks Grandpa is suffering from heat exhaustion," she explained as she bathed Grandpa's face. Mom gave a big sigh. "*Oh, hinh,* Martin. How do you suppose he got here?"

We found out after the doctor's visit. Grandpa was angrily sitting up in bed while Mom tried to feed him some soup.

"Tonight you let Marie feed you, Grandpa," spoke my dad, who had gotten home from work just as the doctor was leaving. "You're not really sick," he said as he gently pushed Grandpa back against the pillows. "The doctor said you just got too tired and hot after your long trip."

Grandpa relaxed, and between sips of soup, he told us of his journey. Soon after our visit to him, Grandpa decided that he would like to see where his only living descendants lived and what our home was like. Besides, he admitted sheepishly, he was lonesome after we left.

I knew that everybody felt as guilty as I did—especially Mom. Mom was all

Grandpa had left. So even after she married my dad, who's a white man and teaches in the college in our city, and after Cheryl and I were born, Mom made sure that every summer we spent a week with Grandpa.

I never thought that Grandpa would be lonely after our visits, and none of us noticed how old and weak he had become. But Grandpa knew, and so he came to us. He had ridden on buses for two and a half days. When he arrived in the city, tired and stiff from sitting for so long, he set out, walking, to find us.

He had stopped to rest on the steps of some building downtown, and a police-man found him. The cop, according to Grandpa, was a good man who took him to the bus stop and waited until the bus came and told the driver to let Grandpa out at Bell View Drive. After Grandpa got off the bus, he started walking again. But he couldn't see the house numbers on the other side when he walked on the side-walk, so he walked in the middle of the street. That's when all the little kids and dogs followed him.

I knew everybody felt as bad as I did. Yet I was so proud of this eighty-six-year-old man, who had never been away from the reservation, having the courage to travel so far alone.

"You found the money in my boots?" he asked Mom.

"Martin did," she answered, and roused herself to scold. "Grandpa, you shouldn't have carried so much money. What if someone had stolen it from you?"

---

thong (THAHNG) a narrow strip of leather

Reading Focus:
Compare and Contrast Character Traits

Ask: What feeling prompted Grand-pa to visit his granddaughter's fam-ily? How do Martin and his family feel when they learn about Grand-pa's feelings? Why does Martin, in addition, feel proud of Grandpa?

Grandpa laughed. "I would've known if anyone tried to take the boots off my feet. The money is what I've saved for a long time—a hundred dollars—for my funeral. But you take it now to buy groceries so that I won't be a burden to you while I am here."

"That won't be necessary, Grandpa," Dad said. "We are honored to have you with us, and you will never be a burden. I am only sorry that we never thought to bring you home with us this summer and spare you the discomfort of a long trip."

Grandpa was pleased. "Thank you," he answered. "But do not feel bad that you didn't bring me with you, for I would not have come then. It was not time." He said this in such a way that no one could argue with him. To Grandpa and the Sioux, he once told me, a thing would be done when it was the right time to do it, and that's the way it was.

"Also," Grandpa went on, looking at me, "I have come because it is soon time for Martin to have the medicine bag."

We all knew what that meant. Grandpa thought he was going to die, and he had to follow the tradition of his family to pass the medicine bag, along with its history, to the oldest male child.

"Even though the boy," he said still looking at me, "bears a white man's name, the medicine bag will be his."

I didn't know what to say. I had the same hot and cold feeling that I had when I first saw Grandpa in the street. The medicine bag was the dirty leather pouch I had found around his neck. "I could never wear such a thing," I almost said aloud. I thought of having my friends see it in gym class or at the swimming pool and could imagine the smart things they would say. But I just swallowed hard and took a step toward the bed. I knew I would have to take it.

But Grandpa was tired. "Not now, Martin," he said, waving his hand in dismissal. "It is not time. Now I will sleep."

So that's how Grandpa came to be with us for two months. My friends kept asking to come see the old man, but I put them off. I told myself that I didn't want them laughing at Grandpa. But even as I made excuses, I knew it wasn't Grandpa that I was afraid they'd laugh at.

Nothing bothered Cheryl about bringing her friends to see Grandpa. Every day after school started, there'd be a crew of giggling little girls or round-eyed little boys crowded around the old man on the patio, where he'd gotten in the habit of sitting every afternoon.

Grandpa would smile in his gentle way and patiently answer their questions, or he'd tell them stories of brave warriors, ghosts, animals; and the kids listened in awed silence. Those little guys thought Grandpa was great.

Finally, one day after school, my friends came home with me because nothing I said stopped them. "We're going to see the great Indian of Bell View Drive," said Hank, who was supposed to be my best friend. "My brother has seen him three times so he oughta be well enough to see us."

When we got to my house, Grandpa was sitting on the patio. He had on his red shirt, but today he also wore a fringed

The Medicine Bag ■ 515

Literary Focus:
Plot
Ask: What does Grandpa want to give Martin? Why? Why does Martin feel "hot and cold" when he learns about Grandpa's plan?

Discussion
Have students discuss why they think the medicine bag was so important to Grandpa. What do they think the medicine bag represents? What traditions and objects pass on from generation to generation in their own families?

Native American painter Amado Peña again depicts the situation of the modern-day Native American. In this case, the artist sits thoughtfully in his studio with an undecorated vase and a ready-to-paint canvas nearby. Both the vase and the patterned rug in the background represent traditional Native American art forms. Other details in the painting, however, such as the Western saddle and cowboy emblem on the painter's scarf, as well as the new form of painting the artist has chosen, suggest the nontraditional world in which the painter also lives. Ask: How do you think Martin's buddies would react to the figure in the painting?

El Pintor, Amado Peña, Jr. El Taller, Inc.

leather vest that was decorated with beads. Instead of his usual cowboy boots, he had solidly beaded moccasins on his feet that stuck out of his black trousers. Of course, he had his old black hat on— he was seldom without it. But it had been brushed, and the feather in the beaded headband was proudly erect, its tip a brighter white. His hair lay in silver strands over the red shirt collar.

I stared just as my friends did, and I heard one of them murmur, "Wow!"

Grandpa looked up, and, when his eyes met mine, they twinkled as if he were laughing inside. He nodded to me, and my face got all hot. I could tell that he had known all along I was afraid he'd embarrass me in front of my friends.

"*Hau, hoksilas,* boys," he greeted and held out his hand.

My buddies passed in a single file and shook his hand as I introduced them. They were so polite I almost laughed. "How, there, Grandpa," and even a "How-do-you-do, sir."

"You look fine, Grandpa," I said as the guys sat on the lawn chairs or on the patio floor.

"*Hanh,* yes," he agreed. "When I woke up this morning, it seemed the right time to dress in the good clothes. I knew that my grandson would be bringing his friends."

"You guys want some lemonade or something?" I offered. No one answered. They were listening to Grandpa as he started telling how he'd killed the deer from which his vest was made.

Grandpa did most of the talking while my friends were there. I was so proud of him and amazed at how respectfully quiet my buddies were. Mom had to chase them home at supper time. As they left, they shook Grandpa's hand again and said to me,

"Martin, he's really great!"

"Yeah, man! Don't blame you for keeping him to yourself."

"Can we come back?"

But after they left, Mom said, "No more visitors for a while, Martin. Grandpa won't admit it, but his strength hasn't returned. He likes having company, but it tires him."

That evening Grandpa called me to his room before he went to sleep. "Tomorrow," he said, "when you come home, it will be time to give you the medicine bag."

I felt a hard squeeze from where my heart is supposed to be and was scared, but I answered, "OK, Grandpa."

All night I had weird dreams about thunder and lightning on a high hill. From a distance I heard the slow beat of a drum. When I woke up in the morning, I felt as if I hadn't slept at all. At school it seemed as if the day would never end and, when it finally did, I ran home.

Grandpa was in his room, sitting on the bed. The shades were down, and the place was dim and cool. I sat on the floor in front of Grandpa, but he didn't even look at me. After what seemed a long time he spoke.

"I sent your mother and sister away. What you will hear today is only for a man's ears. What you will receive is only for a man's hands." He fell silent, and I felt shivers down my back.

The Medicine Bag ■ 517

Reading Focus:
Compare and Contrast Character Traits
Ask: Is Martin embarrassed when his friends finally meet his great-grandfather? Explain.

Literary Focus:
Plot
Ask: What climax do the events of the plot seem to be leading up to?

Critical Thinking:
Analyze
Ask: Why, do you think, is Martin scared about being given the medicine bag?

Background Notes

Grandpa refers to the time when the Sioux were forced to move to reservation lands in the Dakota Territory and Nebraska. The removal came after the Sioux were defeated in a clash with government troops over white violations of treaties.

Literary Focus:
Symbols

Point out that a symbol is a thing that stands for something beyond itself, usually something you cannot see or touch. For example, the ornaments worn by a medicine man (see painting on page 510) could symbolize his healing powers. Have students speculate on what Grandpa's medicine bag might symbolize to its owner.

Reading Focus:
Compare and Contrast Character Traits

Grandpa's father lived during a time of upheaval for Native Americans. Ask: How does he respond to this change? Does Grandpa seem to have the same trait? Does Martin?

"My father in his early manhood," Grandpa began, "made a vision quest to find a spirit guide for his life. You cannot understand how it was in that time, when the great Teton Sioux were first made to stay on the reservation. There was a strong need for guidance from *Wakantanka*, the Great Spirit. But too many of the young men were filled with despair and hatred. They thought it was hopeless to search for a vision when the glorious life was gone and only the hated confines of a reservation lay ahead. But my father held to the old ways.

"He carefully prepared for his quest with a purifying sweat bath, and then he went alone to a high butte top to fast and pray. After three days he received his sacred dream—in which he found, after long searching, the white man's iron. He did not understand his vision of finding something belonging to the white people, for in that time they were the enemy. When he came down from the butte to cleanse himself at the stream below, he found the remains of a campfire and the broken shell of an iron kettle. This was a sign that reinforced his dream. He took a piece of the iron for his medicine bag, which he had made of elk skin years before, to prepare for his quest.

"He returned to his village, where he told his dream to the wise old men of the tribe. They gave him the name *Iron Shell*, but neither did they understand the meaning of the dream. The first Iron Shell kept the piece of iron with him at all times and believed it gave him protection from the evils of those unhappy days.

"Then a terrible thing happened to Iron Shell. He and several other young men were taken from their homes by the soldiers and sent far away to a white man's boarding school. He was angry and lonesome for his parents and the young girl he had wed before he was taken away. At first Iron Shell resisted the teacher's attempts to change him, and he did not try to learn. One day it was his turn to work in the school's blacksmith shop. As he walked into the place, he knew that his medicine had brought him there to learn and work with the white man's iron.

"Iron Shell became a blacksmith and worked at the trade when he returned to the reservation. All of his life he treasured the medicine bag. When he was old, and I was a man, he gave it to me, for no one made the vision quest any more."

Grandpa quit talking, and I stared in disbelief as he covered his face with his hands. His shoulders were shaking with quiet sobs, and I looked away until he began to speak again.

"I kept the bag until my son, your mother's father, was a man and had to leave us to fight in the war across the ocean. I gave him the bag, for I believed

---

vision quest (VIZH un KWEST) a search for a revelation that would aid understanding
Wakantanka (wah kahn TANGK uh) the Sioux religion's most important spirit—the creator of the world
butte (BYOOT) the top of a steep hill standing alone in a plain

518 ■ Unit 6

Deer Rattle/Deer Dancer, Frank La Pend

The Medicine Bag ■ 519

T519

Literary Focus:
Climax and Resolution

Point out that the crisis is often the same event as the climax—the moment where the character overcomes the problem he or she has been facing. Ask: When Grandpa passes the medicine bag on to Martin, why does he say, "You need not wear it"? How does this event allow Martin to overcome the problem he had been facing?

Reading Focus:
Compare and Contrast Character Traits

Ask: What does Martin do two weeks after Grandpa dies? What does his response tell you about his attitude toward his great-grandfather and the medicine bag? What trait do he and his great-grandfather share?

it would protect him in battle, but he did not take it with him. He was afraid that he would lose it. He died in a far-away place."

Again Grandpa was still, and I felt his grief around me.

"My son," he went on after clearing his throat, "had only a daughter, and it is not proper for her to know of these things."

He unbuttoned his shirt, pulled out the leather pouch, and lifted it over his head. He held it in his hand, turning it over and over as if memorizing how it looked.

"In the bag," he said as he opened it and removed two objects, "is the broken shell of the iron kettle, a pebble from the butte, and a piece of the sacred sage." He held the pouch upside down and dust drifted down.

"After the bag is yours you must put a piece of prairie sage within and never open it again until you pass it on to your son." He replaced the pebble and the piece of iron, and tied the bag.

I stood up, somehow knowing I should. Grandpa slowly rose from the bed and stood upright in front of me holding the bag before my face. I closed my eyes and waited for him to slip it over my head. But he spoke.

"No, you need not wear it." He placed the soft leather bag in my right hand and closed my other hand over it. "It would not be right to wear it in this time and place where no one will understand. Put it safely away until you are again on the reservation. Wear it then, when you replace the sacred sage."

Grandpa turned and sat again on the bed. Wearily he leaned his head against the pillow. "Go," he said. "I will sleep now."

"Thank you, Grandpa," I said softly and left with the bag in my hands.

That night Mom and Dad took Grandpa to the hospital. Two weeks later I stood alone on the lonely prairie of the reservation and put the sacred sage in my medicine bag.

---

sage (SAYJ) plant belonging to the mint family

Mini Quiz

Write the following sentences on the chalkboard or overhead projector and call on students to fill in the blanks. Discuss the answers with the class.

1. Martin first saw his great-grandfather surrounded by _____.
2. Grandpa came from _____.
3. Grandpa came to see Martin and his family because _____.
4. It was Grandpa's intention to give Martin _____.
5. Grandpa died shortly after _____.

Answers

1. a group of children and dogs
2. the Rosebud Reservation in South Dakota
3. he knew that he was going to die
4. a medicine bag
5. he gave Martin a medicine bag

Virginia Driving Hawk Sneve (1933–   )

Writer and teacher Virginia Driving Hawk Sneve grew up on a Sioux reservation in South Dakota. Her knowledge of Sioux life and heritage has played an important role in her writings, which include novels, short stories, and nonfiction.

The Sioux history was an oral one, with stories handed down from one generation to another. As a result there are few written records of historical events among the Sioux. Time, the author explains, is less important to the Native Americans than to the white people; Native Americans are more concerned with the dramatic significance of an event and its impact on their lives than with when it occurred.

In addition to several novels and many short stories, Ms. Sneve has written a collection of biographies of Sioux leaders entitled *They Led a Nation*. In this book, she points out an interesting fact, that the word *chief* is not a Native American word. It was coined by non–Native Americans to refer to the leader of a Native American tribe. Yet Sneve often uses the word *chief* in her stories, because she feels that for her readers it evokes "a picture of stoic greatness, unflinching courage, and . . . manly beauty and strength. To use another word for these men would be to rob them of their glory."

Author Biography ■ 521

MORE ABOUT THE AUTHOR

Virginia Driving Hawk Sneve has always viewed writing as an extension of teaching, an activity she has been involved in all her life. She says she has always strived to be honest and accurate in portraying the experiences of Native Americans. Her aim is to show readers "that Native Americans have a proud past, a viable present, and a hopeful future."

The best way to learn how to write, according to Sneve, is to read. "Reading exposes you to the way words are used in good stories," she says. "It builds your vocabulary so that your writing can build images in readers' minds the way great authors have done. Reading is also the way a writer finds out what has been written and what needs to be written."

Additional Works BY VIRGINIA DRIVING HAWK SNEVE

You may wish to suggest these works by Virginia Driving Hawk Sneve for additional reading:

High Elk's Treasure. Holiday House, 1995. A 13-year-old boy finds an object of historical importance. (fiction)

Completing the Circle. Bison Books, 1998. Sneve blends stories and autobiography in this account of her female relatives. (nonfiction)

The Sioux. Holiday House, 1993. Sketches of history, beliefs, and daily life of the Sioux. (nonfiction)

Dancing Teepees: Poems of American Indian Youth. Holiday House, 1991. An anthology including some poems by Sneve. (poetry)

UNDERSTAND THE SELECTION

Answers

1. Martin, a teenage boy
2. Martin's great-grandfather
3. He has exaggerated about Grandpa and is afraid his friends will laugh at him when they see the real thing.
4. He knew that he was not going to live much longer and was lonely for his family.
5. He was embarrassed and angry, and he felt like crying.
6. Men and women had strictly defined roles, with things like the medicine bag not known to the women. The relationships within a family were formal, with little display of affection.
7. He said that it would not be right to wear it in this time and place where no one would understand.
8. Cheryl was glad to see him and readily brought her friends home to meet him. Martin cared for Grandpa but had mixed feelings about his visit and was embarrassed to bring his friends home.
9. Cheryl, being younger, did not feel the peer pressure that Martin did and was less concerned about what other people thought.
10. Before Grandpa's visit, Martin admired Grandpa for his story-telling and tales of adventure. He came to admire Grandpa for his courage to travel to Iowa alone and for his devotion to his family and heritage.

Respond to Literature

Have students think about why many Sioux choose not to continue traditions such as the medicine bag. Remind students that in "Ta-Na-E-Ka," the author mentions that many Kaw had given up Ta-Na-E-Ka ritual. Also ask students in what way Martin's great-grandfather has given up something of the old days.

WRITE ABOUT THE SELECTION

Prewriting

Create a cluster on the chalkboard or overhead transparency.

UNDERSTAND THE SELECTION

Recall

1. Who is the main character and narrator in this story?

2. Who comes to visit?

3. What problem does the visit present for the narrator?

Infer

4. Why did Grandpa travel to Iowa?

5. What different feelings did Martin have when he saw Grandpa walking down the street?

6. What can you infer about the relationship between men and women in the Sioux culture?

7. What indicates that Grandpa knew how Martin felt about wearing the medicine bag?

Apply

8. Compare Cheryl's initial reaction to Grandpa with Martin's reaction.

9. How do you account for the difference?

10. What qualities in Grandpa did Martin admire at the beginning of the story? At the end?

Respond to Literature

Why are Martin and his family especially important to Grandpa in terms of generations?

WRITE ABOUT THE SELECTION

The short story "The Medicine Bag" has several important themes. One of these themes is the importance of family traditions and cultural heritage. Another theme is Martin and Grandpa's successful bridging of a three-generation gap. Yet another theme is the blending of white and Native American cultures, both in terms of the iron shell in the medicine bag and in Martin's mother marrying a white man. Which theme is most meaningful to you? Write a paragraph in which you express your opinion about one of the themes in the story.

Prewriting Reread the story and list any theme you discover that was not mentioned above. Then choose from all the themes the one that has the most meaning for you. Cluster facts, details, and ideas about the theme you chose.

Writing Write a paragraph in which you express your opinion about the theme that you have chosen. Your opinion can be positive or negative; it can be based on your own experiences or the experiences of people you know.

Revising What point of view have you used for your paragraph? If you have written in the first person, try rewriting your paragraph in the third person, and vice versa. Decide which version is more effective.

Proofreading Make sure that all of your sentences have a subject and a verb. Correct any sentence fragments by rewriting them as complete sentences.

Writing

Some students may find it helpful to ask themselves these questions as they write about the theme: What did I learn as a result of reading this story? What did the main character learn? What problems did the main character go through and overcome?

Revising

Have each student trade papers with a partner. Ask students to read both versions of their partner's paragraph, then offer an opinion as to which is better—first- or third-person point of view.

Proofreading

Review the use of subjects and verbs by putting a student's paper on the overhead projector. Have the class identify the subject and verb in each sentence.

THINK ABOUT PLOT

Without a plot, there would be no story. The events that happen in a story make up the plot. The main elements of a plot are **exposition**, **complication**, **crisis**, **climax**, and **resolution**. In a well-written story, every event and action is important and related.

1. What is the exposition of the plot in "The Medicine Bag"? Where in the story does it occur?

2. What complication is introduced into the plot? How does this add to the problem of the main character?

3. What is the crisis of the story?

4. At what point does the climax occur? What is the outcome for the main character?

5. Does the story have a resolution? If so, what do you think it adds to the story?

> ### READING FOCUS
> **Compare and Contrast Character Traits**
> What attitudes does Martin exhibit at the beginning of the story? How has he changed by the end?

DEVELOP YOUR VOCABULARY

Several words in the short story "The Medicine Bag" relate specifically to the Native American culture. Some of the words, such as *moccasins*, have found their way into the English language. Words from other cultures have also found their way into the English language. For example, you are probably familiar with the Eskimo word *igloo*, which is a house built of ice.

Find the meaning of each word. The cultural origin of the word is given in parentheses. Then use each word in an original sentence.

1. tepee (Native American); also teepee

2. siesta (Spanish)

3. amigo (Spanish)

4. cafe (French)

5. cabana (Spanish)

6. pueblo (Spanish)

7. marionette (French)

8. marina (Italian)

Answers

1. Martin has told glamorous tales to his friends about his Sioux great-grandfather, who lives on a reservation. Martin is deeply embarrassed when Grandpa comes to visit because his frail and rumpled appearance does not match the exciting image Martin created. The exposition occurs in the first three paragraphs of the story.

2. Grandpa becomes ill and will be staying with the family for a while.

3. Answers will vary. Some students may feel that the crisis is when Martin's friends come to see Grandpa; others when Martin is told to take the medicine bag.

4. The climax comes when Martin receives the medicine bag in his hands and says thank you to Grandpa.

5. Yes. Shortly after Martin receives the bag, Grandpa dies. Martin goes to the reservation and puts the sacred sage in the bag.

DEVELOP YOUR VOCABULARY

Answers
Sample sentences are given.

1. cone-shaped tent usually made of animal skin; The *teepee* was portable.

2. nap taken in the middle of the afternoon; Don't interrupt my *siesta*.

3. friend; A good *friend* helps you.

4. small restaurant; Let's have lunch at the *cafe*.

5. shelter at the beach or a swimming pool; I'll change in the *cabana*.

6. people; an Indian village in the Southwest; The *pueblo* is my home.

7. wooden puppet with strings; Would you put on a *marionette* show?

8. place where boats are kept; Put your boat at the *marina*.

ESL Activity

Have students identify each item in the medicine bag and explain why it is important. Ask them if a relative or good friend has ever given them something precious to keep throughout their lives. Alternatively, ask them to think of the kinds of special objects that might be passed down in a family from generation to generation. Examples might include a necklace passed down from grandmother to mother to daughter to wear on her wedding day.

READING FOCUS

Sample Answer
At the beginning he had mixed feelings about his Sioux heritage; at the end he embraces it securely. He understands that although he lives in a different world, he can still carry on the traditions of his ancestors.

SELECTION OVERVIEW

SELECTION OBJECTIVES

After completing these selections, students will be able to

- understand form
- used closed form to write a couplet
- discuss relationships between children and grandparents
- write from a different point of view
- analyze the form of a poem
- use adjectives
- identify themes

Lesson Resources

Medicine/Grandfather
- Selection Synopses, Teacher's Edition, p. T483c
- Comprehension and Vocabulary Workbook, pp. 101–102
- Language Enrichment Workbook, p. 105
- Teacher's Resources Reinforcement, p. R50 Test, pp. T97–T98

More About Form

An interesting form of poetry is concrete poetry. In concrete poetry, the arrangement of the words on the page contributes to the meaning of the poem. Sometimes the words form a picture, as in a poem about trees written in the form of a tree. At other times, the arrangement of words simply creates a feeling. In this lesson, the poem "Medicine" uses words in this way.

About the Author

Alice Walker (1944–) is an African American novelist, poet, and short-story writer whose works often deal with personal and family relationships. Walker is the author of the acclaimed novel *The Color Purple*, which won a Pulitzer Prize. Among her writing is a collection of feminist essays, *In Search of Our Mothers' Gardens*.

READING FOCUS

Identify Theme As you read the next two poems, think about the theme, or message, of each one. How does the speaker's feeling toward the subject help you understand the theme?

More About the Unit Theme

In this selection, two poems provide different views of grandparents and grandchildren. In "Medicine," the speaker views the relationship between her grandmother and grandfather. In "Grandfather," the speaker recalls the relationship that she had with her grandfather, who is no longer alive.

Learn About

FORM

The form of a poem is the way the poem is constructed. The two main types of poetic form are **closed** and **open**. Closed form includes most established forms of poetry, such as the couplet, the ballad, and the epigram. A **couplet** is a pair of lines that, together, form a complete unit —either because of their meaning or because of end rhyme. A **ballad** is a short narrative poem that is written in four-line stanzas that rhyme *abcb*. An **epigram** is a short, usually witty, poem, dealing with a single thought or event. Usually, it is composed of either one couplet or two couplets (also called a **quatrain**).

The main type of open poetry is free verse. **Free verse**, as you have already seen in several poems, is verse that has no regular rhythmic pattern.

As you read the poems in this selection, ask yourself:

1. In what form of poetry is "Medicine" written?
2. In what form is "Grandfather" written?

WRITING CONNECTION

Write a couplet that consists of two lines that rhyme. The couplet should express a complete thought; for example, "I'd like to go to bed and rest/But I must study for a test."

Cooperative Group Activity

Have students work in pairs to write two couplets. First, have one student write the first line and the other write the second line. Then have students switch roles to write the second couplet. Ask that they choose the one they like better for class presentation.

Medicine

by Alice Walker

Grandma sleeps with
my sick
    grand-
pa so she
5   can get him
during the night
medicine
to stop
  the pain

10   In
the morning
    clumsily
    I
wake
15   them

Her eyes
look at me
from under-
      neath
20 his withered
arm

    The
medicine
  is all
25   in
her long
  un-
    braided
      hair.

---

clumsily (KLUM zuh lee) ungracefully
withered (WI*TH* urd) powerless; incapable of action

Medicine ■ 525

TEACHING PLAN

INTRODUCE

Motivation
Have students recall the discussion of generations in the opening pages of this unit. Read again, or have a student read, the opening quote by Margaret Walker. Discuss the way the poet views her grandmothers. Then relate the discussion to the poems in this selection.

Purpose-Setting Question
What do children remember most about their grandparents?

READ

Literary Focus:
Form
Hold up the poem "Medicine" so students can more easily see the shape it has on the page. Ask: Does the shape of the poem on this page look like something that is mentioned in the poem? Is the form of the poem open or closed?

Reading Focus:
Identify Theme
Help students identify the theme of each poem. Point out that although the subjects of the two poems are similar, each poet's message may differ. Remind them that the speaker's attitude toward the subject may help reveal the central message. Ask: How does each speaker feel about her grandparent? What does this convey about the theme?

CLOSE

Have students complete Review the Selection on pages 528–529.

Develop Vocabulary Skills
Familiarize students with the vocabulary words footnoted in the selection. Use each word in an original sentence, then ask volunteers to do the same.

ESL Activity

Ask students to think of an older relative or other older person they know, whom they like or admire. Have them list several adjectives that could describe this person. The adjectives could refer to the person's appearance, behavior, or personality. Then invite students to share stories about these older people using the adjectives they listed.

Henry Ossawa Tanner (1859–1937) was an African American artist who spent most of his career painting in Europe. Tanner worked in a traditional style with strong chiaroscuro (light and shadow). In this sentimental picture the figures are accented by the brilliant light behind them and the darkness in front of them. In a color scheme of golden yellows and deep blues and browns, Tanner made an idyllic scene of the simple kitchen setting surrounding the old man teaching a child on his knee. Ask: What might the boy and the old man be thinking? How might these two be like the great-grandfather and great-grandson in *The Medicine Bag*?

The Banjo Lesson, Henry Ossawa Tanner. Hampton University Museum

526 ■ Unit 6

Grandfather

by Shirley Crawford

Grandfather sings, I dance.
Grandfather speaks, I listen.
Now I sing, who will dance?
I speak, who will listen?

5 Grandfather hunts, I learn.
Grandfather fishes, I clean.
Now I hunt, who will learn?
I fish, who will clean?

Grandfather dies, I weep.
10 Grandfather buried, I am left alone.
When I am dead, who will cry?
When I am buried, who will be alone?

Grandfather ■ 527

UNDERSTAND THE SELECTION

Answers

1. The speaker's grandfather is sick, and her grandmother is caring for him.
2. the poet's relationship with her grandfather, and her interest in who her children and grand-children will be
3. the death of the speaker's grandfather
4. probably quite young
5. They are devoted to each other.
6. who will feel for her the way she felt for her grandfather when she is grown
7. They seemed to be close companions and close partners.
8. the relationship between speaker and grandfather; the relationship between the grandmother and grandfather
9. Help students recognize the symbolism here. The grand-mother's hair is the "medicine." It helps the grandfather feel better, perhaps because it reminds him of when they were younger and she wore her hair unbraided.
10. No. One may infer that the speaker does not yet have children or grandchildren since she wonders who will feel for her the way she felt for her grandfather.

Respond to Literature

"Medicine" portrays grandparents as a loving couple. "Grandfather" portrays the relationship of grand-parent and grandchild as most important.

WRITE ABOUT THE SELECTION

Prewriting

Have students get together in small groups to discuss the poems and other possible points of view. After a short time, bring the groups back together and ask one member from each group to summarize the group's discussion.

UNDERSTAND THE SELECTION

Recall

1. What situation is described in the poem "Medicine"?

2. What is the subject of the poem "Grandfather"?

3. In "Grandfather," what event has occurred?

Infer

4. Can you guess the approximate age of the speaker in the poem "Medicine"?

5. What can you infer about the grand-parents in "Medicine"?

6. In "Grandfather," what question is the speaker asking?

7. In "Grandfather," what kind of rela-tionship exists between the poet and her grandfather?

Apply

8. What relationship is most important in "Grandfather"? In "Medicine"?

9. How do you think the medicine got in the grandmother's hair?

10. Do you think that the speaker in "Grandfather" has children? Why?

Respond to Literature

How do these two poems give different views of grandparents and grand-children?

WRITE ABOUT THE SELECTION

The poems "Grandfather" and "Medicine" are both written from the grandchild's point of view. How do you think the same stories might be told from one of the grandparents' point of view? Write a paragraph or poem in which you speak from the point of view of the grandfather in Shirley Crawford's poem or from the point of view of one of the grandparents in Alice Walker's poem.

Prewriting Decide which poem appeals to you more. Then begin to make notes about how the grandparent might tell the story. Ask yourself: What tone would the grandparent use? What aspect of the story would the grandparent empha-size? Take your cues from the details in the poem.

Writing Use your prewriting notes to write from the grandparent's point of view. Be sure to include in your poem or paragraph the grandparent's view of the grandchild.

Revising Try writing in the same form as the original poem. If you are writing based on Crawford's poem, use couplets. If you are writing based on Walker's poem, use free verse.

Proofreading Check your paper for errors in spelling. Then compare your form to the original. If you chose free verse like Alice Walker, for example, you may want to change where a line breaks.

Writing

If students are writing poems, make sure that they have a clear idea of what form they are using. If they are writing paragraphs, make sure they have a clear idea of who the speaker is, and whether the point of view is the first or third person.

Revising

For students who chose to write in the same form as the poem, have them read their poems aloud to a partner. Ask students to evaluate the effectiveness of their partner's use of form.

Proofreading

Choose several students' papers as examples of each type of form. Put the papers on the overhead projector and proofread them as a class exercise.

THINK ABOUT FORM

The **form** of a poem is its outward structure. The two main types of poetic form are closed and open. **Closed** poetry includes such forms as the couplet, ballad, and epigram. **Open** form includes free verse and concrete poetry. In concrete poetry the arrangement of letters and words in the poem relates to the content— for example, a poem about Christmas written in the shape of a Christmas tree.

1. Is the form of "Medicine" closed or open?

2. How does the form the poet uses in "Medicine" reflect the speaker's age?

3. Is the form of "Grandfather" closed or open?

4. Does the poem "Grandfather" resemble a couplet, ballad, or epigram? If so, how?

5. In "Grandfather," what rhythmic relationship exists between various lines of the poem?

READING FOCUS

Identify Theme What is the subject of each poem? How did the speaker of each poem feel about the subject? What does this tell you about the theme of each poem?

DEVELOP YOUR VOCABULARY

An **adjective** is a word that describes a noun or pronoun. An adjective answers one or more of the following questions about the word it describes: What kind? Which one? How many? How much?

In a sentence, an adjective usually comes before the noun it describes. Sometimes, however, an adjective comes after the noun: for example, *Juan is sick.* The adjective *sick* describes Juan.

Review the meaning of each adjective listed below. Then use each adjective in an original sentence.

1. alone
2. sick
3. withered
4. long
5. unbraided
6. sparkling
7. interminable
8. personal
9. fancy
10. exciting
11. weary
12. patient
13. respectful
14. sacred

Review the Selection ■ 529

THINK ABOUT FORM

Answers
1. open
2. Free verse seems more childlike.
3. closed
4. couplet, because each pair of lines is related in meaning
5. The first two lines of each stanza have similar rhythm, and the last two lines of the stanza have similar rhythm.

DEVELOP YOUR VOCABULARY

Sample Answers
1. When my friend is angry at me, I feel very much *alone.*
2. I am *sick* and tired of the way she treats me.
3. He could not lift his *withered* arm.
4. Her skirt was *long* and flowing.
5. Her *unbraided* hair hung loosely around her shoulders.
6. The *sparkling* diamond caught my attention.
7. The train ride seemed *interminable.*
8. I did not want to ask such a *personal* question.
9. The dress was too *fancy* to wear to school.
10. This movie is not very *exciting.*
11. I am *weary* of waiting.
12. I try to be *patient* with her.
13. Children should be *respectful* of their parents.
14. The *sacred* candle was lit.

READING FOCUS

Sample Answer

Grandparents' love for each other is the subject of "Medicine." This reflects the theme of love throughout the ages. A grandparent's relationship with a grandchild is the subject of "Grandfather." This also reflects the theme of love, now between the generations.

ESL Activity

Invite students to write a poem about the person they selected for the activity on page T525. Encourage them to chose one of the two poems they have read as a model. For example, students might imitate the form used in "Grandfather" by using two sentences and two questions in each stanza. Others might feel more comfortable using free verse, as in "Medicine." Some students may wish to experiment with concrete poetry, arranging the words to form a picture that suggests something about the subject.

SELECTION OBJECTIVES

After completing these selections, students will be able to

- understand figures of speech
- use figures of speech to describe a person, place, or thing
- recognize the importance of heritage
- write a fantasy encounter
- analyze figures of speech in a poem
- use figurative expressions
- make inferences about the speaker

Lesson Resources

Some People/My People
- Selection Synopses, Teacher's Edition, pp. T483c–T483d
- Comprehension and Vocabulary Workbook, pp. 103–104
- Language Enrichment Workbook, p. 106
- Teacher's Resources Reinforcement, p. R51 Test, pp. T97–T98

**More About
Figures of Speech**

Figures of speech are words and expressions that are used in ways that are out of the ordinary. While it is true that some figures of speech have become clichés, such as "tower of strength," good poets usually use figures of speech that are original, and that is part of the appeal of their poetry.

READING FOCUS

Make Inferences About the Speaker
When you make an inference, you use details in a poem or story to make a logical guess. The speaker in a poem is the person telling the story. If a line reads, "Matt's chin was on his chest after he heard the news," you might infer that the speaker thinks Matt was probably unhappy or depressed.

As you read the next two poems, look for details that help you make inferences about the speakers' thoughts and feelings.

FIGURES OF SPEECH

Figures of speech are specific forms of figurative language. Most figures of speech compare two unlike things. Two important figures of speech are similes and metaphors.

In a **simile**, the word *like* or *as* is used to make a comparison. For example, you might say, "Riding in Grandpa's old car was like riding in a roller coaster."

In a **metaphor**, a comparison is made directly, without using *like* or *as*. For example, "My father is a tower of strength" is a metaphor. The phrase "tower of strength" describes a quality of the father.

Similes and metaphors add meaning by providing vivid images that describe a person, object, place, or idea.

As you read the poems in the next selection, ask yourself:

1. What similes or metaphors are used by the poets?
2. How do these figures of speech add meaning to the poem?

WRITING CONNECTION

Look around you wherever you happen to be right now. Choose five objects or people that you can see clearly. Write a simile or metaphor to describe each.

Cooperative Group Activity

To extend the Writing Connection activity, divide the class into small groups. Ask each group to think of metaphors and similes that have become part of everyday speech. For example: "pillar of the community," "hard as a rock," "light as a feather." Make a list of these metaphors and similes for class review.

Some People

by Rachel Field

Isn't it strange some people make
    You feel so tired inside,
Your thoughts begin to shrivel up
    Like leaves all brown and dried!

But when you're with some other ones,
    It's stranger still to find
Your thoughts as thick as fireflies
    All shiny in your mind!

My People

by Bernice George

    I am a Navajo, the Navajos are my people.
    They live in the hogans upon the dry desert,
    With a little shade house and a sheep corral.
    It is nice and peaceful there away
5 From the city street.
    There were the sad, dark years for my people,
    But my people didn't disappear.
    They started rebuilding, increasing
    In population.
10 I am proud that the desert floor,
    The lonely hogans,
    Have made me thoughtful and
    Respectful of my people.
    I am proud to be born in my people's land.
15 I shall never forget my home and people.

---

shrivel (SHRIV ul) wither, dry up, become wrinkled
hogans (HOH gunz) Navajo houses made of branches, clay, and sod
corral (kuh RAL) a fenced-in area for keeping livestock

Some People/My People ■ 531

TEACHING PLAN

INTRODUCE

Motivation
Ask students to describe the kinds of people that they enjoy being with. Have them list some of the characteristics of these people, such as sense of humor, optimistic attitude, and so on. Then ask: How do these people make you feel about yourself? Relate students' responses to the poem "Some People."

Purpose-Setting Question
How does cultural heritage affect the way a person feels about himself or herself?

READ

Literary Focus:
Figures of Speech
Have students identify figures of speech in these poems and ask them to visualize the author's words.

Reading Focus:
Make Inferences About the Speaker
Have students put themselves in the place of each speaker in "Some People" and "My People." Ask: Which speaker is most similar to you? Why?

CLOSE

Have students complete Review the Selection on pages 532–533.

Develop Vocabulary Skills
When you preteach the footnoted vocabulary words on this page, ask students to demonstrate *shrivel* and draw a *hogan* and *corral* on the board.

ESL Activity
Have students list people they know or have known. These lists should contain people they like and people they disliked. The key word is *unique*.

Comparing Selections
Have students compare the subject matter of the two poems. Ask: What kinds of people are described in each poem?

UNDERSTAND THE SELECTION

Answers

1. the way different people can make a person feel inside
2. the poet's pride in her heritage as a Navajo
3. a Navajo who was born on Navajo land
4. those who spark creative thoughts in others and those who inhibit them
5. the way the Navajos rebuilt after hard times; the way they live peacefully and simply
6. probably not, although it is not totally clear in the poem
7. Sample answer: She is referring to some period when the Navajo were either persecuted or confined to a reservation.
8. the contrast between people who make you feel good inside and those who do not; the contrast between dry leaves and fireflies
9. Answers will vary. Students should realize that the poet may have met many types of people like the ones she describes.
10. The poem contains many facts about the Navajo, but it also contains some opinion, as the poet presents these facts in a positive light and emphasizes her own pride in and respect for her people.

Respond to Literature

Ask students to think of a group of people outside of their families with whom they feel connected. The group might be friends, neighbors, a club, a sports team. Then have students list the aspects of this group that make them feel happy or proud to be a part of it. Relate the discussion to the poems in the selection.

WRITE ABOUT THE SELECTION

Prewriting

As a class exercise, use students' suggestions to make a prewriting chart on the chalkboard or overhead transparency. Encourage students to share

---

UNDERSTAND THE SELECTION

Recall

1. What is the subject of the poem "Some People"?

2. What is the subject of the poem "My People"?

3. Who is the speaker in "My People"?

Infer

4. What two groups of people does the poet describe in "Some People"?

5. What qualities of her people does the speaker admire in "My People"?

6. Can you infer whether the speaker in "My People" is with her people now?

7. What do you think the speaker means when she speaks of "sad, dark years for my people"?

Apply

8. What contrasts are made in "Some People"?

9. What personal experiences might have led the poet to write "Some People"?

10. Would you say that "My People" contains facts or opinions about the Navajo? Explain your answer.

Respond to Literature

In what way does the poem "My People" speak about generations?

WRITE ABOUT THE SELECTION

The poem "Some People" describes two different types of people. What do you think it would be like to meet each of these people at a party? How would they make you feel? Write one or two paragraphs in which you describe an encounter with each type of person described in the poem.

Prewriting On a sheet of paper, make two columns. At the top of one column, write *Type 1*; at the top of the other, write *Type 2*. Under each heading list characteristics of the imaginary people you are going to describe; or you may, instead, want to base your descriptions on actual people you have met.

Writing Use your prewriting notes to write one or two paragraphs in which you describe meeting at a party the two types of people described in the poem "Some People." Be sure to include details about the setting of the party. You may also wish to include dialogue.

Revising Read over your paper and think about the tone you have used. Is your paper serious or humorous? Try adding specific verbs and vivid descriptions to make your paragraphs more interesting.

Proofreading Make sure that each sentence in your paper begins with a capital letter and ends with a period, question mark, or exclamation point. If you have used dialogue, remember to insert quotation marks.

---

personal experiences about actual people they have met who fit into one of the two categories.

Writing

Encourage students to use dialogue in their paragraphs. Point out that it is largely the things a person says that make us feel a certain way in his or her presence.

Revising

Ask one or two volunteers to share their papers with the class. Place the paper on an overhead projector, then have the class assist in revising.

Proofreading

Have students trade papers with a partner to proofread.

ESL Activity

Have students choose one individual from their lists of unique people and work with a partner to write a paragraph explaining why they liked or disliked this person.

THINK ABOUT FIGURES OF SPEECH

Figures of speech add meaning to a poem by providing vivid images that help you see things in new ways. Two important figures of speech are similes and metaphors. A **simile** compares two different things by using the word *like* or *as*. A **metaphor** compares two different things directly, without using *like* or *as*.

1. Find two similes in "Some People."

2. What two images are conveyed by the use of these similes? Are the images similar, or are they opposite?

3. What other imagery does the author use in "Some People"?

4. What image is conveyed by this description? How does it add meaning to the poem?

5. Does the poem "My People" use similes or metaphors? Can you think of a reason for this?

READING FOCUS

Make Inferences About the Speaker
What can you infer about the speakers of these two poems? How do other people affect the speaker of "Some People"? How does the speaker of "My People" feel about her Navajo heritage? What clues in each poem helped you make these inferences?

DEVELOP YOUR VOCABULARY

A **figurative expression** is a group of words that has a meaning of its own—a meaning that will be different from the meanings of the individual words. For example, you might say, "The answer was on the tip of my tongue." The expression "tip of my tongue" means that you were just about to say the answer.

Identify the figurative expression in each of the sentences below. Then write a sentence explaining the meaning of each figurative expression.

1. He was running around like a chicken with its head cut off.

2. The story was about a woman with shattered hopes and broken dreams.

3. Keep a stiff upper lip.

4. I think it would be best to talk and get it off your chest.

5. Donna decided to go home and curl up with a good book.

Review the Selection ■ 533

THINK ABOUT FIGURES OF SPEECH

Answers

1. "Your thoughts begin to shrivel up like leaves all brown and dried!" and "Your thoughts as thick as fireflies. . ."
2. They are opposite. The first simile implies death or drying up of life, and the second implies brightness and abundance.
3. "fireflies all shiny in your mind"
4. The sparkling brightness of "your mind" illustrates the positive effect that some things have on one's thoughts.
5. No. Possible answer: The poet draws largely on simple information that doesn't need elaboration.

DEVELOP YOUR VOCABULARY

Sample Answers

1. "like a chicken with its head cut off"—He ran around crazily as if he had no brain.
2. "shattered hopes and broken dreams"—The things that the woman had hoped for and dreamed about no longer seemed possible.
3. "stiff upper lip"—Don't let your feelings show.
4. "get it off your chest"—Express your feelings.
5. "curl up with a good book"—Relax and read a good book.

READING FOCUS

Sample Answer
The speakers of these poems both have found people they enjoy being around. Other people affect the speaker's creativity in "Some People." The speaker of "My People" has found strength from her Navajo heritage, such as in the line "I am proud . . . ." The speaker in "Some People" finds strength only in those who help her open up, such as in the line "other ones . . . thoughts as thick as fireflies."

T533

SELECTION OVERVIEW

SELECTION OBJECTIVES

After completing these selections, students will be able to

- understand theme in poetry
- analyze the theme of a poem
- discuss relationships between parent and child and grandparent and child
- write from a different character's point of view
- use nouns and verbs
- compare and contrast poems

Lesson Resources

Otto/Christmas morning i
- Selection Synopses, Teacher's Edition, p. T483c
- Comprehension and Vocabulary Workbook, pp. 105–106
- Language Enrichment Workbook, p. 107
- Teacher's Resources Reinforcement, p. R52 Test, pp. T99–T100

More About Theme in Poetry

Many poets have a particular theme that runs throughout their works. For example, Gwendolyn Brooks has written a number of poems on the theme of positive family relationships. The poems of e. e. cummings often have as an underlying theme the celebration of the individual. Poet and novelist Margaret Atwood likes to write about the irony in male-female relationships.

About the Author

Gwendolyn Brooks is sometimes referred to as a "people's poet" because she writes about the kind of people that one might see on the street any day. Brooks's view of herself is that of an ordinary person, even after many years of fame and literary prizes.

READING FOCUS

Compare and Contrast Poems When you compare two things, you note the features that the two things share. When you contrast two things, you highlight differences between the two things. In poems, you can compare and contrast elements such as theme, style, and point of view. As you read the next two poems, look for ways they are different and ways they are the same.

Learn About

THEME IN POETRY

You have learned about theme in short stories. Theme is also an important element of poetry.

Like storytellers, poets write because they have something to say. The **theme** of a poem may be what the poet values or feels deeply about. Two poems that you will read illustrate the poets' values in a few lines. In "Otto," the theme concerns a child's sensitivity to his father's difficulties. In "Christmas morning i," the theme concerns a child's relationship with a grandparent.

As with a short story, it is important not to confuse the theme of a poem with the subject. The **subject** of a poem is simply the topic. Keep in mind that two poems may have similar subjects but different themes.

As you read the poems "Otto" and "Christmas morning i," ask yourself:
1. What is the theme of each poem?
2. Are these themes similar or different?

WRITING CONNECTION

Review the poems that you have read in this unit and the preceding units. Choose the poem you liked best and discuss the theme.

Develop Vocabulary Skills

Most of the words in these poems will be familiar to students. Discuss the meanings of the two words that are footnoted. Encourage students to ask about any other words that they do not understand.

ESL Activity

Before students read the poems, discuss gifts. Ask: Are there certain times of the year when you look forward to giving or receiving gifts? What is the best gift you ever received? What is the best gift you ever gave? What makes a gift meaningful to the recipient?

Cooperative Group Activity

For the Writing Connection activity, have students get together with others in the class who have chosen the same favorite poem. Then ask each group to prepare a short paragraph in which they describe the theme of the poem and discuss their feelings about it.

OTTO

by Gwendolyn Brooks

It's Christmas Day. I did not get
The presents that I hoped for. Yet,
It is not nice to frown or fret.

To frown or fret would not be fair.
My Dad must never know I care
It's hard enough for him to bear.

Christmas morning i

by Carol Freeman

Christmas morning i
got up before the others and
ran
naked across the plank
floor into the front
room to see grandmama
sewing a new
button on my last year
ragdoll.

---

fret (FRET) become worried or upset
plank (PLANGK) a long, thick board

Otto/Christmas morning i ■ 535

UNDERSTAND THE SELECTION

Answers

1. on Christmas Day
2. a boy named Otto
3. a little girl
4. that the burden of providing Christmas presents is difficult, and that it would be unbearable for his father to know his son's disappointment
5. his father's
6. that she is going to get last year's ragdoll with a new button for Christmas
7. disappointed
8. Both take place on Christmas Day, and express a child's feelings about his or her presents.
9. Yes. Both children are disappointed by their Christmas presents. The first poem, however, expresses the child's understanding of the parent's dilemma.
10. The family could not afford to buy new presents.

Respond to Literature

In each poem, the reader can infer that the speaker's family is not well-to-do. But both the father in "Otto" and the grandmother in "Christmas morning i" knew it was important for a child to have a gift or gifts on Christmas. Both poems show that gifts are important but not all-important in family relationships. The poem "Otto" also shows that a child, when old enough, can think of others' feelings, even when disappointed.

WRITE ABOUT THE SELECTION

Prewriting

As they work on this section, students could freewrite some conversation between the father or the grandmother and other family members.

UNDERSTAND THE SELECTION

Recall

1. When do both poems take place?

2. Who is the speaker in "Otto"?

3. Who is the speaker in "Christmas morning i"?

Infer

4. What does Otto understand about his father?

5. About whose feelings does Otto care most?

6. What does the speaker in the second poem infer when she sees her grandmother sewing?

7. How do you think the speaker will feel about her Christmas present?

Apply

8. In what way are both poems similar?

9. Do both poems express similar feelings? Why or why not?

10. Why do you think that the grandmother in the second poem was sewing a button on last year's ragdoll?

Respond to Literature

What do these poems have to say about the relationships between children and parents, and between children and grandparents?

WRITE ABOUT THE SELECTION

Each poem in this selection is spoken from the child's point of view. What do you think the speaker's father might say in the first poem? What do you think the grandmother would have to say in the second poem? Write a paragraph or poem in which you tell either story from the parent's or grandparent's point of view.

Prewriting Decide which poem you want to write about. Then read the poem several times and try to imagine that you are the father or the grandmother. Write down your ideas about how this person might feel. Also write down any additional details that you might want to add, such as the family's financial circumstances.

Writing Use your prewriting notes to write a poem or paragraph from the father's or grandmother's point of view. Be sure to include the older person's view of the child or grandchild. Take your cues from the details in the story.

Revising As you revise, consider using dialogue in your paragraph or poem. You can also present a character's thoughts in the form of dialogue.

Proofreading If you chose to write a poem, reread it now with careful attention to your punctuation at the end of each line. You may choose whatever you want —a comma, period, nothing at all—as long as you keep in mind that end-of-line punctuation plays an important part in *how* a poem is spoken.

Writing

As students work on their poems or paragraphs, go around the class and help those who are having trouble. Suggest to students that they imagine themselves in the position of the father or grandmother as they write.

Revising

Have students work with a partner. Have each pair role-play conversations between the grandmother or father and other family members. Students can then use ideas from the conversations to write the dialogue.

Proofreading

Have students trade papers with a partner. Ask students to read their partner's poem aloud, paying special attention to punctuation. Then have partners discuss how the punctuation might be changed or corrected to improve the way the poem is spoken.

THINK ABOUT THEME IN POETRY

The **theme** of a poem expresses what the poet values, feels, or thinks. Often a poem communicates an insight that the poet has gained about life, about others, or about self. Like the author of a short story, a poet may state the theme clearly or leave it for you to figure out for yourself. Since poetry usually involves far fewer words than a short story, it is more likely that the theme will be suggested rather than spelled out.

1. What is the theme of "Otto"?

2. What is the theme of "Christmas morning i"?

3. What is the subject of each poem?

4. Are the subjects similar or different?

5. Are the themes similar or different?

READING FOCUS

Compare and Contrast Poems Describe two ways the two poems you have read are alike. Describe two ways they are different. Consider style and point of view.

DEVELOP YOUR VOCABULARY

A **noun** is a word that names a person, place, or thing. A **verb** is a word that describes action or a state of being. Some words can be used as both nouns and verbs. For example, the word *dare* can be a noun: "He took the *dare* and dove into the water." The word *dare* can also be used as a verb: "I *dare* you to tell Father what you told me." The meaning of words that can be used as either nouns or verbs depends on their use in a particular sentence.

Each of the following words can be used as a noun or as a verb. Write original sentences that illustrate both uses of each word.

1. call
2. frown
3. bill
4. care
5. pass
6. throw
7. turn
8. button

Review the Selection ■ 537

THINK ABOUT THEME IN POETRY

Answers
1. that love and understanding for another person are more important than presents
2. that a family's love is often the best gift of all
3. a child's reaction on Christmas morning
4. similar, because both take place on the same day and involve children and their reactions to what they receive
5. The themes are similar in that both poems concern a child's disappointment. However, the main theme of the first poem is the child's sympathy for the parent, while the second focuses on the loving gesture of the grandmother.

DEVELOP YOUR VOCABULARY

Sample Answers
1. I'll *call* you tomorrow. I got a *call* from Aunt Jane.
2. Please don't *frown*. He had a *frown* on his face.
3. You will get a *bill* later. We won't *bill* you until May 1.
4. I *care* about you a lot. I don't have a *care* in the world.
5. *Pass* the butter, please! May I have a *pass* to the office?
6. Do not *throw* that away! That was a great *throw*!
7. *Turn* around! He made a quick left *turn* onto the highway.
8. *Button* down the collar of your shirt. I'm missing a *button* on my dress.

READING FOCUS

Sample Answer
The style of each poem differs in the sentence formation. They are similar in style in that each is free verse with interesting line breaks. The point of view is first-person for both poems.

ESL Activity

Invite students to think of other titles that would be appropriate for each poem. If students need help, point out that titles might suggest the subject matter, the setting, or the feelings of the speaker.

T537

SELECTION OVERVIEW

SELECTION OBJECTIVES

After completing these selections, students will be able to

- understand tone
- use tone to change the meaning of a poem
- evaluate a character's feelings
- write about a childhood memory
- analyze the tone of a poem
- use antonyms
- identify cause and effect

Lesson Resources

Whale Hunting/Luther Leavitt
- Selection Synopses, Teacher's Edition, p. T483d
- Comprehension and Vocabulary Workbook, pp. 107–108
- Language Enrichment Workbook, p. 108
- Teacher's Resources Reinforcement, p. R53 Test, pp. T99–T100

More About Tone

One literary critic says that tone is what colors a poem and gives it atmosphere. Tone is also closely associated with mood. The tone of a poem can convey a mood that is somber, giddy, serious, or light-hearted.

More About the Unit Theme

Both poems in this selection deal with an important aspect of life in Alaska: whaling. The speakers in both poems are children who feel left out of an activity in their family or community.

READING FOCUS

Identify Cause and Effect A cause is something that brings about a certain result, or effect. Thinking about cause and effect when you read can help you understand why events happen or why characters feel as they do. For example, snow can cause roads to become slippery. A harsh remark can cause someone to feel sad. Sometimes several events in a row are linked by cause and effect. For example, snow can cause slippery roads, which can cause car accidents. Asking why as you read can help you discover which events are linked by cause and effect.

538 ■ Unit 6

TONE

The attitude of a poem is called the **tone**. The tone indicates the speaker's feelings toward the subject and sometimes toward the reader.

You can better understand the importance of tone if you think of the way tone of voice can change the meaning of spoken words. For example, if a person says in a friendly tone of voice, "That is a great dress you have on," you know that you are being given a compliment. If someone says the same sentence in a sarcastic tone of voice, you know that you are being insulted.

As you read the poems in this selection, ask yourself:

1. What is the tone of each poem?
2. What does the tone tell about the speaker's attitudes?

WRITING CONNECTION

Read the following sentences silently. Then try reading each sentence aloud using various tones of voice. Write down how the meaning of each sentence is changed by the way it is spoken.

Where are you going?
The weather is supposed to be warm and sunny.
You are an hour early!
I am going out to take a walk.

ESL Activity

Have students list some of their relatives, where they lived, and how they earned their livings. Students may need to interview parents to find information about relatives they have never met.

Develop Vocabulary Skills

As you review the footnoted vocabulary words, have students locate Alaska and the Bering Sea on a map.

Cooperative Group Activity

To extend the Writing Connection activity, divide the class into small groups. Have each group choose a poem or a paragraph from a short story to read aloud. Then ask each member of the group to read the poem or paragraph in a different tone of voice. Have students discuss how the meaning of the piece is changed by the tone.

Whale Hunting

by Sally Nashookpuk

My daddy goes whaling in the Bering Sea
I'm just a girl, he can't take me
My brother joins the whaling group
They caught four this year
For muk-tuk soup.

Luther Leavitt

by Alfred Brower

Luther Leavitt is a whale hunter.
last year
they got a whale
we went
to the blanket toss
I never
got a chance to go
on the blanket
cause there were too many kids.

---

whaling (HWAYL ing) hunting whales
Bering Sea (BIR ing SEE) part of the north Pacific Ocean between Alaska and Siberia

Whale Hunting/Luther Leavitt ■ 539

UNDERSTAND THE SELECTION

Answers

1. near the Bering Sea
2. a celebration after a successful whale hunt
3. whale hunting
4. A blanket toss celebration is held.
5. She does not like being left out because she is a girl.
6. She is not able to do what her father and brother can do.
7. It provides food for her community, and it is a traditional group activity. Students might also speculate that the speaker thinks whaling would be fun or exciting.
8. It is really about the child speaking, because it deals with his or her feelings about the event.
9. Both felt left out of an important event.
10. envious

Respond to Literature

In both poems, a child feels left out of an important event. Have students list the similarities and differences in the situations of the two children. For example, the child in the first poem is excluded because of gender, and this exclusion is probably permanent. The child in the second poem is excluded because a particular event is crowded; he or she may very well not be left out of a similar event in the future. How are both children part of a tradition that may be passed down through the generations?

WRITE ABOUT THE SELECTION

Prewriting

Display a volunteer's prewriting cluster on an overhead projector. Encourage students to ask questions of the person to bring out additional details. Then give students a few more minutes to add to their own clusters.

Writing

Remind students that they are to compare their memory with one of the poems, not just relate an incident. Encourage them to use comparison words such as *like, as,* and *unlike.*

Revising

Have students work in pairs to revise. After students have read their partners' papers, have them suggest adverbs and other descriptive words that can be added.

Proofreading

Have students proofread their papers in groups of three. Ask one member of each group to be the spelling expert, another to be the grammar expert, and the third to be the punctuation expert. Have each expert proofread the group's papers for that particular kind of error.

Review the Selection

UNDERSTAND THE SELECTION

Recall

1. What is the setting of the first poem?

2. What is the setting of the second poem?

3. What occupation is discussed in both poems?

Infer

4. In the second poem, what tells you that catching a whale is an important event?

5. What can you infer from the first poem about the speaker's feelings about being a girl?

6. Why do you think the speaker feels this way?

7. Why is whaling important to the speaker in the first poem?

Apply

8. The second poem is entitled "Luther Leavitt," but who is the poem really about? Explain your answer.

9. In what way do the speakers in both poems have similar feelings?

10. How do you think the speaker in the first poem feels toward her brother?

Respond to Literature

What aspect of the theme of generations is illustrated by these two poems?

---

540 ■ Unit 6

WRITE ABOUT THE SELECTION

In the poems, two children express their observations and feelings about events connected with whale hunting. You may never have lived in a place where people whale hunt, but you may have childhood memories that are similar to those of the speakers in other ways. For example, perhaps you had to stay behind as your brother or sister joined a parent or grandparent in doing something important. Perhaps you were the only child who did not win a prize at a party. Write a paragraph in which you compare a memory from your childhood with one in these poems.

Prewriting   Take a few minutes to cluster incidents that you remember from childhood. Write down your ideas and any details that you can remember.

Writing   Choose the incident that you remember most vividly or about which you feel most strongly. Then use your prewriting cluster to write a paragraph in which you compare and contrast this incident with the incident described in one of the poems.

Revising   As you revise your paragraph, make sure that your feelings about the incident are clearly communicated. Often, adding adverbs can help to communicate feelings. Use parallel structure to make your comparison logical and organized.

Proofreading   Check your paper for correct grammar, spelling, and punctuation. If you are writing in the past tense, make sure that you have used correct verb forms.

ESL Activity

Have students choose one relative from their list compiled earlier and write a paragraph describing the relative's profession and where he or she lived. Have them use at least seven adjectives and adverbs.

THINK ABOUT TONE

The **tone** of a poem indicates the speaker's attitude toward his or her subject. The tone can also indicate the speaker's or poet's attitude toward the reader. Some elements that contribute to the tone are the formality or informality of the poem's language, the rhythm, the choice of certain words, and the energy or pace of the poem. Sometimes, tone will change within a poem, especially if the poem is long.

1. What is the tone of "Whale Hunting"?

2. Which line in "Whale Hunting" displays the tone most clearly?

3. What is the tone of "Luther Leavitt"?

4. In which part of the poem is the tone most evident?

5. How might the tone of the poem be different if the speaker had been able to go on the blanket?

READING FOCUS

Identify Cause and Effect Identify one cause-and-effect relationship in each of the poems.

DEVELOP YOUR VOCABULARY

Antonyms are words that have opposite, or nearly opposite, meanings. *Short* and *tall* are antonyms, as are *thin* and *fat*. In the poem "Luther Leavitt," the speaker says that there were "too many kids." An antonym of the word *many* would be *few*. The phrase would have exactly the opposite meaning if the word *few* were substituted for the word *many*.

Two words in each group below are antonyms. Write the antonyms on a separate sheet of paper. Then write a sentence using the first antonym in each pair. Rewrite each sentence using the second antonym, and see how the meaning of the sentence changes.

1. knowledge, thoughtfulness, ignorance, consideration

2. tired, rude, polite, quick

3. difficult, hidden, confusing, easy

4. politely, hesitantly, eagerly, slowly

THINK ABOUT TONE

Answers
1. familiar, informal, and childlike
2. "I'm just a girl, he can't take me"
3. straightforward, matter-of-fact
4. in the last four lines
5. The tone would have been positive or exuberant.

DEVELOP YOUR VOCABULARY

Answers
Sample sentences are given.
1. *knowledge, ignorance*— His *knowledge* was astounding. His *ignorance* was astounding.
2. *rude, polite*—I could not believe how *rude* he was! I could not believe how *polite* he was!
3. *difficult, easy*—That test was much too *difficult*. That test was much too *easy*.
4. *hesitantly, eagerly*—I reached for the kitten *hesitantly*. I reached for the kitten *eagerly*.

READING FOCUS

Sample Answer
The first speaker cannot go whaling because she is a girl. The second speaker could not go on the blanket because it was too crowded.

WRITING APPLICATIONS

Write About Theme

Ask students to think about the last time their extended family got together. The occasion may have been a holiday, such as Thanksgiving, or it may have been a wedding, funeral, or birthday celebration. Ask students to share some of their experiences, impressions, and feelings about this event. Relate the discussion to the writing assignment in this section.

Cooperative Group Activity

The following activity can be used during the prewriting section, or it can be used after the completion of the writing section. Divide the class into small groups. Ask each group to role-play the conversations that group members have written, as if they were characters in a play.

Writer's Toolkit CD-ROM Encourage students to use the Descriptive Word Bin (Writing Tools, Drafting) to complete the **writing** activity.

WRITING APPLICATIONS

Write About Theme

All of the stories and poems in this unit are about generations. Suppose that four of the characters from this unit meet at a family reunion, and the conversation turns to family history and tradition. What might these characters say to one another? Write their conversation as a dialogue for a story.

Prewriting Choose the four characters that you feel you know best. You will have to decide how the four characters are related. Perhaps one character is the distant cousin of another character or one character has married into the family of another character. Maybe one character comes to the reunion as the boyfriend or girlfriend of another character. Freewrite their conversations, thinking of questions that they might ask one another and the answers that might be given.

Writing Use your freewriting as a basis for your dialogue. Be sure to describe each character's facial expressions and tone of voice. Introduce your dialogue by describing the setting of the reunion.

Revising Make sure that the personality of each character stands out clearly. Add details and descriptive words to make each characterization more vivid.

Proofreading Make sure that you have used quotation marks correctly. Remember that a new paragraph must begin each time the speaker changes.

Write About Genre

You have studied five important elements that can be used to analyze poetry: denotation and connotation, rhythm, sounds, form, and symbolism. Choose two poems from this unit about which you feel strongly. Compare and contrast the works according to the literary elements you have studied.

Prewriting Review the work that you did for the Think About sections for the poems in this unit. Then make a chart that has the name of the two poems that you have chosen at the top and the five literary elements on the side. Fill in the spaces on the chart with details about each element from the poems.

Writing Use your prewriting chart to write a comparison of the two poems. You might enjoy writing your paper as if you were a literary critic writing for a newspaper or magazine.

Revising Try to include in your paper both positive and negative statements about each poem. Add a sentence or two that states how well you think a particular poet uses such devices as symbolism, sounds, or connotation.

Proofreading Check your paper for correct punctuation. If you used colons or semicolons, make sure that they are used correctly. Also check to be certain that you used either a question mark or an exclamation mark at the end of a sentence in which a period would be inappropriate.

Write About Genre

Have students discuss the things that make a particular poem appealing to them. At first, encourage students to express their feelings about what makes a good poem. Then relate the discussion to the literary elements they have studied. Try to help students see that much of what they like in poetry is the effective use of these elements.

Cooperative Group Activity

Divide students into teams of five to eight. Have each team put their papers together to form a small literary magazine. Each team can provide additional copy to introduce or conclude the magazine; teams can also include illustrations or short biographies of authors.

Writer's Toolkit CD-ROM Encourage students to use the Venn Diagram (Writing Tools, Organizing Details) to complete the **prewriting** activity.

Suggest that students copy the sentence and then do the following: (1) circle the conjunction; (2) underline the word groups connected by the conjunction; and (3) state the type of conjunction in parentheses after the sentence.

A sample sentence is given from "Somebody's Son" (p. 504). The faint clink of scissors landing in his half-filled basket came to him (and) then the foreman was bawling at him, "Hey!" (coordinating)

Write these sentences on the chalkboard and ask students to identify the conjunctions:

I will give her either a sweater or a skirt for her birthday.

I will go out, even though it is raining.

In the first sentence, *or* is a coordinating conjunction because it connects similar words. In the second sentence, *even though* is a subordinating conjunction because it connects two ideas by making one idea less important than the other.

Cooperative Group Activity

Have students work in small groups to write original sentences that use conjunctions.

BUILD LANGUAGE SKILLS

Vocabulary

A **prefix** is a letter or letters added to the beginning of a word or word root to change its meaning. A negative prefix acts like the word *not* and changes the meaning of the word from positive to negative. For example, the word *inconsiderate* is formed by adding the prefix *in-* to *considerate*. The word *inconsiderate* means "not considerate." In addition to *in-*, some commonly used negative prefixes include *un-*, *dis-*, *il-*, *ir-*, and *im-*.

Identify the negative prefix and root word for each italicized word below. Then write a definition for each word.

1. It would be *inappropriate* to wear sneakers to graduation.

2. She was wearing a very *unusual* hat.

3. The boy lost something that was *irreplaceable*.

4. Grandfather was *immobilized* by the injury.

5. It would be *impossible* for Roberto to go to school.

6. He *disregarded* his father's remarks and kept on walking.

7. It is *illogical* to wear mittens in the summer.

Grammar, Usage, and Mechanics

A **conjunction** is a part of speech that makes a direct connection between words or groups of words. Some common conjunctions are *and*, *or*, and *because*.

Two kinds of conjunctions are coordinating conjunctions and subordinating conjunctions. **Coordinating conjunctions** connect similar words or word groups. The following are examples:

It was a thoroughly happy *and* relaxed time for everybody.

Should she choose chocolate *or* vanilla?

Subordinating conjunctions connect two complete ideas by making one of the ideas less important than the other. Some subordinating conjunctions are *after*, *as*, *even though*, *since*, *unless*, and *wherever*. Here are some examples:

I cheered loudly for my team *even though* they were losing the game.

I will not go to college *unless* I have enough money to support myself.

Find five sentences from the selections that use conjunctions. Identify the conjunctions and state whether they are coordinating or subordinating. Then identify the words or word groups that the conjunctions connect. Use the five sentences as models to write five original sentences.

Unit Review ■ 543

BUILD LANGUAGE SKILLS

Vocabulary

Answers

1. in + appropriate—not appropriate
2. un + usual—not usual
3. ir + replaceable—not replaceable
4. im + mobilized—not able to move
5. im + possible—not possible
6. dis + regarded—did not pay attention to
7. il + logical—not logical

More About Word Attack: Point out that identifying a negative prefix and root word can help students figure out the meaning of a word. Write this example from "Somebody's Son": *"Is it there?" he asked with an uncontrollable quaver.* The negative prefix changes the meaning of *controllable* to "not controllable."

Motivation

Ask students to recall a speaker they have heard recently who held their attention. This person may have been a teacher, a person on television, or a speaker at a club meeting. Have students discuss what this person did to make the speech effective.

Teaching Strategy

Guide students through the explanation of oral interpretation, paying particular attention to the five steps. Allow students time in class to choose their characters. When students are ready to practice their speeches, you may wish to make tape recorders available so that students can hear their own voices.

Evaluation Criteria

Use the following evaluation code to rate each student's speaking:

NI   needs improvement

A   adequate

G   good

O   outstanding

In all students' speeches, try to find some aspect that was positive and encourage the student in that area.

SPEAKING AND LISTENING

You have read about many interesting real people and some colorful imaginary characters in this unit. If you were asked to name the most notable real person in this unit, whom would it be and why? Also, if you were asked to name the character who seemed the most interesting to you, whom would it be and why? Think about these questions as you prepare to talk about literature.

1. Think about the people you have read about in this unit. Choose two, one real and one imaginary, who seem to stand out from all the others. Write their names on 3 × 5 index cards.

2. On each card, write as much as you can recall about the person or character whose name is on the card. Limit yourself to two minutes per card, but try to remember as many things as you can. Write without stopping if possible, and do not worry about complete sentences.

3. Try to fill up both sides of the card. In writing about the character, you will want to consider memorable qualities, personality, importance in the story, and whether he or she represented a stereotype or was an unusual character. In writing about the real person,

you probably will want to include such information as personal life, personality, and contributions to family or community.

4. After you have filled your cards, work with a group of your classmates. Decide whether you will discuss characters or real people, or a mix of both. Then take turns round-robin style to discuss the characters and real people you have chosen. Use your cards to help you. Limit your dialogue to about one minute.

5. If someone in your group has chosen the same person or character that you have, try not to repeat anything already said. Instead, add to his or her dialogue. You will be surprised how something another person says can jar your memory so that you recall something new about that person or character.

Now that you have read these five steps, go back to the beginning and prepare yourself to talk about characters from literature. Once you meet with your group, you will want to spend enough time together so that everyone has a chance to share ideas.

Career Connection

After reading the poem "My People," students might be interested in a career as an anthropology field-worker. Anthropology is the study of the physical, social, and cultural development of humans. An anthropologist studies a particular people, such as the Navajo, and traces their origin and development throughout history. A field-worker assists an anthropologist by gathering information in the field. A field-worker may work anywhere in the world. Since fieldwork can be difficult, an anthropology field-worker must be in good physical condition. Educational requirements for anthropology field-workers vary according to the particular job; the minimum requirement is a high school diploma. Students who are interested in this career should contact the Anthropology Department of the nearest college or university.

CRITICAL THINKING

Generalization A general conclusion drawn from particular details is called a **generalization**. For example, suppose that all the children on your block play a certain game. You might make the generalization that this game is popular among children.

Sometimes, when you read a piece of literature, you will be tempted to make a generalization based on what you have read. It is important that you recognize whether such a generalization is accurate or inaccurate. For example, after reading the short story "The Medicine Bag," you might come to the conclusion that the Sioux place a great deal of importance on passing traditions from generation to generation. This is an accurate generalization. However, suppose that after reading the story you come to the conclusion that all Sioux children fear that their grandparents might embarrass them. This is an inaccurate generalization.

Choose a selection from this unit that suggests several generalizations. Use the selection to answer the following questions:

1. What generalizations are suggested by this story or poem? What specific details support these generalizations?

2. What inaccurate generalizations might a reader make based on this selection? Why are these generalizations inaccurate?

EFFECTIVE STUDYING

Tests In a matching test, first read the instructions. Notice whether an item in either column can be used more than once. Also, note if some items in a column may not be used at all. Begin by matching the items that you are sure of. If each item is used only once, it is possible to match some of the remaining items by the process of elimination.

In a multiple-choice test, answer the question in your own mind before you look at the choices. Eliminate the choices that are obviously wrong. Then choose the remaining answer that seems best.

In true and false tests, do not mark a statement true unless it is totally true. If you know that a statement is true only in some cases, it is probably false. Be aware of limiting words such as *always*, *never*, or *only*. Also be aware if a statement has two parts joined by a word such as *because*. One or both parts might be true, but the relationship between the two parts might be false.

Test Preparation

On any type of test, it is a good idea to answer all the items you are sure of first. Keep track of the ones you skipped. Then take more time to work on them.

Unit Review ■ 545

Teaching Strategy

Discuss with students the advantages of eliminating obvious wrong choices before choosing their answers.

Have students identify each statement as true or false.

1. In a multiple choice test, only one answer to a question can be correct. (true)

2. You should mark a statement true as long as it is true some of the time. (false)

Read the following questions to the class and have students answer them. Discuss the answers.

1. In a true/false test, you should mark an answer true
   a. when it is true in some cases.
   b. when it is always true. ✓
   c. when it is partly true.
   d. in all of the above cases.

2. In a matching test, the two columns to be matched
   a. always have the same number of items.
   b. never have the same number of items.
   c. sometimes have the same number of items. ✓

3. What types of tests are important to know about?
   a. multiple-choice
   b. true/false
   c. matching
   d. all of the above ✓

CRITICAL THINKING

Sample Answers

Sample answers are for the selection "Bread."

1. Crimes bring punishment. (The speaker is imprisoned for murder.) Small crimes can lead to bigger crimes. (For the speaker, stealing led to killing.) Desperation can drive people to commit crimes. (The man was so poor he could not afford food for his sick child, so he stole some crackers.) Conditions in prison are very unpleasant. (The speaker is given only bread and broth to eat. Time is a burden to him.)

2. All criminals commit crimes with good intentions. (A criminal could commit a crime out of hatred.) All criminals are poor. (Rich people commit crimes too.) All criminals care deeply about their children. (In the real world, some criminals do harm to family members or commit crimes without thinking of the welfare of their children. Many criminals do not have children.)

T545

GLOSSARY

PRONUNCIATION KEY

Accent is the force or stress given to some words or syllables in speech. In this book, accent is indicated by the use of uppercase letters. One syllable words are always shown as accented. Thus, the pronunciation of *hand* is (HAND). In words of more than one syllable, the accented syllable is printed in uppercase letters. The other syllable or syllables are printed in lowercase letters. Thus, the pronunciation of *handbag* is (HAND bag).

Letter(s) in text words	Letter(s) used in respelling	Sample words	Phonetic respelling	Letter(s) in text words	Letter(s) used in respelling	Sample words	Phonetic respelling
a	a	bandit	(BAN dit)	i	uh	possible	(POS uh bul)
a	ay	makeup	(MAYK up)	o	o	bottle	(BOT ul)
a	air	daring	(DAIR ing)	o	u	gallon	(GAL un)
a	ah	dart	(DAHRT)	o	oh	open	(OH pun)
a	uh	about	(uh BOUT)	o	aw	horn	(HAWRN)
a	aw	ball	(BAWL)	oo	oo	move	(MOOV)
e	e	denim	(DEN im)	oo	uu	football	(FUUT bawl)
e	eh	ingest	(in JEHST)	oo	oo	pool	(POOL)
e	ih	delight	(dih LYT)	oi	oi	point	(POINT)
e	u	darken	(DAHR kun)	ou	ou	output	(OUT put)
e	ee	he	(HEE)	u	u	upshot	(UP shot)
i	i	mitten	(MIT un)	u	uh	support	(suh PAWRT)
i	ih	gravity	(GRAV ih tee)	u	oo	ruler	(ROO lur)
i	y	idle	(YD ul)	y	i	rhythm	(RITH um)
i	eye	idea	(eye DEE uh)	y	ee	lazy	(LAY zee)
i	ee	medium	(MEE dee um)	y	y	thyme	(TYM)

A

abhorred (ab HAWRD) hated, dreaded *p. 70*

absurd (ab SURD) unreasonable; ridiculous *p. 169*

acquainted (un KWAYN tid) known to one another *p. 38*

acrid (AK rid) bitter to the tongue *p. 324*

aloof (uh LOOF) at a distance, apart *p. 65*

amorous (AM uh rus) full of love *p. 70*

anatomy (uh NAT uh mee) here, body *p. 158*

apologetic (uh pol uh JET ik) filled with apology; suggesting that one is sorry *p. 120*

ardently (AR dent lee) with great eagerness *p. 13*

attorney (uh TUR nee) lawyer *p. 252*

authorities (uh THAWR uh teez) people with official power *p. 132*

automatically (aw tuh MAT ihk lee) happening in a regular way without planning *p. 43*

avarice (AV uh ris) greed *p. 101*

B

banter (BAN tur) good-natured teasing *p. 324*

barbaric (bahr BAR ik) wild and cruel; not yet civilized *p. 285*

bedlam (BED lum) confusion *p. 416*

belt (BELT) area; region *p. 383*

beseech (bih SEECH) ask earnestly *p. 62*

bifocals (BY foh kulz) eyeglasses with parts to correct both near and far vision *p. 44*

bilingual (by LING gwul) able to use two languages *p. 415*

blare (BLAIR) make a loud noise *p. 414*

blunt (BLUNT) having a rounded point *p. 277*

bogies (BOH geez) real or imaginary things that startle or frighten *p. 171*

bottoms (BAH tumz) low-lying land along a river *p. 37*

brawl (BRAWL) noisy fight *p. 228*

bustle (BUS ul) move about busily *p. 477*

C

caravans (KAR uh vanz) in Great Britain, camping trailers *p. 188*

carcass (KAHR kus) body of dead animal *p. 386*

catastrophe (kuh TAS truh fee) a sudden, horrible disaster *p. 435*

charred (CHAHRD) partly burned *p. 388*

civic (SIV ik) having to do with good citizenship *p. 140*

clarity (KLAR uh tee) clearness *p. 418*

client (KLY unt) person who pays for a duty performed *p. 138*

coincidence (koh IN suh duns) two or more related events accidentally happening at the same time *pp. 144, 173, 243*

companion (kum PAN yun) a friend *p. 274*

comprehension (kom prih HEN shun) understanding or knowledge of something *p. 266*

Confederate (kun FED uh raht) during the Civil War, a supporter of the South *p. 5*

confide (kun FYD) tell as a secret *p. 353*

consolations (KAHN suh LAY shunz) the acts of comforting in time of sorrow *p. 8*

contagion (kun TAY jun) spreading disease *p. 72*

corral (kuh RAL) a fenced-in area for keeping livestock *p. 531*

correspondence (kawr uh SPON duns) exchange of letters *p. 95*

covert (KOH vurt) hidden or disguised *p. 266*

creed (KREED) formal statement of belief *p. 453*

crocus (KROH kus) spring flower *p. 235*

croksack, variation of *croker sack* (KRO kur sak) a bag of rough cloth or burlap *p. 36*

cuddling (KUD ling) holding and petting *p. 381*

cupboard (KUB urd) a closet fitted with shelves for holding cups *p. 256*

D

deception (dih SEP shun) trickery; action intended to fool another person *pp. 97, 201*

deftly (DEFT lee) cleverly *p. 505*

deliberately (dah LIH bur ayt lee) in an unhurried, slow, and steady manner *p. 176*

demonstration (dem un STRAY shun) any happening that can be observed *p. 205*

denouement (day noo MAHN) the final outcome *p. 507*

despite (dih SPYT) in spite of *p. 349*

destination (des tuh NAY shun) a place to which one is going *p. 43*

dignitary (DIG nuh ter ee) important person *p. 414*

dismaying (dis MAY ing) losing courage or confidence *p. 340*

doff (DOF) take off or discard *p. 58*

douse (DOUS) soak with water *p. 388*

E

elimination (ih lim uh NAY shun) in a tournament, dropped out after one loss *p. 410*

emerged (ih MURJD) came out *p. 467*

endure (en DUUR) put up with *p. 92*

entitled (en TYT uld) have as a claim or right; empowered *p. 148*

evade (ee VAYD) to keep away from; avoid *p. 177*

eventually (ih VEN choo ul ee) in the end; at some time *p. 434*

exclusive (ik SKLOO siv) private and expensive *p. 148*

exhausting (eg ZAW sting) very tiring *p. 43*

explicitly (ik SPLIS it lee) very clearly *p. 140*

extreme (ik STREEM) very great *p. 433*

F

facetiously (fuh SEE shus lee) jokingly, especially at an inappropriate time *p. 269*

fanatical (fuh NAT ih kul) incredibly devoted, to the point of being unreasonable *p. 190*

fantasy (FAN tuh see) daydream; idea created by the imagination; something imagined *pp. 157*

faze (FAYZ) confuse; weaken *p. 92*

felon (FEL un) criminal *p. 68*

ferocious (fuh ROH shus) very fierce *pp. 44, 349*

fiancé (fee ahn SAY) husband-to-be *p. 226*

fitful (FIT ful) uneasy; very restless *p. 412*

fortnight (FAWRT nyt) two weeks *p. 192*

frustrations (frus TRAY shunz) unhappy feelings that come from not being able to reach one's goals *p. 453*

G

gables (GAY bulz) the triangular top part of an outer wall between the sides of a sloped roof *p. 169*

gaped (GAYPT) opened wide; yawned *p. 474*

gaudy (GAWD ee) showy; bright-colored *p. 321*

genial (JEEN yul) pleasant; good-natured *p. 285*

gopher (GOH fur) a rodent that digs into the ground *p. 274*

gory (GAWR ee) bloody *p. 71*

greed (GREED) a great desire for wealth or material things *p. 101*

guile (GYL) the use of cunning; slyness *p. 13*

H

habitation (hab ih TAY shun) a building to live in *p. 384*

hamlet (HAM lit) very small village *p. 454*

heritage (HER ih tij) what is handed down to a person from ancestors *p. 353*

homesteaded (HOHM sted id) occupied land as a home *p. 267*

hummocks (HUM uks) areas of fertile, wooded land, higher than the surrounding swamp *p. 277*

I

idle (YD ul) unused; not busy *p. 468*

illustrate (IL uh strayt) to make clear by giving an example *p. 45*

impeach (im PEECH) accuse *p. 75*

improvised (IM pruh vyzd) made up quickly, without planning *p. 414*

indolence (IN dul lens) laziness *p. 321*

inexorable (in EKS uh ruh bul) unable to change or control *p. 67*

insolent (IN suh lunt) deliberately rude or insulting *p. 16*

instinct (IN stingkt) a natural tendency; unconscious skill *p. 258*

invalid (IN vuh lid) sick person *p. 143*

K

knobby (NOB ee) lumpy *p. 129*

L

lagoon (luh GOON) a shallow body of water, usually connected to a larger one *p. 164*

lamentable (LAM un tuh bul) distressing, sorrowful *p. 71*

lest (LEST) for fear that *p. 53*

lust (LUST) powerful desire *p. 412*

M

malignant (muh LIHG nunt) evil *p. 177*

malnutrition (mal noo TRISH un) poor health condition caused by not having enough of the right kinds of food *p. 130*

marina (muh REE nuh) large area set up for docking boats *p. 356*

maw (MAW) stomach *p. 67*

medallion (muh DAL yun) large medal *p. 409*

mingle (MING gul) mix *p. 411*

mortgage (MAWR gij) loan given to purchase a house *p. 227*

motive (MOHT iv) reason to act *p. 237*

murky (MUR kee) clouded; unclear *p. 91*

musket (MUHS kut) an old type of firearm *p. 9*

mute (MYOOT) unable to talk; quiet *p. 418*

N

nimble (NIM bul) quick and accurate *p. 415*

O

oafs (OHFS) stupid, awkward persons *p. 474*

omelet (OM lut) eggs beaten up, fried, and folded in half when done *p. 358*

P

pallet (PAL it) bed *p. 70*

paramour (PAR uh muur) lover *p. 70*

pensively (PEN siv lee) thoughtfully *p. 411*

perpetual (pur PECH oo ul) never stopping; without pause *p. 412*

persevered (pur suh VIRD) kept going by not giving up *p. 467*

perturbed (pur TURBD) greatly disturbed or alarmed *p. 15*

perverse (pur VURS) here, stubbornly difficult or contrary; wrong, improper *pp. 60, 159*

plaited (PLAYT ihd) braided *p. 36*

pleasantries (PLEZ un treez) lively, agreeable talks *p. 266*

pneumonia (noo MOHN yuh) disease of the lungs caused by an infection *pp. 133, 253*

poltergeist (POHL tur gyst) a noisy ghost *p. 201*

portly (PAWRT lee) heavy, but dignified *p. 53*

potion (POH shun) a drink with special powers, such as medicine or poison *p. 75*

presence (PREZ uns) nearness; being there *p. 381*

prodigious (pruh DIJ us) great; huge *pp. 55, 454*

profane (proh FAYN) show disrespect for holy things *p. 53*

purge (PURJ) get rid of *p. 53*

Q

quilt (KWILT) a bed cover made by stitching a layer of cotton between two layers of fabric *p. 261*

R

raggedy (RAG ih dee) tattered or torn *p. 349*

reconnaissance (rih KON uh sens) quick survey of information *p. 189*

reeds (REEDZ) tall grass in a marsh *p. 467*

relent (ruh LEHNT) to become gentler or more compassionate *p. 11*

relentless (rih LENT lis) without pity; harsh and cruel *p. 288*

relic (REH lik) something that remains from what has disappeared or been destroyed *p. 174*

resignation (reh zig NAY shun) patient acceptance *p. 10*

restorative (rih STAWR uh tiv) something that brings back consciousness or health generally; a medicine *p. 72*

righteous (RY chus) morally right, virtuous *p. 70*

rigid (RIH jihd) stiff *p. 177*

ritual (RICH oo ul) ceremony; tradition; a set pattern *pp. 155, 353*

rival (RY vul) one who wants the same things as another person *p. 92*

S

sanctified (SANK tuh fyd) set apart as holy *p. 9*

sarcastic (sahr KAS tik) sneering or ironic, and meant to hurt feelings *p. 260*

scowled (SKOULD) frowned *p. 121*

scullery (SKUL er ee) a room for cleaning and storing dishes and pots *p. 156*

scythe (SYTH) a long, curved blade fixed at an angle to a long, bent handle and used to cut down grass or grain *p. 123*

self-centered (SELF SENT urd) selfish; concerned with oneself *p. 137*

self-conscious (SELF KON shus) very aware of oneself; embarrassed or shy *p. 434*

semblance (SEHM bluns) outward appearance *p. 7*

severity (suh VAIR uh tee) great strictness or harshness *p. 43*

shields (SHEELDZ) defends; protects *pp. 173, 490*

shrewdest (SHROOD ist) cleverest, often in a tricky way *pp. 354, 465*

sluggish (SLUG ish) lacking energy *p. 274*

snatches (SNACH iz) grabs suddenly *p. 269*

somber (SOM bur) gloomy and sad *p. 122*

spellbinding (SPEL bynd ing) fascinating *p. 391*

stammered (STAM urd) in speaking, repeated the same sound without meaning to *p. 15*

stout (STOUT) having a heavy-set body *p. 489*

strides (STRYDZ) long steps *p. 130*

stupor (STOO pur) dazed or dull state *p. 385*

suffused (suh FYOOSD) spread through or over, as with a color, liquid or light *p. 16*

superstitious (soo pur STISH us) too much fear of the unknown *p. 266*

surged (SURJD) rolled; swelled up *p. 182*

T

tarpaulin (tahr PAW lin) a waterproof sheet used to protect *p. 343*

technique (tek NEEK) a way of doing something *pp. 45, 190*

telephoto (TEL uh foht oh) a camera lens that is able to make faraway things appear large *p. 188*

tepee (TEE pee) a cone-shaped tent of animal skins, used by the Plains Indians *p. 511*

theory (THEE uh ree) guess based on reasoning *p. 234*

thrive (THRYV) grow healthy and strong *p. 387*

timid (TIM id) shy *p. 265*

traditional (truh DISH uh nul) following old customs *p. 354*

transmitter (trans MIT ur) radio device that sends out signals *p. 194*

tremor (TREH mur) a quick, constant shaking or trembling *p. 174*

trifles (TRY fulz) anything of little value or importance *p. 257*

turret (TUR it) tower on top of a building *p. 181*

twine (TWYN) a thin rope *p. 37*

U

unnerved (un NURVD) terrified *p. 142*

V

vague (VAYG) not clear, hazy *pp. 144, 226*

varmints (VAHR munts) animals regarded as troublesome *p. 273*

vegetation (vej uh TAY shun) plant life *p. 274*

vestal (VES tul) virtuous, pure *p. 56*

virtuous (VUR choo us) honorable *p. 53*

W

wainscot (WAYNS koht) a facing for the walls in a room, usually made of wood paneling *p. 171*

welterweight (WEL tur wayt) boxer in a weight division between light- and middleweight *p. 411*

woes (WOHZ) misery, sorrows *p. 73*

womb (WOOM) stomach or uterus; any place that holds or generates something else *p. 67*

wryly (RY lee) humorously *p. 504*

Z

zealously (ZEL us lee) eagerly; fanatically *p. 325*

INDEX OF TITLES AND AUTHORS

Index of Titles and Authors ■ 551

INDEX OF SKILLS

Index of Skills ■ 553

INDEX OF FINE ART

Index of Fine Art ■ 555

ACKNOWLEDGMENTS

Unit 1: *The Lucky Stone* by Lucille Clifton. © 1979 by Lucille Clifton. Used by permission in the World excluding the UK by Dell Publishing, a division of Random House. Used by permission in the UK by Curtis Brown Ltd. "First Person Demonstrative" from *Mindscape* by Phyllis Gotlieb edited by Richard Peck. © 1971, 1990 by Richard Peck. Published by Delacorte Press. "Where Have You Gone" from *I am a Black Woman*, published by Wm. Morrow & Co., 1970, used by permission of the author. "Here Hold My Hand" from *I am a Black Woman*, published by Wm. Morrow & Co., 1970, used by permission of the author. "Greyday" from *Oh Pray My Wings Are Gonna Fit Me Well* by Maya Angelou. Copyright © 1975 by Maya Angelou. Reprinted by permission of Random House. "Reflections" by Vanessa Howard from *Soulscript Afro-American Poetry* edited by June Jordan. Copyright © 1970 by June Meyer Jordan. Published by Zenith Books a division of Random House. "Love" from *3000 Years of Black Poetry*. Translated by Raoul Abdul from the Raoul Abdul Collection used by permission of the Buxton National Historic Site & Museum. "Troubled Island" by Langston Hughes and William Grant Still. Copyright © 1976 by Southern Music Publishing Co., Inc. International Copyright Secured. Used by permission. All Rights Reserved. "Housecleaning" from *The Selected Poems of Nikki Giovanni* by Nikki Giovanni compilation copyright © 1996 by Nikki Giovanni. Reprinted by permission of HarperCollins Publishers, Inc./William Morrow. Eight pages from Babyhood by Paul Reiser. Copyright © 1997 by Paul Reiser. Reprinted by permission of HarperCollins Publishers, Inc./William Morrow. "Spring" by Carole Gregory Clemmons from *The Poetry of Black America* edited by Arnold Adoff © 1973 by Arnold Adoff. "Where Are You Now, William Shakespeare?" from *ME, ME, ME, ME, ME: Not a Novel* by M. E. Kerr. Copyright © 1983 by M. E. Kerr. Published by Harper & Row. Reprinted by permission of McIntosh and Otis, Inc. "What Is Once Loved…" by Elizabeth Coatsworth from *Alice-All-By-Herself*. Reprinted with the permission of Simon & Schuster Books for Young Readers, an imprint of Simon & Schuster Children's Publishing Division. Copyright © 1937 Macmillan Publishing Company; copyright renewed © 1965 Elizabeth Coatsworth Beston. **Unit 2:** "hist, whist." Copyright 1923, 1951, © 1991 by the Trustees for the E. E. Cummings Trust. Copyright © 1976 by George James Firmage, from Complete Poems: 1904-1962 by E. E. Cummings, edited by George J. Firmage. Used by permission of Liveright Publishing Corporation. "Incident in a Rose Garden" from *New and Selected Poems* by Donald Justice. Copyright © 1995 by Donald Justice. Reprinted by permission of Alfred A. Knopf, a Division of Random House Inc. "The Listeners" from *The Collected Poems of Walter de la Mare* by Walter de la Mare. The Literary Trustees of Walter de la Mare, and the Society of Authors as their representatives. "Sorry, Wrong Number" from *Sorry, Wrong Number and the Hitch-hiker* by Lucille Fletcher. Copyright © 1948 by Lucille Fletcher. Reprinted by permission of William Morris Agency, Inc. on behalf of the author. "Overheard on a Saltmarsh" from Collected Poems by Harold Monro. Used by permission of Freda McGregor. "Thus I Refute Beelzy" from *The John Collier Reader* by John Collier. Copyright © 1951 by John Collier renewed 1979 by the Estate of John Collier. Permission granted by Harold Matson Co., Inc. on behalf of John George Stafford Collier. "Boy in the Shadows" from *House of Evil* by Margaret Ronan. Copyright © 1977 by Scholastic Inc. Reprinted by permission. "The Great Amherst Mystery by Walter Hubbell from *Tales of Mystery and the Unknown* by Robert Potter. © 1976 by Globe Book Company, Inc. **Unit 3:** Used as unit opener "The Admirals Ghost. . ." from *Collected Poems in One Volume* by Alfred Noyes. Published by J. B. Lippincott. "Trifles" from *Plays by Susan Glaspell*. Copyright 1920 by Dodd, Mead & Company, Inc. Copyright renewed 1948 by Susan Glaspell. "Displays of Skill: The Bat" (first published as "Being a Mammal" in *Nature and Love Poems*), copyright © 1969 by Ruth Hershberger, Eakins Press Foundation. Reproduced with permission. "Earth" by John Hall Wheelock from *Modern American Poetry* by Louis Untermeyer. Published by arrangement with the Estate of Louis Untermeyer, Norma Anchin Untermeyer c/o Professional Publishing Services Company. This permission is expressly granted by Laurence S. Untermeyer. "Bird of Night" from *The Bat-Poet* by Randall Jarrell. Reprinted by permission of Mary Jarrell. "The Getaway" by John Savage from *Saturday Evening Post 5/7/66*. "Ancient Enmity (retitled: The Rattlesnake Hunt from Cross Creek)" excerpted and reprinted with the permission of Scribner, a Division of Simon & Schuster from *Cross Creek* by Marjorie Kinnan Rawlings. Copyright 1942 by Marjorie Kinnan Rawlings; copyright renewed © 1970 by Norton Baskin and Charles Scribner's Sons. "Earth" from *The Gardener and Other Poems* by John Hall Wheelock. Reprinted with the permission of Scribner, a Division of Simon & Schuster. Copyright © 1961 by John Hall Wheelock, renewed 1989 by Sally Wheelock Brayton. "A Secret for Two" by Quentin Reynolds. Published in Collier's magazine. **Unit 4:** "Haiku (Crying Insects…)" by Issa from *An Anthology of Haiku Ancient* *and Modern* translated and annotated by Asataro Miyamori. Published by Greenwood Publishing Group. "Haiku" (Waterfalls...)" by Buson from *An Anthology of Haiku Ancient and Modern* translated and annotated by Asataro Miyamori. Published by Greenwood Publishing Group. "Chee's Daughter" by Juanita Platero and Siyowin Miller, from *Common Ground*, vol. VIII, no. 2 (Winter 1948), pp. 22–31. Reprinted from *Common Ground* with the permission of the Immigration and Refugee Services of America. Used as unit opener from *The Oxford Dictionary of Quotations*, Published by the Oxford University Press. Copyright © 1979, first edition 1941, second edition 1953, third edition 1979, reprinted with corrections 1980. "Hokku Poems" copyright by Richard Wright. "Haiku (Friends that open mouth...)" from *Japanese Haiku*. Copyright © 1955, 1956. Used by permission of Peter Pauper Press. "Starvation Wilderness" by Olive A. Fredrickson from *Outdoor Life*, Vol. 143, No. 6 (June 1969). "Dreams" from *Collected Poems* by Langston Hughes. Copyright © 1994 by the Estate of Langston Hughes. Reprinted by permission of Alfred A. Knopf, a Division of Random House Inc. Reprinted in the UK by permission of Harold Ober. "Ta-Na-E-Ka" by Mary Whitebird from *Scholastic Voice*, Vol. 55, No. 12 (Dec. 13, 1973). Copyright © 1973 Scholastic Inc. Reprinted by permission of Scholastic Inc. "A bee thumps ..." from *Bunch Grass* by Robert Sund. Copyright © 1969 by Robert Sund. Reprinted by permission of the University of Washington Press. "Four Skinny Trees" from *The House on Mango Street* by Sandra Cisneros. Published by Vintage Books a division of Random House © 1989 by Sandra Cisneros. Reprinted by permission in the World excluding Britian by the Susan Bergholz Literary Services, New York Reprinted by permission of Bloomsbury Publishing in Britian. "Dead at Seventeen"used by permission of Solis Creative Services, Inc. "Thank you, M'am" from *Short Stories* by Langston Hughes. Copyright © 1996 by Romona Bass and Arnold Rampersad. Introduction copyright © 1996 by Arnold Rampersad. Compilation and editorial contribution copyright © 1996 by Akiba Sullivan Harper. Reprinted by permission of Hill & Wang, a division of Farrar, Straus and Giroux, LLC. Reprinted outside North America by permission of Harold Ober. "Sympathy" from *Black Writers of America* by Paul Dunbar. Prentice Hall Inc. **Unit 5:** "The Secret Life of Walter Mitty" from the book *My World—and Welcome To It* © 1942 by James Thurber. Copyright © renewed 1971 by Helen Thurber and Rosemary A. Thurber. Reprinted by arrangement with Rosemary A. Thurber and The Barbara Hogenson Agency. All rights reserved. "Song of Failure" "War Song" "Warrior Song I" "Warrior Song II" from *Literature of the American Indians* by Sanders © 1974. Reprinted by permission of Prentice Hall Inc., Upper Saddle River, NJ. . "Terror in the North" from *American Girl Magazine*, 3/66 used by permission of Girl Scouts of the USA. "Ulysses Meets the Cyclops" by Homer. Retold by Alice Delman. From Chapman's Homer © 1956 by Bolingen Foundation. Reprinted by permission of Princeton University Press. "Amigo Brothers" from *Stories from El Barrio* by Piri Thomas Copyright © 1978 by Piri Thomas. Used as unit opener from The Oxford Dictionary of Quotations, Published by the Oxford University Press. Copyright © 1979, first edition 1941, second edition 1953, third edition 1979, reprinted with corrections 1980. **Unit 6:** "Medicine" from *ONCE* by Alice Walker. Copyright © 1968 and renewed 1996. Reprinted by permission of Harcourt, Inc. Reprinted by permission of David Highman Assoc. in the UK. "Andre" from *Bronzeville Boys & Girls*. Copyright © 1956 by Gwendolyn Brooks Blakely. Used by permission of HarperCollins Publishers. "Otto" by Gwendolyn Brooks Blakely from *Bronzeville Boys & Girls*. Published by HarperCollins Publishers. "Bread" by Amado V. Hernandez from *Rice Grains* selected and translated by E. San Juan, Jr. Copyright © 1966 by International Publishers Co. Used by permission. "Family Album" from *Poetry by Diane Stevenson*. Copyright © 1987 by Modern Poetry Association. Reprinted by permission of the Editor of Poetry. "My People" by Bernice George from *Here I Am!* by Virginia Olsen Baron. Copyright © 1969 by Virginia Olsen Baron. Used by permission of Dutton Children's Books, a division of Penguin Putnam Inc. "Whale Hunting" by Sally Nashookpuk from *Here I Am!* by Virginia Olsen Baron. Copyright © 1969 by Virginia Olsen Baron. Used by permission of Dutton Children's Books, a division of Penguin Putnam Inc. "Luther Leavitt" by Alfred Brower from *Here I Am!* by Virginia Olsen Baron. Copyright © 1969 by Virginia Olsen Baron. Used by permission of Dutton Children's Books, a division of Penguin Putnam Inc. Used as unit opener "Lineage" from *For My People* by Margaret Walker. Copyright © 1942 by Yale University Press. "Christmas Morning i" copyright © 1968 by Carol Freeman Reprinted from *Black Fire* edited by LeRoi Jones and Larry Neal (William Morrow & Co) "Some People" reprinted with the permission of Simon & Schuster Books for Young Readers, an imprint of Simon & Schuster Children's Publishing Division from Poems by Rachel Field (Macmillan, NY, 1957).

Note: Every effort has been made to locate the copyright owner of material reprinted in this book. Omissions brought to our attention will be corrected in subsequent editions.

ART CREDITS

Illustrations

Unit 1: pp. 6, 9, 12, 14, 17: Dan Clifford; pp. 34, 35, 36–37, 38, 43, 45: Guy Porfirio; p. 82: Sterling Brown; p. 100: Guy Porfirio. **Unit 2:** p. 112: Guy Porfirio; p. 123: Marlies Merk-Najaka; p. 126: Guy Porfirio; p. 164: David Palladin; pp. 168, 170, 172, 175: Janet Hamlin; p. 183: Michael Bryant; pp. 186, 187, 191: Doug Schneider; pp. 200, 203: Alex Bloch, **Unit 3:** pp. 216, 220: Den Schofield; pp. 224, 227, 230, 235, 237, 240, 246: Bert Dodson/Bookmakers Ltd.; p. 280: Steven Hunt; **Unit 4:** p. 316: David Dircks; p. 332: Eva Auchincloss; pp. 336, 338, 341, 344: Rupert Baxter; pp. 348, 349, 368: Guy Porfirio; pp. 369, 373: Dick Smolinski; p. 376: Gary Underhill; p. 394: Michael Bryant; p. 396: Robert Pasternak; **Unit 5:** pp. 408, 413, 417, 419: Paul Lackner; pp. 442, 445, 447, 449: (tinting) Donna Day; p. 455: Merlies Merk-Najacka; pp. 464: William Hunter-Hicklin; **Unit 6:** p. 489: Robert Martin; p. 496: Jack Stockman; pp. 500, 503, 507: Yoshi Miyake; p. 524: Richard Leonard.

Photographs

Contents: p. v: *The Letter*, Mary Cassatt. Courtesy of the Library of Congress; p. vii: *Allegory*, Ben Shahn. Collection of the Modern Art Museum of Fort Worth. Estate of Ben Shahn/Licensed by VAGA, New York, NY; p. ix: *Tiger*, Edward J. Detmold. The Metropolitan Museum of Art, The Elisha Whittelsey Collection; p. xi: *Familia India*, Amado M. Pena, Jr. El Taller, Inc.; p. xiii: *Buffalo Hunter*, Unknown American. Gift of Harriett Cowles Hammett Grahm in Memory of Buell Hammett; **Unit 1:** p. 20: R. Andrew Odum/Peter Arnold, Inc.; p. 39: Courtesy of Michael Glaser; p. 42: Ed Bock/The Stock Market; pp. 48, 50, 54, 57, 61, 65, 69: The Museum of Modern Art/Film Stills Archive; p. 77: The Granger Collection; p. 83: AP/Wide World Photos; p. 91: Eve Arnold/Magnum; p. 96: Photofest; **Unit 2:** pp. 136, 141, 145: H. Armstrong Roberts; p. 151: Courtesy of Lucille Fletcher; p. 165: UPI/Corbis Bettmann; p. 180: Gregory K. Scott/Photo Researchers, Inc.; p. 195: London Daily Mail/Photo Researchers, Inc.; **Unit 3:** p. 272: Gary Retherford/Photo Researchers, Inc.; p. 276: Juan Manuel Rejifo/Animals Animals; pp. 290–291: A&L Sinibaldi/Stone; p. 294: Mark Boulton/Photo Researchers, Inc.; p. 300: Chris Jones/Photo Researchers, Inc.; p. 302: Eastcott/Momatiuk/Animals Animals; **Unit 4:** p. 397: The Granger Collection; **Unit 5:** p. 432: Will & Deni McIntyre/Photo Researchers Inc.; p. 452: Flip Schulke/Black Star; p. 453: Dennis Brack/Black Star; p. 455: American Stock/Archive Photos; p. 473: Topham/The Image Works; **Unit 6:** p. 488: Stone; p. 491: the Granger Collection; p. 521: Courtesy of Holiday House; p. 530: C.K. Lorenz/Photo Researchers, Inc.; p. 538: Chris Arend/Alaska Stock Images.

Note: Every effort has been made to locate the copyright owner of material reprinted in this book. Omissions brought to our attention will be corrected in subsequent editions.